dition

GUN DIGEST TREASURY

The Best From 40 Years of GUN DIGEST

Edited by Ken Warner

DBI BOOKS, INC.

GUN DIGEST TREASURY STAFF

Editor
Ken Warner

Associate Editors
Harold A. Murtz
Robert S.L. Anderson
Pamela Johnson

Index Editor
Lilo Anderson

Publisher
Sheldon L. Factor

Arms and Armour Press, London, G.B., exclusive licensees and distributors in Britain and Europe; Australia; Nigeria and South Africa and Zimbabwe; India and Pakistan; Singapore, Hong Kong and Japan.

ISBN 0-87349-017-7 **Library of Congress Catalog #61-9610**

CONTENTS

JOHN T. AMBER
1903-1986

THE FIRST FIVE of these TREASURY volumes of GUN DIGEST were edited by John Amber. This, the Sixth TREASURY in the four-decade history of GUN DIGEST, was not edited by John Amber.

The Editor Emeritus of GUN DIGEST died January 1, 1986 at his beloved Creedmoor Farm near Marengo, Illinois. He was 82 and suffered a cardiac arrest. By all accounts, he died peacefully lying on a couch in his study.

He was buried in the Marengo City Cemetery. He left a considerable legacy of memories to old friends and foes alike. Amber was survived by his wife Jean. His outstanding and considerable collection of firearms and kindred artifacts and books was sold at auction, bringing over a million dollars to his estate.

He had a good run, John did, a race he liked if the gleam that rarely left his eyes was any indication. His times and his life were busy with all the wonders a bright and inquiring mind, beginning in the 1920s, could discover. He knew and loved, for examples, jazz music, ballroom dancing and sports cars.

It was, however, a virtually single-minded devotion to guns that brought Amber to his life's work. Above all the fascinations of his life, guns reigned at the center of his attention. In a life of many jobs, GUN DIGEST was the one he made a career.

Along the way there were hundreds and thousands of guns to cherish or test or hunt with, trips to take, parties to enjoy and friends and enemies to make, but the thousands of pages of GUN DIGEST were his first care. He was proud of that work.

He was entitled.

Ken Warner

Photo by Ken Warner, 1973

Already in a heyday to last for decades, a clean-shaven Amber kept a Gatling near his desk. (Kufrin Photo)

Tough talk over good guns could be the highlight of any day John Amber had. (Anderson photo)

Once settled in his place in Marengo, IL, Amber gave little thought to moving and never did. (Murtz photo)

GUN DIGEST AS HISTORY

By Ken Warner

In four decades, the substance of GUN DIGEST has changed greatly, as has its size, but the character of an annual report on all available guns is still with us.

THESE DAYS, when we publish GUN DIGEST, we publish 230 pages of what we have come to call "the best compact catalog" in the business. We used to publish fewer pages of the catalog; it has been enlarged as the number of offerings in the gun field have increased; it is now quite a publication in its own right, all those feature articles and think-pieces and the current reportage from up front notwithstanding.

And it is—our catalog—history, the very stuff of history in and of itself. One way to look at it is to take some reasonably significant development and follow it through. Let us take, for instance, the deservedly important 222 Remington cartridge.

Announced in 1950, the 222 was an all-Remington show, a cartridge case never before seen. It came out that first year in a special version of the 722 Remington rifle, a plain-Jane gun, Model 722A, priced at $74.95. The magazine was blocked short from the rear; it had a 26-inch barrel; and it quite caught the fancy of every varmint hunter there was.

It caught a lot of other fancies, too. In 1954, Sako's L46, at $128.75 in Mannlicher style, had jumped on the bandwagon, and Savage had the under-$50 Model 340 in 222. There was a lot of 222 going on those years. The benchresters were really giving it a go, and, of all people, Winchester-Western was loading the 222.

No wonder about it, really. Here's what GUN DIGEST's Major General Julian S. Hatcher had to say about the new cartridge in the 1951 book:

Latest thing in factory made varmint rifles is the Remington Model 722 bolt-action repeater chambered for the recently announced Remington 222 cartridge which made its appearance early in 1950. This new cartridge is strictly an original development of the Remington Arms Company, and bears little resemblance to any other previous cartridge. It is of the rimless type, looking not unlike a small version of the 30-06. As was stated above, the jacketed soft-point bullet weighs 50 grains and is driven at a speed of 3,200 f.p.s. This new cartridge has much flatter trajectory and greater power than either the Hornet or the Bee, and should give a much longer barrel life than the Swift, which wears out a barrel in from 1,200 to 2,000 rounds. The 222 Remington should be good for 5,000 to 6,000 rounds at least, if the barrel is properly cared for. Another advantage over the Swift is the fact that the 222 gives a considerably softer report, which can be a real advantage in thickly settled communities. But the biggest pulling point is the fact that at present it is the only varmint cartridge that can be had in the ultra modern Remington 722 rifle. The owner of such a combination can feel that he is really up to date.

By 1956, Marlin had a Micro-Grooved 222 on the Sako action at $119.95. And that year it was Gen. Hatcher again. He gave the new Marlin and the 222 cartridge a real boost:

When I got the Model 322 Micro-Groove, I already had available two superbly accurate Finnish Sako rifles in the same caliber, one with heavy barrel and the other with the regular weight barrel. So of course all three were fired together for accuracy, and again the Micro-Groove shot groups slightly smaller than the other two.

Once again I call attention to the fact that the firing of only two or three rifles is not a conclusive test; but the results obtained at the factory provide a much more extensive indication. When Marlin began to get the first production of the Model 322 off the line, they determined to find out the cold truth about all the claims and indications they had about accuracy with the Micro-Groove system. So they made a 100 per cent accuracy test of the first 150 guns to come off the production line. Each rifle was fired for accuracy at 100 yards over sandbag rests, using at least two lots of Winchester and two lots of Remington 222 ammunition, and the standard bead front sight and peep rear sight.

Four 5-shot groups were fired with each rifle, two with Winchester ammunition and two with Remington, or vice versa. The group average for all guns at 100 yards, 20 shots from each gun, with iron sights, was 1.31 inches extreme spread—a remarkable accuracy record.

There was also Sears, weighing in with yet another 222 on the Sako action. That one went for $110. The Savage 340 was up to $62.25. And a Sako heavy barrel in the 60X magazine version eventually to be called Vixen was $145.

There's another thing about that 1956 GUN DIGEST and the times it records. In that year, a list of "U.S. Rifles Now Made and Available—Center Fire" contained 18 models. Seven were Winchesters, four were Remingtons, two were Savages and two were J. C. Higginses and Roy Weatherby was making all the rest.

That is fairly startling, seeing that we're not speaking of the Dark Ages, but of only 30 years ago, when your reporter here was out there buying and trying a lot of them. However, perhaps even more boggling was a 1956 list of "Center Fire Cartridges And The Rifles For Them." There were 19 cartridges in that list. Included among the 19 were 348 Winchester, 32 Winchester Special, the 219 Zipper and the 351 Winchester Self-Loading and those, all will recognize, *are* history.

But we digress.

In the 1958 book, Remington had the 760A in 222—a slide-action varmint rifle. And the number of high-power rifle models was down to 14 and the list of cartridges for them was up to 20, including five new ones—243 Winchester, 244 Remington, 280 Remington, 358 Winchester and 458 Winchester Magnum.

The expansion of the 222 options may go on a long time. There are smaller versions and longer versions and wildcats. One 222 offspring is our standard infantry rifle cartridge. And the whole development can be traced, a year at a time, in GUN DIGEST.

Today, the 222 is a staple and GUN DIGEST for 1987 lists loads from five manufacturers. There is a handgun in 222 and we show over 25 rifles and combination rifle-shotguns in which the 222 Remington is a standard chambering. Rather impressive, considering the cartridge, with 38 years

It is necessary these days to pack a great deal more information into two pages of GUN DIGEST than at the beginning—just one of these pages of the 1986/40th edition shows over 20 different models of revolver.

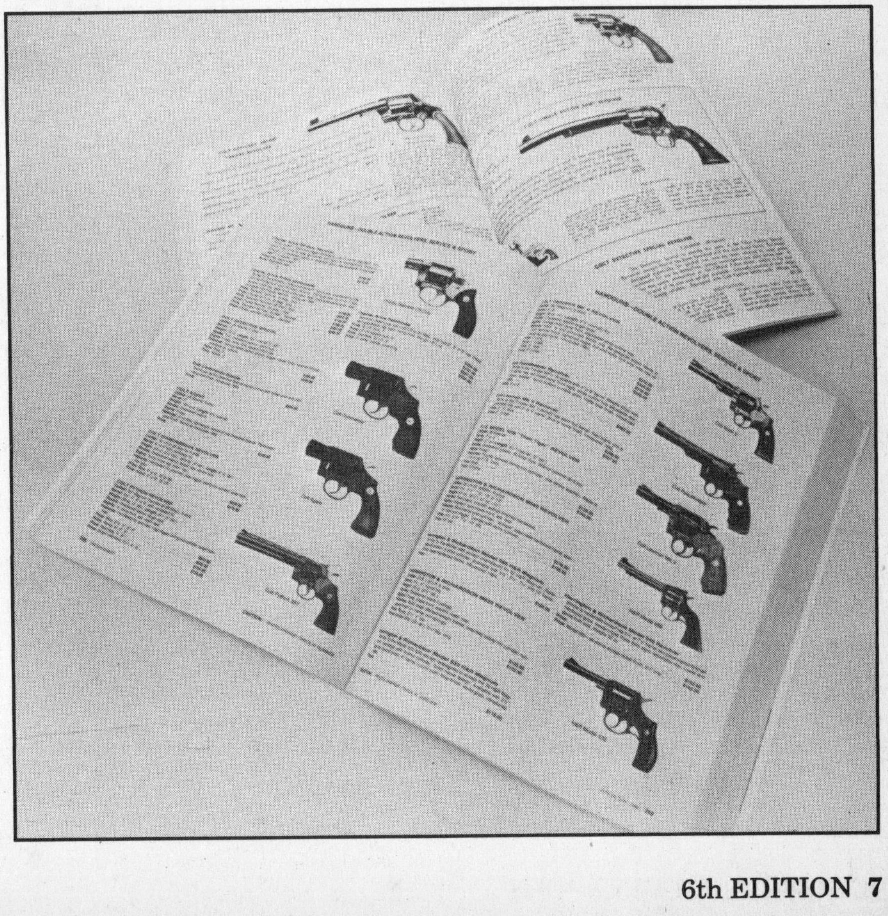

WINCHESTER MODEL 70 HIGH POWER RIFLES

STANDARD GRADE MODEL 70. (Top Illustration) $78.45

Solid frame, bolt action repeating rifle with speed lock. (Put on the market in 1936) Round tapered barrel of Winchester proof-steel. Pistol grip N.R.A. type black walnut stock with semi-beavertail fore-end. Grip, fore-end and steel butt plate checkered. Dimensions: 13½ x 1⅝ x 2⅝". Bead front sight on ramp base with sight cover. Winchester 22G opening sporting rear sight, round top. Flat top rear sight substituted, if desired. Safety operates in horizontal plane. 5 cartridge (4 in .300 and .375 H & H Magnum calibers) magazine with hinged floor plate. 1" swivel bows. Wt. about 8¼ lbs. 24" barrel in following calibers: .22 Hornet, .250-3000 Savage, .270 Win., .30 Gov't '06, 7 M/M, .257 Roberts, .35 Rem., .375 H & H Magnum (has recoil pad). 20" barrel same calibers, excepting .375 H & H Magnum. 26" barrel in calibers .220 Swift and .300 H & H Magnum.

The Standard Model 70 is also equipped with Lyman No. 48WJS receiver sight with blank piece in rear sight slot in place of standard sight. Or with Lyman No. 57W receiver sight. $92.65

MODEL 70 NATIONAL MATCH RIFLE. $120.80

Solid frame. 24" round Winchester Proof Steel barrel, floating type. Marksman design stock with full pistol grip and full fluted comb. Length of pull, 13¼"; drop at comb, 1 9/16"; drop at heel, 1⅞"; pitch down, 3". Lyman No. 77 front sight on forged ramp sight base. Lyman No. 48WH receiver sight. Telescope mount bases. 1¼" Army type leather shooting gun sling on non-detachable bow type swivels. Approx. wt. 9½ lbs. .30 Gov't '06 cal. only.

MODEL 70 TARGET RIFLE. (2nd Illustration) $131.90

Medium weight barrel, solid frame. Same specifications as National Match, except without forged ramp; wt. about 10½ lbs. Same calibers as Standard Grade in 24" and 26" barrel lengths excepting .375 H & H Magnum.

MODEL 70 BULL GUN. (3rd Illustration) $142.70

Made with heavy 28", floating type barrel. In .30 Gov't '06 and .300 H & H Magnum calibers only. Otherwise the same as the Target Model. Wt. about 13¼ lbs.

SUPER GRADE MODEL 70. (Illustrated Above) $107.85

American walnut stock with cheek piece. Pistol grip and field full gold bead front sight on ramp with sight cover. W... sight, round or flat top. 1" Army type leather sling strap wi... specifications same as Standard Grade. Same calibers and ... Magnum comes in 25" barrel with special flat top rear sig... ...checkered. Red- ...rting rear ...Other

19

THE NEW REMINGTON 722 VARMINT RIFLE

Proof of accuracy. An actual size group shot at 100 yds. with the Model 722 and the new cartridge. Bench rest. The 50-grain soft point bullet is encased in a tapered metal jacket thin at the nose for perfect mushrooming and reduced ricochet. The jacket is thick at the base to prevent bullet separation.

BALLISTICS

CARTRIDGE	BULLET		VELOCITY — FEET PER SECOND				ENERGY — FOOT POUNDS				MID-RANGE TRAJECTORY — INCHES		
	Wt. Grains	Style	Muzzle	100 Yds.	200 Yds.	300 Yds.	Muzzle	100 Yds.	200 Yds.	300 Yds.	100 Yds.	200 Yds.	300 Yds.
222 Remington	50	Soft Point	3200	2660	2170	1750	1135	785	520	340	0.5	2.5	7.0

MODEL 722A "STANDARD" GRADE—chambered for 222 Remington cartridge. 26-inch round, tapered barrel of special steel. Carefully bored and rifled for extreme accuracy. High comb stock of genuine American walnut especially designed for use with telescope or receiver sight. Properly shaped pistol grip. Long, full, well rounded fore-end of semi-beavertail type. Shotgun style metal butt plate, checkered to prevent slipping. Rifle cocks on opening movement of bolt. Sensational trigger without back lash—lightning fast let-off. Side placed thumb operated safety. Polished bolt and action. Special bolt stop. Magazine holds 5 cartridges which with one in chamber gives a capacity of 6 shots. White metal bead front sight mounted on matted ramp. Step adjustable sporting rear sight. Receiver drilled and tapped for adaptable scope mounts and standard micrometer receiver sights. Weight about 7½ lbs. Length over-all 45¼". Price $74.95

NO. 722A "STANDARD" GRADE—chambered for 300 Sav. or 257 Roberts cartridge. Magazine holds 4 cartridges which with one in chamber gives a capacity of 5 shots. 24" barrel. Weight about 7 pounds. Length over-all 43¼". Price $74.95

No. 722AC "Standard" Grade with checkered stock .... $ 91.60
No. 722B "Special" Grade with checkered stock and selected wood 103.00
No. 722D "Peerless" Grade 430.00
No. 722F "Premier" Grade 670.00
High Comb Stock for use with telescope (furnished when specified) .... No Extra Charge
1" Leather Sling Strap, Whelen type, with swivel loops, extra 4.00
1" Leather Sling Strap, Whelen type, with quick release swivels, extra 6.70

23

Above—In 1944, there were five models of the Winchester Model 70 available in 11 calibers, provided in those war years one could find any Model 70 at all. Right—In 1951, GUN DIGEST introduced the exciting new 222 Remington cartridge and a short-actioned Remington rifle to go with it with a full catalog page. The standard grade rifle was just $74.95.

of its history recorded, has to be well past the growth curve.

One could also look at a single firearm over a considerable length of time in GUN DIGEST and learn a bit there, too. For instance, the ups and downs and sideways of the deservedly famous Model 70 Winchester rifle.

In 1944, in the GUN DIGEST of the war years, the Model 70 was offered in 10 *calibers*, and 5 *versions*, all of them the venerable 1930s-style sporters and competition guns. There was the standard sporter and the Super Grade, and Model 70 target rifles in National Match, standard target and bull gun. Of course, in that year and in that time, the Model 70 wasn't really offered—it was just listed. There was a war on.

When the war was over, things didn't change very fast. In the years through 1951, the problems for Winchester were not finding new models of the Winchester Model 70 to sell, but filling up a pipeline long-emptied with the rifles they were already making. So they went with identical rifles, and the same cartridges as in 1944.

Finally, in 1954, we listed in GUN DIGEST something new in the Model 70, and it really was. Given a new cartridge—the 308 Winchester—Winchester furnished a new version of the Model 70, the Featherweight. And they banged their drum very hard, as well they should.

The ferment in things military was very active back then. For Winchester to dive in and nail their name onto the cartridge which was to become the 7.62 NATO and the standard small arms round of the U.S. military was a *coup* indeed. They made the most of it.

So did Gen. Hatcher in GUN DIGEST:

Since our last year's review, there haven't been many new developments in the field of sporting rifles and ammunition, but there is one exception, and that is a big one. It is the Model 70 Featherweight, made for a special cartridge—the 308 Winchester. This new gun is about 1½ pounds lighter than the regular 8-pound Model 70. The catalog lists the Featherweight at only 6½ pounds, though the samples that I have used weighed slightly more. This reduction in weight makes all the difference on long hikes or hunting trips in the mountains.

The 308 Winchester is an entirely new item to the trade, for it is actually the Army's new experimental T-65 case loaded as a hunting cartridge.

As everyone who has followed the news for the past few months knows, the Army has been considering some new rifle designs, and the new guns that have been tested most recently have all been made for a cartridge that is a 30 caliber, with the same power as the old 30-06, but with a case ½-inch shorter, called the T-65 case. The reason is that powders have been much improved in the fifty-eight years since that old 30-06 was adopted, and the more efficient and concentrated powders available now do not require so much space for a charge to give the necessary velocity. When the 30-06 case is loaded up to service pressure and velocity, there is a lot of waste space in the case, and this does not make for efficient burning of the powder. Better ballistics are obtained if the case is more nearly filled.

This being so, it seemed to be a fine solution to shorten the case as

New Winchester Model 70 Featherweight Rifle

NEW MODEL 70 FEATHERWEIGHT

To satisfy the sportsman's need for short, lighter, high-powered hunting cartridges and lighter-weight rifles, Winchester announced in August 1952 a new cartridge—the 308 Winchester—and a companion rifle, the Featherweight version of the famous Winchester Model 70.

Made possible by the use of spherically grained Olin smokeless "Ball Powder," which was first used in the U.S. Carbine, caliber 30 M-1 of World War II fame, the new 308 Winchester cartridge makes use of the high-density, high-energy characteristics of this powder. The cartridge is a full half-inch shorter and 10% lighter than the standard 30-06 cartridge. It is offered in the popular 150-grain and 180-grain Silvertip controlled expanding game bullets and in the 110-grain soft point bullet used for varmint and pest shooting.

An outgrowth of the proposed new lightweight T-65, caliber 30 military cartridge, the 308's ballistics are only slightly inferior to those of the standard 30-06 cartridges. The 180-grain 308 has 2610 f.p.s. muzzle velocity; the 150-grain 308 has 2860 f.p.s. MV; and the 110-grain 308 has 3340 f.p.s. MV.

The re-engineered Winchester M-70 rifle has been reduced in weight to 6½ pounds (without sacrifice of the M-70's superb accuracy) by a new 22" barrel contour and by redesign of the stock. The Featherweight M-70 features a free floating barrel and has a rifling twist of one turn in 12 inches, which produces full stability in the three bullet weights of the new 308 cartridge.

An aluminum butt plate, trigger guard, and floor plate help reduce the weight of the new rifle 15 to 20% below the standard M-70 weight.

Standard stock for regular open sights or the high-comb stock for use with telescope sights may be had, and on special order the M-70 Featherweight may be obtained with a 24" barrel. Prices are the same as for the standard Model 70.

Ballistic Data for the 308 Winchester Cartridges

Bullet	Range	Velocity (ft./sec.)	Energy (ft./pounds)	Mid-Range Trajectory (in.)
110-Gr. SP	Muzzle	3340	2730	
	15'	3300		
	100 yds.	2810	1930	.5
	200 yds.	2340	1340	2.2
	300 yds.	1920	900	6.0
	400 yds.	1550	590	13.0
	500 yds.	1260	390	24.0
150-Gr. ST	Muzzle	2860	2730	
	15'	2845		
	100 yds.	2570	2200	.6
	200 yds.	2300	1760	2.6
	300 yds.	2050	1400	6.5
	400 yds.	1810	1090	13.4
	500 yds.	1590	840	23.0
180-Gr. ST	Muzzle	2610	2720	
	15'	2600		
	100 yds.	2390	2280	.8
	200 yds.	2170	1870	3.1
	300 yds.	1970	1540	7.4
	400 yds.	1780	1260	15.0
	500 yds.	1600	1010	26.0

Comparison of 30-06 cartridge with the new 308 Winchester short sporting cartridges.

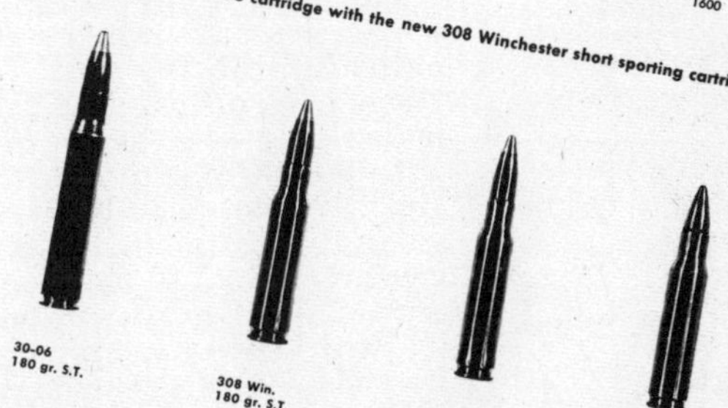

30-06 180 gr. S.T.

308 Win. 180 gr. S.T.

308 Win. 150 gr. S.T.

308 Win. 110 gr. S.P

47

U.S. RIFLES NOW MADE AND AVAILABLE—CENTER

Name	Model	Magazine	Weight	Price	Car
			Self Loader		
Remington	740	Box	7½ lbs.	$124.95	30-06
Winchester	07	Box	8¼ lbs.	140.20	351 Win. Self Loading
			Slide Action		
Remington	760	Box	7½ lbs.	104.40	257 Robt., 270 Win., 300 Sav., 30-06; 35 Rem.
			Lever Action		
Marlin	336	Tubular	7 lbs.	68.95	219 Zipper, 30-30 Win., 35 Rem.
Savage	99	Reel	7½ lbs.	105.65	250 Savage; 300 Savage
Winchester	64	Tubular	7 lbs.	91.60	30-30 Win.; 32 Win. Spl.
Winchester	94	Tubular	6¼ lbs.	69.00	30-30 Win.; 32 Win. Spl.
Winchester	71	Tubular	8 lbs.	100.30	348 Winchester
Winchester	88	Box	6½ lbs.	123.95	308 Winchester
			Bolt Action		
J.C. Higgins	50	Box	7½ lbs.	89.95	30-06; 270 Win.
J. C. Higgins	52	Box	7 lbs.	110.00	222 Remington
Marlin	322	Box	7½ lbs.	119.95	222 Remington
Remington	721	Box	7¼ lbs.	88.35	270 Win.; 30-06; 300 H & H Magnum
Remington	722	Box	7 lbs.	82.80	222 Rem.; 257 Roberts; 300 Savage
Savage	340	Box	6¾ lbs.	49.95	22 Hornet; 222 Rem.; 30-30 Win.
Weatherby	. . .	Box	7½ lbs.	252.75	220 Swift; 257 Roberts; 270 Win.; 7mm Mauser; 30-06
Winchester	70	Box	8 lbs.	120.95	22 Hornet; 220 Swift; 257 Roberts; 270 Win.; 308 Win.; 30-06; 300 H & H Magnum; 375 H & H Magnum
Winchester	43	Box	6 lbs.	60.65	218 Bee; 22 Hornet

CENTER FIRE CARTRIDGES AND THE RIFLES FOR THEM

Name of Cartridge	Muzzle Energy in Foot-pounds	200-Yd. Energy in Foot-pounds	Rifle Made for It
375 H & H Magnum	4500 (270 gr.)	2970	Win. 70; Weatherby
300 H & H Magnum	3400 (180 gr.)	2380	Rem. 721; Win. 70, Weatherby
30-06	2910 (180 gr.)	2020	J. C. Higgins; Rem. 721; Rem. 740; Rem. 760; Win. 70; Weatherby
270 Winchester	2840 (130 gr.)	1920	J. C. Higgins; Rem. 721; Win. 70; Weatherby
308 Winchester	2720 (180 gr.)	1540	Winchester 70, 88
300 Savage	2240 (180 gr.)	1530	Rem. 722; Rem. 760; Savage 99
348 Winchester	2840 (200 gr.)	1470	Winchester 71
7mm Mauser	2410	1400	Weatherby
35 Remington	2170	1050	Marlin 336; Rem. 760
250 Savage	1770 (87 gr.)	1050	Savage 99
32 Win. Spl.	1960 (170 gr.)	1000	Win. 64; Win. 94
30-30 Win.	1860 (170 gr.)	1000	Marlin 336; Savage 340; Win. 64 & 94
257 Roberts	1820 (117 gr.)	985	Rem. 722, 760; Weatherby; Win 70
220 Swift	1800	915	Weatherby; Win. 70
351 Win. S.L.	1307	685	Winchester 07 Self-Loading
222 Remington	1140	520	J. C. H. 52, Marlin 322, Rem. 722; Savage 340
219 Zipper	1200	465	Marlin 336
218 Bee	835	265	Winchester 43
22 Hornet	720	130	Savage 322; Win. 70 & 43

Above—The next really big news in Winchester rifles came in 1954 with the adoption of the new Winchester 308 cartridge and a new Featherweight Model 70 rifle and GUN DIGEST celebrated that with a full page. Left—In a simpler time, 30 and more years ago, a little chart like this could show all the centerfire rifles and their cartridges.

New this year 222 Rem., also 308 Win.

REMINGTON MODEL 760-A GAMEMASTER. Slide action, hammerless, solid frame, side ejection. Rotary multiple-lug breech bolt locks into barrel. 22" barrel. Walnut pistol grip stock and forearm. Cross bolt safety. Bead front sight on matted ramp, open sporting rear sight. 4-shot detachable magazine. Weight 7½ lbs. Calibers: 244 Rem., 257, 270, 300 Sav., 30-06, 35 Rem. Price..$112.45

Sometimes GUN DIGEST just sneaked a little announcement into the catalog, as in 1958 when eight words told the world the Remington 760 rifle is now available in 22 Remington and 308 Winchester.

much as possible and still retain the same ballistics. It was found that ½-inch could be taken from the case length, with several resulting advantages. One was the fact that as stated above, the powder would burn more efficiently, and ballistics could be expected to be more uniform. Another was the fact that the shorter case made possible a shorter and lighter rifle. Still another is the saving in brass, which is a big item when billions of rounds of ammunition are used, as they are by the Army.

This new Army cartridge went through several different versions before the final shape and dimensions were arrived at, in the form of the T-65 case. Based on this case, the Army made several kinds of experimental complete rounds, designated as follows:

T-70	E4	Dummy Round
T-93	E1	Armor Piercing
T-101	E1	Armor Piercing Incendiary
T-102	E1	Tracer
T-103	E1	Spotting Cartridge
T-104	E1	Ball Cartridge (with soft steel core)
T-116	E2	Grenade Launching Cartridge

The progressive Winchester management, noting the good points of this new cartridge, asked permission of the Army to use the case as the basis of a hunting cartridge for their proposed Model 70 Featherweight, and the permission was granted. This is the origin of the 308 Winchester.

Before we go further, note one interesting point about this new cartridge; the fact that although it is called a 308, it is actually a 30 caliber, and uses the same bullets as former 30-caliber loads. If we don't watch these small points, it is very easy to become confused. In the good old days it was usual to name a bullet by the size of the bore before rifling. Thus a 30 caliber means that the bore of the gun is 30 hundredths of an inch in diameter; the rifling is usually about 4 thousandths of an inch deep, making the groove diameter .308 inch.

That system went along fine until the time came when some designer dreamed up a new cartridge or a new gun, and wanted to distinguish it from other cartridges or guns of the same caliber already in existence. The first step was usually to add another zero so that the new 25 became a 250, and the new 30 became a 300, and so on. This was the way the Savage 250-3000 and the 300 Savage were named. However, when another new and different 25 came along, the designer was stuck for a new name, so he called it the 257, naming it for the groove instead of the bore. Thus the '257 Roberts' is actually a 25.

For the same reason this new 30 caliber Winchester will be known as the 308, though it is really a 30.

The new Model 70 Featherweight has a 22-inch barrel, which helps lighten the gun. The cartridge is furnished with three bullet weights—180-grain Silvertip, with 2,610 f.p.s. muzzle velocity and 2,720 foot-pounds energy; 150-grain Silvertip, with 2,860 f.p.s. velocity and 2,730 foot-pounds energy; and 110-grain soft-point bullet, with 3,340 f.p.s. muzzle velocity and 2,730 foot-pounds energy.

This new gun and its cartridge have made a stir in the gun world, and are a fine addition to the Winchester line.

GUN DIGEST in the years that followed registered the changes in the Model 70 and in its cartridges. The listings are a chronicle of good and bad. The 458 Winchester Magnum cartridge made the Model as near the standard elephant rifle as any single firearm could be. The 264 Winchester Magnum and the 358 Winchester, however, petered out pretty quick. The 338 Winchester Magnum was another success; the 225 Winchester was another clunker.

Cartridges weren't the only changes in the Model 70. For 1964, nearly 30 years after its introduction, and about a half-century after the Model 70's technology was developed, the company changed things and hardly anyone liked it, including those who wrote in GUN DIGEST.

The "pre-'64" Model 70 is revered and high priced today. But the post-'64 Model 70 is still with us. There are, in 1987, eight versions, chambered for 14 cartridges at prices from $360 or so for the Ranger to over $800 for the Super Express Magnum model in 375 Holland & Holland Magnum or 458 Winchester Magnum. And these Model 70s are not made by Winchester, but by U.S. Repeating Arms Co., which is yet *another* story one could read from year to year in GUN DIGEST.

The catalog portion of GUN DIGEST is living history. It is prepared entirely by staff people in DBI headquarters, and the mechanics are somewhat interesting.

It really begins with the Directory of the Arms Trade, which is a small marvel all our own. To every name listed in the Directory of the Arms Trade, GUN DIGEST sends a first class letter early in the year. Those who do not answer after a short time receive another letter. Other follow-ups follow.

The formatting; the preparation of the written entries; the choice of illustrations—all the work that makes the catalog visibly what you see before you when you buy GUN DIGEST—is accomplished by Senior Staff Editor Harold A. Murtz. Of his annual chore, Murtz says, more or less fondly:

"Each year we do mailings similar to those for the Directory of the Arms—we ask for corrections to the previous listings, information about new product introductions and deletions of obsolete products, etc. What we show is the information we *have* received from the makers—as up-to-date as we can make it. If a product isn't in there, it is not for lack of trying.

"Putting together this huge catalog takes months of work each year, but it's gratifying to see the finished product because *I* know we've done the best job possible."

We show some samples here so you can see how it went. But then, of course, you are familiar with all that. You rely on it, right? So do we. It is probably true that the most-used reference for the editors of GUN DIGEST is GUN DIGEST.

That is not unusual. We must get 20 letters a year from executives in the firearms industry who take pains to point out that GUN DIGEST is the one book they keep handy and refer to constantly. We hope that's true for you, too, because that is why we do it.

SHOOTING EDITOR

by JACK O'CONNOR

There are many routes to a gun editorship—one of my colleagues was a cowboy, a forest service packer and a guide. Another was a former naval officer and later an ammunition company ballistician. A third was a Harvard graduate and a teacher in a boys' school. This is the rags to riches story of how I became one.

O'Connor wears this stern and noble look because he managed to make a pretty good running shot on this Coues whitetail (Arizona whitetail) in Sonora.

TO ANY WRITER the most fascinating subject in the world is himself—his glorious deeds, his wise and witty sayings, his triumphs and his defeats, even his corns, his back aches and his acid stomach.

This is a piece about me—or at least how I became a gun editor. I am doing this partly because writing about himself in one way or another is a good part of any writer's stock in trade, and partly because a great many young men would like nothing better than to get a job like the one I held on *Outdoor Life* for 31 years.

I haven't kept a record of the number of letters I have received from aspiring gun editors and outdoor writers, but in the years I was with *Outdoor Life* I am sure I received several thousands. I used to get at least 100 requests for such information a year and often I received several such queries in one week.

Many of the letters were from earnest and gifted young men who would probably become good outdoor journalists. Others were from unimaginative lads to whom the job simply looked like a very soft way to make a living. I got some letters that began: "Please tell me how you got your job, how much you make, how many hours a week you work, what vacations you get." Likewise, I get many letters from high school and college students wanting to know what courses to take in order to become gun editors.

There are plenty of routes to a gun editorship. One of my colleagues was a cowboy, a forest service packer, and a guide. I doubt if he finished high school. Another was a former naval officer with an Annapolis background who was for a time a ballistician for one of the big ammunition companies. Yet another was a Harvard graduate and a teacher in a boys' school.

Of the old time gun editors I read when I was growing up, one had been an advertising man, another an oil company executive, another an army officer. Still another was, I believe, a dog trainer and market hunter. Yet another was a sort of society play boy.

None of the practioners of the trade took college courses in gun editing and outdoor writing—such courses didn't exist then. Most of them simply happened to fall into their jobs. One gun editor I know had long been a fishing enthusiast, but was not particularly mad about either guns or hunting. He went to a magazine office, asked for a job as a fishing editor. He was hired as a gun editor instead, and since he is an intelligent and adaptable person, he speedily learned a great deal about guns.

Writing and editing a shooting department or any other department in an outdoor magazine is a branch of the very wide field of journalism—or "communications" as it now seems fashionable to call it. A good gun writer or, for that matter, any kind of writer in the outdoor field is primarily a journalist who knows a good deal about his specialty. But first and foremost, he is a *writer*.

Sports Specialists

The world is full of fine big-bore and small-bore target shots, crack Skeet and trap shots, expert big-game guides, champion bait-casters, erudite ballisticians, shrewed optical engineers. It is also full of excellent writers. But the world is not exactly full of people who know something about rifles and rifle shooting, shotguns, big game hunting, elementary optics, reloading and A.B.C. ballistics, and who can write about these things interestingly, entertainingly, and clearly.

Few genuine specialists in the sports world are able to write well about their specialties. Boxers, golf players, jockeys, baseball pitchers, professional halfbacks, are seldom articulate and the stuff that appears under their by-lines is generally written by ghosts—usually facile newspapermen trying to pick up an extra buck. One big league pitcher is a highly articulate person and an excellent writer, but he is regarded by his fellows as being exceedingly odd if not actually subversive.

Ballisticians, optical engineers, and biologists write for other optical engineers, ballisticians, and biologists. The stuff they turn out would bring the average reader down with chills and fever. If their stuff is presented to the public in understandable form, it generally must be put into English by a journalist.

In some ways, outdoor journalism differs from other forms of sports journalism. The average sports writer cannot throw a down-field block, hit big-league pitching, break 90 at golf, or last one round in the ring with even a third-rate welterweight.

But the outdoor journalist must be able to perform reasonably well and, if he can write, the more he knows about his field the better off he is. He can't tell others how to shoot unless he knows how to shoot himself, how to outwit a whitetail buck unless he has hunted whitetail long and intelligently, how to load ammunition or sight in a rifle unless he himself has worked out the angles. Most outdoor writers are reasonably good at what they write about. If they were not they wouldn't last—their stuff is read by a highly critical, often very well informed, audience of enthusiasts.

But even more than the ability to write, even more than knowledge of the subject, the important thing is enthusiasm. The longer I write, the more convinced I am that no amount of writing skill or knowledge of a subject can make up for a lack of enthusiasm. No man can do well with a subject that bores him, and any writer is most successful when he writes about something about which he feels deeply.

Many people have a great deal of enthusiasm for guns, for hunting, and for fishing, but are they writers? I would say that if a young man has reached the age of 21 and has never written anything he did not have to write, he is probably not an instinctive writer. The man whom God intended to write plays with words as naturally as a Brittany spaniel or a setter points birds or a hound follows a trail. I have a daughter who, I believe, will eventually be a professional writer. When she was 10, she wrote and illustrated a "novel" about a horse and a little girl who by some odd coincidence was also 10 years old.

But first, let us see how I got into this business of being what used to be called gun editor or arms and ammunition editor, but which is now generally called shooting editor.

Early Days in the West

I can hardly remember when I was not a gun nut. I probably became one because I grew up in an atmosphere of guns. My maternal grandfather, who had come west from Kentucky in the 1870s was a big-game hunter, a bird shot, and something of a gun nut himself. When he started a cattle ranch in the Rocky Mountains along the New Mexico-Colorado border, he hunted bighorn sheep, mule deer, black bear, mountain lions, and grizzlies. When he moved to Arizona, he hunted desert bighorn sheep in the mountains around the Salt River Valley and mule deer out on the flats. He was a passion-

O'Connor with a 60-inch greater Kudu shot in Mozambique in 1959 with a 30-06.

O'Connor with urial ram (Iran, 1958).

ate bird hunter, shooting whitewing and mourning doves and Gambel quail. As I've said, he was also something of a gun nut—meaning that he really had more firearms than he had use for. I can remember that he had an old Model 1876 Winchester for some now-obsolete black powder cartridge, a Model 1886 for the 45-70, and a Model 94 Winchester in 30-30. But in his declining years James Wiley Woolf, my grandfather, was more of a shotgun nut than a rifle nut. He had a Parker of good grade, an Ithaca, and a Purdey with two sets of barrels in a fitted oak-and-leather case lined with billiard cloth. All his guns were 12 gauge. He looked upon 20 and 16 gauge guns as playthings for women and children and weaklings, and on pumps and automatics as inventions of the Devil.

My uncle Bill Woolf, his son, was a crack rifle shot and a fine shotgun handler. He competed at Camp Perry. Another uncle is reputed to have awakened one morning to see a desert bighorn ram staring at him from a rocky hillside a couple of hundred yards away. He rolled over in his bedroll, grabbed a 30-30 and bumped the ram off. Another uncle told me in later years that when he'd had a ranch in Nevada he used to shoot desert rams with a 30 caliber Luger pistol. There were a good many sheep in the Southwest in those early days.

Yet another gun nut uncle was from the Irish side—Jim O'Connor, a lawyer, superior court judge and rancher. He owned a whole flock of rifles and shotguns including a Model 92 Winchester 25-20 with which I shot my first coyote, and a 10 gauge Model 1910 Winchester lever action shotgun that I used to sneak out and shoot.

If I had not been allowed to acquire the air rifle I wanted when I was 5 years old, I may not have turned out to be a gun nut. But at that time, my mother was pretty sour on guns. She had just divorced my father and one of the things she held against him was that he was a sucker for good guns and fine watches and he had been known to come home without his pay check but with a new top-grade Uncle Dan Lefever shotgun or a watch that had a filigreed solid gold case, struck the hours, and could even be set to go off like an alarm clock. My good mother was convinced the my precocious interest in air guns was proof that, unless she watched me, I was destined to go waltzing down the primrose path just like my old man. I would have, she thought, a rifle in one hand, a shotgun in the other, a $200 watch in my pocket, but not a dime in cash to my name. She told me that it would be over her dead body if I ever got that air rifle.

But I fooled her. Later on I sold copies of a wild newspaper full of murder, jewel robbery, rape and assorted chicanery called (if my memory serves me correctly) *The Chicago Blade and Sunday Ledger*. I peddled it in Tempe's two saloons, in the pool halls, to my mother's friends, and in what I now know was a house of ill fame in Mexican Town. I got the air gun. It was a break open single shot. It retailed for $1.50. It cocked by breaking and I loaded one BB at the muzzle. With it I shot black birds, sparrows, spun clothespins on my mother's clothes line, and I also shot some of my pals in their derrieres.

Starting at the age of 5, I went along with my Grandfather Woolf to shag birds and when I was 8, he bought me a 20-gauge Iver Johnson single shot. Later I got a Marlin 22 pump. I shot my first deer with a 30-40 Krag army rifle that I bought for $1.50 from a bindle stiff who had a camp down in the river bed. He was at the time in grave need of a quart of sour-mash bourbon.

My grandfather was a devoted reader of *Outdoor Recreation, Field & Stream, Outdoor Life,* and *Hunter, Trader, & Trapper*. So was I. I sent off for gun catalogs of European importers and American manufacturers. I read all the stories of hunting bighorn sheep and elk in Wyoming, Dall sheep and grizzly bears in the Yukon, giant moose and brown bears in Alaska, Stone sheep and caribou in the Cassiar section of British Columbia. I saw the African movies of Paul J. Rainey and read about Teddy Roosevelt's heroic feats in British East Africa.

I also read the early stuff of Capt. E. C. "Ned" Crossman, Col. (then lieutenant) Townsend Whelen, Charles Askins Sr., and Chauncey Thomas. I longed to own a Model 1910 Ross straight-pull rifle or a Newton. Later, by heroic toil and spartan savings, I acquired enough money to buy a deluxe grade 256 Newton. This, I believe, was in 1916, when I was 14. Those were the days when a dollar was a dollar—and mighty hard to come by, I might add. My Newton cost me either

$40 or $45, if I remember correctly. It had a little engraving, a Lyman 1-A cocking piece rear sight, a stock with cheekpiece which was supposed to be made of French walnut. I also bought 100 rounds of ammunition at a cost of about $6. My mother was absolutely certain that I had lost my marbles.

I shot a couple of mule deer and a javelina with the 256. I sold it at a time when I could get no more ammunition and when I was also broke. I hunted later with a remodeled Springfield 30-06, with a Model 95 Winchester lever action in 30-06, with a Model 8 Remington auto in 35 Remington caliber that I bought for $5. Its sheepherder owner had inlaid about 65 coins in the stock. He had hocked it for $5 in Holbrook, Arizona.

I went to college, worked on newspapers, did P.R. work, got a master's degree, fell in love with a cute little broad, married her, got a job teaching and doing publicity at a college in Texas. At the time, I had a Winchester Model 54 in 270, a 12 gauge Winchester Model 12 shotgun with a 30-inch full choke barrel. I got my bride a Model 30 Remington bolt-action rifle in 25 Remington rimless caliber and an Ithaca 20-gauge shotgun. Between us we had a Winchester Model 75 bolt-action 22.

The Writing Begins

I tried my hand at a few short stories and sold most of them. I wrote a novel called *Conquest* and it was accepted by Harpers about the time of the 1929 stock market crash. It came out a year later. It created something of a scandal there in Texas because in it one of the characters called another a son of a bitch. At that time down in Texas the phrase son of a bitch was very useful. It could be used as a pronoun as in "I told the SOB (for him) what he could do with it", or "Don't bother me. Just put the SOB (for it) on the table and get the hell out of here." You could even use it as part of an adverbial phrase as in "as cold as a son of a bitch." But, by golly, you couldn't write it without getting your tail in a crack. I didn't exactly get fired because of that word in the novel, but I beat them to the draw and resigned.

At 29, I had a wife, a baby, a few hundred dollars and a 1929 Chevrolet coupe. No job. The Depression had really struck in the East in 1931, but conditions were not quite so desperate in the West. I returned to my home state of Arizona and luckily managed to get a job teaching and doing publicity at what is now called Northern Arizona University at Flagstaff.

I could hunt mule deer and wild turkey within a few miles of town, shoot quail in the Verde Valley an hour and a half away. My salary was $2,500 a year, and even in those days that was poor pickings. I got a check for a few hundred dollars for English and American royalties on my novel. A bank failure gobbled it up. At the end of my first year at Flagstaff I, along with the other members of the faculty, got a 10 per cent salary cut, and at the end of my second year, I got another 10 per cent cut. The state couldn't collect its taxes and instead of cash we state employees got warrants. Magazines were not buying fiction. All of them were almost broke and were living on the stuff they had bought previously.

The O'Connors were pretty hard up for cash. What to do? Since I had been a hunter and a gun nut all my life, I decided to try my hand at the outdoor field. I wrote a piece called "Rifles & Cartridges for Southwestern Game." Turned down by *The American Rifleman,* it was bought by *Sports Afield.* I wrote a piece on mule deer and sent it to *Field & Stream.* Ray P. Holland, then editor, liked it, bought it, sent me a check for $50. The check was printed on buff-colored paper and had a wild duck on it. Ah, a lovely thing! In those days, 50 bucks was like 500 today. I was launched in a new and supplementary career. By today's standards, the checks I got were not big, but they enabled me to balance the budget and to buy a new rifle now and then.

I wrote for *National Sportsman* and *Hunting and Fishing* as well as for *Sports Afield, Field & Stream,* and *Outdoor Life.* Popular Science Publishing Company then bought *Outdoor Life* and the new editor, Ray Brown, encouraged me to write some gun stuff for the front of the magazine.

The Old Magazines

Today it is hard to turn around without falling over a magazine that publishes articles about guns and shooting, but in those days such magazines were scarce. Capt. Paul Curtis was the gun editor of *Field & Stream.* For a time, Major Charles Askins (father of Col. Charles Askins Jr.) and Col. Townsend Whelen wrote shotgun and rifle stuff for *Outdoor Life.* Capt. E. C. "Ned" Crossman was freelancing when I first got into the business, but sometime in the 1930s he was hired to do gun departments in *Hunting & Fishing* and *National Sportsman.* Both magazines are now unhappily defunct, largely because the publisher could never convince himself that he ought to pay anything more than a pittance for contributions. I sold a few pieces to Bill Foster, the editor and, incidentally, the guy who invented Skeet, for $35. Then he sent me a check for $15 for a piece. I sent the check back to Foster and told him to return the manuscript. He did so and explained that the owners of the magazine had told him he could pay no more than 15 bucks for anything. Eventually, the two magazines bought

O'Connor (right) and his son Bradford, with trophies taken by their party in northern British Columbia in 1967.

no material at all. Instead, they simply published letters from readers. When they were in their death throes, they were dreadful to contemplate.

Back in the 1930s, Russell Annabel, who was and is a very good writer, was getting some of those little checks. Archibald Rutledge killed a monster South Carolina buck or a wild turkey regularly in *Field & Stream.* Askins and Whelen both wrote regularly for the *American Rifleman.* Bob Nichols replaced Capt. Paul Curtis as gun editor of *Field & Stream.* Monroe Goode edited a very interesting shooting department for *Sports Afield.* Elmer Keith was writing for the *Rifleman* and now and then he had a piece in *Outdoor Life.*

By 1934, I was to some extent getting established as an outdoor writer. *Field & Stream* was putting my name on the cover and had raised my remuneration to $75 a story. The market for short stories had opened up and I was peddling one now and then.

Hundreds of people have written me asking how to get a story in an outdoor magazine. The only way I know of is to write the tale up and send it to the editor with suitable pictures. It helps if the story is neatly typed, the sentences make sense, and the pictures are good. Most magazines have a story read by about three sub-editors. These write reports on each manuscript. If the verdict is unfavorable, the story is returned. If the sub-editors like the yarn, it goes to the editor's desk. He either buys it or turns it down.

O'Connor (right) with his last ram, a Stone shot in northern B.C. in 1973.

Selling a Story

An editor turns down a manuscript for various reasons: (1) It isn't any good. (2) He has bought something too much like it. (3) He is running out of budget money and he would have to hold the script too long before he published it. (4) Or he is hung over and feels like hell.

If, on the other hand, the editor buys it, the reason may be that (1) it is a good story and he likes it, (2) that he is short of whitetail stories and this will fit in, (3) he hopes to encourage the writer, (4) the story stinks but the writer has a following, (5) the story stinks but the poor bastard who wrote it needs the money.

In the fall of 1934, I went to the University of Arizona as professor of journalism and promptly incurred the enmity of my immediate superior when he found that I had got the then fabulous sum of $750 for a short story that came out about that time in what was then known as a Big Slick.

At the same time, I was doing a lot of hunting in Mexico, working on a novel and balancing the budget by writing outdoor stuff. In 1936, I got a proposition to write for no other outdoor magazine except *Outdoor Life.* I accepted it. That same year, Townsend Whelen resigned as rifle editor for *Outdoor Life* and Ned Crossman was hired to take his place. By this time I had written perhaps a dozen gun and shooting articles for the front section of *Outdoor Life.* Then, in 1939, Ned Crossman committed suicide. Ray Brown put me in his place as a columnist and in 1941, he promoted me to Arms & Ammunition Editor, as the job was then called, and Major Charles Askins Sr. went to *Sports Afield.*

The Hardy Perennials

I once told an aspiring outdoor writer that I had told all I knew in my first four or five articles as a gun columnist and had been repeating myself ever since. That was jest to some extent, but the number of suitable shooting department subjects is limited. Perennial subjects include: How to Sight in a Rifle, Cartridges for Whitetails, What Choke in a Shotgun Is, How to Lead Birds and Clay Targets. All of these subjects are old and all the gun writer can do is to dish them up in a frisky and ingratiating manner. He should attempt to write so he can be understood by those who are just beginning and know little and entertain those who know as much or more than he does. I have probably written How to Sight in a Rifle a dozen times. The gun editor should not forget that he writes for an ever-changing audience. Old readers die off or quit. New ones come in!

Bill Rae, the former editor of *Outdoor Life,* and I were having lunch not long ago, and Bill commented that he had been the editor of an outdoor magazine for 20 years and that there were fewer good outdoor writers now than there were when he got into the business. I am inclined to agree with him. For that reason of little competition and many magazines, I think it is even easier to break into the field now than when I was starting out.

I read the young gun editors with considerable interest. Some, alas, can't write their way out of a paper bag. Others have had almost no experience, don't know much, and try to cover their ignorance with bluff and baloney. But now and then I bump into the writings of some youngster who can write, who knows something, and who can communicate his experience.

Such a lad can go a long way and lead a good life if he works hard and is smart. He should curb his natural tendency to larceny and fat headedness, be honest with himself, remember that he is working for the magazine and only incidentally for himself. If he does all this, he may pick up some extra bread by writing books. He will be able to charge the hunts that produce his copy off on his income tax. Men will admire him and beautiful maidens will warm him with their smiles. It's a good life for the industrious and gifted. ●

My Triumphs In
GUN COLLECTING

The fun, the furor and the fantastic deals of 40 years.

by JOHN T. AMBER

PHOTOS: ROBERT S. L. ANDERSON

IMMEDIATELY after World War II, when Marshall Field & Company marketed antique and collectors' firearms—1944-1946—a woman came up to me one day and spoke about a large lot of 45-70 Springfield rifles she controlled. These 750-plus single shot military rifles, Models 1873 and later, were in storage at the Navy's Great Lakes Training Station, north of Chicago.

When the war broke out, she told me, the National 4-H Clubs, anxious to do their bit, had obtained these rifles from the Minnesota National Guard and delivered them to Great Lakes. Intended to supplant more modern rifles for sentry duties there, the 45-70s had not been used. The Navy wanted to get rid of them, and had asked the 4-H Club to remove them. "Would the Gun Shop," she asked, "be interested in buying them?" Thinking quickly about the amount of money that would be tied up if we bought them, and of how long it might take to sell them, I told the woman we would prefer to handle them on consignment. She agreed.

A week or so later we received the first shipment, some 200 45-70 rifles and their accoutrements. All, surprisingly, were in very good to excellent condition (most had never been fired, I was sure). The next Friday we ran a small illustrated ad in the Chicago *Daily News,* now defunct. Reaching a price had been difficult—we had no previous experience to go on, and some 750 rifles was a lot! We wanted to sell them quickly, if we could, so I set a price of $5.00 or $7.50 per rifle, including bayonet and scabbard, cartridge belt (blue-colored Mills web), sling strap and 25 rounds of blank cartridges—those were among the Great Lakes shipment, too.

We were not open on Saturday, but on Monday morning all hell broke loose. Hundreds of people, mostly men, were jammed against our street level doors, clamoring to get in, jostling for position. Our ad had not mentioned how many we had. Once the doors opened, our 5th floor was soon overflowing with customers for the 45-70 rifles. Men were packed 6 and 7 deep along our long counters, money waving in their hands, shouting to be waited on. I was aghast, as were my several fellow salesmen, not to mention the bevy of executives who had come over from their main store offices to investigate the near-riot.

I was severely criticized by the brass, but I wasn't taking any of that. Sure, we were faced with an unruly mob, but the sale was a success, a hell of a success. Gradually a semblance of order was achieved, and we moved out all the 200-odd rifles on hand. Advance orders were taken, pending delivery of the rest from Great Lakes. By the end of the day we had all but sold the entire lot, and the next morning saw those disposed of.

In the days and weeks following, mail orders for the 45-70s came in from all over the country, but the rifles were gone. The store returned checks to over 600 would-be buyers, so I'm certain we could have easily sold 1500 rifles had they been available.

Amber and Ken Warner with an unbelievable gun: A three-barrel Lefever with the rifle barrel on top.

Perhaps the gun which comes closest to pleasing Amber most is his accidentally gold-inlaid Billinghurst buggy rifle.

I was kidded about that inept pricing job for a long time, but we had had a *sale!* I wonder—could we have got $10 and $15?

During the mid-1940s I managed Field's antique arms section, a part of their famed Gun Shop. Later on, a well-dressed man, 40 years old or so, approached me. Opening a large briefcase, he produced a pair of flintlock pistols, the like of which I'd never handled before, though I'd seen the type at the Metropolitan Museum in New York, and pictured in auction catalogs. What could I tell him about them—their origin, their current value?

Obviously of the late Renaissance period, these pistols were deeply carved—not engraved as such—in the rococo style typical of their time. Each had several grotesque masks (heads of gargoyles and other monsters), and the general theme was one of monkeys—another sign of their period. The metal was generally black or nearly so. They had never been cleaned, I felt—the chiseling was so sharp that an unwary grasping of them could cut the thumb. The barrels were Spanish, each showing the sunken mark in gold of Nicolas Bis, royal gunmaker to the Spanish court in 1690-1710 or so. Spanish barrels were famed for their quality at that period, so their use was not amiss on these Italinate pistols. In addition, both barrels carried the engraved symbols of two noble orders—the Knights of Malta and the Order of the Golden Fleece.

Gently removing one of the lockplates, I read inside the name: Pietro Manani. I knew something of that name; a superb craftsman, by all accounts, but relatively unknown and uncollected, perhaps because his output was limited. I told the gentleman before me most of what I've just put down here. He was, he told me, an ex-colonel of artillery, and he'd "found" the pistols in Europe during the late war. Were they for sale, I asked. No, not just now, he said—he might call me later. Reluctantly I handed the pistols to him; I'd never held such magnificent quality before. They were gone forever, I feared.

Some 18 months later the red-legged colonel called me. Did I remember him and did I still want the Manani pistols? I did—I'd thought about them endlessly. After a brief bit of haggling, I bought them. I won't say what the cost was, but it was more by far than I'd ever paid before. They remain my most valuable flintlocks, monetarily and otherwise.

Dr. Prentice D. Cheney, long since dead, was a charming and affable gentleman, a native of Jerseyville, Ill. Doc was, rumor had it, a devotee of John Barleycorn—his periodical benders, some lasting for weeks, it was said, were legend. We were long-time friends, if only casually so, and fellow members of the Ohio Gun Collectors

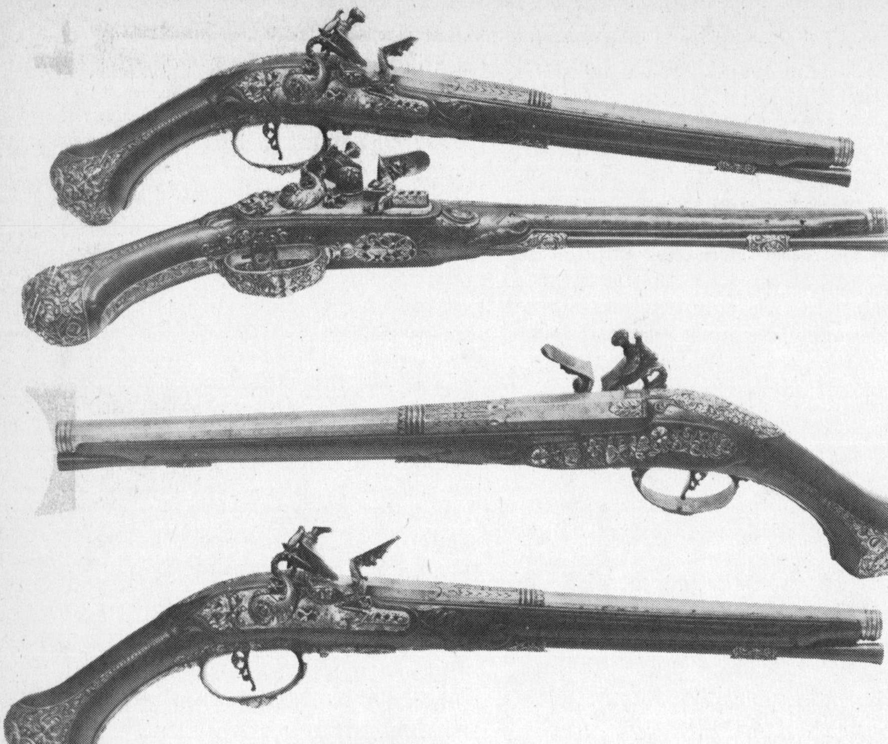

Pietro Manani made these pistols, most likely in Italy, and owning them has been a triumph, Amber thinks.

They are 17th Century, with barrels by Nicolas Bis, Spanish royal gunmaker. Everything about them, and especially their condition bespeaks the collector's joy. Noteworthy: the monkey motif, the grotesque faces, the engraved orders of noble groups, the deep rococo metal carving, and, beyond these, something you can discover only by handling the guns —they point very well.

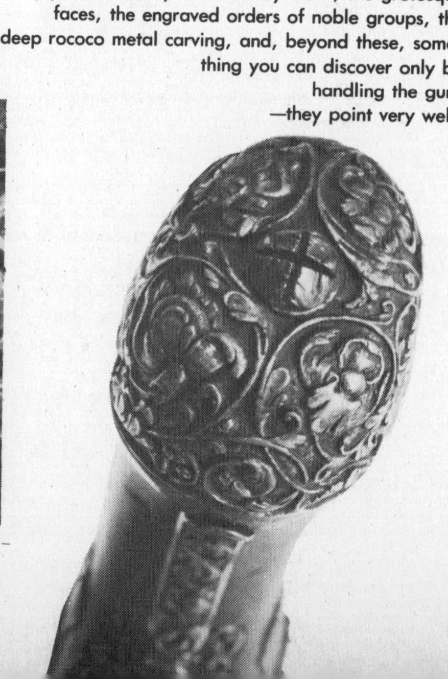

Assn. Doc's collecting aims were catholic—no specialist whatever, he bought or traded for anything, as long as the guns were in mint condition, or nearly so, and of the very best quality.

One Friday night, in the mid-1950s, I went to a weekend OGCA meeting at Columbus, Ohio. Walking into the hotel's coffee shop on Saturday morning, there sat the amiable Dr. Cheney, across from him his latest wife—his third or fourth, I'd heard. It was also being bruited about that Doc was in need of cash—he spent money wildly when in his cups, and he was, reportedly, paying stiff alimony to his earlier wives.

Doc asked me to sit down. He then told me—confirming the current gossip—that he was going to sell "a lot of guns" that weekend, among them his Gatling gun. I hadn't known he owned one. That sparked a memory, for I'd long wanted to have a Gatling, though it wasn't a high-priority desire.

A year or so before I'd been one of a party of eight or nine hunters at a Maine camp. Among the gang was Herb Glass, then and now a well-known dealer in collectors arms. One evening during that hardly-successful whitetail hunt, Glass revealed that he had been quietly gathering together an array of Gatling guns. (All of us were in the gun world, one way or other—a younger Bill Ruger was there, Mike Walker of Remington, Warren Page, Harry Sefried, a Ruger designer, so gun talk was natural if not mandatory—after or before girls and fast cars I'm not sure.)

Glass had now, he told us, some 25 Gatlings stashed away. The late Lucian Cary, he said, had written a story on Gatlings that would soon appear in *True* magazine—which it did. I asked Herb if, in that many Gatlings, did he have duplicate models? Sure, he said, he'd several such on hand. Would he sell me one, I wanted to know? No way, he replied—the Cary piece would quickly elevate Gatling prices and he was going to cash in grandly. Gatlings, it was true, had not been widely traded, scarcity alone preventing that. There was, therefore, little solid price information available on them—they were, at that time, an unknown quantity.

All right, I said, you greedy S.O.B., or words to that effect, and I put Gatling guns out of my mind.

"Doc," I said, just as he rose to go upstairs, "how about giving me first refusal on the Gatling?"

"Of course," he told me, as I sat on and waited for my breakfast, "and I'll

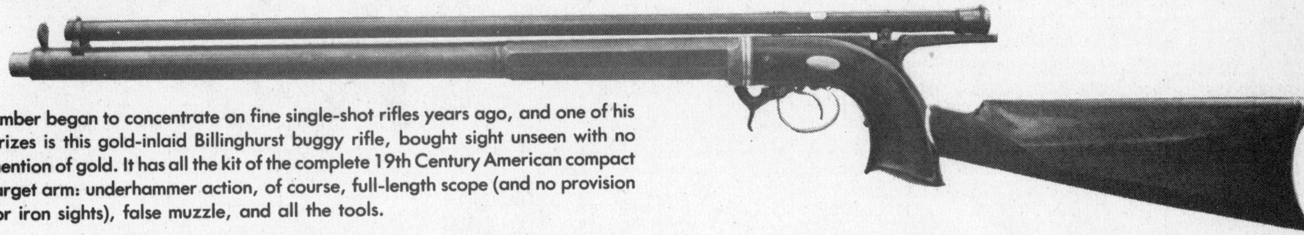

Amber began to concentrate on fine single-shot rifles years ago, and one of his prizes is this gold-inlaid Billinghurst buggy rifle, bought sight unseen with no mention of gold. It has all the kit of the complete 19th Century American compact target arm: underhammer action, of course, full-length scope (and no provision for iron sights), false muzzle, and all the tools.

Under the oaks at Creedmoor Farm, Amber can't help grinning over owning what is probably his favorite—an unexpected triumph.

The Billinghurst false muzzle slides satisfyingly into place on its four pins. Note the blinder that blocks the scope view to ensure the muzzle is not shot off the gun by any aimed shot.

Packed in the case when Amber got the Billinghurst were bullets and patches and wound cotton cleaning bobs.

The 45-caliber arch punch in the Gibbs' kit is marked with Japanese ideograms. As can be seen, it is in new condition.

(Top) Regally gloating over a regal rifle, Amber handles what he regards as one of the pinnacles of the art of the long-range target rifle, his Gibbs Farquharson apparently built for or presented to the royal family of Japan 100 or more years ago. It is also shown above as it arrived, full-length in a case.

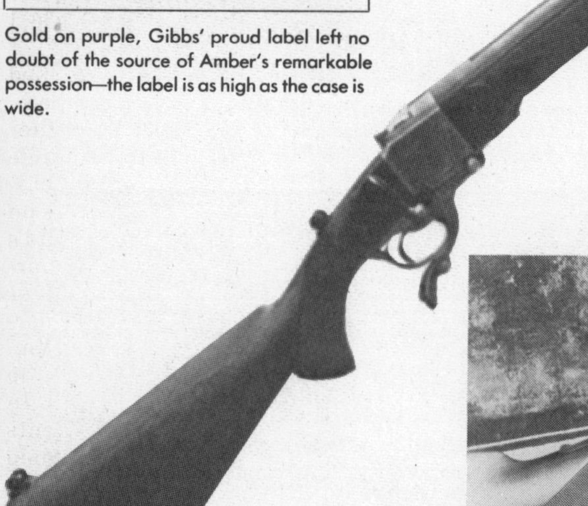

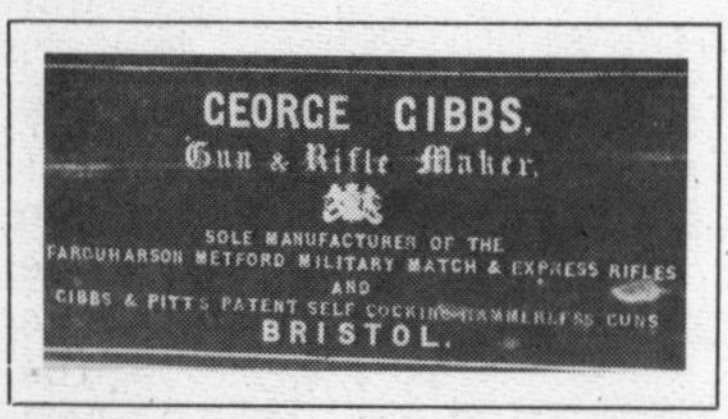

Gold on purple, Gibbs' proud label left no doubt of the source of Amber's remarkable possession—the label is as high as the case is wide.

Gibbs is fitted for the several sorts of sighting favored at long range, including this vernier heel sight for the supine position.

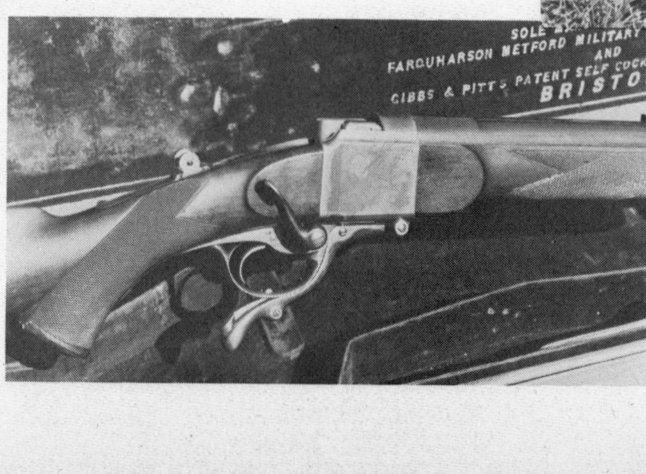

To add to Amber's joy, this Japanese Gibbs is a scarce version of the Farquharson action, the type with a separate side-cocking lever. Note the anchor for a tang sight.

see you later."

I walked into the display room, filled with gun-loaded tables already. Doc Cheney stood behind two tables, reaching down into assorted bags and cartons for the guns he'd brought to the show. Behind him stood the Gatling gun on its brass-and-steel tripod, the brass sleeve over its 6 barrels gleaming. Atop the breech was an 1883-patent Accles cartridge drum, its all-brass exterior also glowing warmly. I'd seen a photograph, I recalled, of a like small Gatling gun in Chinn's* book on machineguns—was this the same type? Inspection showed the typical "Colt Pat. F.A. Mfg. Co." marking, hand engraved in big bold letters, and—a thrilling shock— "No. 1" in equally big size.

Hurriedly, I tried to gain Doc's attention, tapping him on the back as he talked and bargained with the large group crowded in front of his tables—now loaded with guns.

He turned to me at last and I said "Doc, the Gatling—how much?"

He hesitated for a moment or two, then said "I've got to have $400 or I'll take it home."

At that very moment I could see Herb Glass approaching Doc's display, so I had to act *now*—yet I didn't know whether I was getting a bargain—"stealing it," as the jargon has it, or paying 'way too much.

"Doc," I said, folly or not, "you've just sold your Gatling. I'll give you a check later."

At that moment Glass had reached the edges of the crowd standing before Cheney. He stood on tiptoe, pointed at the small 45-70 caliber Gatling, and pantomimed "Mine," pointing at himself.

O frabjous day! Making no effort to conceal my glee and malice, I thumbed my nose at old friend Herb and silently mouthed "No, mine."

Herb Glass followed me all over the show floor that memorable weekend, cajoling me, pleading with me to sell him the Gatling. I think tears came to his eyes once—crocodile, of course.

"No," I said repeatedly, "I won't sell it to you," even though by this time he had raised his offer to well over my cost.

I was adamant Amber now, and I reminded Herb of our talk in Maine and his smug refusal to sell me a Gatling, even a fairly common 10-barrel Army type. I'm afraid I was a little sadistic. I hope so.

Giving Doc Cheney my $400 check later, I had a small but pleasurable shock. "John," he said, thanking me for the money, "I'll send the other 5 magazines to you later."

Harvey Brandt wrote about this baby Gatling and its shooting in the 1958/12th edition of GUN DIGEST, pages 20-29.

One of the most interesting and valuable pieces in my collection is the type commonly called, for some obscure reason, a buggy rifle. These are quite short-barreled (10 inches to 14 inches or so) "rifles," usually with detachable buttstocks. They often look like long-barreled pistols, and they're usually found cased, with an array of loading tools, sometimes with false-muzzled barrels. Calibers were, for their day—the 1850s-1870s—small; 30 or 32 caliber is a common size. They're caplock muzzleloaders, of course.

Mine is by Wm. Billinghurst of Rochester, New York, better known for his heavy-barreled match rifles, one of which I also have in "picket ball" form—conical lead bullets with no cylindrical section—with which I won several matches or was well-placed in them.

Billinghurst was partial to the understriker ignition system, which he pioneered, and justly so. Many modern made slug rifles used in the stiffest competitions use the same system—the trigger guard acts as main spring and sear, driving the hammer against the underside nipple of these front-loading rifles. The train of fire, obviously, runs directly and straight to the main charge of black powder.

Shortly after Marshall Field & Co. closed out the antique arms section I got a phone call from a man in Virginia. He had seen one of our brochures, in which were listed several cased sets of English duelling flintlock pistols. They were priced at about $250-$350, I recall, and my caller wanted to know if I would trade him a set for what he offered, a buggy rifle. I explained that all such sets had been sold, and that his buggy rifle—which I assumed to be the common, average type, then selling for $100 or so—could hardly be traded even for a pair of flint duellers in case.

What I'd said was true, he agreed, but he thought he might achieve his desire at less than the figures I'd cited. Well, I said, why not try that, and if he'd put a price on the Billinghurst pistol, I might buy it—I explained that rifled arms of any type interested me. "Give me $150, and it's yours," he told me.

Some two weeks later, after some correspondence between us, the heavy carton reached me. There, lying in its beautifully-figured rosewood veneer case, lay a buggy rifle the likes of which I'd never seen, never dreamed of, and in virtually new condition. This Billinghurst had to be truly unique, I felt.

Reverently picking up the pistol-gripped rifle, I started counting the several gold inlays and appliques—one lay athwart the full-length telescope sight, reading MALCOLM; two were let into the sides of the pistol grip and another—reading RAWSON—was on the S-curved bottom of the grip. Two gold bands lay around the barrel breech and, of all places, the top of the false muzzle carried a section of gold a sixteenth-inch thick! To ward off rust, I'd guess. The buttstock, of fancy reddish English walnut (as is the hand grip) is holed for a through-bolt, used to fit the butt to the rear of the grip. Yet another gold band surrounds the area of the joint.

Not *once,* during our phone talk or in his letters, did my Virginian mention the gold inlays—perhaps he thought they were all made that way. I was tempted to send him a few hundred more dollars, Confederate money, that is.

Postscript: I've said that I deemed this superb Billinghurst unique. A few years later I saw another Billinghurst buggy rifle almost identical with mine. Not a duplicate, but one of the same high quality with, again, numerous gold inlays.

The 1951 Meeting of the NRA was held in San Francisco. GUN DIGEST had a booth there and I went out to manage it. One day Elmer Keith came by, carrying a long-barreled rifle to show me. We were very busy at the time, and, hardly looking at the rifle, I told Elmer I'd see him later.

The next day, during a lull, I walked over to where it was displayed. There, now lying in its long oak-and-leather case, was a magnificent long range target rifle, with "George Gibbs, Bristol," emblazoned in big gold letters on the purple velvet covering the lid's interior. The action was a Farquharson of scarce form, a *cocking* lever along the side in addition to the normal underlever. The barrel, of Wm. Metford's patented design, was 36 inches long, its rich blue flawless. In fact, the rifle and the case's contents were in new condition. Two domed leather boxes held the sights—short and long Vernier tangs, an even 20 front sight apertures, etc. A false muzzle, which at the time I'd never seen before, was among the tools. Among

*Col. G.M. Chinn, *The Machine Gun* Vol. 1. (Washington, D.C. 1951).

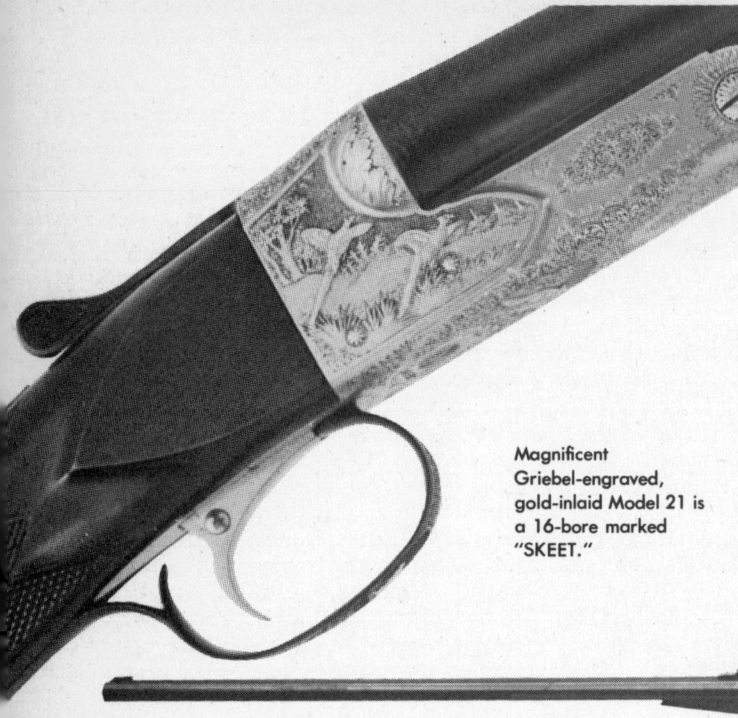

Magnificent Griebel-engraved, gold-inlaid Model 21 is a 16-bore marked "SKEET."

Amber explains on oval-bored nitro-proved Lancaster double rifle's working to colleague Harold Murtz.

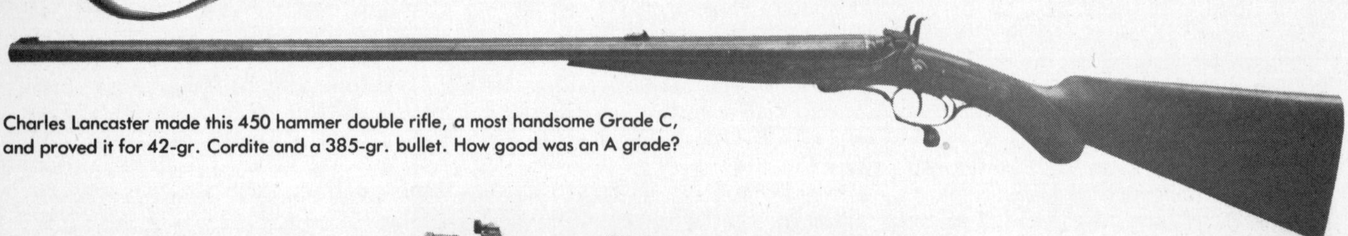

Charles Lancaster made this 450 hammer double rifle, a most handsome Grade C, and proved it for 42-gr. Cordite and a 385-gr. bullet. How good was an A grade?

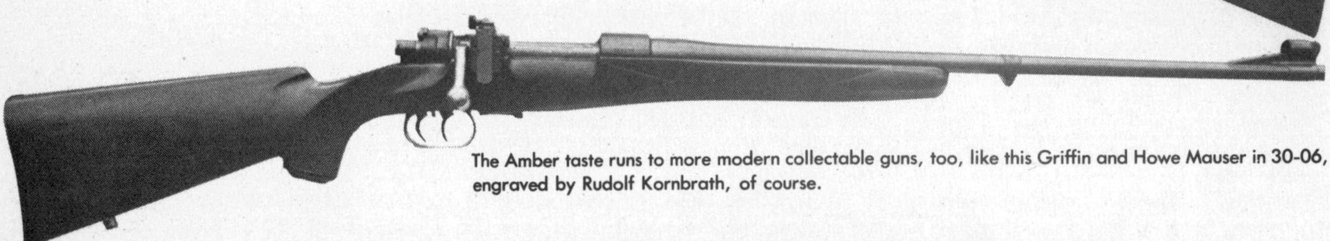

The Amber taste runs to more modern collectable guns, too, like this Griffin and Howe Mauser in 30-06, engraved by Rudolf Kornbrath, of course.

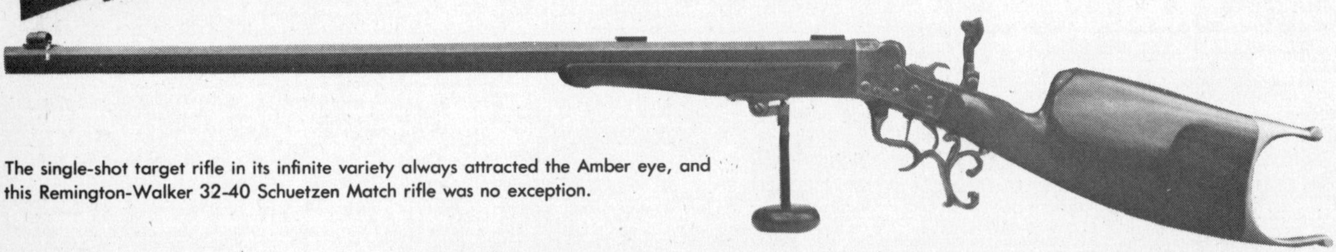

The single-shot target rifle in its infinite variety always attracted the Amber eye, and this Remington-Walker 32-40 Schuetzen Match rifle was no exception.

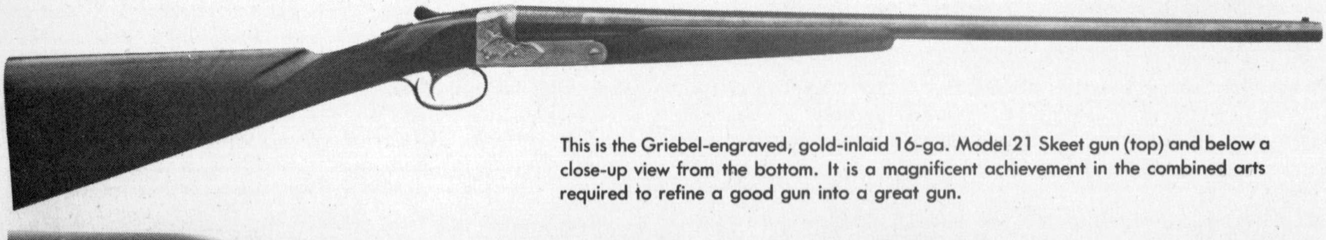

This is the Griebel-engraved, gold-inlaid 16-ga. Model 21 Skeet gun (top) and below a close-up view from the bottom. It is a magnificent achievement in the combined arts required to refine a good gun into a great gun.

these was an arch punch in 45 caliber, marked on both sides of its shank in Japanese ideographs.

The owner, one Capt. G., told me he had bought the outfit in Tokyo at the end of the war. He'd take the highest offer bid on it during the show—if sufficient. I wouldn't do that, I said, but if he would get in touch with me after the meeting I thought I might be able to top his best offer. I knew that all too frequently such bidding was used by the owner to successively raise each bidder's price.

I left for home, worried about who would get the rifle, convinced that I'd never hear from Capt. G. Elmer Keith, of course, was well known as a single shot rifle collector/shooter.

But my guardian angel prevailed. About a month later Capt. G called me, and I bought the Gibbs-Farquharson-Metford rifle. Sure, I had to beat what he said was a firm, legitimate offer, but I've never regretted it.

Today, almost 30 years later, this remarkable rifle and its many fittings is, arguably, the best single shot rifle I own, perhaps the most valuable. A translation of the archaic Japanese characters reads, roughly: Corridor 3, Number XX of the Royal Household. I wrote about this rifle at length in the GUN DIGEST for 1954/12th ed., the story called "Tokyo Treasure."

Our 25th/1971 edition of the GUN DIGEST carried a splendid story by John T. Dutcher called "George Schoyen—Riflemaker Extraordinary." No one better deserved that praise; his barrels were the prime choice of numerous top level marksmen.

A few years before the article appeared I had received a letter from a man in Iowa. He had, he said, a muzzle-loading Schoyen rifle, caliber about 30—small indeed for a front loader. I was highly skeptical—Schoyen was known for metallic cartridge barrels, 32-40, 38-55 and the like. No, said the Iowan, the barrel was clearly marked Schoyen and it was indeed a muzzleloader. After a few phone talks and a couple of letters, the rifle was shipped to me. There, in a roughly-made but old pine case, was a profusely engraved, gold-inlaid Schuetzen rifle in excellent condition. As with the Billinghurst gold-embellished buggy rifle described earlier, my man in Iowa had failed to make any mention of the gold work or the engraving!

A careful inspection revealed several things. The rifle had been made originally by Edwin Phillips of New York City, sometime before 1868. A gold plaque, let into the buttstock, shows that it was a prize awarded at the "Third Union Shooting Festival," held in July, 1868 in New York. Sometime subsequently George Schoyen had rebarreled the rifle to 32-40 size, and had included the false muzzle and bullet starter normally supplied with his cartridge barrels; the original caliber was, most likely, 45 or larger.

The engraving and gold work was done by the famed L.D. Nimschke; the patterns (rubbings) of the work are shown in the Nimschke pattern book published by John J. Malloy.

I included detailed notes on this Phillips-Schoyen rifle, plus seven photographs of it, with the Dutcher story mentioned above. I'm glad my curiosity overcame my skepticism—very glad. •

A three-barrel gun is not so rare, and even one with the rifle bore centered at the top is understandable, but when it is marked Lefever and is this handsomely gotten up, one can truly marvel.

A splendid gold setter and a splendid woodcock grace the left side of the receiver of the Griebel-finished Model 21 16-ga. Skeet gun.

Apart from the fun of getting and shooting guns, Amber loves to talk of them and here does so with successor Ken Warner. Such talk can be heady stuff for a confirmed enthusiast.

Right on the

A well aimed shot for the quick- kill spot – boy, meat in the pot!

by WARREN PAGE

SUGAR RAY ROBINSON, about as scientific a fighter as the modern ring has produced, on TV the other night was demonstrating with precision fist just those spots where one punch knocks a man wobbly-kneed. The solar plexus, the kidneys, those handy buttons either side of the chin. For the judo expert we humans have even more killing or crippling "buttons." But game animals, though we hit them with flesh-ripping bullets rather than padded fist or edged palm, show fewer sudden-death spots. Moving far out or ducking through timber, their vital buttons are harder to tag even with a precision rifle. Yet that is what every sportsman wants, the execution-fast kill. He craves to hit 'em right on the button.

Sometimes he needs to do just that if he is to keep his own life. I've never been charged by a grizzly or a brown bear, not even while acquiring enough rugs to clutter a dance hall, but it does happen. In British Columbia a few years ago, in the process of trailing up a grizzly that had been wounded—with a 375 Magnum—anywhere but in a vital spot, Wenzel Dvorak was out ahead of his winded sportsman, no rifleman, when he met the bear. Not a big bear, really, but just a medium grizzly has power and vitality enough to maul a man to ribbons even after its heart and lungs are smashed up. Wenzel had only a battered Model 54 rifle in 270 caliber. But he hit the button, in this case the spine where it joins the neck, exposed when the bear came in with its head low. It dropped at ten feet. A vital *area* hit could have let the grizzly live long enough to make Wenzel's wife a widow. He *had* to connect with the button.

Actually, there are two types of kill-points on a game animal. One is the vital area or areas, where a hit with a bullet of reasonable caliber and energy will cause sure but not necessarily instant death. The term vital area covers considerable anatomy; its definition depends in good part on the construction and speed of the bullet we're driving at the animal, and a vital area hit is normally all we need or hope for on non-dangerous game. With critters that properly qualify in the dangerous group—and the North American continent properly has two; under certain circumstances the moose and the *Ursus* tribe of bears, the grizzlies and their assorted cousins—the second style of button becomes the important instant-kill point.

Oddly enough, in the bear-killing business until and unless bruin is actually charging, the average hunter taking a shot under most bear-hunting conditions is well-advised not to try for such obvious quick-kill spots as the head, the neck, and the spine. I deliberately except the blackies from the dangerous group save when they are completely cornered, at which point any wild animal, even normally of Casper Milquetoast disposition, turns vicious. On grizzly or brown bear the head shot is a very poor bet, for the reasons that the target is small, usually moving, and if you should happen to stick a 220-grain slug right in bruin's ear you'd execute him, but you'd also smash to smithereens the skull, which is his only true measure as a trophy. A poor head-hit means trouble. A skilled surgeon friend of mine, when his son mistakenly tried for a fast headshot kill but succeeded only in smashing the grizzly's jaw, got into a mauling brawl with the bear in a Yukon Territory alder patch. It could have ended his surgical career, or any other, quite permanently, since the bruin was slightly out of the medico's class! And seldom if ever will the Alaska guide easing his sportsman into dead-sure range of a big brownie let him try the head shot.

The trouble with neck and spine tries on bear—and on many other animals—is the difficulty of locating the true line of the vertebrae in the outlines of shaggy hair and hump. As with a sea lion, for example, the backbone sets several inches lower in both neck and body than with, as the opposite type of example, the tiger. Going away, the backbone of bruin or any animal is unmistakable. When a bear is standing on hind feet looking over the country-side, not starting a two-footed charge as the nature-fakers would have us think, hitting spine by centering the upper chest is not a hard shot, tough only in that it takes a tough-jacketed bullet to go the complete distance.

The Best Buttons

The most practical "button" on a big bear as with most rugged critters is the shoulder. Smash that and you'll have ample time to throw in the finisher, which is a common sense precaution on any grizzly. It won't hurt the rug any. Compared to the black bears the *Ursus* tribe will go down after the lightest sort of wounding hit, but they can absorb a lot of lead and still get up to go or come at you. Sloshing back down an Admiralty Island creek one afternoon, guide Ralph Young and I were annoyed because we hadn't been able to come up with the heavy old boar brownie whose tracks we'd found. To ease the tension, I grumbled jokingly that from the three trophy bears I had killed in his bailiwick we'd never had a charge How could I write hair-raising tales of bloody-fanged near-maulings with no charges? Ralph grunted in disgust at such foolishness. "You just keep smacking 'em in the shoulder with that 300 Weatherby, Bub, and we won't

BUTTON

Only long study of the peculiar anatomy of the Indian gaur or sladang made possible a one-shot spine-break, on vertebrae located strangely far below the odd hump. The tiger, however, carries his backbone normally high. Anatomical study pays off for hunters as well as surgeons.

have any charges—which is just fine by me!" Ten minutes later I had brownie No. 4 with a shoulder shot. There haven't been charges, either, not from a small herd of shoulder-smashed grizzlies, even the record boar I snowshoed in on back of Rainy Pass last spring. Belted once with a 275-grain slug from a 35 Mashburn Magnum, he went down with both shoulders broken, but his vital steam wasn't shut off until I drove in another two tons of bullet energy.

The same reasoning and experience applies to other dangerous game, whether on this continuent or overseas. On two occasions, however, I can recall taking spine shots that turned out well. The first tiger I killed in India hesitated in a clear *nullah* or dry wash. He gave me a clean 90-pace shot at a downward angle into the spine at the withers, if indeed a tiger has withers. No hump or long black hair there to disguise the line of backbone. The 300-grain Silvertip, traveling some 200 foot-seconds faster than factory-rated speeds since it was ahead of an 82-grain charge of 4064 in 375 Weatherby brass, smashed the bone—and itself—into a melon-sized bulge of jelly. Stripes never knew what hit him.

But on the gaur or sladang, a critter whose spine line is completely camouflaged by an amazing hump of fat and muscle over vertebrae that fin up a foot over his normal back line, I got away with it for only one reason. Hearing that this type of bison, a quick-footed beast standing well over six feet and weighing a full ton, had most peculiar anatomy, I'd spent hours studying a museum specimen from every angle. Knowing then that his spine actually ran well over a foot below the ridge of hump, a full third down his body, when I met the gaur in a Chanda jungle at fifty or sixty yards the shot was easy. One Kynoch solid on the button and he was down, out. Shooting for the backbone located as in a normal anatomy would only have stunned the great beast—and messing with a wounded sladang in an Asiastic jungle is not a procedure recommended by the Metropolitan Life Insurance Company.

The Tricky Neck Shot

Even such familiar and normally constructed animals as deer and elk can fool us on neck shots, in that the neatly fatal bones of neck and forward spine are carried a little lower in the buck or bull's body than we think. The same is true of moose, perhaps even more so in that the humping withers and deep neck of *alces* kid us into mis-spotting the spine line even more than do the swell or the shaggy neck hair of a rutting elk. Seven or eight years ago I knocked a big Quebec bull flat with a 180-grain pill from a 300 Weatherby. As we

Charging head on, a mad grizzly or brownie offers a head shot, but that's a trophy-ruiner. If bruin's head is low enough his spine can be smashed. Head high, his chest area shows. But the smart bear hunter breaks up a shoulder first, to anchor his bear, kill a charge before it starts.

Drawings by Bob Kuhn

strolled nonchalantly in on him the moose, apparently just stunned from a hit that was a shade high and merely clipped the spine, got up and left for Ontario. A spike bull elk, hit high in the neck by a 270 bullet fired by a New Mexico friend of mine went down too. But he got up and traveled over half the mountains of that rugged state before we came up on him. Only then did we discover that the 130-grain open point expanding, a bullet too lightly constructed for the job, had blasted off a wad of muscle but hadn't touched the vital spine.

Where the circumstances call for a neck shot, it's better to err by holding a trifle low than too high. In the Wapiti Range of Wyoming last fall, the elk I wanted for his massive rack was standing about three hundred yards across the park, stern-to. His neck and head were craned to look back in my direction. Bellied into the snow behind a handy log, with a 7 x 61 Sharpe & Hart rifle in my hands that I knew like a brother, I had a chance for a neck shot and for only that unless I wanted to bust him in the stern. I pulled the cross-hairs down a shade from the original guess. At the lash of the shot the bull went flat, done. Smash the spine? No, the front end of the 160-grain Nosler bullet had broken up fast. In the process it had slashed up windpipe and the whole jugular and arterial plumbing for an immediate though not instant kill.

For the meat-saver there's no better execution spot than the neck, provided you don't make the over-shooting error. In the course of trimming a privately owned herd of whitetail a New Jersey warden, so I have it on good authority, popped fifty-two animals with a 222, losing none, all with standing neck shots. No great depth of bullet penetration was needed under the circumstances, and nothing but prospective hamburger was blood-shot. This past fall, trying out some special 6mm bullets that proved entirely too tough in the jacket, I dropped three whitetail with neck-bone hits where the bullets expanded not at all. Those deer might have been lost, using that same bullet, had I experimented with hits back in the rib area. The neck shot on our antlered animals may not call for as much care in bullet and caliber choice, but it can't be instantly effective with sloppy hit placement. On running deer, unless you happen to be strictly a shot-with-luck type of character, I've always figured the neck try as a good one chiefly because it assures enough lead for a smash back in the lung area of the animal.

That is where, on the non-dangerous game that ninety-nine per cent of us hunt, the average man figures to put his bullet —into the heart and lungs. And he is right for most such circumstances. The rib cage gives him a sizeable target; it's possible to get a slug into the breathing and blood-pumping apparatus from a great variety of angles; and the lung area offers the biggest target. But never figure that the rib cage is an instant-kill "button." That it is not, necessarily.

There isn't a serious whitetail hunter living who hasn't gutted out a buck from one to three hundred yards beyond the spot where he took a heart-smashing bullet. I've known moose to absorb three handsomely placed low-chest hits from the 220-grain 30-06 load and still stagger around for long yardage and time. Doc Smith made a perfect heart shot on a Baranof grizzly, yet the bear traveled over three hundred yards minus any semblance of a blood pump—and those three hundred yards could have been in Doc's direction. In India I pranged a hundred and fifty pound chital or spotted deer with a 375 slug straight through his ticker—and stood there with my mouth open in amazement while the handsome little buck bounced nearly a furlong through the teak. Every Wyoming antelope hunter has seen antelope sprinting across the sage for many times as far as they *should* travel with only a bullet-burst blob to keep up blood pressure. For whatever freakish reason of vitality, game critters can travel amazing distances after heart shots—even admitting that what the happy hunter tends to call a perfect heart shot is likely to be anything else but. Especially if the critter is spooked beforehand, doped up with its own adrenalin, do they run out that last breath.

Yet for the average hunter such as you and I the lung area, a vital area rather than an instant-kill point, is the place where the bull's-eye should be painted on. But let's qualify that in at least one respect.

The High Lung Shot

For my own dough—and this is a conclusion I've come to only slowly—the center of the imaginary bull's-eye should *not* be dead on heart, where it nestles just behind the foreleg "elbow" in the lower third of the chest. It should be higher, about a fat third of the way down the back line and well forward, in what is, by most, termed the high lung section. With today's styles of cartridge, which drive bullets for impact velocities of anywhere from 2000 foot-seconds on up, and usually well up, that high lung spot has become a better sudden-death area than the lower aiming point.

The high lung hit really does the business. For example, a sizeable British Columbia moose showed me, through the alders, only that area for an aiming point. The 175-grain slug from my 7mm Mashburn Magnum went in, drove perhaps thirty inches toward the off shoulder, and the bull went down. Last fall a muley smacked with a 270 caliber Hornady pill in the same place, slightly different angle, was kaput in milli-

Heavy hair on a bull elk's neck may fool you as to location of the "sudden-death" spinal column, but the high lung hit or heart shot in the vital forward thorax area will quickly put down a winter meat supply.

seconds; a whitetail hit with a 100-grain 6mm bullet managed to flounder thirty yards. A fine white billy goat jabbed with the 7mm not far below his spine never got off his narrow ledge in British Columbia. On the other side of the world, Iraqi pigs, long-tusked Asiatic boars hefting four or five hundred pounds, ran out of steam pronto after hits in the same area. So did elk-sized sambhar deer. The journals I keep on my hunts are loaded with high lung area kills.

How come? For one thing—and this is especially true of hits from an angle off the broadside—the ribs are close enough there so that hitting bone at full impact velocity is almost certain. That means the bullet has started expanding as it enters the lung cavity, with a resultant broad wound channel. For another, if the bullet blows up as a result of too great impact speed for its jacketing, pieces not only blast down into the heart and lower lung but also upward into the complex of nerves on the underside of the spine. Major arteries feeding into the top side of the heart are likely to be smashed up, and that is as effective as ripping the heart muscle itself. Finally, if on the high lung shot you happen to hold off a bit all is not lost.

A handspan too high and your slug will crack into the spine. Too far forward and it will smash up the shoulder articulation that keeps a beast's front end under control. A shade aft or angling that way and the bullet may channel through the liver. That will ruin your next day's breakfast plans, but the liver is also the only abdominal organ behind the diaphragm muscle where a hit means a kill in any decent time. Impact a shade low drives your slug into the classical heart-kill area. When we're using a load adequate for the game, and are dealing with non-dangerous game, the high lung offers maximum room for sighting error and in most cases a mercifully certain kill.

Quartering Shots

The hunter's life would be far easier if game animals stood around in casual broadside poses, or if they carried built-in aiming markers like the white throat patches common on black bears. They do neither, and all too often the shot must be taken at a body that is at an angle to us, either quartering on as the trophy moves closer, all unsuspecting, or quartering off as it leaves for the next county. Then the same shooter will revert to the shoulder as an aiming point. Quartering on, a buck, bull, or bear hit in the nigh shoulder, at the point or moving around toward the base of the neck as the quartering angle slims, should also develop an acute case of lead destruction in his bellows-and-blood-pump area. Quartering away, the aiming point shifts to the further shoulder, that is to where your imagination and knowledge of animal anatomy tells you it should be, and a bullet of adequate penetration ability will tear through thorax and into offside bone structure.

But there are two distinct gimmicks in that very obvious piece of reasoning. First, you must have some understanding of the way an animal is made, of what the wound lines are that will surely smash up vital tissue. Spend an hour at the local zoo, peering at the caged sample of the critter you're going to hunt. The attendant may think you've gone off your wheezer when you squat down to observe the south end of a tame moose going north—but the zoo keeper isn't heading into Canada to shoot himself a hatrack. You are. The moose you meet up there may be standing at just that angle. And second, there's no logic in making shallow quartering shots on game with a rifle and load incapable of penetration into the shielded boiler works.

The new Winchester Model 88 short-throw lever action is a fine choice for those quick, now-or-never snapshots.

On "soft" light-framed animals of our continent such as deer, antelope, or sheep there isn't much of a penetration problem unless we're trying to bump a buck with a woodchuck load. But on the harder heavier-framed critters whose nerves don't come all unhooked with high-velocity hits in the tonneau, lead-carriers like elk for example, there is a penetration problem. Trying to bring down a six-pointer with an antelope pellet is a sporting misdemeanor. It verges on felony when that bull is angling so that your bullet must either smash through heavy shoulder hide, muscle, and bone to spend itself in his lung cavity or must slice forward toward the off shoulder from some point behind the rib cage.

From a 25 caliber no bullets lighter than 117 grains will give anything like such big animal penetration, and the 125-grain Barnes or Al Cosentino's 130- and 140-grain longsters for quick-twist barrels make it surer. About ninety per cent of the criticism of the estimable and efficient 270 caliber has come from set-ups where a fast-opening 130-grain pill was fired at a slant into a critter whose bone and muscle toughness demanded the longer 150-grain numbers by Sierra, Hornady, and Speer, or Fred Barnes' copper-jacketed 160-grain. It's likewise folly to expect a 150-grain 30 caliber blow-up bullet like the Bronze Point to go through a bull endways. This whole subject of which bullets give deepest penetration, or expand slowest or most surely at various impact speeds and on various animals is one so big it will have to be treated elsewhere. But suffice it to say that no matter how carefully—and how correctly—a projectile is chosen for a given hunting job, it cannot do that job properly if it isn't driven to the right spot, to the kill button—or mighty close to it.

The 7.65mm Vienna-made Little Tom pistol, right side.

The Little Tom Pistols of Alois Tomiška

Patented in 1910, these pocket automatic pistols were the first of their type made in double action form. Here's a thorough-going account—models, markings, variations and serial number data are included.

by J. B. WOOD

SOME OF THE earliest self-loading pistols had double-action firing systems. The 1894 Mannlicher, for example, could be fired by a long pull on the trigger or by thumb-cocking the hammer for single action firing. All of these pre-1900 automatics, however, were quite large. None could be called a "pocket pistol" in the usual sense of the term. When the smaller self-loaders arrived, via John M. Browning's 7.65mm Model 1900, no designer thought to include a double-action feature in any of the first pocket pistols.

No one, that is, until Alois Tomiška of Pilsen, Czechoslovakia, created the "Little Tom" automatic. Produced in 6.35mm (25 ACP) and 7.65mm (32 ACP), its double-action system differs from today's pistol of this type in one respect. When the hammer is cocked the trigger is not retracted to the rear of the guard. Whether single or double action, the stroke starts from full forward position of the trigger. The connecting bar is mounted on the hammer, and the sear is a non-moving part on the frame side near the trigger. In single-action firing a pivoting lever on the trigger simply pushes the bar upward to free it from the stationary sear. The magazine is also unusual, having no forward floorplate extension and being inserted and withdrawn from the *top,* with the slide locked in open position. While some magazines were made with steel bodies, the majority are of brass, apparently with the idea of rust prevention for this often-handled component. The top-loading feature was apparently intended for easy operation by those familiar with the Austrian military pistols of that time. The Roth-Steyr and Steyr-Hahn did not have removable magazines, of course, but did load from the top.

As is usually the case, the earliest prototypes were quite different from the production guns. German patent number 218897, dated February 11th, 1910, shows the pistol with a barrel-encircling recoil spring, separate trigger spring in the frame, and a hammer-block safety at the rear of the slide. Also, the hammer spring is shown spanning the magazine well on the right side. The magazine is a conventional type, removable from the bottom of the grip frame. It's a sleeker-looking pistol than the production model, but there must have been manufacturing problems, as this version was never made in quantity.

French patent number 421.509, dated October 15th, 1910, refers only to the method of barrel mounting, a slide-in-from-the-rear system akin to the Beretta pistols. The illustrations, however, are much closer to the production Little Tom. The recoil spring is now below the barrel, its guide bearing on the trigger so that it doubles as a trigger spring. The hammer-block safety is no longer shown. There is no cut-away view of the magazine, but it appears that it is now the top-insertion type. The only obvious differences from the production model are the grip angle, the tongue-and-groove mounting of the sideplate, and the shape of the hammer.

Prototypes

On both patents the inventor's name is spelled "Tomischka," the "sch" replacing the Slavic "s," which has no exact equivalent in Western European usage. The pistol's name, of course, was derived from the designer's last name which, translated from the Czech, is just that—"Little Tom." After obtaining these patents—and others—Tomiška apparently produced no more than a few prototypes at Pilsen over the next 3 or 4 years. At this point World War I intervened, and the 44-year-old inventor was a *Büchsenmacher* (riflemaker) in Vienna, Austria, until the War's end. In late 1919 or early 1920, Tomiška formed a partnership with Camillo Frank of the Wiener Waffenfabrik to produce the Little Tom pistols in Vienna. As made by the Wiener factory, there are a few differences between the two calibers, the most obvious being the grips. Most of their 25 pistols have panels of moulded hard rubber, with a "WWF" monogram in an oval at the center. The 32 grips are of a light-colored wood, and carry the "WWF" monogram on a round brass medallion, slightly above center. Just above this, in the vicinity of the upper screw, there is a shallow depression in each grip, as if for a minimum thumb-rest.

On most 32 Little Toms, there is a small front sight, integral with the

Asian copy of the 7.65mm Little Tom. The only major departure from original design is in the lipped, bottom-removal magazine.

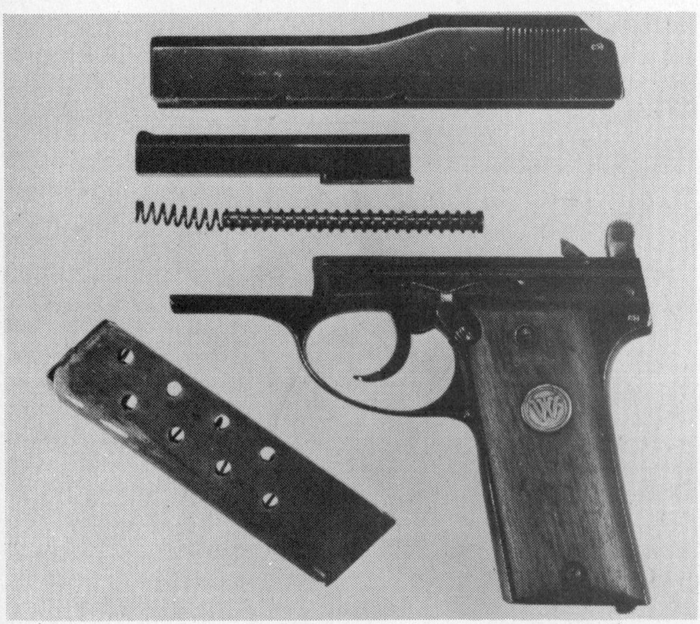

The 7.65mm Wiener Little Tom pistol, field stripped.

The 6.35mm Little Tom pistol, showing method of magazine insertion and removal.

barrel, and the slide top is grooved to form a rear sight. The 25 pistols usually have no provision for sights. There is also a difference in the mounting of the sideplate on the right side of the frame. The 32 plate has two slots in its lower edge which fit over the shaft of the top grip screw, and a separate screw or stud on the frame behind the grip. The screw, or screws, must be loosened before the plate can be slid upward and off. The 25 plate also has two slots, but they are spaced differently, and fit over fixed studs on the frame. After the slide is removed, the plate can be lifted off, exposing the firing mechanism.

Aside from these differences between the 25 and 32 pistols, Little Toms of both calibers have shape variations in three areas—the trigger, trigger guard opening, and the top rear of the slide. Two trigger shapes have been noted—a deeply curved type, and a slightly curved type, almost straight by comparison.

There is no particular chronological pattern to the trigger types. In the 32 pistols observed number 32338 has the deeply-curved trigger, while the later number 33406 has the slightly-curved type. In the 25 pistols several in the 26- and 27-thousand range have the slightly curved trigger, while only three observed—numbers 26867, 27029, and 43500—have the deeply curved type. Because of this random application, and the fact that the examples ran 7 to 4 in favor of the "straight" trigger, perhaps the deeply curved type was offered as an optional feature. If so, this might explain its relative scarcity, since it is rather uncomfortable for all but the slimmest fingers.

At top—Little Tom 6.35mm with sideplate removed and held. Note sideplate studs on frame and rounded cut to clear grip screw. Center—same as above, parts shown in position for double-action firing. Bottom—as above, parts positioned for single-action shooting. Note—trigger was moved rearward, away from its normal mid-position.

Varations and Marks

On the earliest pistols the trigger guard opening is a true oval, its upper line curving into the frame to the lower edge of the slide. In later production, the opening is more egg-shaped, its upper line conforming to a straight projection from the lower front of the frame extension to the rear, and not reaching the lower edge of the slide. In the same production range, the shape of the safety lever was altered, and its button was changed from cross-checkering to simple milled cross-grooves.

The other variable shape, the top rear of the slide, underwent changes to expose more of the hammer top, to make thumb-cocking easier. An early Wiener example in 32 has a very shallow "scoop" in that area, barely exposing the hammer top. In later Vienna production, the slide shape seems to have been somewhat standardized. The 32 pistols are deeply scooped at that point, the hammer top exposed, while the 25 pistols have the shallow scoop, with most of the hammer hidden. One variation observed between mid-production and late 25 pistols is the number and size of the slide serrations or finger grooves. Earlier guns have 15 larger serrations, measuring 22mm (⅞-inch) from front to rear. A quite late example has 14 very small serrations, measuring only 13mm (17/32-inch).

There are two types of slide markings on the Wiener pistols. On most of the 25 automatics the left slide-flat has two lines: WIENER WAFFENFABRIK and MADE IN AUSTRIA. At the center, near the top, are the Vienna proof marks and date. On the left frame, safety positions are marked S and F. On the right slide flat, in one line, is WIENER WAFFENFABRIK, PATENT, LITTLE TOM, 6.35MM (25). Serial number is near the top, just below the extractor. On most of the 32 pistols the left slide-flat has a single line, very small and lightly stamped: WIENER WAFFENFABRIK, PATENT, LITTLE TOM, CAL. 7.65MM. Proof marks, date, and safety markings are identical with the 25 locations. The right slide-flat has the serial number, just below the extractor, and one line at center: MADE IN AUSTRIA. Some late-numbered 25 pistols are also marked in this pattern. A third grip style has also been seen on some early pistols. Of moulded hard rubber, they have a diagonal banner with the words LITTLE TOM.

During the production years of the Wiener Little Tom pistols, Alois Tomiška was also doing design work for Jihočeská Zbrojovka in Pilsen, Czechoslovakia. He is credited with the design of their little "Fox" pistol, made from 1919 to 1921. Collectors will remember this as one of the two small Czech pistols which have a folding trigger and no guard.

Czech Models

The last proof date noted on a Vienna-made Little Tom is 1925, so it was sometime after that year that Camillo Frank sold the production equipment to the inventor, and Tomiška moved the tools to Pilsen, where he began making the last of the Little Tom pistols. On some of these late models the top rear of the slide is rounded off, rather than "scooped", achieving the same purpose – exposure of the hammer top for easier cocking. The Pilsen-made pistols are marked on the left slide flat, in a single line, ALOIS TOMIŠKA-PLZEN-PATENT-LITTLE TOM - 7.65 (32), or 6.35 (25), depending on caliber. On the right slide-flat, in a single line, is MADE IN CZECHOSLOVAKIA. Grips are smooth wood, plain or with a small brass medallion bearing an "AT" monogram.

I've recorded only *one* certain serial number of a Pilsen-made pistol – a 32, number 2065. If the numbering began with "1", then we can assume that at least that many were made. The Pilsen guns are quite scarce, so the

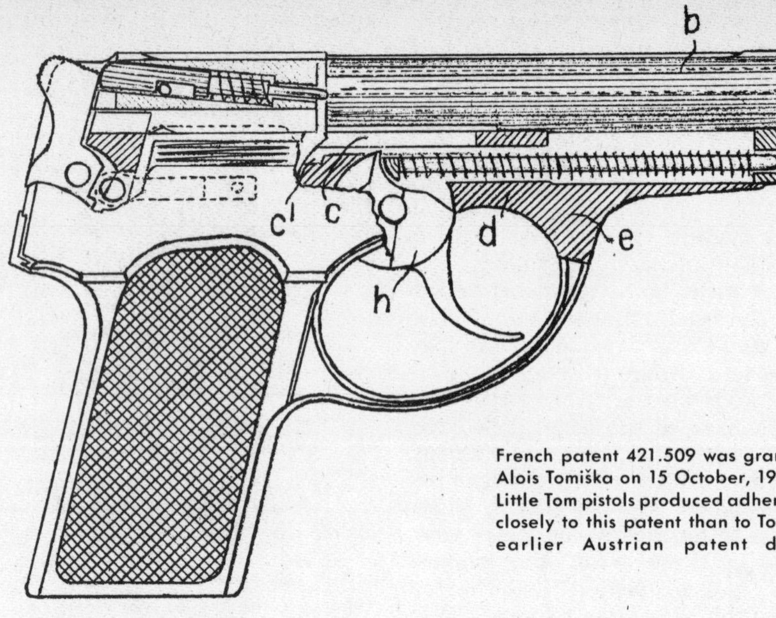

French patent 421.509 was granted to Alois Tomiška on 15 October, 1910. The Little Tom pistols produced adhere more closely to this patent than to Tomiška's earlier Austrian patent design.

One of the Little Tom 6.5mm pistols made originally with a longer than normal barrel – the barrel was later reduced to the size seen.

total production could not have been large.

Although the Wiener firm was apparently still in business as late as 1944, its records, like those of many European companies, did not survive the war. In an effort to arrive at an approximate production figure, I wrote the *Beschussamt Wien* (Government Proof House) in Vienna. In their reply they indicated that their records, also, were disorganized by the war. They did, however, estimate that they had proved "around 17,000" of the Little Tom pistols in both calibers. I believe that the 32 pistols were a separate numbering block *within* the 25-caliber number range, with the 32 beginning at 30 thousand, and fewer than 5,000 being made. They are certainly scarcer than the 25 pistols. I think the regular production numbering of the 25 Wieners began at "1", stopped at 10,000, then jumped to 25,000. I base this number-hiatus theory on the fact that no serials between 10,000 and 25,000 have been seen. Counting from this point to the highest number observed – 43560 – and adding the first group, we arrive at a round figure of 28,000, considerably more than the estimate by *Beschussamt Wien*. Keep in mind, of course, that the later Pilsen production was not proved in Vienna. I estimate that the total from both factories was less than 35 thousand pieces, most in 25 caliber.

Asian Copy

Many readers will be familiar with the Asian copies of well-known European guns. The Browning Model 1900, for example, was a particular favorite of these primitive "manufacturers." Considering the crude hand tools they used, it's amazing how closely they managed to copy the original guns in detail, if not in quality. While gathering representative pistols for this article, I was surprised to find an Asiatic copy of the 7.65mm Little Tom! It is slightly larger than a genuine pistol, but otherwise it's a very close copy of a Vienna-made 32 with the deeply curved trigger. Total length is 5⅝ inches, height 4⅝ inches and barrel length 3³⁄₁₆ inches. Magazine capacity, 8 rounds. Since the native workmen had little knowledge of any language other than their own, markings on Asian copies are often fanciful and amusing. On the Little Tom copy, the left slide flat has AUTQNJG JSTQL DCEL 24, DANTQN PTET 70724 TESTED, and a number, 5042. The left rear frame has RUS and a large 8 near the grip. Safety positions are marked B for off, R for on. The right slide-flat carries a reversal of the number, 2405, and one line at center, WADE IM RUSSIA. Grips are smooth wood, with a round brass medallion bearing a man's head. One departure from the original design is the magazine, which has a floorplate extension and withdraws from the bottom of the grip. Certain aspects of the gun's markings and the workmanship point to fabrication in the Khyber Pass area of India (now, West Pakistan), rather than the Far East.

There are also some interesting individual pieces among the genuine Little Tom pistols examined for this article. Number 43500 has a longer barrel, one which protrudes ⅜-inch beyond the front of slide and frame. There is an easy explanation for this – a law, in effect in that part of Europe until the late 1920's, required that any handgun not made for export must have an over-all length of at least 18 centimeters (7.09 inches). To comply with this ridiculous regulation many manufacturers simply extended the barrel to the required length. Little Tom number 43500 was one of these, and someone later cut off 5½ centimeters (2⅛ inches) of the barrel for more convenience in carrying. Two other pistols observed, numbers 43560 and 2065, had extra long barrels.

Another odd pistol is my own

The Little Tom 25 pistol (left) with hammer cocked. Note that trigger is not retracted • Left side of same pistol.

Wiener 32, number 32338. Except for the deeply curved trigger, it is typical of most Little Toms in this caliber. It has, however, *no* Austrian proof marks. Instead, the top of the barrel carries the English view, definitive, and smokeless powder marks of the London proofhouse! The view proof also appears on the left rear flats of slide and frame. On the right slide flat, just forward of the words MADE IN AUSTRIA, is a mark formerly used on all guns imported into England—a small, bordered rectangle containing the words NOT ENGLISH MAKE. In this particular case, a rather redundant application. English marks are not particularly unusual, on this or any other "foreign" gun. The question is, why no Austrian proofs?

At the age of 79, Alois Tomiška died on December 29th, 1946, in Prague, Czechoslovakia. He lived to see his idea perfected by Walther, Sauer, and Mauser. It has long been the opinion of many authorities that the Little Tom pistols were the inspiration for Walther's excellent Model PP. Perhaps, in the principle of applying double action to a pocket pistol design, this may be true. The mechanical application, however, is very different. Walther's famous "horseshoe" sear and single-action trigger retraction have no parallel in the Tomiška dedesign. There is, though, one direct relation between the two: When the sophisticated Walther PP appeared in 1929, the days of the Little Tom were numbered. ●

The 7.65mm (left) and 6.35mm Little Toms, a rear view showing the hammer shapes and slide cuts. The 32 is much easier to cock and has a sight cut.

Specifications

	6.35mm	7.65mm
Weight:	12¾ ozs.	21½ ozs.
Length:	4½ in.	5⁵⁄₁₆ in.
Height:	3¼ in.	4⁷⁄₁₆ in.
Width:	¾ in.	1¹⁄₁₆ in.
Barrel:	2⁵⁄₁₆ in.	3¹⁄₁₆ in.
Mag. cap.:	7	8

Note: Measurements taken from a 25 (26605) and a 32 (32338), both by Wiener Waffenfabrik.

Serial numbers observed: Wiener—4304, 9441, 26087, 26605, 26668, 26867, 27029, 27052, 30194, 32338, 32589, 33406, 41409, 43500, 43560. Tomiska—2065.

For technical assistance, the writer would like to thank James B. Stewart, Jan Stevenson, Lucien Scrandour, Dan Byrne, Ernie Lang, Al Snaper, and Don Crews. Without their co-operation, this article would not have been possible.

Bibliography

Col. Robert E. Gardner, *Small Arms Makers,* Bonanza (Crown), New York, 1963, p. 329.

Dr. J. Howard Mathews, *Firearms Identification,* Charles C. Thomas, Springfield, IL., 1973. Vol. I, pp. 223, 224. Vol. II, pp. 58, 122, 386, 387. Vol. III, pp. 185, 243.

James B. Stewart, "Those Collectable 25 Auto Pistols" *Guns Magazine,* Jan., 1972, p. 40.

James B. Stewart, "Why the Double-Action Semi-Auto Pistol," *The American Rifleman,* June, 1973, p. 22.

James B. Stewart, "Those Long Barrel 25s," *Gun Collector's Digest,* Digest Books, Inc., Northfield, IL., 1974, p. 106.

James B. Stewart, "10cm Automatics," *Gun Collector's Digest,* Digest Books, Inc., Northfield, IL., 1974, p. 276.

RIFLES FOR THE WILDER

THE MAJORITY of big game hunters are either trophy hunters or meat hunters, and they are not particularly in love with the wilderness or life in the open. This is shown clearly in the books and articles they write, which describe their many kills, how they killed, and with what rifles they killed. There is a complete lack of description of the country through which they hunted. Almost always it is glorious, beautiful country, for big game are most discriminating, and do not dwell in lands despoiled and poisoned by man. And almost invariably these hunters, when they have obtained their trophy or meat, beat it back to the city "where brick and mortar breed filth and crime."

Although 113 head of big game have fallen to my rifle, including almost all of the North American species, I do not like to be classed as a "big game hunter." I have, it is true, a few nice trophies on the walls of my hearth-room, the windows of which look out over a glorious panorama of mountains. And I have shot game for meat, eating more birds and small mammals than large animals, practically always consuming them in the wilds to enable me to subsist there longer.

I adore to live in the wilderness, and to wander through it alone; to view its glories, and to feel the inexpressible thrill of winning my way through it alone. I love the forested hills and rounded mountains, the little lily-choked ponds and the canoe lakes and rivers of the East—the limitless plains, vast distances, the haze and the deep canyons of the Southwest—the high, snow-capped and buttressed peaks, the deep valleys with rivers that rush like express trains, and the smell of sage and of quaking aspen in the fall in the Rockies and the Northwest. As much as I love camp life, I do not particularly care to loaf or live around the usual camp amid such surroundings. I want to be out in the wilderness, worshiping it all the time, night as well as day, in storm or sunshine, and always with a favorite rifle and a little equipment so as to be able to care for myself.

There are two classes of big game hunters in this country. The first is the "one week a year" hunter who goes out into a deer forest to get vension for home consumption. The other is the wealthy man who employs a guide and goes farther afield. The former may sometimes be a hunter. The latter rarely is. Rather the guide, to whose apron strings he is tied, is the hunter, and entitled to all the credit. Both are interested almost exclusively in big game, and in big game rifles. There is endless discussion as to killing power and velocity. Their discussions in print show lack of field experience, a failure to realize that many of the weapons they unhesitatingly criticize will invariably kill well if the bullet is properly placed.

The placing of the bullet is everything. The most powerful weapon made will not make up for lack of skill in marksmanship. The only sense I see in the discussion of small bore, high velocity, light bullet weapons *vs.* big bores and heavy bullets is that the former are more properly open country—Western—rifles where the game is seen clearly at a long distance and the hunter can usually wait an instant or two until he can place his bullet in a truly vital spot. The bigger calibers are weapons for thick woods where the only glimpse of game may be at its north end headed south, and the bullet must drive surely through hind quarters into the vitals. But even in the latter instance marksmanship is paramount, and no one can shoot well with an arm whose recoil he dreads.

I look on the rifle from a different standpoint. My trip is not ruined if I fail to kill, for I still have my beloved country, and I can afford to pass up chances that are not fairly sure. But I do want a weapon of fairly flat trajectory, of superb accuracy, which will maintain its zero all the time, so I can place my bullet exactly even at sensibly long ranges. And I also demand a rifle that will take a load suitable for small game, for I often have to subsist on such game.

The usual big game hunter leaves his base camp or his hunting resort considerably after the cook has given him and his guide a substantial breakfast, and he returns to that camp before pitch dark. Thus he is not really hunting, for the productive hunting hours are just after dawn, and just before or at dusk, and when he starts out for the day he is traversing for the first hours the unproductive country close to his camp where game has been disturbed by the smell and noise of that camp.

It is only in the more open Northwest, where sheep, goat, caribou, and moose largely feed and bed in the open during mid-day, and can be seen from afar with binoculars and stalked, that hunting in the middle of the day is profitable.

In the wilder and little-known regions that I have penetrated, I have usually gone alone, or in later years as I have grown older, I have taken a combined horse wrangler and cook, or a canoe man. My camp impedimenta and store grub have always been reduced to the minimum in favor of easy transport into such remote areas, and hence I have done a remarkable amount of "living off the country." Subsistence has been quite as much from small as from big game. Crazy to be out in it all, and realizing that the early and late hours, and often more distant terrain is both more interesting and more profitable, it has been my habit to breakfast long before dawn. Just as soon as the gray of the morning makes it possible to avoid running into bushes or stepping into holes, I leave my little base camp, and by the time rifle sights and animals can be seen I am in undisturbed country, where I linger, hunt, observe, or invite my soul until the last moment when return is advisable. And very often, toward dusk I see ahead a basin, a valley, or a range that looks like good and interesting country, and decide to bed down there for the night and wander in it the next day, for I could never reach it on one day from my camp. Or it may be that in the late afternoon I see game far off with my binoculars and want to reach them the next day. Or again I may kill a large animal near sunset, and the dressing and butchering of it to save the good meat and trophy will take me into pitch darkness, and again I must remain where I am for the night. And if I investigate the good and distant country that has called me, the chances are that I shall have to remain out a second night.

My Hunting Pack

So I almost always start out with a little hunter's pack that I have evolved over the years by experience, and with some assistance from alpine climbers, that will keep me comfortable and in vigor for several days if need be. This is nothing very elaborate, but it contains nothing that is not absolutely

Photo courtesy of Arthur Jackson

NESS LOVER

The grandest old gentleman of them all—the affable, amiable, knowledgeable, and gentle Colonel Townsend Whelen, at his shooting bench. The "old, disabled veteran is still at it despite hell and high water," to quote the Colonel himself. Long, long may he flourish.

by COLONEL TOWNSEND WHELEN

essential, and it has been pared down to the last ounce. It is carried in a small rucksack, on my back, snuggled down so the weight rests mainly on my hips; with center of gravity low, it does not make me unsteady or topheavy. Nor is it any burden at all, for it seldom weighs as much as ten pounds. The contents of the pack include those essential for successful hunting—extra ammunition, skinning knife, whetstone, compass, waterproof matches, etc. A small assortment of water-free grub in small cloth (now plastic) bags, such as oatmeal, corn meal, milk powder, salt, sugar, tea, bacon, dates, figs, and sweet chocolate. To prepare the grub there is a little one-quart aluminum kettle, an Army mess pan, a cup, and a spoon. I have also a little camera, and a binocular is strung around my neck by its thong. There is likewise a little, extremely light tarp, in recent years a Koroseal poncho weighing only a pound and bulking up not larger than a bandana handkerchief, and serving for both raincoat and night shelter.

To bring weight and bulk down to the minimum, the grub, the heaviest item, is pared down to the bone, hence the desirability of picking up some edible game in the days I spend away from camp. Of course one does not shoot a large animal to provide only two or three meals, and in my wanderings free and footloose I have subsisted on an astonishing assortment of small game—grouse, and fish mostly, but often on porcupine, ground hogs, rabbits, squirrels, muskrats, beaver, etc. Of these the most delectable is beaver. Out is all the weasel tribe—mink and otter particularly. Not even a whiskey jack will touch these.

Of course you might say a good little 22 target pistol or revolver should serve for this small stuff, but its weight, bulk, and uncertainty make it impossible from my point of view—that is, away from the base camp—and besides they are prohibited in the Canadian North where much of my wandering has been done. So a really effective small game load that will not ruin meat enters into my choice of a weapon, and so at last we come to the preferred rifles for the wilderness lover.

Accuracy Important

I place accuracy as the first consideration, and with it I include maintenance of zero. The dependable rifle should both make a small group, and the location of the center of impact should not change from month to month. You don't have any sighting shots in the game fields. So far as trajectory is concerned, if the height of the bullet's flight is not more than 3½ inches at 100 yards when sighted for 200 yards, that is ample. That means that, when sighted for 200, if you aim at the top of the back of an animal at 300 yards, the bullet will strike in the center of the chest cavity—the "boiler room." If that bullet weighs 100 grains or over in 25 caliber, or 150 grains in 30 caliber, and is well constructed, at the velocity which gives the above trajectory, it will invariably smash through the chest walls or shoulder into the chest cavity and give a quickly fatal kill. Then all that is needed is marksmanship sufficient to insure a shot in the boiler room, and that rifle and cartridge are suitable for big game.

I never had a really accurate rifle, suitable for long-range game shooting, in my hands until I began to shoot the Krag rifle in 1902. The only commercially made rifle in those days that would compare with it was the Winchester single shot for the same 30-40 Krag cartridge. Where accuracy and maintenance of zero were concerned there were no high-power rifles of those days that would even begin to compare with these two. About this time Horace Kephart developed a finely accurate, reduced, small game load for the 30-40 Winchester single shot rifle, using a 125-grain lead bullet. So I adopted it for my wilderness rifle, and it served me well up until 1912, when I found a repeating rifle that would shoot as well. The only trouble even today with this single shot rifle is that you cannot reload it fast enough when your hands are numb with cold. I shot a lot of big game with it—deer, goats, and sheep—with its 220-grain soft point bullet at M.V. 1960 f.s., and a whole pile of small game with the reduced load.

Along about 1911 a number of our rifle cranks began to experiment with our 30-06 Springfield 1903 rifle, remodelling it into sporting type, and soon we had developed it into an accurate and reliable rifle, with superior full charges and small game loads. I adopted it for my wilderness hunting in 1912, using it first on a two months trip in a primitive area in Montana. Since then I used it steadily until 1927, and have used it in the wilderness more than any other rifle, because in those days I had more opportunity to get out into wild country than I have had since. My first Springfield had a Lyman rear sight on the cocking piece, and when turning from the big game load to the small game load it was easy to elevate that sight 1-3/4 graduations. Any small game load that will have such a trajectory that it will center its hits 1 inch above aim at 50 yards and 1 inch below aim at 100 yards will be perfectly satisfactory. My first reduced load employed a 154-grain lead bullet, but about 1915 I worked out a load consisting of the 150-grain pointed, full jacketed military bullet and 18 grains of du Pont No. 80 powder which was so satisfactory that I have used it ever since. The modern loading for this bullet is 18 grains of du Pont No. 4759 powder, with the Federal No. 210 primer.

Custom 270 Rifle with Pfeifer barrel chambered by Al Marciante, and Springfield 1903 action. Stock by the late William L. Humphrey from a Circassian walnut blank liberated in Berlin just after the capture of that city, where it had been seasoning for 25 years. 4X Bear Cub Double scope in G. & H. mount. The slide for the Lyman 48 receiver sight is in trap under butt-plate.

Telescope Sights

About 1920 hunting telescope sights had been developed to the point where they became suitable and dependable for hunting, and I then had a new Springfield rifle fitted with a 2¼X Zeiss Zielklein scope, a very fine scope which was well adapted to wilderness use and to quick catching of aim. Griffin & Howe graduated to reticle dials on this scope so it was easy to turn them quickly from full charged to reduced load zeros. This rifle in my hands accounted for a vast amount of big and small game, from the Far North to the tropics, including grizzly, moose, elk, caribou, sheep, goats, and four species of our deer. It never failed me a single time. Today I think it is more powerful than is necessary for the wilderness lover, and not quite as accurate or as suitable for reduced small game loads as two other calibers.

A student of rifles wrote me that he thought the 257 Roberts rifle and cartridge were on their way out. I do not think so. Probably he based his opinion on the recent volumes of *factory* ammunition sold. This rifle with factory ammunition, while it is good, is not in any way outstanding. Ned Roberts was a personal friend, and we were together many months on the range and in the chuck pastures when he was developing his cartridge. He thought of it only as a woodchuck cartridge. When he had it perfected, I got a rifle similar to his, with a heavy Niedner barrel, Springfield action, and fine Shelhamer stock, weighing 12 pounds. With properly loaded ammunition it is a very accurate arm. I have shot many chucks with it, some at very long ranges, and with one load in particular it would make a very respectable 300-meter match rifle. But it is just too heavy to carry in rough country.

When the Winchester Model 70 rifle was produced in 257 Roberts caliber, I began to get letters about its excellence from riflemen all over the country, and particularly from Western hunters who were finding it eminently satisfactory for all big game, even elk and moose. So I immediately got one of these rifles, just a standard non-selected one, and had it fitted with a 2½X Lyman Alaskan scope, one of the first models of these scopes without the "all-weather" caps, and with the reticle dials clearly graduated, and zero lines on the housing, so you could easily read and record the adjustments in terms of minutes. Despite the handicap of this low-power scope as compared with the Lyman 10X scope on the Niedner, it gave just as small groups with all loads as the latter rifle, and maintained its zeros always—still does after sixteen years of use.

I have noted that the 257 Roberts does not set the world afire with factory ammunition, all of which seems to be rather lightly loaded, all with round nosed bullets, and with bullets seated so deeply in the case that when fired they have to jump a considerable distance before taking the rifling. To add insult to injury, the magazines are only long enough to take this factory ammunition with its deeply seated bullets. But correction with the Model 70 rifle was pie to any rifleman. I yanked the filler plate out of the magazine, and substituted a 30-06 follower and bolt stop. Then I began seating the bullets farther out of the case so their ogive just missed contacting the lands by perhaps 1/32 inch, and increasing the powder charges. The increase in accuracy and the flattening of the trajectory was very marked.

I have not myself shot any large game with this rifle. It just happens that my wanderings were confined for some years to the summer season when big game was not legal, and this is the rifle I took along, and it certainly gave a splendid performance on varmints and small game. I think I have carried it farther afoot than any rifle I have owned, and it certainly shows it, for the metal parts lack most of their blue, and the stock its polish.

Load for the 257 Roberts

My records show that I have to date made 72 separate accuracy and trajectory tests of this 257 Roberts Model 70 rifle with many different loads. In the past two years I have been testing it with modern bullets and powders, and I give the dope on the most successful loads.

100-grain Sierra spitzer bullet. 46 grains du Pont No. 4350 powder. Winchester cases. Winchester No. 120 primers. Bullet seated to an overall cartridge length of 2.90 inch, or to almost touch lands in your rifle. Muzzle velocity 3034 f.s. Bench rest accuracy at 100 yards with 2½X scope, 5 shot groups—smallest 1.00″, largest 2.10″, average for seven groups 1.39″. Sighted for 200 yards with above scope, bullets average 2 inches above aim at 100, and drop 5 inches below aim at 300 yards. The 100-grain Hornady and 100-grain Gardiner bullets are also excellent and give about the same accuracy.

117-grain Sierra spitzer boat-tail bullet. 45 grains of du Pont No. 4350 powder. Winchester cases. Winchester No. 120 primer. Overall length 2.90 inches. M.V. 2975 f.s. Five-shot groups at 100 yards were: smallest 1.30″, largest 1.85″, average for seven groups 1.60″. (Note: In the Niedner rifle this load gave three groups: 1.45″, 1.60″, and 1.25″.) Sighted for 200 yards with Alaskan scope, center of impact was 2″ above aim at 100, and 4½″ below aim at 300 yards.

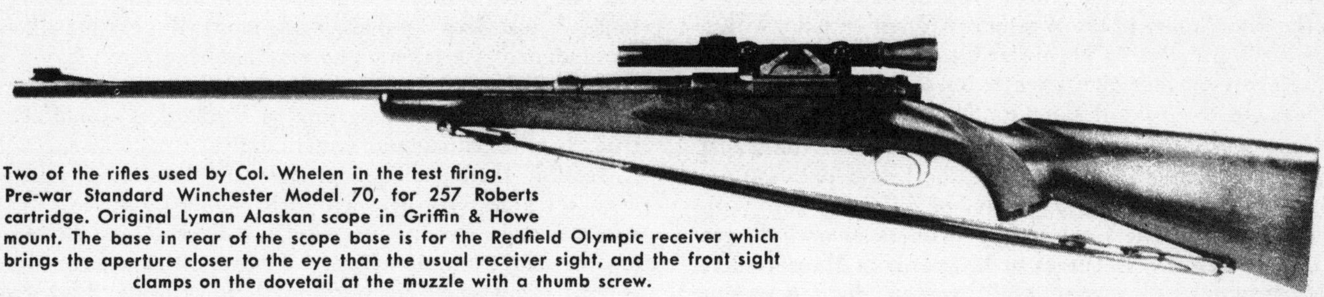

Two of the rifles used by Col. Whelen in the test firing. Pre-war Standard Winchester Model 70, for 257 Roberts cartridge. Original Lyman Alaskan scope in Griffin & Howe mount. The base in rear of the scope base is for the Redfield Olympic receiver which brings the aperture closer to the eye than the usual receiver sight, and the front sight clamps on the dovetail at the muzzle with a thumb screw.

Small Game Load. Bond Loverin gas check bullet No. 257730—94 grains, or Ideal Loverin gas check bullet No. 257464—97 grains, cast of No. 2 Ideal alloy or 1 to 10 tin and lead, lubricated and sized to .258″. 14 grains du Pont No. 4759 powder. Winchester cases expanded with .258″ expander, Federal No. 210 primer. (This primer I consider important with this load.) Bullet seated with two lubricated grooves outside case mouth. An elevation on the Alaskan scope 6 minutes or clicks above that required for 200 yards with above full loads causes this load to center 1 inch above aim at 50 yards and 1 inch below aim at 100 yards. M.V. is about 1600 f.s. Groups steadily under 2 inches at 100 yards. Besides small game, I use it for offhand target practice, and am now on my sixth box of 100 bullets. It will kill small game neatly without spoiling meat or pelts. It is not an altogether satisfactory varmint load, for several chucks struck in the belly have gotten into their holes. The best varmint load is the above 100-grain full load, much more accurate and with a flatter trajectory than any of the 87-grain bullets.

I think that the 257 Roberts is as sweet a rifle as any wilderness lover would want, provided he is not hunting in elk, moose, or grizzly country. Seemingly the 250-3000 Savage would almost equal it, but the Savage will not handle 117-grain bullets, which experience in the game fields seems to show are desirable to get through the shoulders on the larger animals. Of course there are many wildcat 25's that much excel the 257 Roberts in velocity, and may equal it in accuracy, but one and all, these large capacity cases will not do at all well with reduced and small game loads. It will do its work well anywhere in America if the bullets are placed well, and if they are not so placed the most powerful rifle made will fail just as badly. Jack O'Connor wrote me recently that he was sick and tired over all this discussion on killing power. He said he had a mind, on his next trip into the Far North to take a 257 Roberts rifle, and he bet he would get all his game, including grizzlies and moose, just as well and in just as few shots as with any rifle. But please remember—I am not writing about big game rifles, and most certainly not about thick woods big game rifles, but about rifles for the wilderness lover and loafer.

The Superb 270 W.C.F.

And now we come to my present favorite rifle, one I have used pretty exclusively on trips into the West and North for the past twenty-seven years. In 1925, shortly before it was announced to the public, Winchester sent me one of their Model 54 rifles for the 270 W.C.F. cartridge. I put a Zeiss Zielklein scope on it, with dial graduated by Griffin & Howe, and it shot beautifully; was more accurate with the 130-grain factory cartridge than any 30-06 with any factory hunting load, and it had a much flatter trajectory. Continued use of it on combat ranges at Fort Benning showed that I could make sure hits with it at long *estimated* ranges better than with any rifle I had owned to that date. At first, with my previous 30-06 experience I was skeptical about its suitability for the larger animals, but I need not have worried for it was not long before reports from the game fields by the bushel came in indicating its entire suitability for any American game. The first shot I got on big game with it was at a bull moose, an instantaneous kill as it stood in a beaver dam at about 75 yards. I had three sportsmen friends and two guides to feed, and we had been without meat for two weeks. Since then I have shot another moose, caribou, and a number of deer with it, all killed instantaneously with one properly placed shot. One caribou was shot at 325 yards and ran a mad race for 50 yards before dropping. Also it has bagged much small game for food, and countless woodchucks.

This Winchester rifle always gave splendid accuracy with any good loads except the 100-grain factory loads with which it was just mediocre. In fact all of the many 270 Model 70 rifles with which I am familiar have been noted for accuracy. My rifle has now been fired at least 2,500 rounds with full charges, and I am expecting it to lose some of its accuracy any time, but so far it is as good as ever. Therefore I have acquired two other 270 rifles. One is an FN Mauser supplied by the Firearms International Corporation, and the other has a Pfeifer barrel, chamber by Al Marciante, a Springfield 1903 breech action, and a fine Circassian walnut stock by William L. Humphrey. Both have 10-inch twist, and both are sighted with 4X Bear Cub Double scopes with flat top post reticles. During the past four years I have been testing these two rifles for accuracy and trajectory with both factory and hand loads, using for the latter the more modern bullets and powders. Factory ammunition of various weights and kinds of bullets, and all makes, gave 100-yard 5-shot groups running all the way from .90" to 3.5". Apparently no one make or bullet was outstandingly better than others. The .90" group was followed immediately with one 1.70", same ammunition. The outstanding performance with special bullets and powder was as follows:

140-grain Modern Gun Shop, 2-diameter, spire point bullet. This is the bullet that has proved most accurate in the majority of 270 rifles. 57 grains of du Pont 4350 powder, Winchester cases, Winchester No. 120 primer. Overall length 3.35". Muzzle velocity about 3100 f.s. Bench rest accuracy at 100 yards, 5-shot groups. In the Mauser rifle: smallest .80", largest 1.87", average for nine groups 1.29". Two 5-shot groups at 200 yards went into 2.52" and 2.82". In the Pfeifer barrel: two 5-shot groups measuring 1.70" and 1.32". The late Al. Barr shot this load for trajectory, sights set for 200 yards, height at 100 yards 1.60", and drop at 300 yards 7.20". With the same bullet in the Weatherby Magnum rifle, with a charge of 67 grains of 4350 powder his drop at 300 yards was 6.05". Hardly a material difference, but look at the difference in expense of the two rifles and ammunition.

130-grain Hornady spire point bullet. This is the bullet which, to date, seems to have made the best reputation for killing power. Charge was 57 grains of 4350 powder, Winchester cases, Winchester No. 120 primers, overall length 3.35". M.V. 3140 f.s. Accuracy at 100 yards in Mauser rifle; smallest group 1.22", largest 2.50", average for ten groups 1.89". In the Pfeifer barrel; smallest 1.50", largest 2.35", average for five groups 1.77". My own trajectory test, sights set for 200 yards, gave height at 100 yards 1¼", and drop at 300 yards 6½".

150-grain Sierra soft point boat-tail bullet. This is a favorite among California deer hunters, and should give the flattest trajectory beyond 300 yards. Powder charge 54 grains of 4350 powder. Winchester cases, Winchester No. 120 primers, overall length 3.35". M.V. about 2950 f.s. 100-yard accuracy in Mauser rifle; smallest 1.2", largest 2.2", average for six groups 1.64". In the Pfeifer barrel three groups were fired, smallest 2.15", largest 3.55". Apparently this bullet is not particularly suited to this barrel, but it gave one 5-shot group at 200 yards measuring 2.65". Trajectory height at 100 yards 1¼", and drop at 300 yards only 5½".

Varmint load. A number of my friends tell me that the most accurate load of all in 270 rifles is the 110-grain Sierra spitzer bullet with a charge of 59 grains of 4350 powder, muzzle velocity over 3300 f.s. I have not tried this load, being perfectly satisfied with the 130- and 140-grain loads for varmints. It is easier to have to remember only two elevations, one for the full load and one for the small game load.

Small Game Load. I have developed a number of these loads for these two rifles. Either the Modern Bond gas check bullet No. 280780 of 111.5 grains, or the Ideal Bullet No. 280468-S weighing 103 grains, is very satisfactory with 16 grains of 4759 powder, and the Federal No. 210 primer. But the load I like best has been the 110-grain Sierra pointed soft point bullet with 16 grains of 4759 powder, Winchester cases, and Federal No. 210 primer. This primer seems to give much better accuracy with 4759 powder than any others. Overall length 3.35 inches. M.V. about 1700 f.s. When the reticle dial is set 6 minutes above that required for the above full loads for 200 yards, bullets strike .3 inch below aim at 25 yards, 1 inch above aim at 50 yards, and ¾ inch above aim at 100 yards. 100 yard 5-shot groups average 1.80". The soft point of this bullet seldom expands at the low velocity and does not spoil meat or pelts.

It is easy to make the change between the full and the reduced load elevations on the reticle dials of the Bear Cub scopes because they are so clearly marked in minutes, and have a clear zero mark, all plainly visible even in poor lights. And here I would like to digress a little on these graduations. Of all the modern hunting scopes made since World War II that I have seen, the Bear Cub Doubles and the Bushnells are the only ones with clear, unmistakable graduations and zero marks. The others, even the more expensive ones, have reticle dial graduations that are hard to see, unnumbered, or merely serrations and clicks, and none of them have zero marks, and most have no place on the reticle dial housing where you can scratch a zero mark. Probably you are not supposed to adjust them for the various loads and distances, but just to sight them in for one particular load and one distance. It just does not make sense to a real, old-time rifleman. Reminds me of a friend who was motoring through Vermont and stopped to ask a farmer the way to Rutland. The farmer said; "Mister, if I was going to Rutland, I wouldn't start from here." Both about equally silly.

Possibly the casual reader may not think so much of the accuracy here recorded for the 257 Roberts and the 270 rifles and the loads given, being used to all this loose talk running around about minute of angle accuracy. But believe me, this is very exceptional accuracy for light hunting rifles sighted suitably for big game shooting. I have never seen any such rifles, with the exception of purely target rifles and heavy 22 high power varmint rifles that would average minute of angle groups or anything like it.

The wildcatters have tried their best to "improve" the 270 Winchester cartridge. They claim great things for their super-duper 270's, but when you try them on the chronograph and a bench rest range these extravagant claims are not substantiated. In some cases there is 100 to 150 feet greater velocity, and perhaps one inch less drop at 300 yards, but what is that from a practical point of view? And look what you pay—double the cost of rifle and cartridges, very much shorter accuracy life of barrel, greater report and recoil, factory ammunition unusable in an emergency, spare parts for the rifle cannot be obtained, and with these large capacity cases it is utterly impossible to work up a suitable small game load. Again I think of the mother who was trying to induce her three-year-old son to eat a new vegetable. She said, "That's broccoli, Tom, and I want you to try it." Tom said, "I say it's spinach, and I say to hell with it!"

I think a good 270, with good loads, is the finest weapon a wilderness lover can get for wandering all over this continent. Remember, please, I am not talking about big game rifles for the largest game in thick cover. That is an entirely different story, and for such use I will agree with the "big bores" that nothing less than a 275-grain bullet with a sectional density of at least 275 will command our largest big game regardless of its position when shot.

All the loads mentioned herein are such that they will be safe in any normal standard bolt action rifle of these calibers, their breech pressures having been determined by careful tests conducted by the National Rifle Assc. in cooperation with the H. P. White Company.

Individual rifles may differ in the way their barrels vibrate or jump with various loads. Differences in elevation (and occasionally in windage), for the different loads may vary slightly from those I found in my own shooting. The rifleman should always verify these differences in zero elevations by range shooting with his own rifle and loadings.

JOHN M. BROWNING: THE MAN AND HIS PATENTS

The inventor with his Auto-5 above; the patent drawing for his wildly successful Model 1911 pistol at right.

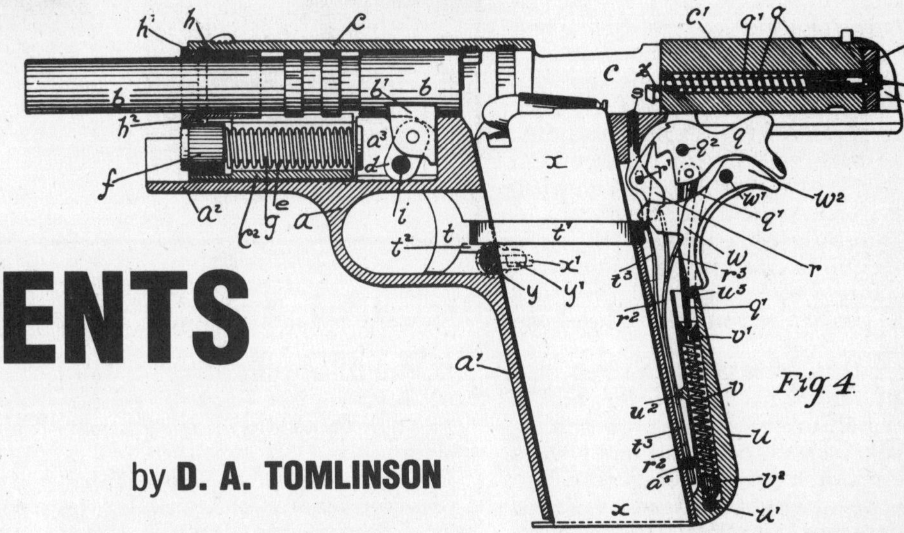

by **D. A. TOMLINSON**

AS I WALKED through the small museum in Ogden, Utah, I was awestruck by what I was seeing. Only a small fraction of John M. Browning's life's work is on display there, but that small part is enough to astound anyone who knows what he's seeing.

No gun designer in the history of the world approaches John Browning; his guns have stood the test of time, the test of war, the test of customer tastes, and the tests of increasing pressure in more modern cartridges. He died on the 26th of November, 1926, over a half-century ago, but many of his guns are still in production.

For anyone interested in guns, the story of John Moses Browning holds fascinating information.

Are you an IPSC shooter? Browning designed both the 45 Colt and the Browning Hi-Power 9mm: the two pistols most commonly used in your sport.

Are you a World War II vet? John designed the 30-06 and 50-caliber Browning machine guns and the Browning Automatic Rifle (BAR). That means that every standard-issue machine gun used by the U.S. Army, Navy, Marines, and Air Corps in that war was designed by him. So were the 303-cal. machine guns that won the Battle of Britain from the wings of the Spitfire and Hurricane fighters of the Royal Air Force.

Are you a gun collector? John designed the Winchester High-Wall, Low-Wall, 1886, 1887, 1890, 1892, 1893, 1894, 1895, 1897, 1906 and more, all the basic Colt automatic pistols, and many other fine collector's items.

I am a Canadian, and I'm astonished at the American neglect of John M. Browing. What you're reading is just a sketch of the life and work of the American who became The Master, the greatest gun designer the world has ever known. It isn't enough. There should be books, copies of all his patents gathered together into one volume, research . . . such material would be most valuable in the library of any arms designer, and an object of long study for anyone interested in fine guns, or in American military history. There should be commentary on his guns and on the production history of his guns. There should be research, collecting, and study.

The importance of this man, both to the firearms world and to the cause of freedom, can't be seen in scattered bits. It is only by taking it step by step, patent by patent, that we can see the sheer size and importance of his work. He was such a quiet man, so reasonable and unpretentious, that his accomplishments are often unrecognized and unremembered. Perhaps if he had been as flamboyant as Samuel Colt, he would be better remembered by those of us who owe him so much.

John's father was a Mormon, a gunsmith and an inventor named Johnathan Browning. Johnathan invented and built repeating cap-and-ball rifles, both in revolver and in the seldom-seen harmonica type. His revolving rifles were fine specimens, and the harmonicas were cheap, effective, and easy to repair; ideal for the early Mormon settlers of the 1830s and 40s. Like most working-class percussion rifles, few of Johnathan's making survived into the 20th century.

Johnathan brought 11 children with him to Utah in 1852, and sired 10 more after he arrived. The story deals with the younger, Utah-born family.

As John grew up, he worked with his younger brother Matt, and his four half-brothers. The oldest of the group, he was the leader and always the senior, even with Matt. The sign over the door of their business seems to indicate the relationship; though all six worked there, it said: "J. M. Browning & Bro."

Johnathan's inventiveness may have started John as an inventor, but Johnathan's trade certainly made John a craftsman. John first realized this at the age of 13 when a wagon freighter gave him a crushed and broken caplock shotgun. He disassembled it, and realized that there was no part, except the barrel, he couldn't make himself. The barrel was almost the only undamaged part, and the boy soon had the gun repaired, re-stocked, and shooting again.

At the tender age of 15, John was advised by the local schoolteacher that he'd graduated; he'd learned all that the teacher had to teach. He became a full-time gunsmith, but business was bad and the shop was run down. John built up the business, and gradually became the gunsmith in residence as his father gradually retired.

A remark by his father caused the next major shift in his life; John was cussing at a single shot rifle he was working on because it was complex and badly designed. He growled that he could design a better rifle himself. Old Johnathan calmly replied, "I know you could, John Mose, and I wish you'd get at it. I'd like to live to see you do it."

During that year of 1878, John built his first two Browning guns, both single shot rifles for metallic cartridges.

One of the rifles (unpatented?) had a reversed lever that lay under the rear of the forearm, and was pulled back and down to load; the other (U.S. Patent 220,271) is familiar to anyone who has ever handled a Winchester Hi-Wall, a Winchester Lo-Wall, or an FN/Browning B-78 single shot rifle. He applied for a patent on this one in May of 1879, and U.S. Patent 220,271 was his first.

Another important aspect of his career began here. He didn't design guns on paper; he built working firearms and then patented them by making the drawings from the guns. Bear it in mind, because each "design" I will talk about was a working, shooting, well-made and durable custom-made firearm.

Winchester, at this time, was in trouble. The Model 1873 repeater was selling well, but the '73 wasn't strong enough for heavier cartridges such as the 45-70. Winchester had no good single shot rifle for these heavy cartridges, either.

John was also in trouble; he disliked the dogwork of business, but he was ambitious. He'd bought a little five-horsepower steam engine, and set up a miniature arms factory. Matt and the four half brothers were his workers. He also employed Frank Rushton, an English Mormon who'd arrived on the day they began setting up the factory. Rushton had worked in the big English gun factories, and he knew machine tools and gunmaking. John hired him and learned from him.

Their Browning Single Shot, today a collector's item, was a good seller. It sold as fast as they could make it, which wasn't very fast. On a good day, they could make three rifles. The brothers also ran a sporting goods store in the front room of the little arms factory, and they sold their rifles there.

As the rifles spread around the area, the inevitable happened; early in 1883, a Winchester representative bought one second hand and sent it to the Winchester factory for their examination. If it was wise of Andrew McAusland to send it, it was doubly wise of Thomas G. Bennett, Winchester's General Manager, to recognize what it implied. The serial number, 463, was not too impressive; but it was a production gun. Somewhere,

In July of 1896, Browning showed this gun and three others to Colt. Patent 580,923 (opposite) was granted April 20, 1897. It's gas-operated.

out in the wilds of Utah Territory, there was a new competitor—it said, "BROWNING BROS. OGDEN UTAH" on the barrel of the best single shot rifle he'd ever seen.

Bennett was an active man. He boarded a train for Ogden. On arrival, he found the factory and the 25-year-old inventor. He promptly bought the patent for $8,000 and a promise to put J. M. Browning & Bro. on Winchester's jobber list.

The deal was a happy one for both sides. For Bennett, it was an important new product for Winchester; for John, it was a lump sum of much-needed capital, and some hope of earning important money by his brains instead of by production and administration.

It is probable that Bennett saw two more guns of John's design, because Browning had already patented two repeaters. One was a bolt action with a tubular magazine (261,667), which does not survive; the other was a very simple lever action repeater, also with a tube magazine (282,839). That one may rank as the simplest lever action repeater ever constructed. It was probably intended for production in the little factory, and it's now in the Ogden museum. While it may have been suitable for small scale production, John was apparently unsatisfied with it; he had a better design in mind, and Bennett asked to see that when it was ready.

Relieved by Bennett's $8000 of the daily business of running a factory, John radically revised his business. The store in Ogden, thanks to Winchester's jobber list, became a major sporting goods store, employing three of John's half-brothers, partly run by Matt, John's only full brother.

Bennet had taken a train back east on the same day he arrived in Ogden, but with John's comments about a heavy cartridge repeater design stirring his interest in the young inventor. Bennett's day in Utah was in the spring of 1883; in October, 1884, John was ready with the rifle some call the finest lever action of them all—the smooth, slick action that was to become the Model 1886 Winchester (306,557) and later the Model 71.

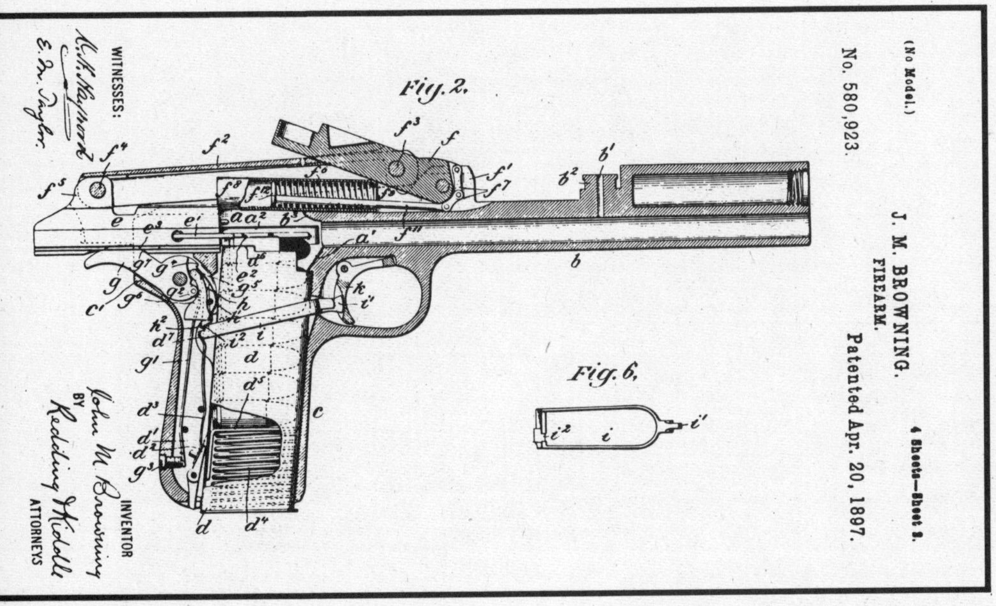

John applied for the patent on the new repeater himself, on May 26, 1884. He didn't take it east to Winchester until the patent was actually granted, in October, 1884. While waiting for the patent, he designed and built two attractive lever-action repeating rifles, one in 38 caliber (312,183), and one recorded by Browning and Gentry as in 30-40 Krag (324,296). This second caliber seems dubious, as 1884 is very early for it, but may be correct. The rifle is still in existence, in the Winchester museum, so I hope someone will check it. Personally, I'm dubious about many of the calibers attributed to Browning prototypes, as little hands-on research has been done in the last 50 years.

The 1886 was a beautiful piece of design. The lever pulled the twin locking bars down, while pivoting on its front end; then it pivoted on its middle and racked the bolt back to cock, extract and eject. Snapping the lever up fed a fresh cartridge, as smoothly as sliding cold butter on a hot stove. There were other lever-action repeaters on the market, but none were in the class of John's design for strength, smoothness of action, and simple beauty—the beauty of a well-designed machine with perfect functioning.

John and Matt went east for the first time in October of 1884, taking the prototype of the Model 1886 with them. They stopped off in New York, partly to see the sights, and partly to visit Schoverling, Daly, and Gales, the jobbing house that was their chief supplier of sporting goods. They toured the city with a Schoverling salesman whom they knew from his visits to Ogden, then returned to their hotel.

To Matt's surprise, John invited the salesman up to see the new rifle. John figured that the salesman knew guns, and he knew the gun business; his opinions could be a valuable clue to the importance of the new design. After handling it, the salesman pronounced it the finest rifle he'd ever seen, and commented that John probably held the future of the Winchester company in his hands. The worry that he was bringing a design already surpassed by someone else faded from John's mind.

Partly as a result of the salesman's comments, John felt free to ask for a steep price for the design. It is believed that he got $50,000 for it—and Winchester got a bargain. Some 203,261 rifles were made under this patent as the Model 1886 and the Model 71, a slight redesign introduced in 1935. It was in production for 71 years.

As a result of the new way of making money (selling guns to Winchester), a design team was assembled in Utah: John, the designer and inventor; Matt, the businessman; and half-brother Johnathan Edward (Ed), the machinist and model maker.

John would make sketches and sheetmetal models of parts to study working relationships. Once the relationships were clear in his mind, Ed would be brought in to do the heavy machining of parts for the working firearm, under John's direction. Later still, he and John would do the fine fitting and trimming. Once the firearm was complete, working, and ready to patent, Matt Browning would handle the paperwork and financial end of the business.

Winchester's Bennett was a man who liked to control his business. He bought John's patents outright, for flat sums. John got no royalties on the firearms he sold to Winchester, which was a pity. With royalties, the returns would have been slower but much greater. In the end, this system led to his final break with Winchester, but for the first 16 years of his career, all his long arms were sold to Winchester on similar terms.

When he bought the Model 1886, in late 1884, Bennett asked for a lever-action shotgun design. John proposed a pump action as better adapted to the larger shotgun shells, but Bennett felt that the public associated Winchester with lever actions. That's why John's next production design was the lever-action shotgun now known as the Winchester Models 1887 and 1901 (336,287). The request was made in October, 1884, and the patent was applied for (by Winchester!) on June 15, 1885. Bennett also bought the two rifles (324,296 and 324,297) mentioned above in 1885.

The patent procedure was worth noting: John designed and built firearms, but the company which bought the design often arranged for the patent in his name. This was apparently a convenience step, as the companies had legal departments and draftsmen and engineers, while John disliked paperwork. He used this system with several companies. He supplied working, tested firearms; they made production and patent drawings from the guns.

Bennett was a shrewd businessman. He bought all of John's long arm designs, some for production and others, apparently, to prevent his competitors from buying them. These patents for firearms that weren't manufactured also made it more difficult for lesser designers to design new firearms without infringing on patents owned by Winchester. As you'll see when we get to 1900, gun makers may be missing a bonanza by not studying the patents for John's guns, both produced and never produced. He was so productive that many excellent designs were never made, simply because they could only have competed with the ones that were produced; and what maker competes with himself?

The effects so far were incredible. In 1885, Winchester announced the Single Shot; in 1886, the heavy caliber Model 1886 repeater; and in 1887, the Model 1887 lever-action shotgun. These were the best available firearms in three widely differing fields.

In 1886, John sold Bennett three more designs, in the form of five working guns. There were two versions of one design of pump-action shotgun (356,271), two versions of the completely different pump-action shotgun (345,882), and a 22-caliber rifle (385,238). The shotguns were never produced, but the 22 became the first really successful 22 repeater. Issued by Winchester as the Model 1890, it became famous for rugged durability. It was the common rifle found in public shooting galleries for decades for that reason. Re-issued as the Model 06 and 62 and 62A, the total production reached 2,106,475 from Winchester alone. I have no way of totalling the numerous copies made by other makers, such as Rossi.

The success of the 22 must have been embarrassing for Winchester's

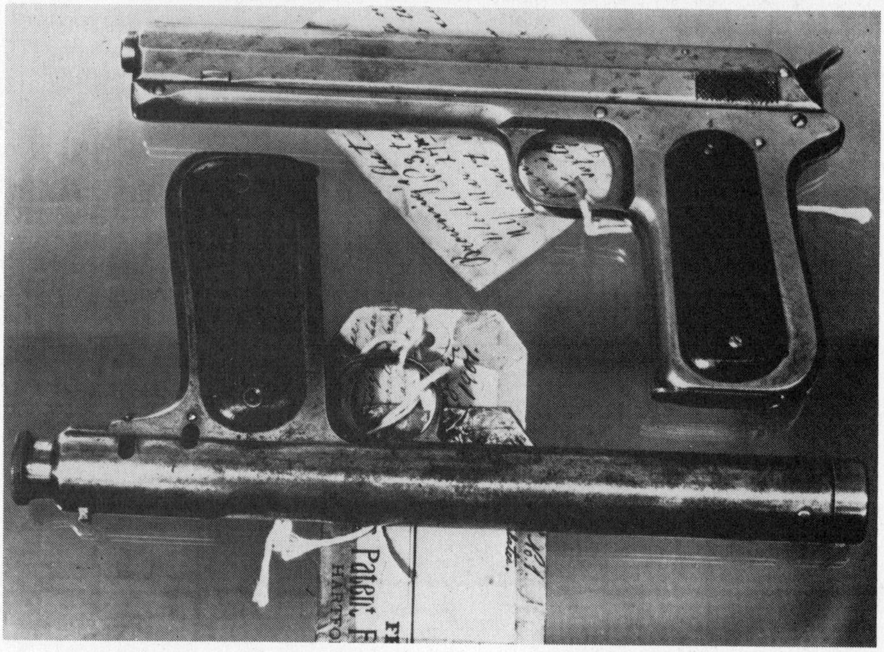

in-plant experts. It was a design requested by Bennett, and, pushed for time, John sent drawings instead of a working model. The experts told Bennett the design could not possibly work, and he notified John. John made a rifle and sent it in; the rest is history.

John sold no guns to Winchester in 1888. He was out on the road, drafted as a missionary by the Mormon church. He was 32 and married; today, the church selects only unmarried men for this duty, but in the 1880s John was eligible, and he was called. On his return, he went back to work.

In 1889, he sold Winchester only one design, in the form of two working rifles. It was an unusual repeater (428,887) that held its cartridges inside a one-piece breech block lever magazine, nose down. John often used one piece to do several jobs, which accounts for some of the simplicity of his works, but this seems to be going a bit too far—having all three major components of a lever-action repeater in just ONE piece!? One suspects that the design was a bit tongue-in-cheek, but the two rifles made to this patent (a 45-70 and a 44-40) are not at all odd-looking.

In the autumn of 1889, a minor event stirred Browning into a new path. At a shoot of the Ogden Rifle Club, he noticed that the weeds in front of a competitor's rifle swayed away from the muzzle when he fired. Probably already thinking about automatic firearms (the Maxim machine gun became available in 1888), he immediately gathered Matt and Ed and headed for the shop. There, he fired a 44-40 1873 Winchester through a hole in a bit of two-by-four. As the muzzle blast hit its rear suface, the wood was thrown violently forward, away from the muzzle.

By the next day, the same rifle had had its lever shortened, its trigger lengthened, and a crude "flapper" attached to the muzzle. In action, the flapper swung down and away from the muzzle when hit by muzzle blast. Actuated by the flapper's movement via a thin rod running from flapper to lever, the lever worked as though a hand had moved it. This extracted and ejected the empty. A spring returned the flapper to the pre-blast position, moving the lever to feed another cartridge. At the moment of final bolt closure, the short lever contacted the trigger, and the piece fired again. The work, from initial concept to a working 44-40 black powder machine carbine firing about 1000 cartridges per minute, had taken one day.

On January 6th, 1890, he applied for a patent (417,782) on the first gas-operated automatic firearm in the world. By that time, he had made several working automatic guns, of which only two survive. They are in the Ogden museum. Automatic arms now began to play an increasing role in the Browning story.

He did not stop his work for Winchester; the automatic arms were not ready to be considered for sale or production. In June of 1890, he sold Bennett the design now known as the Winchester Models 1893 and 1897 pump-action shotguns (441,390). The Model 1893 was replaced in the line by the Model 1897, in 1897. Total production ran to 1,274,750. It was discontinued in 1957 after a 64-year run.

In 1890, Bennett requested a design for a small rifle, as similar as possible to the Model 1886, but for the 25-20, 32-20, 38-40, and 44-40 family of cartridges. Winchester had tried to miniaturize the Model 1886 in the plant, but had failed. Impatient for once, Bennett offered $10,000 for a design delivered in three months, or $15,000 for one delivered in two months. Browning, wanting to see the look on Bennett's face, offered to have the rifle in Bennett's hands within thirty days for $20,000, or give it to him for nothing. This would give him six days to get back to Ogden by train, 18 days to design and build the rifle, and six days to get it to Bennett in New Haven, Connecticut. A contract was drawn, citing the three possible dates and corresponding fees, but with the gift idea omitted. Browning collected the $20,000. It was another bargain for Winchester; the Model 1892 Winchester (465,339; 499,005; 306,577) had a production run of 1,034,687. It was put back into production as the B-92 by FN of Belgium and Browning Arms a few years ago. It was also widely copied elsewhere, as the El Tigre and under other names.

Examination of the prototype in the Ogden museum startled me; knowing the history of its incredibly rapid development, I did not expect to see any major change from the Model 1886, but there is one. The prototype has the locking bars hidden under the top surface of the bolt, so the bolt top is smooth. Winchester deleted this feature on the production guns.

If this feat wasn't enough, John sold Bennett two more rifle designs in 1891, a 22 pull-apart rifle (465,340) (sort of a reverse direction pump action), and a lever-action hammerless box magazine rifle (465,339) in 45 caliber. This rifle is stocked in military fashion, and may have had something to do with the trials that led to the adoption of the 30-40 Krag by the U.S. Army in 1892.

Now, let's back up a year. This was a busy time for John, who was branching out. On November 22, 1890, Matt wrote to Colt's Patent Firearms Mfg. Co., and informed them that the Browning Bros. had a 40-pound machine gun (471,783) in 45-70 caliber, capable of firing government black powder cartridges at the rate of six shots per second. Was Colt's interested? Colt's replied that they had been making and selling Gatling hand-cranked machine guns, but Gatlings were expensive and sales were poor. They would, however, like to see the gun. They would also like to meet the inventor of all those superb Winchesters, if he cared to come to Hartford.

John and Matt arrived in early 1891. The gun they took to Colt's still exists in the Ogden museum. It bears the marks of the forge and is highly unattractive to the eye, but the visit was not an attempt to sell a finished design. John just wanted to know if he was completely wasting his time in the machine gun area. Kindly received by John Hall, the President of Colt's, the brothers asked for a place to demonstrate the gun. They had four belts of fifty each, and the gun hammered them all through without a hitch.

The talks with Hall after the demonstration were inconclusive; Colt's was interested, but, lacking a war, the market for a new type of machine gun did not exist. Hall showed them a Colt's-made Gatling, and John and Matt surprised him when they admitted that it was the first machine gun they'd ever seen, except for their own.

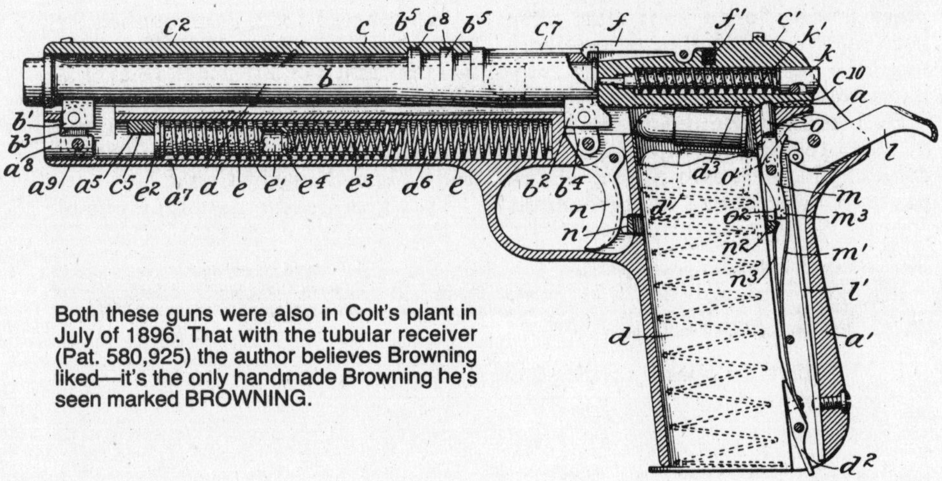

Both these guns were also in Colt's plant in July of 1896. That with the tubular receiver (Pat. 580,925) the author believes Browning liked—it's the only handmade Browning he's seen marked BROWNING.

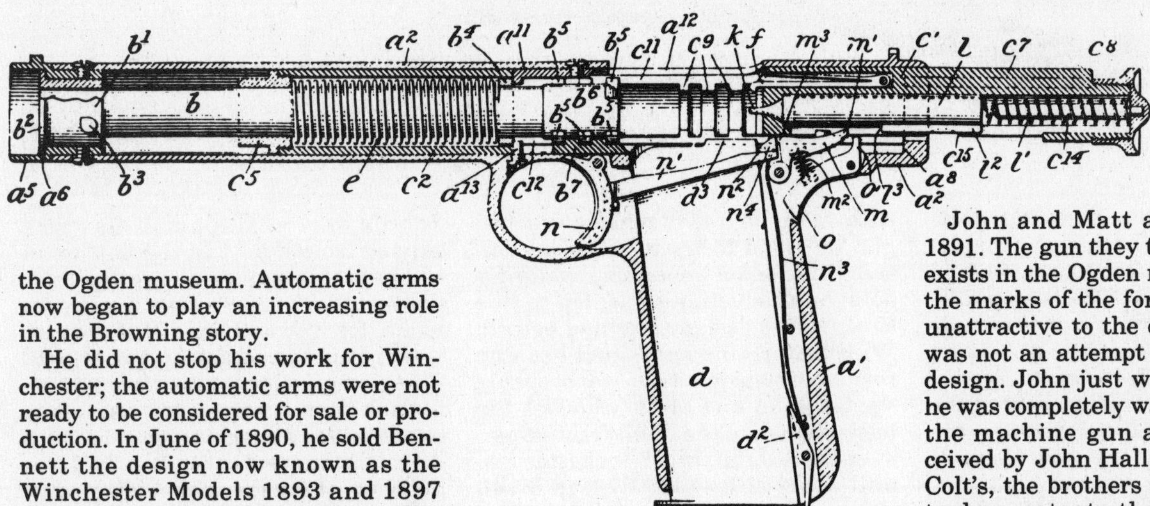

During this visit, John's reticence was bypassed by Matt's cheerful explanations of John's history and inventions. A shrewd businessman, Hall decided that this young inventor should be encouraged to develop his connection with Colt's. It was the beginning of a relationship that made both Colt's and the Brownings much wealthier. It seems probable that the patenting of this machine gun (471,783) was the first of many patents secured via the Colt's legal and drafting departments for the Brownings, as it was applied for in August of 1891.

Hall arranged an unofficial military test later in 1891, and John returned alone with the gun. The Naval Ordnance Department wanted to see the gun try for three minutes of continuous fire. They thought that ships in battle might get within small arms range of one another for up to three minutes, so that was their test. John was appalled; he had the gun firing at 600 cartridges per minute, and he knew that the heat effects would be terrific. It was a lot to ask of a crude prototype, and he didn't really expect perfect success. Hall, however, said that the point had been made that the gun was not fully developed and the officers would be forgiving of small failures.

Late one afternoon in 1891, John sat down behind the gun. He had nine boxes, each with a 200-round belt. He sat on a bicycle seat he'd attached to the gun's tripod. Earnestly watched by Hall, two Navy officers, and the works manager, he fed in the first belt and worked the action once. Twenty roaring seconds later, he tossed off an empty box, slapped a fresh one on, and started another belt. He lost count of the boxes very early, and swore as the flapper fanned droplets of molten lead back in his face. The bullets were melting in the barrel! Shoot, change belts, shoot . . . The barrel turned blue. Then it turned red. John thought about the tiny extractor, touching that red-hot barrel 600 times a minute. It would soften and break, he knew it . . . silence. For a moment, he thought the extractor had broken, but the smoke dissipated and he became aware that the belt was empty and there were no boxes left. He'd done it!

I doubt that anyone can watch three minutes of uninterrupted fire roaring through a machine gun without being impressed. Browning was using 45-70 black powder loads, so it must have been really spectacular, especially to men who had never seen a fully automatic weapon in action before.

Hall took Browning and the Naval officers to dinner that night, and John had his first-ever glass of champagne. Colt's signed an agreement with John; he was to make a finished gun for them to try to sell. The contract included a generous royalty for John on production guns. Up to this time, all his design sales had been to Winchester, and there had been no royalty provisions. This deal probably started John and Matt (who was the businessman of the family) thinking.

In 1892, John sold Winchester two pull-apart rifles (486,273) in 30-40 Krag, a pull-apart shotgun (487-659), two lever-action rifles (486-272 and 492-459) in 30-40, and an odd rifle with a lever that swung back and down (499,007) instead of forward and down, also in 30-40.

1892 was the year that the U.S. Army adopted the 30-40 Krag rifle. Three of these rifles had military style stocks, and the two pairs were a full-stocked rifle and a carbine (for cavalry?) each. Were Browning and Winchester competing against the Krag to supply the next U.S. Army rifle, or was Browning just jumping on the bandwagon of the next U.S. military cartridge?

Still in 1892, John sold Bennett a rifle (499,005) which was a minor variant on the Model 1892 patent in 44-40 caliber. He patented, but did not sell, the simplest 22 single shot rifle ever made, with ONE spring and ONE moving part. We will return to it later—in 1900.

In addition, he applied for one more machine gun patent. It covered a machine rifle (502,549) of small size, low power and light weight which was never produced.

In 1892 and 1893, John applied for four patents (544,658; 544,659; 544,660; and 543,567) for the machine gun now known as the Model 1895 Colt "Potato Digger." It was later manufactured in 30-40 Krag, 30-06, and 236 Lee Navy by Colt's.

This gun used a development of John's early "flapper." Gas was tapped from a port in the bottom of the barrel to push a swinging lever downward. The lever gave the gun its name, for it would dig dirt if the gun was mounted too low on the tripod. This swinging lever deserves more attention than it ever got; its action is excellent for a machine gun, because its initial movement is mostly down but slowly to the rear, providing enormous strength for the crucial initial movement of the bolt, followed by speed for the rest of the travel, and slow, positive closure on return. The prototype preserved in Ogden is one of the smoothest firearms I have ever handled, and swinging that big lever is like operating a well-oiled 1886 Winchester.

Belt-fed, and quite reliable, the Colt 1895's were bought by the U.S. armed forces in small numbers. They were used in the Spanish American War, and also in the Boxer Rebellion

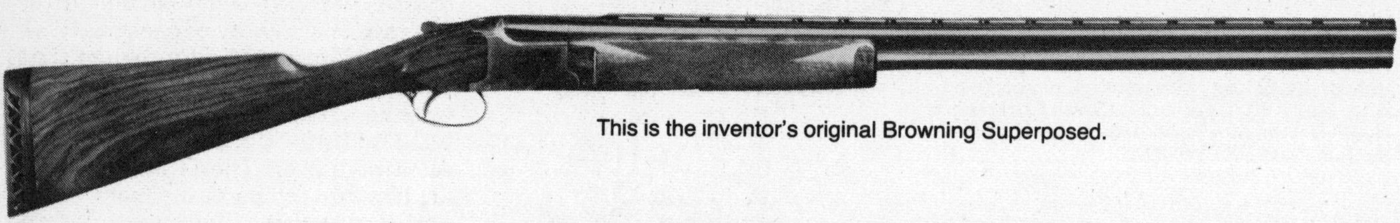

This is the inventor's original Browning Superposed.

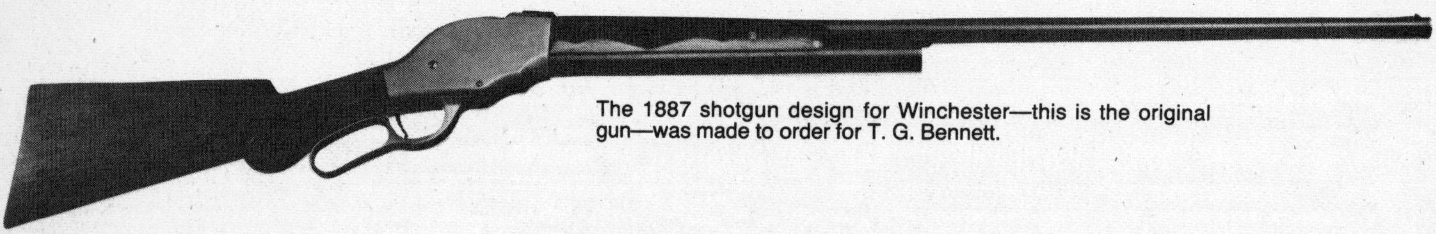

The 1887 shotgun design for Winchester—this is the original gun—was made to order for T. G. Bennett.

in China, where they were credited with saving the foreign legations from massacre.

Only a few thousand M1895's were ever made, but Marlin made some with conventional fore-and-aft pistons during the First World War, for use in aircraft and tanks. Though this redesign is usually credited to the Marlin factory, it was actually present as a possible variant in Browning's original patent.

For serious students of firearms design, it should be noted that a frequently-used photograph of the M1895 is in error; properly, a belt enters the gun below the breech from the left, and exits, empty, from a short slit on the right. Ejection is from the right rear of the breech. The photograph shows a short, loaded belt stuck into the ejection port from the wrong side of the gun!

A fluke of timing and a lot of hard work led to the large number of patents applied for in 1892. They came in two lots, one early in the year and one quite late. He applied for few in 1893, but in that year he designed the most famous lever gun of them all—the Model 1894 Winchester (524,702), still in production.

Designed for the family of black powder intermediate cartridges, the 32-40 and 38-55, the Model 1894 was immediately adapted to the 30-30 Winchester. The designation stood for 30 caliber and 30 grains of SMOKELESS powder. It was a revolution. The big 45's and 50's thinned out quickly, as the superior ballistics and power of the world's first sporting smokeless powder cartridge rendered them, and the heavy rifles they needed, obsolete. It is noteworthy that the Model 1894 required *no* changes in the action design to withstand the doubled pressure of the smokeless loads; designed for black powder, it ate smokeless without a murmur. John always designed for both durability and strength. In fact, none of his black powder guns were rendered obsolete by the coming of smokeless powder. The extra stress of doubled pressure was within Browning's designed-in safety factors, without any modifications being required.

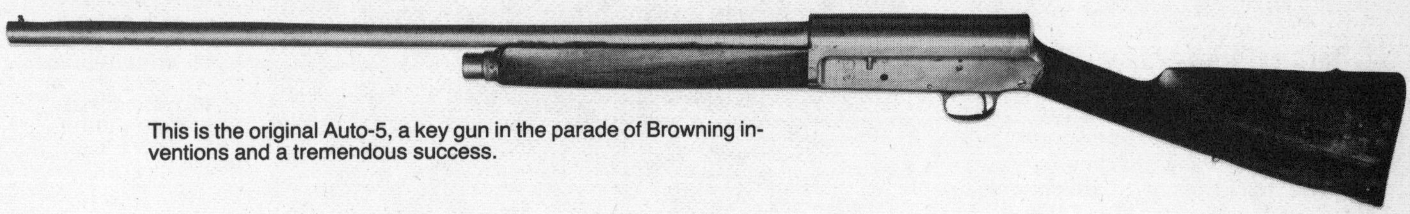

This is the original Auto-5, a key gun in the parade of Browning inventions and a tremendous success.

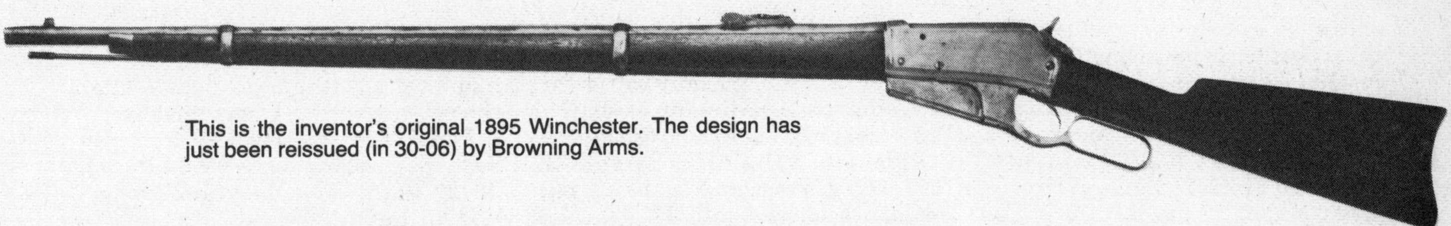

This is the inventor's original 1895 Winchester. The design has just been reissued (in 30-06) by Browning Arms.

In 1894, the design of the Model 1895 Winchester (549,345) was completed and sold to Winchester. It was the first production lever gun with a box magazine, which made it suitable for sharp-nosed hardpoint ammunition of military type. Made in 30-40 Krag, 30-06, and 405 Winchester (among others), it was produced from 1895 to 1931 for a total of 425,881.

Patented in 1894 were also: a pump-action shotgun (552,864), sold to Winchester, and a small automatic rifle (544,461), never sold and apparently made only to test and demonstrate some ideas for automatic arms. Also in 1894, he designed and tested a gas operated semi-automatic pistol with a potato digger-type swinging lever which swung upward instead of downwards.

In 1895, John sold Winchester another pump-action shotgun (550,778) which externally resembles the Stevens Model 520, a gun he designed for Stevens in 1903. In 1896, he sold Winchester another (577,281), externally similar but internally quite different. He also designed and made several more semi-automatic pistols.

Sometime during or before July of 1896, John arrived at the Colt's plant with four semi-automatic pistols. There were a few semi-auto pistols on the world market in 1896, but only the 1896 Mauser and a heavily modified version of the 1893 Borchardt are still remembered (as the Luger or P.08) as successful designs. He had:

1. A gas-operated pistol (580,923) with outside hammer, detachable magazine in the butt, and locked action.
2. A hammer-fired dropping barrel-locked action pistol (580,924), with similar magazine, obviously the prototype M1900 Colt, and the direct ancestor of the M1905 and M1911 Colts.
3. A striker-fired, rotating barrel-locked action pistol (580,925), with similar magazine and a grip safety.
4. A hammer-fired blowback pistol (580,926), with similar magazine, obviously the direct ancestor of the M1900 FN pistol.

One may be forgiven for taking a serious look at recognizing him as The Master, a title given him later by the workers of FN, when one realizes that the patented features included in this lot include the grip safety, the slide, the dropping barrel lock, the detachable magazine in the grip and the slide return spring placed under, over, and around the barrel!

Try and think of a semi-auto pistol that does not use at least one of these key patented features.

John signed an agreement (24 July 1896) with Colt's which licensed Colt's to produce his pistols and promised licenses for any improvements to come, in exchange for royalties. It included Colt's being responsible for patenting the four pistols, at Colt's expense.

In 1896, he built a modified version of the blowback pistol (#4), and patented it (621,747) via Colt's.

A chance meeting with Hart O. Berg at Colt's in 1897 proved a major turning point in John's life. Berg was a representative of Fabrique Nationale d'Armes de Guerre of Belgium, a large plant originally set up to make M1889 Mauser rifles to re-equip the Belgian Army. With the Army contract fulfilled, they had nothing to make!

Ludwig Loewe and Co., a German firm, had sold FN their Mauser manufacturing tooling. By 1896, Loewe owned DWM, Mauser, the big Steyr plant called Osterreich Waffenfabrik (probably; this relationship is unclear), and Fegyver es Gepgyar of Hungary (which made Roths and Roth-Steyrs). In early 1896, they bought control of the financially troubled FN. After the purchase, FN got a 15% share in any military contracts for Mauser rifles, but it wasn't enough; most of the plant was idle. The local FN managers did have the right to make anything they could find, except the designs controlled by other companies, and were desperately hunting for products.

Berg returned to Belgium with John's modified blowback pistol (621,747) and a license for FN to make it for the European market. Smaller than the 1896 type. it was in 32 ACP or 7.65mm caliber, pocket sized, and very slim. The FN managers tested it, and it fired 500 rounds without a bobble, an excellent performance even by today's standards. Put into production as the Model 1899 and immediately slightly modified, it was renamed the Model 1900 (to take advantage of the turn of the century?), it sold like hot cakes. It also gave a new word to the French language: browning—an automatic pistol.

There was a complex Browning-Colt-FN agreement, dating from July, 1897, which gave the European market to FN, the Americas to Colt, and shared the British areas; John licensed each of them to make his designs, and each decided what to produce. They paid each other royalties for sales infringing on each other's exclusive territories. This agreement, with minor modifications from time to time, ran at least to the start of World War I, and probably later. The two companies co-operated and communicated, as we shall see.

In 1897, John sold Bennett a box magazine lever-action rifle (599,595) in 236 Lee Navy caliber. It had an incredibly short receiver. He sold Winchester another (619,132), in 30 caliber, in 1898. There were two differing rifles made to this basic design, one with a one-piece stock and the other with a flush magazine. Both had extremely short receivers, and triggers that moved with the lever like a modern Browning BLR.

In 1899, Bennett requested a single shot 22 to compete with the cheap European Flobert rifles then flooding the U.S. market. John designed the bolt-action Model 1900 Winchester

This is Lt. Val Browning posing, in 1917, with an early BAR. The modified 1892 Winchester above, probably a 44-40, was originally a full-auto potato-digger, now is semi-auto.

(632,094) for him, the only bolt-action gun, other than his first repeater, that I can find record of him designing.

Remember the ultra-simple 22 (511,677) I mentioned as being patented, but not sold, in 1892? John did. It was even simpler than the hinged breech Flobert—so John sold it to Bennett. He knew that Bennett would not make it, because it was a mechanical joke, and Bennett took his company's prestige seriously. Equally, he knew Bennett would have to buy it—if someone else started producing it, nothing could be made cheaper or easier. There were four working rifles of this design, with minor variations in the extraction method. They are now in the Winchester museum, and the patent has expired. Does anyone want to produce the world's cheapest 22?

This tiny rifle worked like this: The rifle has no trigger in the trigger guard, so put your thumb on top of the breech block and push it down against spring tension. As it slides down, the apparently missing trigger (which is just a section of the block) appears, coming downward into the trigger guard. Fully down, the block hooks onto the trigger guard. Push a 22 shell into the open breech, aim, and pull the trigger. This unhooks the block. The spring tosses the block upward, behind the shell, and the trigger vanishes upward. Disconcerting at first, no doubt! As the block gets to the top of its travel, a fixed firing pin digs in and fires the shell. Push the block down, and pluck out the empty. Why no enterprising small businessman ever put it into production after the patent expired, I can't imagine!

The bolt-action Model 1900 22 sold well, reappearing as the 02, 04, 99, 36, 58, 60, and 68 over the years. Production hit 1,458,606.

By March of 1899, John had a semi-automatic shotgun ready for Winchester. While no one else had figured out how to make an auto shotgun, John had made two! One is now known as the Browning Auto-5 (659,507; 689,283; 710,094; and 812,326), the Remington Model 11, and under several other names; the other was never produced, but used a Luger-style toggle action.

A large caliber semi-auto rifle (659,786) was patented at this time too, probably through Winchester. Its history is a bit obscure; patented in 1900, it did not appear as a commercial production gun until 1906, when it became the Remington Model 8, in 25, 30, and 35 Remington; in 1936 it became the Model 81. Remington halted production in 1950. It was also produced by FN, but did not prove popular in Europe. Its relationship to the Auto-5 quarrel are obscure.

The Auto-5 was the cause of the

break with Winchester. Bennett was, apparently, afraid of it. He wasn't sure that automatic firearms were here to stay, and he stalled for two years. He refused to buy it or produce it, and he refused to state definitely that he would not buy it or produce it. The prototypes were kept at Winchester for trials and patenting.

One day in 1902, an angry John Browning stalked into Bennett's office, determined to force a showdown. He demanded a huge fee for the Auto-5, but the killer was that he demanded royalties as well. Bennett stated that Winchester didn't pay royalties, and John stated that he no longer sold without getting royalties. John picked up his prototypes from the drafting room and left.

Winchester did the patent work (in John's name) on the Auto-5, but hadn't bought it, so John went to Remington to try and sell it. On January 8th, 1902, while he was waiting to see Marcellus Hartley, President of Remington, Hartley dropped dead of a heart attack. This resulted in John making a trip to Belgium, where he arranged for FN to produce the Auto-5. He also signed a contract to purchase 10,000 Auto-5's marked "Browning Automatic Arms Company" for the American market, which he reserved for his own company. This was the real start of the FN-Browning manufacturing and selling business partnership that brought America so many fine firearms.

Interestingly enough, the Auto-5 was so good that no other really successful semi-auto shotgun design appeared until 1957, when the first gas-operated shotguns hit the market. The two keys to this situation were the bronze friction brake he invented, which handled the heavy recoil forces by dragging on the magazine tube, and the cocking handle. It was the only really good place to put a cocking handle, and he not only patented that point, he patented nearly every other place one *could* put it!

The Auto-5 has been made by FN, Remington, Savage, Daiwa, and, with minor modifications, by many others. It is still in production, and likely to stay in production. Millions have been made, in Belgium, America, Italy, and Japan.

It seems probable that John also took to FN, on this trip, the large prototype of the pistol (747,585) that became the 1903 FN in 9mm Browning Long caliber. It was a partial success as a military pistol. The FN version was adopted by seven countries, but only about 150,000 were ever made, and more than half of those were made by Husqvarna in Sweden for the Swedish armed forces.

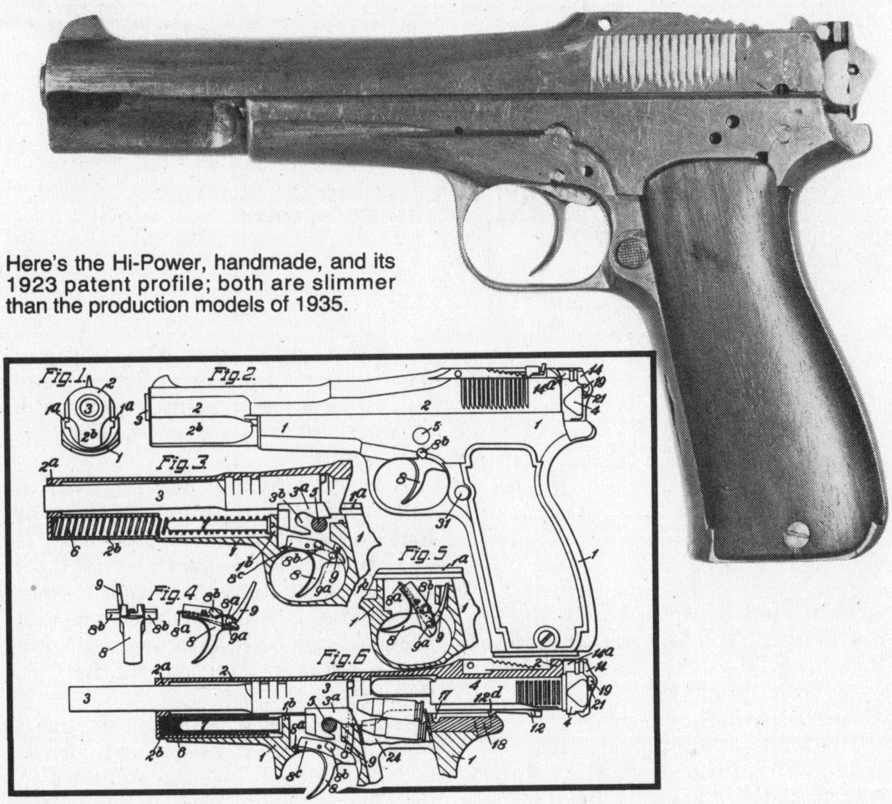

Here's the Hi-Power, handmade, and its 1923 patent profile; both are slimmer than the production models of 1935.

This design was simultaneously produced as the Colt 32ACP and (later) 380ACP pocket pistols, based on a smaller handmade prototype. The pocket Colts were more successful, about 572,215 being made in 32 and about 150,000 in 380, with production running from 1902 to 1945. In 1903, John sold a pump shotgun (781,765) to Stevens, who produced it as the Model 520 for many years.

In 1904 or 05, John designed a really small pistol; the 25ACP Colt or 6.35mm FN. It was patented in Belgium through FN in 1905, and production began there in that year. From 1905 to 1940, some 1,080,408 6.35mm FN's were made in Belgium.

Colt decided to produce a 25 in 1906. American patent laws did not allow patenting John's design for FN in the U.S., since it had been patented elsewhere. This prevented a cottage industry in re-patenting foreign patents, but left the 25 unprotected in the U.S. FN provided drawings and a sample pistol to Colt's, and we have a problem. Colt's made a toolroom prototype with a hammer instead of a striker firing system like the FN; we know that, but was this John producing another type for Colt's, or Colt's re-doing the 25 nearer to the 32 by themselves?

In any case, Colt's actually manufactured a duplicate of the FN, starting production in 1909. Three patents were listed on the slide, but none of them are relevant to the pistol; it was an attempt to pretend it was covered by U.S. patents, apparently. In 1910, a real U.S. patent was applied as well; it covered John's new safety catch (947,478) for the 25, which doubled as a takedown latch. The 25 Colt was discontinued in 1946, after 500,000 had been made.

The series of heavy caliber Colt Brownings began with the original four from the 1896 contact. The M1900 38ACP (a longer and more powerful cartridge than the 380ACP) with two-link dropping barrel lockup was disappointing in commercial sales, but it was sold in small test quantities to the U.S. Army and Navy in 1900. Complaints about the 38-caliber and design problems led to John's patent 708,794 for a slide lock to hold the pistol open when empty, and to experiments in 41 and 45 calibers.

The 41 experiments died out, but John designed a 45 pistol (808,003) in 1905, and Colt's produced it. A hammerless (internal hammer) example of this pistol still exists.

The U.S. Army insisted on using a heavier bullet than the M1905's 200-

grain, so the pistol was beefed up for the trials of 1906-07. It did well enough to be bought in test quantities for 1908 field trials, but Browning wasn't happy with it. He produced an almost totally new pistol (984,519) for the tests of 1909. This pistol, never produced, is basically an M1911 with the grip at 84 degrees to the slide instead of 74 degrees, and no manual safety. Complaints about grip angle caused John to make his 1910 version, recognizably an M1911, but still with no manual safety. The 1910 prototype is in Ogden.

The final, triumphantly successful M1911 I will leave to others to sing about; Lord knows there were enough people doing it, and have been for the last 70-plus years. I will add, however, mention of two little-known pistols from this series. There was a hammerless prototype of the 1909, and it's in Ogden. It looks just like a giant version of the Colt 32ACP pocket pistol, with an external slide locking lever added to the left side, and a safety catch. Even the grip safety looks like the 32ACP's.

There was also a 9.8mm toolroom version of the 1910 design fabricated at Colt's. It had features from both the 1910 and the 1911 prototypes, and wasn't quite either. Eugene Reising of Colt's claimed to have demonstrated it in Rumania, Serbia, and Bulgaria in 1911 and 1912. It probably died because Colt's had their plate running over, mass-producing M1911s for the U.S. armed forces.

Now, we back up a tad to 1910. John designed a 32ACP and 380ACP pistol for FN that year. It went into production as the M1910. With extended slide, barrel, magazine, and butt, it later became the military and police version, the M1922. About 572,590 M1910's and 396,865 M1922's were made by FN; there were the usual unlicensed copies everywhere, and a true copy made by DWM in Germany. Several European forces were equipped with the M1922, including the Yugoslav and Dutch armies, and the Belgian, Danish, French, Swedish, and Czech police. FN's still making M1910s.

In late 1912, Browning patented a lovely little takedown 22 semi-auto rifle. It was produced by FN, and by Remington as the Model 24 and 241, for many years. Barely a yard long, it breaks into two parts of equal length for storage and backpacking. It also had the best takedown system ever devised; it was adjustable. The chief fault of takedown rifles is that they get loose in their old age, but the Browning has an adjustment that takes up the slack. It's nearly impossible to wear one out. Its only fault is its bottom ejection; I hate those hot cases entering my cuffs.

A request from the U.S. Army for a practice pistol in 22 caliber caused Colt's to try a 22 conversion unit for the M1911, but it was not a success. No records survive, except for a 1911 letter from Colt's, stating that a 22 version had proved impossible, and they were trying a 25ACP version of the M1911. As this would have defeated the purpose of cheap practice with rimfire cartridges, we understandably know of no further developments in this line. We don't know if John was involved; Colt's had other inventors in its string.

Springfield Armory did make a prototype M1911 look-alike in 22 Short rimfire, but it also died very young. Browning may have produced a 22 rimfire pistol in 1911, or did he? Bady has a photo (Fig. 91) of a pistol that is clearly a Browning handmade; he labels it as an internal bolt 22, and he's wrong. That prototype is in Ogden; it's related to the first prototype of the Browning Hi-Power, and it probably dates from about 1923. It isn't a 22; it's probably in 9mm Luger.

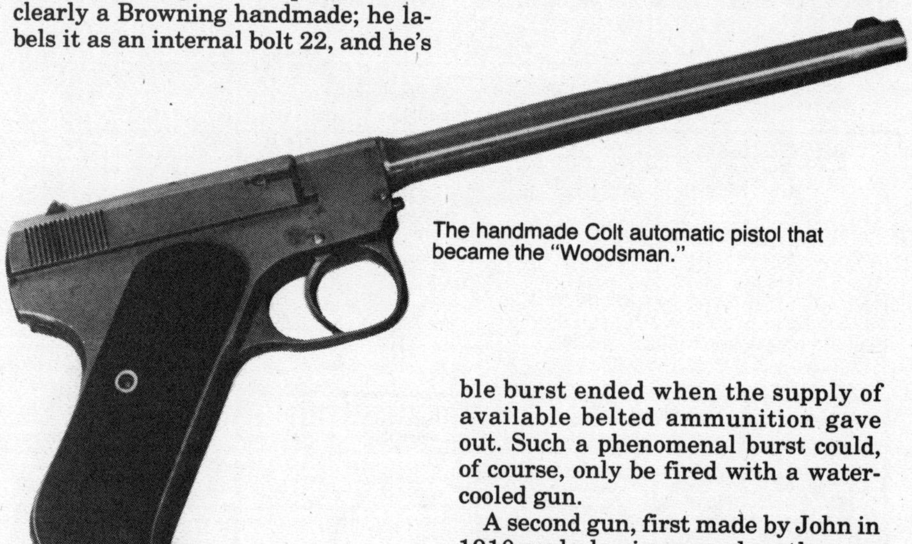

The handmade Colt automatic pistol that became the "Woodsman."

The Master did produce a 22 prototype in 1915, Bady's Fig. 92, and it was tested and rejected by the U.S. Army in 1916. He made several other 22 pistols in 1914 and 1915, but only one (1,276,716) made it into production. That one was to become known as the Colt Woodsman, and it was made from 1915 to the late 1970s with minor variations. Some 540,000 were made. It was also copied, as in the Tala from Argentina.

By this time, World War I was raging, but the U.S. wasn't in it—yet. John knew that the U.S. might get in, and then there would be a mighty rush to make arms. He already had a better machine gun (678,934) than the M1895, patented in 1900. The war in Europe, plus his own inventiveness, had spurred him to make improvements which were patented (1,293,021) in 1916. Tested at Springfield Armory in May, 1917, the water-cooled Browning in 30-06 fired 20,000 rounds without a malfunction or a broken part. It was then fired for a further 20,000 rounds, with the same result.

The test was so spectacularly successful that there were murmurs of disbelief; was the test gun rigged in some way? Ignoring the silliness of that idea, John felt obliged to answer it. A second toolroom gun was brought out, and it not only duplicated the performance of the first one, it actually fired a continuous burst lasting 48 minutes and 12 seconds. This incredible burst ended when the supply of available belted ammunition gave out. Such a phenomenal burst could, of course, only be fired with a water-cooled gun.

A second gun, first made by John in 1910 and also improved as the war loomed closer, was tested during the 1917 trials. This was a 15-pound light machine gun, in 30-06, with a 20-shot magazine. It was gas operated, and became known as the Browning Automatic Rifle (BAR). It served the U.S. through the 1950s.

Both guns were later manufactured in quantity by FN and others; for example, the BAR became standard in the Swedish army, and FN-made 30's are still used by the Israeli army.

Although it is not generally recognized, the FN General Purpose Machine Gun, now standard for many armies including the British, is a heavily modified, belt-fed BAR.

In late 1917, an American Army officer called on Browning to settle details of the government's rights to produce the M1911 Colt pistol, the BAR, and the M1917 machine gun for the duration of the war. The chief detail was the price; the officer made one bid, a flat cash sum for all rights. He stated that he knew the sum offered was only a fraction of what would go to John if he wanted royalties on the guns, even if only those already ordered for production were considered, so negotiations would probably be necessary. Browning didn't hesitate; he simply said: "Major, if that suits Uncle Sam, it's all right with me."

John M. Browning deserves to be remembered for that moment of patriotism. He actually received $750,000 for that contract; if he had insisted on the standard royalties he could have had for the asking, he would have received $12,704,350.

In 1917, John took an apartment in Hartford, and supervised the making of drawings and toolroom models of his guns. He checked the work of all the factories making his pistols, BAR, and M1917 machine guns (Colt in Hartford and Meriden, Conn; Westinghouse in Springfield, Mass; Marlin-Rockwell and Winchester in New Haven, Conn; and Remington in Ilion, NY). He cut red tape and worked quiet miracles, but there was a lesson to be dearly learned. The U.S. went to war with exactly 1100 obsolescent machine guns on hand; and it took time to tool up and produce all the guns that were needed. That war was over before the Army could be fully equipped with Browning guns, but they were ready for World War II.

General Pershing, commander of the U.S. Army in France, was faced by the first primitive German tanks. He promptly requested a gun, firing bullets of 670 grains minimum weight at a velocity of 2700 fps minimum. Springfield Armory tried and failed to produce such a gun, so John was called in. He made the 50-caliber Browning machine gun, and had it firing by September, 1918. It was scheduled for formal government acceptance trials on 11 Nov 1918. The armistice delayed the tests until the 15th, when John fired bursts of 100 to 150, and had no malfunctions in 877 rounds.

The 50 looks like a scaled-up 30-06, but it's more than that. It incorporates a hydraulic buffer to handle the massive recoil of the 50 BMG cartridge.

Both the 30 and the 50 developed into weapons systems as time rolled on. Water-cooled and air-cooled, light-barrelled and heavy-barrelled, one side feeding or either side feeding, slow fire or rapid fire, bipod, tripod, pedestal, or turret mounts, in aircraft at 30,000 feet and 40-below temperatures, in the mud of Viet Nam, in the desert of North Africa, the Brownings went with the troops and the Brownings worked.

In one interesting area, the 50 was scaled up to become a 20mm aircraft cannon. Unfortunately, it was the Japanese who did this, and 20mm Brownings (which American experts said couldn't be made) were used against America from the wings of Japanese fighters. That was much later.

In 1918, somehow, Browning found time to prepare a little-known firearm, the Browning 30-18. It looked like an infantry rifle of the period, with a long stick magazine hanging out the bottom. From the magazine size, I think it may have been a development spurred by the idea of the Pedersen device. The Pedersen device temporarily converted the Springfield bolt-action rifle into a semi-auto firing a cartridge like a long 32 pistol cartridge. The 30-18 is associated with FN, and the action reappeared in a line of French (MAS 38, etc.) submachine guns. The action used a bolt that moved at a slight angle to the bore to retard the bolt opening by friction.

By 26 July 1919, John was back at his normal trade. He applied for a patent (1,424,553) on a pump-action 22 rifle, and FN produced it for many years.

In the years 1920 through 1923, he had a big project; the U.S. Army had been asking him for a 37mm machine cannon. They had been trying to produce one for several years, with no success, and General C.C. Williams, Chief or Ordnance, finally decided only Browning could do it. John begged off, pleading that his work on sporting arms had him tied up. In 1920, though, he finally agreed, mostly because he knew he could do it. He also knew he'd never make a dime out of it in peacetime.

The Army sent him a few dummy cartridges, and noted that it would have to make up some solid-projectile ammunition; the only ammo they had on hand had explosive projectiles. John finished the gun in three months; the ammunition wasn't ready yet.

The 37mm was as usual a reliable, strong, and workmanlike gun. The Army promptly asked if it could be made more powerful, as the muzzle velocity of 1400 fps was a bit pathetic. John pointed out that that was the cartridge they supplied and asked to have the gun made for, then made a gun for 37mm cartridges producing 2000 fps, as requested. He then made another, for 37mm cartridges producing 3050 fps, again on request. The patents (1,525,065 to 1525,067) date from 1923 and 1924, but the guns did not go into production until 1935, nine years after John's death.

As the M4 and M9, the 37mm machine cannons were used in the Bell P-39 Airacobra and a few other planes. The Russians used the high velocity M9 in Lend-Lease Airacobras as a tank destroyer. Today, it would be an excellent weapon for Armored Personnel Carriers.

In 1923, the Superposed shotgun (1,578,638 and 1,578,639) was patented. Also in 1923, Browning patented the Hi-Power pistol (1,618,510). This final development in a line from the Colt M1900, M1905, M1911 family featured a double column magazine, cam unlocking, and a tangent elevating rear sight. It may have been designed to cash in on the lucrative Chinese market for shoulder-stocked pistols with large magazines, the result of Chinese laws banning ownership of rifles, but silent on pistols. Mauser, Astra, and others were selling well there; probably FN wanted a piece of the action. One feature in the patent drawings for the Hi-Power that doesn't appear in the finished gun is a trigger safety; the pistol could be put on safe by swinging the trigger forward and up. It was his last patent, and it's still in production.

John Moses Browning died of heart failure in the office of his son, Val Browning, at FN on the twenty-sixth of November, 1926. The Master is gone, but his guns still proclaim his mastery. No one has taken his place. It is unlikely anyone ever will. Honor his memory; we owe him much. ●

Editor's Note: GUN DIGEST thanks the Browning Arms Co. for the photos used here. K.W.

BIBLIOGRAPHY

John M. Browning, American Gunmaker; Doubleday & Co. Inc; John Browning and Curt Gentry, 1964

Handguns of the World; Stackpole Books; Edward C. Ezell, 1981

Colt Automatic Pistols; Borden Publishing Co; Donald B. Bady, 1973

The World's Assault Rifles; TBN Enterprises, Daniel O. Musgrave and Thomas B Nelson

The World's Machine Pistols and Submachine Guns, Vol IIa; TBN Enterprises; Thomas B. Nelson and Daniel O. Musgrave, 1980

Mauser Bolt Rifles, Third Edition; F. Brownell & Son, Publishers, Inc; Ludwig Olsen, 1976

IT MAY dumbfound those fascinated by the glamorous age of American pioneering to learn that many fabulous long rifles never were rifles at all. Technically they were smoothbores, smoothbores of special kinds, not oddities or rebores or rarities. We speak of traditional firearms created as far back as early colonial times. Ancestrally, these long American smoothbores deserve a place of distinction akin to that of their far more famous relatives, the long rifles.

As a class, surviving long smoothbores have come down to us through the years as unnoticed as wallflowers at a dance. Much of their obscurity may be blamed on mistaken identity. They look like long rifles; they often served as shotguns; they were not exactly either. Because of this ambiguity, they never had a real name all their own.

For nearly two centuries now, the few people who recognized these guns as a distinct type have groped for a satisfactory name for them. Most tries went wide of the mark. For example: Everyone knows that a rifle has rifling and a smoothbore hasn't, yet these long guns were dubbed with such contradictions as "smoothbore rifles," a misnomer adopted by the U.S. Army before 1800. The phrase that best describes their function would be "ball-or-shot guns," but that is cumbersome. For our purposes here, then, let us christen them American *long smoothbores*. All the early ones were flintlocks, but the type continued well

Look Again At... Long Rifles With Smooth Bores

by **ASHLEY HALSEY, JR.**

Author with his probable favorite smoothbored rifle: a 1780 Jacobus Schuler.

into the percussion period.

To arrive at a clearer understanding of the long smoothbores and their correct status among American firearms, consider their salient features and how they came into being:

At the start of gunsmithing in the 13 American colonies, there were two basic kinds of civilian shoulder arms: The light smoothbore fowling piece or bird gun, principally English in origin, and the heavy hunting rifle of Germanic derivation. The two stood extremes apart in both appearance and performance. The fowling piece, graceful and thin if not frail, threw shot. In the flintlock period, it served as the predecessor of the modern shotgun. The rifle, stubby and weighty by comparison, fired a substantial round ball. Rifle fodder ran as big as 60 to 70 caliber. Several colonial American versions of English fowlers that I have examined, by contrast, gauged the smoothbore equivalent of less than half that caliber.

In the inevitable American process of change and progress, the rifles stretched out very nearly to fowling piece length and slimness without surrendering their rifling. Some indigenous fowlers also appeared, notably the Hudson River type with their extra-long smoothbore barrels suitable for pass shooting in that majestic valley. Largely lost to sight in the transition period, however, was the development of a combination-purpose long smoothbore.

Like all new things in the New World, the long smoothbore was invented in response to a need and a demand. In this instance the cry was for a hard-hitting large caliber gun that could be loaded with a choice of shot or unpatched balls faster than a patched-ball rifle could swallow its single projectile. The new arm offered this versatility and what passed in muzzle-loading days for speedy loading. It fit neatly into its time and place.

Look backward a moment to that time and place. Most Americans today harbor a tidy notion that the frontier advanced almost in a line from east to west over all obstacles, climbing mountains and fording rivers. Actually it was a wavering process. It began on the brink of the Atlantic in the 1600's. From there it marched "by the left flank, right flank" and in grim times such as Indian massacres, "double-to-the-rear." It flowed through the gaps and valleys, bypassing the highlands. In those areas—Adirondacks, Poconos, Alleghenies, Appalachians, Ozarks, in turn—the larger game lurked in the fastnesses and forayed around the settlements. Wildlife biologists tell of elk and bison roving east of the Mississippi and infiltrating the Atlantic coastal plain. Wolves prowled in plenty. Bears in their deceptively lumbering way wandered widely in the East and some still do. Hunting in the settled areas, however, gradually turned more to mixed bags including squirrels, rabbits and fowl.

During the period from the late 1600's through the mid 1700's, meanwhile, the rifle underwent its transformation from Germanic short hunting arm to the legendary American long rifle, although it kept such jaeger features as the octagon barrel and patchbox. Essentially it emerged as the "big game" rifle of its time. As such, it lacked the capability of a shotgun in taking small game. To overcome this, some 18th and 19th century gunsmiths produced over-and-under muzzleloaders with one barrel rifled, one smooth. These proved relatively heavy in the field and expensive to make. They obviously were not the best answer.

Meanwhile, enter quietly the long smoothbore. It is impossible to say just when it established itself. Probably it was known by word-of-mouth by the third quarter of the 1700's. The Verner long smoothbore illustrated herewith may have been one of the first of its kind fabricated in America.

To fulfill the double need for a ball-or-shot gun, the new firearm had to be more than a lightweight fowling piece and it was. For one thing, its octagon breech section was usually heavier and stronger than most fowlers and some rifles. To save weight and simplify barrel production, however, its barrel was round for most of its length from breech section to muzzle. In this respect the barrel followed the pattern of the fowler barrel. Some other characteristics are typical of the long rifle.

The veil over the identity of the new gun was due in part to its birthplace. Like the famous long rifles, the long smoothbores came first from the hands and forges of the Teutonic immigrants who settled in eastern Pennsylvania before 1750. In creating the long smoothbores they naturally utilized many proven features of the rifles. This is highly visible in at least three respects. In a half-dozen other ways, they fashioned the new arms with differences, some evident and some not.

Nearly all of the dozens of long smoothbores that I have owned or examined over some 50 years shared these features in common with the long rifles:

- Front and rear open sights, Kentucky rifle style.
- Cheekpieces, also usually found only on rifled arms.
- Patchboxes, many of them as elaborate as on the long rifles.

The differences were more numerous though sometimes less noticeable. The smoothbores featured:

- Broader, less curved butts than rifles as a rule.
- Plain triggers, not double-set or "hair" triggers such as appeared particularly on the later Kentucky rifles.
- Barrels not over one-third octagonal and the rest round, instead of being entirely octagonal.
- Bores almost invariably above 50 caliber where the rifles, with early exceptions, ranged around 45 caliber or below.
- Barrels averaging several inches longer than rifles.
- Lighter over-all weight than rifles despite the longer barrels.

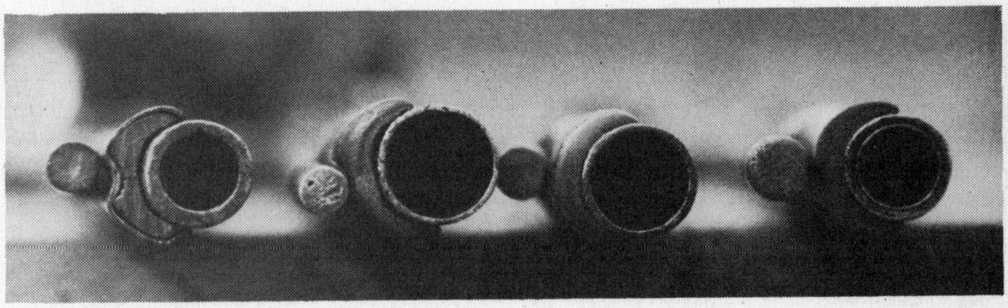

Nary a groove infects the barrels of these four original rifle-styled smoothbores, all with half-octagon, half-round barrels and none of them re-bored.

Each of these points deserves discussion. Let us take up first what an old Pennsylvania Dutch gunsmith might have called "the alikes":

The smoothbores' rifle sights and cheekpieces played useful roles in firing ball instead of shot. They surely helped in aiming and holding. Antique fowlers and modern shotguns alike carry only bead front sights. The long

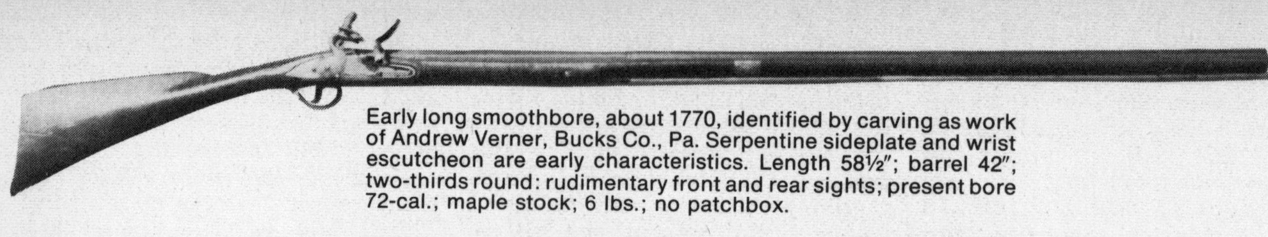

Early long smoothbore, about 1770, identified by carving as work of Andrew Verner, Bucks Co., Pa. Serpentine sideplate and wrist escutcheon are early characteristics. Length 58½"; barrel 42"; two-thirds round: rudimentary front and rear sights; present bore 72-cal.; maple stock; 6 lbs.; no patchbox.

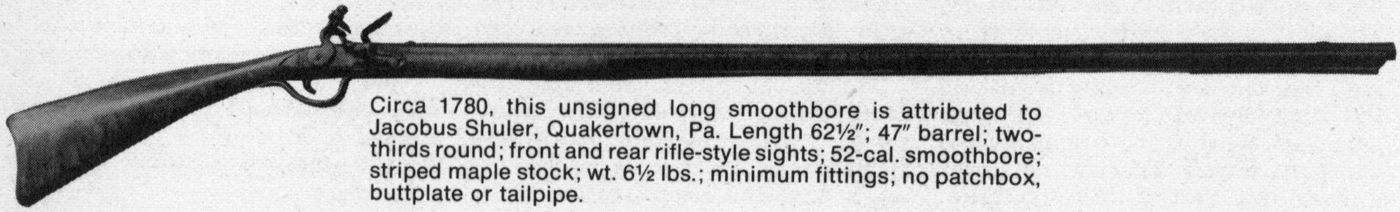

Circa 1780, this unsigned long smoothbore is attributed to Jacobus Shuler, Quakertown, Pa. Length 62½"; 47" barrel; two-thirds round; front and rear rifle-style sights; 52-cal. smoothbore; striped maple stock; wt. 6½ lbs.; minimum fittings; no patchbox, buttplate or tailpipe.

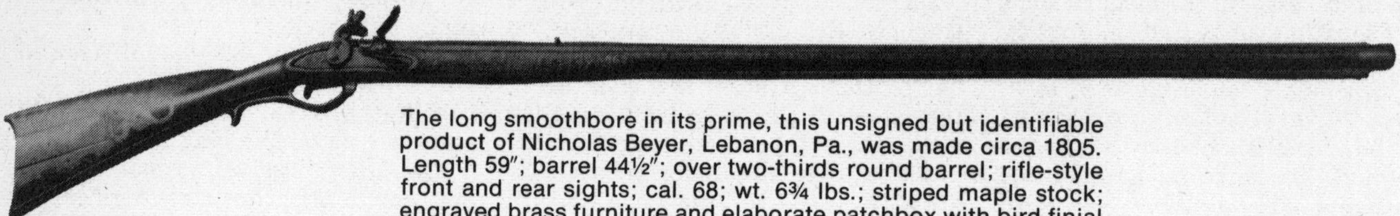

The long smoothbore in its prime, this unsigned but identifiable product of Nicholas Beyer, Lebanon, Pa., was made circa 1805. Length 59"; barrel 44½"; over two-thirds round barrel; rifle-style front and rear sights; cal. 68; wt. 6¾ lbs.; striped maple stock; engraved brass furniture and elaborate patchbox with bird finial recognized as Beyer design.

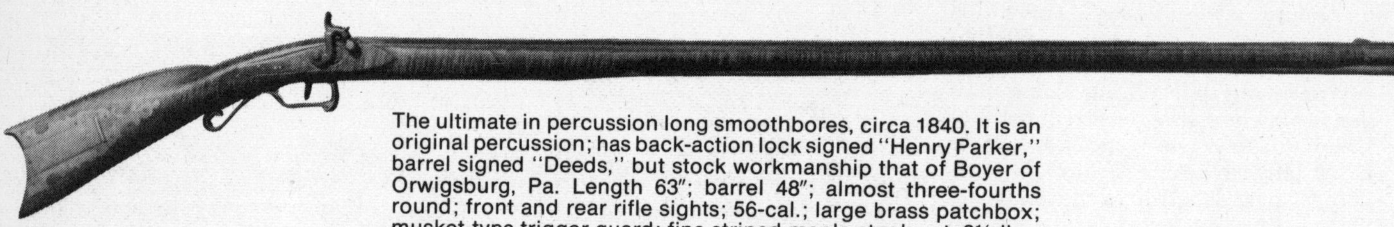

The ultimate in percussion long smoothbores, circa 1840. It is an original percussion; has back-action lock signed "Henry Parker," barrel signed "Deeds," but stock workmanship that of Boyer of Orwigsburg, Pa. Length 63"; barrel 48"; almost three-fourths round; front and rear rifle sights; 56-cal.; large brass patchbox; musket-type trigger guard; fine striped maple stock; wt. 8½ lbs.

smoothbores, however, mounted lengthy blade front sights like the rifles—what else?

The predilection for patchboxes on long smoothbores is harder to explain in retrospect. Part of it could have been traditional appearance. Quality rifles sported patchboxes, so . . . Even today, Kentucky rifle experts, of whom there are many and more a-making, dispute the purpose of these ornate brass creations. But it is fair to assume that if they were handy in loading patched-ball rifles, as their widespread acceptance suggests, they no doubt helped in fitting a patched ball snugly into a smoothbore.

Aside from personal experience, my own evidence on that score is slight but affirmative. I just once found aged cloth patches, but to the correct caliber, in the box of a long percussion smoothbore from Pennsylvania. I have detected smears and remnants of grease in other boxes. But more often, some collectors now theorize, the patchboxes held bullets, vent picks, spare flints or percussion caps.

"They were like a lady's handbag," one said.

So much for the characteristics that the long smoothbore shared with the long rifle. Now let us review the differences between the two types.

Colonial American gun butts were thick with little in-curve. Some measured as much as two inches across, leading certain advanced collectors to describe them as "clubby." As American rifles grew elongated, their butts became thinner and more crescent-shaped. These changes were far less pronounced in the smoothbores. Their butts retained a slight curve but more nearly resembled those of modern shotguns.

As for double-set or hair triggers, never have I seen them either in fact or in photograph on a long muzzleloader manufactured as a smoothbore. They would serve no purpose on such a gun and in truth could prove a handicap. Some remained on long rifles that were bored out smooth, but that is another story. Modern set triggers are found mainly on European hunting rifles fired from stands or on target handguns and rifles. They simply do not go with shotgunning techniques, old or new.

The four remaining differences all have to do with barrels and can be discussed together:

The preference for the octagon-to-round barrels arose from several advantages. They were easier to make. Barrels of the period were hammered out of long flat strips of iron called skelps. These were laboriously turned and welded around rod-like mandrels to create bores. In making barrels round for most of their length, the smoothbore manufacturers eliminated beating out and finishing the eight full-length flats required for octagonal rifle barrels. And, of course, the slow, painstaking process of rifling the smoothbore by hand became unnecessary. All this added up to a sizeable labor saving.

To function as shotguns, the long smoothbores were given larger bores than their contemporary rifles. That left less metal in the barrel and enabled the gunsmiths to lengthen barrels without adding weight. Employment of mostly round barrels further reduced the weight. The resulting long smoothbore could reach out well with shot or ball without overburdening its shooter in the field.

The earlier musket-like smoothbores weighed six to six and a half pounds, not heavy even by today's aluminized standards. Later ones reached above seven pounds. But they still must have seemed as feathery light as fairy wands in a day when true long rifles often weighed in at eight to ten pounds or more.

As for comparative calibers, a few early Pennsylvania rifles revealed their Germanic jaeger descent in having bores of .50-in. or more. Nearly all of the more typical ones made, say, from 1790 to 1820, gauged 45 caliber or under. Compare that with my statistical sampling of 26 old guns of the period which can be indisputably classified as original long smoothbores. All except one measured above 50 caliber and that exception gauged 48. Four of the others were 60 or above and one reached 70.

From its inception the long smoothbore must have been a joy to the frontiersmen and others who carried it. An outstanding advantage was that the proper size of round ball gave fair accuracy without patching. This happily bypassed the bothersome and time-consuming chore of greasing or spit-moistening a patch, placing it on the muzzle, centering the bullet on it, patch-cutting or trimming off the excess cloth, and starting it down the bore usually with a special short starter. While an experienced rifleman could do this faster than it takes to tell, patching nevertheless consumed precious time. In extremes of desperation, beset by a charging bear or rampaging Indians, it remained possible to fire an unpatched ball from a rifle bore. At close range in a crisis, the loss of velocity due to the deep open rifling scarcely mattered.

But the long smoothbores afforded shooters a better option in firing round bullets. Circumstances permitting, their users probably preferred to patch the balls. This increased obturation—perhaps saving a little powder—and improved accuracy. If a shooter did not want to pause to patch, the absence of rifling assured a better bullet fit and less waste of pressure.

There is reason to believe that some devotees of the long smoothbore carried two sizes of balls for the same gun: One for use with patches and a slightly fatter one to be slipped down the bore bare. If so, that would answer questions as to a minor mystery in antique arms collecting. There exist a number of old double-cavity round ball moulds with only a slight difference in the calibers they cast. One of these moulds would throw, say, one ball of 535 caliber and another miking .54" or .545". Collectors have conjectured over these moulds for years. A theory that they were for over-and-under muzzleloaders with two rifled barrels of nearly identical caliber fails to hold up well. With such close calibers in a rifle, it has been pointed out, a thicker patch on the smaller ball almost certainly would turn the trick. But with the long smoothbore, the larger ball cast by these double moulds would be ideal for loading bare. The other, of course, would be reserved to be put down patched. It's an interesting speculation.

The long smoothbore possessed another virtue that was even more valuable at times. It could be quickly charged with two round bullets, loaded bare one on top of the other. Capt. John G.W. Dillin, the pioneer writer on long rifles, reported coming upon an old hunter in the Pennsylvania hills in 1891 who had just shot a good buck with a smoothbore heavily loaded with two balls. Both passed through the neck. Dillin testified that such double loads were frequently used. A latter-day authority and master maker of long flintlock rifles, Carl Pippert, a Marylander, told this writer the same thing recently. There is ample testimony to back up the custom.

Anyone unfamiliar with muzzleloader shooting may reasonably ask: Why wouldn't the regular, deep-groove Kentucky rifle, or at least a shallow-groove version of it, serve equally well when double-loading is desired?

To most who have fired muzzleloader rifles, either antique or reproduction, the answer should be fairly evident. It takes long enough to load and ram down a single patched ball under most conditions, especially in a foul bore. To double that loading time and more than double the risk of balls jamming on their way down the bore invites a plight. Certainly it must have been highly undesirable within range of a fleeting deer or disgruntled bear. By contrast, I have seen experienced muzzleloader shooters literally pop two balls into a smoothbore in an instant. One, in fact, got the nickname "Bullfrog" because he carried (for short periods) several balls bulging in his mouth and spat them into the muzzle.

Back in the prime of the long smoothbores, moreover, "double-shotted" arms were in common use. To appreciate this fully, it is essential to know the military smallarms and ordnance of the muzzleloader period. At one time, say 1750-1825, all artillery and standard-issue muskets consisted of smoothbores. A recognized U.S. Infantry load from the Revolutionary War into the Civil War consisted of "buck and ball," three buckshot and a large ball packaged for the 69 caliber musket. Cannon, especially naval ones, were crammed on occasion with a weird assortment of projectiles. That mention refers not to fiction writers' fanciful assertions that such guns were loaded with a "keg of nails"—a precious commodity back then—but to carefully-designed multiple projectiles.

The armies used grapeshot and canister to mow down advancing ranks of infantry and bombshells to explode inside fortifications and enemy ships. Naval ammunition in the square-rigger days was even more exotic. U.S. warships fired chain shot (two big balls linked by chain), bar shot (two balls connected by a bar), expanding bar shot (two balls each on a bar, the bars linked by chain) and an anti-personnel load called langrage, a fancy name for a canvas bag of scrap iron. British Navy variations included star, faggot and three-piece chain shot calculated to lash out in every direction.

So it took no stretch of the imagination to charge a long smoothbore hunting arm with two or more balls or any one of several combinations of buckshot and smaller shot. I have several times in past years pried combinations of No. 6 and No. 9 shot, or the like, from the reluctant chambers of old muzzleloaders. Other mixtures were even stranger, suggesting that shooters might have run out of one size of shot and topped off the load with another.

While the versatility of the long smoothbore passed proof beyond question, what did remain in question was its true identity—a situation that continues to this day. The slow passage of the years further obscured this distinctive American arm. Another simple and logical firearms evolution almost sank it from sight.

Guns a century and more ago were too prized to be casually discarded. Due to hard and long use, many octagon-barrel long rifles eroded their bores. These "rocky roads" became pitted traps for bullets. Patched balls hung up in them. Ramrods snapped. So, no doubt, did tempers.

Hence the worn rifle barrels were reamed out smooth to facilitate further use of the arms. Where the barrel walls remained thick enough,

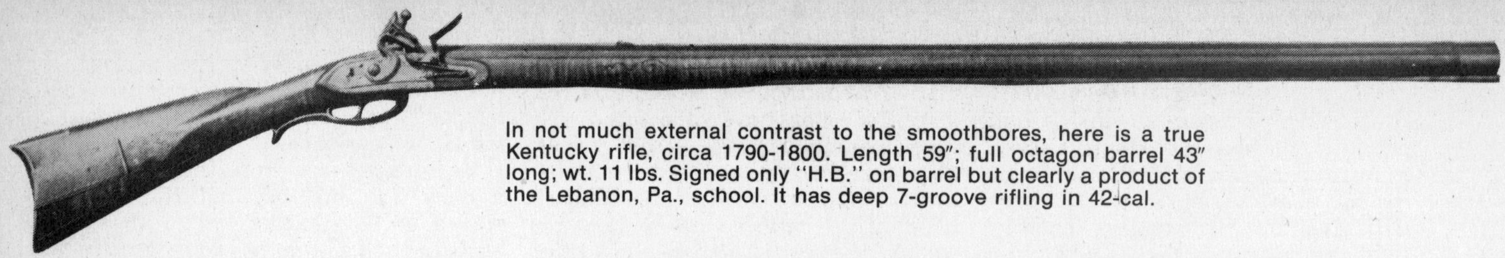

In not much external contrast to the smoothbores, here is a true Kentucky rifle, circa 1790-1800. Length 59"; full octagon barrel 43" long; wt. 11 lbs. Signed only "H.B." on barrel but clearly a product of the Lebanon, Pa., school. It has deep 7-groove rifling in 42-cal.

rifling could be recut to a larger caliber. But that took time and money and not everyone wanted to expend these on old rifles. To judge by the considerable number of fine flintlock rifles that have turned up in original form—with the significant exception of smoothbored barrels—many gun owners must have said, "Don't bother with rerifling it" after reboring. What's more, the altered rifles could perform smoothbore tricks such as readily accepting double-shotted loads.

The alterations confront collectors and historians today with not two but three variations in American long muzzleloaders. We have:

1. The long rifle in its pristine form, say, deeply rifled with seven grooves in 45 caliber and with a full-octagon barrel—currently regarded as the most desirable by collectors.

2. The smoothbore conversion of the long rifle by reaming and possibly reboring it into a gun that would ungrudgingly take shot or ball and which otherwise looked identical to an original rifle.

3. The increasingly obscured long smoothbore, built as such from the start but displaying the rifle features discussed here.

To what extent, then, were original long smoothbores produced? Like most such questions, there is no pat answer. There are some clear indications.

The Kentucky Rifle Association, certainly the foremost organization in the world specializing in this firearm, published books in 1967 and 1976. These reveal considerable progress in recent years in assembling hard facts on Kentucky rifles and stand as milestones in the collecting field.

The first volume presented photographs and details of 100 long arms. Of the 100 that I counted there, 13 are smoothbores, but ten of these very likely began life rifled. Only three displayed the distinguishable features of the long smoothbore. These, then, would represent 3% of the whole.

Publication of the 1976 KRA volume with data and photographs of some 279 fine representative long arms enabled me to make a study on a larger scale. Of the total in that volume, no fewer than 26 met my strict definition of original smoothbores. That, then, would amount to nearly 10% as compared with 3% detected in the previous volume.

What emerges between those lines appears to be a growing perception of the status of the smoothbore. They've been there all along, but more have come to light and won the attention of advanced collectors.

The long smoothbore has received occasional recognition in a growing bibliography on Kentuckies. Included are such basic books as John Dillin's volume, first issued in 1920; Joe Kindig, Jr.'s monumental meditation in print over his personal collection of 500 of these firearms, not one of which did he ever shoot; the Kentucky Rifle Association's aforementioned definitive works of love on the subject, and the scholarly perceptions published by George Shumway, Roy F. Chandler, James R. Johnston, Henry J. Kauffman, Merrill Lindsay and others.

Dillin (pages 39-40), 1946 edition) reports that his exhaustive research of "several hundred" smoothbore long guns revealed only six which could be classified as original smoothbores with certainty. The rest presumably were bored-out rifles. At least one "old man" in the Lehigh County area of Pennsylvania, Dillin recalled, was said to have specialized in converting aged rifles to smoothbores in the mid-1800's. That, be it noted, is just about when many of the fine old long rifles would have worn out.

The same source reveals that an original smoothbore by a Pennsylvania maker of the 1780's named Reading was "called a smoothbore rifle" and that such guns were uncommon then. The term "smooth rifle" also crops up in a U.S. Army Ordnance report of arms repaired at West Point, N.Y., in 1783-92, as quoted by William Guthman in his "March to Massacre." Among some 15,000 firearms of all kinds repaired, the report lists "smooth rifles" as a separate category.

In his massive book *Thoughts on the Kentucky Rifle in Its Golden Age,* Joe Kindig, Jr., dismisses the smoothbore in rifle form with a paragraph on page 36. Joe, long preeminent in the Kentucky or Pennsylvania rifle field, comments that guns with part octagon and part round barrels "are generally smoothbore" although he found about one in ten of this type rifled. He explains that the smoothbores were made "to shoot shot or a ball" and lets it go at that.

A fuller definition appears in "Longrifles of Note, Pennsylvania," a monograph by author-publisher George Shumway, of York, Pa. In discussing a long smoothbore made by John Noll, who worked in Pennsylvania about 1780 to 1820, Shumway comments that the gun was not a "true rifle" but "rather a smoothbore rifle with a barrel part octagon and part round." He adds that the phrase "smooth rifle" came into currency to designate flintlocks with rifle front and rear sights, cheekpieces, patchboxes, and "rifle-type trigger guards." Shumway also attempted to rescue the long smoothbore from anonymity by coining a one-word name for it. After referring to "longrifles"—one word—he terms the lengthy smoothbores "longfowlers," also one word. A capacity for discharging several 50-plus-caliber balls at a time, however, would seem to lift them out of the bird-hunting fowler category.

In a scholarly introduction to the second KRA volume, Member George H. Carroll points out that the Allentown-Bethlehem gunsmiths of Pennsylvania, who contributed importantly to long arm evolution, produced relatively few rifles. So many were smoothbores that Carroll comments: "A preference of smoothbore weapons was probably more in evidence throughout Pennsylvania than popular imagination now concedes."

As for myself, as author and longtime collector and shooter, let me make clear that I no more claim to have discovered the long smoothbore than Columbus laid claim to having discovered North America. The firearm, like the continent, has been there all along. Others have glimpsed it and reported on it as I have noted. Here I only attempt to amplify, analyze and publicize the facts of its existence. It is time to bring this distinctive firearm out of the shadows and into the campfire light as a proudly American arm in its own—the American long smoothbore. ●

SIXGUNS

by ELMER KEITH

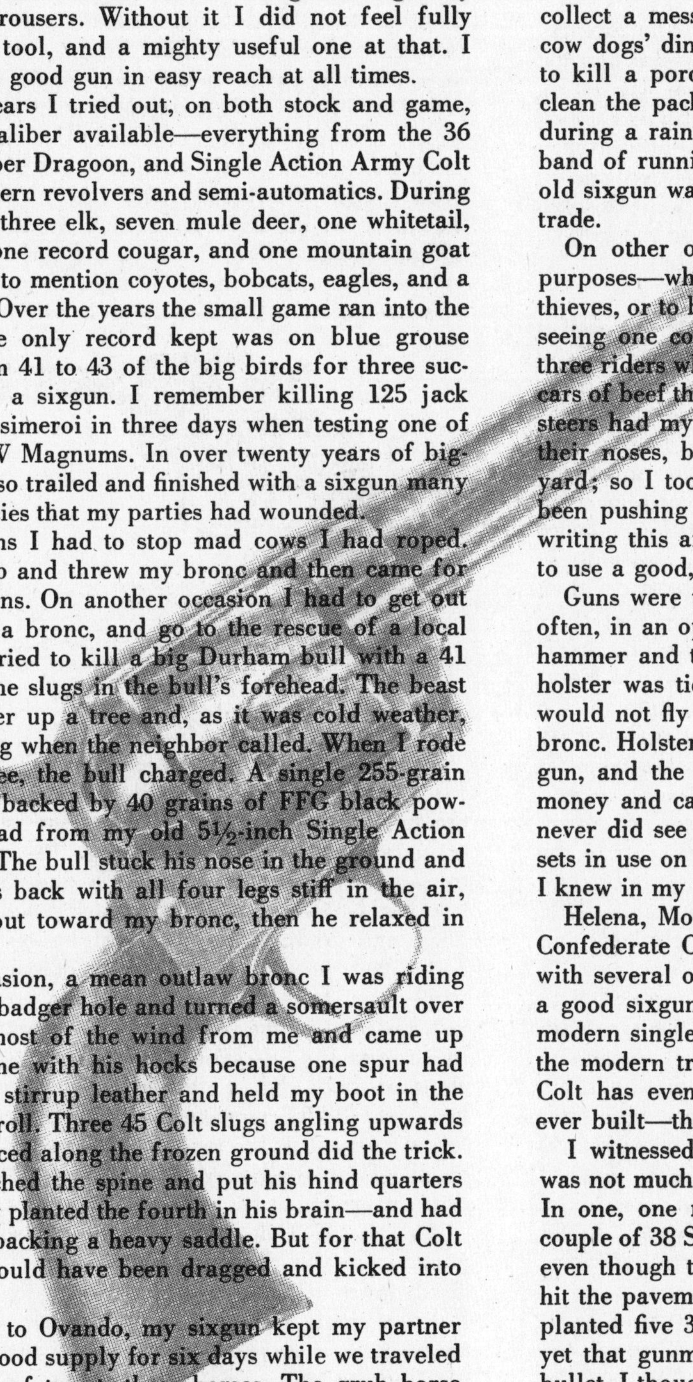

FOR OVER THIRTY YEARS I wore a sixgun as regularly as I did my trousers. Without it I did not feel fully dressed. It was a tool, and a mighty useful one at that. I still like to have a good gun in easy reach at all times.

During those years I tried out, on both stock and game, every make and caliber available—everything from the 36 Navy Colt, 44 caliber Dragoon, and Single Action Army Colt down through modern revolvers and semi-automatics. During that time I killed three elk, seven mule deer, one whitetail, three black bear, one record cougar, and one mountain goat with a sixgun, not to mention coyotes, bobcats, eagles, and a Mexican javelina. Over the years the small game ran into the thousands, but the only record kept was on blue grouse when I killed from 41 to 43 of the big birds for three successive years with a sixgun. I remember killing 125 jack rabbits on the Pahsimeroi in three days when testing one of the first 357 S & W Magnums. In over twenty years of big-game guiding, I also trailed and finished with a sixgun many animals of all species that my parties had wounded.

On two occasions I had to stop mad cows I had roped. They wound me up and threw my bronc and then came for me with sharp horns. On another occasion I had to get out of bed, saddle up a bronc, and go to the rescue of a local butcher who had tried to kill a big Durham bull with a 41 Colt by planting the slugs in the bull's forehead. The beast had put the butcher up a tree and, as it was cold weather, he was fast freezing when the neighbor called. When I rode up close to the tree, the bull charged. A single 255-grain 45-cal. Ideal slug, backed by 40 grains of FFG black powder, in the forehead from my old $5\frac{1}{2}$-inch Single Action Colt did the trick. The bull stuck his nose in the ground and turned over on his back with all four legs stiff in the air, his tail stretched out toward my bronc, then he relaxed in death.

On another occasion, a mean outlaw bronc I was riding stuck his foot in a badger hole and turned a somersault over me. He knocked most of the wind from me and came up running, kicking me with his hocks because one spur had caught around the stirrup leather and held my boot in the stirrup during the roll. Three 45 Colt slugs angling upwards from where I bounced along the frozen ground did the trick. The third one reached the spine and put his hind quarters down, and I simply planted the fourth in his brain—and had a long hike home packing a heavy saddle. But for that Colt Single Action, I would have been dragged and kicked into doll rags.

On one trip out to Ovando, my sixgun kept my partner and me in meager food supply for six days while we traveled with a pack string of twenty-three horses. The grub horse had busted a yellow-jackets' nest and bucked off down the mountain and across a river. When we found her, there was no food left in the pack. We lived by that sixgun alone for those six days.

Far more often the sixgun was needed to kill a rattler, collect a mess of grouse or sage hens, or a rabbit for the cow dogs' dinner. Whether I had to roll out of the blanket to kill a porcupine that was eating up the pack outfit, or clean the pack rats out of some cabin I wished to sleep in during a rainy night, or simply heave a slug in front of a band of running horses to turn them toward the corral, the old sixgun was always near and handy. It was a tool of the trade.

On other occasions the old gun was packed for social purposes—when serving on sheriff's posses, hunting cow thieves, or to back our honor and judgment. I still remember seeing one cow thief squirm when I watched him and his three riders while my partner cut four of my steers from two cars of beef that he was preparing to load on the train. Those steers had my brand, badly blotched, and the wattle cut off their noses, but I would have known their hides in a tan yard; so I took them by force. Suffice to say, I would have been pushing up daisies over twenty years ago instead of writing this article now, had I not carried and known how to use a good, heavy sixgun.

Guns were usually carried in a shoulder holster or, more often, in an open-top, quick-draw belt holster that left both hammer and trigger fully exposed. The bottom of the belt holster was tied to the leg or to the chaps so that the gun would not fly up and hit the elbow when riding a pitching bronc. Holsters were just large enough to accommodate the gun, and the belts were more often than not combination money and cartridge belts of double-soft chap leather. We never did see any of those huge *buscadero* Hollywood corsets in use on the range, nor did any of the old gun fighters I knew in my younger days use such an outfit.

Helena, Mont., was settled in the late sixties, largely by Confederate Civil War veterans. I knew, lived, and hunted with several of these men, most of whom owned or carried a good sixgun, either an old cap and ball Colt or a more modern single action. Now they are all dead and gone, and the modern trend seems more to small-caliber target guns. Colt has even stopped manufacture of the best gun they ever built—the Single Action Army.

I witnessed three gun fights when a kid in Helena and was not much impressed by the results from the 38 Special. In one, one man proved the quicker on the draw and a couple of 38 Specials through the heart stopped his opponent even though the opponent did draw and fire two shots that hit the pavement short of his executioner. In another, a cop planted five 38 Specials in a gunman's chest, about center, yet that gunman emptied his break-top 32 at the cop. One bullet, I thought the first, hit the cop right over the heart but went through a notebook and lodged in the bottom of his blouse pocket. One more went through a kid's leg as he was peacefully engaged in eating noodles in his booth, and the rest came through the front window over my head and

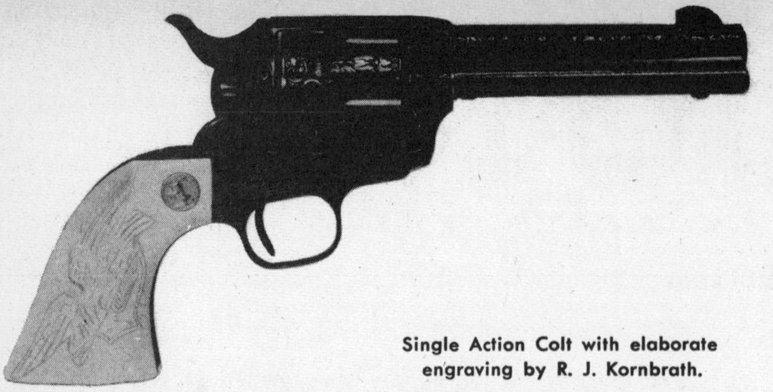

Single Action Colt with elaborate engraving by R. J. Kornbrath.

flattened against a building across the street. The gunman then threw his gun at the cop, and it also went through the window and across the street. He died as he was carried up the hospital steps. Another time my friend Bill O'Connel, the night cop around the N.P. Depot, killed two holdup men who had stuck up a saloon, with one shot each from his 45 Colt Single Action. Their one return shot only went through a transom window over Bill's head as he entered the saloon.

Small-Caliber Pistols

The 22-caliber sixguns and semi-auto pistols are useful for just one thing—target practice and competition. They may also be used effectively on very small game with high-speed hollow points occasionally. The 32-20 and 38 Special factory loads are far better small-game loads as a whole, but both lack power for any serious social purposes, for shooting game of any size, or for use against mean stock.

I have killed three mule deer with the 32-20 low-velocity smokeless soft-point load, and the cartridge proved entirely inadequate. I have also killed a couple of muleys with a K-22 S & W at close range, working on the backs of their heads double action. I had walked out on the edge of a small cliff and a big buck and a doe appeared just under me at about six yards range. A quick shot, double action, to the back of each head put both of them down, but each got up on its feet almost instantly. Two more shots were taken at each, and then the gun was empty. Both were down and kicking, but I had hardly reloaded when both were up again. Then I started shooting at the back of the neck, just to the rear of the skull. When the gun was again empty, both were dead, but I will never try that stunt again. Another time, I had put two 172-grain 30-06 slugs in a big mule buck and he went down. Not wanting to shoot him up any more, I borrowed Jim Robbin's Colt Woodsman and proceeded to empty the gun in him. I hit the deer between the eyes with the first shot and heard the tiny slug whine as it ricocheted away. As the buck ran past, I put the rest of the magazine in close behind the shoulder. The buck went a couple hundred yards and again lay down. I approached to within 30 yards as he lay in the sagebrush watching me. I bounced most of another magazine off his skull before one bullet went through the tiny nerve hole over the left eye and killed him. No more 22's for me on anything bigger than bullfrogs, squirrels, or cottontails.

Contrary to popular opinion, the 32-20, 38-40, and 44-40 factory soft-point low-velocity loads will expand very well on deer and, if bones are struck, turn wrong side out. Yet the bullets will not expand in pine wood, simply smearing off the soft point and leaving the jacket intact. I wore out completely one 32-20 barrel with both factory loads and handloads in game shooting. I have also shot a 38-40 and a 44-40 a great deal. All three cartridges are bottlenecked and the chambers are much too long for the body of the case. When fired, the cases expand nearly to the mouth, leaving only about half of the original neck and requiring considerable resizing to reload them. I used to use No. 80 powder and the 260-grain 40-82 Winchester bullet sized down to fit in the 38-40. The combination was superbly accurate from a 5½-inch Single Action Colt, and a real killer on anything, but constant resizing made for short case life and I finally gave it up. The 44-40 is by far the best of these three rifle cartridges, and it was old-timer Ashley Haines' favorite sixgun load, but the 44-40 does its best work from a long 7¼-inch barrel owing to being loaded with rifle powder. I never could get much penetration with factory 38-40 or 44-40 loads from a sixgun, and soon came to prefer longer, heavier bullets that would give better penetration on stock or big game when the necessity for such use arose. A factory 38-40 load almost cost me my life while monkeying with a wounded bull elk. The bullet simply splattered on the elk's skull, and did not penetrate. Had the cylinder not been loaded alternately with heavy black powder loads, that bull would have ended my hunting. With both cartridges, the case body is large and the neck short for short bullets. The charge must be held down religiously to safe pressures or it will bulge the bolt cuts in the cylinder.

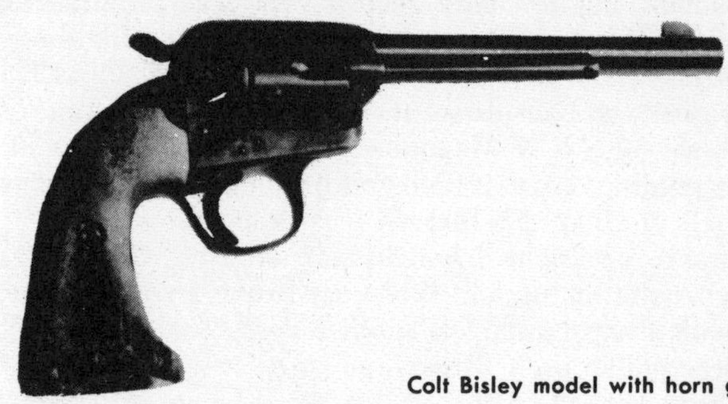

Colt Bisley model with horn grips.

My Preferences

I much prefer the 44 Special and the 45 Colt cartridges for sixgun use. For the handloader, the 44 Special is by far the best of all sixgun cartridges for serious work, either target, defense, or game killing. The cylinder walls are thicker over the case body than in the 45, and the cartridge is superbly accurate. The old black powder loads with 250-, 255-, and 260-grain government bullets and 40 grains of FFG black powder gave 900 feet in the 45 Colt and would surely penetrate. I planted a 250-grain Remington black powder load in the seat of a goat's pants and it penetrated through to the left shoulder, which it broke. On broadside shots on both elk and goats, it went clean through unless heavy shoulder bones were hit. The 38-40 and 44-40 factory loads stopped under the skin on the off side on lung shots on elk. With the heavy 260-grain 38-40 handload, penetration was excellent.

Another 45 Colt load that gave excellent accuracy and penetration was the Winchester 300-grain 45-90 lead bullet sized down to .454 inch and backed by 35 grain of FFG. It killed mule deer and wounded elk well and was very accurate. I once had a case head separate with this load, blowing the loading gate out of the gun and cutting through the side of my trigger finger. That case had been reloaded many times, however, and the load was safe enough in good cases.

The factory 45 Colt pointed bullet punched a rather small hole through game and would not expand unless it hit a heavy bone. With that bullet I shot a great many grouse with little damage to the meat. In search of the best sixgun bullet, I designed a blunt-nosed bullet (No. 454260) for Belding & Mull but found that it or the same design worked out for the 44 Special in 260- and 280-grain was not accurate at any great range, so we dropped them and designed another bullet for Lyman. First in 44 Special, 250-grain solid and 235-grain hollow base or hollow point, then in 45 Colt 250-grain, later in 45 semi-auto rim 240-grain, and still later in 173-grain solid and 160-grain hollow base or hollow point 38 Special, these Keith bullets have proven ideal, for me at least, for all sixgun work in twenty years of continuous use. They cut full caliber holes in anything and penetrate almost as well as the old pointed 45 Colt black powder load in solid persuasion. In hollow-point design, they will expand at velocities of 1,000 feet or more, and at 1,200 feet are very destructive to all game and ruinous to small game.

The Keith 160-grain 38 Special hollow point, backed by 13.5 grains of 2400, from the Colt Single Action or Shooting Master, or the S & W Heavy Duty or Outdoorsman will simply blow a grouse to bits and wings. The legs and neck will fly off at all angles when the bird is centered. The Keith 235-grain 44 Special hollow point, backed by 18.5 grains of 2400, is even worse in its destruction of living tissue. It's certain death on either elk or deer if placed in the lungs broadside at close range, but it will not penetrate quite as well as the 250-grain solid in bone or when meaty portions of an animal are struck. Bob Hagel killed eight treed cougar last winter with a 44 Special 4¾-inch barrel Single Action Colt using these loads. He said the hollow point was much the best for a chest or lung shot and the solid bullet best for shoulder shots to break the big cats down so that they would not fall out of the tree full of fight.

I have tried both the Super 38's and the 9 mm Lugers on game, also the 45 semi-auto, for many years and they are one and all far inferior in actual knockdown power to the heavy revolver loads. A friend emptied a Super 38 Colt into a cougar's chest at close range in a tree, but the big cat jumped out and ran a short distance. One heavy 44 Special or 357 Magnum or 45 Colt in the same place would have done the business. Metal-patched bullets from the semi-auto pistols are simply not as good stoppers as are the soft lead bullets of the revolver, but the 45 Colt semi-auto has more actual shock on game than either the Luger or the Super 38. I have shot enough game with all three to prove the point, to my own satisfaction at least.

Guns for Self Defense

For a defense gun against man, the 1917 S & W semi-auto rim is a fine, fast gun, and one can carry a couple of the three-shot clips loaded with 45 auto ammo, preferably of the new Remington and Peters 185-grain wadcutter type, and have a very quick reload.

The late Frank Waterman carried a nickel-plated 7¼-inch Single Action Colt 45 all his life. His dad had given it to him new when Frank was a kid in Wyoming. Frank was past seventy when he died last year. That old Peacemaker had killed all species of game in Wyoming, Montana, and Idaho except buffalo. When on a Wyoming elk hunt, a sportsman had downed a big bull elk and the guide borrowed Frank's 45 Colt to go back and pack out the elk as he did not want to bother with a rifle that day. They were working up a brushy creek bed to the kill, and the sportsman was some one hundred yards to the rear as usual, when the guide turned around a big willow bush and found the elk. A big grizzly was eating on the carcass. The bear instantly rose to its full height, and the guide drew Frank's old Peacemaker. Aiming just under the chin of the big grizzly, he squeezed the trigger. The heavy 260-grain bullet backed by Frank's 40-grain black powder load went in under the chin and broke the grizzly's neck, and the bear went down like a sack of beans.

I once loaded some 44 Specials with the Keith 250-grain solid and 12 grains of No. 80 for Charley Stauffenberg. He carried a New Service Colt for that cartridge. One fall, when in need of his winter's meat, Charley ran onto a bull moose standing broadside. Holding his gun with both hands, he aimed for the heart and shot once. The bull lurched away but went only one hundred yards and lay down and was soon ready for the knife. The flat-point Keith bullet went through the middle of the heart and bled him out nicely.

Some nineteen years ago I loaded a large quantity of the very same load for James T. Maxwell, of Omaha, Neb., for use in Africa in a 6½-inch S & W. Maxwell later reported that he had no trouble at all supplying twelve men with all the antelope meat they could eat by using that gun and load alone. He said it killed the small and medium antelope about as well as a rifle during a six-week period of African hunting in Kenya and Tanganyika. Recently I had another letter from the good doctor saying he had just tested some of these same loads after all these years and they still shot as well as ever.

With the advent of Hercules 2400 powder I dropped the use of No. 80 entirely, as 2400 proved a much better propellant, giving far less pressure than No. 80 and even higher velocity.

Throughout the West and North, many men—prospectors, surveyors, cowpunchers, trappers, and woods' loafers—who must make long trips into the back country, often by back pack only, and who cannot carry a rifle handily, need a good dependable heavy sixgun. The best guns for the purpose today are the Colt Single Action and the S & W 357 Magnum and 1926 44 Special target models.[1] The guns should have accurate target sights which suit individual preference as to width of blade or bead and general type, but the sights should be adjustable so that they may be correctly zeroed for any desired load. If the Colt Single Action is preferred, then it should be target sighted by King Gunsight Co., Pachmayr, or some other reliable gunsmith. The best rear sight is the S & W click adjustment target rear, with a suit-

[1] Now being produced as the Model 1950 with improved shorter action, etc.—Editor.

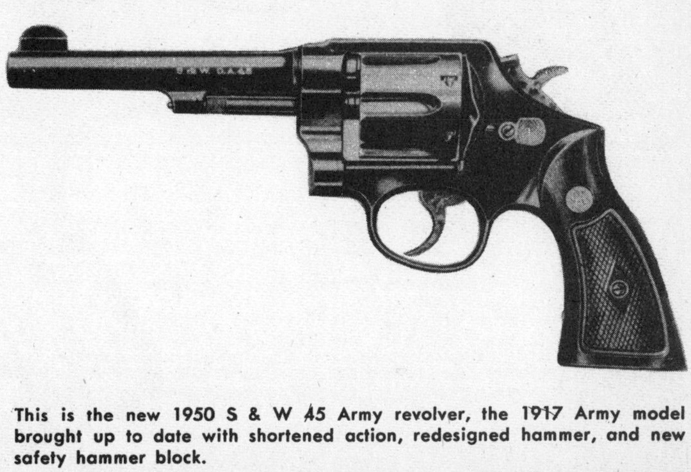

This is the new 1950 S & W 45 Army revolver, the 1917 Army model brought up to date with shortened action, redesigned hammer, and new safety hammer block.

able band or ramp front sight base and blade sight. The S & W target guns, both the Magnums and the 1926, come equipped with perfect sights, and front beads or blades to suit individual preference can be had to order.

For loads, I believe the 357 S & W Magnum and 45 Colt to be the best in factory loads, and the 44-40 is not so far behind, some shooters preferring it to the others. If the shooter is also a handloader, or wishes to purchase heavy handloads from Moody's Custom Loads, Helena, Mont., or another custom loader, the best caliber is the 44 Special. The factory 44 Special makes a fine grouse and small-game load and is also an ideal target load. The Keith 250-grain solid bullet or the 235-grain hollow base or hollow point can be loaded with 18.5 grains of Hercules 2400 and bullets sized to .001 inch larger than groove diameter and cast 1 part tin to 16 parts lead for solids, and 1 to 20 for hollow points, and you have the most powerful handgun loads in existence.

The factory 357 Magnum is very good but it is not nearly as good a killer as the above-mentioned 44 Special handloads. Col. Doug Wesson killed elk, antelope, moose, and grizzly with the 357 Magnum, but the fact remains that the heavy Keith 44 Special loads are a lot more powerful. The factory 38 Special can also be used in the Magnum as a grouse or small-game load; wadcutters in full charge are particularly good small-game loads. If you want to reload for the Magnum, use 13.5 grains of 2400 behind the Keith 173-grain solid bullet or the 160-grain Keith hollow point in 38 Special cases. For the longer Magnum case, use 14 grains of 2400 with the 160-grain hollow point or 13.5 grains with the 173-grain Keith solid and barely crimp the case over the front band of the bullet. The fact remains, however, that the 38 Special case, with Keith bullet and 13.5 grains of 2400, is a more accurate load at any range, even to 600 yards, than is the factory 357 Magnum or the Keith bullet from the Magnum case when the case is crimped over the forward band. Bullets should be of same temper as above for the 44 Special and should be sized to not over .001 inch above groove diameter.

In the 45 Colt, the standard factory smokeless load is a good one though at only about 800 feet velocity. It is accurate and will penetrate well. The old Remington 40-grain black powder load was much more powerful, and handloads can be made up with the Keith 250-grain Ideal bullet and 18 to 20 grains of Hercules 2400, always keeping bullets sized to not over .001 inch above groove diameter and crimping in the beveled crimp groove. In the 45 Colt, we have much thinner cylinder walls than in the 44 Special and for that reason the 44 Special has a much greater margin of safety. The bullet, being the same weight as for the 45, also has more sectional density and will penetrate better, so for the handloader the 44 Special is absolutely tops. The factory 44 Special 146-grain bullet is loaded to only 750 feet velocity, and both the 357 Magnum and the 45 Colt, as well as the 44-40, beat it badly for killing power in factory loads. But carefully handloaded, the 44 Special comes to life. For all social purposes, when a gun is needed in self defense against man targets, the 357 Magnum is the smallest cartridge I would consider. The heavy Keith handloads described above are, however, much better stoppers, and a man hit anywhere between the top of the skull and the pelvic bone with one of them in 44 Special or 45 Colt will not shoot back.

Automatics are totally dependent on perfect ammunition for certain functioning and are, for that reason, a second choice for a defense gun. If a jam or a misfire occurs, then two hands are needed to clear the jam and get the gun in action again. For that reason, they are never as reliable as a good cylinder gun when one's life is at stake.

(Reprinted by courtesy of *The American Rifleman.*)

Colt Single Action fitted with hand-finished sterling silver grips by Mac Lester of New York City. These are furnished with a Flying Eagle, a Stag, or plain finish at $25.00. Grips for the Colt 45 Auto and old style Woodsman are available at $20.00 a pair.

AFTER WE WON THE WAR

The next 30 years were a lot easier.

by **ROY DUNLAP**

AFTER WE saved the world for the democrats the second time, calling it World War Two—the last one we won—99 percent of the two million in uniform wanted out now, and most did not want to go back to the old pre-war jobs, which screwed up things a bit. The incredible total-war organization stopped; the old workers, men and women, wanted out; reconversion to peace-time production meant changing equipment and training workers to replace the ex-soldiers who wanted different occupations now. Everything was in short supply up into 1948—if you wanted a new car, a stove, a Winchester Model 70, forget it for now, get on the list, find a friend in the business. Stores were empty.

I wrote a book for Tom Samworth (Small Arms Publishing Co.) called *Ordnance Up Front*. I think it was his title, not mine. I wrote it while waiting for my new car that my service-manager buddy in Chicago was getting me. Sam proudly showed the manuscript to an army general friend, who confiscated it and held for over a year as having too much information for the public. When it was published, it became a text in all the assorted military survival schools.

Finally, I got the car, accumulated tools, rented a garage in Chicago to work in, made a couple rifles for army friends, and then took off west looking for a climate like that in Egypt. Like, for example, southern Arizona. I took a store gunsmith job in Tucson, rented a room next door to Jack O'Connor's home, traded him out of a 22-250 with one of Keith Stegall's first stocks, and took up varmint hunting, meaning I learned to shoot running jackrabbits at 200 yards and further. It's not as hard as it sounds. I got so I hit one out of three first shot, which broke Jack of his habit of sitting down to shoot. By the time he was planted, I had fired three shots and anything I got three shots at was hit.

The factories were slow getting back into sporting arms and ammunition production, having few experienced workmen. I must have made a few thousand 8x57mm cartridges from 30-06 cases and Vernon Speer's first bullets for the Mausers brought back by the soldiers. Lots of actions used for sporters, of course. Parker Ackley was making barrels in 1947 and had a batch of GI trainee gunsmith students. Some of whom were good stock men, including John Hearn who was very good. He was a young veteran with some war disabilities and quit stock work for health reasons after a few years. I remember shortening a Springfield action to 250-3000 length so he could make himself a small-scale deer rifle in the early 1950s.

The BRNO (Czech) sporters were first imports, I believe—available in 1947. They were very good rifles, first to have integral dovetails on receivers for scope mounting. Lots of ex-servicemen were interested in gunsmithing, so Ackley, Pfeifer, a few others started GI Bill training deals. I think P.O. started the first college program at Trinidad State Junior College in Colorado, which is still one of the very best gunsmithing schools.

I rented a room next to Jack O'Connor's house, traded him out of a 22-250 . . .

Samworth wanted me to update Baker's *Modern Gunsmithing*, which was the only usable gunsmithing text; Howe's fine two-volume job was nice to look at, but nearly worthless to the average shop or to the amateur. Only, from experience, I knew Baker's book was not so good. Formula might say '30 minutes' when correct time was about 45 seconds. Clyde Baker was never a professional. He was a good amateur, greatly interested, and an advertising writer by trade. I refused to compound the errors, and spent several months writing my own book *Gunsmithing* which pretty well covered the subject. It must be OK as it's now in about the 12th printing. I wish I had royalties on it, but I sold it outright to Samworth for $5,000 in advance, good money in 1948. I was just married and broke.

After 1950, we were in pretty good shape. Fabrique Nationale, Husqvarna, other European makers were sending in good rifles; Beretta was furnishing pistols; U.S. makers were back in production. Remington brought out the 721 and 722 rifles, their first self-designed bolt actions. The 722 was instantly popular, being the first medium-length since the Savage 1920, long gone. Both lengths sold well having good triggers, not too heavy, and the price was right. I found I could remodel the hinged forged trigger guards from Japanese 6.5mm Arisaka rifles to fit the 722 and made a few presentable custom rifles from them.

Foreign surplus came in an ever-increasing flood. Rifles, actions, were $15 to $25, retail. Handguns were $14 to $40, all sorts, from Colt revolvers to Broomhandle Mausers. Lots of custom rifles were made, many not too great in style or finish. And lots of barrel makers started up, learning on the job.

From a weak start in 1948, International shooting slowly grew. I looked at it, and—after realizing that I was probably the best-known gunsmith in the U.S. at the moment and was averaging about $65 a week—said goodbye to the metal work and the sporters and went into target equipment. I went to the world matches in Venezuela in 1954, wrote them up for *The American Rifleman* (February, 1955). However, the *Rifleman* did not print the second half of my writeup, which proved a mistake. In it, I foresaw the building boom around cities and recommended that all shooters—handgun, rifle, shotgun—form associations, financed to buy large tracts of land so that all types of safe ranges could be built with recreational facilities for family participation.

The Great Western firm in California put out a copy of the Colt Single Action Army revolver, a very good copy of very good steel, which I believe eventually prompted Colt to get back into production on the model.

Ruger was making his 22 auto and 22 single action, getting set to become one of the great arms makers. High Standard was flourishing, showing new models yearly. Smith & Wesson began their good revolvers again, and target shooting boomed. I was a Referee on pistol, smallbore, and high power except when I was shooting myself. I was mainly in high power, fighting with top experts twenty years younger than I, with better eyes to begin with. I set a few national records, but on the whole, I was the country's top second-rater for twenty years.

Foreign surplus came in an ever-increasing flood. Rifles, actions, were $15 to $25 . . .

In the middle 1950s, the National Matches became very popular, and the service rifle, then the M1 Garand, was lacking somewhat in accuracy. So everybody—the Army, the Marines and me—began working on it. I picked the brains of all the experimenting armorers, put those things together, and started from there. I worked out a good system with glass bedding, tight handguards, waterproofed stocks, clearance on metal parts, and so on. I could make the M1's shoot nearly as good as bolt actions.

Ft. Benning sent their shop chief, WO/Glenn Baker, to me for three weeks; the Air Force decided to get into shooting, found a sergeant in Japan who was a good amateur gunsmith on his own time, and sent him in to me. Leon Johnson was head of the Lackland shop until he retired from service and went promptly to Remington's custom shop to make beautiful stocks on the special-order arms. The Marines had their own shop training.

We all swapped information, tools, and parts. My principal point was knowing the shrinkage of the fiberglass resins and milling wood surfaces away to uniform depths so there would be full support when the bedding shrank a little. You couldn't allow high and low spots.

At one and the same time, I was accurizing M1s for service units, base teams, and civilians; I was making free rifles, match rifles and accessories; I was importing from Europe, everything from Finnish leather coats to Russian rapid-fire pistols.

Colt made match auto pistols in 38 Special and 38 AMU as well as 45 caliber that would really shoot. The revolvers faded from the firing lines. Smith & Wesson came out with a 22 match pistol that was good; High Standard had several models, too; and the Colt 22s could not compete. Today a Match Woodsman is just a plinking pistol or an item for a Colt collector.

Winchester began to go downhill in the '60s. Sales people evidently dominated the engineers. There were a lot of new and not-so-good 22s. In 1964, the Model 70 was discontinued, but the model number kept for a cheaper replacement type. They weren't selling as many rifles as was Remington, and it did not occur to the idiots to keep the old 70, double the price, make it a premium rifle, like the deluxe FN's, and such.

. . . it did not occur to the idiots to keep the old 70, double the price . . .

Cheaper materials were experimented with and there are people now wondering why their 94 won't take a reblue job, or why the carbine they bought at the discount house has some stamped parts inside while the ones from the gun store have forged ones. Today, under new management, it appears that the good features of the original M70 rifle are slowly returning. The feeble extractor on the Winchester post-64 70—and Remington 700, for that matter—have finally surfaced through the advertising to reach public awareness. The old M70 Winchester rifle was not perfect, but it was the highest development of the Mauser system, with locking, extractor and trigger system superior to any other manually-operated rifle.

The companies have a spotty track record for service as well as products. Around 1949 or 1950 they decided that reloading was cutting into their profits too much, so Winchester, Remington, Western all quit selling primers and other components. Dick Speer immediately announced he was preparing to make cases and primers. And did. The company is now CCI. Federal started selling primers, too.

The late 1960s saw the 1968 restrictive gun law come into effect, the start of inflation in Europe and the beginning of steady raises in gun and ammunition prices. The Viet Nam war went on for a decade, influenced the military small-arms thinking of the world, and made a generation of young men believe in paramilitary weapons and firepower. Witness the vast number of semi-auto military type "rifles" such as the AR-15, Mini-14, the countless foreign-made ones, even the AK-47, available. And all these arms sell—we got a lot of weekend commandoes and survival types buying them. Personally, I don't think survival necessarily means guerilla warfare.

Personally, I don't think survival necessarily means guerilla warfare.

Scope sights became universal on everything, even handguns for hunting, and metallic silhouette shooting. In April, 1968, I ran a Mexican-type Metallic Silhouette rifle match in Tucson. Today the sport has more competitors than all other rifle and pistol shooting sports combined. Now rifles, handguns and scopes are made especially for it.

Except for the high cost of everything, resulting from the worldwide inflation, I think the shooter of the 1980s pretty well off. He has by far the greatest variety of arms of all types available since modern shooting began. Even loading equipment gives so many choices everyone can be confused. Superb optical equipment like the positive-adjusting Weaver T system, imported scopes like the matchless Kahles and Zeiss models, and the vast choice of U.S.-made scopes make catalog-browsing a pleasure. On mounts, we ain't so well off. Nothing as good as the Tilden of 25 years ago is being made. We have a half-dozen or more skilled barrelmakers, plus even more specializing in muzzleloader barrels.

In gunsmithing, I think we have a bad gap. We have many, many more top-grade custom men, such as Fred Wells, who can actually make actions and complete rifles of superb quality, custom makers of all sorts of modern arms, and in the muzzle-loading field, men such as Bivens, Mandarino, Alexander and a half-dozen others are artists equal if not superior to Manton, Nock and Egg, the original English masters, and far better than the American colonial gunsmiths who, after all, weren't trying to be artists, just gunmakers. There are a hundred men in the country who can make top-quality "using" replica antiques. We got better tools and better barrels than the old-timers had.

We have so many super-good custom stockmakers and gun engravers I wouldn't try to mention even one. Prices on both engraving and stock work are high, but not out of reason. Consider that a union carpenter makes over $16 per hour, that a custom stock can take 100 hours of highly-skilled labor. And an engraver's pay-per-hour isn't going to figure out a hell of a lot more than a tool and die man, or even a master machinist.

I mentioned a gap: We have a great shortage of good everyday gunshop repair gunsmiths, men who can put a broken gun back into using condition, fix trigger pulls on all types of arms, make repeaters repeat. I was both, and I think it takes longer to learn general gunsmithing than custom work. You work on old, often unfamiliar rifles, pistols, shotguns. And make parts that cannot be bought. You make flat springs.

The gunsmithing schools turn out capable smiths, but we have a new semi-pro would-be gunsmith type that often doesn't even buy gunsmithing books. They don't even know how to take an unfamiliar arm apart, or where to find obsolete parts or make them. Or even where to get gunsmithing tools and supplies. They scar up a lot of good guns: The post-WW II gunsmith population of 1950-60-70 working years, like me, just died off or retired.

Shooting for fun—plinking, groups from bench, etc., is a big thing now. Formal target shooting has become a very expensive game—match 22 cartridges can cost you fourteen cents each, for example. Hunting is not too great in most areas of the country, as of course it is seasonal, and the number of hunters increases yearly, making good hunting grounds pretty crowded. The metallic silhouette game, (high-power rifle, 22 rifle and handgun of many types) seems a great outlet, and does not have to cost as much as many of its participants believe—custom equipment is not really needed.

One thing the handgun silhouette program has done is to produce some hitherto unheard-of power. Rifle calibers, no limit, come in bolt action and single-shot type arms; now there are super-magnum revolver and auto cartridges. I'm not sure if they are really worthwhile, but they sure can be fun to try! It all was before. ●

Matchlocks i

DURING THE FINAL decade of the 15th century, two portentous events took place in Spain, heralding the rapid ascendancy of that nation as a powerful influence on the ever dramatic, often enigmatic course of history. On January 2, 1492, the indomitable Christian armies of the Catholic sovereigns, Ferdinand and Isabella, crushed Moorish resistance in Granada, terminating nearly 800 years of Islamic dominance on the Iberian Peninsula. Then on March 15, 1493, the intrepid Genoese mariner, Christopher Columbus, sailed into bustling Palos harbor with the astounding news that a "new world" had been discovered across the capricious Atlantic.

With colonies in the West Indies relatively secure by about 1500, Spanish exploration intensified in what could be called the Age of the Conquistador. Juan Ponce de León, following the loss of his Puerto Rican governorship, petitioned the Crown for permission to seek other lands for colonization. King Ferdinand approved and granted him a patent for the exploration and colonization of Bimini. Ponce failed to discover Bimini but, on April 2, 1513, the winds of fortune guided him to what would eventually become part of the continental United States. He called it Florida.

A paucity of documentation surrounds Ponce de León's first and second expeditions to Florida, a then vast, vaguely delineated region. That his ships mounted cannon is unquestioned; that bloody conflicts with the Indians occurred is undeniable, and that the venerable crossbow accompanied both expeditions is beyond debate. But particularly lacking is any concrete data specifically referring to firearms. Consequently, until authenticated documentation is unearthed, if ever, this question remains moot and invites speculation.

Firearms had been used in the conquest and colonization of the Indies since the time of Columbus. Indeed, the Admiral of the Ocean Sea, himself, on January 30, 1495, requested from the Crown 100 crossbows, 200 cuirasses, an undetermined quantity of ammunition and 100 *espingardas* to equip a complement of 200 infantry.[1] Two months after the discovery of Florida, on May 31, 1513, Pedro Arias de Avila, preparing an expedition to the Indies, ordered from the artillery factory at Málaga 200 *espingardas* for infantry use, supplemented by 35 *hacabuches* "...each of 30 lb (sic).."[2] to serve as rampart guns.

A soldier of Ponce de Leon's infantry (left center) is firing an *espingarda* during a skirmish with unidentified Florida Indians early in the 16th century. This illustration is from the title page of the "Decada Segunda" (Second Decade) portion of Antonio Herrera's rare *Descripcion de las Indias Occidentales*, published in Madrid in 1726. *Photo courtesy Library of Congress.*

A reasonable assumption is that since *Adelantado* (Governor) Juan Ponce de León was an experienced conquistador, he certainly would have been aware of firearms, while the very nature of an expedition to a strange land with equally strange inhabitants called for numerous arms of various kinds. In any case, while attempting to establish a colony on the Florida Gulf coast in 1521, Ponce de León was severely wounded by a Calusa arrow and returned to Cuba, where he died.

The term *espingarda* is somewhat ambiguous. In 15th century Spanish literature it appears to be synonymous with *hacabuche,* earliest known Spanish variant of the Middle High German *hakenbüchse* (hook gun); those early Germanic firearms displayed an iron hook beneath the barrel and near the muzzle, the purpose of which remains obscure.

In essence the *espingarda* of the early 15th century was a refined hand cannon cast of brass, bronze or, infrequently, iron. These smoothbore, muzzle-loading weapons had no breech plug;* although variations appeared with breech chambers; that is, the breech section was of smaller diameter than the barrel proper (plate I, fig. 1). A wooden tiller or handle was attached to the barrel by bands or pins, and a length of slow match, applied manually to the rudimentary priming pan, served as the ignition agent. There was no standardization of barrel length, caliber or weight. A wooden ramrod was used for loading and a bullet mould of metal or stone was a common accessory. Reference is also made to *espingardas* employing arrow-like projectiles similar to those used in early cannon.[3]

A late 15th century *hacabuche* in the Alcázar of Segovia (fig. 2) has an iron barrel fitted with front and rear sights. The bore is about one inch in diameter. Again, there is no separate, removable breech plug. An integrally cast priming pan, surrounding the

*The early specimens were cast, with the breech closure integral. Later barrels were forged closed, before the breech plug as we know it appeared.

Spanish Florida

Though contemporary documentation is scarce and incomplete, the author's diligent research has discovered much fresh information on these primitive firearms, their use and abuse in a strange and unfriendly land.

by M. L. BROWN

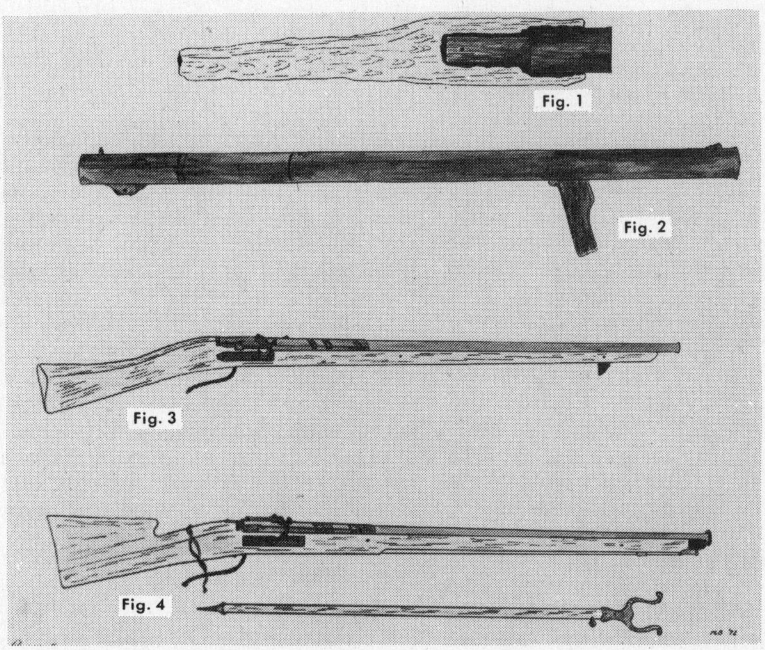

Plate 1. Spanish match-ignition firearms from about 1450 to 1550 or so: Fig. 1, *espingarda* or early hand cannon. Fig. 2, *hacabuche* (late hand cannon). Fig. 3, *arcabuz* or arquebus. Fig. 4, *mosquete* (musket) with aiming fork or rest *(horquilla)*.

Sketch by the author.

touchhole, is found to the right of the breech, slightly below the center line of the barrel. Although this specimen has no stock, it doubtless was equipped originally with a pin-fastened type, having two lugs beneath the barrel for that purpose. The larger lug near the muzzle served as a hook.

During the first quarter of the 16th century, there is an indication that the *espingarda* differed slightly from the *hacabuche*. That the weight of the latter is specifically mentioned by Pedro Arias (which see), suggests that the *espingardas* requested for infantry use were somewhat lighter; however, most contemporary sources refer to the *hacabuche* serving as both infantry weapon and rampart piece.

There had emerged in Spain about 1490 an advanced form of *hacabuche* with a mechanical rather than manual method of applying the match to the priming. This revolutionary mechanism, forerunner of the true gunlock, probably originated in Germany about 1450 and had been applied to firearms throughout most of Western Europe by 1525. These were what is termed today a matchlock.

The most common matchlock mechanism found in Spain and her American colonies during the 16th and 17th centuries was the sear type. This was a remarkably simple device with but two operating parts—the serpentine and sear—attached to a rectangular metal lockplate secured to the stock by two long screws which entered the stock from the left side. The serpentine derives its name from an early matchlock form having an S-shaped or "serpent-like" metal arm, pivoting on a pin, which held the slow match in its upper curve, while the lower rear end served as an operating lever or trigger.

In the sear-type matchlock arquebus (fig. 3) only the upper half of the serpentine was used, gripping the match in adjustable jaws tightened by a small turnscrew. A stud at the opposite end of the serpentine passed through the lockplate and was attached to a slotted tumbler. The nose of the long, pivotal sear engaged the tumbler slot, while a curved lever extending beneath the stock was fitted to the heel. A leaf spring mounted inside the lockplate exerted pressure on the sear. The lever, drawn upward, pivoted the sear nose down, compressing the spring and simultaneously rotating the serpentine rearward. This action carried the match to the priming powder, which then flashed through the touchhole, igniting the main charge. When the lever was released, pressure from the spring, bearing on the sear, returned the serpentine to its pre-firing position.

The matchlock was clearly an improvement over manual ignition, for the soldier now had both hands available to steady the gun when aiming. The simple mechanism was also relatively easy to make and inexpensive. These considerations doubtlessly were responsible for its popularity and longevity as a military weapon despite the introduction of more sophisticated ignition systems in the interim.

Barrels and Barrelmaking

By the start of the 16th century, barrels no longer were cast; the tube was fashioned by shaping rectangular iron plates, heated to a malleable state, around a cylindrical mandrel or rod and hammering the edges to join the seam. A threaded breechplug with a tang sealed the rear end. The simple tiller was supplanted by a shorter, broader stock cut from a single board, curving slightly downward from the breech and terminating in a flat butt. The breechplug tang and lockplate were let into the stock, which was usually walnut in martial specimens although cherry, poplar, serbal, agnus castus, fruitwood and oak also were used.

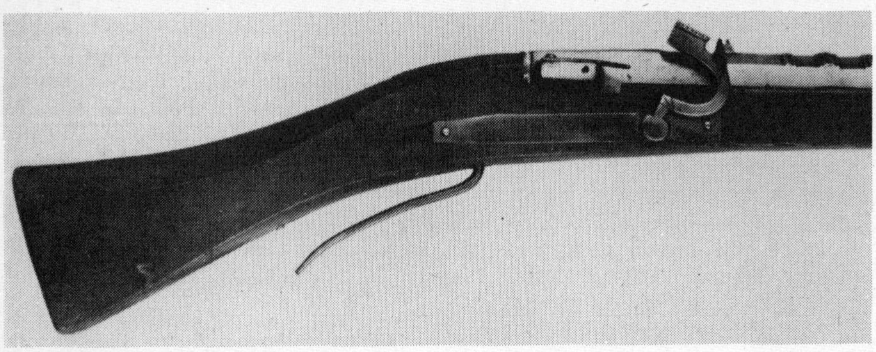

This early 16th century Spanish *Hacabuche* is in the Museo del Ejercito, Madrid. Just over 60" long, it weighs over 20 lbs., and its iron barrel has a hook near the muzzle.
Photo courtesy James D. Lavin.

Barrels of most Spanish matchlocks were slightly over 60 inches long and of about 80 caliber, commonly loaded with 3½ to 4 drams of powder—and more brown than black. The massive, usually octagonal, breech section became round after a foot or so, although fully round barrels are also encountered. The stock was normally fastened by two cross pins, and additional support was provided by a long screw passing vertically through the wrist to the breech plug tang. The ramrod, often tipped with brass or bronze, was located on the left side of the long stock, secured by a metal loop (thimble) near the muzzle and fastened to a threaded hook opposite the lock by merely screwing the tip a few turns into it.

A rectangular, shallow-cupped priming pan, welded to the breech, was fitted with a lateral-moving, manually-operated cover. This allowed the arm to be pre-primed, the cover keeping the priming powder fairly dry and intact; it also served as a safety device, for the glowing match could not reach the powder in the pan with the cover over the charge. By about 1546 a "fence," projecting upward from the rear of the pan, shielded the gunner's eyes from ignition flash and flying particles of burning powder.

An aiming fork or rest was used to support these massive 30- to 35-pound weapons. However, this accessory seems to have been discarded early in the 16th century when less cumbrous guns emerged, only to reappear with the introduction of the heavy martial matchlock musket. The Spanish are generally credited with originating the practice of firing the arquebus with the stock held to the shoulder rather than pressed against the cheek or chest, as was customary elsewhere, although it cannot be precisely learned when this method was introduced.

Powders and Ignition

A coarse (corned) powder was used for loading and a finely ground (serpentine) powder, easier to ignite, was used for priming; consequently two powder flasks were normally used. Other accessories included a brush to clean the pan and a pick (or "pricker") to clear the touchhole; a "worm" to remove an unfired ball from the bore; a "wipe" (scraper) to swab the bore, and a match case. This last was a cylindrical brass or tin tube about a foot long, the sides perforated at one end for air circulation, into which a 1½- or 2-foot length of lighted match was coiled to protect it from the elements.

Generally lighted at both ends, the match used as the ignition agent was made of cotton, flax or hemp fibers soaked in a saltpeter/water solution, twisted into a cord and dried. The amount of saltpeter determined the burning rate, which was generally about 4 or 5 inches per hour. Balls were carried in a cloth or leather bag secured by a drawstring, although when action was anticipated one or two were placed in the mouth to facilitate loading.

In addition to the myriad developments seen in the evolution of the Spanish *hacabuche,* there were also changes in terminology. A variant spelling appeared about 1525 as *arcabuche,* and shortly after the word was rendered *arcabuz.* Compounding the etymological confusion is the term *escopeta,* often used synonymously during this era, although it early fell from popular usage; it emerged later with a more precise connotation. It is used today to describe a shotgun.*

The Crossbow

The military crossbow was superior to the matchlock arquebus in range, accuracy and rapidity of fire during the first half of the 16th century. On a clear calm day the effective range of the arquebus was roughly 80 to 100 yards. Accuracy with the round ball beyond that distance was dismal, even with the best powder and a relatively straight barrel. By contemporary standards an *arcubucero* capable of loading and firing 2 shots in 3 minutes was exceptional.

By about 1550 the martial arquebus had supplanted the crossbow, especially in the New World, where warfare was conducted by more unorthodox methods than on the ancient battlefields of Europe, due primarily to the guerrilla tactics used by the Indians.

An excellent description of a military matchlock arquebus is provided

*In 1519, during the conquest of Mexico, Bernal Díaz del Castillo referred to the arquebus as an *escopeta.* This briefly popular term re-emerged in Spain about 1650, where it was used to describe an unrifled sporting firearm; however, in the Spanish colonies of North America, *escopeta* evidently meant a smoothbore military flintlock musket.

by an arms contract accepted by Biscayan gunsmith Anton de Urquizu in 1535 wherein he undertook "...the manufacture of 2,000 arquebuses of the length and shape and walnut stocks and powder flasks and priming flasks and mould and ramrod and barrel cleaner and bullet worm and all other tools as had the sample arquebus that was given him at the time he took with him the contract that was made at moncon (Monzon) the past year of 533 (1533) for the 4,000 arquebuses which he took to malaga (Málaga) which (sample) weighs 14 pounds and three-quarters weight of *castilla* which are 16 ounces to the pound (.) the said arquebuses must be well and cleanly bored and the balls for each three-quarters of an ounce and half a silver *real* weight of *castilla* and the locks of the said arquebuses the same as those that he delivered in malaga and each one of them must carry seven turns to the breech plug which must be very tight and well made and at the time the said anton de urquicu received the said arquebus from the masters who are to make them he must prove each with two charges of fine arquebus powder and its ball of lead and each charge must be of the weight of its ball for in this manner they are used and all must be made in this same way with charge and ball conforming to the said sample so that in time of necessity the charges and balls of one arquebus can be used in others and the powder flasks and priming flasks are to be made as the last ones that were taken to malaga..."[4]

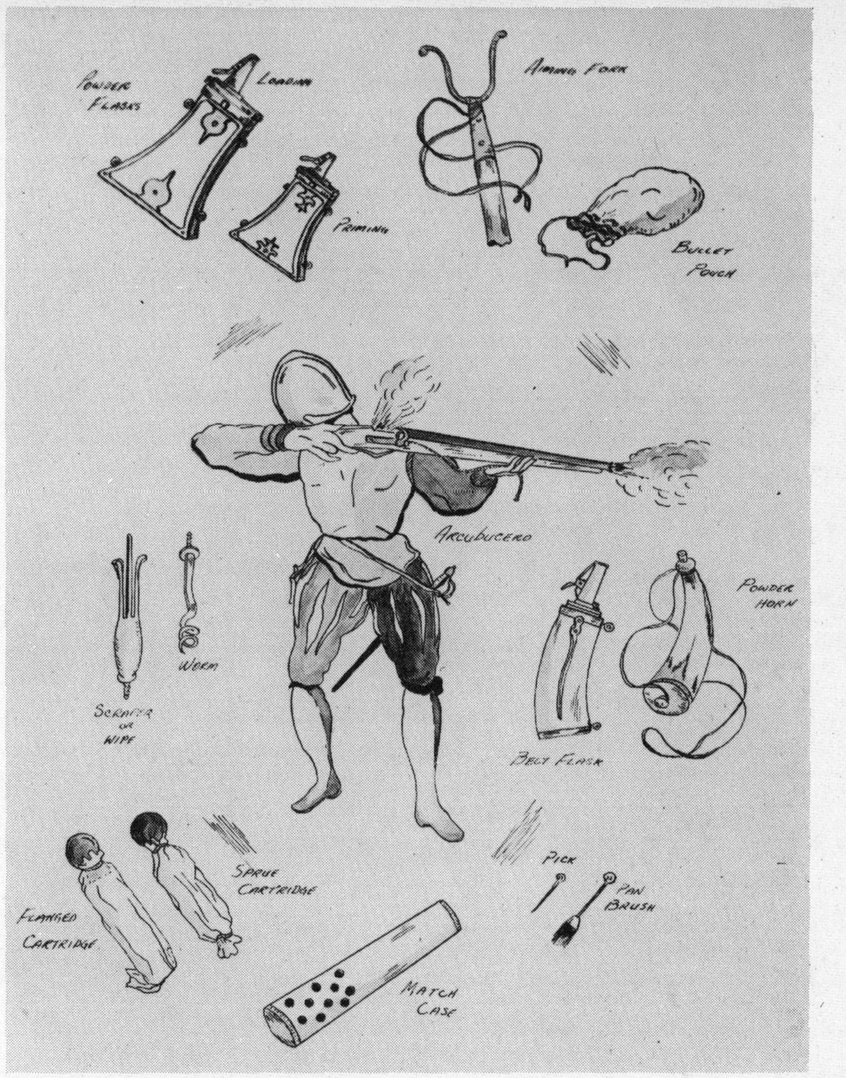

A Spanish arcabucero of about 1558, after a mural in the *Sala de Battalas*, the Escorial, Madrid, framed by accouterments common to the period.
Sketched by the author.

Arquebuses similar to those made by Urquizu probably accompanied Hernando de Soto's 1539 Florida expedition. As were his predecessors, De Soto was continually attacked by hostile Indians. Both crossbow and arquebus left much to be desired as defensive weapons for, as one participant lamented, the Indians "...never stand still, but are alwaies running and traversing from one place to another: by reason whereof neither crossebow nor arcubuse can aime at them: and before one crossebowman can make one shot (not to mention the arcubucero), an Indian will discharge three or foure arrowes; and he seldome misseth what he shooteth at."[5]

Colonial Ventures

At least four determined attempts to colonize Florida had failed by 1543, yet in 1559 another venture was mounted, this time from Nueva España (New Mexico). Led by Ristán de Luna y Arellano, 1,000 colonists and 500 soldiers left Vera Cruz on June 11, landing at Pensacola Bay on August 14. The colony was abandoned in 1561. Significant data concerning the firearms and accouterments used during that period are outlined by correspondence dated May 6, 1560, between Luis de Velasco, Viceroy of New Spain, and De Luna.

"...Luis Daza is taking (to the colony) 200 helmets covered with tin. I think they will be stronger and last longer than those you took with you. He is also taking 110 or 120 horn flasks which will preserve the powder better in a damp cold country than wooden ones; they will last longer, and be useful for loading and priming. If they work well, let me know, and I will send more. He is also taking I do not know how many *arrobas* (a weight of about 25 pounds) of matchcord. It did not turn out as well as I could have wished. It will (need to be) twisted and pulled again there, and if this is done, it will serve. It pained me to learn what you write me about the little care which the men take to conserve their offensive and defensive arms, for, aside from the fact that they are necessary, they cost a great deal and much time and labor is spent in making them. You will give strict orders how to care for and preserve the arquebuses which came from Spain. I have ordered that 100 of them be given to Luis Daza in Vera Cruz, together with their powder horns and small flasks and iron helmets. They write me that these are very good munitions...Please tell me whether more munitions than these are needed, that they may be sent." He goes on: "You ask me to send you two Indians who

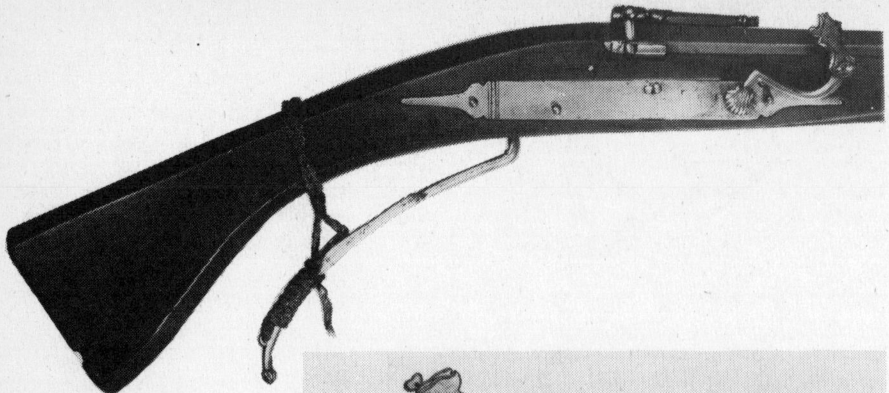

This late 16th century Spanish *arcabuz* weighs 12 lbs., its 39.5" barrel is about 60 caliber. Length over-all is 55". It has a match guide, fence and pan cover. The cord seen kept the lever from unscrewing out of the sear bar.
James D. Lavin collection.

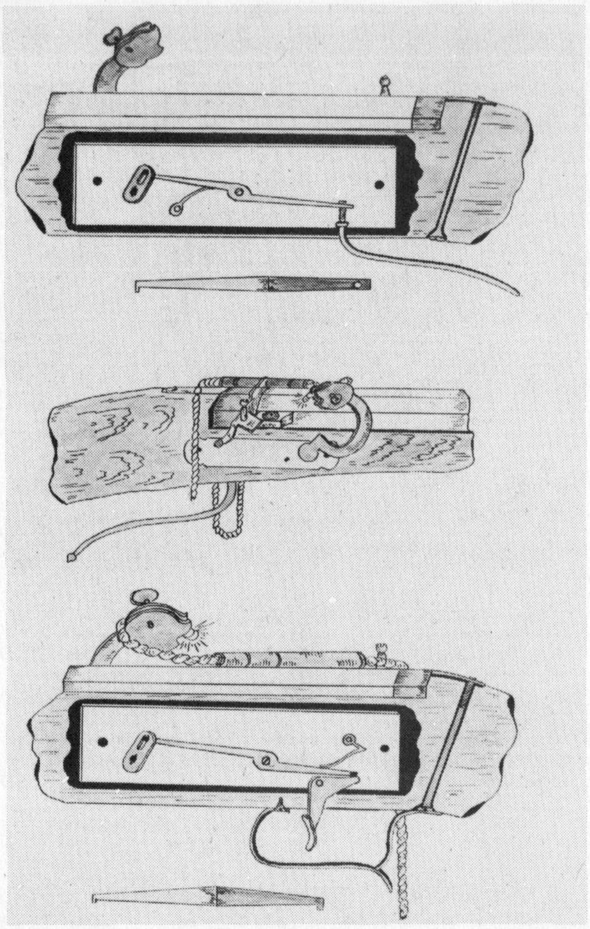

European sear-type matchlock mechanisms. Top—interior of lever form, about 1525. Middle—exterior of lever form, about 1585. Bottom—interior of trigger type, about 1600. Diagrams represent simplified version of usual styles; variations were common. Author's sketch.

know now to make arquebus stocks. Until now I have not been able to finish with two or three who are making them here, and not one of them wants to go. I think they may be excused for the time being, considering the munitions now being sent which have come from Spain. There are 130 or 140 arquebuses with powder horns and flasks and iron helmets. If there is no one who knows how to make the stocks or who can repair the broken ones which cannot be used, you will order them sent here and they will be repaired or others will be sent."[6]

De Luna's unfortunate experience and the earlier failures prompted King Philip II, on September 23, 1561, to terminate all Spanish attempts to colonize Florida. However, events in Europe soon dictated a reversal of Crown policy. In 1562 French Protestants (Huguenots), led by Jean Ribault, fled to North America to escape the horrors of the Inquisition. Ribault's colony also failed, but an attempt by Rene Goulaine de Laudonniere in 1564 established Fort Caroline on the St. Johns River near present-day Jacksonville, Fla.

Philip viewed both French incursions with justified alarm; not only had heretics encroached upon Spanish soil, but also there now was a French colony intolerably situated on the flank of the Spanish treasure fleet route from the Indies. He immediately dispatched *Adelantado* Pedro Menéndez de Avilés with 500 soldiers to destroy the Huguenots, plus more than 2,000 colonists to start yet another Spanish settlement. Arriving in Florida, on St. Augustine's Day (August 28), 1565, Menéndez located a suitable harbor about 35 miles south of the French fort.

At dawn on September 20, Menéndez attacked Fort Caroline. The resulting battle revealed one of the principal disadvantages of matchcord ignition. Five hundred Spaniards, at least two-thirds of them *arcubuceros,* had made a 4-day forced march through a severe tropical storm to reach the French position. Torrential rain ruined both powder and match. However, the attack was vigorously pressed forward with the sword and Menéndez' victory temporarily halted French colonial aspirations in Florida.

On an expedition to Guale (northeast Florida and Georgia) in 1566, Menéndez again was frustrated during an encounter with the Timucuan Indians when he was forced to withdraw because a sudden shower doused the *arcubuceros'* matches. Further problems were revealed by a Timucuan attack on the fort at St. Augustine that same year. Although the attack failed, the Indians succeeded in killing many of the sentries because they were betrayed at night by their glowing matches.

Ordnance Supplies

Some idea of the firearms, munitions and related ordnance available in St. Augustine and at Fort San Felipe in Santa Elena (near Port Royal, S.C.) during the 1565-1572 period can be derived from the following testimony of several witnesses questioned in the investigation of the Florida provinces made by *Licentiate* (Judge) Gamboa in Madrid on February 4, 1573.

"...On being questioned as to how many arms, and how much artillery and ammunition there are in the said two forts and in the said province, and in what order and with what care they keep them, he (Alonzo Ruiz) said that in the fort of St. Augustine there are about 20 pieces of artillery, large and small, some of bronze and others of iron; and, as it appeared to this witness, there was a quantity of powder, fuses (match) and balls, that which was necessary for its defense; and there may be an extra supply of about 20 or 30 arquebuses, of the large ones, and all the soldiers had their complete outfits of arms and arquebuses. And this witness knows that in the fort of Santa Elena there were about four pieces of mounted artillery, and there were others to be mounted which were in an old fort; and this witness does not know how many arquebuses, nor how much ammunition they had, further than that he heard it said that the soldiers that were there had the needed supply of arms and munitions, and it was well managed and in order."[7]

Pedro Gonzales of Escalona, another witness, said that in addition to the artillery at the fort in St. Augustine there were "....16 large arquebuses, 30 small ones, all in good condition...and much powder and lead, many balls and fuses, and other things in good order and well guarded..."[8]

One Juan Lopez de Paredes disclosed that in the fort at St. Augustine there were "...as many as 24 arquebuses for a reserve supply..."[9] and he also noted that each soldier had an arquebus, while there was an unspecified amount of powder, lead and match.

The arms and munitions intended for the Spanish settlements in the Florida provinces came directly from Spain or were trans-shipped via Havana, Vera Cruz or elsewhere in the Indies. Diego de Velasco, writing to the Crown from St. Augustine in August, 1575, complained that "...there is such a need of providing the pay and sustenance of the soldiers who are here at present, that I doubt if they can be maintained in conformity with what your Majesty command; because, as the supplies and munitions wherewith they are provided, are bought in Havana and other parts of these Indies, they are so expensive..."[10]

Arquebuses were fabricated at the Royal Artillery Factory at Málaga and possibly sub-contracted by that facility, while the Crown also contracted for firearms from independent gunsmiths in the arms-making centers of Cordova, Madrid, Orio, Ricla, Salamanca, Seville, Soria and Vizcaya (Biscay). At St. Augustine a plain arquebus cost three *ducados* in 1565[11] (current equivalent U.S. value not known).

A new fort, San Marcos, was built at Santa Elena in 1576, and it was near there that Spanish avarice, coupled with Indian perfidy, precipitated a full-scale conflict. Ensign Hernando Moyano with 21 *arcubuceros* entered a Cusabo village and seized provisions needed at the fort. The Indians promised an abundant supply of food if the Spaniards would show their peaceful intent by smothering their matches. Moyano's detachment complied. The Indians attacked, and only one Spaniard, Andres Calderon, survived the ensuing battle and escaped to warn the colony.

An Inspector Arrives

Alvaro Flores, *visitador* (inspector) of the Florida provinces, came to St. Augustine on September 27, 1578, to inspect the fort and garrison, visiting Santa Elena on October 12 for the same purpose. Flores was an ordnance expert authorized to report on the number and condition of the weapons and equipment held and used in those fortifications. The inspection was typically thorough and, in addition to the artillery at the fort in St. Augustine, Flores found "...at the door...whereby one enters this platform and the fort, 25 arquebuses, primed and loaded, laid on a long table ..., (while) in the sentry-box of the said platform, where the sentinel mounts guard, (were) two pikes and his arquebus in order that with it, if need be, he can give the alarm; with its fuse lighted, as it is, in fact, by day and by night."[12]

Nails had been driven in the walls of the building where the guard slept and, hanging from these Flores perceived "...12 muskets, and many other arquebuses of the soldiers; there were 14 arquebuses..."[13] Inspecting the many cots where the soldiers slept, he found above each two nails "...where were (hung) the arquebuses of the soldiers, and a few muskets among them."[14] In another sentry-box on the platform "...were six pikes, four half-pikes, six muskets, and a few soldiers' arquebuses..."[15]

An inspection of the magazine disclosed "...a house built of boards where the powder and the arquebus fuses are kept, with its key and sliding door, wherein were 12 barrels each containing one *quintal* (a hundredweight) of powder for arquebuses, ten *quintals* of fuses for arquebuses from Palnuch (Palmicha?) and New Spain; six bars of lead, four of them weighing five *arrobas* and two of them, six; and 1,500 bullets made for arquebuses, and 500 for muskets."[16]

Flores' inspection of the St. Augustine garrison determined the kinds of arms and accouterments then available to the soldiers of the Florida provinces, exemplified by those presented by Andres Calderon, a native of Cordova, including: "...an arquebus, a sword, powder flasks and bullets."[17]

Accompanied by Gov. Pedro Menéndez Marqués, Flores arrived at Santa Elena via frigate. Entering Fort San Marcos, he discovered "...30 soldiers, and a table on which were the arquebuses of the said soldiers, primed and loaded; and they had their arms: swords, powder-flasks, bullets, and munitions pouches."[18]

On the wall of the platform above the artillery, Flores saw "...8 muskets, 12 pikes, and 20 half-pikes hanging on their nails; and on the same platform, at the end of it, a sentry-box where they keep a sentinel, wherein were two pikes, and an arquebus...with its fuse lighted."[19] Inspecting the bastion on the south side of the fort, Flores noted "...6 muskets and 10 arquebuses...,"[20] while "...6 muskets, 8 pikes, 16 half-pikes, and one dozen arquebuses..."[21] were found at another bastion.

In the magazine Flores discovered "...8 barrels, each of the capacity of one *quintal* of arquebus powder; 8 *quintals* of fuses...6 bars of lead weighing 5 or 6 *arrobas* each one, 500 bullets of lead for muskets and 1,000 for arquebuses."[22]

The Matchlock Musket

Though no mention is made of the martial matchlock musket (fig. 4) during De Luna's temporary stay in Florida, and while it cannot positively be established that muskets accompanied the 1565 Menéndez expedition, testimony from Gamboa's 1573 investigation refers to *large* and *small* arquebuses, indicating that either muskets or similar firearms were available in Florida before 1572, when most of the witnesses departed for Spain. The Flores report leaves no doubt that muskets served in Florida before 1578.

Some firearms historians have expressed the opinion that the only distinction between the Spanish musket and arquebus was weight; however, there is ample evidence clearly indicating a distinct difference in caliber also. The 1578 Flores report states that in the magazines at St. Augustine and Santa Elena were "...bullets made for arquebuses and ...muskets." Unfortunately, Flores does not mention the caliber of either.

The Spanish term *mosquete* appeared in the late 16th century, probably derived from the contemporary Italian *moschetto* (sparrow hawk), originating from the ancient practice of naming cannon and firearms for birds of prey. Sebastián de Covarrubias, writing in 1611, described the musket as "...a type of reinforced *escopeta* (which see), a terrible arm and heavy to the one who carries it; but with the employment of forks its use had been facilitated. It is called a *mosquete* (or) *quasi-muscovete,* for having invented it, so it is understood, the Muscovites."[23]

Spanish documents relating to the arms and accouterments in the Florida provinces are curiously silent regarding the bandolier, popular throughout most of Europe during this period. The bandolier was a leather baldric or strap worn across the shoulder and chest, and strung with from 12 to 20 wood or leather chargers, each containing a single, predetermined load. It is likely that the bandolier found little favor in Florida due to its predilection to tangle in the dense undergrowth, the rattle the chargers might make when covert movement was attempted, or the susceptibility of the chargers to the priming flash. In any event the Flores report indicates that paper cartridges, containing both powder and ball, had been introduced to the Florida provinces before 1578, for by this time "munitions pouches" are mentioned as part of the equipment of the Santa Elena garrison.

Matchlock Improvements

By about 1575, the sear-type ignition mechanism had been improved by the introduction of a conventional trigger with a guard, and the lockplate assumed a form subsequently found on early snapping-type flintlock firearms. Other developments include a match guide atop the breech, which kept the match from fouling the serpentine, while the ramrod was relocated in a channel cut into the stock beneath the barrel and secured by a thimble. By about 1580 the arquebus stock had been somewhat slimmed, particularly at the wrist, while the butt flared conspicuously in what is termed a fishtail design; however, variations were the rule.

European martial matchlocks of the late 16th century, despite their origin, had similar characteristics which would generally remain constant thereafter. A typical musket weighed 15 to 20 pounds, was at least 70 inches over-all, and of a caliber between 80 and 92. Capable of penetrating the heaviest armor up to 125 yards, the musket was effective at 200 yards if the heavy ball struck its intended target. In comparison, the martial arquebus of the period weighed 12 to 15 pounds, was between 40 and 65 inches over-all, and of a caliber ranging from 60 to 79. It was effective against light armor to some 40 yards and could fell man or beast at 125 yards.

The English early learned to respect the effectiveness of the Spanish martial arquebus. When in 1586 Sir Francis Drake attacked St. Augustine, destroying Fort San Juan de los Pinnillos and burning the town, Juan de Contreras kept the enemy awake throughout the night by intermittently discharging his arquebus at their position. The next morning the plucky Spaniard killed English Sergeant-Major Anthony Powell with a shot through the head, and then managed to elude his pursuers via a nearby thicket.

The Wheel-Lock

During the final decade of the 16th century, numerous wheel-lock firearms were used by the Spaniards in the Indies. With the emergence of the wheel-lock came terms to distinguish them from the matchlock and vice versa. The matchlock arquebus became an *arcabuz de cuerda* (cord) or *arcabuz de mecha* (match), while the wheel-lock arquebus was termed an *arcabuz de pedernal* (flint) or *arcabuz de rueda* (wheel). In the late 17th century the matchlock and wheel-lock were distinguished from snapping-type flintlock arms by the suffix *rastrillo* (rake), which described the action of the cock against the battery (frizzen).

Although the wheel-lock was superior to the matchlock in several respects, its more complex and therefore more fragile mechanism was expensive to make and difficult to repair, especially in the New World where such facilities were few and widely scattered. Experienced conquistadors generally preferred the strong, simple, inexpensive matchlock. This was the case in 1596, when Pedro Ponce de León requested from the Crown 500 arquebuses, 100 muskets, 60 *quintals* of match and a large supply of powder and lead for his expedition to the Indies.[24]

The advent of the 17th century saw the presidio of St. Augustine become the focal point of Spanish activity in the Florida provinces. Santa Elena had been abandoned in 1587, and the defeat of the Royal Armada in the English Channel the following year marked the beginning of Spain's decline as a world power.

In 1592 lightning struck the fort's powder magazine at St. Augustine, causing severe damage, while in 1597 another Indian revolt in Guale abruptly terminated missionary activity there, shunting the movement westward toward Apalache province. Philip III, assuming the monarchy in 1598, inherited a disintegrating Florida and did little to prevent total collapse. St. Augustine, fighting for its life in 1602, managed to survive all attempts to abandon it and, by 1640, became the single permanent colony in the Florida provinces, supporting a few small, far-flung military outposts and a handful of struggling missions.

When in 1653 Crown officials arrived to inspect the fort and settlement at St. Augustine, conditions were hardly improved. The rapidly decaying fort contained 10 bronze cannon, two without carriages, and 20 other artillery pieces with only 9 mounted. There were 6 arquebuses beyond redemption and all 178 muskets needed repairs, while the powder for both the artillery and small-arms had been spoiled by dampness and deterioration.[25]

During that tumultuous epoch the matchlock arquebus and musket saw further improvement. By about 1650, stronger barrels were made by lapping the edges of the seam, and by 1665 the addition of a sideplate provided more support for the lock mechanism. The stock, particularly the butt, manifested a more conventional pattern and most of the iron parts of those weapons, heretofore finished bright, were blued by about 1675.

On May 29, 1668, English pirate Robert Searles launched a night attack against St. Augustine. Several *arcubuceros* were slain when the pirates, armed with flintlocks, fired at their glowing match. The need for better arms was graphically demonstrated and prompted Gov. Francisco de la Guerra y de la Vega to order 50 *escopetas* from Vera Cruz.[26] In December, 24 arrived, each costing 22 pesos (about $35 U.S.). These weapons had an over-all length of 50 inches and were of a larger caliber and had a greater range than the *arcabuz*.[27] They were probably the first Spanish snapping-type (now commonly termed a *miquelet*) flintlock arms employed in Florida.

Spain's policy of not arming the Indians in her dominions, inaugurated during the initial stages of conquest and colonization, was strictly adhered to for obvious reasons. However, both colonists and mission Indians were at a disadvantage when, about 1670, French exploitation along the Gulf of Mexico and English encroachments from the Carolinas, each assisted by Indian allies armed with flintlocks, seriously began to erode the Spanish position in the Florida provinces.

Those incursions stimulated the Crown to bolster the defenses at St. Augustine. In 1672 construction began on the Castillo de San Marcos, the first stone fort in the Florida provinces. (Nine wooden forts preceded the Castillo.) It was from there on May 14, 1680, that a worried Gov. Pablo de Hita Salazar wrote the Crown that "...there are not 200 firearms in the armory nor among the soldiers and natives."[28]

Salazar's comments inspired results, for in December an arms shipment reached St. Augustine. It consisted of 100 muskets with their flasks and rests; 100 arquebuses with their flasks; and 75 *carabinas vizcáinas* (Biscayan carbines) with their flasks, slings and springs.[29] These wheel-lock carbines, perhaps the first to arrive in Florida, were of unspecified length, weight and caliber. Ten were issued to the garrison's mounted infantry, 16 were stored in the armory and 49 were unserviceable due to locks broken by metal fatigue and stocks riddled by termites.[30]

French *harquebusiers* of 1564 assisting Chief Outina of Timucuas against his rival, Potanou. Engraving by Theodor de Bry from a painting by Jacques Le Moyne fails to show the match cords. Weapons have flared muzzles, in background, others a common barrel style. *N.Y. Public Library photo.*

The disturbing shortage of firearms was met, with varying degrees of success, by obtaining them from other than official sources. Sergeant-Major Juan Márquez Cabrera, Governor and Captain-General of Florida, bought 7 flintlock muskets from trader John Grantland at 8 *pesos* each in 1683,[31] while later that year he bought from another source 20 more at the same price.[32] In 1684, another 8 flintlock muskets were captured from English pirates.[33] Gov. Márquez also described an additional method of procurement: "It was a fixed custom here that, when a soldier died, his wife or kinswoman felt they had a right to sell the arms, but I have taken away from them those that I have been able to locate..." (and) "a few of these (women) used to sell the arms to the crewmen of vessels calling at this port."[34] When Gov. Márquez left Florida on April 13, 1687, 13 flintlock muskets were among the items accompanying him.[35]

Crown policy regarding Indian procurement of firearms apparently relaxed in 1686, or perhaps the local situation demanded a change. This is indicated by a letter of instructions from Gov. Márquez to Marcos Delgado in Apalache province on June 18. Delgado was ordered to personally select "...12 soldiers...armed with their muskets or *carabinas* and also 20 Indians with firearms and 20 with bows and arrows..."[36] for a mission to Mexico.

Of the 232 firearms among two infantry companies stationed at the Castillo de San Marcos in February, 1686, 228 were matchlocks and 4 were flintlocks.[37] Seven years later an inventory of the armory disclosed 111 serviceable and 100 unserviceable matchlock muskets, 16 unserviceable matchlock arquebuses, 9 unserviceable carbines (no distinction as to type), 9 unserviceable flintlock muskets and a pair of serviceable flintlock blunderbuses.[38]

A 1694 report of the firearms intended for shipment to the proposed presidio of Pensacola reveals a greater percentage of flintlock arms than had previous inventories. It lists 300 matchlock muskets, 100 flintlock muskets, 50 pairs of pistols (type unspecified), and 50 hundredweight of musket balls, half for the flintlocks.[39]

St. Augustine continued to receive shipments of matchlock arms as late as 1697, when 100 arquebuses and 100 pairs of flasks were delivered in May.[40] Five years later, in 1702, when English Gov. James Moore of the Carolina Colony attacked St. Augustine, the Spanish defenders were predominately armed with matchlocks, while the enemy was provided

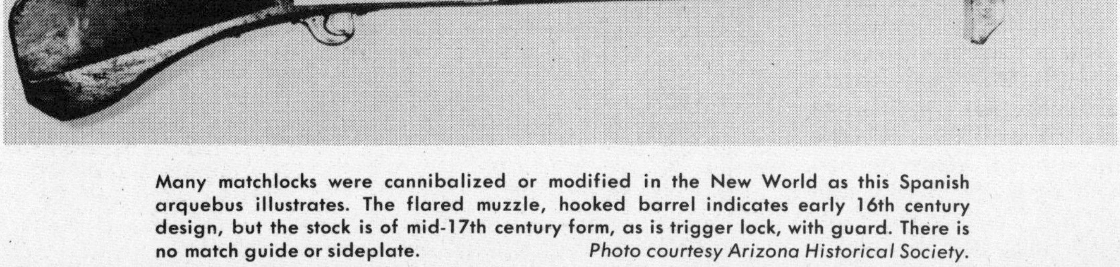

Many matchlocks were cannibalized or modified in the New World as this Spanish arquebus illustrates. The flared muzzle, hooked barrel indicates early 16th century design, but the stock is of mid-17th century form, as is trigger lock, with guard. There is no match guide or sideplate. *Photo courtesy Arizona Historical Society.*

with superior flintlock muskets.[41]

The martial matchlock in various forms served the Spanish in the Florida provinces for more than 200 years. However, it can be seen that from about 1690 those already obsolescent firearms gradually began to be replaced by the more sophisticated flintlock. The military transition from match to flint ignition was much slower in Spain than elsewhere in Europe and, consequently, the practically orphaned Florida provinces received flintlock arms in smaller numbers and considerably later than rival English and French colonies in North America.

Not until 1703 did Spain officially adopt the snapping-type flintlock musket as the standard military arm,[42] and the transition was finally accomplished in Florida 37 years later. The armory of the Castillo de San Marcos on September 12, 1740, listed an inventory of 550 flintlock muskets. Of these, 400 had been issued to the garrison and inhabitants of St. Augustine to defend the presidio during the War of Jenkins' Ear (1740-1743). The remainder was stored in the armory.[43]

Eighty-one years after the Spanish matchlock passed from the historical scene, Florida became part of the United States. Of the literally thousands of matchlock firearms carried on the numerous Spanish expeditions to Florida or sent to the various settlements there in the two centuries prior to the acceptance of the flintlock, only a handful survive and are preserved in a few public and private collections. The fate of the rest is cloaked by the mantle of the ages. ●

Conjectural drawing by Capt. S. Eastman, USA, engraved by James Smillie, depicts Hernando de Soto's 1539 expedition disembarking at Tampa Bay. Like his predecessors, De Soto was constantly harassed by hostile Indians.
Library of Congress photo.

Castillo de San Marcos, the first stone fort in Spanish Florida, was the center of its military activity from 1672 to 1821. Six strong efforts to capture the fort failed, and it withstood several lesser attacks by pirates and Indians. *Photo courtesy National Park Service.*

Notes

1. James D. Lavin, *A History of Spanish Firearms* (New York, 1965), p. 43.
2. Ibid., p. 46.
3. Ibid., p. 43.
4. Ibid., pp. 48-49, n. 23.
5. Harold L. Peterson, *Arms and Armor in Colonial America, 1526-1783* (New York, 1956), p. 11.
6. Herbert Ingram Priestley (ed. and trans.), *The Luna Papers,* Vol. I (DeLand, Fla., 1928), pp. 107-109, 117.
7. Jeanette Thurber Conner (ed. and trans.), *Colonial Records of Spanish Florida,* Vol. I (DeLand, Fla., 1925), pp. 89-91.

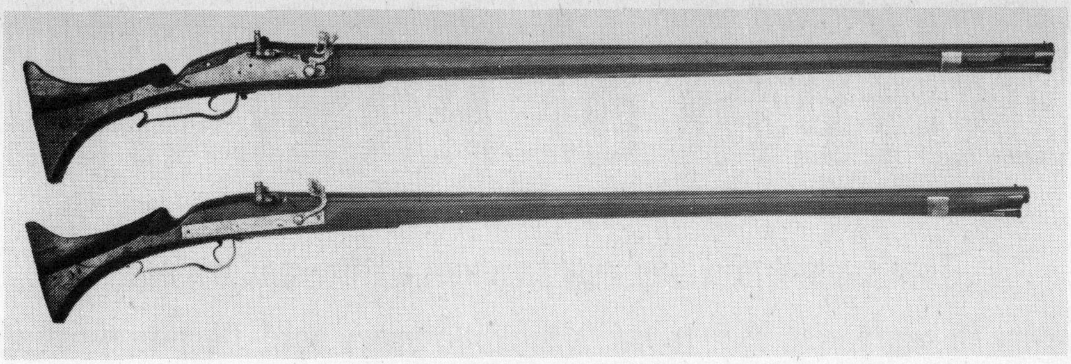

English matchlock muskets. Top specimen (about 1638) has pan attached to lockplate as in early flintlock types. The other, of about 1577, is like those used by Sir Francis Drake during his attack on St. Augustine in 1586.
Photo courtesy H.M. Tower of London Armouries.

8. Ibid., p. 97.
9. Ibid., p. 101.
10. Ibid., p. 307.
11. Charles W. Arnade, *Florida On Trial* Coral Gables, Fla., 1959, p. v.
12. Conner, p. 125, 127.
13. Ibid., p. 127.
14. Ibid., p. 129.
15. Ibid., p. 131.
16. Ibid., p. 131.
17. Ibid., p. 137.
18. Ibid., pp. 153-155.
19. Ibid., p. 157.
20. Ibid., p. 157.
21. Ibid., p. 159.
22. Ibid., p. 161.
23. Lavin, p. 48, n. 22.
24. Ibid., p. 47, n. 18.
25. Verne E. Chatelain, *The Defenses of Spanish Florida, 1565 to 1763* (Washington, D.C., 1941), p. 56.
26. North Carolina Spanish Records Collection, Department of Archives and History, Raleigh (hereafter NC), Archivo General de Indias, Sevilla (hereafter AGI) 58-2-2/14, Viceroy Marquess de Mancera of Nueva España to the crown, Mexico, April 20, 1669, 89 fols., fol. 27.
27. Stetson Collection, P. K. Yonge Library of Florida History, University of Florida (hereafter SC), AGI 58-2-2/15, Mancera to the crown, October 28, 1669, 35 ff., 14.
28. Chatelain, *op. cit.*, p. 160, n. 23.
29. NC, AGI 54-5-11/71, Royal officials of Florida to the crown, St. Augustine, December 12, 1680, 7 ff.
30. SC, AGI 58-2-2/38, 12.
31. SC, AGI 58-2-2/38, 2, 8.
32. NC, AGI 54-5-11/111, Governor Juan Márquez Cabrera to the crown, October 8, 1683, 51 ff., 44.
33. SC, AGI 58-2-2/38, 8.
34. SC, AGI 58-2-2/38, Governor Márquez to the crown, March 20, 1686, 24 ff., 1, 2.
35. Luis R. Arana, "The Day Governor Cabrera Left Florida," *Florida Historical Quarterly,* XL (1961), pp. 154-163.
36. Mark F. Boyd, "The Expedition of Marcos Delgado from Apalache to the Upper Creek Country in 1686," *Florida Historical Quarterly,* XVI (1937), pp. 9-11.
37. SC, AGI 58-2-2/38, 22.
38. SC, AGI 54-5-13/60, Royal officials to the crown, December 22, 1693, 9 ff., 7.
39. SC, AGI 61-6-21/38, Count of Montellano to Don Juan de la Rea, Sevilla, June 15, 1694, 11 ff., 6.
40. SC, AGI 54-5-15/128, Royal officials to the crown, August 12, 1697, 2 ff., 1.
41. Charles W. Arnade, *The Siege of St. Augustine in 1702* (Gainesville, Fla., 1959), passim.
42. Francisco Barado, *Museo militar-Historia del ejército español,* (Barcelona, Spain, 1889), 3 vols., III, p. 543.
43. SC, AGI 58-1-32/23, Governor and Royal officials to the crown, September 25, 1740, 41 ff., 10-11.

Sources

Books

Arnade, Charles W. *Florida On Trial.* Coral Gables, Fla.: 1959.

________. *The Siege of St. Augustine in 1702.* Gainesville, Fla.: 1959.

Blackmore, Howard L. *Guns and Rifles of the World.* New York & London: 1965.

Chatelain, Verne E. *The Defenses of Spanish Florida, 1565 to 1763.* Washington, D.C.: 1941.

Conner, Jeanette Thurber. *Colonial Records of Spanish Florida.* 2 vols. DeLand, Fla.: 1925, 1930.

Greener, W. W. *The Gun and Its Development.* 9th ed. (fac.), New York: 1967.

Held, Robert. *The Age of Firearms.* New York: 1957.

Lavin, James D. *A History of Spanish Firearms.* New York: 1965.

Lawson, Edward W. *The Discovery of Florida and It's Discoverer, Juan Ponce de Léon.* St. Augustine, Fla.: 1946.

Lowery, Woodbury. *The Spanish Settlements Within the Present Limits of the United States.* 2 vols. New York & London: 1901, 1905.

Peterson, Harold L. *Arms and Armor In Colonial America, 1526 to 1783.* New York: 1956.

Preistley, Herbert Ingram. *The Luna Papers.* 2 vols. Deland, Fla.: 1928.

Periodicals

Arana, Luis R. "The Day Governor Cabrera Left Florida," *Florida Historical Quarterly,* Vol. XL (1961).

________. "The Exploration of Florida and Sources on the Founding of St. Augustine," *Florida Historical Quarterly,* Vol. XLIV (1965).

Bennett, Charles E. "A 16th Century French Manuscript and a 16th Century French 'Mug Book'," *Florida Historical Quarterly,* Vol. XXXIX (1961).

Covington, James W. "Drake Destroys St. Augustine: 1586," *Florida Historical Quarterly,* Vol. XLIV (1961).

Davis, Frederick T. "History of Juan Ponce de León's Voyages to Florida," *Florida Historical Quarterly,* Vol. XIV (1935).

Ehrmann, W. W. "The Timucua Indians of Sixteenth-Century Florida," *Florida Historical Quarterly,* Vol. XVIII (1939-1940).

Gorman, M. Adele Francis. "Jean Ribault's Colonies in Florida," *Florida Historical Quarterly,* Vol. XLIV (1965).

Held, Ray. "Hernando de Miranda, Governor of Florida, 1576-1577," *Florida Historical Quarterly,* Vol. XXVIII (1949-1950).

Higgs, Charles D. "Spanish Contacts with the Ais (Indian River) Country," *Florida Historical Quarterly,* Vol. XXI (1942-1943).

Hoffman, Paul E., and Lyon, Eugene. "Accounts of the Real Hacienda, Florida, 1565-1602," *Florida Historical Quarterly,* Vol. XLVIII (1969).

Lyon, Eugene. "Captives of Florida," *Florida Historical Quarterly,* Vol. L (1971).

Manucy, Albert. "The Man Who Was Pedro Menendez," *Florida Historical Quarterly.* Vol. XLIV (1965).

Wright, J. Leitch, Jr. "Sixteenth Century English-Spanish Rivalry in La Florida," *Florida Historical Quarterly,* Vol. XXXVIII (1960).

Acknowledgement

The author gratefully acknowledges the generous and invaluable assistance rendered in the preparation of this article by Mr. James D. Lavin, Ph.D., College of William and Mary, Williamsburg, Va.; Mr. Luis Rafael Arana, Chief Park Historian, Castillo de San Marcos National Monument, St. Augustine, Fla.; and Mr. William Scollard of Anaheim, California.

SHOOTING at 1000 YARDS

That's a hell of a long way to shoot a rifle—and it's not much easier to score well than it was a hundred years ago! Despite great advances in the making of barrels and bullets, the over-all group averages aren't all that much smaller than they were at Creedmoor. The top shooters? They do a lot better.

BY BOB BELL

IF YOUR EYESIGHT is good and the weather is better, you might not need optical aid to see that 12-inch bullseye 'way out there on the mountain. That bull on the military A target forms the basic aiming point for riflemen in these matches. However, a good target scope is a necessity for defining and aiming at the 4-inch white square thumbtacked to the middle. The reason such big targets are so hard to see is their distance from the shooting benches—to be precise, 1022 yards, for the range was deliberately fixed by survey at this odd distance so no one could accuse these competitors of shooting a "short 1000."

Now, 1000 yards—honest-to-God, three-feet-to-the-yard yards—is one helluva distance to shoot at anything with a rifle. It's well over half a mile, and the first time a garden-variety deer shooter or self-deluding antelope hunter gazes downrange toward those distant specks of black (which happen to approximate the vital area of a pronghorn or whitetail) his long-bragged-on tales of 700- or 800-yard kills—on running game!—suddenly begin sliding toward more realistic estimates, perhaps parelleling the sinking feeling in his stomach.

Yet all summer long, at roughly two-week intervals, some 100 shooters pile ponderous bench rifles, boxes of precisely handloaded ammo and assorted scopes, sandbags, etc., into their cars and make the trek to a mountaintop, leased from Irvin E. Plants, about 24 miles northeast of Williamsport, Pa.—the site of the Original Pennsylvania 1000-Yard Benchrest Club, Inc. Some of them drive hundreds of miles to compete. Most are from Pennsylvania, of course, but others come from the surrounding states and others not so near. Occasionally some gifted rifleman, unable to go on not knowing how his skill stacks up against these top rifles, makes the long trip from perhaps the other side of the continent, doubtless driven by the same urge that sent gunslingers of our frontier days toward Abilene, Dodge or Tombstone—wherever the current No. One Gun hung out.

During the actual 1000-yd. match competition, coaching is not allowed and shots are not spotted. When conditions change—as they often do during the 10-minute period—the shooter must dope them as best he can and make his own allowances.

Results aren't as final here. A second-place finisher can come back next match and maybe take all the marbles. In fact, there are two first-place winners in every shootout here, for there are in effect two objectives in each—smallest group and highest score—and one shooter cannot win both in a given match. That is, if the smallest group happens to be so well centered that it also scores the highest, that shooter wins for group (in earlier years he took top score), but the next-highest score wins that category.

A day's competition is called a "shoot," and each relay of 10 shooters (the range currently has 10 covered benches) is termed a "match." The riflemen turning in the smallest group and highest score in each match compete in a shootoff at the end of the day to determine the day's two over-all winners.

Simple Rules

Basic rules are simple. Before each match there's a 6-minute period during which an unlimited number of shots may be fired. Each shot is spotted as it's fired with a military-type disc that's visible through the scope, and coaching is permitted. The objectives at this time are to get zeroed and do some doping of wind and mirage.

A match consists of 10 shots fired for record during a 10-minute period. No sighters are permitted and shots are not spotted. If conditions change—as they usually do, for there are two small valleys between the benches and the butts, and sometimes the wind is blowing in opposite directions in each—it's up to the shooter to make corrections based on his own experience and ability. This often leads to a beautiful 9-shot group.

Pit personnel (everyone takes turns pulling targets) make a small replica of each target on which they locate and number every shot as it's fired. This is taped to the real target, which is rough scored and signed by the pit men, and returned to the rear for official scoring. Targets are given to the shooters, along with the replica which shows him how his group formed. Integrated with notes he makes during firing, this helps him build up a backlog of data during a summer. This keeping track of range conditions, "holds," etc., can be vitally important.

Long-range riflemen Bill Theis and Dave Troxell, of Williamsport, and George Reeder, of Cogan Station, Pa., organized the club in 1967, and it was incorporated in August of 1968. It seemed a logical extension of the bench shooting game which has fascinated so many dedicated shooters since the end of World War II. If little round holes in targets at 100 and 200 yards were interesting, they should be even more so at 5 or 10 times those distances, right? Too, the long range would not only permit, but even make almost necessary, the Magnum cartridges which intrigue many shooters nowadays—those oversize powder-gobblers so out of place at the short distances.

The concept gained an immediate following. In the first year of competition attendance averaged over 50 riflemen per shoot, with a total of 121 different entrants. Almost twice that number of shooters is average now (see Table I), and 173 different shooters competed in 1973. It should be mentioned right now that a significant percentage of these "riflemen" are women. There's nothing at all uncommon about somebody's wife or daughter using Pop's big gun (or maybe her own) during the day, and typical female scores fit right into the males' avergaes. In fact, the smallest group fired in competition to date is the 7.687-incher turned in by Mary Louise DeVito in 1970 with her 7mm-300 Weatherby.

The 1000-yd. firing line in 1973.

Rifles and Barrels

There are few restrictions on equipment. Each rifle must be mechanically safe and no return-to-battery machine-rest type rigs are allowed. The rifle must be rested on sandbags front and rear. Otherwise, the sky's the limit, but the truth is, most rifles are conventional in appearance to anyone used to bull barrels, thumbhole laminated stocks and target scopes. Turnbolt actions are the only logical choice for the Magnum cartridges used by most, and all common models are seen. Remington M700s and 40Xs, Winchester 70s and FN Mausers are the most numerous among commercial actions. Military Mausers and Springfields are chosen by many, the crude but strong M38 Japanese Arisaka by a few, and the big beautifully built custom actions of Howard Wolfe, Bob Hart and Ed Shilen by others. Most actions are used as single shots, the lack of a magazine well permitting a more rigid stock, and many are sleeved, which stiffens the action and gets the scope bases off the barrel.

Barrels by such top custom makers as Hart, Douglas and Shilen are used by the majority, though some have found commercial outfits, particularly from the Remington custom shop, deliver equivalent accuracy. Whereas many 200-yard benchresters have gone to short barrels for various reasons, longer ones—28 to 30 inches usually—are favored here, as they give more velocity from the slow-burning powders needed in Magnum cases, and cut down muzzle blast. Full diameters are common, the weight helping to reduce recoil and making precise holding easier.

Stocks tend to be king-size, laminated to reduce warping, flat-bottomed for easier control, with a thumbhole to allow straight-back trigger movement. Glass or metal bedding is used around the action and the first few inches of the barrel. Occasionally barrels are glassed full length. Various bedding techniques have been tried in addition to "normal" glassing, especially by Mechanicsburg, Pa., rifle-builder Al Wardrop, a longtime contender in these shoots and for several decades a competitor in conventional rifle matches.

Wardrop's Methods

Wardrop sleeves most of the rifles he builds, and has several ways of doing it. His sleeves are seamless steel tubing having .250" wall thickness with an inside diameter about ¼" greater than the barrel diameter; this gives ⅛" clearance all around the barrel. By one method, a 9" length of sleeve is centered over the barrel with the sleeve's rear end near the front of the receiver ring. The inside of the sleeve and the portion of barrel it encloses are slighly roughened. The space between the barrel and sleeve is then filled with glass. The outside of the sleeve is also glassed and screwed into the stock, but the receiver and the unsleeved section of the barrel float completely—no guard screws are used in the action. The rear face of the sleeve, trued up earlier, acts as a recoil shoulder. This face has three or four times the area of a conventional recoil shoulder. Some riflemen might feel concern that the sleeve will let go under recoil, but this has never happened to Wardrop's knowledge. Once, when he wanted to remove a sleeve, he tried heating, twisting, etc., with no noticeable effect, and ended up turning it off on the lathe. In some versions, a slightly longer sleeve also encloses the receiver ring.

A different operation encloses the entire action, the sleeve being epoxied to the receiver and extending forward over some 6 inches of the barrel. Sometimes the sleeve clears the barrel completely, but Al prefers to pour glass to give about a half-inch collar around the barrel at the front of the sleeve. In his testing, this has always given better accuracy than a fully floating barrel. Some gunsmiths who sleeve actions completely enclose them, making it necessary to remove the bolt to extract a case and insert a cartridge, but Wardrop prefers to cut a loading port into the sleeve, perhaps sacrificing a little stiffness but making it easier to remove a case that's suffered a head separation. With the sleeved action, he usually installs several ¼" allen screws through the sleeve and into the action, to increase the safety factor if by some chance the glass should let go during firing. Again, the rear face of the sleeve acts as the recoil shoulder, though in some cases he has added another one by soldering a ¼"-thick piece of metal, about one-third the circumference of the sleeve, to the bottom of the sleeve.

This is Al Wardrop, Mechanicsburg, Pa., gunsmith who has built many of the rifles used in the 1000-yd. matches, and is himself a top competitor. Al has done a lot of experimenting with bedding techniques (described in text). Rifle seen is typical of the type used—laminated stock, broad flat fore-end, heavy barrel, target scope.

Table 1
Average Number of Competitors per Shoot

Year		Competitors
1969	–	83
1970	–	81
1971	–	91
1972	–	94
1973	–	90

High—121 at Shoot 6, Aug. 13, 1972

In all cases described above, the sleeves are glassed into the stocks and held by three or four ¼ x 28 allen head cap screws. To allow these to be pulled up firmly, Al makes 1-¼"-diameter, ½"-thick washers, and counter-sinks and epoxies them into the wood, to secure the screw heads.

A newer bedding system Wardrop has been trying consists of two steel blocks each measuring about 2" on a side. These are drilled and contoured to fit the barrel, split into halves, and installed on the barrel on 7¼" centers (which permits scope block mounting on top). Four ¼ x 28 allen head cap screws bind the halves together. The bottom halves are glassed into the stock, while everything else floats.

Some of these systems seem unconventional, but Wardrop-built rifles have been among the winners for years.

Target scopes are used almost universally in these matches, to take advantage of their comparatively precise adjustments (a quarter-minute click gives a 2½" change at 1000 yards!) and good optics. Medium magnifications, 15x to 20x, are generally preferred, as they give less mirage trouble than the 24x to 30x models popular with the short range bench shooters. As weight is no worry, the 2" Unertl is a favorite of many, with others choosing the solidly mounted 3200 Redfield or the older Lyman Super Targetspot. A few old 6-24x Bausch & Lombs are seen (usually with Unertl type mounts), the variable power making it easy to choose a magnification to suit conditions.

Choice of Calibers

In the early days of the club, the most popular cartridge was the 6.5 WWH (Weatherby-Wright-Hoyer) Magnum (Table 2), an impressive design made by necking the 300 Weatherby case down to 6.5mm. Col. Paul Wright, a skilled long-range rifleman, fathered this creation, with the mechanical work being done by the late Al Hoyer. This Mifflintown, Pa., gunsmith, a big, quiet, kindly man, was long recognized as a leader in the extreme-range shooting game, both from the bench and in the field. It's one of the tragedies of the shooting world that he didn't take time to assemble and publish the countless facts he learned through his decades of shooting.

The 6.5 WWH seemed to be the

Calibers Winning Over-all Match or Shootoff, 1969-1973

	1969	1970	1971	1972	1973
6.5-300 WWH	5	4	2	2	0
7mm Wby. Mag.	1	0	1	0	0
7mm Rem. Mag.	0	0	0	0	1
7mm-300 Mag.	0	1	2	2	6
308 Norma Mag.	2	4	2	2	1
30-338 Mag.	0	0	0	1	0
300 Win. Mag.	2	0	2	3	2
300 Wby. Mag.	0	0	1	0	0
30-378 Mag.	0	1	0	0	0

ultimate in long-range efficiency. It won many matches, made many excellent groups. Yet after being the overwhelming choice to start with (330 matches were shot with it in 1969), it steadily dropped in favor until it was used in only 107 matches in 1973 (Table 3). By comparison, the 300 Winchester Magnum rose from 120 matches to 218 in the same period; the somewhat smaller 308 Norma Magnum held its own at around the 125 mark most of this time, and the wildcat 7mm-300, the 300 Weatherby case necked down to 284-cal., skyrocketed from a mere 17 matches in 1969 to 199 in 1973. The smaller 7mm Remington Magnum also gained a fine following after a slow start.

Different factors might be involved in the rating changes among these cartridges (many cartridges, from 6mm up through such monsters as the 30-378, are regularly shot in these 1000-yard competitions, but the 5 just named are the leaders), but the most important seems to be bullets... and perhaps an intangible known as shooter gossip.

Top-quality, properly bedded barrels and near perfect bullets are absolute necessities for all benchrest shooting. Since barrels of similar quality are available in all calibers and there is little bedding variation, at least within a given string of shots, bullet quality inherits by default most of the blame, or credit, for groups. The 6.5, for some reason, did not seem to have consistently good bullets. An inordinate amount of flyers appeared in groups fired with this caliber, many shooters said. Pit workers reported watching 8 or 9 bullets snap into a volleyball-size group, with the other shot or two wandering far out. They felt this occured too often, when compared with the 30-calibers being fired in the same match, say, to be blamed on wind or shooter error, and concluded that poor projectiles were to blame. The theory gained reinforcement when occasional shooters got supplies of "better" bullets and turned in fine groups with them. Since such bullets couldn't regularly be found, many shooters gave up on the 6.5 and turned largely to the big 30 calibers. The success of Paul Kempfer, who won the 1968 aggregate with a 12.8" average using a 308 Norma, probably had some influence on their thinking, as did the ready availability of the excellent Sierra Matchking bullets. These bullets had made the various 30-cal. Magnums hot contenders from the first, and over the long haul they gained followers as the 6.5-300 lost them.

Mary Louise DeVito with her 7mm-300. She currently holds the record for the smallest 10-shot group ever fired at the 1000-yd. range—7.687".

The Surging 7mms

Another factor was the surging 7mms, particularly the 7mm-300. This load started slowly (Table 2), then almost tripled its popularity between the end of the 1970 matches and the following season. The reasons are obvious. First, Sierra had marketed the highly efficient 168-gr. spitzer boat-tail in 7mm, and on October 11, 1970, Mary Louise De Vito put 10 of these Matchkings, kicked out by 87 grains of H570, into a 7.687" group, for a record not equaled to date, though Boydell Theis came within .188" of it in 1971, with a 7.875" group shot with a 300 Weatherby. Mrs. DeVito's effort followed by a few months a Wimbledon Cup record fired in the National Matches by Tom Treinen, who used the same bullet in a custom 7mm Remington Magnum for his win. Treinen went clean for the 20 shots of his match, putting them all into the 20-inch V-ring of the 1000-yard target, then drilled in 12 more to break a record which had been set in 1939. With examples like these, the Big 7s had to gain followers, and the trend was reinforced in 1971 when Mary Louise's husband, Guido DeVito, took the year's aggregate with a 13.5" average using the 7mm-300.

Not all shooters gave up on the 6.5-300, and more than a few were convinced that the specific cartridge had little to do with winning, reasoning that most of the top choices, regardless of caliber, used bullets of similar ballistic coefficients at similar velocities, thus should deliver similar results if the shooters did their part. They pointed out that the 6.5/140-gr., the 7mm/168-gr., and the 30/190-gr. Sierra spitzer boattails had ballistic coefficients (BCs) closer than kissin' cousins (.54-.62). All other things being equal, it seemed logical to assume that the 6.5-300 would have a little edge because it delivered higher velocity.

Looking for more of that edge based on velocity, Tom Drummond, Sr., of Williamsport, developed two series of long range cartridges. Those of most interest to the 1000-yard shooters are based on the Weatherby 300 and 378 cases. Each design

1969 Group Winners

Shoot	Name	Rifle	Group
1	Lawrence Wog	6.5-300 WWH	13.8
2	Richard Kepp	6.5-300 WWH	12.6
3	Lance Heller	7mm Wby. Magnum	9.2
4*	Walter Bryan	308 Norma Magnum	9.7
5	Art Mackey	6.5-300 WWH	11.7
6	Lee Hocker	300 Win. Magnum	8.4
7	Ray Rink	6.5-300 WWH	10.9
8	Ritchie Moorhead	300 Win. Magnum	11.1
9	Ted Mackey	6.5-300 WWH	9.6
10	Jerry Stocum	308 Norma Magnum	12.3

*Cliff Hocker shot a 9.1 group in this match, but also shot the top score—a possible 50—and under regulations then prevailing took top score rather than best group. An individual shooter is not awarded top place for both group and score in a given match.

1970 Group Winners

Shoot	Name	Rifle	Group
1	Richard Beaver	308 Norma Magnum	12.9
2	Guy Mitchell	6.5-300 WWH	12.4
3	Bob Tillinghast	308 Norma Magnum	13.4
4	Bob Longley	6.5-300 WWH	12.3
5	Earl Chronister	308 Norma Magnum	9.98
6	Frank Weber	6.5-300 WWH	10.2
7	Earl Chronister	308 Norma Magnum	9.1
8	Frank Weber	6.5-300 WWH	8.5
9	Mary Louise DeVito	7mm-300 Magnum	7.687
10	Howard Wolfe	30-378 Magnum	8.75

1971 Shootoff Winners*

Shoot	Name	Rifle	Group
1	Tom Drummond, Sr.	6.5-300	17.8
2	Joe Reitz	6.5-300	11.1
3	Guido DeVito	7mm-300 Magnum	16.3
4	Boydell Theis	300 Wby. Magnum	8.7
5	Bob Bitner	308 Norma Magnum	12.1
6	Guido DeVito	7mm-300 Magnum	12.0
7	Nick Leach	300 Win. Magnum	10.4
8	George Miller	308 Norma	12.4
9	Leonard Heller	7mm Wby. Magnum	12.7
10	Craig Steinmetz	300 Win. Magnum	17.8

*Beginning in 1971, a shootoff match was held at the end of each day, competitors being the group and score winners of the 10 matches held earlier, rather than the two men having the top score and best group out of the entire day's shooting being over-all winners, as had been done in earlier years.

1972 Shootoff Winners

Shoot	Name	Rifle	Group
1	Tony Mariano	30-378 Magnum	29.0
2	Guy Mitchell	6.5-300 WWH	13.75
3	Ken Madeira	6.5-300 WWH	12.5
4	Bill Jodun	7mm-300 Magnum	21.6
5	Clair Peters	308 Norma Magnum	13.6
6	Clair Peters	308 Norma Magnum	13.6
7	Cliff Hocker	308 Norma Magnum	19.25
8	George Reeder	300 Win. Magnum	19.0
9	(Not shot—fog)	—	—
10	Ritchie Moorhead	300 Win. Magnum	10.5

1973 Shootoff Winners

Shoot	Name	Rifle	Group
1	Eileen Baskin*	7mm-300 Magnum	11.6
2	Bob Bitner	308 Norma Magnum	12.6
3	Pete Romani	7mm-300 Magnum	11.9
4	Chet Leach	300 Win. Magnum	11.1
5	George Stephanis	7mm Rem. Magnum	8.9
6	Les Wilcox	300 Win. Magnum	11.6
7	Pete Romani	7mm-300 Magnum	19.4
8	Bill Hagerman	7mm-300 Magnum	11.9
9	Les Wilcox	7mm-300 Magnum	16.7
10	Clarence Palmer	7mm-300 Magnum	14.6

*Eileen Baskin, in this match, was the first woman to win a shootoff.

features a 60-degree shoulder, intended to give maximum powder capacity, with three calibers on each case, the 6.5mm, 7mm and 30. (For long range hunting and bench shooting at less than 1000 yards, Drummond offers 257, 264, 270, 7mm and 30-cal. cartridges, all with a 60-degree shoulder, based on the 270 Weatherby Magnum case, and for extreme-range varmint shooters 60-degree shouldered 22 and 6mm cartridges based on 240 Weatherby brass.) Drummond sells heavy bench guns and heavy sporters, all chambered by Harry Keiser and featuring stainless steel Douglas barrels. Supreme FN Mauser single shot actions are used for the bench jobs, Sako Finnbear Magnum actions for the hunting models. Actions are glass bedded, the barrels floated.

Long Range Chronographing

The Drummonds—Tom Sr. and Jr.—have done a great deal of test shooting with these loads, including chronographing for instrumental velocities and, of great interest, chronographing of remaining velocity at 1000 yards. (See table.) Avtron models K233 and T973 were used for this, with special screens for the 1000-yard shooting. These screens, 7½ x 14 inches, are custom made of plastic with metallic ink as a conductor. A 5-foot spacing was used for the 1000-yard testing, with a minimum of 3 shots (usually 5) for average. At this range, it normally was necessary to fire far more shots than that to get the requisite hits, but it was less expensive to shoot up the ammo than to pay for larger screens.

Drummond told me he thought that the comparatively new 162-gr. Hornady boat-tail HP 7mm bullet, with an advertised ballistic coefficient of .725, was the greatest long range projectile he had found, the first bullet he felt was superior to the 6.5mm. However, many longtime Big 7 shooters, including the DeVitos, stick with the 168-gr. Sierra Matchking, which has a BC of .628.*

The Drummond cartridges came into common use during the 1971 season, and a number of fine groups have been made with them since. However, they have not, at this

*In recent test firing with a Remington 40X 7mm Rem. Magnum, 27½" barrel, Drummond got the following results: Hornady 162-gr., 68½/N205, Fed. 215—muzzle velocity 3245 fps, remaining velocity at 1000 yds. 1852, loss 1393; Sierra 168-gr., 67½/N205, Fed. 215—MV 3180 fps, remaining velocity at 1000 yds. 1760, loss 1420. Since the Sierra bullet lost only 27 fs more than the Hornady over 1000 yards, I'm dubious whether the ballistic coefficients actually are as different as indicated. B.B.

writing, proved more accurate than smaller, more-conventional Magnums. Their higher velocity should be a benefit, but possibly their speed requires bullets even more perfect than those now available. One thing is certain: even this group of shooters, to whom the roar of a Magnum is routine, notices when one of these big Drummonds blasts off.

Rifle nut Cliff Hocker, of Camp Hill, Pa. who has long believed that any cartridge in this general class of Magnums can do the job, proved this to his own satisfaction by taking the 1972 aggregate with a 15.4" average compiled with 4 or 5 different rifles—6.5-300, a couple of Big 7s and several

Each shooter takes his turn pulling and marking targets in the pits. A 4" white square is thumbtacked to the center of the black bull to provide a better aiming point for the scope—on those shots where the shooter actually aims at the bull. Sometimes he might be holding several feet off.

1969 Score Winners

Shoot	Name	Rifle	Score
1	Leonard Heller	7mm Wby.	45
2	Mike Grove	6.5-300	46
3	Craig Wilkin	6.5-300	47
4	Cliff Hocker	300 Win.	50
5	Ted Mackey	6.5-300	48
6	Trudy Miller	300 Win.	48
7	Larry Wog	6.5-300	47
8	Ted Mackey	6.5-300	48
9	Tony Hopkins	308 Norma	48
10	Jon Smeigh	300 Win.	47

1970 Score Winners

Shoot	Name	Rifle	Score
1	Gene Plants	6.5-300	44
2	Jon Smeigh	300 Win.	47
3	Lance Heller	7mm Wby.	47
4	Al Wardrop	300 Win.	46
5	Bill Theis	300 Win.	48
6	Earl Chronister	308 Norma	46
7	Mary Louise DeVito	7mm-300	46
8	Earl Chronister	308 Norma	48
9	Joe Reitz	6.5-300	48
10	Bob Brown	6.5-300	48

1971 Score Shootoff Winners

Shoot	Name	Rifle	Score
1	John Smith	30-378	38
2	Tom Drummond, Sr.	30-378	43
3	Clyde Bonnell	308 Norma	39
4	George Horton	7mm Rem.	46
5	Lois Kertesz	7mm-300	41
6	Bill Miller	300 Win.	47
7	Willard Nelson	30-338	43
8	Trudy Miller	300 Win.	42
9	Tony Mariano	30-338	40
10	Joe Reitz	6.5-378	44

1972 Score Shootoff Winners

Shoot	Name	Rifle	Score
1	Bill Miller	300 Win.	35
2	Don Bower	7mm-300	46
3	Joe Reitz	6.5-378	43
4	Frank Popp, Sr.	6.5-300	40
5	Ken Madeira	6.5-300 Imp.	45
6	Lee Aunkst	300 Win.	43
7	Arlan Laity	6.5-300	3*
8	Ken Reeder	7mm-300	46
9	(No contest---fog)		
10	Cleon Bradley	7mm Rem.	46

*It was windy!

1973 Score Shootoff Winners*

Shoot	Name	Rifle	Score
1	Gene Stephanis	7mm Rem.	75
2	Judy Smith	308 Norma	88
3	Clair Peters	308 Norma	91
4	Eileen Baskin	7mm-300	84
5	Dot Kerstetter	6.5-300	86
6	Joe Doebler	264 Win.	86
7	Sue Dewalt	300 Win.	88
8	Dave Jarrell	7mm Rem.	85
9	Ray Guinther	7mm-300	75
10	Bill Theis	264 Win.	79

*Beginning in 1973 a possible was 100 rather than 50, through an unavoidable change in targets. The black center of the new target measured 13 inches instead of 12, with a 7-inch 10 ring.

30s. He occasionally won a match with one rifle and then fired a different one in the day's shootoff.

Cartridges Compared

The similarity of results is best illustrated in Table 3, where all cartridges used during the 5-year period of 1969 through 1973 are listed.
(Complete data on earlier matches could not be obtained, so this survey was limited to these 5 years.) Every group fired by each cartridge in the regular shoots of these years is shown in this table, with a yearly average for each. (Groups which did not have 10 shots on the paper are listed, but of course don't figure in the averages.) Perhaps the most interesting conclusion to be drawn is that, as Hocker claims, there is little to choose among them, if we eliminate the few obvious non-contenders, such as the 22-250. Aggregate average group size is about 25 inches, or 2½ MOA. This is considerably larger than the winning aggregate for each year—or even the Top 20 aggregate—but it should be pointed out that the Club's aggregates are figured on 6 shoots per year, with competitors who fire more than that being permitted to discard their worst scores—up to 4, in the case of those who compete in all 10 shoots. This is a fair regulation so far as the shooters are concerned, as it benefits these who make the effort to take part in all matches, but we included all groups in the averages in order to better reflect the total picture of what is being done by this group at this time.

Aggregate Winners and Data

1968	Paul Kempfer	308 Norma Magnum	12.810
1969	Richard Kepp	6.5-300 WWH Magnum	13.880
1970	Earl Chronister	308 Norma Magnum	11.369
1971	Guido DeVito	7mm-300 Magnum	13.531
1972	Cliff Hocker	7mm-300 Magnum	15.417
1973	Chet Leach	300 Winchester Magnum	13.479

This aggregate is based on the best 6 matches out of a possible ten.

Some cartridges might appear to be well under the general 2½ MOA level—for instance, if we consider the average group size only, the 7x61 Sharpe & Hart came up with 13". However, this was used only in one match, so that doesn't prove anything. As more groups are fired, the tendency is to enlarge the average, for one wild shot can foul up everything, while it takes a lot of good 10-shotters to decrease an average significantly.

That being the case, the performances of such Big 30s as the 308 Norma, its near-twin, the 30-338, and the 300 Winchester; the Big 7s like the Remington Magnum and the 7mm-300, are outstanding. They keep plugging along, even with many different shooters using them in a helluva lot of matches. Looking back a bit, an even more impressive record was compiled by the now-somewhat maligned 6.5-300. In 1969, when this load was used for 279 groups, each of what registered 10 shots on the paper, its average was 22.6"—better than any of the Big 30s above, despite the fact they were used for fewer matches. It continued to hold an edge the following year, but dropped off slightly since then, though it's still very close. Such averages make one wonder if those 6.5's fliers that some shooters talked about so much a few years back, actually occurred any more often with that caliber than with others, or if they simply wanted to believe that...

Handloading

Handloading for 1000-yard matches is mechanically the same as for the 100-yard shoots, the most noticeable difference being how quickly a powder hopper empties when it's dumping 105-gr. charges instead of 20-gr. ones. Basically, you simply resize, decap, and reprime a case, drop a powder charge and seat a bullet. Some 1000-yarders go to most of the extremes practiced by the short-range experts—segregating cases by make, volume, flash-hole diameter, times fired, etc., trimming to a given length, perhaps weighing powder charges, spinning bullets and seating them in some pre-

Many competitors arrive with campers and vans to spend the weekend. This is a behind-the-line shot. The spotting scopes cannot pick up bullet holes at this 1000-yd. range, but conditions can be studied—mirage, wind, etc.

cise relationship to the bore throat, and so on. Few if any make their own bullets or use handmade ones; apparently in the larger calibers used here, large quantity custom makers such as Sierra and Hornady offer acceptable projectiles.

Many competitors are more casual about their loading. They pay attention to ordinary details and safety, but usually load bullets straight from the box, measure powder charges (as most short-range benchresters also do), etc. They argue, perhaps correctly, that any improvements accruing from such minutiae are so small they simply get lost in the winds that sweep that long, long range. In general, this argument prevails, for the less picky loaders seem to do as well as their more persnickety brothers...yet when a given group comes within a fraction of an inch of taking a shoot or a fifth of an inch of breaking a record, it would be surprising if that also-ran rifleman didn't give at least a fleeting thought to his loading techniques, perhaps wondering if attention to some minor detail might have made him Number 1.

Table 2
Number of Times 5 Most Popular Cartridges Were Used in 1969-1973 Shoots

Cartridge	1969	1970	1971	1972	1973
6.5-300 WWH Mag.	279 (51)	186 (48)	149 (24)	106 (21)	91 (16)
7mm Rem. Mag.	23 (9)	23 (2)	63 (14)	54 (17)	76 (11)
7mm-300 Mag.	17 (--)	21 (3)	81 (8)	113 (9)	175 (24)
308 Norma Mag.	112 (24)	133 (20)	114 (29)	97 (26)	102 (17)
300 Win. Mag.	97 (23)	173 (31)	173 (25)	183 (34)	193 (25)

Note: Numbers in parentheses are groups which didn't have 10 shots on target.

Getting ready to score a target. Only official scorers are allowed inside scoring area during this operation.

Ranges Compared

Shooters who have never fired a rifle at 1000 yards may or may not be impressed with the 2-foot groups we've been talking about. They sound awfully big when you're used to seeing nickel-size clusters from ordinary varmint rifles. But 1000 yards is an awful lot farther than 100 yards, which is where most chuck shooters do their load testing. Mathematically, it's just 10 times as far, but unless you're shooting in a vacuum problems don't increase in simple proportion with the range, but at some accelerating ratio as the distance increases. There's a psychological aspect to this long-range shooting, too. Gazing way down there into the hazy distance where those tiny black bulls stand defiantly, the distance simply *seems* like more than 10 times as far as the old familiar 100-yard butt. Even the 2-foot circle needed to enclose a more or less average group doesn't look very big at all when viewed from well over a half-mile away.

It's inevitable that some will try to compare this 1000-yard shooting with the shorter range bench stuff. This can't be done directly, as identical matches aren't shot in both. In a general sense, it's obvious that the 100/200-yard shooters turn in tighter groups. Quarter-minute groups are common here, while even full MOA groups are still rare at 1000, and those in the ¾-minute category are records. Still, the 1000-yarders have no reason to feel like second-raters. It's possible for a 100-yard bench shooter to turn in a ¾-minute group from an outfit that has almost no measurable recoil, and even worse groups are fairly common.

Recoil is a factor of some importance in the Magnums. In rifles weighing 20 to 40 pounds it's nothing to be afraid of it in a physical sense, but there's no doubt that a 190-gr. 30-cal. bullet propelled by 109 grains of H570, will be more difficult to control, shot after shot, than a 22-cal. 52-gr. squirted downrange by 20 gr. of 4198.

Wind and Mirage

The big problem with this 1000-yard shooting, through, are the same ones which give the short-rangers fits—wind and mirage. It takes a genuine expert to dope these factors closely at 100 yards; at 10 times that distance it's doubtful if anyone can really do a topnotch job. Some obviously are better at it than others, for

Calibers and Groups 1969-1970

Caliber	1969 1st	1969 2nd	1970 1st	1970 2nd
6.5-300 WWH	5	5	4	2
7mm Wby.	1	0	0	0
7mm-300	0	0	1	1
308 Norma	2	2	4	3
300 Win.	2	2	0	4
300 Super	0	1	0	0
30-378	0	0	1	0

In 1969-70, there were no shootoffs to determine the overall group and score winners of the day. Each competitor fired one 10-shot group which was judged against all others for size and score. This table shows the times in those two years that the calibers listed turned in the first- and second-place groups. No other calibers placed in those positions.

Cartridges Compared

Beginning in 1971, each relay of ten shooters was termed a match, and the winners of these matches fired in a shootoff at the end of the day to determine the over-all winners (group and score) of the shoot. To give some idea of how the various cartridges compared with each other, this table shows the total number of times each won an individual match in the 1971-72-73 competitions. Shootoff winners are shown in other tables.

Cartridge	Match Wins	Cartridge	Match Wins
25-06	2	7mm-378 Dr.	1
264 Win. Mag.	10	308 Win.	1
6.5-257 Wby.	1	30-338	9
6.5-270 Wby.	1	308 Norma	43
6.5-300 WWH	42	300 Win. Mag.	77
6.5-300 Imp.	2	300 Wby. Mag.	9
6.5-300 Dr.	4	300 Dr.	1
284 Win.	1	300 Super	3
7mm Wby. Mag.	2	30-378	12
7mm Rem. Mag.	21	30-378 Dr.	1
7mm-300	56	Not specified	2
7mm-300 Dr.	6		

their names keep cropping up among the Top 20 riflemen, shoot after shoot, year after year. But even they have not reached the level of consistency that the best 100/200-yard shooters show. It's unlikely that they will, at least in the foreseeable future, for nobody has the time it would take to spend on the 1000-yard range, firing under all conditions, studying every sign of change between the bench and the butts, constantly tuning rifles, adjusting loads... replacing barrels. It's easy to find a 100-yard range to practice on, but not so a 1000-yarder. Yet, until something like this takes place, it's hard to believe that anyone will start to shoot 2½-inch groups at that distance, to equal the quarter-minute level of the short-range groups.

The results of other long-range shooting reinforce these views. *Hatcher's Notebook* gives data on test firing of 30-06 ammo for the National Matches in the years 1919 to 1930, and for Palma Match ammo in about the same period. The former gave a mean radius averaging some 7 inches, for a group diameter of approximately 22 inches, while the Palma Match ammo went about 5½ inches mean radius, or about 18 inches group diameter.

Mary Louise DeVito updating scoreboard. Results are posted immediately after final scoring, which is done as targets are brought back.

An article in the July 1967 *American Rifleman* indicates testing of National Match ammo at 600 yards in the 1957-61 period averaged about 3 inches mean radius, and 2-plus during 1962-66.

This is not greatly different than the results achieved by the Original Benchrest Club shooters, though the ammo testing covered more groups, acceptance being based on 27 consecutive 10-shot groups divided among 3 test barrels. That being the case, it might be argued that no progress has been made in over a half-century, since in 1919, using a 30-06 with 150-gr. flat base bullet and 46.5 gr. Pyro 1406, a mean radius of 9.65 inches was recorded, and many of today's bench shooters don't surpass that regularly. However, this conclusion is not necessarily correct. Conditions under which the firing takes place must be considered. The government ammunition testing was by machine rest under weather conditions we can assume were decent if not necessarily perfect. Furthermore, since the machine rest eliminates the necessity for recovering from recoil, moving the gun back into position, and aiming, shots can be fired at an extremely fast rate. The 10 rounds of a given

Typical Loads Used for 1000-Yard Matches

Cartridge	Bullet	Load	Primer
25-06	117 gr. Sierra	53/4831	CCI Mag.
264 Win. Mag.	140 gr. Sierra MK	64/4831	Fed. 215
6.5-300 WWH	139 gr. Norma	82/H870	Fed. 215
6.5-300 Drummond	139 gr. Norma	86/H870	Fed. 215
6.5-378 Drummond	139 gr. Norma	98/H570	Fed. 215
	140 gr. Sierra MK	95/H570	Fed. 215
7mm Rem. Mag.	162 gr. Hornady	69/4831	Rem. 9½M
7mm-300	162 gr. Hornady	87/H570	Rem. 9½M
	168 gr. Sierra MK	85/H570	Rem. 9½M
7mm-300 Drummond	162 gr. Hornady	90/H570	Fed. 215
	168 gr. Sierra MK	83/H570	Fed. 215
7mm-378 Drummond	162 gr. Hornady	104/H570	Fed. 215
	168 gr. Sierra MK	101/H570	Fed. 215
308 Norma	190 gr. Sierra	75/4831	Fed. 215
	190 gr. Sierra	73/4831	Rem. 9½M
300 Win. Mag.	190 gr. Sierra MK	69/4350	Win. 120
	190 gr. Sierra MK	70/4350	Win. 120
	190 gr. Sierra MK	75/4831	Fed. 215
	190 gr. Sierra MK	78/4831	Rem. 9½M
300 Drummond	168 gr. Sierra MK	82/4831	Fed. 215
30-378 Mag.	190 gr. Sierra MK	105/H570	Rem. 9½M
30-378 Drummond	168 gr. Sierra MK	112/H570	Fed. 215
	190 gr. Sierra MK	108/H570	Fed. 215

Table 3

Caliber	1969 Groups Shot*	1969 Average Spread (ins.)	1970 Groups Shot*	1970 Average Spread (ins.)	1971 Groups Shot*	1971 Average Spread (ins.)	1972 Groups Shot*	1972 Average Spread (ins.)	1973 Groups Shot*	1973 Average Spread (ins.)
22-250	1 —	32.5	— —	—	— —	—	— —	—	— —	—
6mm	— (1)	—	— (1)	—	— —	—	— —	—	— —	—
257	7	22.4	1 —	46.2	— —	—	— —	—	— —	—
25-06	14 (8)	24.7	5 (3)	21.7	20 (2)	25.3	4 (9)	30.1	11 (5)	22.1
25-06 Imp.	— (1)	—	— —	—	— —	—	— —	—	— —	—
6.5-06	— —	—	2 (2)	31.7	2 —	26.3	— —	—	— —	—
6.5 Rem. Magnum	— (1)	—	— (2)	—	6 —	29.2	— —	—	— —	—
6.5-257 Wby. Magnum	— —	—	— —	—	— —	—	— —	—	8 —	19.6
6.5-270 Wby. Dr. Magnum	— —	—	— —	—	— (1)	—	— —	—	4 —	17.4
264 Win. Magnum	34 (12)	26.9	2 (3)	33.5	19 (6)	26.3	15 (7)	19.0	20 (2)	19.6
6.5-300 Win. Magnum	— —	—	— —	—	— (2)	—	— —	—	— —	—
6.5-300 Imp.	— —	—	— —	—	— —	—	16 (2)	20.4	— —	—
6.5-300 WWH	279 (51)	22.6	186 (48)	21.6	149 (24)	25.5	106 (21)	24.1	91 (16)	24.2
6.5-300 Drummond	— —	—	— —	—	11 (3)	26.9	16 (2)	24.5	6 (4)	19.7
6.5-378 Magnum	— —	—	— —	—	— —	—	7 —	24.2	1 —	26.3
6.5-378 Drummond	— —	—	— —	—	2 —	21.9	4 (2)	24.4	— —	—
270 Win.	1 (1)	29.1	3 (1)	17.0	— —	—	— —	—	— —	—
270 Wby. Magnum	— (3)	—	— —	—	— —	—	— —	—	— —	—
284 Win.	— —	—	— —	—	— —	—	— —	—	1 —	17.6
7x61 S & H Magnum	— —	—	— —	—	— —	—	1 —	13.0	— —	—
7x67 Wardrop	— —	—	— —	—	— —	—	2 —	28.1	— —	—
7mm Wby. Magnum	12 (5)	21.9	5 (2)	34.1	7 (4)	23.0	3 (3)	28.7	8 —	22.9
7mm Rem. Magnum	23 (9)	26.5	23 (2)	23.3	63 (14)	21.1	54 (17)	25.8	76 (11)	20.4
7mm-300 Magnum	17 —	24.9	21 (3)	19.8	81 (8)	23.7	113 (9)	23.7	175 (24)	21.1
7mm-300 Imp. Magnum	— —	—	— —	—	— —	—	— —	—	1 —	23.7
7mm-300 Drummond	— —	—	— —	—	5 (1)	27.3	15 (3)	23.5	16 (3)	20.8
7mm-378 Magnum	— —	—	— —	—	— —	—	15 —	22.8	— —	—
7mm-378 Drummond	— —	—	— —	—	5 (1)	26.4	16 (3)	21.7	— —	—
308 Win.	— (2)	—	— —	—	4 (1)	23.5	— —	—	— —	—
30-284	5 (2)	22.3	— —	—	— —	—	— —	—	— —	—
30-350	— —	—	— —	—	— —	—	1 (2)	38.6	— —	—
30-06	5 (3)	30.2	— —	—	3 (4)	26.4	1 (1)	39.1	2 (2)	34.9
30-06 Imp.	— —	—	2 (3)	28.5	— —	—	— —	—	— —	—
300 H & H Magnum	1 —	46.9	4 —	35.1	— —	—	— —	—	— —	—
30-338 Magnum	3 (2)	23.8	28 (1)	19.9	32 (9)	24.9	29 (8)	21.0	18 (5)	22.7
308 Norma	112 (24)	23.5	133 (20)	22.1	114 (29)	23.4	97 (26)	23.5	102 (17)	24.2
30 Belted Newton	4 —	27.7	— —	—	— —	—	— —	—	— —	—
300 Win. Magnum	97 (23)	24.5	173 (31)	22.6	173 (25)	23.9	183 (34)	23.8	193 (25)	24.5
30-375 Magnum	— —	—	— —	—	— —	—	— (1)	—	— —	—
300 Wby. Magnum	13 (2)	27.1	30 (6)	18.6	33 (3)	21.9	14 (4)	27.7	4 (4)	23.0
300 Ackley Magnum	15 (4)	29.0	12 (2)	26.1	— —	—	— (1)	—	6 (2)	26.1
300 Super Magnum	7 —	22.6	9 (2)	23.8	8 (1)	22.5	6 —	23.2	3 (1)	17.4
300 Drummond	— —	—	— —	—	4 (2)	19.1	2 (1)	27.6	— —	—
30-378 Magnum	19 (3)	20.0	26 (4)	19.3	55 (1)	22.4	39 (7)	23.9	14 (4)	20.9
30-378 Drummond	— —	—	— —	—	4 —	18.8	5 (1)	24.1	4 —	27.7
Not Specified	— —	—	— —	—	19 —	—	3 —	—	8 —	—

*Numbers in parentheses are groups which didn't have 10 shots on target.

This table is based on five years' shooting as reported in official bulletins. There is some inevitable error, as shooters are not always precise or complete in their caliber listings, sometimes listing only 6.5-300 instead of 6.5-300 Drummond, for instance; however, it is believed this table is accurate enough to give a good over-all picture of results during this period.

group often were fired in 5 to 8 seconds, according to Col. E. H. Harrison of the NRA technical staff, who was directly involved in the testing in the 1960s. This had the great advantage of getting all shots off under essentially the same conditions of wind.

By comparison, these 1000-yard benchrest competitors do all their shooting in a normal manner, and they do it under whatever conditions happen to be prevailing when they're called to the line. It might be so hazy, or raining so hard, that the targets are barely visible; the wind might be of gale proportions; it might even be snowing, for a winter match is scheduled at this writing. Regardless, when the command to commence firing is given, they commence.

The proof that they don't do very badly is shown by an accident of a few years back. Apparently intrigued by the reports trickling out of those north-Pennsylvania hills, some shooters who earn their daily bread in the technical shops of one of the country's great gun building companies, arrived on the scene, weighted down with all the goodies at their command. It was their intention, obvious if unstated, to show the local hillbillies just how 10 bullets should be neatly placed in those far-off bullseyes. Alas'n'alack, things somehow didn't turn out as expected. At the end of that day's shoot those newly-educated New Englanders—expert riflemen all, truly—packed their gear like the Arabs, and silently stole away.

Well...who ever said it was supposed to be *easy* to put 10 shots in a grapefruit size group at 1000? A *challenge?* It's all of that. So why not get your gear together, head up back of Williamsport, ask for Irv Plants' place—or just listen for the shooting—and sign up. Who knows—maybe the barrel and 10 bullets which are going to give that first 2½-inch, 1000-yard group are yours. ●

U.S. Pocket

A detailed, critical and definitive survey of these long-gone handguns. The entire spectrum is broken into types and major variations for ready and clear identification by the collector. Included are serial numbers and a table showing quantities produced and today's average market prices. Drawings and photographs by the author.

by DONALD M. SIMMONS, JR.

ONE OF THE hardest things to get across to the media-conditioned public is this: there is nothing basically wrong or unhealthy in collecting guns. We collectors find it hard to believe the contention that there is an underlying Freudian sexual symbolism exhibited by gun collectors. Taking this theory to the ridiculous ultimate, this would have to mean that all gun collections would consist of long, high powered rifles. I think the motivation springs from caveman days, when the male was responsible for his family's protection and, by hunting for game, its survival. Because of this dual responsibility he came to appreciate those devices which made his task easier, less dangerous. With the disappearance of both his responsibility and his sport, he now finds solace in collecting those inanimate instruments which served his forefathers so faithfully. We have now hurdled the "why" of collecting guns, let's look at the "why" of collecting a particular type.

In firearms collecting specialization comes very quickly from a purely economic standpoint. As one who had a very general collection years ago I can readily appreciate the desire, but you just can't have a good collection without some specialization. Even granted unlimited finances, one can't buy or build a really great general collection. As a classic example, take the gun collection of the late multi-millionaire William Randolph Hearst — it covered every facet of guns, yet to me, at least, it lacked the stature of a great collection. I truly believe that a few good pieces tied to a lot of research makes a better collection, even though channeled, than any huge amassing of everything called a gun.

Pocket Automatics

In 1900 firearms genius John M. Browning introduced the pocket automatic pistol. The word "automatic" in this context really means a self-loading pistol, that is, an arm requiring a separate pull of the trigger to fire each shot. The word "pocket," though seeming to designate specifically where the arm was carried (such as pants or overcoat), in fact merely means that a certain degree of concealment was possible with them. In reality most such pistols were kept in the home for protection or, when carried, in holsters. They have 3″ to 4½″ barrels, their weight (empty) varies from the light Savage 1907 32 at 19.4 ozs. to the Smith & Wesson 32 at 25.5 ozs. Their magazines carry 7 to 10 rounds, and over-all length plus height is usually around 10″. Those figures have been spotlighted by the 1968 Gun Control Act, and most of the famous pistols discussed here could not, for one reason or another, be imported into the U.S. today because of failure to conform to some portion of the act's "Importation Criteria." The U.S. pocket automatic's caliber is 32 Automatic Colt Pistol (ACP) or 380 ACP. The identical cartridges in the metric system are respectively 7.65mm Browning or 9mm Browing short. There are a few other types of ammunition which have been used in this class of arms but, with the exception of the special 35 Smith & Wesson, they have no bearing on the field of U.S. pocket automatics. One last thing needs an explanation — the distinction between a pocket automatic and a *vest* pocket, pistol. The latter is found in caliber 25 ACP and 22 rimfire. They are characterized by a much shorter barrel and a much shorter length-plus-height measurement.

Era of the Pocket Automatic Pistol

The pocket automatic was probably first produced by the Bergmann Industrial Works in Germany in 1896, these pioneer pistols the design of Louis Schmeisser. The Bergmanns, made in small numbers, are extremely rare today. The first successful mass-produced pocket automatic was designed by John M. Browning. Starting in 1900, these popular pistols were made by the Belgian firm of Fabrique National d'Armes de Guerre (F.N.). These 1900 Brownings were so instantly popular in Europe that all U.S. firearms makers must have started their own design programs to produce a similar, saleable item. It is these U.S. pocket automatics, made in the next half-century, that offer the collector such a rich field.

Strangely, the American public never took to the pocket automatic to the degree that the rest of the world did. From the first American one made in 1903 to the last produced, just after World War II, only a few more than one million were made in the U.S. F.N., by 1912, had made a million pocket automatics! This lack of interest in the U.S. has been generally considered a negative reaction to a rash of anti-gun laws written in the 1930s, but I feel that it can be more accurately traced to a disinterest on the part of most Americans. The average citizen here, with his eye on U.S. police handguns, really believes that the revolver is supreme. Yet world-wide today, as a service or police arm, the revolver is all but extinct.

Automatic Pistols

Top—one of the oldest pocket automatics in the world, the FN Browning Model 1900 in 32 ACP, SN 5071 (made in 1900). Bottom—the latest U.S. pocket automatic, Sterling's Model PPL 380 ACP, SN 003733 (made in the 1970s). This most recent offering does little to enhance the image of U.S. pocket automatics.

Strangely, though, there are still far more small revolvers made and sold in this country than small automatics. The American Firearms Manufacturing Co., Sterling Arms Corp. and Clerke, doubtless others, all make or plan to make a pocket automatic pistol.

Golden Age of U.S. Pocket Automatics

The Golden Age of the U.S.-made pocket automatic pistol started around 1910 and extended through World War I. From that halcyon decade until today there has been a growing hiatus of native-made pocket automatics. From the time when every domestic handgun maker marketed or planned to market a pocket automatic, today only a few new and small firms are even considering making such a gun. In order to help new collectors enter this field I've broken down the entire spectrum of these arms into 26 different major variations. I choose to call these "types," reserving the word "model" for those so-called by the company. Few "models" are to be found but, beyond my "types," myriads of variations exist.

Colt Patent Firearms Mfg. Co.

Starting in 1903, Colt led the way in the development of all semi-automatic pistols. From 1900 Colt made and sold Browning-designed automatic pistols but, though FN had sold Browning's blowback-operated pocket pistols, Colt had made the recoil-operated heavier military pistols. It was obvious to Colt that FN's 1900

Brownings were selling 10 times as fast as their larger automatics. When Çolt consulted Browning he offered them an upgraded 32-caliber pistol. This was Browning's patent 747,585, filed April 3, 1902 and issued Dec. 22, 1903. This is so basic a patent that all pocket autos made since look — and most actually operate — as described in Browning's brilliant disclosure.

Colt 32 ACP Hammerless Automatic

There are four basic and different types of Colt 32 ACP pistols.

1. The original Type 1 has a 4" barrel; later-issued types having only a 3¾" barrel. These long barreled 32s started with serial number (SN) 1 and ended at SN 71,999. They were sold from 1903 until 1908.

2. Type 2, which followed, had the 3¾" barrel noted and a correspondingly shorter frame. Type 2s, numbered from 72,000 to 105,050, were made from 1908 to 1910. This block of 33,050 makes Type 2 the rarest 32 Colt.

3. Type 3 did away with the barrel bushing characteristic of Types 1 and 2. These Type 3s started at SN 105,051 and went to SN 468,096. Produced from 1910 to 1926, 363,045 were manfactured. A Colt Type 3 is the most common of all the models and types. In any budding collection of automatic pistols this Type Colt 32 is a good opener. The collector with luck can still find these, new in the box.

4. The last Colt 32 is Type 4, which have a magazine-safety device to distinguish them from the other types. To determine if this device is present, pull the slide back and hold it back with the manual safety. By dropping the magazine down you can look into the ejector port of the slide and see, in the magazine well, the characteristic plunger and yoke of the magazine safety. To confirm this let the slide go forward (magazine still dropped) and pull the trigger. If the hammer drops it is Type 3 or earlier; if not it is Type 4. Type 4s started at SN 468,097 in 1926 and ended with the last Colt pocket automatic made — SN 572,214 in 1946. It is doubtful that Colt actually made these pistols in 1946, but they exhausted their stock of finished pistols in that year. There were 104,117 Type 4 Colt 32s made, which makes the entire Colt line of 32 automatics the most common of all U.S. pocket automatics, with a total 572,214 manufactured.

Colt pocket automatics. Top — Colt 32 ACP Type 1, SN 852. Bottom — Colt 380 ACP Type 4 (U.S. Property), SN 137295.

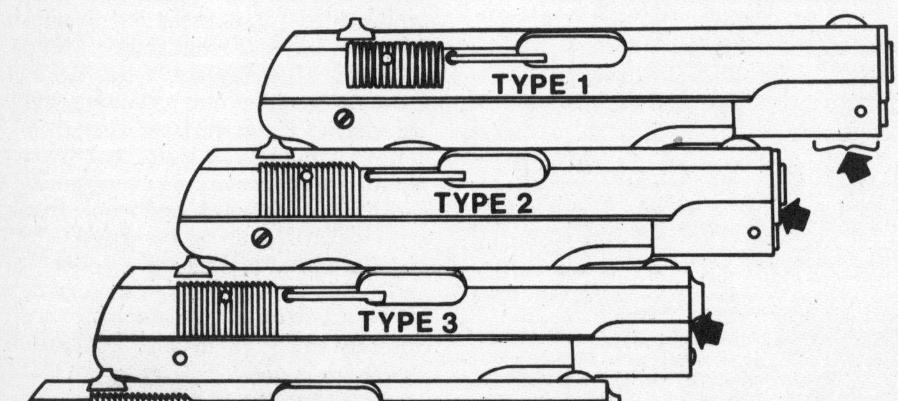

Colt pocket automatic pistols by types. Note — Type 4 has the magazine safety, not easily seen from outside the pistol. See text for arrow-indicated details.

Colt 380 ACP Hammerless Automatic

Probably because of the relatively-low stopping power of the 32 ACP cartridge, Colt asked Browning in 1906 to see if he could come up with a more potent round. Browning, in turn, consulted William "UMC" Thomas of Union Metallic Cartridge Co./Remington Arms. The result was the 380 ACP. Browning, in 1907-1908, worked on adapting the new round to the Colt 32 pistol.

5. In 1908 Colt announced their new pocket automatic. Because production of the 32s then was of the 2nd type, the 380s were also of Type 2 and its 3¾" barrel and barrel bushing. These 2nd type Colt 380s started with SN 1 and went to SN 6251. Manufacturing dates were the same as the 32s, 1908 to 1910. These 6251 pistols are the rarest Colt pocket automatic type and they're rare in their own right as U.S. pockets.

6. The 2nd type gave way to Type 3 at SN 6,252 in 1910, and lasted until 1926 and SN 92,893. These are characterized by having *no* barrel bushing, just like the Type 3 Colt 32s. These 86,641 pistols are the most common of all U.S. made 380s.

7. The Type 4 Colt 380, like its counterpart in 32, had a magazine safety. Type 4s started at SN 92,894 and terminated at SN 138,000, when the gun was discontinued. These pistols were sold from 1926 to 1945. Colt exhausted the supply of 380s a year earlier than the 32s. Type 4 380 Colts totalled 45,106; collectively, all Colt 380s represent 138,000 pistols, making them 4 times rarer than Colt's 32s. Oddly enough the 380 Colt usually commands no higher price than a 32. (This is not a testimonial to the good heartedness of used-gun dealers but rather to their ignorance.)

Savage Arms Corporation

Elbert H. Searle applied for a patent on his newly designed automatic pistol in 1904. It was received (patent 804,985) on November 21, 1905. Sometime later he made an agreement with Savage Arms Company to produce his pistol. The first version was made in a very limited quantity in 45 ACP caliber for a field test by the U.S. Army in 1908-1909, but the Army, after evaluating the 288 Savages, decided on the Colt as the Army sidearm. Searle had also been working on a pocket model on the same principle, which Savage decided to make. Savage, unlike most of the other American firms we will study, did break their run of automatics into models, therefore we'll call them models rather than types.

Savage pocket automatics. Top—Model 1907, 32 ACP, SN 124. Bottom—Model 1917, 380 ACP, SN 29185B.

Savage 32 ACP Automatics

The first model 1907 Savage pocket automatic, caliber 32 ACP, was not sold until 1908. (The Savage is the only U.S.-made pocket automatic that really rivaled the Colt in the quantity sold.) Searle's design consisted of a semi-locked breech, the barrel locked to the slide. Without any backward motion by the barrel, when it had twisted through only 5 degrees, the slide unlocked and was free to travel to the rear. Resisting this unlocking was the torque of the bullet driving down the barrel, spinning in the opposite direction. All in all, the Savage was a well made and high grade pistol. As a bonus, its staggered magazine gave it a 10-round capacity over Colt's 8.

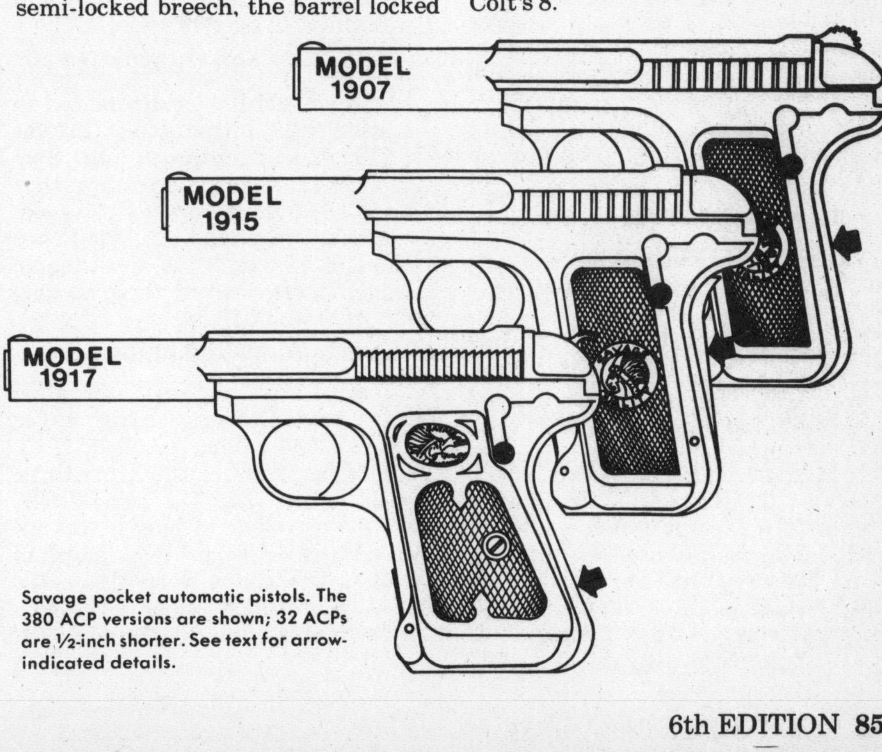

Savage pocket automatic pistols. The 380 ACP versions are shown; 32 ACPs are ½-inch shorter. See text for arrow-indicated details.

Harrington & Richardson pocket automatics. Top—32 ACP Type 1, SN 363. Bottom—32 ACP Type 2, SN 32282.

8. The model 1907 started at SN 1 and ran to SN 229,800 in 1920. A block of numbers, 130,000 to 150,000, was skipped, these being reserved for the model 1915, as will be explained later. There were thus some 209,201 1907s made. The pistol can be distinguished by the rather straight backstrap of the grip and the fact that it apparently has a hammer—actually this is a cocking piece attached to a spring-loaded striker, a unique system. It is the only U.S.-made pocket automatic which offered an external device for cocking the arm—a cocking method considered almost mandatory in modern high class pocket automatics.

Savage 32 ACP Model 1915

9. The second Savage 32 was the model 1915 hammerless, made right within the 1907 series, taking numbers from 1907's serial numbers. Thus we find a model within another model. The 1915 differs from the 1907 in that the cocking piece (the so-called hammer) is concealed like the Colt's. Also like the Colt it has a grip safety, which won't let the pistol to be fired unless the safety is depressed, as when gripped by the palm of the shooting hand. Thirdly, it had a slide hold-open device which operated when the magazine was empty. It was the only U.S. pocket automatic with this desirable feature, one found in the larger military automatic pistols. The 1915 was only made in that year. Serial numbers started with 130,000 and went to 136,520, using part of that block from 130,000 to 150,000 set aside for the 1915, but only 6,520 were ever made. Very few collectors realize how rare these "hammerless" Savages are. The 1907's production resumed at SN 150,000 and rolled until the 1907 was discontinued at SN 229,800.

Savage 32 ACP Model 1917

10. The model 1907 was replaced by the model 1917, introduced in 1920 at SN 229,801 and continued until 1928 at SN 259,472. The factory knows that a block of 600 numbers was skipped, these from 246,020 to 246,620, hence a total of 89,671 1917s were made. Total production of all three models in 32 ACP was 245,391.

Savage Arms 380 Automatic

Savage Arms Company (later called Savage Arms Corporation) decided to market a 380 caliber pistol in 1913. These were made in the same three models as the 32s. The basic difference was that barrel length was increased to 4⁵⁄₁₆" from 3¹³⁄₁₆" length of the 32s. The slides were also made this same half-inch longer in the 380s—all else was virtually the same externally.

Savage 380 ACP Model 1907

11. The 1907 380s started with SN B2001 in 1913 and went to SN 15,748B by 1920, less a block of numbers, from 10,000B to 13,902B, used for the model 1915 in 380. Note that only the first 400 pistols had the letter "B" in front of the serial number. This "B" is often misread as an "8", thus giving the pistol a serial number much too high. This 1907 was discontinued in 1920 at SN 15,748B, thus only 10,046 of these 1907 Savage 380s were made.

Savage 380 ACP Model 1915

12. As noted above, a block of 1907 serial numbers was set aside for the model 1915 "hammerless," the SNs running from 10,000B to 13,902B. The entire run was made in 1915. These 3,902 pistols are rare.

Savage 380 ACP Model 1917

13. The 1907s in 380 ACP were superseded by the model 1917. These last started with SN 15,749B and terminated at SN 29,862B. The factory knows that 757 serial numbers were not used in this run, these from SN 25,243B to SN 26,000B. Thus a total of 15,157 were made from 1920 to 1928. Collectively the Savage production of 380s was a mere 29,105 pistols. The total number of Savage pocket automatics made was 274,496 pistols. More interesting is the fact that the combined total of both Colt and Savage pocket automatics equals 89.41%, just under 90% of the grand total. Thus in a group of 20 U.S. pocket automatic pistols, selected at random, 18 of them should be either a Colt or a Savage, with the split mathematically 13 Colts to 5 Savages. These statistics mean that the 4 remaining U.S. manufacturers of pocket automatics had a combined production which represents just 10% of the total U.S. output, therefore all of these 4 makes are relatively rare arms.

Harrington & Richardson, Inc.

H&R entered the pocket automatic pistol market by making an agreement with the long-established English firm of Webley & Scott, Ltd., for the U.S. rights to their pistols. Webley's superintendent, William John Whiting, was a designer as well—he designed the entire Webley line of automatics. Whiting was granted 3 patents in the United States, and it was these which were used to develop H&R's automatics. The dates of the above patents are found on each H&R 32. Whiting held many more patents, but these were not cited by H&R. The most basic of the 3 Whiting patents is 863,770, issued August 20, 1907. Though this patent shows a typical hammered Webley, it was the essential design for the hammerless blowback H&R also. H&R, unlike all other U.S. manufacturers, made a small vest pocket 25 ACP before producing their 32. The 32 made by H&R was a quality firearm. I emphasize this because H&R is well known for its inexpensive solid-frame revolvers. The H&R 32 was well made and well designed, with many highly advanced features. From the very beginning of their 32 series, all H&Rs had a magazine safety, a grip safety, and a manual safety. All had a loaded-chamber indicator, a much more valuable feature than the more common "cocked" indicator. These H&Rs take down fast for cleaning, controlled by a multi-functioned trigger guard. This guard further acts as a slide motion buffer during full recoil, saving wear on other parts. All in all, these 32 H&Rs were fine automatics but, judging from their low sales, were greatly unappreciated by the public.

H&R Self-Loading 32 ACP

14. The Type 1 H&R pocket is characterized by its 12 broad slide pull grooves, these starting with SN 1 and continued to about SN 2000. The actual break-off point is unknown by the factory. These 2000 (approximately) early pistols were made in 1916 and 1917.

15. The Type 2 has 16 narrower pull grooves, but covering the same area of the slide as did those on Type 1. These started at about SN 2001; the model was discontinued at about SN 35,000. These Type 2s were sold from 1917 until 1940, but production must have stopped back in the 1920s, and those sold after that time just inventory being marketed. There were 33,000 finely-grooved H&Rs made and, counting both types, a total of about 35,000.

A word here about this long-time holding of guns in inventory and how it poses an additional problem for the collector. The people in the shipping room don't follow any chronological method of selecting which pistol is to be shipped. First in may be last out, so we have a paradox. The serial number books at H&R show that a 32 automatic with SN 101 wasn't shipped until July 1939, yet I own the later SN 363, which is marked as having been carried by an Australian soldier in World War I. H&R also knows that the 32 shipped last was SN 1099, shipped in July 1940. At that late date we would have expected serials in the 34,000 or at least a Type 2 pistol.

Remington Arms Company

Just as a parent loves all his children, so must a collector love all his treasures but, like the parent, the collector has a pet that he will only admit to when pressed. I like my Remington 51s the best of all my U.S. pocket automatics—there, I said it! Some of this preference may have sprung from working at Remington in Ilion as a teenager before World War II. But, beyond such sentimental reasons, I really believe that this pistol, initially made before I was borne, was way ahead of its time. Even today, the much heralded German Walthers PP and PPK, the Sauer (38)M and Mauser HSC pocket automatics owe something to this fine Remington. The 51 was designed by John D. Pedersen of Wyoming—an engineer, not a "seat of the pants" inventor. He analysed the entire principle of the automatic pistol and came up with a superb example in the 51. Pedersen took out many patents in his lifetime but the most basic to the Remington 51 was patent 1,348,-733, issued on August 3, 1920. Running to over 100 pages, it is the most detailed patent description of any automatic arm of which I am aware. For the cost of the patent, the collector can get an education in the field of firearms design. The Remington 51, unlike most other pocket automatic pistols, was first made in 380 ACP. The 51 also introduced a unique type of action, a design which is neither the usual blowback nor a recoil-operated pistol. I have called the Pedersen action "blowback/recoil," since at various times in its functional cycle it shows features of both. To understand the 51's design, first consider what a pistol cartridge case looks like in cross-section. The side walls taper inside as they approach the base, the flash-hole area, becoming much thicker in section at that point. Because of the strength of the lower part of the case a small amount of set-back during firing can be tolerated. When a 51 is fired the case moves about 3/32" to the rear, carrying the slide and its separate breechblock with it. This is the blowback phase of the cycle. At this point the breechblock locks to the frame while the slide, driven by the momentum of the breechblock, continues rearward. This represents the locked or recoil stage of the cycle. The slide, as it moves rearward, cams the breechblock out of its locked position, the slide and breechblock traveling to full open position together. Pedersen's action allows—with perfect safety to the shooter—a lighter slide than

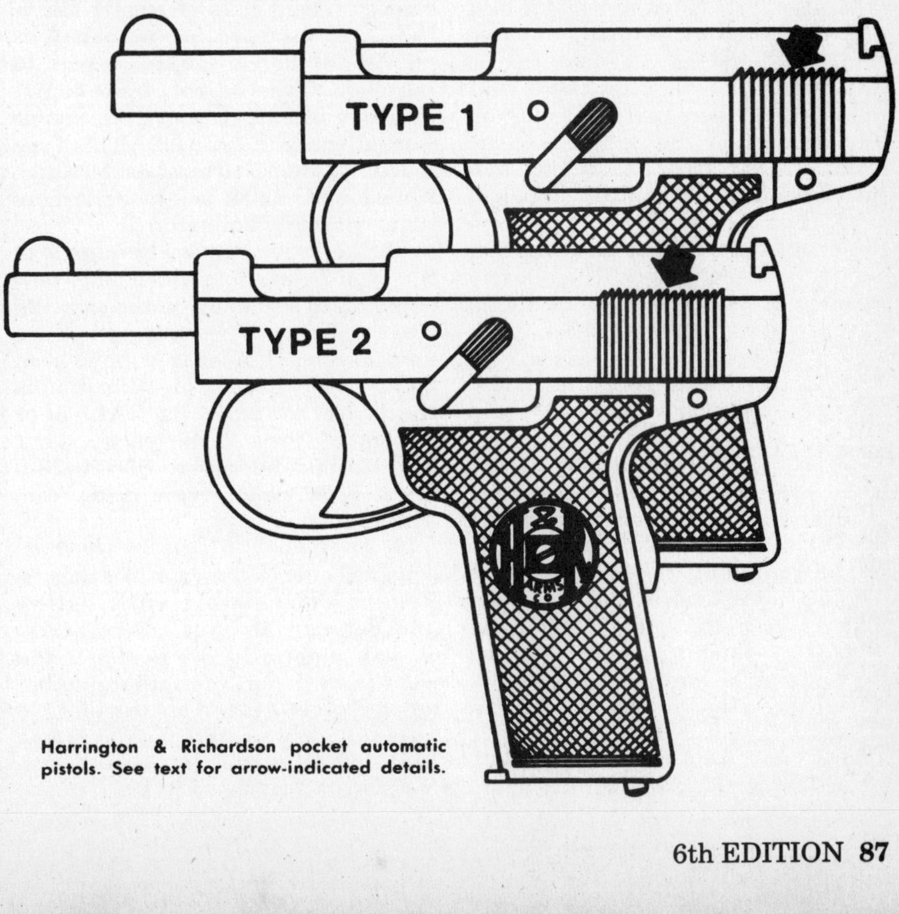

Harrington & Richardson pocket automatic pistols. See text for arrow-indicated details.

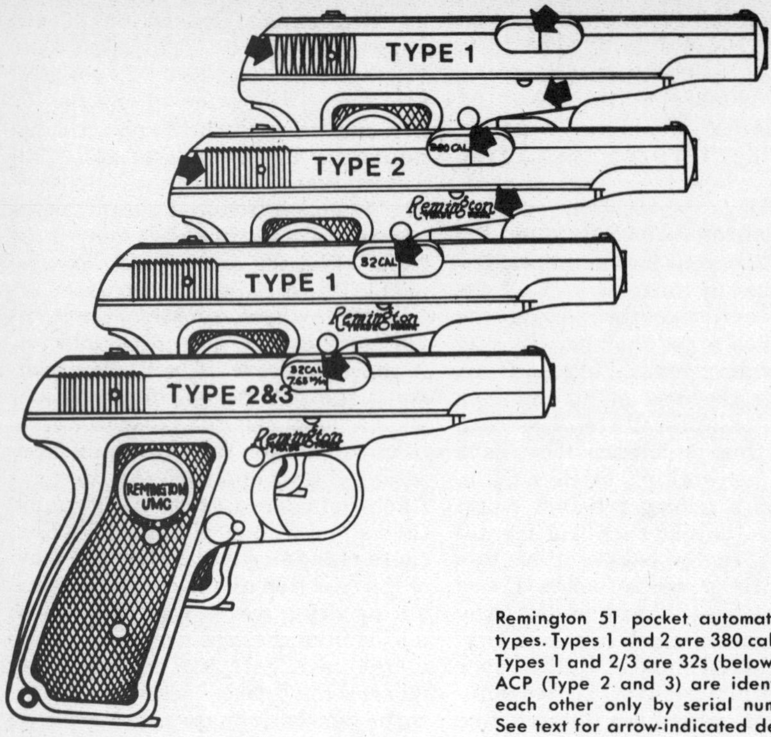

Remington 51 pocket automatic pistols by types. Types 1 and 2 are 380 caliber (at top). Types 1 and 2/3 are 32s (below). Caliber 32 ACP (Type 2 and 3) are identifiable from each other only by serial number ranges. See text for arrow-indicated details.

would be found in other well-designed, full blowback pistols. As an example, the recoiling parts of a Remington 51 weigh only 6.97 ounces compared to the blowback Colt, whose parts weigh 8.90 ounces.

Remington 380 ACP Model 51

16. The Type 1 Remington 51 is best distinguished by pointing out two things it didn't have. There was *no* caliber mark visible through the ejection port and there was *no* Remington logo stamped on the right side of the pistol. As a further identifying feature, the slide-retracting grooves had a "U" cross section. These 3 areas represent all the external identification points between types. These early Remington 380s started with SN 25 in 1919 and went to SN 38,000 in 1921.

17. The Type 2 did not replace Type 1 at one particular period in time—changes between the two would appear only to disappear. I have selected SN 38,001 arbitrarily as the point when all changes were firmly established. Caliber marking on the barrel started to appear first at serials in the 14,000 to 15,000 range, but with no consistency. Next, the Remington logo on the frame began in the mid-20,000 range. Finally, by 38,000 the slide pulls were changed from a "U" cross-section to the more usual "V" form. The fully modified Type 2s extend then from 38,000 to 60,800, from 1921 until 1934. There are many serial number blanks in this block of numbers, so instead of an apparent 22,800 automatics made, there were about 15,206.

Remington 32 ACP Model 51

18. The Type 1 32s have *no* patent dates stamped on the slide top, making them identical to the 380s in this respect. Their chief characteristic is "32 CAL" stamped on the barrel as viewed through the ejection port in the slide. Type 1s run from 60,801 to about 61,999. These 1,198 pistols were all made in 1921-1922. This Type 1 32 is unknown to most dealers and, when found, can be bought for no more than a normal Remington 51.

19. The Type 1s gave way quickly to the Type 2 variation, which had a new patent date stamping on the sighting rib of the slide. These stampings are hard to read because they have been matted over. Easiest identification is the barrel stamp—"32 CAL" over "7.65mm." Type 2 started at about SN 62,000 and ran to SN 70,280. These 8,281 pistols were made from 1921 to 1926.

20. The Type 3 51s in 32 are characterized only by their serial numbers. Remington, possible anticipating another run of 380s above serial 70,280, jumped the 32s to 90,501 and went from there to terminal number for the 32 of 92,626. This run of 2,126 automatics was sold from 1926 to 1934, but all production of both calibers virtually stopped in 1927.

Smith & Wesson, Inc.

Long-established Smith & Wesson had watched most of their competition in revolver manufacture come up with a pocket automatic design. In the first decade of the 20th century S&W still counted on the reputation of their fine revolvers to combat the sales inroads that the upstart automatic pistol was making. By mid-1909 the sales people at S&W must have seen that the automatic was here to stay, if that was so they would have to develop one to stay competitive. With this late start, and looking for a design they could quickly produce, Smith & Wesson turned to the small Belgian firm of Charles Clement in Liege. S&W received U. S. rights to Clement's pistol, patent number 970,307 issued on September 13, 1910. Clement pistols were in 25 ACP and 5mm Clement, both producing low chamber pressures. Smith & Wesson's engineers and designers were not content to use these relatively ineffective rounds. They also had the revolver fancier's phobia of the lead bullet's advantage in extending barrel life. Because of these two concepts they came up with a new 35 caliber cartridge, its projectile having a gilding metal cap for ease of feeding, but with lead below the cap to engage the rifling. This 35 S&W was less powerful than the 32 ACP. Unfortunately Clement's design was inadequate for the 35 S&W cartridge. Even worse, the more powerful 32 ACP could be used in the 35 S&W pistol. This weakness was that where the Browning 1900

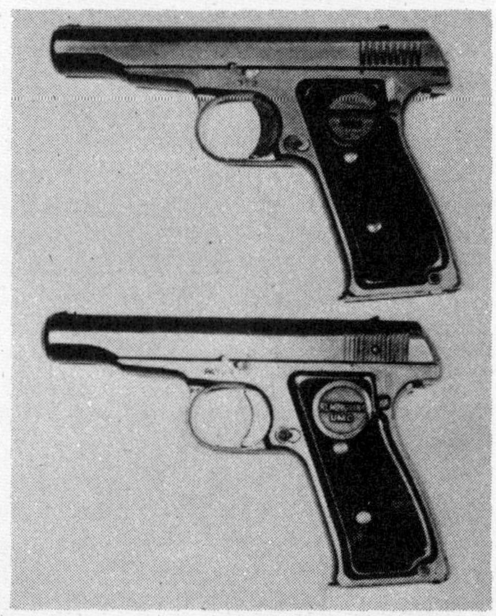

Remington pocket automatics. Top—Model 51, 380 ACP, SN 312. Bottom—Model 51, 32 ACP, SN 92475.

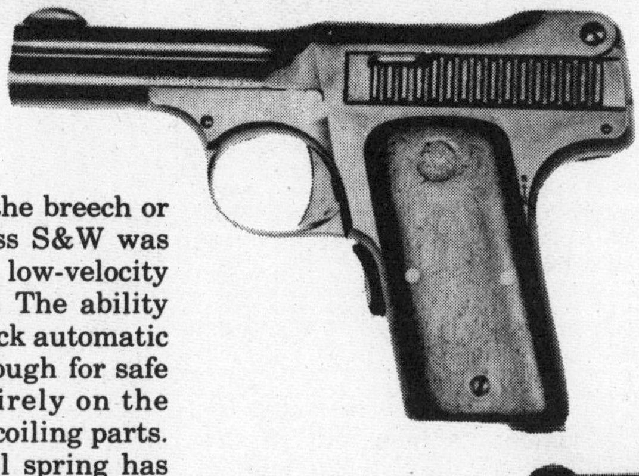

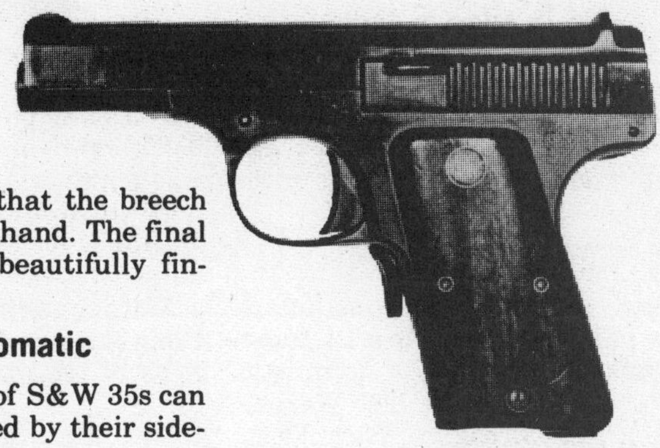

Smith & Wesson pocket automatics. Top — 35 S&W Type 1, SN 263. Middle — 35 S&W Type 2, SN 8279. Bottom — 32 ACP, SN 263. (Note that the first and third pistols have the same serial number, making them a one in a million pair!)

had a full weight slide, the breech or bolt piece of the slideless S&W was much too light for the low-velocity recoil the bolt required. The ability of the breech of a blowback automatic pistol to open slowly enough for safe operation depends entirely on the weight or mass of the recoiling parts. The tension of the recoil spring has virtually *no* function in retarding the slide or breech piece's opening except by its mass. The Browning 1900 and most other successful blowback automatics have recoiling parts which have an aggregate weight of 6 to 9 ounces in both the 32 and 380 class. Like 35 S&W parts weigh a scant 4½ ounces. This deficiency haunted the 35 S&W all through its unsuccessful life.

The Smith & Wesson, though badly designed, was made like a Swiss watch and beautifully finished in the tradition of the S&W company. S&W spent an incredible 3 years putting together one of the worst-designed guns ever made. Starting with its ill-starred 35 caliber and a too-high-velocity breech bolt, they added a palm-operated manual safety, a middle-finger-operated safety, and a side-operated magazine release. As they tried (erroneously) to correct the breech piece's deficiency by stiffening the recoil spring, they had to have a disconnect device so that the breech could be retracted by hand. The final product came out a beautifully finished nightmare.

S&W 35 Automatic

21. The first group of S&W 35s can be immediately spotted by their side-operating magazine catch. Type 1s started with SN 1 and proceeded to about SN 3,300, and were manufactured from 1913 to 1916.

22. Type 2 S&W 35s exhibit many small changes over the Type 1, but the obvious change was elimination of the side-operating magazine catch to the more conventional rearward-moving one. Starting about SN 3,300 and continuing to SN 8,350, 5,050 Type 2 pistols were made for 1916 to 1921.

These S&W 35s have also been lately called the Model of 1913, but this is not a factory designation and, since the caliber alone is sufficient identification, I see no value in the date term being used also. Total 35 S&W production was 8,350, only ¾ of one per cent of all U. S. pockets made, so they are rare today.

S&W 32 ACP Automatic

S&W, by 1924, decided to try again. They redesigned the 35 S&W in an attempt to correct its basic faults. The new S&W 32 ACP pistol had a conventional slide of the required mass (8 ounces) but it also retained a separately movable breech piece for loading, a very good feature for operating by weaker hands. The finger safety remained but the manual wheel-safety went, replaced by nothing. Quality of finish was maintained and the pistol was outstandingly attractive. It had only two "faults" — it was expensive and it came too late to participate in the heyday of U. S. pocket automatic sales.

23. There is only one type of S&W 32 ACP pistol. The SNs started at 1 and went only to 957. These rare pistols were sold from 1924 to 1927, but obviously they were all made at one time, probably, in one run in 1924 and were sold as long as stocks lasted.

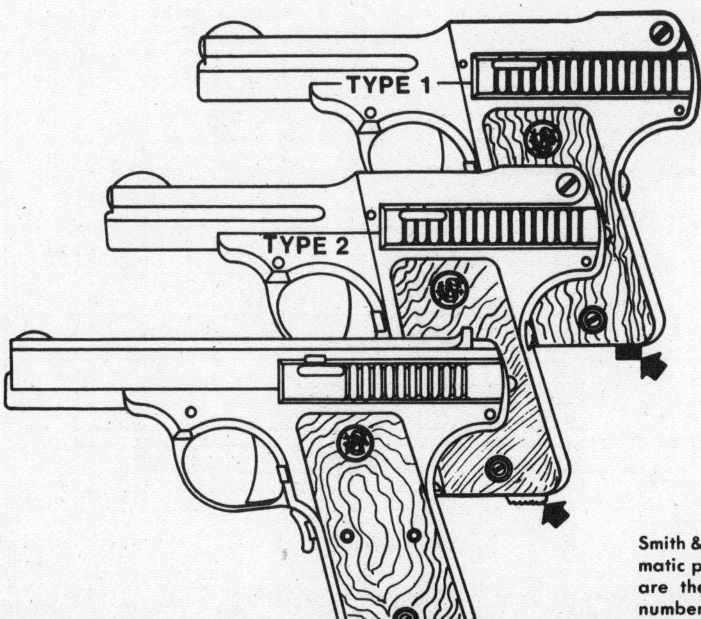

Smith & Wesson pocket automatic pistols. Types 1 and 2 are the S&W 35. The unnumbered pistol is the rare 32 ACP. See text for arrow-indicated details.

"The Infallible" pocket automatics. Top—Warner Arms Corp. 32 ACP, SN 1365. Bottom—Warner Arms Corp. 32 ACP, SN 6859.

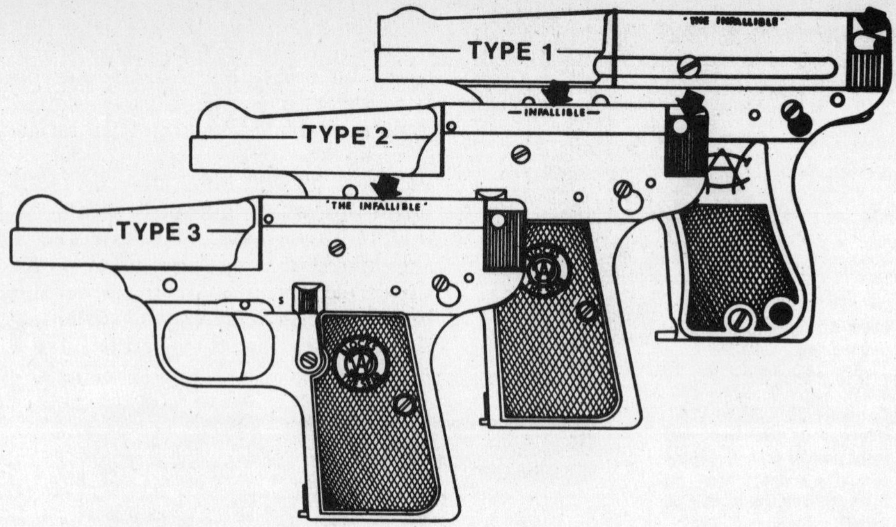

"Infallible" pocket automatic pistols. Early Warner Arms, Type 1; Warner-Davis Arms, Type 2; late Warner Arms, Type 3. See text for arrow-indicated details.

This small number makes them the rarest production pocket automatic pistol made in the United States. They're a highly desired pistol both by the automatic collector and the S&W collector. This dual interest has made these pistols today's most expensive production U. S. pocket automatics.

The Infallibles

Rather than use their manufacturer's name, I prefer to call these next pocket autos by the optimistic model name—Infallible. The Warner Arms Corp. of Brooklyn, New York, had started business as an importer of the German-made Schwarzlose blow-forward pistol. When this weird automatic failed (predictably) to capture any share of the U. S. market, Warner turned to a domestically-designed automatic to arrest their sagging sales curve. Warner selected a design of inventer Andrew Fyrberg for their next offering. Fyrberg's most basic automatic pistol patent is numbered 1,131,360, issued March 9, 1915. Though this is the second patent date found stamped on some of these pistols, it does show graphically the danger of his system. His ambitious blowback 32 ACP pistol was called the Infallible. Like the S&W 35, the Infallible suffered from a misconception—that a strong spring or two strong springs can materially delay the opening of the breech in a blowback automatic. Unlike the S&W pistol, Fyrberg's design had a breech or bolt which disassembled from the rear. Not only did it disassemble toward the shooter's face, but in the earliest examples the bolt had a lever that disconnected the twin recoil-spring guides from the bolt. This left only a small piece of steel to arrest the bolt's rearward motion if the lever was accidently left open. This design was *not safe*, and these Infallibles should be looked on as collector items only, *not* to be fired.

Warner Arms (now in Norwich, Conn.) merged with N.R. Davis & Sons of Assonet, Mass., forming the Davis-Warner Arms Corp. there. This merger occurred early in the run of Infallible automatics. Toward the end of the Infallible run, the Davis family withdrew from the firm and it went back to Warner Arms Corp., at Norwich, Conn. These changes in the firm's name make identification between the various types easy.

24. The Infallible Type 1 is identifiable by its "Warner Arms Corp. Norwich, Connecticut" logo, accompanied by a tell-tale disconnect lever at the end of the bolt. These early type Infallibles, with their many other inter-type variations, make a fascinating example of a product already being sold to the public yet still being designed. The Type 1 Infallibles start with either SN 1 or 500. I've never

U.S. POCKET AUTOMATICS

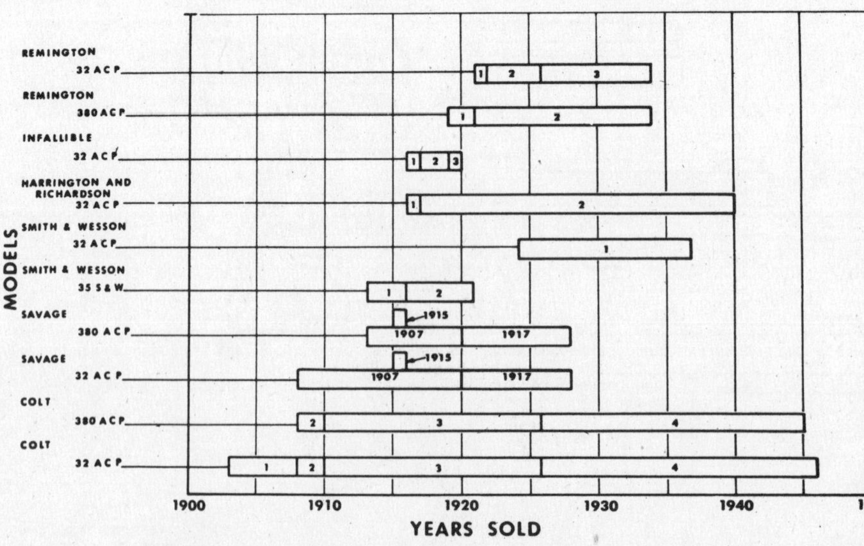

Chart showing the years the various U.S. pocket automatics were sold. Note that almost all types and makers appear in the decade from 1910 to 1920. (Type numbers are inside bars.)

seen any serial below 529 but this doesn't mean that there couldn't be some. They run to SN 2,299 or thereabout, date of manufacture 1916 to 1917.

25. Type 2s show the corporate logo of "Davis-Warner Arms Corporation, Assonet, Massachusetts." Too, the disconnector lever was replaced by a spring locked pin. These pistols started at about SN 2,300 and ran to about SN 5,299. These 3000 pistols, made from 1917 to 1919, contain the largest number of Infallibles made.

26. The last Infallibles can be recognized by the lack of a takedown lever, and the return to the original side stamping, "Warner Arms Corporation, Norwich, Massachusetts." These Type 3s started at about SN 5,300 and lasted to serial numbers in the 7300s, which is where the Infallibles stopped. Period of manufacture would be from 1919 to 1920, although they were still being sold new in the mid-1930s.

Total production of the 3 types represents only ⅔ds of one per cent of the U.S. grand total, therefore Infallibles are the rarest of all.

There it is, a sort of welcome to my world – no phallic symbolism – just an interesting slice of history showing American ingenuity. You now have reached the first plateau of U.S. automatic collectors but, to avoid any feeling that this is the whole package, let me point out that the Savage 32 has 90 minor variations to my knowledge – and there are probably that many more again. Good hunting, but remember that some dealers can read, too. Go get 'em before they're all gone or, worse, called home by Big Brother!

Acknowledgements

H. Milton Every*, Sidney Aberman, Richard Baker, Ara P. Burgess, James R. Carr, Charles Engle*, Paul Hendel (photography), J. Howard Mathews*, W. H. McCrillis, Fred H. Miller, Nicholas Niles, Jr., Doris S. Simmons (typing/editing), Daniel K. Stern, Ronald H. Wagner and to Charles W. Walker, special thanks.

*Deceased

Notes for Pocket Auto Collectors

THE BEST WAY to start a collection of U.S. pocket autos is – *don't* buy one! Not yet anyway. First, I suggest investing about 10 dollars in what, I feel, will clearly help determine if this is your particular field. Get a copy of some of the patents mentioned in the box accompanying this article. For 50¢ each they'll give you a good idea of what pocket automatics are all about. Next, get the *Book of Pistols and Revolvers* by W. H. B. Smith, published by Stackpole of Harrisburg, about $6.00. This one, a reprint of the NRA published book in 1946, was one of the few books we had in the early days on collecting automatics. Next, get the NRA *Illustrated Firearms Assembly Handbook,* Vol. I, and *The Gun Digest Book of Exploded Drawings,* published by Digest Books, Inc., 1974. Both show exploded views and disassembly drawings of many pocket autos, U.S. and foreign. Some statements made in the NRA book and in Smith's book are now known to be incorrect, but as basic textbooks they are invaluable.

After the written material has been studied and the new collector finds that he really likes the field, I suggest a visit to a gun show, but don't take along any big money. You're still not going to buy anything unless it's a secondhand book, maybe a firearms instruction manual or an original catalog showing some American pocket automatic. If you like this show it would make good sense to apply for membership in the sponsoring club and then find out which of its members are automatic collectors and, more specifically, U.S. pocket automatic collectors. Most advanced collectors will help the beginner if he asks for help and doesn't become too frequent a questioner. I also suggest membership in the National Automatic Pistol Collectors Assn., P.O. Box 272, Cayce, SC 29033. It publishes an excellent monthly "question and answer" magazine.

Now, having touched all of the preliminary bases, you're ready to buy your first pocket automatic. If, after a few gun shows, you've not found any of the more rare ones for sale, buy a Colt 32, Type 3. Because it's so common, you should look for a very good to excellent specimen, preferably one in the original box with the instruction manual and cleaning brush – the works. This is going to cost, depending on condition, about $140 to $160, but it will be the cornerstone of the collection and should therefore be a beauty. Now, when this prize is home, comes the purpose of all the books and reading and preliminary work. TAKE THE AUTOMATIC APART – all the way. Do it slowly, laying out the pieces in an orderly way, using only a screwdriver (one that fits) a drift punch or two and, if necessary, a small brass hammer. Now see if you can understand the function of each piece, down to the purpose of each hole in the metal. Look at the patent and follow the function and see how the original idea has been modified by manufacturing experience. This beginning phase of collecting from the first interest to the purchase of the first pistol might take as much as a year. There is really no hurry and, the more one learns about this first pistol, the more interesting each successive one will become.

In the early days of automatic collecting there were so few of us that exchange of knowledge was rare, printed information was almost nonexistent, and questions to the manufacturers, then as now, invariably elicited the reply (if any), "All the men who had anything to do with this pistol are dead or have left our employ." So we perforce learned slowly, but in the long run, we worked hard for what we learned and most of us share it with some reserve. In spite of this reservation, there are now enough of us who write and do know our subject, that new collectors can gain much by reading the many magazines that cater to the gun collecting fraternity.

Walter Smith, H.B.C. Pollard, and R.K. Wilson all covered the subject of automatic pistols with a broad brush. These pioneers were followed by the detail men, each of whom took a single type of arm and found a variation potential produced at every shift change at the manufacturer's plant. This nitpicking has led to the current Luger situation in which there are

Selected U.S. Pocket Pistol Patents

J.M. Browning, Dec. 22, 1903, No. 747, 585. (Colt)
E.H. Searle, Nov. 21, 1905, No. 804, 985. (Savage)
W.J. Whiting, Aug. 20, 1907, No. 863, 770. (Webley & Scott – H&R)
J.D. Pedersen, Aug. 3, 1920, No. 1,348,733. (Rem. 51)
Chas. Clement, Sept. 13, 1910, No. 970, 307. (S&W)
A. Fyrbert, March 9, 1915, No. 1,131,360. (Infallible)

almost as many variations as there were Lugers. Incidentally, a Luger is a relatively common pistol – 2 million were made in World War I by only two firms, DWM and Erfurt. The proliferation of variations, though fun for the expert, has made life very tough for a novice pistol collector.

Next, study the gun-oriented periodicals to learn who writes about your newly-chosen field and, even more importantly, who writes from a background of research and in some depth. Beware of the writer who overwhelms you with minute detail, minutiae that's germane to only one particular example, the one he's holding in his hand. Beware of articles that spend most of their verbiage on how to assemble/disassemble a particular piece.

Having sifted out these deadwood experts, you will have gathered a few authors who have answers to your questions, or to some of them. If you have additional questions write to these men in care of the magazine, and my guess is you'll get a concise answer. Don't put a raft of questions in one letter. As you become more familiar with your subject you may be able to help the expert and it will become a two-way street.

The second automatic to buy, if a rare one still hasn't been found, should be a Savage – of all U.S. pocket automatic pistols, none has better written detail than this pistol. Again, with this second basic, try for a boxed Savage Model 1907 caliber 32 with accessories; these can be found in new condition, and at a cost a little less than that first Colt, though for no good reason.

Pocket Auto Values

I know that between writing this next section and its being printed, things will change. However, I feel that some basic values should be given to a beginner and, if I've been able to hold his attention this long, I owe him some price information. You now know what the relative rarity of each basic model is, but this rarity factor has little or no influence on the market price. Imagine yourself a full time dealer in the broad subject of firearms – you would be swamped if you tried to memorize or even file the manufactured quantities of every type arm ever made. So they, like most of us, put a high price on some previously unseen model and see what happens. Unfortunately, some one new to the arms field sees this high "fishing" price and thinks that it is really today's value. Guard against this.

A relative rarity list and rational list of values for all the types discussed appears nearby, based on show prices and prices that I have been offered for that particular gun.

From this point on, the collector is on his own. As a last word of warning, *don't* buy a refinished example unless you have really given up finding the real thing – a rublued pistol to fill a gap is better than the gap. If a reblued S&W 32 ACP pistol were offered to me, I would take it at a reblued price, hoping to trade it off later for the real thing, at no loss, to some other gap-filling collector. Today both the H&R 32 and the Infallible 32 are sold for much under their relative-rarity value, so if you find one in collectable condition, grab it! S&W 35s are getting more and more expensive, so get one as soon as a very good or better one comes by.

– Donald M. Simmons, Jr.

Relative Rarity and Values of U.S. Pocket Automatics

Ref. No.	Maker	Cal.	Type, Model	Quantity	Percent. U.S. Total	Price*
1	Colt	32	1	71,999	6.57	$125
2	Colt	32	2	30,050	2.74	100
3	Colt	32	3	363,045	33.06	75
4	Colt	32	4	104,117	9.48	100
5	Colt	380	2	6,251	0.57	150
6	Colt	380	3	86,641	7.89	100
7	Colt	380	4	45,106	4.11	125
8	Savage	32	1907	209,201	19.05	75
9	Savage	32	1915	6,520	0.59	150
10	Savage	32	1917	29,671	2.70	100
11	Savage	380	1907	10,046	0.91	100
12	Savage	380	1915	3,902	0.36	150
13	Savage	380	1917	15,157	1.38	100
14	H&R	32	1	2,000	0.18	100
15	H&R	32	2	33,000	3.01	75
16	Rem. 51	380	1	37,975	3.46	100
17	Rem. 51	380	2	15,206	1.38	100
18	Rem. 51	32	1	1,198	0.11	150
19	Rem. 51	32	2	8,281	0.75	100
20	Rem. 51	32	3	2,126	0.19	125
21	S&W	35	1	3,300	0.30	250
22	S&W	35	2	5,050	0.46	250
23	S&W	32		957	0.09	550
24	Infall.	32	1	2,300	0.21	100
25	Infall.	32	2	3,000	0.27	75
26	Infall.	32	3	2,000	0.18	80
			Total	1,098,099	100.00	

*In Very Good (VG) condition, plus 10%.

Basic Collectors Library

Smith & Wesson Handguns, McHenry & Roper, Standard Publ's., Inc., Huntington WV, 1945.

Remington Arms (in American History), Alden Hatch. Rinehart & Co., Inc., N.Y.C., 1956.

The NRA Book of Small Arms, Vol. I, Pistols & Revolvers, W.H.B. Smith. The National Rifle Assn. of America and The Military Service Publishing Co., Washington D.C., and Harrisburg, PA, 1946 et seq.

A History of the Colt Revolver, Charles T. Haven & Frank A. Belden. William Morrow & Co., N.Y.C., 1940.

10 Shots Quick, Daniel K. Stern. Globe Printing Co., San Jose, CA, 1967.

Savage Automatic Pistols, James R. Carr. Privately printed by author, no place, no date.

Remington Handguns, Charles Lee Karr, Jr. & Carroll Robbins Karr. The Military Service Publishing Co., Harrisburg, PA, 1947.

Automatic Pistols, Captain Hugh B.C. Pollard, reprinted by WE, Old Greenwich, CT, 1970.

Automatic Arms, Melvin M. Johnson, Jr. & Charles T. Haven. William Morrow & Co., N.Y.C., 1941.

Automatic Firearm Pistols, Elmer Swanson. Wesmore Book Co., Weehawken, NJ, 1955.

A Catalog of Firearms for the Collector, L.D. Satterlee. Privately printed, Detroit, MI, 1927.

Colt Automatic Pistols 1896-1955, Donald B. Bady. Fadco Publishing Co., Hollywood, CA, 1956.

Collector's Guide to American Cartridge Handguns, DeWitt E. Sell. The Stackpole Co., Harrisburg, PA, 1963.

Textbook of Automatic Pistols 1884-1935, R.K. Wilson. Small-Arms Technical Publishing Co., Plantersville, SC, 1943.

Firearms Identification, Vols. I & II. J. Howard Mathews. The University of Wisconsin Press, Madison, WI, 1962.

Firearms Identification, Vol. II. J. Howard Mathews. Charles C. Thomas, Springfield, IL, 1973.

Illustrated Firearms Assembly Handbook, Vols. I & II. Various authors. The National Rifle Assn. of America, 5th printing., Washington, D.C., 1961.

Annual Publications – *Gun Digest, Guns Illustrated, Gun Collector's Digest, Guns Annual,* Stoeger catalogs, et al.

Periodical publications – Guns, American Rifleman, Guns & Ammo, Shooting Times, Gun Sport & Gun Collector, National Defense, Shotgun News, Gun Week.

THE SCOUT RIFLE IDEA

by **JEFF COOPER**

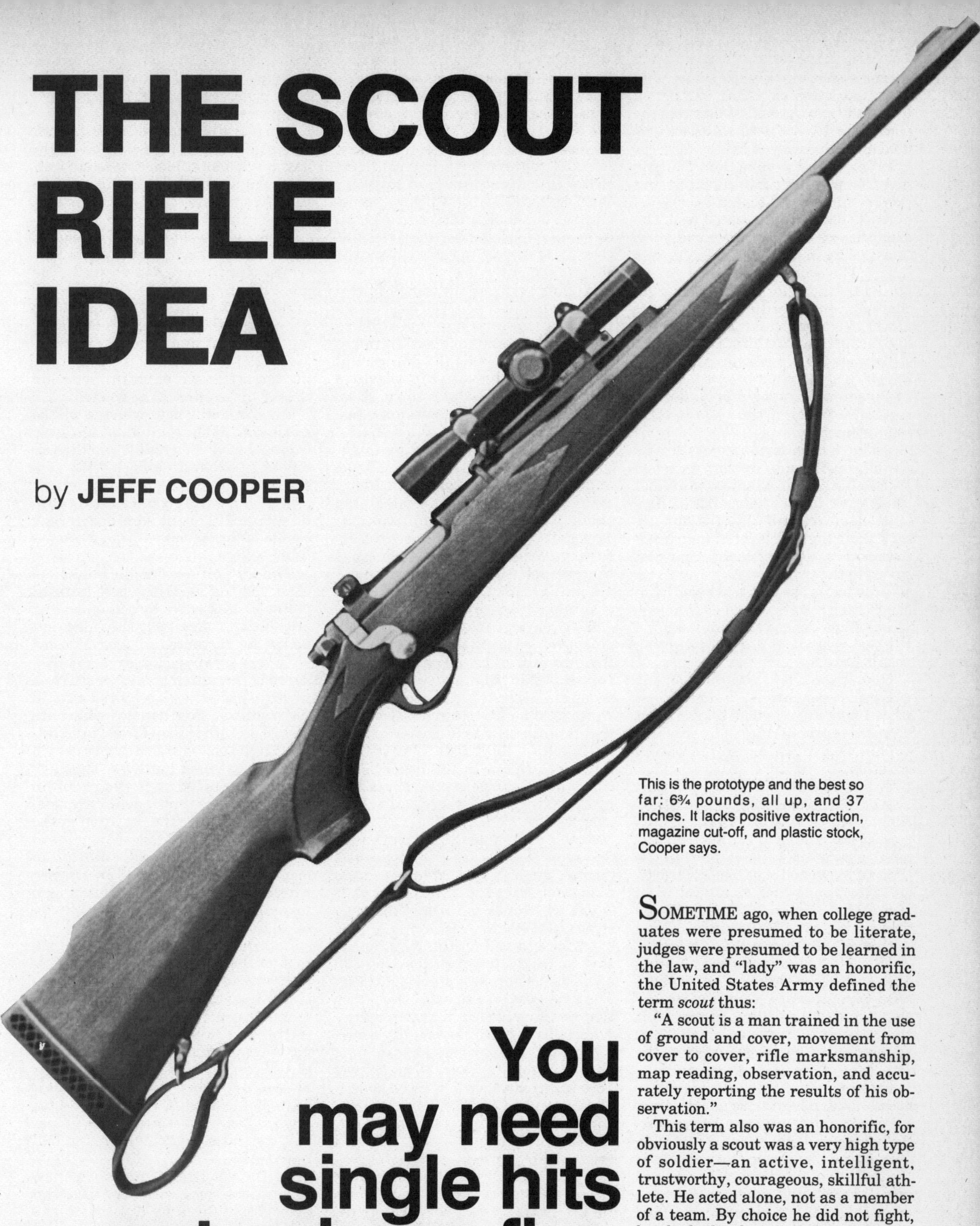

This is the prototype and the best so far: 6¾ pounds, all up, and 37 inches. It lacks positive extraction, magazine cut-off, and plastic stock, Cooper says.

You may need single hits not volume fire.

SOMETIME ago, when college graduates were presumed to be literate, judges were presumed to be learned in the law, and "lady" was an honorific, the United States Army defined the term *scout* thus:

"A scout is a man trained in the use of ground and cover, movement from cover to cover, rifle marksmanship, map reading, observation, and accurately reporting the results of his observation."

This term also was an honorific, for obviously a scout was a very high type of soldier—an active, intelligent, trustworthy, courageous, skillful athlete. He acted alone, not as a member of a team. By choice he did not fight, but he had to be an expert at the hit-and-run art of single combat. By choice he did not shoot, but if forced to shoot he shot quickly, carefully, and as little as possible. "One round, one hit—and then vanish!"—that was his motto. He did not need an assault rifle. He needed a *scout rifle*.

Times have changed, and the true scout is no longer found (Or, at any rate, *cataloged:* Editor) in today's armies. The enemy is located from the air, pinned by artillery, and then smashed by mechanized infantry and tanks. The scout's rifle has been replaced by the *Sturmgewehr,* and the character and qualities of the rifle for use by a lone rifleman have been all but forgotten. The hunter-rifleman still exists (in diminishing number), but since he does not hunt to save his life, even he loses sight of certain essentials which a true scout rifle should embody.

We have been fortunate at Gunsite Ranch, in Arizona, in that we teach practical riflery to clients who are not likely ever to use their rifles as fireteam members, and who consequently seek their highest level of *individual* competence, with the instrument best suited to the task.

But what *is* the task of a rifle? In an age of specialization it is easy to say, "Just tell me what you want it for and I'll tell you what sort of rifle you should have."

That is too easy. What do you say when the response is, "I don't know what I may want to do with it. I want a *general purpose* rifle?"

That is a much more interesting question.

One of the Eternal Truths is this: *The purpose of shooting is hitting*. By extension we may say that the purpose of the rifle is to enable the rifleman to strike a decisive blow to the limit of his vision. Let us call a "decisive blow" one which can be relied on instantly to incapacitate any unarmored animal of 500 pounds or less, with one solid hit in the vital zone. Such a blow will provide good probability to twice that weight, or more with careful placement. Let us further say that the "limit of vision" is the greatest distance at which 20-20 eyes, unaided, can clearly discern the vital zone of the animal engaged.

These parameters suffice well for both human adversaries and medium big game, and there are all sorts of rifles which will suit them. That, however, is not the whole story. There is the quality of handiness. We work so much at the target range (to which we drive in motor vehicles) that we tend to forget that the natural habitat of the general-purpose rifle is the field, the forest, the desert and the mountain—not the shooting shed with its bench rest. To be really useful a rifle must be as short, light and quick to use as is technically compatible with adequate power and useful accuracy. Adequate power may be had with any of the 20-caliber family of military cartridges, the best of which was probably the 30-06, now largely pre-empted by its compacted offspring the 308. Useful accuracy is that which the shooter can put to use.

We properly use the bench to test the intrinsic accuracy of barrel, action, bedding, cartridge, and sighting system. And we often forget that what matters is not what the equipment can do, but rather what it will do in the hands of its operator under field, rather than laboratory, conditions. One enlightening test is a series of five two-shot pairs, standing-to-sitting, 100 yards, Option target, 10 seconds per pair. Any combination of man and rifle which can keep all ten shots in five inches in this exercise demonstrates excellent *practical* accuracy. Whether the equipment is bench-capable of a one-inch group or a 1½-inch group or a two-inch group at that range is irrelevant.

If we consider that the "range probable error" of a rifle—the distance of the best 50% of hits from the mathematical point of aim—is one-fourth group diameter, it is clear that the advantage of a one-minute rifle over a two-minute rifle is a matter of one-half inch at 200 yards. Under field conditions this is insignificant. Thus the general-purpose rifle should be good for two minutes, and 2½ will do very well.

At this point a certain kind of purist will snort that we are talking about a "scatter gun." Not so. We are talking about accuracy we can use, for that which we cannot use is only theoretically interesting.

Let us proceed on the assumption that we need a two-inch-shooting 308 as a base. There are plenty of those. The next goal is compactness, and for that we think at once of a short barrel. A short barrel reduces velocity somewhat, and it increases blast. The shortest popular barrel measures 18½-inches. In such a barrel a charge of 43 grains of IMR3031 will start a 150-gr. bullet at right about 2700 fps. Those were the ballistics of the old original 30-06 in a 24-inch barrel, and they sufficed very well for Theodore Roosevelt and Stewart Edward White in Africa. A 30-caliber, 150-grain spitzer at 2700 fps may not be a "magnum," but it has been logging one-shot kills all over the world for so long that one may well ask why anything more is necessary, unless one's target weighs over 1000 pounds.

It is true that the blast of an 18-inch 308 is impressive, especially on a dark day, but a lone rifleman need not worry much about tell-tale flash. If he shoots carefully—once—and moves, it doesn't matter.

Along with a short barrel we should have a short action, both as to cartridge length and also over-all. The most compact actions that come to mind are the new Remington Model Seven and the Remington 600, now out of production, and the curious Mauser also called 600. By compressing the action, an extra inch or more of over-all length can be deleted.

The scout rifle now evolving will be a bolt gun, as the semi-autos are overly long, heavy, and bulky, and the volume of fire they afford is of little consequence to a true scout. One might construct a quite good scout rifle with a Savage 99, but it would still be a couple of inches longer than a comparable bolt gun.

Modern bolt actions all fall somewhat short of ideal, the best features of some being offset by corresponding drawbacks. Completely shrouded case heads, for instance, all seem to come with weak extraction systems. Reduced bolt rotation makes for stiff bolt work, especially with a fired case in the chamber. Bolt handles which are tacked on rather than forged integrally with the bolt will sometimes detach themselves under hard use. This may produce an elegant dueling scar on the right cheek, but it definitely sidelines the rifle for the duration of the game. Actions which are enclosed against foreign matter are difficult to load from the top, eyes off, in a hurry; whereas those that facilitate single loading do not feature a magazine cutoff to take full advantage thereof.

Detachable box magazines are, except for the Mannlicher, of reduced capacity, and experimental modifications taking the 20-round M-14 magazine are awfully clumsy with the big box in place. At this time nobody except Mannlicher offers point protection for reserve rounds in the magazine. Nearly all modern bolt guns come with a roughened bolt knob, when what is needed for proper bolt work is a smooth and round ball bearing.

On the good side, most of the new bolt actions come with very nice triggers. Though many are set on the heavy side for reasons of product-liability intimidation, they normally can be reduced down to a marksman-

Scouts move and a scout rifle needs to be easy in the grasp for tough-country hurrying.

The forward scope permits eyes-off loading and manipulation, and alternate iron sights as well.

like three pounds. The consensus of the masters is that a fine trigger is the single most important *desideratum* in any rifle.

A short bolt action, in combination with a short barrel, can bring over-all length down to about 37 inches without serious loss in performance. For optimum handiness and portability we should now seek a weight ceiling of seven pounds, all up. The scout rifle should weigh less than seven pounds, with scope and sling in place, but unloaded. The best way to meet this limit is by means of a plastic stock. There are all sorts of plastics, but the best sort can produce a stock that is both lighter and stronger than wood. Fine wood is prohibitive in price and common wood is no prettier than plastic, so plastic would seem to be the wave of the future. Stamped checkering is rather like instant wine (better than nothing, but not much), so perhaps some sort of blast-roughening is the answer.

In styling the stock should be plain and straight, a "classic" without bumps, flanges, notches, or cheekpieces, since the gun must be comfortably operable from either shoulder. It should be high enough at comb to support a low scope line. No butt cushion is necessary, but the heel should be rounded to encourage quick mounting for a snap shot. A thin rubber skidplate should finish the butt.

The short, light barrel of the scout rifle heats up quickly. This is no problem in the field but has been known to blister hands during practice. It can be partially shrouded by a full-length stock of the pattern popularly termed "Mannlicher"—which need not, incidentally, have any adverse affect upon accuracy, contrary to rumor. (I have a Model L that shoots like a match rifle.)

The sling fittings should be of the Pachmayr flush design, metal reinforced, and the sling itself must provide loop support. Bipods are certainly helpful under certain conditions but they constitute a dangerous crutch if a shooter comes to depend on them. On the range they work fine, but in rough and broken terrain they are almost useless, and those presently available are ugly. The loop sling remains more generally useful than the bipod, and no bipod design should interfere with proper sling mounting.

To this point the scout rifle is fairly easy to assemble. Sights, however, are another matter. A scout rifle should be equipped with both iron and optical sights, but neither is easily available at this time in a configuration which suits it for the scout rifle concept.

The iron sights for a scout should consist of a square front post, possibly red filled, and a large-aperture, small-rim rear sight mounted on the receiver bridge—popularly referred to as a "ghost ring." Most over-the-counter rifles come with a front bead and a rear notch, since it is assumed that they will be quickly fitted with a telescope and therefore nothing very good in the way of iron sights is necessary or desirable. It is no great problem to knock out the gold bead and install a proper front post. The square post gives all the speed afforded by a bead, plus a distinctly better index of elevation in precise shooting.

On the other hand, rear aperture sights are rarely fitted to rifles at the factory, and those available as accessories are often both bulky and unsightly. Possibly the best option was the integral and retractable rear aperture that came as standard equipment on the ZKK 600 Series actions from Brno in Czechoslovakia. The aperture in this sight was too small, but it could be easily drilled out, and the neatness and compactness of the entire assembly are not duplicable with currently available accessory equipment.

Those who do not understand the ghost ring or its usages should try it sometime, on both paper targets and thrown clay birds. Locations where one can shoot trap with the rifle with safety are scarce, but the skeptic is well advised to try this, even at considerable difficulty, in order to learn how the rifle is properly used in a hurry.

The vast majority of currently available telescope sights are too big and have too little eye relief for proper use as we are learning to use a scout rifle. And most mounting systems place the sight axis too high above the bore. The best combination so far was available only for a short time during which Leupold produced a 2x compact glass of ten-inch eye relief, and Buehler produced a mount which would fit this glass very low over the bore of the Remington 600 series and mounted so as to place the ocular lens directly flush with the front end of the magazine well. This combination, sight and mount, is the fastest ever to appear at Gunsite, and it loses nothing in precision when used for careful shots at long range. We have even heard it dubbed "unfair," and no higher compliment can ever be paid to any piece of equipment than that.

The virtues of this sight system are three:

First, it obscures very little of the shooter's vision as the piece is cheeked. This enables him to keep both eyes open while mounting the rifle, with a full view of his entire target area, and to place the cross wires instantly with his shooting eye while keeping track of the target with his non-shooting eye. The closer the glass is to the eye, the more of the shooter's field of view is obscured.

Second, the forward-mounted scope allows instantaneous eyes-off loading from the top, without obstruction by the scope tube.

Third, the forward-mounted glass allows the rifle to be grasped at the balance during running, jumping and violent exercise much more conveniently than any weapon with the glass mounted rearward.

There are several extended-eye-relief telescopes available, but they are primarily designed for pistols and come with an eye relief of about 14 inches, making it necessary to place them so far forward on the piece that no secure portion of the action is available for a base. The classic quarter-rib sometimes found on venerable bolt action rifles forms an excellent base for a forward-mounted telescope, but only if the glass may be mounted far enough to the rear to take advantage of it. Of course, until there is perfection, a good low conventional scope will serve.

The notion that a rifle must be long and heavy in order to suit it for any sort of serious work at distance is a myth which has been with us for a long time. The most frequent comment heard about the prototype scout rifles is that they are all very well as brush guns, but are not suited for general use. This charge is best met by taking the rifles to a field trial exercise and examining the results. It is clearly true that smaller groups may be fired at 500 meters with a properly designed bull gun than with a scout rifle. But the difference is less than one might think, and certainly too little to matter when the goal is achieving hits in the vital zones of big game animals, or in human adversaries.

Long testing has led to the conclusion that the ability to achieve a first-shot hit, on a 10-inch disc at ranges varying from 50 to 550 yards, is far more a matter of the skill of the shooter than of the size or weight of his rifle. The scouts hold their own with the big guns on any practical field test we have been able to devise, and they are so much easier to pack around and to use quickly, that our more traditional rifles are spending more and more time on the rack.

Consider this observation from H. W. McBride, quoted from his classic, *A Rifleman Went to War:*

> "The neatest and handiest military rifle I have ever seen was one I took from one of these German *Jägers,* and when I held it up beside my Ross for comparison, the cocky little rascal actually laughed in my face, and he had a bullet through his arm at that. It did look ridiculous, I admit—that is, the Ross did; a great big long heavy club beside the trim little sporter which he had been using. His rifle had been made for something other than a handle for a bayonet."

At this time it would seem that the best cartridges for the scout rifle are three, with possibly one more if extra power is important. We have already discussed the virtues of the 308, and nearly all of our experimental and pioneer models are made for this cartridge. For those who are recoil shy, or lightly built, the 243 is an acceptable option, although since the 243 is a "velocity cartridge" its barrel should not probably be cut much under 22-inches in order to retain the virtues of the round. The 7mm-08 may be of no particular interest to the American shooting public, but it has much to recommend it in those jurisdictions where the 308 cartridge is forbidden as a "military caliber." There are more places like this than you might suspect. All three—the 308, the 7mm-08, and the 243—are of the same length on the same basic case.

Conventional scope placement obscures a lot of country and covers the best place to grab the piece.

Steyr's quick-switch potential means a lot in the scout concept, but the forward scope can't be had easily.

The additional cartridge in the scout family, which makes up into what may be called a "super scout," is the 350 Remington Magnum. This is one of the very few *short* magnum cartridges, and is certainly useful in places where its 250-grain bullet may be desirable for extra knockdown effect on large animals. I have taken my own to many strange and far-away places, and always my host wanted to buy it from me. The super scout, incidentally, runs to 7½ pounds, and 39 inches.

The scouts, as now built in prototype form, do have certain drawbacks. They heat up quickly, they are noisy, and they kick somewhat more than conventional rifles of similar type. Also, finding sights for them is a frustrating enterprise. Their virtues, however, outnumber their vices, or so it seems to me.

In C. S. Forester's heroic tale, *Brown on Resolution,* one Able Seaman Brown, on the beach with a Mauser rifle in a battle port, is able to forestall the repairs necessary on a German cruiser for long enough for the British fleet to arrive, thus winning the battle:

> "But Brown was only powerful in consequence of his rifle; the handiest, neatest, most efficient piece of machinery ever devised by man."

That was in 1915, and, though fictional, realistically drawn from life. Now we have a handier, neater, and more efficient piece of machinery than that. Actually, of course, we don't quite have it, but there are designs, prototypes and ideas. When we are satisfied with our concept, we may prevail upon some established maker to produce it.

Perhaps some year soon, you will be able to walk into a store and buy a scout rifle over the counter. As Max Beerbohm says, "It is a contingency furiously to be hoped." ●

Kentucky Rifle

fact – and fiction

by ROBERT HELD

Graceful and handsome Pennsylvania rifle, marked JL on top of the 42½-inch octagon barrel. Made about 1760 by James Long (?), the caliber is 50, the rifling seven narrow grooves making one turn in 60 inches. Stocked in fiddle-back maple, it carries the thicker wrist and shallow-curved butt of the earlier "Kentuckys." 58½" over-all, the weight is 9 lbs.

NOT VERY long ago we had occasion to visit the classroom of our 12-year-old nephew. A history lesson was in progress and, to the delight of our antique-gun-collector's ears, we were just in time to hear a bright young particle of America's future read his composition on the armaments of the War of Independence. It wasn't long before he came to the Kentucky rifle. Quite accurately, he explained that it had originated in Pennsylvania but that it was called a "Kentucky" rifle because "Kentucky" used to mean all the vast wilderness west of the Alleghenies; he spoke of its German ancestry, and correctly sketched its evolution between 1720 and 1760. We found ourselves inordinately pleased.

But suddenly he veered sharply from the paths of truth. With growing horror we heard him warble: "... and it was American frontiersmen who first introduced greased patches for loading rifle bullets." We sighed and resigned ourselves to what we knew would now inevitably follow – as indeed it did an instant later. "Kentucky rifles were the finest and most accurate in the world. They were also ...."

We didn't have to listen. He had obviously been to the town library and had done a good deal of studying in most of the standard reference works, as well as in half a dozen specialized gun books, and assorted articles in various gun periodicals. He had no doubt also sought the advice of local collectors. We knew only too well the myths he had unearthed – and which he was now passing on as matters of historical fact: that Kentuckys were the most accurate and most effective rifles ever known up to the middle 1800's; that they were the most beautiful, the best-made, the most ingenious; that without them the War of Independence would have been lost before it had hardly got started; that European rifles prior to and contemporary with Kentuckys were clumsy, woefully inaccurate; in fact, scarcely better than smoothbore muskets; that the making of Kentuckys was a skill confined to American riflesmiths, envied but never equalled or even approximated by the gunmakers of the Old World.

All this folderol the boy had dutifully copied down and accepted as truth; indeed, what else could he have done? He had got it, after all, from the "best authorities." We decided then and there that the time had come – in fact, that it was long overdue – for a thoughtful review of Kentucky rifles in accordance with reality.

Now, let us make one point very clear right at the start: *we hold deep*

Mr. Held is the author of the well-known work *The Age of Firearms* (see The Arms Library pages).

affection and great respect for that magnificent species of weaponry, the American Long Rifle of the 18th and early 19th centuries! We have owned, shot and lovingly restored a good many of them; we have defended them vehemently against the condescension and derision prevalent among fellow-members of a couple of European gun collectors' associations. Let no man charge us with proceeding from a bias of dislike or that we simply want to muckrake. We are out to restore objectivity – a viewpoint long now lost among much or most of American collectordom in the matter of Kentuckys (also of Colts, but that's another story); we have come to praise Kentuckys, not to bury them – but to praise them in the light of historical truth.

And so, let us begin with the beginning: the European rifles out of which the American variety evolved.

Emergence of Rifling

Despite the invention of rifling having been credited to certain people in certain places at certain dates (notably to Köllner or Zöllner at Vienna in 1498), the fact is that no one really knows, and that no one place, time or man can be given credit. All we know for certain is that by about 1475 it had become obvious to gunmakers and shooters that bullets made to spin by means of spiraling grooves in the bores were more accurate than those which were shot out of smoothbored pieces. No one understood the reason for this phenomenon until the British physicist Benjamin Robins published his famous paper *Observations on the Nature and Advantages of Rifled Barrel Pieces* in 1747; Robins explained it all very correctly (in fact, he founded the modern science of ballistics). Gunmakers and shooters of earlier ages ascribed the effect to demons, devils, witches, angels, the "elastic fluid of the air," the "harmony of the rotation of the universe" and other such theories were (a) that a spinning bullet "drilled" its way through the air, and (b) that the retardation exercised by rifling upon the ball ensured more forceful combustion of the powder.

In any event, rifles were not rarities on the gun cabinets of the well-to-do and the aristocracy by 1540. Wheel-lock rifles of splendid ornamentation ranged from light 35 to 40 caliber small-game weapons to 70 and even 85 caliber thundermakers designed to stop any living creature dead or lame by sheer impact (a necessity for many European hunting conditions, of which more will be said anon). Rifling abounded in a profusion of experimental styles, some very successful, some very unsuccessful. By about 1650, however, two main types had become stable; the 20- to 50-groove star system, lands and grooves of equal width and triangular in cross-section (essentially the same as our modern (?) "micro-groove" weapons) and the seven- to 10-groove flat system, the lands ranging from a width equal to that of the grooves to about twice that of the grooves. Pitches varied from one turn in about 48 inches to one in about 70 or more, but by far the greater number were held close to one in 48.

The Patched Ball

There were two methods of loading rifles in those days (in fact, right up to the end of the muzzle-loading era some eighty years ago). One, as most American gun enthusiasts know, was by means of a ball of the same size as the diameter between two opposite grooves – not lands – hammered down from muzzle to powder by hard blows of a wooden mallet upon an iron ramrod. The oversized ball naturally adapted itself to the lands, filled or nearly filled the grooves and, upon being propelled forward by the burning gases, was gripped so firmly by the spiral as to be virtually strip-proof. Most American collectors – and several writers who should know better – seem to think that this laborious and time-consuming (but effective) method was the *only* one known in Europe. Now, it is true that until the middle 1700's it was more widely employed *among those shooters who believed that the greater the retardation of the ball, the greater the force of the shot* – as noted, a not-unreasonable theory in pre-Robins days. Moreover, this method also permitted very sharp pitches – one turn in 30 inches was not infrequent among rifles designed for this type of loading. But there was another method: viz., the use of an undersized ball wrapped in a greased leather or cloth patch, the rifling gripping the patch, the patch in turn obturating the grooves and gripping the ball, and the whole charge rammed by a relatively light push of a wooden rod. Contrary to the opinions of most American collectors – and of some writers – the greased-patch method was emphatically *not* the discovery of American frontiersmen. It was old stuff in Europe at least a full century before the first Pennsylvania rifle had taken on its own identity in the 1730's. Diego Espinar* describes it in detail, and the simple evidence among pre-1580 rifles of grease-filled patchboxes and light wooden ramrods (*original,* not later additions, as is made clear by the size of the ramrod ferrules and the horn tip ornamentations) proves that patch-loading was nothing new in Shakespeare's time. Let this article contribute to the final explosion – with a resounding BANG! – of the myth that greased patches originated in America.

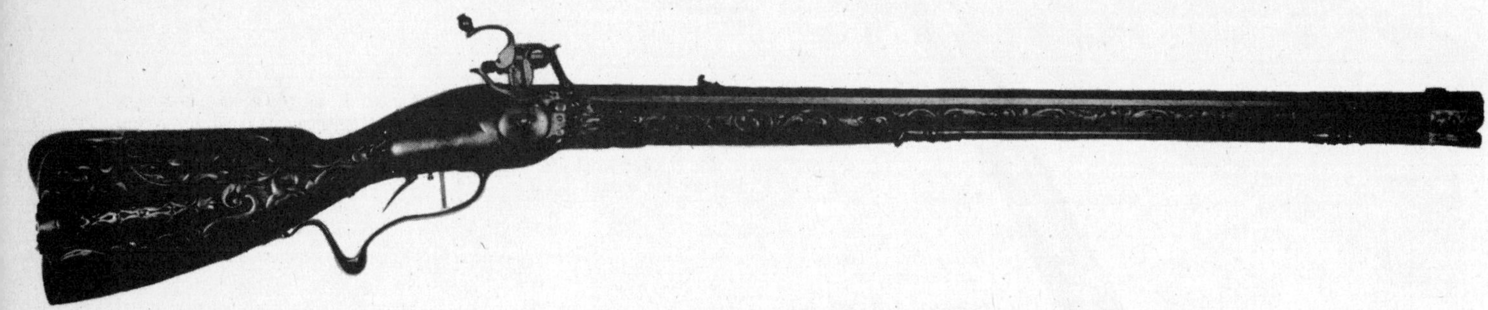

German wheel-lock hunting rifle, dated 1738. Wheel-locks were much more reliable and faster-firing than flintlocks, but also vastly more expensive and difficult to repair—two drawbacks which disqualified them from American frontier usage. Rifling has seven grooves and lands of equal width making one turn in 44 inches in the 56-caliber bore. 7-lb. weight, a carrying sling (not shown) and short 31-inch barrel make it convenient to carry in all sorts of terrain. It will put four balls through the same hole at 40 yards, clover-leaf them at 70 and hold 4-inch groups at 100. Although not of the very finest, its quality of woodwork, lock, rifling, and ornamentations is typically excellent.

Thus far, then our picture of European rifledom is roughly one of aristocratic sporting weapons, exclusively wheel-locks until the middle of the 17th century, thereafter flintlocks (but with many wheel-locks still about) into the 18th century and a bit beyond. For the most part they were made on a level of craftsmanship never, not to this very day, attained in America. Quite aside from the gold, silver, ivory and ebony inlays – the intricate sculptures in steel and iron – the bas-relief and engraved hunting scenes – quite aside from these (which naturally could not possibly have been duplicated in a frontier society struggling for survival), there was the watch-like precision of the 47-odd parts required to make a wheel-lock, the mirror surfaces of talcum-polished bores, lockplates and bar-

*Arte de Ballesteria y Monteria (Madrid, 1644).

rel flats, the six-stage set- and hair-triggers, the masterful perfection of mechanics and aesthetics attainable only through the patient apprentice-master journeyman system of European guilds, and through the existence of an affluent class willing and able to pay for it all. Yet even among the lower-class rifles of, say, 1650-1700 – the relatively humble "working" rifles of semi-professional hunters and mountaineers – the excellence of mechanical fit, finish and polish were almost invariably there. The rifle shown here, circa 1700, is typical of such non-aristocratic pieces in its shape, style, craftsmanship and ornamentation; it is the best pre-1750 medium-bore rifle we've ever fired; it is perfectly representative of the rifles brought to America by the early German settlers – it is the Kentucky's immediate ancestor. Yet in respect to workmanship it defies comparison with virtually any Kentucky; in respect to accuracy it compares favorably with most.

Why, then, if so many virtues were embodied in the European species, didn't the frontiersmen of America simply use them in the forms in which they arrived?

The Jäger Rifle

Because European terrain and wildlife differed vastly from those of the New World, so that rifles specifically developed for one set of conditions were not found suitable for the other. In the first place, the forests of continental Europe (especially southern Germany, the principal domain of the rifle) abounded with razor-tusked boars weighing up to 400 pounds and fond of charging suddenly from nearby bushes in ghastly onslaught. Secondly, hunters in the craggy alpine regions of Bavaria, Austria and Switzerland often found themselves removed from their quarry by perhaps only 100 or 200 yards in a straight horizontal line, but with a thousand-foot chasm in between. Both of these circumstances demanded the use of quite large bullets – say, between 55 and 75 caliber – so that the boar might be stopped in mid-charge by such a projectile's stunning blow even if it should glance off the mammoth skull, and also to lame or otherwise disable a mountain ram by sheer impact, so that the wounded animal could not flee far during the four or five hours that might be required to

Examples of rifling in pre-percussion days. Top to bottom: "star" form; polygrooving; wide-land styles (2) and last, shallow, late-Kentucky type. The first four are of poor design, the last quite close to modern rifling.

reach it. Moreover, the rifles had to be relatively short, not only to permit a quick swing on a boar, but because a hunter often needed both hands for climbing while his rifle was strap-slung across his back. The fact that the lead ball for an average rifle of, say, 66 caliber weighed fully an ounce (and required 75 to 125 grains of powder), was of no concern to its user – he rarely carried more than a dozen loadings for a one- or two-day prowl, at the end of which he went home to his town or village. He could also afford to use a wheel-lock – vastly more reliable and quick-firing than even the best of flintlocks – because if anything should go out of order among its 45 to 50 parts, he had merely to take it to a nearby master gunsmith for repair. (After about 1650, however, many flintlocks were in use because of the high initial cost of wheel-locks.) Finally, the European hunter didn't much care that his big bullets flew in rather high, arched trajectories, for he had learned from boyhood on to estimate distances carefully, to elevate his line of sight accordingly, and to hit squarely even at 200 yards; there was no great rush about shooting (except for the throw-away shot at a charging boar) because Indian warfare, in which rapid aim and fire were vital to the survival of entire communities, did not exist.

The first thing learned, following the appearance of such rifles on the American frontier around 1700-1720, was that there was no need for box-car, boar-stopper missiles. There was no dangerous game in America save a few black- and brown-bear (or Indians); both could be felled by half-inch balls and, as was discovered by the middle of the 18th century, even by 45's and 40's. Thus a reduction in caliber was possible; more than that, it was absolutely essential, for American pioneers were often away from civilization for six months and more, and had to carry all their supplies along – a circumstance in which it was very important indeed to have rifles firing bullets weighing not 10 or 15 but 40 and 50 to the pound, propelled not by 75 to more than 100 grains of powder but by 30 to 60. Even in fairly well-established communities this economy factor was an essential consideration, for lead and powder were (unlike in Europe) expensive and in scant supply. Thus the earliest "American" rifles made for American conditions by the German gunsmiths of Pennsylvania were in all respects European save for the reduced bores. The fact that the smaller projectiles flew in flatter trajectories was an incidental effect, not a primary one – it was, of course, highly welcome since it permitted the use of one fixed set of sights and one line of aim for all normal hunting ranges up to 75 yards or so, with only little holding over being necessary for those a bit beyond. It is important to note here (we'll come back to it) that neither early-, middle- or late-period Kentuckys were more accurate than European rifles in terms of the latter's ability to consistently place bullets at the same or nearly same point of impact – but the flatter-trajectory American rifles required less shooter judgment for long distances, which is not the same as the often-alleged "more accurate." But without a doubt, one of the huge Kentucky advantages was the lesser need for a lifetime of practice and experience, so that accurate fire could be delivered against Indians and animals by nearly every steady-eyed, steady-handed man, boy and woman on the frontier (some of whom, obviously, would be better shots than others).

The Long Barrels

Now, having effectively reduced the calibers – not much at first, the early Kentuckys running between 50 and 58 – the German-Pennsylvanian riflesmiths went off the deep end and proceeded to another change, one which was ultimately proved to be based on error: they lengthened barrels from the usual European 30 to 36 inches to somewhere between 40 (short among 18th-century Kentuckys) to 55 inches. Why? *Not,* as is thought by many collectors, to achieve greater accuracy; rifle barrel lengths beyond a certain point do not contribute to greater accuracy – with patch-loaded black powder rifles, about 30 to 36 inches mark that point, depending on caliber and style of rifling. This is simply a fact, and American black powder muzzle-loading rifles after about 1835-40 fell

Patchboxes of American long rifles, invariably brass, constitute a pure species of American folk art. Made in a vast profusion of patterns and details, the basic form has no antecedents among European patchboxes, which were almost always wood, and sliding rather than hinged. Specimen shown stems from region around Lancaster, Penna., dates from about 1780-1800. (In the collection of Mr. Joel Gross, Los Angeles, Calif.)

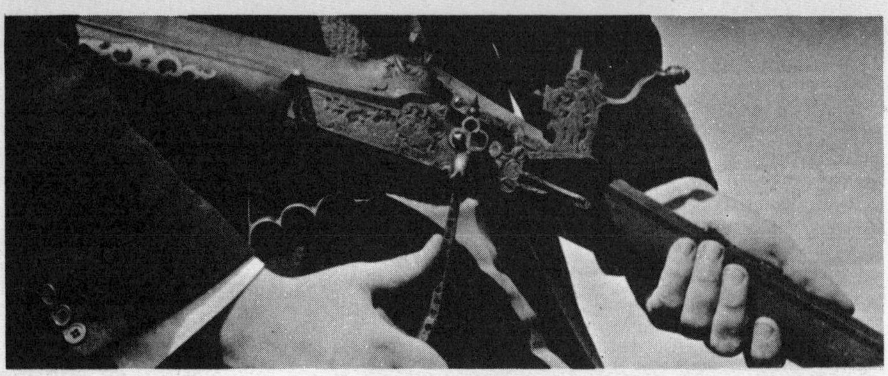

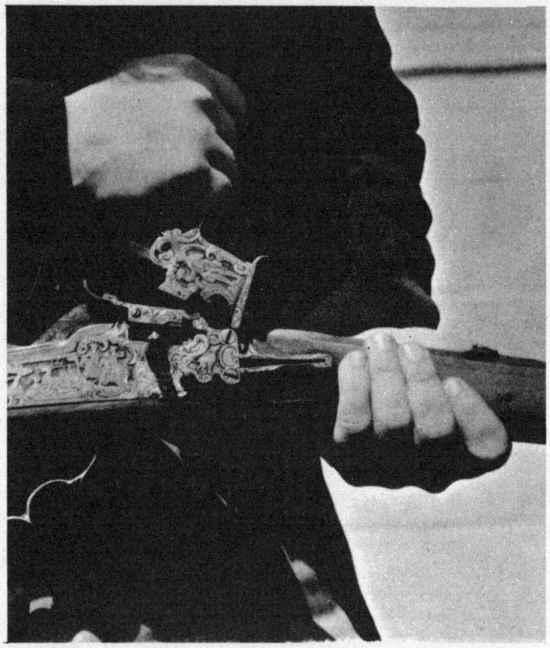

Wheel-lock rifles were superbly reliable and quick-firing, but far too complicated and costly for American conditions. Top picture shows wheel of a German rifle, circa 1725, being wound with spanner prior to priming; middle, shooter swings pyrites-holding doghead down onto the closed cover of the primed flash-pan. Last picture catches dramatic eruption of smoke and fire. German gunmakers must have brought such weapons to Pennsylvania around 1700-1710, but very few have survived in America; most seem to have been abandoned, first in favor of flintlock Jäger rifles of the type shown elsewhere on these pages, then of the slowly-emerging, simple, economical-to-use Pennsylvania rifles.

back to barrels of 36 inches and less. Did the Pennsylvania riflesmiths of the early 1700's know this? Clearly they did, since they had inherited their trade at a time when the efficiency of relatively short barrels had been established for well over a century. It was also perfectly obvious that a very long rifle was (and still is) considerably more clumsy and cumbersome to load, aim and tote about than a very short one of approximately equal weight. Again, then: why did these experienced craftsmen take the weight they had saved by slimming the barrels and add it back in the form of unnecessary length? Simply because the entire 17th- and most of the 18th century shooting world was under the unshakable conviction that (as has been noted earlier) the greater the retardation of the projectile in its path down the tube, the more complete the combustion of the powder and consequently the more forceful the shot. In the iron-ramrod-and-mallet-loaded rifles, the retardation was enormous, consequently such weapons could be made with barrels as short as 26 inches and still satisfy the prevailing theory. In the case of the old patch-loaded bigbores, it was felt that the initial inertia of the large lead spheres was sufficient to create adequate retardation. But when it came to the new smallbore (or at least *smaller*-bore) pieces, it was thought by riflesmith and rifleman alike that the loss of inertia had to be compensated by a longer path down a longer barrel. Hence – and for no better reasons except one, perhaps – the length of our Kentuckys.

Now, the theory rested on error. Combustion was not materially improved, nor velocity materially increased. The efficient, short barrels of smallbore rifles (50 caliber and less) re-discovered in America in the percussion period would have served equally well a hundred years earlier. But mistaken or not, the theory *did* exist and was almost universally believed, and the men of the times acted accordingly – they could hardly have done otherwise. Yet this does not entirely exonerate the middle- and late-period American Kentucky makers, for they persisted in their beliefs long after Europeans had learned that the theory was wrong.

Which brings us to the other reason hinted at above – fashion! Once the belief in long barrels was implanted, however mistakenly, barrels grew in length to ridiculous extremes – just as some fashions in attire became ludicrous in time.

The Kentucky Rifle

Let us now look at the Kentucky rifle in the distinct form it had taken by about 1740. We needn't dwell on the well-known characteristics familiar to all who cherish fine old guns: the use of lovely native woods, chiefly striped maple (occasionally cherry and sometimes, but atypically, walnut and others); the brass furniture; the browned octagonal barrels (sometimes, but chiefly in the early period and even then atypically, one-third octagonal at the breech-end, then round to the muzzle); the extremely beautiful mellowness of the wood finish, the result of patient oil-and-soot treatments; in short, all that lends a good Kentucky rifle its unmistakable identity. And what do we have?

In the first place, a weapon that *looks* extremely graceful and slender, light and elegant, rich in simple dignity – but which was, in fact, unnecessarily long, clumsier than nineteen out of every twenty European rifles, unwieldy to load and carry, nonsensically muzzle-heavy, and (just speaking of design now) woefully inefficient by 18th century European standards ("European" here means primarily German, Swiss and Austrian, since other nations – including the British, who were the world's finest gunmakers after 1750 in terms of superb craftsmanship – were given mostly to smoothbores).

One great failing was that Americans were forever compelled to carry their rifles in one hand – the great length did not permit the use of across-the-back carrying straps (again, a sensible feature reintroduced after about 1835-40). In terms of aesthetics, Kentucky proportions were magnificent; in terms of practical use, they were ridiculous. Now, what about that "master craftsmanship of our forefathers" so often and so jubilantly spoken of (and written about) today? A simple comparison, a bit of effortless research will prove beyond all question (a) that by far the greater number of Kentuckys were very crudely forged and primitively stocked, and (b) that the makers of even the best examples would not have got their apprentice papers had they submitted a sample to the Munich, Geneva or Vienna riflemakers' guilds. Locks, stocks and barrels were made and assembled with a view toward minimally adequate working efficiency; American conditions neither required nor permitted more. The fact is that American riflemakers of the 18th- and early-19th centuries, working with primitive tools under primitive circumstances far removed from the European mainstream of art, science and progress, were *not* particularly skillful and did *not* know very much about good design, execution and performance in the matter of riflery.

Indeed, it is this very characteristic of rugged, unpolished self-reliance that lends Kentuckys their charm and appeal — but to speak of this as the result of "masterful skills" is absurd. A simple, rough-hewn colonial ladder-back pine chair and a hardy cobbler's bench also have their charm and appeal, but they can hardly be classed as examples of fine, or even good, cabinetmaking. The honor and dignity of surviving Kentuckys would be served far better if collectors and many writers referred to naive but distinctly colonial and young-American-style workmanship, rather than wax ecstatic in lavishing superlatives where none are deserving nor were originally called for.

Lock Work

When it comes to locks, the picture grows so dim that even the most ardent partisans of Kentuckys are forced to admit that this was any American long rifle's weakest point. Anyone who thinks that an American-made Kentucky flintlock was good is just not acquainted with good flintlocks. The frontier products were, as a rule, horrible: rough, crude, ill-fitted. A correspondent to a recent issue of a magazine devoted to American muzzle-loading shooting expressed great satisfaction in having got as many as 16 shots before his Kentucky's lock missed fire! Sixteen! We shall be pleased to demonstrate whenever called upon that any good-quality European flintlock can be relied upon to fire 200 times without a miss under reasonably dry conditions, while a top-quality London lock of 1780 and after can reach a thousand and more. Moreover, the lock times (i.e., speed of ignition) among good European locks will run from an imperceptible 3/100ths of a second to a barely perceptible 6/100ths, while most American-made locks discharge their rifles with an easily heard click-hisss-BANG sequence. If a good flintlock is snapped "dry," the thick profusion of sparks should make a clearly audible whirring sound as they dance in the pan; few Kentucky locks will do this. Few Kentucky locks will fire as unfailingly upside-down as right-side-up (a standard test used by European buyers). When it comes to the imported locks found on so many Kentuckys, these are not much better than the frontier-made specimens, for they were the cheapest available, disgorged in great quantities and slip-shod fashion by Birmingham mass-production factories (such as Ketland & Company); like the rifles they were destined to discharge in America. they were minimally adequate — no Bavarian hunter, let alone an English sportsman, would have paid ten pfennigs or a shilling for a dozen of them. (Here it must be noted that naturally there were also poor European locks, stocks and barrels, made for undemanding or impoverished customers — these were so infrequent, though, among hunting rifles, that they cannot be fairly reckoned in a comparative discussion of Kentuckys.)

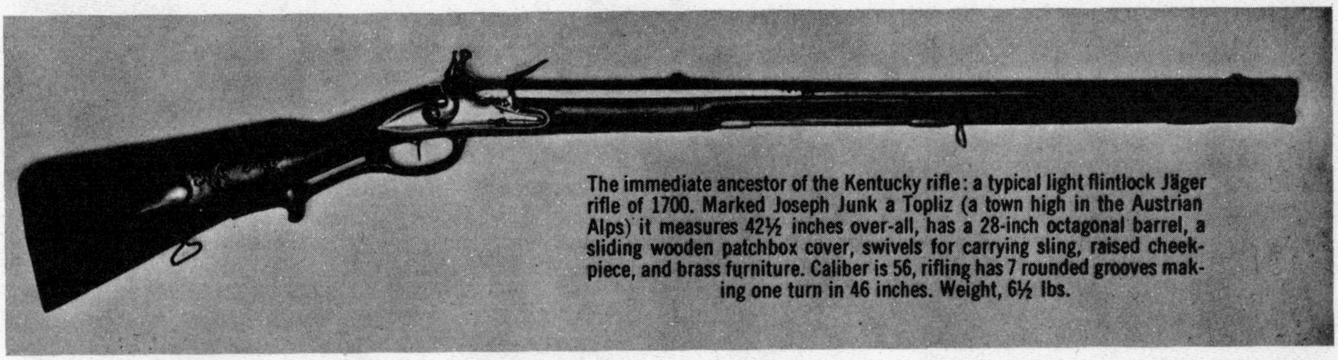

The immediate ancestor of the Kentucky rifle: a typical light flintlock Jäger rifle of 1700. Marked Joseph Junk a Topliz (a town high in the Austrian Alps) it measures 42½ inches over-all, has a 28-inch octagonal barrel, a sliding wooden patchbox cover, swivels for carrying sling, raised cheekpiece, and brass furniture. Caliber is 56, rifling has 7 rounded grooves making one turn in 46 inches. Weight, 6½ lbs.

Ornamentation

Next we come to that feature of Kentucky rifles which is the second-most-widely and wildly exaggerated: their ornamentation. No one familiar with good — not even the best, mind you, just *good* — European rifles of the same period will seriously consider a comparison. So far as the scrollwork or raised carving is concerned (that which is sometimes found around the cheekpieces, wrists and lower ramrod thimbles of early- and middle-period Kentuckys), it should be clear that there is nothing American about it; it is no more than a continuation of the very basic, very conventional ornamentation of virtually every European rifle, even the plainest. It is true that brass patchboxes were an American innovation and often were made with that same primitive attempt at quality craftsmanship that marked the rifles themselves and, in fact, most early American products; but if an apprentice of, say a Nuremberg master brass-worker had produced the rude sawing and scratching characteristic of even the best American patchboxes, he would have had his ears boxed.

The simple brass or German-silver half-moons, stars, fishes, eagles or ovals inlaid to a greater or lesser degree in the stocks of many Kentuckys simply cannot be compared with the ornamentation of most European weapons from lower-medium quality on up. Now, American rifle decorations, in particular some (but not nearly all) patchboxes, *did* have one marvelous characteristic: the unjaded freshness and imaginative vigor of folk-art. The appeal of this is large and warm and lively. Morever, the meticulous, delicate, precise ornamentation of many French, German and English guns had become stereotyped and lifeless by 1750, no matter how well done technically. Thus to speak of Kentucky decoration as "exquisite" or even "beautifully made" is to deny the very spirit that makes it great.

Long Rifle Accuracy

Finally, we come to the most widely and wildly exaggerated Kentucky virtue, one already touched upon: the alleged super-accuracy and super-performance. This reputation rests on three supports: 1) contemporary American sources; 2) modern American accounts; 3) revolutionary-period British military sources. These seem at first most impressive — until one remembers: 1) American backwoods riflemen after about 1740 had no basis for comparison with good European rifles; 2) modern American Kentucky-shooting devotees usually know little or nothing about good European muzzle-loading rifles, do much of their shooting with modern-rebored barrels or even modern precision-rifled liners slipped into reamed-out antique hulls, and for the most part are in any event so prejudiced as to be unapproachable; 3) the British officers who wrote in awed terms of American rifle performance would have written thus about *any* rifle-armed opponent, for rifles were then little-used and little-known in musket-shotgun-and-pistol-conscious Britain, so that the British, too, had no basis for comparison (the so-called "Hessian riflemen" in the British service were, of course, not riflemen at all, but decrepit conscripts sold like cattle and equipped with decrepit, worn-out wrecks of mostly unserviceable rifles*).

Now, it should be obvious to everyone that the only trustworthy sources of information in this matter are those based on extensive experimental comparisons, both antique and modern. When the alleged Kentucky accuracy is

A splendid original flintlock Kentucky rifle (that is, a true Pennsylvania rifle) of circa 1780, and contemporary accoutrements: square and round greased patches, maple-handled hunting knife, bullet mould, two bullets, wooden loading block, two spare flints, small horn for priming powder, large horn (with attached measure) for propellant powder, and corkscrew-like "jag" at end of ramrod for attaching bore-wiping tow or rag. This rifle is still deadly accurate at well beyond 200 yards, has bagged several deer in the hands of its present owner, Mr. Joel Gross of Los Angeles, Calif. Its 50-caliber bore is fairly large by Kentucky standards, but still too small to be of much use to European mountain hunters; its 62-inch over-all length, muzzle-heaviness and lack of carrying sling would have made it unserviceable in Alps and other European mountains.

examined in this light the allegations of fabulous, unerring American rifle shooting are groundless, American frontiersmen shot no better than European riflemen, and the performance of Kentuckys was different from, *but not better than,* their European counterparts. Old records and modern experiments prove, as said earlier, that the difference was primarily one of the shooter's experience and training. It has been shown again and again that, in the hands of an expert marksman (one capable of rather precise distance judgment in 50-yard steps from 50 to 300 yards), European 50- to 65-caliber rifles will shoot as accurately as any Kentucky, yard for yard; they will do so, too, with a much lower rate of misfires and hang-fires, and with an instantaneousness of trigger pull and shot matched by only few Kentuckys.

European hunters were trained for

---

*J. N. George: *English Guns and Rifles* (Plantersville, S. C., 1947).

such distance estimating, which was not necessary — or at least not nearly so critical — in the case of our 35 (19th-century squirrel size) to 48 (mid-18th-century average) weapons. Since Europeans *did*, after all, bring home the game most of the time, it is not unreasonable to conjecture that a Swiss or Austrian rifleman could quite easily have managed to shoot well with a Kentucky had he suddenly found himself plunked down into the middle of Ohio. An American frontiersman on the contrary, would not have been able to do conspicuously well with a Swiss or Austrian rifle without many months of practice.

There appears to be a common impression today that any 18th century American clad in buckskin and moccasins was *ipsco facto* an eagle-eyed, steely-nerved champion marksman; there is, of course, no reason whatever for supposing that such virtuosos should have been more frequent among a random sampling of a thousand frontiersmen than they would be among a similar sampling taken anywhere at any time among men who must rely on rifles for their livelihoods, or who shoot devotedly for target sport.

Thus, in view of the human factor, it must be said that the American long rifles were, in terms of daily usefulness to thousands of ordinary people, the most accurate *long-range, high-velocity small-bore* weapons in the world. But these virtues were purchased at great sacrifice of other desirable rifle qualities. If the smaller bullets flew faster and more nearly straight, they were also subject to much greater deflection by wind and small twigs and branches. so that any discussion of Kentucky accuracy (especially at the vaunted long ranges) must pre-suppose a relatively windless day and a line of sight free of thickets and foliage. Obviously the heavier European spheres stayed more nearly on course in strong breezes and bushy terrain.

Kentucky balls were capable of stopping only thin-skinned game, and to kill efficiently only if they struck direcly into a vital organ. Their impact power beyond 40 or 50 yards was little, and indeed — a fact not often mentioned by Kentucky enthusiasts — among the post-1800 rifles it was *so* slight that Kentuckys were found useless against the grizzlies, bison, moose and elk of the Middle- and Far West. It may be said — in large part correctly — that this was no disadvantage to eastern hunters who required no grizzly-stopping guns; but it is not very often said that the return of westward-moving Americans to relatively short, bigbore rifles after about 1830 was in effect a return to European-principle rifles — a piece of *de facto* evidence that, a hundred years earlier, Kentuckys had not been developed as any improvements upon European rifles, but solely in response to highly specialized needs which prevailed nowhere else.

It is a matter of recorded fact that European riflemakers were thoroughly familiar with Kenuckys — by 1765, German authors* were pointing out the fact that American long rifles would have been more useless in the alps and forests of Central Europe than the European rifles had proved in Pennsylvania and Ohio (and one need not even discuss the usefulness of Kentuckys against tigers and other big game in British India and in Africa).

Kentuckys in Perspective

What, then, is left of American long rifles? What is the true perspective in which a reasonable arms lover must, or should, regard them? Well, first and above all, as a weapon designed so specifically for, and so specifically under, American wilderness - taming conditions that it is as close to a national historical implement-emblem as we shall ever have. One thoughtful writer has said that the long rifle is to America what the quadrant and marine chronometer are to Great Britain (British seafaring instruments were, however, of unequalled excellence on an *absolute* basis, which is not true of American rifles). No reasonable man can deny that for all their shortcomings, Kentuckys did, after all, perform their specialized functions in their unique environs so well that the seemingly unconquerable continent *was* achieved — and very handsomely at that. Our long rifles must be accorded the very highest honors in any appraisal of folk-art and folk-craft. They are uniquely American; they fairly exude the real and legendary spirit of the frontiers of colonial and early-republican America; they are mellow and lovely, they deserve painstaking care by modern collectors and perpetual enshrinement in the American heritage. They did their job right properly, never mind how much better it might have been done had Americans been supplied by workmen like Freund, Egg, Pitout, Svoboda *et al.*

Seen in this light, the greatly superior mechanical construction, ballistic efficiency and elaborate ornamentation of Old World rifles no longer militate to the Kentucky's detraction. If all these considerations are soberly evaluated, the native weapons emerge as things of inordinate merit and pride.

*Chris Beutel: *Das Buchenschiessen . . . und Praktisch Betrachet* (Munich, 1765).

German engraving of 1740 shows rugged Alpine hunting terrain which made it absolutely essential that rifles not only be reasonably short and fitted with carrying slings, but that they fire large bullets which would lame by sheer impact an animal on a distant ledge. Long, unwieldy, sling-less small-bore Kentuckys would have been unserviceable under such conditions.

HOW CHOKE WORKS

by ARVID B. PEDERSEN

This is simple, so simple it deceives: you have never read it before.

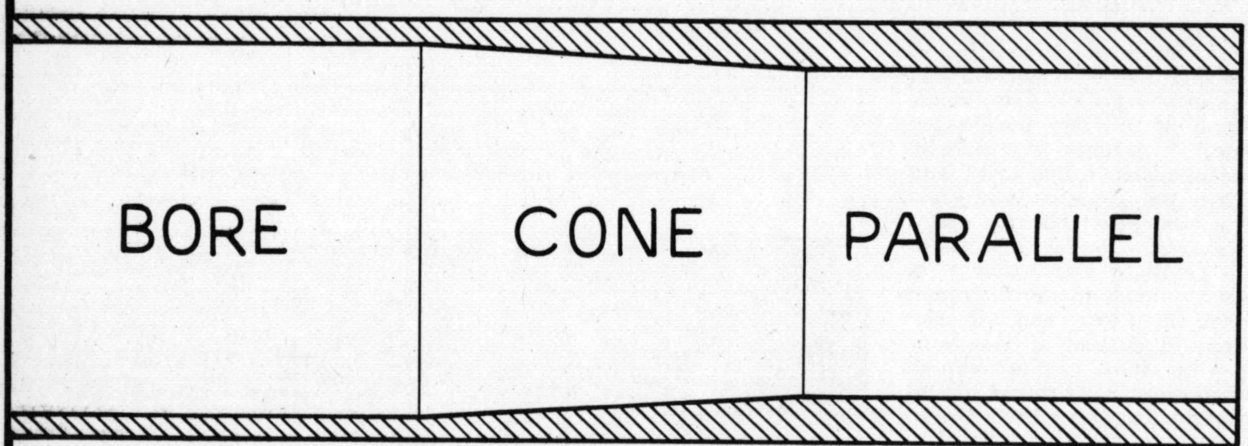

Typical choke design. Schematic.

THE ART OF shooting by virtue of a multiple pellet charge may not have been long established before ever-complaining mankind noticed the reduced range when compared to the single bullet. Now the ideal became the shot barrel delivering its charge most bullet-like, and every possible—and impossible—way of boring was tried out for the purpose.

Late in the 18th century there appear to have been a few individual successes in increasing the range of shotgunning by some sort of choke, but choke boring as a regular feature did not evolve until 100 years later with W. W. Greener in the center of the final development. After him, only minor deviations have appeared and, in fact, no definite improvement can be claimed.

How the choke actually managed to control the pellets remained obscure. It was accepted without much reasoning that constriction of the muzzle meant constriction of the flow of pellets all the way, as it is even today. At the end of the 19th century, however, when the great French authority General Journée advanced into the problems of shotgunning, he was just not the man to relax on practical proof of choke function.

The Journée Theory

After circling the problem theoretically and by numerous experiments, he ventured a conclusion shown in our drawing, which is faithfully redrawn from his celebrated treatise *"Tir des fusils de chasse."*

His accompanying text is not very

specific, but apparently he attributes the concentrating effect to the inward-acting impulses on the pellets striking the sloping wall of the choke cone. The force directs the pellets toward the axis of the bore, and this concentrating effect is supposed to remain effective at shooting range. He himself acknowledged that the drawing was schematic to a degree making it misleading, and doubt probably made him refrain from a detailed verbal description.

Despite this vagueness but on the weight of his authority, the Journée theory has greatly influenced later views on choke function. Even in our day the spell of the old Frenchman is still unmistakeable. And a spell it must be, as the weaknesses of the concept are grave indeed.

deflecting forces. He also states that the dispersal shown in his drawing was grossly exaggerated, and from an adjacent simplified calculation estimates pellet layers to be separated little more than .01″ ($1/_{100}$th-inch) when the column has just passed the choke's cone. This separation, however, does not provide the free lateral movement essential to the theory. Thus, if his calculation holds, the principle expressed in his drawing does not.

Now, the probability of pellets jumping during the choke passage may be settled by calculations of unquestionable validity. Let us consider a modest jump carrying a No. 7 pellet half a diameter ahead during the time when the column itself has moved one pellet diameter. The reality of this jump is that our froggy pellet must gain 50% in velocity and more than double its kinetic energy in about six millionths of a second! The achievement requires an accelerating force on this single pellet amounting to 900 pounds.

The example shows the futility of thinking in "sudden jumps" when the pellets are already travelling at 1300 fps. Even the front pellets are not all moving freely in that sense, and they are much more readily deformed than separated noticeably from the column. Without jumping pellets, there can be no free lateral movement.

Furthermore, the Journée theory has no role for the parallel. Only the cone is acting and directing the pellets. Yet, numerous experiments had already proved that the parallel did a job in concentrating the pattern. If the charge was directed only by the cone, a distorted pattern should be expected if the parallel was set askew, making the charge rub onesidedly against its wall. Journée had himself tested eccentrically bored choke barrels made by M. Breuil, a barrelmaker of St. Etienne, and he found no abnormality of pattern, even when the displacement made one side of the parallel flush with the bore.

Both the acknowledgement of the shot column to be fairly compact following the choke passage and the performance of the eccentric choke points to the charge being guided by the parallel and not by the cone. We have to leave the Journée concept behind as a gallant try, but indeed a blind alley.

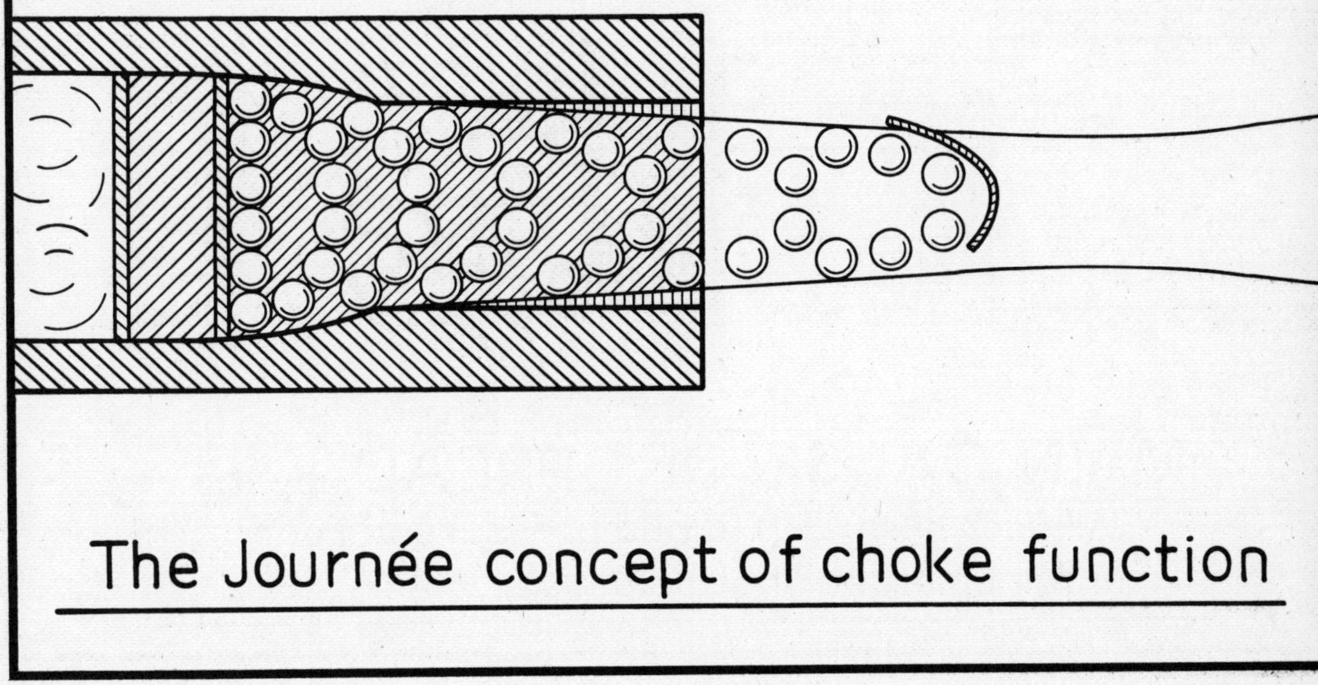

The Journée concept of choke function

Failure of the Journée Theory

To respond to the inward-acting force, the pellets need freedom of movement laterally, otherwise, the radial forces acting from all sides on a compact shot column would largely cancel each other, and no general movement toward the pattern center could prevail.

Journée implies the central pellets in the squeezed column jump ahead creating freedom of movement allowing the outer pellets to respond to the

Starting Afresh

While Journée authority decidedly has been a block on the road to a workable choke theory, another obstacle has been the general approach to the problem. We ask quite naturally why the choke works, as that is our question to be answered, but this is in

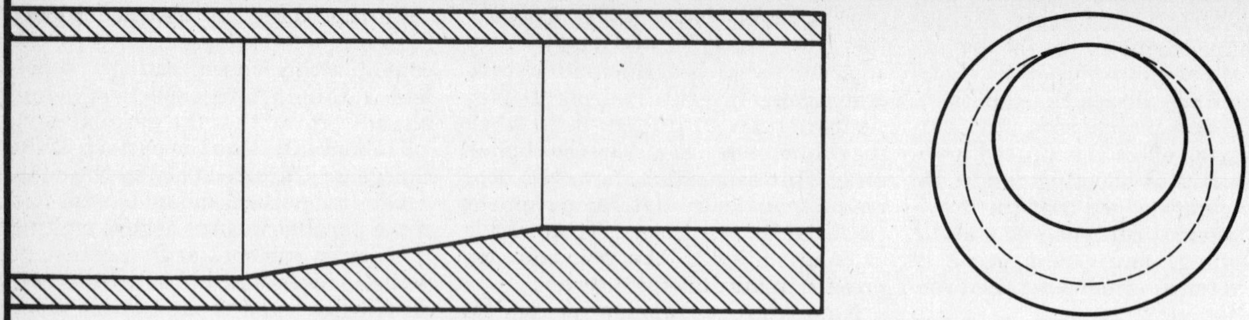

ECCENTRIC CHOKE
Pattern performance equals that of similar concentric choke

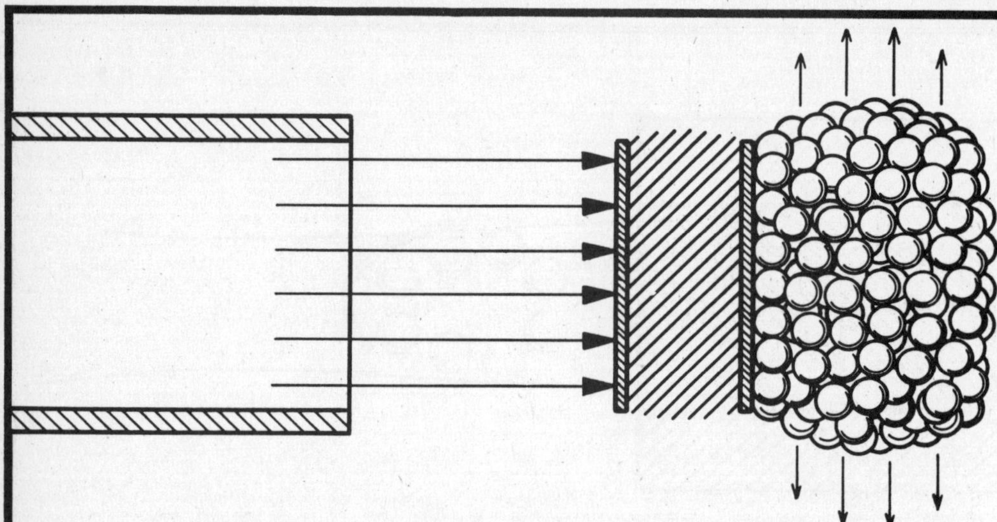

MAIN CAUSE OF SPREAD by the cylinder bore: Sustained pressure at rear of the emerged shot column.

fact a bad start almost bound to lead us astray. It makes us look for "inward-acting impulses," and in the end we cannot much better Journée.

The key to success is to recognize that our ignorance does not start at the choke. Let us forget for the moment why the choke provides a dense pattern and ask why the cylinder throws an open one. Why does the shot charge not just travel along in the neat column formed by the cylindric barrel?

Or: Why does the shot charge spread?

When we inspect the pattern from a cylinder-bored barrel, spread may be related to the following causes:

1. The emerged shot column is not stable to the pressure still acting at the rear. A push starting at more than 200 pounds results in a collapse and the pellets start moving outward, bulging the column to disc shape. Once such a radial velocity component has been imparted, the pellet formation is bound to open up along the route.
2. Pellet deformation may cause erratic flight.
3. Differing air resistance due to differences in size and sphericity make some pellets fly faster than others. Collisions between the faster and the slower moving pellets may cause diversions.
4. Pellet spin may alter the course.
5. The blast from the outstreaming powder gases behind the charge may create an outward suction, when they are diverted around the charge at a much higher

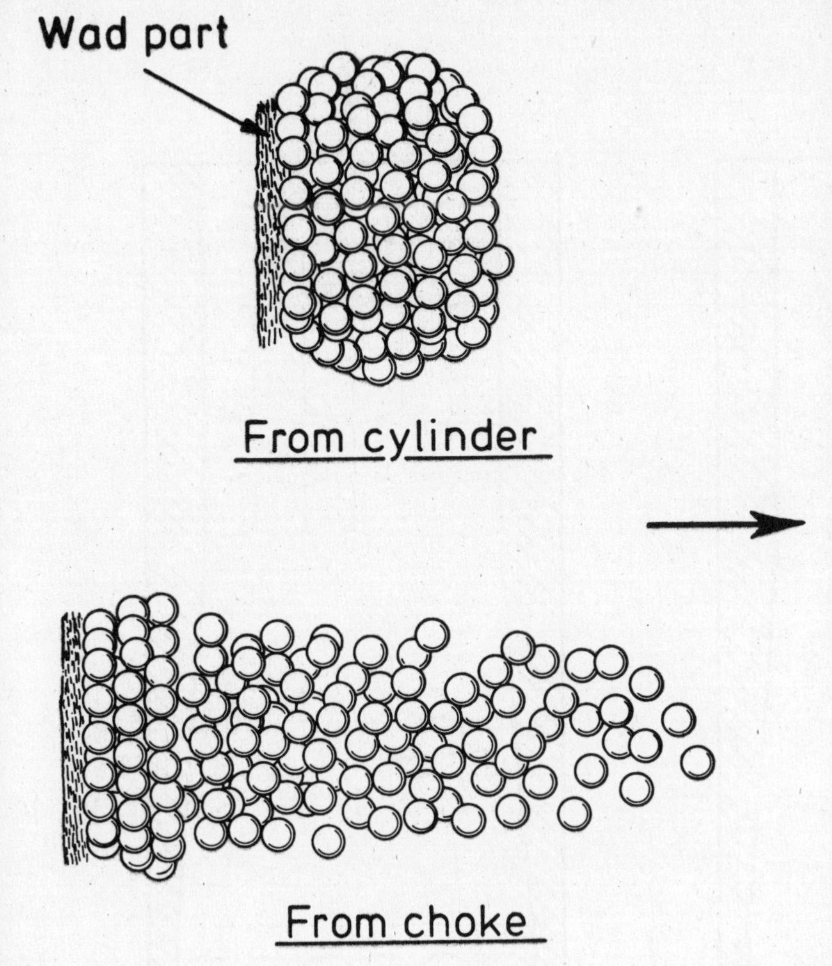

Shape of shot charge 24" from muzzle

speed than the charge itself.

6. Air resistance may force the pellets at the rim at the front of the column outwards.
7. If a top wad is present, it causes some spread when colliding with pellets taking over the lead.

That looks rather confusing but more consideration shortens the list. Calculations indicate Numbers 3, 4, 5 and 6 to be of minor importance, and Number 7 is eliminated entirely in modern crimped cartridges.

That leaves us with Numbers 1 and 2. Number 2 is of some consequence, as we know "fliers" form the outskirt of the pattern, and deliberately deformed pellets are utilized in scatter loads. But we may say for certain that deformation as a cause of spread is a secondary factor in the performance of ordinary loads. This is proved by the denser pattern thrown by the choke, even though the choke definitely adds to pellet deformity.

So, we end at the simple conclusion—the spread of the shot charge is principally caused by the pressure still exerted on the column following its emergence from the muzzle.

And this is the indispensable ballast allowing us to proceed to the main theme:

What Happens In the Choke?

An obvious result of constricting the muzzle is the stretching of the shot column to accommodate the volume in the smaller section of the parallel. In practice, a full choke constriction may demand a $\frac{1}{10}$th inch (.1") elongation of the column. Then, the foremost pellets have gained the $\frac{1}{10}$th inch (.1") over the rearmost pellets during the choke passage.

This may look insignificant until it is realized that the transition has taken place in $\frac{1}{10,000}$ of a second. The $\frac{1}{10}$th inch (.1") change of position in this short time equals a difference in velocity of roundly 80 feet per second. So, following the choke passage, the front pellets must travel at 80 fps higher speed than the rearmost pellets to form the new elongated column.

Now, over the assumed 1½" length of the choke passage, the remaining barrel pressure is adding little to the speed of the charge. A 1½" difference in barrel length means a difference in muzzle velocity of approximately 10 fps only, and furthermore the turmoil in the choke absorbs a substantial amount of energy. Journée states a 1% loss in muzzle energy from this cause.

So, the differing velocities in the column are obtained by transfer of kinetic energy from the rear to the front of the column. In other words, the rear part of the column forces the front part to a higher speed through the constriction and is itself retarded in the process. Journée experimented with abnormally heavy chokes, where the rear part of the charge stuck in the choke as a solid mass, while the front part emerged at 1300 fps.

Likewise the indefatigable Journée fired solid cylindrical lead bullets in heavily choked barrels and found them likely to separate due to the difference in speed attained by the front and the rear part during the choke passage. In the normal full choke we may expect a grading of the total velocity spread of 80 fps from plus-40 fps in front of the column to minus-40 fps at rear, while the speed remains constant at the center.

When we pursue the progressing velocity differentiation during the choke passage more carefully by calculation, we find a surplus acceleration in the cone causing higher velocities than necessary to accommodate

THE O & T PROBLEM —
Role of friction in cone

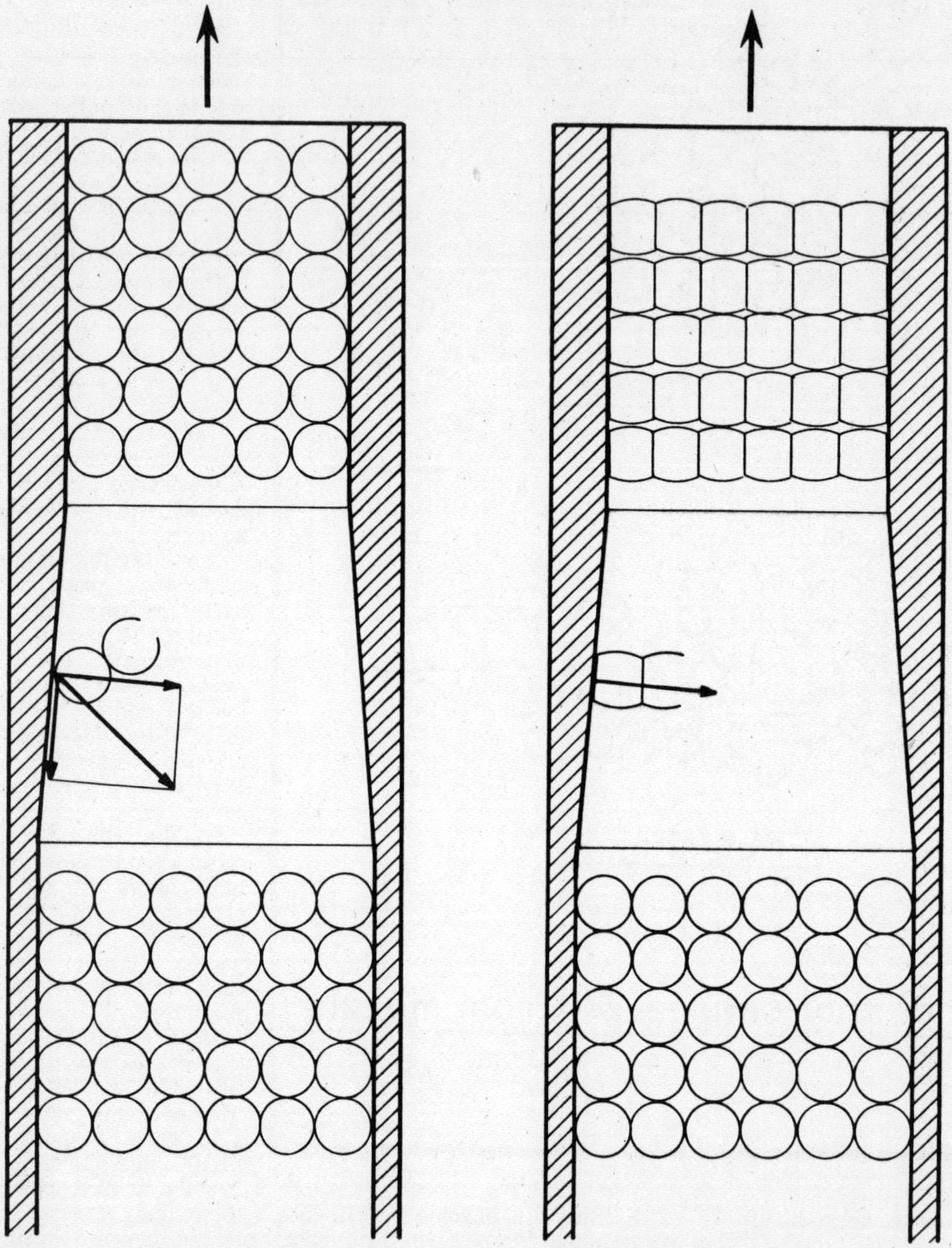

Left: Friction breaks up original column, thereby helping in restacking a new elongated column implying the velocity differentiation basic to choke-effect.

Right: In the absence of friction the charge may adjust to the smaller section of the Parallel by deformation of the pellets, and velocity remains uniform throughout the charge. Then the barrel does perform almost like a cylinder bore but spreading even more due to pellet deformation.

In reality both restacking and deformation may be expected at a balance determined by the amount of friction.

the charge in the parallel. The result is a separation of the column lengthwise. Each layer of pellets is disconnected at the entrance to the parallel and, although the separation is very slight, this allows the differing velocities that are to disperse the column lengthwise still more throughout its flight.

When the complete shot charge has passed into the parallel, the calculated separation between adjacent pellet layers is approximately .004". That is not much, but the column is in fact disconnected, and we may realize our main cause of spread to be eliminated. Pressure acting through the wad just outside the muzzle cannot affect the longer unconnected column as it can the compact one from the cylinder bore. Only a few pellet layers are caught by the wad due to last-stage acceleration by the gas pressure in the parallel and just outside the muzzle, and they form a shorter and more stable column. Also, the spread from the Number 3 and 6 causes in our list is reduced, though they are of little consequence.

So: **the paramount feature of the choke is the disconnection of the shot column relieving the emerged charge of the spreading influence from the gas pressure.** The degree of choke determines the length of the compact rear part comprising the layers caught by the wad at the last stage of acceleration. The longer the compact part, the less stability and the more bulging and spread.

The theory here described accords perfectly with electronic flash photographs showing emerged shot charges. The collapsing column from the cylinder bore expands to form a discoid, while the longitudinally dispersed column from the choke is unaffected by pressure from behind improving the chance of the pellets to end in the pattern center.

Role of the Parallel

Contrary to the Journée theory, we have no use for lasting radial movements of the pellets. They are most likely to give spread. And while the radial forces from the cone wall are largely balancing each other when acting on the near-compact column, the symmetry is not perfect as this would imply a non-existing perfectly symmetrical stack of pellets. Some unbalance and tendency to "turbulence" must be expected. The disturbance shall live to give spread unless it is suppressed in the parallel, and the "laminar" flow is restored. But as the wad is catching up in the parallel due to continued accelerating gas pressure, the choke effect is suffering, and a happy compromise in length of the parallel must be chosen.

Choke Designation

To specify a choke by stating the amount of constriction is not satisfactory as the choke effect is dependent on the length of the cone as well.

The deciding figure is theoretically **the rate of relative change in the sectional area of the bore.**

This quantity could be represented by a figure reasonably nominated as "Choke Power."

$$\text{Choke Power} = \frac{1 - (D_2/D_1)^2}{L}$$

L is length of cone, and D_1 and D_2 are the diameters of bore and parallel respectively.

Choke Power should enable us to compare choke-effect of different bores at different lengths of cones, but there is still a factor which in some cases may obscure Choke Power as a reliable measure of choke-effect:

The Stacking Problem

The process of column elongation demands a restacking of the pellets and we cannot expect a very short cone to behave like the more common lengths during the transition. Furthermore, the problem of stacking efficiency enters.

In the densest stack, spheres occupy $^{74}/_{100}$ths of the volume. This is not realizable in a bore, and if the perfect stack represents 100% stacking efficiency, we may as example find a stacking efficiency in the bore of 85%. The stacking efficiency is obviously dependent on the relation between pellet diameter and bore diameter. The smaller the bore, relatively, the less is the chance of arranging the pellets in a near-perfect stack.

But the stacking efficiency is not continuously dependent on the bore-diameter relation. It is a matter of *fit*, too. If the pellets are stacking more efficiently in the parallel than in the bore, then the column does not elongate to the degree expected from the Choke Power figure, and choke-effect is reduced, perhaps even to the verge of disappearance. On the other hand a slight choke that happens to reduce the stacking efficiency materially may result in a denser pattern than expected.

Role of Friction in the Cone

A fine surface finish of the cone wall has been observed by Oberfell and Thompson to detract from choke-effect, as related in their book *The Mysteries Of Shotgun Patterns*. Likewise, it has been the experience, especially in trapshooting, that the first shot from an oily barrel made a more open pattern. These phenomena are easily explained by the present theory.

Imagine a column of men marching in ranks along a road narrowing into an entrance, under orders to keep the formation as far as possible. The entrance hardly accommodates the original width of the column but as the gateway is flanked by smooth marble walls, the ranks are kept, though somewhat jammed, and no elongation of the column takes place! But if the flanking walls are rough and do not allow the men on the outside to slide along? Then friction forces them back, breaking up the formation, reforming it into a longer column.

And so with pellets. The purely radial forces from the friction-free cone wall are just deforming the pellets and not breaking up the layers. The result is a much reduced column elongation and choke-effect. Moreover, the deformation is a source of spread in itself.

(Here at last is a practical gain from the lesson: If you are shooting an open bore, there is no need to remove a reasonable oil protection from the barrels before shooting. There will be no practical difference in pattern of the first and succeeding shots, and frequently I have observed a higher quality pattern from the oily bore. And the oil protects as long as it stays.)

Epilogue

While the idea of the choke not acting directly was revolutionary to me when it first grew out of the considerations, it was not new to mankind. Credit should be given to W. Borland of the British EC Powder Company, whose analysis of early spark photographs was published in "The Field" in 1908. Unfortunately, his work attracted little attention, though he was quoted by W. W. Greener in the 1910 edition of *The Gun and its Development*. Borland acknowledged the function of the choke as a prevention of spread due to delaying the wad. Unlike Journée, he did not grasp the delaying mechanism, and attributed the delay to friction.

If these two good men had joined their efforts, they could hardly have failed in settling the matter well over 70 years ago. ●

THE M16A2: New World Standard For Infantry Rifles . . .

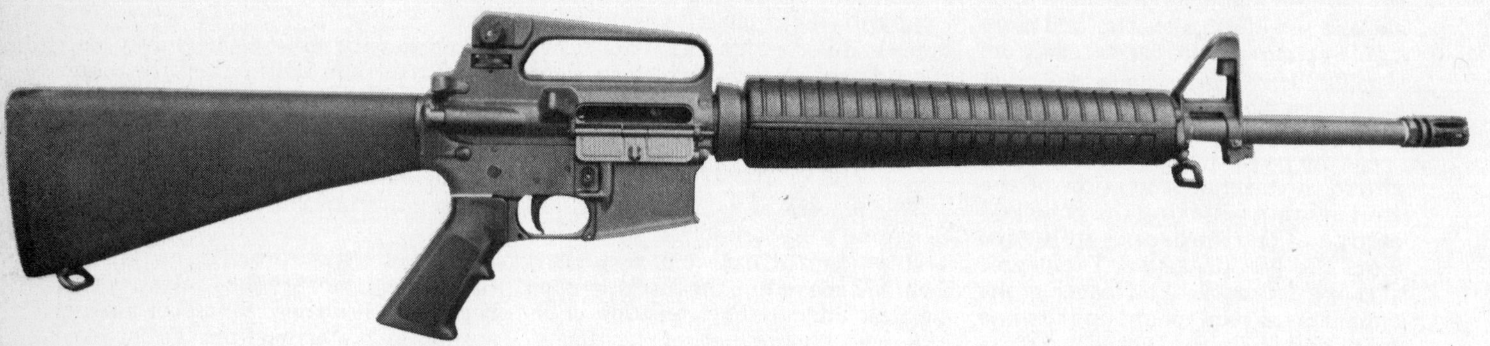

. . . out-penetrates the M1 rifle shooting M2 ball at 800 yards.

THE M16A2 is the new standard to which past and future military rifles will be compared. This second-generation 5.56mm rifle is the product of cooperation between industry and U.S. forces to develop, test and field a product-improved rifle which should meet their needs to the end of this century. The M16A2, standardized in November, 1983, is a wonderful example of how the military development and procurement system is *supposed* to work. The efficiency with which this work proceeded from concept to production and fielding is a tribute to military-industrial cooperation.

When the M16A1 rifle was first adopted by U.S. troops in 1967, the Marines were the most vocal opponent of a "small caliber" rifle. At that time there were valid complaints about the reliability of the M16 and its M193 ammunition and its range and lethality. Although changes in the rifle and ammunition corrected the functional problems, by 1970 it was apparent the sights and the ballistics of the 55-gr. M193 cartridge reached their limits in combat at

M16A2 barrel marking gives caliber and twist as "1/7."

by C.E. HARRIS

The AK74 5.45mm cartridge and the AK47 7.62mm cartridge—the competitors—are shown to the left of the 5.56mm NATO M855 cartridge, our new standard.

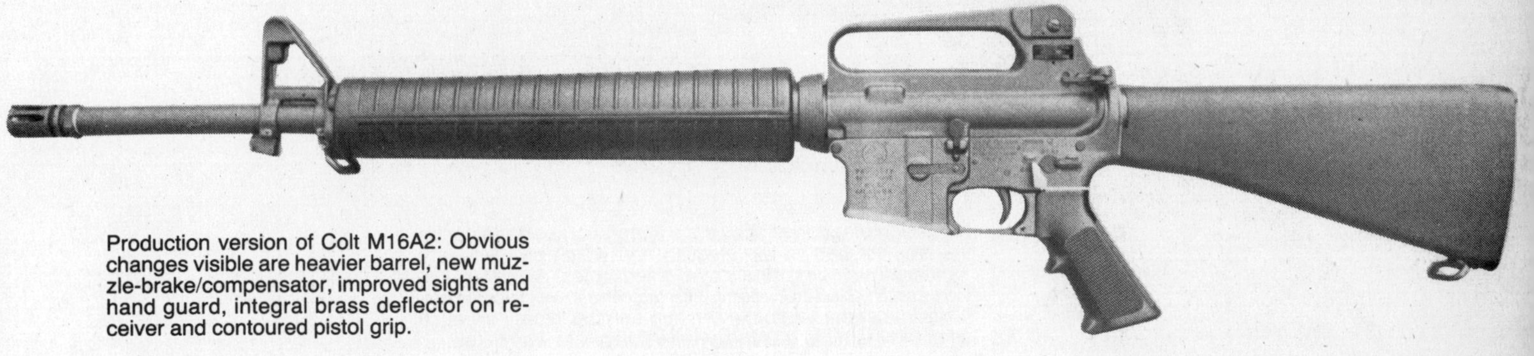

Production version of Colt M16A2: Obvious changes visible are heavier barrel, new muzzle-brake/compensator, improved sights and hand guard, integral brass deflector on receiver and contoured pistol grip.

about 500 yards. To many critics, even 500 yards pushed credibility.

Adopting the 5.56mm NATO SS109/M855 cartridge in 1977 brought ammunition effective to well beyond 600 yards in lethality and accuracy and penetration. Standardization of this NATO cartridge brought a need to adapt the M16 rifle to it, and provided the opportunity to correct the known tactical deficiencies in the M16A1. The USMC Firepower Division, at Quantico, VA, was tasked with this development in cooperation with Colt Industries, under supervision of the Joint Services Small Arms Program (JSSAP).

The product-improved rifle was identified as M16A1E1 during operational testing which preceded formal type classification. Operational testing of 30 M16A1E1 rifles served to evaluate the changes and provide input for further refinements which would be incorporated in the production version of the M16A2. The Modified Operation Test (MOT) began on November 23, 1981, and was completed on December 11, 1981. Supplemental tests continued through August, 1982, to confirm the validity of some proposed improvements and to confirm their production feasibility.

The M16A2 is now in full production, having been adopted by the U.S. Marines to replace their entire complement of M16A1 rifles within the next five years. The Army has also decided to adopt the M16A2. The Canadians are also adopting it, but without the new sights or burst control, as the C7.

The test findings summarized in the MOT Final Report conclude the M16A2 performs as well or better than the M16A1 in all areas. The advantages of the M16A2 over the M16A1 are listed below:

- *Increased effectiveness*: higher hit probability, greater lethality and penetration, improved range through use of NATO standard SS109/M855 ammunition.
- *Better durability and handling* with improved, stronger handguard, and buttstock, longer buttstock, new buttcap, contoured pistol grip.
- *Reduced barrel jump and muzzle climb* during full automatic or sustained semi-automatic fire with new muzzle-brake-compensator.
- *Reduced dust signature* as well when fired over sandy or dusty ground.
- *Heavier, stronger barrel*, to resist bending, with 7-inch twist to exploit advantages of new NATO ammunition.
- *Better sights*: improved contrast and less glare with square post front sight, faster target acquisition of moving targets, better detection of targets in low light, and improved accuracy at long range by use of two optimized rear sight apertures.
- *Better fire control* and more effective use of ammunition with 3-shot burst option.

Operational firepower effectiveness was evaluated by comparing the M16A1 and M16A2 in tactical scenarios. These included base of fire, assault and counterattack, ambush, long range and mid-range defensive fires, final protective fires, defense against ambush, area target suppression, and night firing.

Right side of receiver shows the integral brass deflector on the receiver behind the ejection port which prevents left-handers from being struck by ejected cases. Aluminum device sandwiched between pistol grip and lower receiver inhibits inadvertent automatic in non-combat situations, such as marksmanship training, where this photo was taken.

There was no appreciable difference in base of fire effectiveness between the M16A1 and M16A2, but in the assault and counterattack, test results from the Small Arms Remoted Target System (SARTS) showed the A2 obtained a significantly greater percentage of hits in burst fire. When fired semi-automatic on the field range and Infantry Tactical Training (ITT) course simulations, no significant difference was noted. In the ambush scenario, using high volume semi-automatic fire no appreciable difference was noted. Firing in the burst mode at night the data were inconclusive, but when the same course of fire was fired in daylight on the area target suppression test, the A2 delivered 7 percent more hits at 100 meters than did the M16A1.

When firing in the burst mode at multiple targets at 100 meters the A2 gave a significantly higher number of hits, but at 50 meters this difference was not apparent. All persons firing the M16A1 used for comparison were firing short bursts of 2 or 3 rounds, which may or may not be what would happen in the high stress of actual combat. In the simulation of a patrol being ambushed, requiring quick reaction, immediate action and firing in bursts or automatic fire, the A2 obtained 19 percent hits, compared to only 12 percent for the M16A1.

The A2's increased ruggedness was evaluated through user assessments and inspection of rifles for damage after an exercise in which several squads conducted an operation clearing seven buildings in "combat town." Rifles were used as steps and to gain access to second stories of buildings. Each participant attacked a rubber dummy stabilized by ropes, executing the vertical butt stroke, smash, parry and horizontal butt stroke, in the same sequence with each weapon. Participants also fixed bayonets and attacked a simulated enemy, bayonetting and slashing it twice. The handguards of the A2 were more durable and appeared to offer better control in close combat, and for urban or built-up area operations.

Portability of each weapon was compared for tactical and non-tactical methods of carry, including the manual of arms while marching. Test par-

The contoured pistol grip is intended to provide more secure grasping; backstrap is deeply grooved, and frontstrap has deep finger groove to provide secure hold. Selector lever offers choice of semi-auto or 3-shot bursts. Rear sight has minute of angle clicks for windage and elevation, matched to M855 or SS109 ammunition.

ticipants marched to and from the range with both weapons, and carried them through the combat town course, day movement course and other subtests which included a forced march. User comments indicated no preference for carrying either the M16A1 or A2.

Vulnerability of the weapons to detection and countermeasures were assessed by comparing the noise generated when being carried, and while being operated, as well as the muzzle flash and/or dust signature produced when each weapon fired in day or night conditions. Photographic presentations of the muzzle flash or dust produced were obtained to provide an accurate assessment. Personnel in the butts also answered questionnaires assessing their ability to identify which weapons were being fired based on sounds heard in the butts.

Conclusions indicated no difference in the amount of noise generated by either weapon when being carried or operated. No difference was indicated in muzzle flash in day or night conditions. No significant dust signature was noted due to cold weather conditions, although when firing over new snow less disturbance was noted under the muzzles of the A2s. No essential difference in shape that could be used as a characteristic to identify units can be noted at any distance without the aid of binoculars or a telescope. Personnel in the butts could distinguish which ammunition was being fired at ranges beyond 600 meters, because the NATO SS109 and M855 ammunition remains supersonic to a far greater range, producing a distinct crack as it passes overhead, whereas the 55-grain M193 bullet goes subsonic shortly beyond 600 meters, producing only a muffled pop.

A limited test compared the M16A1 and the new A2 as to any interference generated while carrying the weapons caused by changes in center of gravity, or methods of carry when engaged in airborne, amphibious or helicopter operations. Participants carried both rifles in operation scenarios wearing full combat gear. There was no meaningful difference between weapons regarding their compatibility or suitability while entering or exiting landing craft, vehicles or air-

M16A2 front sight is square in cross-section with parallel sides to provide a more distinct sight picture. After first zero adjustment, rear sight offers all adjustments normally required.

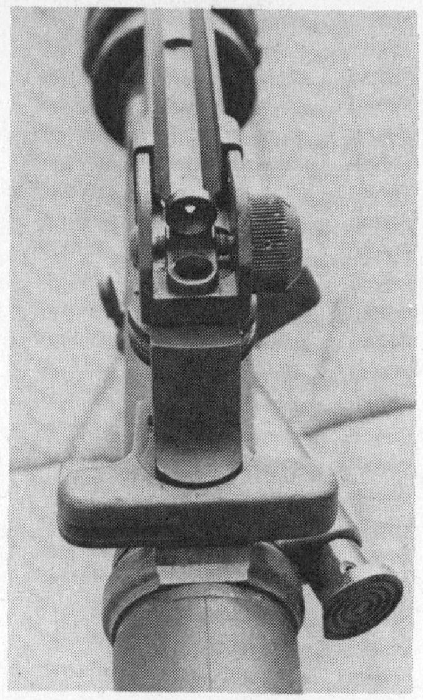

The small aperture leg is used for precision daylight fire at ranges beyond 200 meters. The large aperture is used for snap shooting at ranges less than 200 meters and for low light level use near dawn or dusk. Elevation drum moves sight in minute of angle clicks.

Table I

Accuracy Comparison of M16A2 vs. AK-74

Weapon/Ammunition	Range (yds.)				
M16A2 with 55-gr. M193	100	300	600	800	1000
Mean Radius (ins.)	1.87	4.18	13.2	18.3	no hits
Extreme Spread (ins.)	5.25	13.4	31.4	46.5	no hits
Hits On "E" Silhouette 39" high x 19" wide	20x20	20x20	11x20	10x20	no hits
Score on NRA decimal target SR and MR	99-6X	93-1X	81-1X	79	no hits
M16A2 with M855/SS109					
Mean Radius (ins.)	1.95	5.22	10.98	11.78	15.95
Extreme Spread (ins.)	5.5	15.75	32.75	43.0	73.9
Hits on "E" Silhouette	20x20	20x20	15x20	12x20	6x10
Score on NRA decimal target SR and MR	99-5X	90-1X	91-2X	82-1X	79-1X
AK-74 with 5.45 mm PS					
Mean Radius (ins.)	1.87	8.47	15.9	20.3	no hits
Extreme Spread (ins.)	7.25	21.6	44.0	74.5	no hits
Hits on "E" Silhouette	20x20	17x20	9x20	7x20	no hits
Score on NRA decimal target SR and MR	99-6X	79-0X	69-0X	57	no hits

craft.

The human factors evaluation, or "man-machine interface" characteristics of the two rifles were compared as they might affect operating safety (including hot or sharp parts), useability and adjustability of sights and controls in terms of speed, accessibility, and accuracy of adjustment; and recoil, as it affects recovery time, in burst fire or sustained rapid semiautomatic fire, accuracy in precision fire, comfort and confidence. The effects of the redesigned handguard and buttstock were also evaluated as they affected accuracy, control in automatic fire and hand to hand combat.

Test participants preferred the sights on the M16A2 to those on the M16A1 because they were easier to adjust and provided a greater range of adjustment, which effectively doubles the useful engagement range of this rifle with SS109/M855-type ammunition compared to the M16A1 with M193-type ammunition. The sights on the A2 are safer to adjust when the weapon is loaded than those on the M16A1, because the front sight is not used for routine sight changes. Ranging adjustments are made on the elevation dial of the rear sight after the front sight is initially adjusted to obtain a battlesight zero. Refinements were made in the size of the front sight post and rear sight apertures based on these tests to optimize precision of fire in daylight conditions, and target acquisition for close range snap shooting and firing in morning or evening nautical twilight conditions.

The M16A2 production sight is adjustable from 300 to 800 meters and has indexing marks on the dial and receiver which align when the sight is turned all the way down or within one click. The 300- and 800-meter settings are co-located on the same position, marked with an indexing line on the top of the dial. Remaining ranges are marked on the dial in 100m increments: i.e., 4, 5, 6, 7. Range markings on the elevation dial align with the following detents 8/3 (800/300 meters) at 0 or 25th click, 4 - 3rd click, 5 - 7th click, 6 - 12th click, 7 - 18th click. The short range rear sight aperture is used for ranges up to 200m, has an outside diameter of .375-in. and an inside diameter of .20-in. It is marked "0-2" at the base and has a windage reference point at the top which is used for precision fire with the long range aperture.

The long range aperture is used for firing beyond 200m and has an outside diameter of .375-in. with an inside diameter of .070-in. It is marked "3-8" at the base. The rear faces of both sight apertures are concave and heavily phosphated to reduce glare. One quarter-revolution (one movement/detent) of the front sight moves point of impact approximately 1.4 moa, one click of the elevation dial on the rear sight moves point of impact approximately 1 moa, and one click of the windage knob on the rear sight moves point of impact approximately ½ moa. Firing tests indicate that point of impact is not significantly different with M193 or SS109/M855 ammunition when using the same sight settings at ranges less than 500 meters.

Accuracy and penetration of the M16A1 with M193, the A2 with M193 and SS109/M855 and the Soviet AK-74 with 5.45mm Type PS ammunition were compared at ranges from 100 to 900 meters. The Soviet AK-74 was found to be reliable and accurate at short ranges, but its sights were a limiting factor beyond about 200 meters—it has a short sighting radius, open rear notch sight and no windage adjustments. The M193 ammunition was found most accurate at ranges less than 300 meters, but the SS109 most accurate at ranges beyond 500 meters. The most accurate rifle overall was the M16A2 with SS109 ammunition; the next most accurate was the M16A2 with M193, followed by the M16A1 with M193 and finally the AK-74 with Type PS ammunition. Accuracy results for the various weapons and types of ammunition tested are summarized in the accompanying tables.

In penetration tests the M16A1 rifle with M193 ammunition, the M16A2 with SS109, M855, M193 and Olin Penetrator (commercial approximation of the SS109), and the AK-74 with Type PS ammunition were fired against 3.5mm thick mild steel plates at various ranges. In addition, the 7.62mm M40A1 Remington sniper rifle with M118 Special Ball (Match, 175-2.0 gr. bullet at 2575 fps) and M80 standard Ball (148.0-2.0 bullet at 2750 fps) were fired for comparison. Maximum ranges at which penetrations of the test plate occurred were 500 yards for the M193, 600 for the AK-74 and 7.62mm M80, and 800 for the 7.62mm M118, 5.56mm SS109, M855 and Olin Penetrator. Results are summarized in an accompanying table.

The question of lethality and effectiveness of the M193 cartridge fired from the fast twist rifling in the M16A2 was of concern because existing stocks of M193 ammunition will

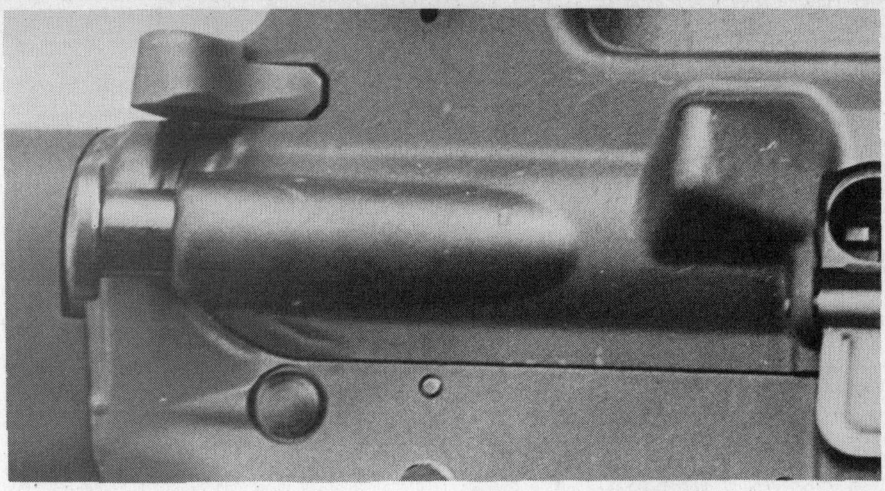

Familiar M16A1 features such as take-down mechanism and bolt-assist knob coexist with new things like brass deflector at right on M16A2.

New muzzle-brake/compensator has closed bottom to reduce dust signature produced when rifle is fired from prone position. It also dramatically improves hit probability in burst fire by reducing muzzle climb.

Table II

Performance Of Typical Military Rifles Against NATO 3.5mm Thick Mild Steel Test Plate

Weapon	Cartridge	Range (yds.)	Performance*
Carbine, M1	Ball, M1	100	CP
		200	FP
AKM	7.62x39 PS (steel core)	300	CP
		400	50% CP, 50% PP
M16A1	Ball, M193	400	CP
		500	50% CP, 50% PP
		600	FP
M16A2	Ball, M855	600	CP
		700	CP
		800	50% CP, 50% PP
		1000	FP
AK-74	5.45x39 PS	600	CP
		800	FP
Rifle, M1	Ball M2	500	CP
		600	FP
Rifle, M14	Ball M80	700	CP
		800	FP
Rifle, M21/M40	Ball M118	800	CP
		900	50% CP, 50% PP
		1000	FP

*Explanation of terms:
CP - complete perforation in which major portion of the projectile exits the armor
PP - partial penetration in which a hole is generated but the major portion of the projectile does not exit the armor
FP - failure to penetrate, the plate may be dented but is intact

Extensive testing of the M16A2 from machine rests indicates that it compares very favorably to the 7.62mm M14 and earlier M1 rifles at ranges beyond 500 yards. Scoped M16A2 was fired in terminal ballistic tests; M40A1 is in no danger of replacement, but there may be scoped M16A2s.

Writer Harris is well-known as a shooter who will shoot all of what's handy anytime there's a chance. Here he shoots an Egyptian AKM; he has fired the AR15 and the various M16 options in about all the variations there are and created some of them himself. Indeed, the USMC officially commended Harris for his work with them on the M16A2.

be used until sufficient supplies of type M855 ammunition can be produced to replace it. Previous testing had already established there was no loss of precision when M193 ammunition was fired in the M16A2. However, since some nations had adopted faster twists of rifling for supposed humanitarian reasons, this factor had to be investigated. Test firings were conducted with M193 ammunition in both the M16A2 and M16A1 at ranges of 100, 300 and 500 yards, shooting into 20 percent gelatin blocks of U.S. DoD standards, 50cm thick. Testing indicated there was no significant difference in the lethality of M193 ammunition in the M16A2 as compared to the M16A1 at any range fired. The SS109/M855 was equivalent to the M193 at ranges up to 300 yards, and it was significantly more effective at longer ranges, such as 500 yards.

Brief tests were conducted to determine the compatibility of the M16A2 barrel with 22 rimfire ammunition used in the M261 Conversion Unit. This sub-caliber training device is used by Army and Air Force units for preliminary training and by reserve units not having year-round ranges. The conversion unit replaces the standard bolt carrier assembly and converts the weapon to blowback operation, firing 22 LR ammunition from 10-round magazine inserts which are loaded into standard M16 magazines. The device is made under contract to the U.S. Army by Saco Defense Systems, Inc., Saco, Maine, USA.

The normal accuracy expected of 10-shot groups with 22 rimfire ammunition fired from the M16A1 with M261 Conversion unit is about 4 MOA at ranges up to 50 meters. Although this is about twice the dispersion of M193 or SS109 type ammunition, it is deemed adequate for training purposes. Side-by-side comparisons with two M16A2 and M16A1 upper receivers, used alternately on the same lower receivers, firing the same M261 unit showed no significant difference in precision, the mean extreme spread of ten consecutive 10-shot groups with each being 2.25-in. and 2.37-in., respectively, at 50 yards.

Testing to date indicates that the M16A2 preserves the strong points of the M16A1 system, while correcting most, if not all of its deficiencies. Since the M16A2 has been adopted by the U.S. Army and U.S. Marine Corps, as well as by the Canadian Forces, it is sure to become a new standard against which future generations of small caliber weapons will be compared. ●

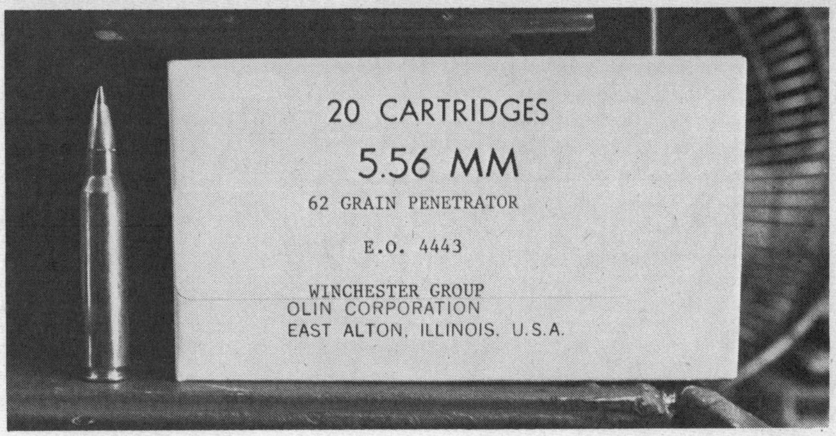

NATO 5.56mm ammunition is made in the U.S. by Olin Corp. and by Lake City Ammunition Plant. FN production is the standard by which others are compared. Ballistics are approximately 3100 fps for a 62-gr. steel core bullet from the M16A2, capable of perforating a 3.5mm steel plate at 700 yards, and capable of defeating soft body armor to 1000 yards. Accuracy of this ammunition from the M16A2 is approximately 2 minutes of angle at ranges less than 300, and about 3 minutes to 1000 yards.

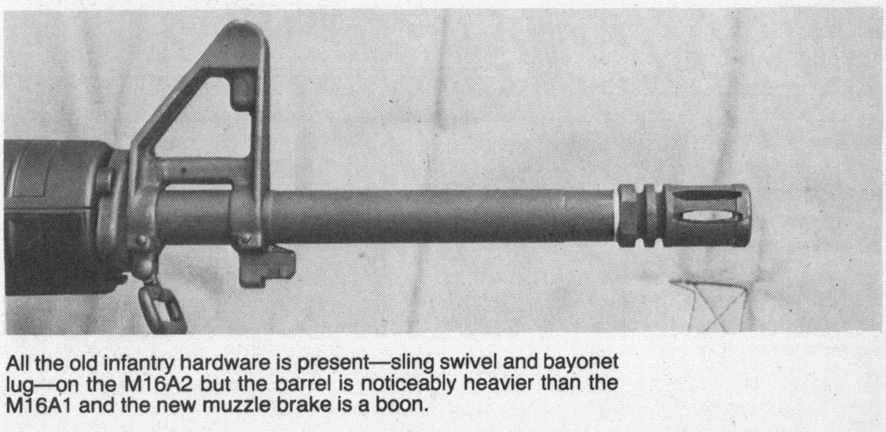

All the old infantry hardware is present—sling swivel and bayonet lug—on the M16A2 but the barrel is noticeably heavier than the M16A1 and the new muzzle brake is a boon.

This graceful and handsome G&H rifle, caliber 30-06, was built on a Sauer Mauser 98 action, color case-hardened, the bolt handle not altered for scope mounting. A long-slide Lyman 48 micro rear sight was fitted (the base engraved to match other areas on the rifle) and a matted-ramp band front sight with hood. Contrary to what's often been said, the double set triggers on this rifle work excellently, set or unset. The checkering covers an ample area, running fully around the pistol grip and fore-end.

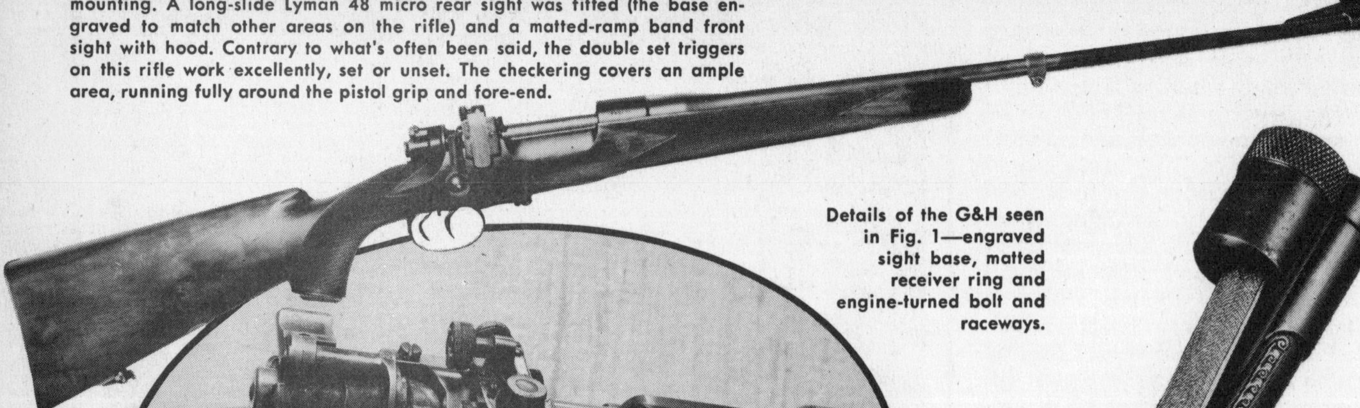

Details of the G&H seen in Fig. 1—engraved sight base, matted receiver ring and engine-turned bolt and raceways.

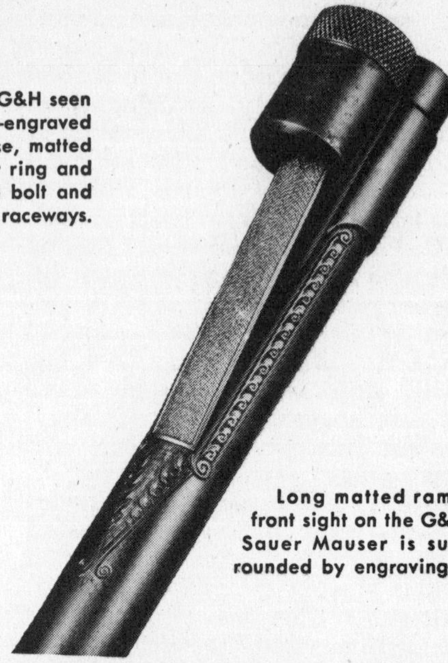

Long matted ramp front sight on the G&H Sauer Mauser is surrounded by engraving.

GRIFFIN & HOWE –

GRIFFIN AND HOWE are custom gunsmiths. The company, founded some 50 years ago, soon became famous for building big game rifles of high quality. No similar company has gained or maintained as much prestige.

I think, looking back over the years and remembering what I have observed and what I have learned from others, that the story of Griffin and Howe is primarily the story of Seymour Griffin. As a young cabinetmaker who loved rifles but didn't have any, he read Theodore Roosevelt's *African Game Trails*. That was in 1910. Roosevelt had taken a sizable battery of rifles to Africa the year before. One was a slightly modified Springfield Armory rifle, Model of 1903, for the 30-06 cartridge. Roosevelt spoke well of the 30-06. Griffin had to have one stocked as a sporting rifle.

He got a Springfield and went hunting for a blank from which to make a stock. He told me that he found a fine piece of French walnut in the store of Von Lengerke and Detmold, a company later absorbed by Abercrombie & Fitch. He paid $5 for the blank as against the $100-$200 that such a blank would cost today. When he had inletted and shaped the stock he spent many hours of hard work—mostly hand work—polishing the metal parts. Finally he found a man who could blue the barrel and action.

For 13 years after that, Griffin made stocks for Springfield rifles in the time he could spare from his regular job. He also made some valuable friends. The late Col. Townsend Whelen was one of these. In the spring of 1923 Col. Whelen, who was then in charge of Frankford Arsenal, wrote Griffin that the Arsenal had a particularly fine workman in metal. His name was James V. Howe. Col. Whelen got the two men together. Not long afterward Griffin and Howe formed a company. Griffin got enough backing to buy the necessary machine tools and supplies. The company began work on June 1, 1923.

The late Lucian Cary wrote this article several years ago, but we were unable, for a variety of reasons, to print it until now. This material represents, we believe, the last unpublished story by Mr. Cary. Ed.

Sunburst engraving of the steel grip cap on the G&H Sauer Mauser.

Engraved steel buttplate of the G&H Sauer 98 has trapdoor.

In many ways the time was favorable. Capt. E. C. Crossman, then one of the most highly regarded gun writers, had published a good deal on the merits of the Springfield rifle and the 30-06 cartridge.* So had Col. Whelen. About 1910 Crossman had got a Los Angeles gunsmith, Louis Wundhammer, to make up four sporting Springfield rifles.† Stewart Edward White, famed writer on the outdoors, took one of these to Africa. He killed a great many lions on his several trips to Africa and came to prefer the Springfield to the Winchester Model 95 in 405 caliber. He decided that the Springfield was more accurate, pleasanter to shoot, and killed just as well. It was with the Springfield that White earned the reputation—for that day—of being the best shot who ever came to Africa. There probably weren't a dozen truly competent gunsmiths in the country in 1923. The commercial arms companies were not producing bolt action big game rifles. If you wanted a bolt action rifle, as the most knowledgeable big game hunters did, you chose a Springfield or imported something from Germany. Hunting scopes made in Germany were beginning to appear but there was no good mount for them.

There was, however, what promised to be a worthy rival to Griffin and Howe. This was the Hoffman

---

*Notably *The Book of the Springfield* (Marines, N.C., 1931), and *Military and Sporting Rifle Shooting* (Marines, N.C., 1932); the former was issued in an edition updated by Roy C. Dunlap in 1951. One of the first of these Wundhammer Springfield sporters appears on p. 55 *et seq.*, and it is described as well.

†Crossman calls his specimen of this group "the first sporter Springfield ever made. The two others for whom these sporters were made were named Rodgers and Colby. While Roosevelt's Springfield rifle was used by him a bit earlier than 1910, the T.R. rifle was not a full-fledged sporter, in the sense that a new stock was fitted to it.

As it happens, the Wundhammer sporter in this group of four that was made for White was added to Editor John Amber's collection some years ago. As Crossman points out *(op. cit.)* the fore-end is a somewhat spindly affair, a fault later to be well-corrected by Wundhammer. The buttstock dimensions of 13¾ x 1⅝ x 2½ show a drop at heel greater than Crossman later advocated, and the pistol grip is, perhaps, of greater radius than we prefer today. This rifle weighs 8 lbs. The original Armory barrel is used (this one dated Feb., 1910), and the rear sight base remains on the barrel though a Lyman peep receiver sight—not the later Lyman 48—is fitted also.

a history and a tribute

This famed firm, makers under the guiding hands of Seymour Griffin of the finest in firearms, flourished even in the dark days of the depression. The sportsman who owned a rifle custom made by G&H had the ultimate in craftsmanship, grace and shooting qualities.

by LUCIAN CARY

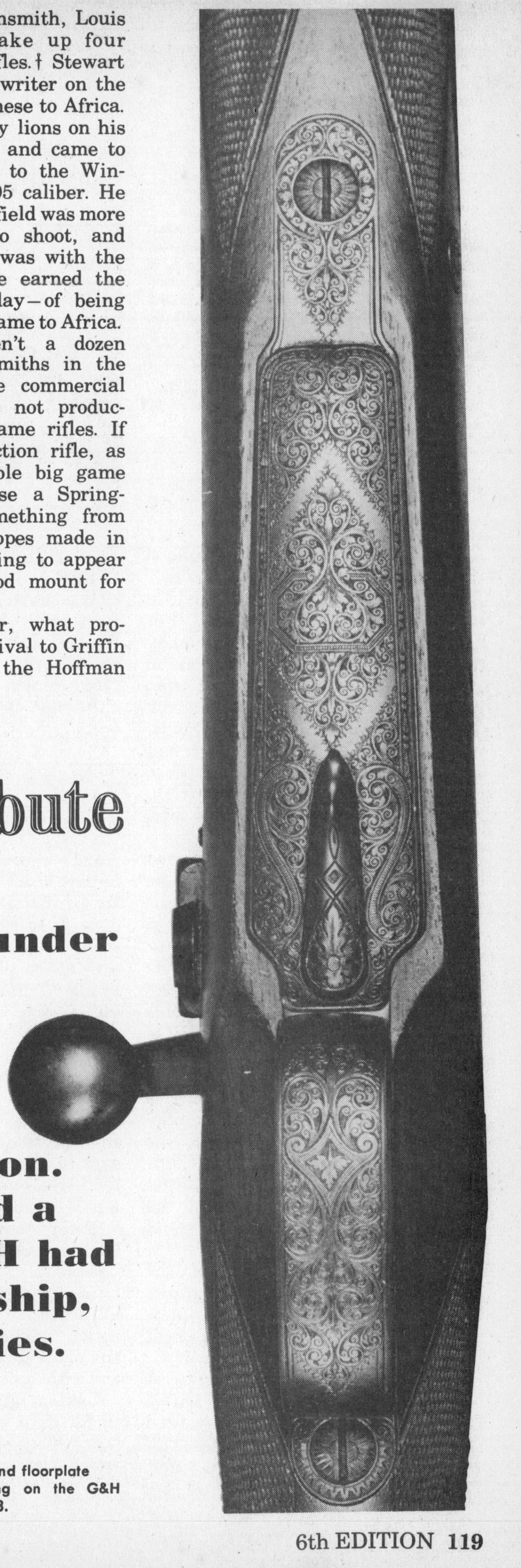

Guard and floorplate engraving on the G&H Sauer 98.

The G&H single shot rifle seen here, serial number 1413, is a Krag that was given unusual treatment. Both sideplate and magazine feed were removed, but enough of the feed mechanism were retained to eject the fired case and to offer a loading platform, semi-circular in section. The rounded wood inside appears as if moulded to the metal pieces. Caliber is 25 Niedner Magnum, a rimmed cartridge in the performance class of the 219 Zipper or 22 Savage Hi-Power. The medium-heavy barrel is 28 inches, rifle weight empty is 10 lbs.

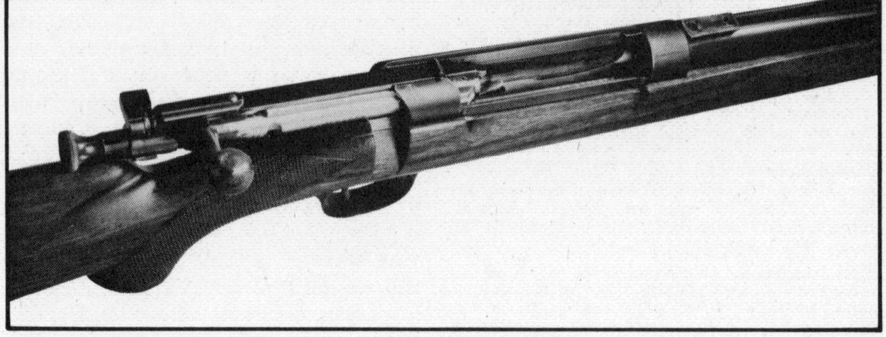

Interior of the G&H Krag shown above.

Arms Co. of Cleveland. It was founded the same day as Griffin and Howe. After a few months Howe left Griffin in order to work for Hoffman. For nearly seven years Griffin held on by himself. He was able to find trained gunsmiths who came over here from Europe, chiefly Germany and Austria. One of these, the late George Hyde, was as accomplished a gunsmith as I ever knew. He left Griffin in order to found his own shop in Brooklyn, where he did some remarkable jobs. Griffin had the reputation of being a hard driver, but his men respected him. He drove himself harder than he drove any of them.

Griffin told me that in those first years he worked seven days a week except for one Sunday a month. He spent that Sunday in Harry Pope's Jersey City shop. Pope, then in his 60's, was well-known as the maker of the most accurate rifle barrels obtainable. For years Pope's specialty was making muzzle-loading barrels with false muzzles for such single-shot, breech-loading actions as the Winchester, Ballard and Sharps Borchardt, but he made 22-cal. target barrels that outshot anything the commercial arms companies could produce at that time. He also made some 30-cal. barrels, first for the Krag and then for the Springfield. It was widely held that Pope knew more about what makes rifles shoot than any other man in the country.

Pope told me that Griffin came over one Sunday with a barrel blank that a customer wanted turned down to three diameters, all within a thousandth of an inch. Pope thought this was nonsense, but he did the job. On another Sunday Griffin arrived with a 30-cal. barrel that a customer wanted chambered for the 300 Magnum cartridge. Griffin had had some trouble with the chambering. Pope helped him complete the job—the first 300 Magnum rifle that Griffin and Howe turned out.

Early Days

Like most of us, Griffin had his foibles. Carl Estey, who once worked for Griffin and later was a salesman on Abercrombie's seventh floor (which contains more new guns than any other place I know of, here or abroad), told me of the time an emissary of the White House came in to order a rifle to be presented to some Eastern potentate. The rifle had to be made in one week. Griffin was out to lunch. When he came back he blew a gasket. Harry Truman was then president and Griffin, for whatever reason, or no reason, hated Truman. He said he would not make up a rifle for Harry Truman.

Estey waited until he thought Griffin had calmed down, then said: "After all, the President of the United States has chosen you above all others to build a rifle for presentation." Griffin yielded and turned the shop upside down in order to get the rifle out in the specified time.

Custom gunsmiths commonly try to fill their orders in rotation. I say "try." Being human, they do sometimes yield to a favorite customer. One of Griffin's customers—not a favorite—once appeared with a bottle of whisky and the suggestion that he was in a hurry for his rifle. Griffin refused the whisky. Then turned to Estey and said: "I don't think you'll take it either, will you, Carl?"

I first met Seymour Griffin in 1928 or 1929. The shop was then on East 44th Street. You entered a room that was full of guns and accessories. This was a retail store. The much larger room behind the store contained the shop. You weren't free to go into the shop except by invitation. In the fall the store was rather a madhouse. Many men seem not to know that the time to order a new gun or have an old one repaired is quite a few months before the hunting season opens rather than the week before. I saw a man bring in a beat up pump shotgun that had a bad dent in the barrel. He was told that the job could be done in three weeks. He said: "I can't wait three weeks. I want to shoot ducks three days from now."

Griffin and Howe had some most unusual customers. One was a man who often ordered two or three rifles at a time. When asked what calibers he wanted his stock reply was: "Any I haven't got."

Finally he reported that he had gone hunting. Phil Johnstone, the then manager, asked him which of his Griffin and Howe rifles he had used. The man shook his head. He hadn't used any of his fine custom made rifles. He had used a factory 30-30 carbine. Johnstone asked what luck he'd had. The man answered that he had hit three tin cans in five shots.

Griffin and Howe finally ran out of calibers for this man, who then began to collect Purdey shotguns. Even second-hand these are likely to cost $3500-$4000 today!

Surprising Lady Customer

Another surprising customer was a little lady who looked as if she were crowding 70. Her chauffeur came in behind her carrying a rifle in a leather case. When he took the rifle out of the case it proved to be one made by Gibbs of Bristol on a magnum Mauser action for an elephant cartridge. Gibbs was one of the best English makers of rifles, maybe the best. The factory was bombed out by the Germans during World War II. When Griffin looked the rifle over he saw signs of use—dents and scratches on the stock and blueing was worn off toward the muzzle.

The little old lady said that she wanted a similar rifle as a present for her husband. Griffin was concerned. How many women know what kind of rifle would please a big game hunting husband?

"You see," the lady said, "my husband has always used a big double for buffalo and rhinoceros and elephant. But I had such luck with the Gibbs that he wants a rifle like mine when we go to Africa again."

Griffin was amazed. He couldn't picture the lady, who didn't weigh 110 pounds, swinging that Gibbs elephant rifle and taking its recoil.

The rather early G&H rifle shown here, made on a Springfield 1903 action, its serial number 827, has handling and balance qualities superior to any other rifle I've owned or used. Its stock dimensions are about normal (13⅝x1⅞x2⅝ inches) for iron sights, but it's the lean, slenderness of the pistol grip and fore-end, the in-the-hands balance that its tapering 23¼-inch barrel contributes to, that make this rifle come alive. Chambered for the 7x57 Mauser cartridge, the rifle weighs 7½ lbs. empty. The bolt has not been altered for scope use. Sights are a Lyman 48 micro rear and a matted-ramp front with hood.

The oil finished stock, now too dark, shows good figure. Grip cap and buttplate—the latter engraved and with trap-door—are of steel. The fore-end tip is genuine buffalo horn, with not a check or crack in it. The checkering all but covers the fore-end, and runs from top edge to top edge. Checkering on the pistol grip goes across the top, though it doesn't join perfectly there.

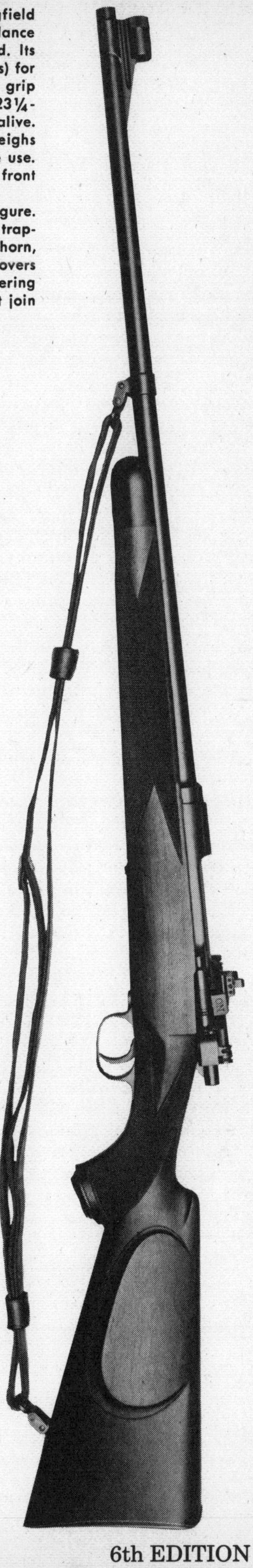

"What about the stock dimensions?" Griffin asked.

"Make the stock the same as mine only an inch longer and not so much cast off. A man doesn't need as much cast off as I do."

After the lady left, Griffin picked up the telephone and called a customer who had hunted more than once in Africa and told him about the order. When he gave the lady's name the man said: "Oh, yes. She is as good a hunter as her husband. No white hunter shoots her game for her. If he tried to, he'd get fired on the spot. She has killed the Big Five without help from any other shooter."

By the Big Five the man meant elephant, rhinoceros, buffalo, lion and leopard.

A Gold Canary

Another customer who gave the place a surprise was the man who

The G&H 7x57mm Springfield, right and left side views. Note G&H's stock styling at this period—the raised ridge, rising out of the grip checkering, then falling away in a trajectory-like arc forward.

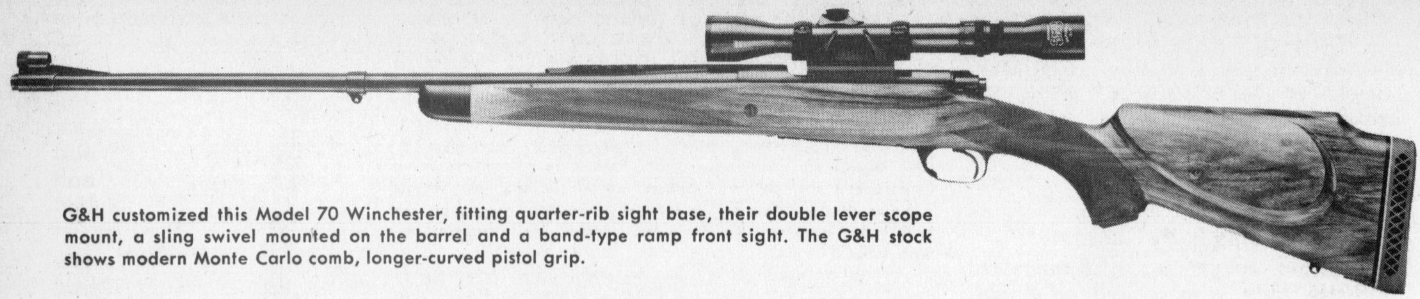

G&H customized this Model 70 Winchester, fitting quarter-rib sight base, their double lever scope mount, a sling swivel mounted on the barrel and a band-type ramp front sight. The G&H stock shows modern Monte Carlo comb, longer-curved pistol grip.

wanted a canary engraved on the top tang of a double barreled elephant rifle. This was so odd that Phil Johnstone asked him why.

"My pet canary just died," the man said. "I want a monument for him."

The job went to Joe Fugger, who studied art in Austria and has been with the company for many years. He's one of the best engravers of guns in the country. Maybe the best. I saw an engraving he did on the sidelocks of a double barrel Purdey elephant rifle. Three elephants were followed by an elephant calf, while beyond them a cheetah pursued an impala. The mountain in the background may have been Kilimanjaro. The animals were beautifully lifelike, the whole a magnificent composition. A coiled cobra in gold relief decorated the top lever. The engraving took 200 hours and cost the man who ordered it—back then—$1500 in addition to the cost of the rifle, which was more than $2000.

I asked Joe Fugger about the canary. He remembered it well. He said it was three-eighths of an inch high, a gold inlay. No doubt gold is the proper color for a canary.

Griffin and his crew designed a scope mount that is still highly regarded because the scope can be removed and replaced without changing the sighting of the rifle. This is rare in scope mounts. The Griffin and Howe mount is in two parts. The base, screwed and pinned to the receiver of the rifle, has a male dovetail along the top. The other part, in which the scope is held, has a female dovetail. After the two parts are slid together, they are clamped by two levers that operate half-round rods. When the two levers are rotated back half a turn or so, the scope can be slid off.

Many of us remember that when Winchester first produced the 22 Hornet cartridge there was no rifle for it on the market. Griffin's answer was to adapt the Springfield rifle made in those days for the 22 long rifle cartridge to take the Hornet. Later a wildcat cartridge, much superior to the Hornet, came along. This was known as the 2R Lovell. It used the 25-20 single shot case necked down to take a 22 bullet. Griffin chambered rifles for the cartridge. The 25-20 single shot was obsolete and the cases were in short supply. Griffin got Winchester to make up some thousands of the cases. The rifle I had for the 2R, on a Sharps Borchardt single shot action, was, up to 200 yards, the most dependably accurate rifle I had ever shot. It averaged 1.70″ for seven successive 10-shot groups at that distance. This was away back—some 35 years ago. We have much better bullets today, and the results are better. The 2R Lovell is now obsolete. Newer woodchuck cartridges have surpassed it.

Griffin also produced a 350-cal. cartridge at the suggestion of an American, Leslie Simpson, who hunted a great deal in Africa. It was the 375 H&H Magnum case necked down. If the slow burning powders we have now had been available in those days, the 350 might have been a considerable success. As it was, it reportedly gave a 250-gr. bullet 2740 fs velocity and a 275-gr. bullet 2600 fs.

To Shoot or Not to Shoot...

In the early years Griffin and Howe were said to make big game rifles for Park Avenue nobs and other toffs, and that the owners, not being hunters, never shot their rifles but used them as conversation pieces. There was some truth in this allegation. Not much, but some.

Actually, Griffin and Howe have made rifles for many big game hunters. The late Grancel Fitz, who was the first man to kill all 25 of the legal varieties of big game on the North American continent, used a Griffin and Howe 30-06 for practically all of his hunting. The list of big game hunters who used Griffin and Howe rifles includes Ernest Hemingway, Russel Aitkin, Townsend Whelen, Edward Queeny, the Maharajah of Bikaner, Michael Lerner and Donald Hopkins. Col. Whelen told me, a few years before his death, that he believed Hopkins had more experience in big game hunting than any other living American. He has hunted in this country, in Alaska, Canada and on many long trips to Africa. The last I heard, Hopkins was in Africa hunting for a particular bull elephant said to have bigger tusks than any other. On one occasion when I visited the Griffin and Howe shop, Hopkins had six rifles in there to be restocked.

In 1930 Griffin and Howe became the subsidiary of Abercrombie & Fitch that it still is. Griffin con-

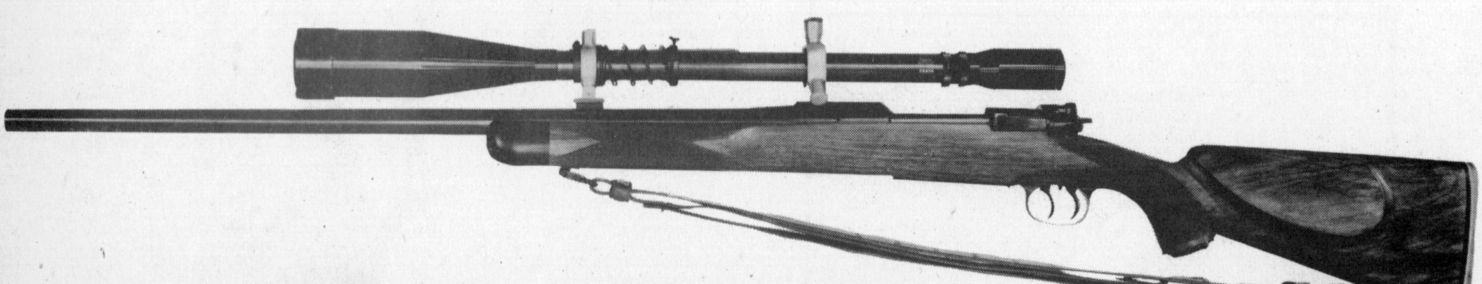

G&H built this Mauser 98-actioned rifle in 225 Winchester-caliber as a varmint rifle. Fore-end is heavier, more full, yet Monte Carlo comb is absent. Double set triggers were fitted, a good choice on a varmint rifle.

tinued in charge until his retirement a few years ago. Today the G&H shop is located at 589 Eighth Avenue. No retail business is done now, as it was on 44th street.

One of the problems of a custom gunsmith is the man who comes in early and stays around all day. One custom gunsmith I know put up a sign saying: "Conversation $5 an hour. Argument $10 an hour." Griffin and Howe's answer was to divorce the shop from the retail store. Whether you want a new recoil pad or a complete Griffin and Howe rifle you go to Abercrombie & Fitch at 45th Street and Madison Avenue, go up to the seventh floor and see John Realmuto, who is now the manager of Griffin and Howe. If you want a particularly fine piece of wood for a stock, John will arrange for you to look over the supply. The shop has some beautiful French walnut. Abercrombie & Fitch once put on exhibition an outstanding piece with the proviso that it was not for sale. However, a man came along and offered $200 for it. He got the piece. Such a blank weighs around eight pounds, so the man paid about $25 a pound for it. By the time the stock is finished it will weigh only a fraction of what it weighed in the blank, of course.

I am inclined to be cautious about using a fancy blank for a bolt action rifle where it is important that the grain run right in the grip and in the fore-end. The buttstock of a single shot rifle or a shotgun can be as fancy as you care to pay for, however.

In the 44th Street days Griffin and Howe had a strange machine that looked a little like a wide ladder. When I first saw it I didn't know what it was for. It was a machine for shaping and inletting rifle stocks. A stock maker did the final fitting. Commercial stocks now are made by a much improved variety of the old Griffin and Howe machine. Even so, they need an amount of hand fitting that they seldom get. Most top stock makers prefer to start with the solid blank and do all the work with hand tools. This is sometimes called "block stocking".

Griffin and Howe discarded the old machine for shaping and inletting stocks when the company moved down to East 13th Street. All of their stocks now are made entirely by hand. This has greatly increased the price. Individual custom stockmakers today often charge $250 to over $500, plus the cost of the wood and the fittings. This may seem like a high price, but if a stock maker spends many hours in making a stock he is not getting rich. Stock making is the poorest paid part of a gunsmith's trade.

Griffin & Howe Check List

G&H rifles have long been collected by enthusiasts for the classic sporting rifle, and of course G&H made some few rifles in target grade or form also.

We are pleased to present here, through the courtesy of Abercrombie & Fitch, a check list of G&H serial numbers. We regret that the numbers for the 1923-1929 period inclusive are no longer available, but serial numbers started with 1 in 1923, and some 820 rifles were made through 1929. Thus an average of some 117 rifles were made each of those seven years. A rather high figure, it would seem in comparison with the near-60 average for the following ten years (1930-1939), but it must be remembered that the pre-depression period was one of prosperity and high *real* income, while the next ten years saw luxuries much less indulged in.

Please do do not write to Abercrombie & Fitch or to G&H for further information on a G&H rifle you may have. They will not reveal the names of the original purchasers under any circumstances, and neither do they have time to correspond on other aspects of G&H rifles.

Year	Serial Numbers
1930	1001 - 1053
1931	1054 - 1109
1932	1110 - 1168
1933	1169 - 1228
1934	1229 - 1348
1935	1349 - 1462
1936	1463 - 1536
1937	1537 - 1599
1938	1600 - 1623
1939	1624 - 1659
1940	1660 - 1678
1941	1679 - 1707
1942	1708 - 1737
1943	none
1944	none
1945	1738 - 1767
1946	1768 - 1797
1947	1798 - 1828
1948	1829 - 1947
1949	1948 - 2007
1950	2008 - 2034
1951	2035 - 2066
1952	2067 - 2096
1953	2097 - 2126
1954	2127 - 2156
1955	2157 - 2186
1956	2187 - 2216
1957	2217 - 2246
1958	2247 - 2276
1959	2277 - 2306
1960	2307 - 2336
1961	2337 - 2426
1962	2427 - 2456
1963	2457 - 2504
1964	2505 - 2519
1965	2520 - 2534
1966	2535 - 2542

G&H is unable to supply exact figures for each year after 1966, but the total number of rifles made for 1967-1972 inclusive was about 42, and the last rifle made (as of February 1973) bears serial number 2584.

Stock Is Classic

Your typical Griffin and Howe stock is of a design I shall call classic. In recent years many stocks have been made, particularly on the West Coast, that I would call elaborate. They have deeply hooked pistol grips, oddly shaped fore-end tips, a variety of inlays made of plastic or contrasting wood, and finally the extreme Monte Carlo comb that is—sadly—on the way to becoming universal.

Now a rifle is a tool. As such it must be designed to suit its purpose, but there is no necessity for making it ugly. I have had two stocks made with the Monte Carlo combs. Then I discovered that this excrescence was entirely unnecessary. The same goes for a deeply hooked pistol grip. There never was any excuse for decorating a rifle stock with contrasting inlays. They merely distract the eye from something that should be seen as a whole.

The typical Griffin and Howe stock does not go in for nonsense. It is a clean, racy job, good to feel in shooting and good to look at. Griffin and Howe would undoubtedly make a stock with a restrained Monte Carlo comb for a man who wanted it, but I don't know what they would do if somebody came along who wanted a white diamond inlay the size of a postcard on one side of the stock and maybe a few more inlays scattered around.

The day of the Springfield is gone. The Director of Civilian Marksmanship no longer sells it. So also is the day when no other bolt action rifles for big game shooting were made in this country. Winchester, Remington

These are some of the fine shotguns marketed today and in years past by Abercrombie & Fitch of New York, Chicago and points West. From the top—Made in England, the Boss over-under; a Holland & Holland side-by-side double; a Purdey, also a lateral double gun. Next, an A&F Mark III made in Italy, and a Perazzi, both over-under. Last, another Italian, the A&F single barrel trap gun.

The G&H rifle pictured here is a complicated—and probably costly—alteration of a Springfield Model 1922 rimfire (22 Long Rifle) action to handle the 25-20 Single Shot cartridge. Discarding the detachable 22 rimfire magazine necessarily, G&H converted the action to conventional centerfire—1903 style floorplate, cartridge follower with W-spring, etc.

Fitted with a medium-heavy 26-inch barrel, making for a total weight of 9½ lbs. empty, this G&H rifle is arche-typical of their work in the Springfield period. The stock is classic—no Monte Carlo, not even a cheekpiece, and the multi-diamond checkering is ample indeed. The wood, probably American, is well figured in the butt section. The pistol grip cap and buttplate are of steel, a band-type ramp, matted, finishes off the muzzle, there's a genuine horn fore-end tip, and the bolt knob, flatted underneath, is fully checkered. Serial number of this well-made rifle is 1379.

The bolt body, follower and receiver raceways are engine turned.

This action close-up shows the conversion from clip magazine to cartridge follower system of the G&H 25-20 S.S. rifle.

and Savage make them now, and so do H&R, Mossberg, et al. In addition, bolt action rifles are made in Finland, Sweden, Germany, Belgium, England and probably elsewhere. I had an excellent Springfield action and I toyed with the idea of having it made up into a sporting rifle. This requires a good deal of expensive work. I finally decided against the project for a reason that may seem odd to guncranks. The reason was that I didn't need it. I already had three excellent custom stocked big game rifles.

How Much Do They Cost?

Like the price of everything else, that of a Griffin and Howe rifle has gone up. The base price is $850. This does not include such things as a trap buttplate. That costs $25 extra. A Griffin and Howe scope mount fitted to the rifle costs $50 or more. A scope costs anywhere from about $40 to over $100. Engraving costs almost anything you care to pay. I saw some years ago a Winchester Model 70 that Griffin and Howe had restocked and engraved. The price was $1350. A similar job would cost much more today.

You can buy a good commercial bolt action big game rifle for from about $115 to $175. What does a man gain by paying Griffin and Howe several times as much? You might ask a man what he gains by paying $350 apiece for his suits when ready made suits are available at one-third that price or less. If he answered you truly he would probably be reduced to saying: "I just like them better."

Griffin and Howe is not a large company. As of last January 1 it employed 12 men in the shop. For years the company has turned out from about 30 to 75 or more rifles a year. Because the company's production ceased during World War II when it went over to war work, its current serial number isn't much over 2600.

It is in the nature of things that a custom gun shop doing fine work cannot be big.

A custom gunsmith has done nice work for me over 15 years. I went to his shop at first because it was only an hour away by car from where I was living in northwestern Connecticut. I continued to go because his work was so good. He works alone. His charges are not much different from those of Griffin and Howe. He is critical. He knows the work of Griffin and Howe. He has had occasion to examine many examples of it.

I asked him when I was writing this what he thought of Griffin and Howe. He said: "If I needed some work that I couldn't do for myself I would go to Griffin and Howe."

I consider that statement, coming from the man who made it, a high tribute to Griffin and Howe. An accolade. ●

The Twenty Comes of Age

The author makes a strong case for the modern three-inch 20 bore, refuting its detractors and supporting its excellence even for long range waterfowl shooting.

by FRANCIS E. SELL

My shooting partner, Dr. Elek of Beverly Hills, California, holds a 20 gauge over-under Perazzi, custom built to his dimensions. The 28" barrels carry my 1½-inch long forcing cones, recommended .620" bore diameter and choke constrictions. The double seen is the author's 20 gauge, custom stocked by him. We were pass shooting in Oregon.

Gunning for snipe with my 6¾" lb. custom-stocked 20 gauge Magnum, chambered for 3" shells. The 30" barrels are choked left .025", right .020". This gun, using 1⅛ ounces of 8s, delivers 70% left, and 58% right barrel with regular reloads. With my special reloads it produces 94% left and 81% right at 40 yards—an excellent pass shooting gun for geese to 75-80 yards and to 60 yards for ducks, using 2s and 4s respectively.

VERSATILITY! Ask a gunner what the chief attraction is of the modern 20 gauge he uses, and that'll be his answer. It's a good one, too. The modern 20 gauge, using shot weights of ⅞, 1, 1⅛, 1³⁄₁₆, and 1¼ ounces, is at home in upland cover, field shooting, swampland and bay shooting. In addition the modern 20 gauge, chambered for 3-inch shells, is an excellent pass shooting gun, ducks and geese the quarry.

The 1-ounce, 1⅛-ounce, and 1¼-ounce shot charges, it should be pointed out, are the same ones that the 12 gauge took over when it displaced the 10 gauge in gunner popularity. Now, with the modern 20 gauge becoming increasingly popular, about the same arguments are heard vis-a-vis the 20 and 12 gauge as were heard during the time the 12 gauge displaced the heavier, more cumbersome 10 gauge. Some of these present day arguments about the short-comings of the modern 20 gauge are downright amusing. They are often taken seriously enough, however, to keep otherwise well-informed shooters from turning to the modern 20 bore, the most versatile gauge currently available.

In one book on shotgunning, supposed to be right out of the hoss's mouth, the author insists that a 20 gauge, in the very nature of things, cannot handle any shot size larger than 6s. Recently, as reported in a shooting mag, to settle the question of 12 gauge superiority for all time, an expert dumped several 20 gauge Magnum loadings of 1¼-ounce shot charges into 12 gauge shells, using the same powder, same shot, and same type of wad column found in the smaller bore. The 12 gauge, citizens, delivered 40-yard patterns above the 80% mark, but the original 1¼-ounce factory loadings in the 20 gauge also reached 80%—out and out proof of 12 gauge superiority.

Next on the list of persistent contentions is that the 20 gauge, with its longer shot column, deforms more pellets than does any of the larger gauges. Topping this, perhaps is the argument that you can always give a 12 gauge a tighter choke constriction and consequently higher density patterns than those achieved in the 20 gauge. Pressures in the 20 are supposed to be higher, too.

Yet, the top prize among all these contentions must be divided—there's the English expert who proclaims that the recoil is more noticeable in the 20 gauge than in the 12 because it has a slower, more push-like effort, through the use of the slower, more progressive-burning powders used (for the same weight shot charges) in the smaller bore. Crowding this very closely for the best award is the assertion by two writers that a 12 gauge gun can be made lighter than the 20 gauge!

Assailing the Arguments

Taking these contentions in turn, let's—as the politicians say—look at the record. First, about the inability of the 20 gauge to effectively use the larger shot sizes. Tests made here, using the same size buckshot in a 12 and a 20 gauge found the smaller bore averaging 3% more pellets in a 30-inch circle than did the 12 gauge—even Stephen, if you ask me!

Getting down to a more practical field-shooting shot size, I have several 20 gauges in my gunrack that deliver 90-95% 40-yard patterns with 2s. These modern 20s reach the 75/80-yard mark with goose killing patterns, their loadings 1¼ ounces of 2s. At 75 yards they deliver an average of 55 pellets to a 30-inch circle, and 50 such pellets at 80 yards. With 4s, an excellent all-round wildfowling shot size, the extreme range on ducks with several of my 20 bores is indicated at the steel pattern plates as being 60/65 yards.

Using the smaller shot sizes, from 9s to 5s, including that size 6 the previously-mentioned expert claimed as the top limit on size in the 20 gauge, I have yet to see *any* gauge larger that will deliver more uniform patterns than will a well-bored 20 gauge.

The expert dumping the 1¼-ounce 20 gauge loads in 12 gauge shells got 40-yard patterns in the mid-80s percentage range. But when I asked a large manufacturer of powder to duplicate these tests with their slow-burning 20 gauge Magnum powders, the results were not unexpected. Out of 10 shells used with these 20 gauge components, 3 were complete flame-outs—bloopers! The muzzle velocity of the 7 other shells, those that actually pushed the shot charges out of the barrel checked out at 650-700 feet a second. Pressures were non-existent—or at least not measurable on the crusher type pressure gun used.

While I have always advocated less than maximum velocities in both the 12 and 20 gauge, a muzzle velocity of 650-700 feet a second, while unquestionably delivering high pattern percentages, is for the birds. Wait a minute, that doesn't sound right, does

A limit of sprig and two wildfowling guns—at left my special-bored Magnum side-by-side double, the other a Model 101 Winchester 12 bore over-under. Both are equally effective with the proper loads.

it? Well, you know what I mean.

Let's examine the controversial longer shot column in the modern 20 gauge chambered for 3 inch shells—and it is longer than the 12 gauge shot column for a given weight, have no doubt of that. A 1¼-ounce loading of 5s in the 20 gauge has a column length of 1.110 inches. This same weight loading in the 12 gauge has a column length of .758 inches. The area of bore contact in the 20 gauge is 2.144 square inches, and in the 12 it's 1.735. This is about 20% more bore contact for the 20 gauge—disregarding a small fraction.

A 12 gauge, with its 20% less bore contact, requires a bore constriction of at least .032-inch for full choke patterns. But because the same shot charge weight in the modern 20 gauge has more bore contact (by 20%), more pellets come in direct contact with the choke. A full choke pattern in the 20 requires about 22% less choke than does the 12 gauge. A choke constriction of .024-inch in the 20 gauge Magnum, handling all shot charges from ⅞- to 1¼-ounces, is sufficient for good full choke patterns. Indeed, in my rack of 20 gauge doubles, this constriction always produces 89/95% patterns with 4s and 2s.

This, of course, is the answer about the 12 gauge being *capable* of using more choke than the 20 gauge. It must, in the ballistic nature of the two gauges, use more choke than the smaller bore.

Shot Deformation

As for the added shot deformation via increased bore contact, this is of no great moment in the 20. For the same velocity level, and the same shot charge weight, the 20 gauge always uses a slower, more progressive-burning powder than does the 12 bore. Such powders in the smaller bore handle the shot charge less violently than the more abrupt, faster-burning powders in the 12 gauge.

A good example of this occurs with Hercules powders. A 1⅛-ounce 20 gauge loading is pushed by 20.5 grains of Herco for a velocity of 1220 feet a second (fps). This powder is actually too slow for this weight of shot in the 12 gauge. The 1⅛-ounce shot package in the 12 gauge is more suitably handled by the faster-burning Hercules Green Dot or Hercules Red Dot. Shot cups, of course, keep practically all pellets out of actual bore contact in both gauges; the shot deformation is caused by the initial combustion, when the inertia of the shot charge is overcome. Here, again, the slower-burning, more progressive powder has something going for it, moving the 20 bore shot charge more gently than the faster-burning powders.

As for the working pressures being higher in the 20 gauge than in the 12, this is mostly myth. Having put hundreds of 20 gauge shells through a ballistic laboratory, I find that most of the more-often used 20 gauge loads operate at a pressure of 8500 to 10,500 psi or, in today's parlance, "lead units of pressure" (LUP). The pressures in the 20 gauge, for the same weight shot charges, peak slower than those in the 12 gauges, too. If you want more reassurance about safety, the 20 gauge wins hands down. A pressure that would take a 12 gauge apart would have no effect on a 20 bore. It requires about 50% more pressure to blow up a 20 gauge than it does a 12 gauge double, assuming the *same* barrel thickness at the breech. (Calculated by using the *Gun Maker's Formula**)

Now we come to the statement of our English authority, who maintains in his well-written book that the slower recoil of the 20 bore is more noticeable and punishing than the same amount of recoil in the 12-gauge—because of the faster recoil of the larger gauge, same-weight guns. If this is so, then the use of a recoil pad should *emphasize* recoil, for all it does is spread recoil over a longer time period by its cushioning action.

Some 12 gauges, according to the authors of another book, weigh less than some 20 gauges. True! This conclusion, however, comes of comparing the weights of light 12 gauge doubles with the weight of a 20 gauge autoloader. Straight across the board, with

*Derived from Major Sir Gerald Burrard's *The Modern Shotgun,* Vol. III (London, 1932, 1st ed.).

the same types of actions and barrel lengths, the 20 gauge is usually about a pound or so lighter than a 12.

The Modern 20 Bore

At present the modern 20 gauge, chambered for 3-inch shells, is available in pump, autoloader, over-under and side-by-side double guns. Any range this side of 60 yards is beautifully covered with the modern 20 gauge, ducks the target. Any range this side of 70 yards is also beautifully covered by this versatile gauge for geese, using the heavier loadings. With special long range handloads, these goose ranges are very handily extended to 75 yards.

There is one domestic 20 gauge double at present available, the Savage-Fox. This is a very sturdy gun, even though the workmanship is a bit rough. In addition, the Winchester Model 21, but strictly as a custom job, is also available.

The imported 20 gauge side-by-side or over-under double, custom made, is receiving more and more attention. Indeed, these custom-made 20s as well as the higher class production imports, are in more demand today than the 12 gauge import.

I've devoted a lot of time during the past two decades doing design and development work on 20 gauge doubles—striving to bring this smaller gauge out from under the shadow of the 12 bore. Prior to this the 20 was a scaled-down model of the 12 gauge—with the same forcing cones and the same choke cones, with choke adjustments achieved by using ⅞-ounce of 7½ size shot. All this, of course, indicated a gun designed for upland, short-range shooting, barrels choke modified and improved cylinder. When the 20 gauge slipped out of this peculiar classification, it was very responsive to changes in chokes and forcing cones. Using the same weight shot charges as the 12 gauge, up to and including 1¼ ounces, the 20 gauge very effectively nipped into *all* 12 gauge activities, as well as dominating upland gunning.

Topping this, and moving beyond the reach of the average factory 12 gauge gun, those 20 gauges carrying my barrel design work and using my long range loads, can take their place beside the *average* 10 gauge Magnum on the goose and duck passes.

A customized 20 gauge double I recently received from Bill Knight (of Knight & Knight, 5030 S.W. 48th St., Miami, FL 33155), a Bernardelli double with two sets of barrels, very solidly underscores these changes. First, and perhaps foremost, is one set of 30-inch long range barrels. Why not 28-inch barrels for pass shooting? One very simple reason. Other factors being equal, the longer barrels will deliver higher pattern percentages. This has nothing to do with the difference in *velocity* between a set of 30-inch and 26-inch barrels, but it does have plenty to do with patterns. The 30-inch barrels have much less gas turbulence at the launch of the shot charge than do the shorter barrels. Also, for the same choke constriction, I found that the 30-inch barrels delivered an average of about 5% greater pattern density.

These barrels carry my 1½-inch forcing cones (38mm), and they're polished to a mirror-smooth finish. The choke cones are also 1¼-inches long, with the right barrel carrying

The author, caught flatfooted by another mallard coming in to the decoys—but not caught with the wrong load, thanks to previous testing. Gun is a 20 gauge Magnum double, the loading used here 1⅛ ounces of 6s delivering 58% with the modified barrel, 72% with the full choke. Ranges were from 35 to 45 yards—a perfect matching of loading to expected shooting that paid off with a limit of 6 ducks with as many shots.

.020-inch and the left barrel .025-inch constrictions. Bore diameter is .620-inch—an overbore of .005-inch from the usual .615-inch found in most factory 20s. The choke parallels measure 1.110 inches from the end of the cones to the muzzle. This, gunners, is sufficient length to contain the heaviest shot charge (1¼ ounces) used in the 20 gauge Magnum—and where one is reaching for the highest pattern percentages at maximum ranges, these long choke parallels are essential. They also produce exceptionally uniform patterns—something proven here by several years of testing to find the elements that contributed to such 20 gauge performance.

Sell's Special

These chokes of .025-inch and .020-inch are usually reversed when using 2s, unless these long forcing and choke cones are used, complemented with the above mentioned long choke parallels. My gun, using the .025-inch choke left barrel, delivers 92% 40-yard patterns, with 50 pellets in the 30-inch circle at 80 yards.

Using 4s the .025-inch choke delivers 94% 40-yard patterns, and 58% patterns at 60 yards, where it averages about 100 pellets in the 30-inch circle.

The other set of barrels, 28 inches long, are bored left .015-inch and right .010-inch, or about half- and quarter-choke—slightly more than modified and a very tight improved cylinder. In many ways, this is the English game gun, though the barrels are a bit more choked than usual. I had chukar, western quail and ruffed grouse in mind for this set of barrels. With either set of barrels the gun balances beautifully—the "strike" is at the knuckle of the action with the 28-inch barrels, a fraction of an inch forward of this with the 30-inch set.

Complementing both sets of barrels is a special raised Knight rib carrying my specifications—6/16-inch wide at the breech, 3/16-inch at the muzzle. File cut to present a dead black level pointing plane. This tapered rib reaches infinity at about 40 yards where it seemingly converges on target. Both sets carry a 1/16-inch front sight that, with the slender taper, makes them seem much longer than their actual length. Gun weight with the 30-inch barrels is a bit under 7 pounds—6 pounds 13 ounces. Remember, this is a wildfowling gun, a pass-shooting gun weighing less than 7 pounds—compared to the usual 8½/9-pound 12 gauge Magnum or the 11/12-pound 10 gauge Magnum.

When you think of a 12 gauge double wildfowler with 30-inch barrels, you picture a heavy, bulky gun—and you're usually right. Place the calipers on those barrels at the breech and you'll find them about 2 5/16 inches wide. At the muzzle they are about 1⅝ inches. A 20 gauge double, such as the Bernardelli described, measures an even 2 inches across the barrels at the breech, at the muzzle 1⅜ inches. This 20 gauge not only sloughs off a pound or so, it is also a slimmer, trimmer gun.

The modern 20 gauge, it seems to me, is at its best in a fine side-by-side double. It complements this classic design with a balance and handling quality out of this world—as more and more gunners are discovering. Make mine with the conventional two triggers, even though most 20 gauge side-by-sides are made with a selective single trigger. This, of course, is a personal preference, but the classic side-by-side with a single trigger always seems to lack something for me.

The over-under 20 gauge is becoming increasingly popular—Winchester has their Model 101, Ithaca now offers side-by-side and over-under 20 gauges, with Browning, Savage and others having a selection of stack barrels.

Light 12 or Light 20?

There is a "yes, but" question to be answered at this point—how about those 6½-pound 12 gauge doubles currently available. No soap, unless you

The author on a goose pass at Tulelake, California. These cackler geese were taken with a 6½-lb. Marlin 20 gauge over-under, ranges about 55-60 yards.

are content to load 'em with the lightest loads. A 6½-pound 12 gauge, handling a 1¼-ounce shot charge at 1330 feet a second, has 37 foot pounds of recoil. Slip in one of those 1½-ounce Magnum loads and you come up with a whopping recoil of 52 foot pounds.

The 20 gauge 3-inch Magnum, weighing 6.5 pounds and using the standard factory 1¼-ounce loading at a velocity of 1220 fps turns out 32 foot pounds of recoil. In short, using the same 1¼-ounce shot charges in the 12 and 20 gauge, with the so-called high velocity factory loading in each case, you can have a 1 pound lighter gun in the 20 gauge for the *same* recoil found in the 12 gauge loading—32 foot pounds.

The news gets around. The 20 gauge double is becoming increasingly popular. One importer told me that the bulk of his imports are 20 gauge guns. Another importer wrote that his over-under and side-by-side doubles, made in 20 gauge and chambered for 3-inch shells, are his most popular offerings.

These custom-made doubles exemplify a trend toward the modern 20 gauge. You'll lay quite a few iron men on the line to acquire one, but they are well worth the price. The basic Bernardelli side-by-side 20 is $625 with very modest engraving. An extra set of barrels will stand you $225 more. Delivery can be within 8 months—something of a record for imported custom guns.

Another import receiving more attention is the 20 gauge Perazzi over-under. Made only in their better grade, and with two sets of barrels, the price rubs $2000. Delivery is a little slow—about 18 months from the time of the order.

The resurgence in general of the double gun in these United States is very closely tied in with the 20 gauge chambered for 3-inch shells. The modern 20 gauge has come of age. It has taken over the more commonly used shot charges in the 28 gauge, the standard 20, the 16 and the 12 gauge—⅞-ounce, 1-ounce, 1⅛ ounces, 1³⁄₁₆ ounces, and 1¼-ounces—covering all gunning from upland to swampland. There is nothing its equal from the standpoint of gunning versatility, balance in hand, proper gun weight and natural pointing ability. ●

Sell's streamlined, custom-bored Bernardelli 20, here with its 28" barrels, 3 inch chambers. Left barrel is bored .015", a very tight modified, the other tube .010" for a tight improved cylinder. These chokes serve well for all shooting to 50 yards with suitable shot charge weights and sizes. The other 30" barrels, bored .020" left and .025" right for long-range wildfowling, produce 90% patterns with 2s and 4s in Sell's special handloads.

WHAT CAN YOU learn about a rifle's accuracy if you only have one box of cartridges to shoot?

This is an important question to the hunter who is not a handloader. With prices as they are today many might justify one extra box of cartridges for sighting-in a new rifle and to determine its potential, but draw the line at that point.

The question is also important if you have just one box of a particular cartridge to test for accuracy. This happened to me recently and was what started me on the way to writing this article. I was rearranging things in my gun cabinet and ran across a box of Norma 22-250 50-grain soft point ammunition that was at least 12 years old. I thought it would be interesting to find out how well it would shoot after sitting on the shelf that long. My varmint rifle, a Remington Model 700 with 26-inch Douglas premium heavy barrel, a Canjar set trigger and Redfield 12x scope was clearly the perfect test instrument. The real problem was to get the most information from this very limited supply of ammunition.

My first inclination was to fire four 5-shot groups. But then I got to thinking about the hunter with his single box of ammunition. He really has only 15 cartridges available for accuracy testing because it will probably take two shots to be sure he is hitting the target more or less where he wants at 100 yards. After firing 15 cartridges for accuracy and making final sight adjustments this leaves three shots for a final group to check that the center of the bullet pattern is where he wants it.

So what to fire? One 15-shot group, three 5-shot groups or five 3-shot groups? A little more thought showed that I could do all of these! The trick is to have three targets, one behind the other, with the edges carefully lined up. This presents the view of a single target to the shooter. All 15 shots are fired at the front target. However, the back target is changed after every three shots and the middle target after each fifth shot.

The single 15-shot group is particularly useful in determining the center of impact of the bullet pattern. The 3-shot and 5-shot groups give a good estimate of the relative accuracy of the rifle/cartridge combination compared to other rifles for which groups of the same number of shots have been fired.

For the hunter the most important thing is to know the center of impact and how far his bullets disperse around it. After all the name of the game is to hit the game, not to make neat patterns in the thin air. As you will see from the groups I shot—and may well have realized from your own shooting experience—the center of impact of each of several 3-shot (or 5-shot) groups are at quite different locations on the target. The smaller the number of shots in the group, the

This is the author with a new rifle, discovering

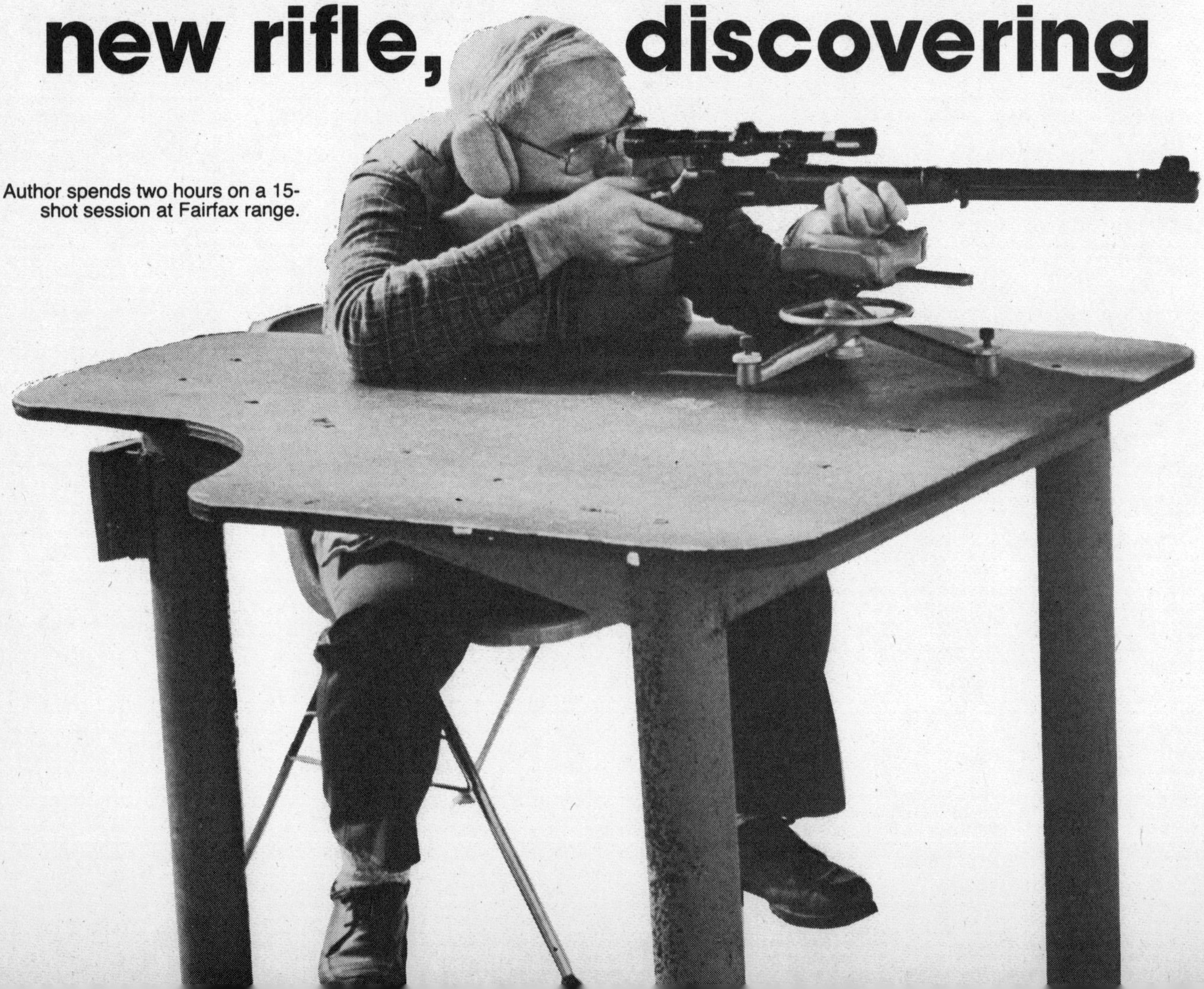

Author spends two hours on a 15-shot session at Fairfax range.

more varied is the position of the center of impact.

I now knew exactly what to do. But did I just take my varmint rifle and the old ammunition out to the range and proceed? Well, yes, I did. But I was getting so interested in the problem of the hunter with his new rifle that in the interests of ballistic science I went out and bought one of the new Winchester Model 94 Angle Eject rifles in 307 Winchester.

The 307 Winchester cartridge is clearly capable out to at least 200 yards. Therefore, I opted for a four-power Redfield Widefield scope and counted on the Widefield feature for adequate field-of-view close-in. After mounting the scope, I went out one weekday morning to the Fairfax Rod & Gun Club ranges. No one else was there, so it was no problem to take all those walks down to the 100-yard target frame to change the middle and back targets.

The first thing I did was cover the whole cardboard target backer with

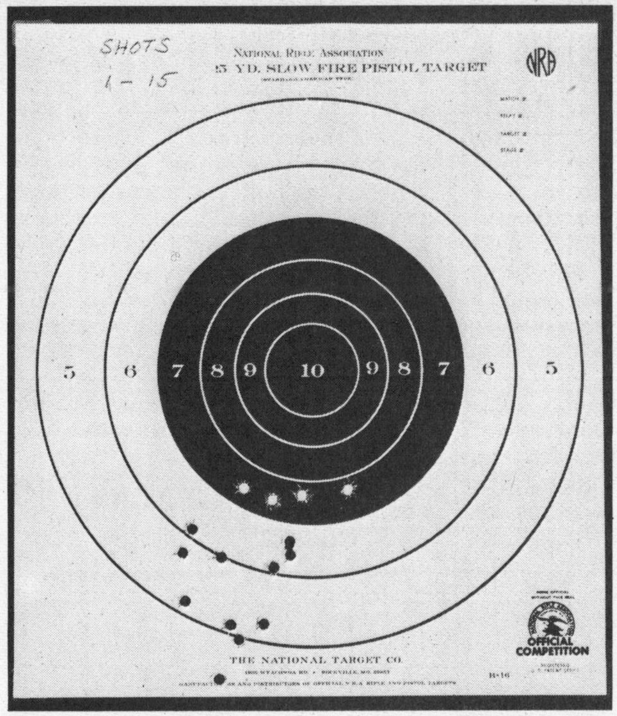

Figure 1

WHAT ONE BOX OF AMMUNITION CAN TELL YOU

by **DAVID LEESTMA**

brown wrapping paper to avoid confusion with all the existing bullet holes. Then I mounted the sighting-in target. The first bullet through the rifle was fired from 25 yards. The bullet hole was above the target and I sure was glad I put the brown paper up or I would never have been able to figure where that first shot went. After adjusting the sights the next shot was fired from 100 yards. It hit the target reasonably close to where I wanted it, so I proceeded to fire for accuracy.

The weather was hot, but I had the whole morning. To avoid shooter fatigue or the effects of a hot barrel, I allotted two hours to shoot the 15 shots, all fired off the benchrest. Since the center of impact was one of the things to be determined, I held the rifle quite like I would if I were hunting. My left hand gripped the forend and the back of that hand rested on the sandbag. The butt of the rifle was pulled tightly into my shoulder. The rear of the stock did *not* rest on a sandbag, but my right elbow did rest on the bench. I've found that this technique not only gives me a center of impact corresponding to what I'd get from normal hunting positions, but also gives very good accuracy.

Now for some heresy. I found that this technique also works for the light kickers like my varmint rifle. With my favorite varmint load—53-grain Sierra benchrest bullet, 35 grains 4064, Remington 9½ primers and Norma brass loaded with one of the old Lee Target Loaders—I consistently get 5-shot groups at 300 yards under two inches. The only rifle I've ever had which did not work best with this method was a Shilen heavy varmint rifle in 222 Remington. It worked best with the classic technique of sandbag support fore and aft and a very light hold. With the classic technique it gave groups around 0.3 inches at 100 yards, while with my usual technique it gave groups around 0.6 inches.

One other thing worth mentioning: Recoil from the Model 94 in 307 Winchester is not bothersome from normal hunting positions, but it is noticeable when shooting off the bench. Since I was looking for the best possible group rather than to prove I was macho, I folded a towel and placed it between the rifle butt and my shoulder. This eliminated any recoil problems as far as I was concerned.

Having done all this, the shooting conditions were ideal. I decided not to allow any alibis. Each shot fired—even if it looked like a flyer—would be part of the group because such a flyer probably would also happen in a hunting situation.

Now let's look at the results. Figure 1 shows the 15-shot group. Figures 2 and 3 are the 3-shot and 5-shot groups, respectively. Things start to get revealing when figure 4 is examined. It shows how the center of impacts of all the groups are distributed.

Determining the center of impact of a group is quite simple. Measure the vertical distance from the bottom edge of the target to the centers of all the bullet holes—that is, from the center of the bullet hole straight down to the bottom edge—and add these numbers together and divide by the number of shots in the group (for a 15-shot group divide by 15, for a 5-shot group divide by 5, etc.). This gives the *average* vertical distance of the group from the bottom edge of the target. It is the same as the vertical measurement of the center of impact of the group.

Now choose one side of the target and measure the horizontal distance from that edge to the centers of all the bullet holes—from the center of the bullet hole straight across to the edge. Proceed exactly as before to obtain the average horizontal distance. Table 1 shows these measurements for the 15-shot target. They are listed in the order in which they were fired.

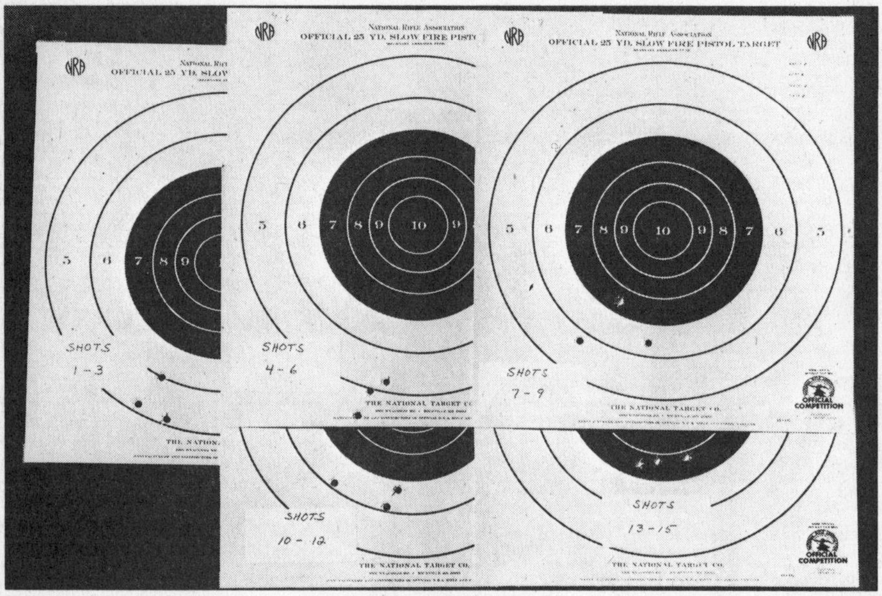

Figure 2

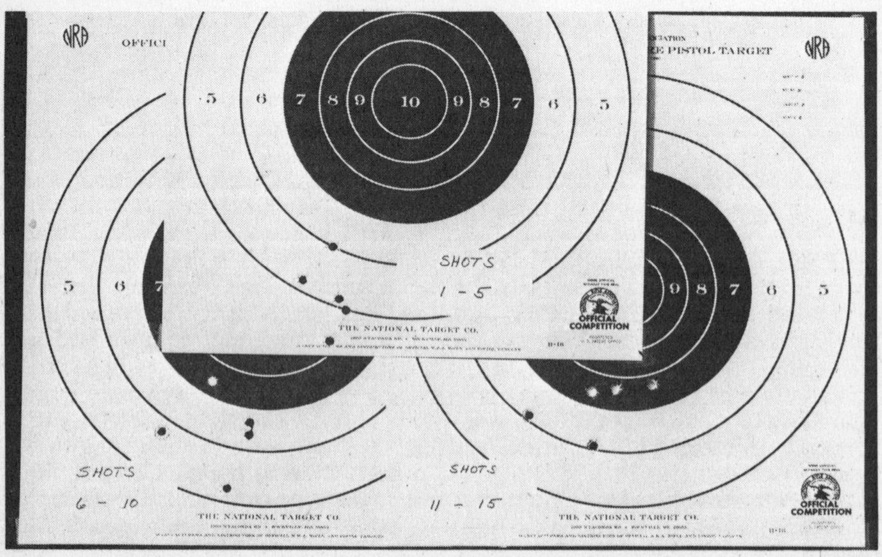

Figure 3

To locate the center of impact of the group just draw a line parallel to the bottom edge of the target at average vertical distance, and another line parallel to the side of the target to the average horizontal distance. Where the two lines cross is the center of the group.

To know the true center of impact of a rifle/cartridge combination would involve firing a group with an infinite number of shots. This could get to be expensive, to say nothing about it taking an eternity to finish all the shooting. However, the center of impact of a 15-shot group gives a pretty good estimate of where the center of impact of a rifle/cartridge combination is really located.

By using statistical techniques involving what is called Chi-Square distribution, it turns out that to a high degree of confidence the true center of impact is located within a box centered on the 15-shot center of impact and with sides equal to 1.5 times the standard deviation in the vertical measurements and 1.5 times the standard deviation in the horizontal measurements. For a 5-shot group the factor is 4.6 instead of 1.5. For a 3-shot group the factor is 12.2

It is relatively easy, though somewhat tedious, to obtain the standard deviations. A hand calculator which takes square roots makes things manageable. Let's look at how to get the standard deviation of the vertical measurements for the 15-shot group in Table 1. Start by taking the first vertical measurement (1.27) and subtracting from it the *average* vertical measurement (2.34). The answer is −1.07. Now square this number, i.e., multiply it by itself. This gives 1.1449. Write this number down. Repeat this process for the remaining 14 vertical measurements. When you are finished, add the numbers you have written down. This gives 15.4984. Now divide by one less than the number of shots in the group. (15.4984 divided by 14 gives 1.1070285) Finally take the square root of the result. To two decimal places this gives 1.05. This is the standard deviation of the vertical measurements. The standard deviation in the horizontal mesurements is obtained in the corresponding way.

Table 2 shows the vertical and horizontal standard deviations obtained by this method for all groups. Table 3 displays the dimensions of the box which contains—with a high degree of confidence—the true center of impact of the rifle/cartridge combination.

Note how large the uncertainty in the location of the true center of impact is for a single 3-shot group as compared to the 15-shot group. That's why shooting a 15-shot group is so valuable. It gives a very good approximation of the true center of impact. The hunter can then adjust his sights based on the 15-shot center of impact and have high confidence that he has put the true center of impact where he wants it.

Now let's examine how the bullet holes are dispersed about the center of impact. To do that we need to know the distance of each bullet hole from the center of impact of the group. This is easily found using the information in Table 1. Pick one of the shots. Subtract the *average* vertical measurement from the actual vertical measurement and square the answer. Now subtract the *average* horizontal measurement from the actual horizontal measurement and square this answer. Add the two squares and take the square root of the result. This is the distance of the bullet hole from the center of impact of the group. The results for all 15 shots are shown in Table 4.

Note that 13 out of 15 shots (87%) are within nearly 1½ inches of the center of impact at 100 yards, and all the shots are within 2¼ inches.

All the above gives, in my estimation, the really important information about the accuracy of a rifle/cartridge combination. However, since most people are used to thinking in terms of group size, it is useful to present that information. I've included the group size information on that 22-250 Norma ammo in case you are curious. The results are given in Table 5.

The really surprising thing to me was how well the Model 94 grouped. Average 3-shot groups under 1½ inches at 100 yards from a lever action rifle was not what I expected, but I surely was pleased. This is as good or better than the groups I have obtained from many bolt action rifles which have passed through my hands over the years. This particular Model 94 will take a prominent place in my gun cabinet.

As you can see, I like accurate rifles. Having a rifle which groups tightly means that as practice improves my holding ability from a field position, I will increase the consistency of my hitting small targets.

But to put things in perspective, consider the problem of hitting a deer in the kill zone at 100 yards. The kill zone of a deer is about 10 inches in diameter, which is pretty big. If from a field position I can shoot a 15-shot group at 100 yards which is 10 inches in extreme spread, then I have a very high confidence that I can put a shot in the kill zone of a deer when shooting from that field position.

The group shot from field position can be considered to consist of two parts: (1)) the rifle's contribution, i.e., the group that would be obtained shooting that rifle from benchrest, and (2) the shooter's contribution, i.e., the size of the group the shooter would get using a perfect one-holer rifle

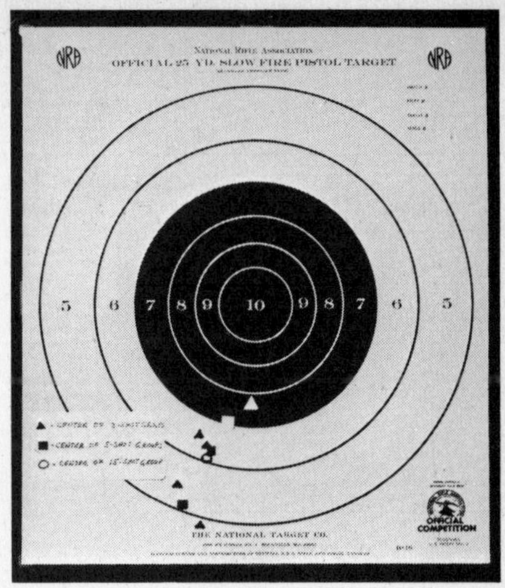

Figure 4

TABLE 1

Location of Bullet Holes in 15-Shot Group Fired From Model 94 in 307 Winchester (180 grain)		
Shot	**Vertical**	**Horizontal**
1	1.27	3.81
2	1.65	3.03
3	2.44	3.65
4	0.31	3.63
5	0.99	3.97
6	1.26	4.40
7	2.50	3.00
8	2.47	4.91
9	3.66	4.08
10	2.72	4.86
11	2.23	4.56
12	2.92	3.12
13	3.48	4.55
14	3.55	5.08
15	3.65	5.91
Average	2.34	4.17

Note: All measurements are in inches. Horizontal measurements are from left edge of target. Measurements made with vernier caliper.

TABLE 2

Standard Deviations For 307 Winchester (180 grain)				
Shots	**Average Vertical**	**Average Horizontal**	**S.D. Vertical**	**S.D. Horizontal**
1 - 3	1.79	3.50	0.60	0.41
4 - 6	0.85	4.00	0.49	0.39
7 - 9	2.88	4.00	0.68	0.96
10 - 12	2.62	4.18	0.36	0.93
13 -15	3.56	5.18	0.09	0.69
1- 5	1.33	3.62	0.79	0.36
6-10	2.52	4.25	0.86	0.78
11-15	3.17	4.64	0.60	1.02
1 -15	2.34	4.17	1.05	0.83

TABLE 3

Location of True Center of Impact For 307 Winchester (180 grain)				
	Dimensions of Box		Center of Box	
Shots	Vertical	Horizontal	Vertical	Horizontal
1 - 3	7.3	5.0	1.79	3.50
4 - 6	6.0	4.8	0.85	4.00
7 - 9	8.3	11.7	2.88	4.00
10-12	4.4	11.3	2.62	4.18
13-15	1.1	8.4	3.56	5.18
1 - 5	3.6	1.7	1.33	3.62
6 -10	4.0	3.6	2.52	4.25
11-15	2.8	4.7	3.17	4.64
1 -15	1.6	1.2	2.34	4.17

TABLE 4

Distance of Bullet Holes From Center of Impact For 15-Shot Group with 307 Winchester (180 grain)			
Shot	Vertical minus Avg. Vert.	Horizontal minus Avg. Horiz.	Distance
1	−1.07	−0.36	1.13
2	−0.69	−1.14	1.33
3	0.10	−0.52	0.53
4	−2.03	−0.54	2.10
5	−1.35	−0.20	1.36
6	−1.08	0.23	1.10
7	0.16	−1.17	1.18
8	0.13	0.74	0.75
9	1.32	−0.09	1.32
10	0.38	0.69	0.79
11	−0.11	0.39	0.41
12	0.58	−1.05	1.20
13	1.14	0.38	1.20
14	1.21	0.91	1.51
15	1.31	1.74	2.18

TABLE 5

Group Sizes		
Shots	307 Winchester	22-250 Norma
1-3	1.18	1.02
4-6	1.22	0.52
7-9	1.91	1.05
10-12	1.74	0.70
13-15	1.37	0.40
Average 3-shot	1.48	0.74
1-5	2.13	1.06
6-10	2.42	1.15
11-15	2.88	0.70
Average 5-shot	2.48	0.97
1-15	4.04	1.41

from the field position. The field group size is just the square root of the sum of the squares of these two parts. Table 6 illustrates some combinations which can be expected to produce a 10-inch field group.

Note that if I can hold well enough to shoot a 4.4-inch group at 100 yards with a perfect rifle, I would still have a very high confidence of killing a deer if I used a rifle that was only capable of 9-inch groups at 100 yards! Also it is evident from Table 6 that a shooter has nearly the same confidence in hitting the kill zone of a deer with a rifle which shoots 5-inch groups as with one that shoots 1-inch groups. This is because the shooter's holding ability needed to get a 10-inch field group is about the same in both of these cases.

Still and all, I subscribe to Townsend Whelen's comment, "Only accurate rifles are interesting."

A final word in closing. Throughout this article I have made some assumptions about the statistical nature of the groups produced by shooter and rifle. Principal among these assumptions are that for both the rifle's contribution and the shooter's contribution the distributions in the horizontal and vertical directions are independent and that these distributions are normal (or Gaussian). In most cases these are pretty good assumptions. Even if for your rifle or holding ability they are not completely accurate assumptions, nevertheless the results obtained by using them are a good guide to the accuracy of your rifle.

Now go out and buy a box of cartridges and learn and have fun! ●

EDITOR'S NOTE: When a physical scientist and serious computer user like this writer uses words here like "confidence," he is using them in the same statistical sense he used them in examining and reporting on heavy weapons systems for our government. *K.W.*

TABLE 6

Combinations Producing A 10-Inch Group From Field Position	
Rifle's Contribution	Shooter's Contribution
1.0	9.95
2.0	9.8
3.0	9.5
4.0	9.2
5.0	8.7
6.0	8.0
7.0	7.1
8.0	6.0
9.0	4.4

Hunting jaguar in the Nayarit region of Mexico, Askins for 10 days lugged a 44-40 "El Tigre" carbine, never got to shoot it — just as well, for it wouldn't group in a foot circle at 40 yards!

GAME FIELD GOOFS

by Colonel CHARLES ASKINS

A few lucky men spend their lives hunting. They roam from Alaska to Mexico to Africa to New Zealand — wherever game awaits. Deadly are their rifles, tremendous their trophies. Unlike you and I (if printed reports are true), they never seem to miss. Never? Well, hardly ever . . .

THE OTHER DAY I dropped a 280 cartridge into a 7mm Magnum chamber and fired it. It was unintentional, the end result of a piece of damfool stupidity. Mine. It did not take the rifle apart but I don't know why. The casing was split from end to end and hot gas spewed out into the action and jetted back into my face. Fortunately for me, the musket was one of the strongest, the Remington M700. Had it been any lesser gun, I reckon I'd have had a lot of iron to comb out of my whiskers.

That piece of knucklebrained fumblebum stuff set me to counting the number of guns and hunting booboos I've pulled over the years. When I finished the tally I felt myself over real careful-like to see if I was still all in one piece. Surprisingly, I was.

They say the Lord looks after fools and drunks, so that must account for my luck, as there have been times when I could qualify on both scores. Let me describe a few of them.

Before I took to fighting wars I was a U.S. Border Patrolman, stationed about 20 miles west of El Paso, Texas. Just at daylight one morning I was tracking a couple of *contrabandista* through a little waterstop on the north line of the Southern Pacific. The pueblo was called Strauss. It is in New Mexico and about 6 miles from the International boundary. It was raining, a rare happening on the desert, and I was in a half-run to keep the tracks in sight before the shower puddled them out.

I loped through the tiny settlement hot on the spoor. The pair quit the railroad tracks above the two-bit hamlet and struck out across the desert. I followed them not more than a quarter-mile and found them sacked out under a rag of a tarp.

Sixgun in hand, I Injuned forward, intending to snatch the tarp off the pair and have them cold turkey. As I leaned forward to grab the tarp, the renegade on the far side reared up on his elbows, a carbine in his hands. I let drive at him with the New Service 44-40 I was packing—and missed. The bullet cut the dirt at his shoulder.

The smuggler did not fire and I let the one shot suffice. It was a good thing I did. The pair were not *contrabandista* at all. They were two old willies and the "carbine" was a pick handle. I'd had my narrowest escape from committing manslaughter.

In Vietnam, one day, I wheeled my battered old jeep up to a Chinaman's little farm and looked the place over. Beside his flimsy corral lay a dead heifer. The farmer was a Nung Chinese. The Nung are soldiers who elected to come south out of the border country between North Vietnam and Red China, and fight the Commies beside the South Vietnamese. This particular Nung had grown too old for the wars and had commenced to farm the land.

This Vietnamese tiger didn't get away, but another — posing in the moonlight at a mere 60 feet — did, to Askins' discomfiture.

The writer, looking slightly goggle-eyed after finding he has bashed a second waterbuck, twin to the one below, but has a license for only one.

He told me a tiger had killed the cow the night before. I wanted to sit up over the bovine and give the cat his lumps that night, but the farmer would have none of that. The cow, he explained, belonged to his landlord and he would have to skin and butcher the critter and peddle the meat to the Third Nung Division which was encamped some 4 miles away, near the village of Song Mao.

I couldn't let this little inconvenience keep me from that cat. I scouted around and purchased a goat and, come the evening, tethered the blatting nanny on a nearby terrace hard by the creek which an inspection during daylight hours had showed the huge feline was using. When the sun went down, I put my back to a mighty Dao tree and felt pretty certain Old Stripes would be along sooner or later.

Directly after sundown two things came out. The mosquitoes and a big fat yellow moon which came boiling up out of the South China Sea. It was almost as light as day. I could see my goat some 50 feet below me. With some premonition that she was on an exposed flank, the goat blatted incessantly. I liked that. The tiger should be back for the heifer but he knew all about nanny goats, too.

At about 9:30 I looked over at the trail coming up out of the nullah and it was bare in the moonlight. At 9:31 I glanced over there again, impelled by the sudden taut silence of my bait. There stood the biggest, most handsome tiger in the jungle! He was simply magnificent there in the moon's brilliant glow, the black stripes on his tawny hide so distinct I could have counted every one of them.

Stripes, Stripes, Stripes——

I was in a sitting position, my elbows on my knees, my rifle in my hands. The shooting iron was a mite on the light side for Asia's toughest carnivore, but I reckoned it would do. Especially at 60 feet. I had a 1x scope on the rifle—a scope with a lot of field, no magnification, and unhappily blessed with these infernally worthless crosshairs. I swung the glass over on the tiger—he seemed in no hurry—and what I saw made me the unhappiest GI in all Vietnam.

All the scope showed at the 20-yard distance was stripes. Stripes in the top of the glass, the bottom, and on all sides. I just could not see the crosswires. But time was a'wastin' and I didn't know how long he'd stay. I squared the cat's shoulder off in the glass and worked on the trigger.

On the shot, the animal reared straight up and fell over backward in the nullah. I went forward with a torch and shined it into the tules, looking for my prize. He had done a lot of thrashing around after he fell and I wasn't exactly surprised not to find him. But there would be a lot of blood. Buckets of it. A good spoor to follow and I was positive he could not go far.

When daylight came, I set out to track down my Mr. Stripes. Well, not only was there no blood, there was no tiger. As a matter of fact, the tiger had gone a mile across the paddy and raided another Chinese farmer, taking off a 2-year old buffalo. I had missed that tiger, big as a Missouri mule, or so he seemed there in the moonlight, at the ignominious distance of 60 feet! I'll never live that one down.

In Africa a few years ago to give the 338 Magnum a wring-out test before it was placed on the market, I got into a band of Grant's gazelle. I had Capt. Allen Pope, our leading soldier of fortune, with me, and we had a little pow-wow as to who would shoot first. "Aw, go ahead," Pope said magnanimously, "I'll take the next one."

Tony Dyer, one of the better white hunters in Africa, motioned and I came up beside him and we commenced to stalk the animals. We moved up for a half-mile and finally could get no closer. The shot was a long one. Too far for a poor hitter like me, but there was no help for it. The Granti were getting fidgety and would take it on the lam any minute. I'd have to shoot. I did.

The buck Dyer had picked out for me dropped. But it was up again and off, limping, immediately. "You've hit him fair enough, but I think too far back," Dyer commented. "I'll go back and get the safari car. You follow him up."

A Grant to Spare

I found the blood-flecked spoor—not easy, what with the tracks of others in and over it—and took it through a patch of thorn. When I broke out on the other side, there stood my Grant, not more than 80 yards distant. We saw each other at the same time and he decided he still had some go left in him. On my second shot he did a cartwheel.

I went up to him and had a look at the horns. This wasn't my buck. Certainly not the trophy Dyer and I had selected from the band. Those horns had been in the record class, these were quite ordinary. About this time Dyer tooled the old Willys safari wagon around the bush and had a look.

"Hell's blood!" he exploded, "You've done it! You've bashed in two Grant." Not more than 60 yards away we found the first buck, piled up and deader than Farouk. The horns were good for the Rowland Ward record book. Some 31¼ inches. Tony took the second buck on his license and I took a ribbing for a piece of typical dumb dude shooting.

You'd think these kind of booboos would sink in, but not on old Askins. On another safari, Bill Jenvey, white hunter from Down Under, and I were scouting for buffalo. This was along the Uaso Nyero River of the Northern Frontier and I had taken a bull but he wasn't much for horn. Returning to camp in the dusk of the evening, we bumped into a gaggle of waterbuck. I had only the 458 Winchester with me and no cartridges save full metal patch. Nothing daunted, we fell out of the safari car and in the gathering gloom minced forward.

At fully 300 yards I let drive at the biggest bull in the band. The slug struck the ground at the critter's feet. I held over his back and on the third shot I got blood. The bull fell, arighted himself, and limped off slowly, weaving like a drunken Sam Salt. He went over a slight rise and out of sight. "Follow him." Jenvey directed. "I'll go back and bring the safari car forward. There are several more buck over that rise. Don't shoot unless you see your buck limping." I nodded, already in a run.

I galloped up the hill, peeked over the crest and there stood my waterbuck. He was a handsome rascal and although I knew he was badly hit he had his head up and looked quite alert. I knifed 500 grains of hard metal into his brisket and he went down like he'd been struck by nuclear reaction.

The distance was about 90 yards and in the thickening gloom I had trouble threading my way forward. I had scarcely gone 40 yards before I stumbled onto a waterbuck stone dead. It was my first one.

Tardily, I remembered Jenvey's admonition, "Don't shoot unless you see him limping." I had two waterbuck and the limit was one. I gave my second prize to a hunting mate who had licensed for the game but hadn't had the luck to see one. What Bill Jenvey told me when he arrived with the safari car and discovered we had two buck instead of the regular quota cannot be published, not even in a book with the liberal unexpunged editorial policy of this one!

One spring I took one of the hot new 300 Magnums to Alaska with me. It was a conversion from the standard right hand bolt action to the port side. I am a southpaw and while I can reach over the bridge pretty well and grab the bolt, I would rather have it mounted on the handy side. Especially when I am going to be hubbing up against the biggest of our bears. The conversion of the action had been done by a reputable guns-tinker and I was satisfied with it.

When I checked the rifle out for zero on the ice in front of guide Nelson Walker's quarters in Kotzebue, sometimes it would fire and other times it would not. I attributed this to a drop or two of oil. The mercury was hanging around minus 35 degrees and this causes some gun oils to solidify. I sloshed the bolt around in a can of airplane gas and reassembled it. There was the same off-again on-again routine. I took the rifle over to Al Guthrie, who is a good amateur gunsmith, and Al put in a driving spring from Walker's old Model 70. That fixed it. I belted a whale of a big white bear, a record book stud, and came away for a go at walrus down on St. Lawrence Island.

The fall following, I was out on the Alaska Peninsula with John Swiss. John is a ring-tailed tooter on hunting the giant Alaska brown bear, and on moose, too. I had shot a lot of the bruin so I went out with Swiss for a big moose.

White hunter Bill Jenvey, here supervising skinning of a zebra, was put on the spot when Askins walloped the second waterbuck.

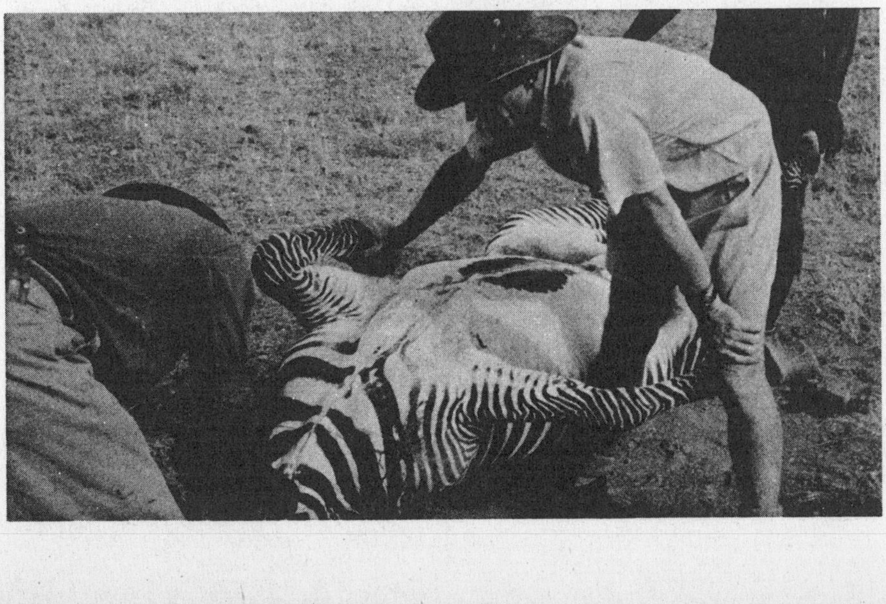

Askins' big Alaskan moose, bagged despite a rifle which fired only twice in four attempts.

We found him all right. And the stalk was a good one. We got up to 60 yards. The first shot was a killing one, but these old lunker bulls like you find out on the peninsula can pack a lot of lead. The bull went down but he got right up again and started off. The second shot was a misfire. So, too, was the third. I finally got the fourth to go bang. It decked the game. "I thought you had fixed that dam' rifle last spring." Swiss growled. "We'd have sure been in a helluva fix if that moose had been a 10-foot brownie." And so we would, for John was packing only a six-gun, his 338 left back in the boat a couple of miles to the rear. The moose went 70½ inches.

When I got back to home base, I gave that musket a real going over. The conversion was strictly a Rube Goldberg. Sometimes the striker would fall freely, other times it was partially caught by the bolt. Anyone with the acumen of a 10-year-old would have checked out these possibilities before going out to joust with the biggest game on the continent, but not me!

During 10 years in the Border Patrol I got into quite a few gunfights with the *contrabandista* along the Tex-Mex frontier. These powder-flecked fisticuffs resulted in a pretty high casualty rate. In fact, it seemed like more of the opposition cashed in their chips than ever regained their health. As a result of this, I got so I seldom ventured out unless all gussied up with a sixgun in my pants.

Trigger Trouble

One fine spring evening I was jogging up Mesa Street, in El Paso, and had along not only my best girlfriend but her mama as well. I was packing a gun in a half-breed rig. It was, of all things, a 22 automatic, and although it might look like middlin' poor ordnance for self-defense, these little stingers shoot 11 times quick-like and point better than any other handgun made.

This was a real special gun. I had sent it to Berdon, who in those days was the gee-whiz guns tinker, and he'd put one of his go-to-hell triggers on it. This trigger was a new development, designed to break clean as glass, with no backlash, and pulled at about 2 pounds. As I say, I had this 4-inch cutter in a shoulder rig and I sorta slapped my arm against the gun to move it into a more comfortable position. The slap was enough for that hair trigger Berdon had whumped up. The gun fired. I was driving at the time and the hollow-point high-speed slug went boring down through my hip.

It was only a few blocks to the hospital so I drove over there, found I could walk okay and so bounced up to the desk and announced I had shot myself. This sort of shook up the reception committee but the gal recovered and soon had me shunted in and ready for first aid.

Doc Gallagher, who I had known for a long time, soaked a pull-through in iodine and swabbed out the bullet channel. The slug had missed the hipbone and gone out through the buttock. About 7 inches of penetration, which I thought was pretty good for a 22. When that wound channel got well filled with iodine it felt a hell of a lot worse than the bullet did boring its way downward, I'll tell you!

I took the gun apart next day and had a look at the Berdon masterpiece. His bearing surfaces between sear nose and notch were so infinitesimally small that any sudden jar could set the gun off, safety or no safety. These are the kind of things a feller should explore before he gets to shooting holes in the seat of his pants.

Another time, hunting jaguar in Nayarit, I whipped into Mazatlan and sat around a couple of days waiting for my guides. They eventually showed up and we pushed off for the hunting camp, 150 miles to the south. It is a bloody nuisance to carry a shooting iron into Mexico so I had permitted my head guide to talk me into coming down gunless. He'd have a good rifle for me, he said. I had with me my old hunting partner, Earl "Tex" Jones of Abilene. He would need some kind of a powder burner, too.

Jonesy was sort of my guest on this one. I had talked him into the hunt, so when it came to a selection of the rifles I gave him a good-looking Springfield. It had been sporterized, made into a Mannlicher style actually, and had an excellent set of Williams sights. It was an Improved '06 and was more than adequate for the biggest *tigre* south of the Rio Grande. My cat-killer was something else again!

It was a Spanish-made 44-40, built before the Spanish Civil War by Garate Anitua y Cia, Eibar. Dubbed the "El Tigre," it was the spitting image of the old Winchester 1892 carbine. I glanced through the barrel. It looked like the inside of a rusty length of sewer pipe. I shot the little snapper. Of the 10 rounds fired, 7 went through the target as keyholes. The group measured 14 inches at 40 yards.

Now, shooting jaguar is a serious business of plunking the great cat spang through the heart. If he is in a tree you absolutely must drop him cold turkey. If he tumbles out with any life remaining in him he is dangerously apt to disembowel a dog or two. It does not take any great degree of shooting skill to slice his heart in two—that is, provided you have a decent gun. With my venerable 44-40 and its tumbling slugs, I wondered if maybe like Sasha Kemal I should just make a spear and go for the feline with that.

We hunted 10 days and never started a jaguar. It wasn't for lack of hard work. But as it turned out I did not have to turn my thoroughly worn old clunk on one of the monster cats. Some good came of that, for all its lack of action. I learned right there never to go into the gamefields without my own ordnance. Regardless of what the outfitter may tell me about his for-hire artillery, hereafter I'll just fetch along a gun I know is capable of pitching all the slugs through the target point foremost.

* * *

These confessionals are seldom related by gents like me who go knocking around the gamelands across the world. Mostly we just keep our booboos top secret. There ought to be a moral to this saga somewhere. The least, I reckon, I can say is that having gotten this account of these utterly stupid dumbcluck stunts off my chest, I'll hold up my hand and solemnly affirm I ain't gonna do 'em anymore. I'd like to say that, but in all honesty I am not so sure. •

COP-PROOF

by COLIN GREENWOOD

Sturm, Ruger's Police Service-Six.

Put down one reasoned British vote for the revolver and don't argue — he makes sense

THE NAME OF Walter Winans is not as well known as it should be amongst the shooters of today. Born of the Russian upper classes, he spent many years in the United States and in England as well as having strong connections with a number of other countries. He sponsored, promoted and took part in handgun competitions in many parts of the world. His shooting skill is well proven and many of today's better shots would find difficulty in improving on his performances.

In 1900 Winans became one of the first to write about handgun shooting techniques. His book *The Art of Revolver Shooting* can be read today with both interest and profit. A second book, *Hints on Revolver Shooting,* was followed by works on rifle shooting and, in 1919, by *The Modern Pistol and How to Shoot It.* Winans should be recognized as one of the father figures of both competitive and practical pistol shooting. But even Winans could be wrong. Chapter I of *The Modern Pistol and How to Shoot It* begins:

"There is now no use learning revolver shooting. That form of pistol is obsolete except in the few instances where it survives for target shooting, or is carried for defense; just as flintlock muskets even now survive in out-of-the-way parts of the world."

In the sixty years or so which have passed since Winans made his pronouncement, the revolver has gone from strength to strength. New manufacturers are in business and new models have come from both old and new makers. This obsolete old wheelgun keeps going and going. Its devotees claim it to be superior in some respects, or even in all respects, to the self-loading pistols (which we will call automatic in this article to conform with popular usage). Much as been written on the "revolver v. automatic" argument and it seems that little remains to be said. Unfortunately, there has been a lack of objectivity and logic and the debate has suffered from over-generalization. Perhaps there is *something* to be said.

It must be conceded at once that Winans' pronouncement was true as it relates to military sidearms. The British clung to the revolver longer than any other major power, but this arose more from a disregard for the handgun than from any conscious decision about the type to be used. No major power now uses the revolver as its standard military sidearm, though the wheel-gun often survives in specialized roles. The dictates of the military and the circumstances in which an army operates are not necessarily applicable in other spheres. With police forces the revolver finds strong supporters. The majority of police in the United States, Canada and many other countries, as well as England, still favor the revolver over the automatic. And there are very good reasons for this. In the context of the reequipping of the British police, I was closely involved with this question at both local and national levels, and had to present and counter the various arguments raised. It might be worthwhile to study these arguments to see whether or not some further light can be shed on the controversy.

British Police

In the not too distant past the firearms used by the British Police were a weird mixture of long obsolete weapons. Some of the smaller forces had just a few handguns salvaged from confiscated weapons. Yorkshire's West Riding Constabulary, which I joined in 1954, had a small stock of 380 Webley Revolvers of the civilian Mark III pattern which had been

bought in the early 1920s. At a few major stations, four or six of these handguns would be securely locked in a safe in the Divisional Commander's office along with six shells per gun. Firearms training then consisted of sending a circular around the 3,000 man force asking who thought himself fit to carry a gun. If your name was on the list, you were officially trained. During my first twelve years of police service no one in the force was issued a gun and not one single round was fired in training. There was a very active and very successful pistol team, but shooting was a sport and not really connected with the business of policing.

This total ignorance of firearms was common throughout England. The best trained forces in the country allowed a very small number of men to fire up to twelve shots per year and one force—far and away the most lavish in this respect—allowed thirty rounds of ammunition per year to the very small number of "trained" men. The fact is that this level of weaponry and training was perfectly adequate for the needs of the day. In London in 1954 there were just *four* robberies in which a firearm was used. Records of such rare events were not kept outside London but there can be no doubt that in the whole of England the total number of robberies involving firearms would rarely exceed twenty per year. That situation has now deteriorated to the point where London expects robberies involving firearms to approach the one thousand mark per year. By international standards that is small stuff, but when compared to England in the 50s it represents an appalling decline. Add to that the growth in international terrorism and the British Police faced a new problem. Their small armories of obsolete weapons were not only inadequate, they were dangerous. The total lack of training created a situation in which armed police were probably a greater danger to the public than armed criminals.

Progressively from the mid-1960s police forces began to look to their armories and by 1970 the problem was receiving attention at national level. The advocates of the automatic pistol had their say and some autos were in use in a number of police forces. The general lack of experience within the English police meant that the few hobby shooters had a great deal of influence. Much of the argument advanced arose from the individual experience and personal preferences of committed enthusiasts who tried to translate their ideas into policy recommendations. Arguments tended to be in abstract terms about which was the "best" weapon, but the arguers failed to establish the precise role which would be filled by a police handgun.

The Role

In police use, a handgun will be carried in its holster day in and day out, year after year. The officer will be involved in a wide range of activities during which he will not give his gun a second thought. Even in the most hectic parts of the world, the gun will rarely be drawn and even more rarely fired. The armed police officer will have many things on his mind and the mere fact of being armed will warrant little thought in his day to day routine. In most cases he will have ample warning of any need to use his gun, but occasionally he will have to bring it into play very quickly and with no warning.

Contrast this with the sportsman or hobby shooter, even with the practical pistolman. The period for which the latter will carry a gun is very limited and he will be well aware of the requirement to use it. The mere fact that he is carrying a gun will be uppermost in his mind. Contrast the policeman's

Author's grandfather (upper left) in 1904 knew little of guns in his time on the forces. The author (at left) as a village constable riding a bike in the 1950's also served in such a gunless era. By the mid-'70's, the author (below) as a Superintendent had official occasion to explain to HRH the Duke of Kent the reasons a short-barreled double shotgun had advantages for police use.

role with that of the soldier who, acting under orders, is committed to a combat situation in a state of preparedness. The police pistol will stay in its holster for every working day of perhaps thirty years, ready to go at any second but actually being fired only once or twice in that thirty year spell.

The police handgun will be carried by a working cop in any one of several branches of a force. He will not be a committed firearms enthusiast. He will not spend countless hours of his free time perfecting his shooting and weapon handling techniques. The odds are that he will be uninterested in his gun, regarding it as a necessary nuisance. He will undergo his training and then his periodic retraining.

During those periods he will be conscious of and interested in his gun, otherwise he will not. He will usually be working alone and unsupervised, with many complex problems on his mind. No matter what country he is from, his basic training will almost certainly be inadequate and his retraining too infrequent to maintain his weapon handling skills at a level where he will deal with all the problems rapidly and without conscious thought. Even in the few forces which provide really good firearms training, it is virtually impossible to keep a busy operational policeman at peak efficiency with his gun unless he is personally interested.

If the arguments about revolver v. automatic pistol are re-examined in this light, many aspects take on a very different complexion.

State of Readiness

The problem of carrying the gun in a holster, unused but ready for instant action, over a thirty year stretch militates against most automatics.

Single action autos carried with the hammer cocked for such a period might eventually suffer from a weakened spring and the less-than-interested cop may not recognize the fact until a fire fight is in progress. Despite the various systems of using holster straps as safety barriers, accidents are likely when cocked autos are drawn rapidly by men whose skills have rusted. Such handguns carried uncocked, or with an empty breech are much less likely to discharge accidentally but the average policeman in a panic situation can still wind up with an uncocked or unloaded gun after performing juggling feats which would mystify Houdini.

Double action autos have their own problems. They can be carried safely with a cartridge in the chamber and the hammer down, but the requirement which must cause most concern is that for drawing and firing a couple of shots at high speed. The first shot on a double action auto requires a long, heavy pull on the trigger; but the second requires much less effort. The average cop will not be able to cope with this rapid change in trigger pressures. In a series of tests it was found that this feature alone reduced the probability of hit by 20% when the subjects were officers with some experience of handguns.

The double action revolver can be fully loaded yet have all the working parts at rest. With no strain on any part, and with very low accident potential, it can be carried in a state of instant readiness for thirty years. When it has to be brought into action there is no fumbling with safeties and the like. The double action trigger pull will be constant from shot to shot and is relatively easily mastered. From the point of carrying in a state of readiness, the revolver is much safer and much more likely to prove effective for the average policeman.

Malfunctions

It is sometimes said that the automatic pistol is more prone to malfunction than a revolver and that malfunctions or misfires are more difficult to clear. In fact, modern automatics are very reliable and if the gun is well cared for, malfunctions are so rare as to merit little consideration. For the individual gun owner, this factor is of no consequence. But the less-than-interested policeman will not give his gun the sort of attention which the individual owner might lavish on it. One of the major causes of malfunctions with automatics in the field is distortion of the magazine lips caused by dropping a magazine on a hard surface. The knowledgeable gun handler will see the damage and correct it. The average cop will not. Clearing a malfunction in a revolver may not be as simple as the hobby shooter expects. Watching policemen struggling with the consequences of a raised primer does nothing to improve confidence. Despite that, it remains beyond question that the rapid clearing of a malfunction or misfire in an auto requires a degree of knowledge, dexterity and practice that police training rarely supplies. In terms of reliability the revolver scores over the auto for the average policeman.

In the hands of a competent shot whose mind is on his gun, the modern automatic pistol is a safe weapon; but the busy policeman with much on his mind can be less than totally attentive to his sidearm. The presence of a round in the breech after the magazine had been removed can and does cause accidents with autos. A magazine safety does not entirely remove this danger because of the chance of replacing an empty magazine without clearing the breech. In a perfect world there would be no accidents, but in the harsh and busy world of the operational policeman, the revolver is more "cop-proof."

Firepower

On magazine capacity the automatic must score. So many of the modern weapons have double column mags with more than a dozen shots in hand. In a military context this could be vital and combat competitions are often devised to give great advantage to the big magazine. The advantage is a dubious one for our average policeman whose average fire fight is likely to involve 2.6 shots. When reloading is required, there is usually plenty of time. The rare instances which indicate a need for rapid reloading in a police combat situation are usually a product of bad tactics. The marginal advantage given by the auto on this score does not balance its disadvantages. Police departments and those individuals who have to provide their own guns will also want to take account of the differences in effective lifetime. A self-loader shooting a serious man-stopping round will be unlikely to survive many more than 5,000 shots. A revolver will happily digest four times that number of cartridges without problems.

Cop-Proof

For the individual gun owner the revolver v. automatic pistol argument is academic and should be resolved on the basis of personal preference. Either type will serve him well if he looks after it, and each has its special features and advantages. For the military, the self-loader is unarguably superior to the revolver in a battle situation. For the average working policeman the revolver has the edge for simplicity, reliability, safety and the general ability to be more "cop-proof." In a service working under constant pressure these factors will allow for a higher standard of training in a given time scale. Overwhelmingly, the British police settled on revolvers in their re-equipping program. Though examined again and again, that decision still seems right. ●

Hammers

A concise history of the many and varied forms that these two elements of a gun—or of most guns—have taken some five centuries of design and execution.

by GOUGH THOMAS

Photographs and captions by Roger Barlow

This Belgin pinfire (shown out of chronology) has most interesting hammers—slightly mad, certainly furious and decorative as well as doing the job that hammers are put on guns to do.

THERE IS AN eternal fascination in observing the evolutionary stages through which various forms of life have passed—the emergence of features to meet newly-arising needs and their progressive adaptation to those needs. In this we can almost see the hand of the Great Designer. Something of the same fascination arises from human artifacts, especially in much-handled objects, such as utensils, implements and weapons. They start in some crude form to satisfy an arising need on the lowest terms; then they progress in functional efficiency; later, in many instances, their esthetic potential is realized and exploited—all this with considerable overlapping of the successive stages.

In this article I want to consider two assoicated features which have accompanied guns throughout their long evolution; aspects which conspicuously mark the stages of that evolution, and which exhibit the sort of evolutionary changes already noted. These features are the hammers and fences of portable firearms.

Hand Gonnes

The father of all firearms of this sort was the late Medieval *hand gonne,* which appeared as a military weapon in the mid-14th century. As depicted in contemporary manuscripts it consisted simply of a short muzzle-loading barrel of cast metal—a miniature cannon—affixed as a prolongation to a stout wooden shaft, by which it was held and manipulated. There was no firing mechanism. The soldier appears to have held the wooden shaft with his left hand and, perhaps, under his left arm, and to have fired the gun with his right hand, by applying a light linstock, tipped with some smouldering substance, to the touch-hole.

The Matchlock

It surely needed nothing more than a recognition of the military potential of the primitive hand-gun to inspire the means for converting it into an effective arm for regular troops. Thus arose the bent stock with a butt, whereby the gun could be shouldered and aimed in substantially the modern manner. At the same time the touch-hole was moved from the barrel's top to one side, and a pan (often with a swinging cover) was fixed alongside it to hold the priming powder. Most important of all, the user's right hand was freed—the match, now a length of saltpeter-soaked cord, was held in a clamp at the head of a pivoted lever, the latter controlled by an external sear or "tricker" (trigger). On pulling the trigger the burning match was swung down mechanically into contact with the priming powder in the pan.

The pivoted lever, then called a *serpentine,* was the first instance of a "hammer" as herein contemplated and, since the flash of the priming powder could now menace the shooter's eye, a piece of metal, often rectangular, was fixed vertically or nearly so behind the pan, acting as a shield. This was the first simple "fence." Our matchlock illustration shows these essential elements as applied to a late matchlock, made about 1590, by which date the matchlock had deposed the mounted man-at-arms for his preeminence in the battle hierarchy.

The Wheellock

The dawn of the 16th century saw

Mr. Thomas is the gun editor of *Shooting Times and Country Magazine,* a British weekly. Mr. Barlow, author and filmmaker, has appeared in these pages before.

and Fences

The simple match lock, our earliest practical firearm, sometimes had a fence of the simplest soft—a cruid baffle to deflect burning powder grains of the priming charge and prevent them from blowing back into the shooter's face and eyes. (This gun in the NRA Museum).

This Spanish matchlock has a crude vestigial fence.

Some wheel-locks depended upon the cock and/or the pyrites in its jaws to prevent any burning grains of the priming charge from coming back toward the shooter's face; many others fitted a true fence to insure protection, as here. (This gun in the NRA Museum).

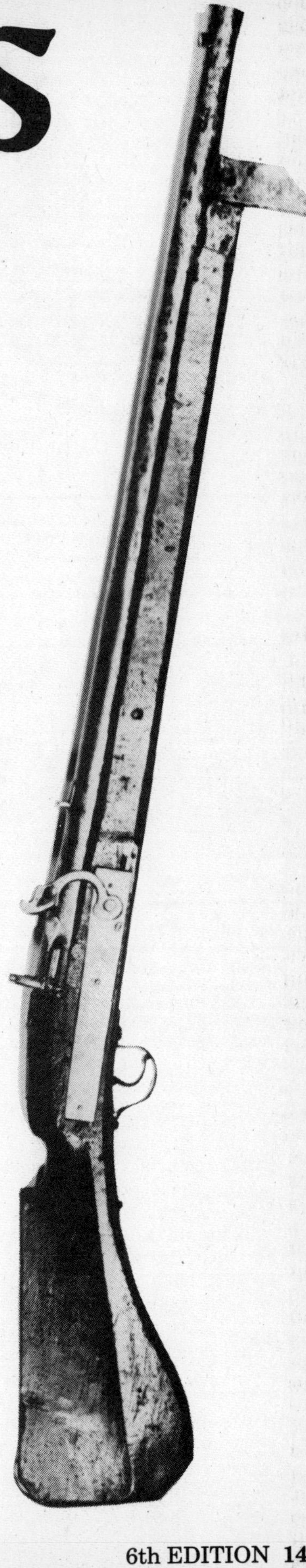

The earliest flint guns seemed to depend upon the hammer (which wasn't even called that, it was the "cock") to keep burning powder grains out of the shooter's face. In later guns, as in this John Manton lock, the compact "V" pan is partially surrounded by sides which aid the hammer in shielding the shooter's face.

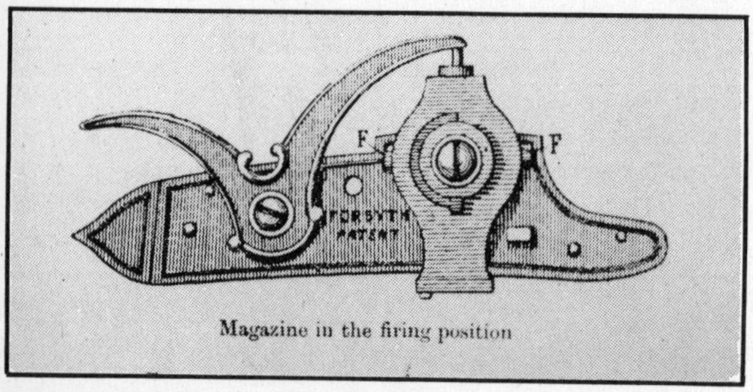

With the advent of Forsyth's percussion priming compound the hammer, in the early 1800s, finally became an actual "hammer" for it now was designed to strike a sharp blow on a firing pin which detonated the priming material by *impact*. This drawing of the famous Forsyth "scent bottle" lock shows an oddly shaped but graceful hammer. As there should be no escape of the flash of the priming compound, no fence is needed.

the introduction of the first modern gun, in the sense of a weapon with self-contained means for igniting the powder charge at the touch of a trigger. This was the wheellock, the invention of which has been attributed, with something less than absolute certainty, to Leonardo da Vinci. The principle was simple: the mechanism complex. A torrent of sparks was generated in the midst of the priming powder by a rapidly-moving, serrated steel wheel, on to which was pressed a piece of iron-pyrites held in the jaws of a spring-loaded clamp. The wheel was made to rotate—though only through a few degrees of arc—by a powerful spring. It was cocked or "spanned" by an external, detachable key—the original spanner. Rapidity and reliability of ignition were remarkable—greater, I would say, than those of the flintlock which in due course superseded it. No less remarkable was the outburst of gunmaking genius which this brilliant invention touched off, as testified to by the arms museums of the world, which display many and wide variations on the original theme.

One of the most constant features of the wheellock was the large hinged clamp holding the pyrites. This was not a true hammer, for it did not move when the gun was fired, but it held that role until the advent of the hammer of the flintlock. Its function of holding something in its jaw inspired many decorative *motifs*, among which dogs, dragons and other fabled monstors were conspicuous.

The fences of wheellocks are not particularly interesting. Sometimes they took the form of a strip-like piece of metal curving upwards to the rear from the pan but, perhaps more often than not, they were omited. One concludes that the flash from the pan of the wheellock did not tend to embarrass the shooter.

It is an odd thing, not entirely to be ascribed to the relatively backward state of gunmaking in England in the 16th and 17th centuries, that the wheellock appears never to have been made there. Germany and Central Europe were its strongholds, where it survived long after the use of the flintlock became general. An eminent Austrian maker, Josef Hamerl, was still producing wheellocks as late as 1735.

The Flintlock

The flintlock had a diverse and obscure origin of uncertain date, though unmistakable references to locks of this type go back to 1547. As finally developed it comprised a spring-operated hammer or cock, holding in its jaws a piece of flint. When the trigger was pulled the flint struck an L-shaped steel "frizzen," the horizontal part of which acted as a cover to the priming pan. The frizzen, transversely pivoted at its lower, forward end and under spring control, was thrown back when struck by the flint. This action exposed the priming powder, to a shower of sparks generated by the flint as it scraped down the vertical face of the frizzen.

In this admirable invention the hammer or cock, so much smaller and neater than the corresponding part of the wheellock, became an object of beauty, chiefly by virtue of the elegant shape it finally acquired.

Fences, however, remained in more or less eclipse, though a vestigial type, comprising an upturned lip to the rearward edge of the priming pan, are not infrequent.

The Percussion Gun

The original percussion guns, made in accordance with the 1805 revolutionary invention of the Scottish pas-

As with the English "dolphin" hammers, these hawk-like hammers of a fine Austrian (1840s) double have deeply recessed faces able to retain most of the flying fragments of the percussion cap. The main job of the fence of this gun was not the protection of the shooter's face but to keep those downward deflected fragments from the shooter's hand!

When the copper (sometimes steel) percussion cap was invented the fence was called back into service to protect the shooter's eyes. Not so much from burning powder or priming compound but from the far more dangerous bits of metal often sent flying by the exploding percussion cap. The fence of this Joseph Manton of the 1820s is, though practical, far less graceful than the shape hammers had already taken.

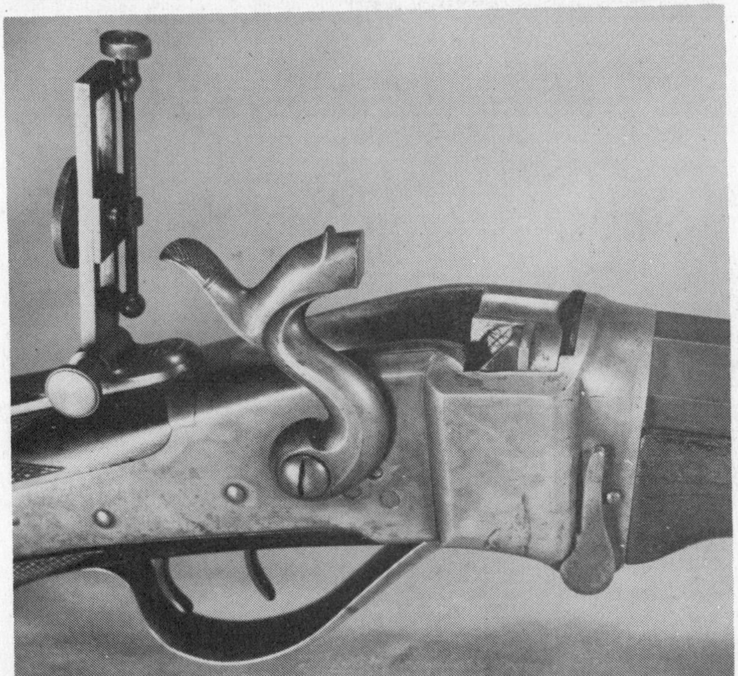

The hammer of the Manton above had already taken on the "dolphin" form which was to become widely copied during the ensuing percussion period.

This side hammer Sharps target rifle (left), sometimes called the 1877 or English model, has a dolphin-like hammer—probably made in Birmingham, England. The breechblock top has a low, integral L-shaped fence of sorts close to the hammer nose.

tor, the Reverend A. J. Forsyth, brought with them a new look. In place of the cock and frizzen there was a graceful, light hammer and the curious, pivoted "scent-bottle" magazine containing the percussion powder. This kind of gun, expensive to build and embodying the bad principle of containing detonating powder in bulk, did not long survive. The percussion cap rightly struck it dead and, incidentally, gave rise to a generation of guns in which fences acquired a new importance for the protection of the shooter's eyes from flying cap fragments. Many of the early caplock guns were ugly affairs, but in the final development the best specimens, with their shapely, cupped hammers and nipples deeply sunk in the delicately curved "shell" fences were highly satisfying to the eye, and depended not at all for their effect on any embellishment.

The Breechloader

It was the French Lefaucheux drop-down gun, using the pinfire cartridge, which launched sporting guns firmly into the breech-loading era. This revolutionary change, best dated here from the appearance of the gun in London at the Great Exhibition of 1851, but matured over the two preceding decades, did nothing to deprive those components, whose history we have been following for nearly five centuries, of their essential functions. The pinfire hammer, at its best, was no more than a graceful variant of its immediate predecessor, whilst the outer part or shoulders of the standing breech took on the now-vital duty and, in English usage, the name "fence."

The supersession of the pinfire by the central-fire breechloader, notably that of G. H. Daw in 1861, saw the restoration of the hammer and shell fence of the caplock muzzleloader; and, in the best specimens of this latest period, the gun arguably attained a peak of elegance and beauty never surpassed.

The introduction of the "hammerless" principle did not, of course, do away with hammers: it merely moved them from the outside to the inside of the gun. But this removal of a centuries-old feature, though it grossly affronted many conservative sportsmen, opened up new opportunities for decorative display. The now-unencumbered surface of the lockplates,

Although there was often a slight escape of gas around the pin of the very early pinfire cartridges (before the base wad was invented by Houllier) no fence was really needed, but they were often there in vestigial form for decoration; and possibly because shooters and gunmakers were so used to seeing them that a gun would simply not have looked right without them! These hammers of a Bastin-Lepage sliding-barrel gun also served as extractors after driving the pin down into the percussion cap inside the base.

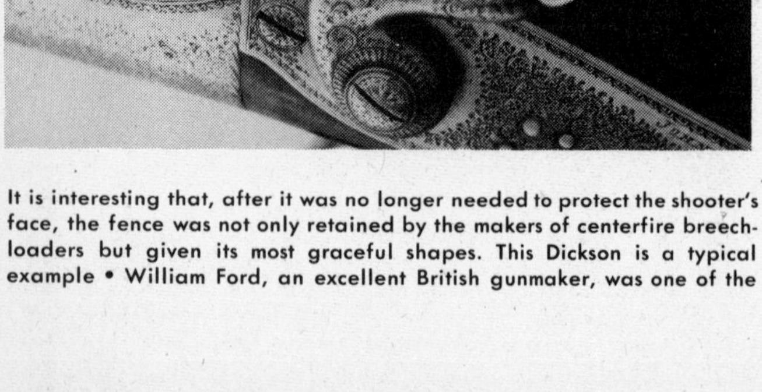

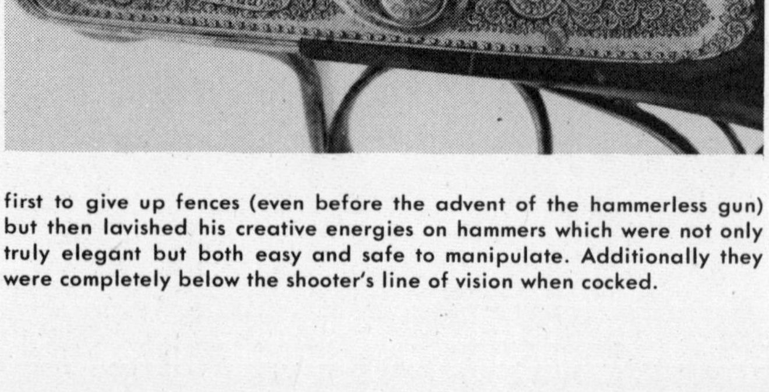

It is interesting that, after it was no longer needed to protect the shooter's face, the fence was not only retained by the makers of centerfire breechloaders but given its most graceful shapes. This Dickson is a typical example • William Ford, an excellent British gunmaker, was one of the first to give up fences (even before the advent of the hammerless gun) but then lavished his creative energies on hammers which were not only truly elegant but both easy and safe to manipulate. Additionally they were completely below the shooter's line of vision when cocked.

and the conspicuous and attractive fences, afforded engravers and other artists in the decorative treatment of metals splendid and unrestricted opportunities for the display of their skills. Best of all, in the view of many heirs to the English tradition of restrained elegance, is that the orthodox, double-barrelled sporting gun had at last come to acquire a naked beauty incapable of being improved by any embellishment whatsoever.

I should add that, in coming to the end of the narrow track I set out to follow in this article, I am chiefly conscious of the size of the forest through which I have passed, and the need I have felt to keep my eyes on the ground, and to ignore the many fascinating side-vistas which have opened up as I went along. ●

With the development of the hammerless gun the fences had to become things of the past. However, the English, apparently loath to relinquish the name, applied it to the rounded outer portions or shoulders of the standing breech. This Thomas Turner 10 bore shows that some shooters and gunmakers found it very hard to completely give up hammers after the firing pins and tumblers were already inside. These odd, thin "hammers" are no more than highly visible cocking indicators, the locks being actually cocked by the long top lever as the gun is opened.

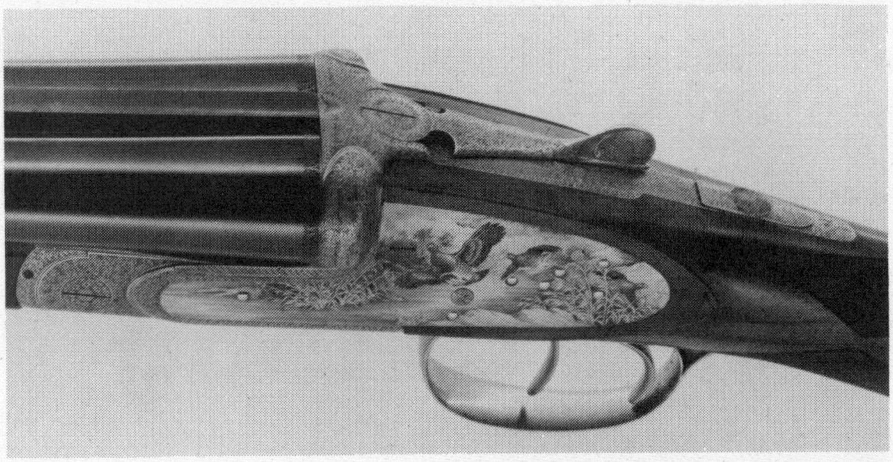

The modern hammerless sidelock gun offers the engraver a variety of shapes and surfaces for an equally varied display of engraving techniques. This Italian double by Feraghli gave the great Angelo Galeazzi the opportunity to display his skill in executing traditional scroll engraving on the frame of the gun and his special ability to depict partridges in flight on the lockplates.

But hammers and fences are not entirely relics of the 19th century. Hammer guns are being manufactured today in Belgium, Spain, the USSR, Brazil and Italy. Especially Italy! For Italy is the home of Famars, whose speciality for some years has been a program of hammer guns featuring flowing, sculptured fences and highly ornate hammers. At various times the Famars oval fences have had their top surfaces flat, convex or concave—a striking contrast to the baroque or rococo hammers.

MODEL 1911 COLT: SIX DECADES OF SERVICE

"It stands quite alone as a standard of excellence among military pistols"

by DENNIS RIORDAN

IN THE PASSING years since the adoption of the Browning/Colt Model of 1911, the development of military pistols has been influenced by three major factors: advances in firearms design, gradual changes in military requirements, and the introduction of new materials and manufacturing methods. All of the Colt's contemporaries have long since disappeared from the martial arsenals of the world, but the 1911 still retains its position as the standard service pistol of the United States. The only military handgun in history to compare with this record was Britain's 455 Webley revolver, which passed through 6 Marks and broached the transition from black to smokeless powder in its long and stormy career. However, even the great Webley has been far outstripped by the Browning/Colt, both in length of service and in actual battle use.

The reasons for the Colt automatic's longevity are various and complex. Unquestionably the basic excellence of the gun and of its unique cartridge have always been paramount, but many other contributory factors may also be cited, whose total leverage has proved irresistable.

A historically related series of events began in 1892, when the Double Action 38 New Army Revolver replaced the 45 Single Action Army, which had been standard issue since 1875. The new revolver appeared to hold great potential, since its swing-out cylinder offered simultaneous ejection and fast reloading, its double-action mechanism increased

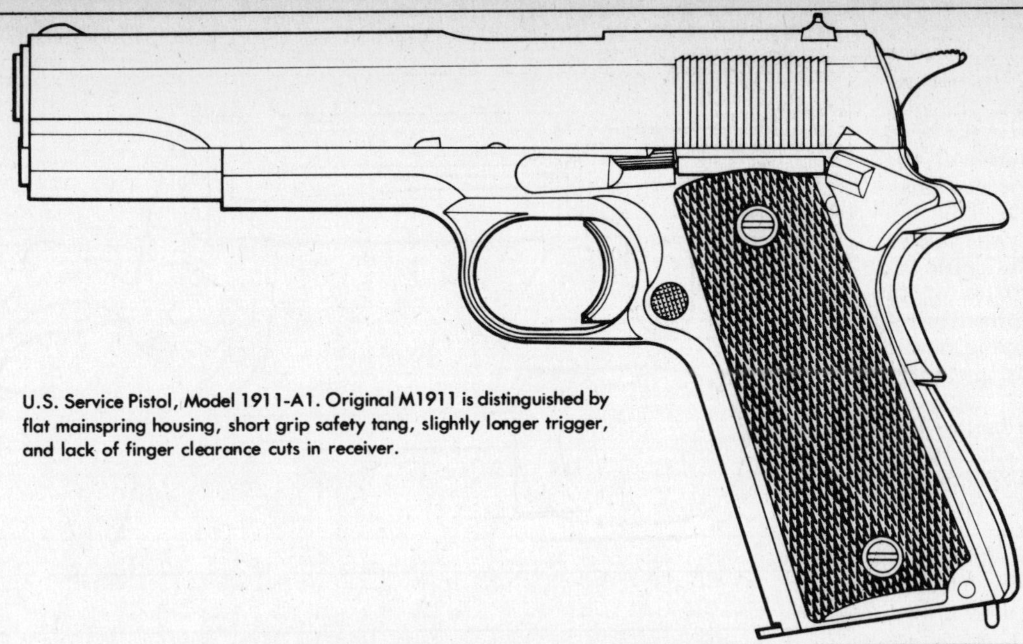

U.S. Service Pistol, Model 1911-A1. Original M1911 is distinguished by flat mainspring housing, short grip safety tang, slightly longer trigger, and lack of finger clearance cuts in receiver.

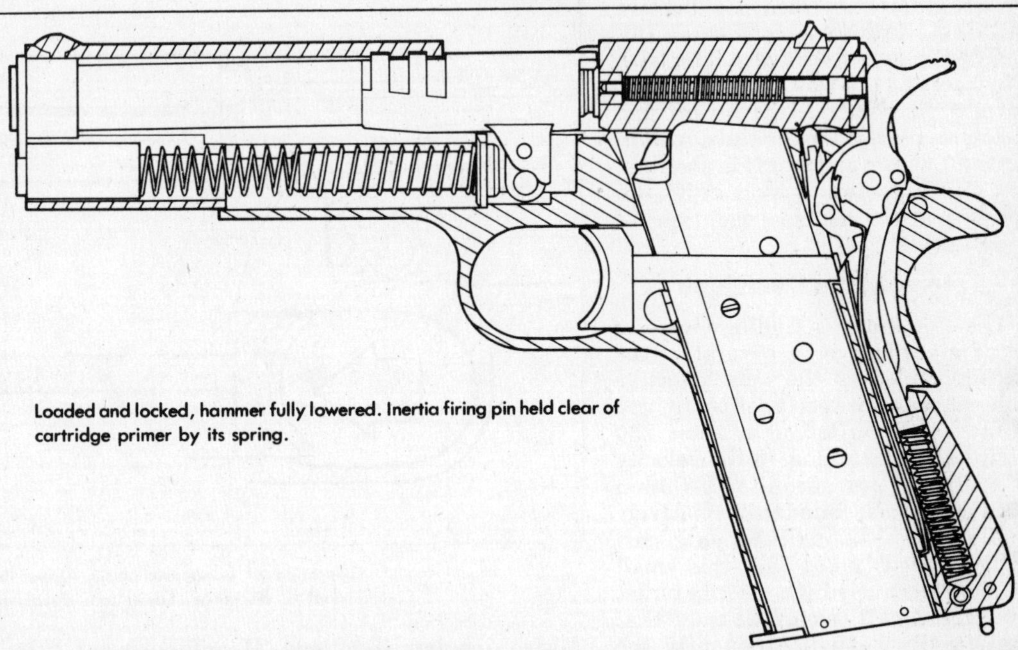

Loaded and locked, hammer fully lowered. Inertia firing pin held clear of cartridge primer by its spring.

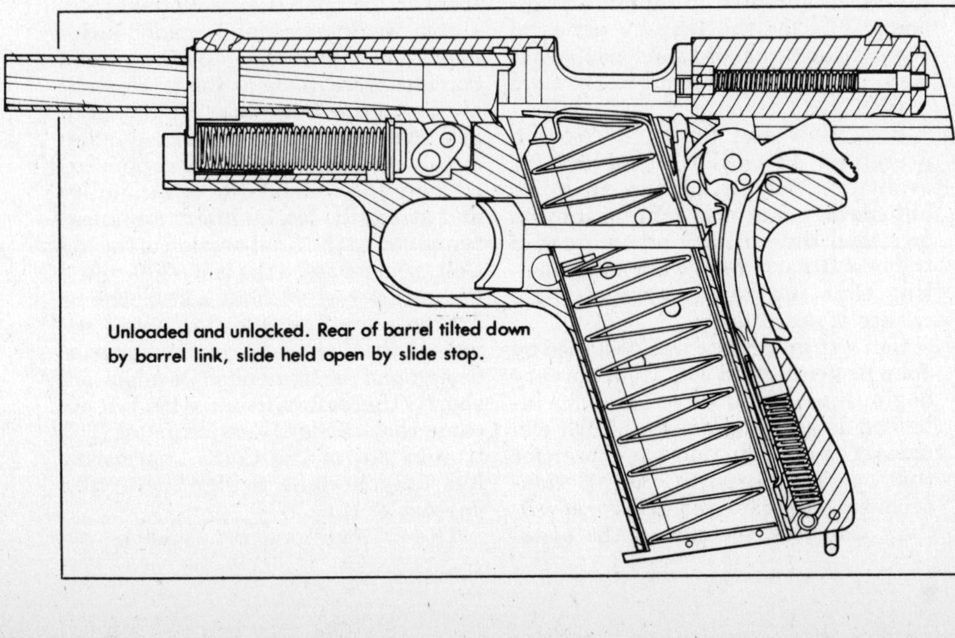

Unloaded and unlocked. Rear of barrel tilted down by barrel link, slide held open by slide stop.

Author's Note

When I once did some drawings on the derivative Model B Star, I began to see the strong points of the basic Model 1911 design. The features of the Star that I disliked, the extractor, firing pin, and disconnector, were departures from the original concept, which began to look very good indeed. This chain of thought was confirmed when I finally obtained a specimen 1911-A1. I then reviewed every objection to the gun that I could find in my files, and found precious little substance in any of them. On the contrary, I found a gun that stands quite alone as a standard of excellence among military pistols.

the rate of fire, and the greatly reduced level of recoil made the gun pleasant to shoot. Whatever the good qualities of the revolver, however, the 38 Long Colt cartridge proved woefully inadequate in battle. This became evident during the close-quarter encounters of the 1899 Philippine Insurrection, where quantities of 45 Single Action Colts were hastily reissued to supply the stopping power that the newer handgun patently lacked.

In 1904, the Army's Ordnance Department assigned Col. (later Brigadier-General) John T. Thompson of Ordnance and Col. La Garde of the Medical Corps, to conduct an investigation into the hitherto shadowy subject of stopping power. The Thompson-La Garde Committee determined the nature of wounds and shock effect by the empiric method. Exhaustive shooting trials were conducted, initially with human cadavers, later with live steers at the Chicago stockyards. Several then-current revolvers and pistols were used for the tests, including the 7.65mm and 9mm Parabellum, and Colt automatic pistols in 38, 45, and 476 caliber, using various types of ammunition.

Momentous Decisions

The Committee's findings were of great significance in several areas. Recommended as the most effective man-stopper was the 45 caliber, with a blunt nosed bullet of at least 230 grains and a minimum initial velocity of 800 feet per second. The 9mm Parabellum was found to be relatively ineffective as a man-stopping cartridge. It was noted that this small caliber, relatively high velocity bullet inflicted small, clean wounds that were easily healed. Frequently the body was completely penetrated without instantaneous damage, and apparent damage was occasionally delayed for hours. The tests proved conclusively that the often quoted muzzle energy figure (kinetic energy of the bullet, derived solely from its mass and velocity and expressed in ft. lbs.) has no direct bearing on the relative stopping power, since it does not consider the cross-sectional area of the bullet (frontal area) nor the factor of bullet shape. (Stopping power is also influenced by expanding bullets, but these have been outlawed for military use since the Second Hague Conference of 1907).

On receipt of the Thompson-La Garde report the Ordnance Department determined to adopt a new service pistol in accord with the Committee's recommendations. Manufacturers were invited to submit 45 caliber pistols for the lengthy series of comparison tests and field trials that were to proceed intermittantly from 1906 to 1911.

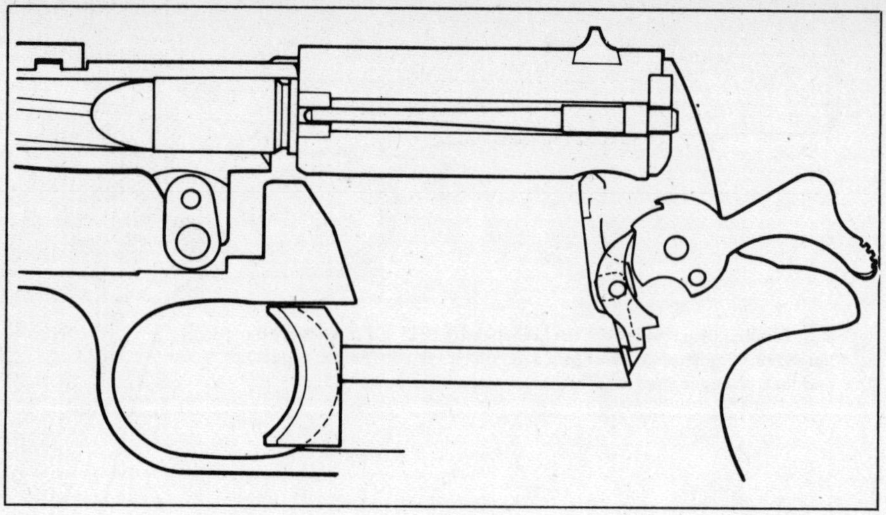

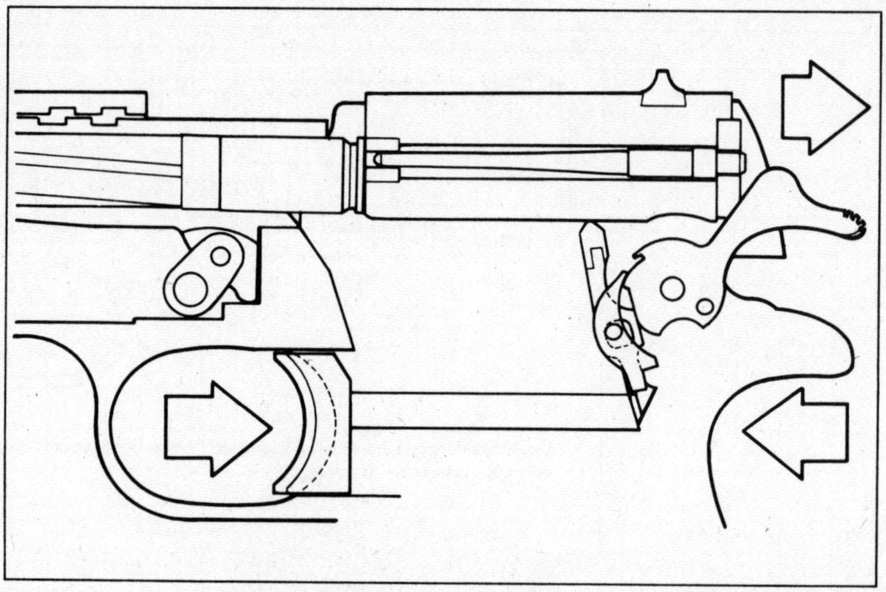

Operation of firing mechanism. Upper left: ready position. Upper right: instant of discharge. Lower left: disconnection of sear. Lower right: return

Both Colt and Smith & Wesson presented 45 caliber revolvers for evaluation, but during these years the automatic pistol was coming into its own, and the military advantages of the new firearm type were so compelling that the revolvers had little chance of acceptance.

Colt's 45 automatic was designed by John Browning and was, from the very beginnings of its development, intended as a military pistol. Each element of its construction was chosen for that specific purpose, and all compromises were resolved in favor of military use. Nonetheless, as the pistol went through the Army's gruelling tests in competition with rival designs, weaknesses and inadequacies appeared within the prototypes, and changes were made as the trials went on. Since the tests were conducted in peacetime, the Army proceeded in leisurely fashion, insisting upon extremely high standards of reliability and strength. No inherent weakness remained in the final version of the big Colt, which passed the last 6000-round endurance test without a stoppage or broken part. The selection board adjudged the Colt as a clearly superior design and recommended its adoption; shortly thereafter, in early 1911, it became the standard service pistol. The true extent of the Colt's superiority has only become evident with the passage of time.

The 45 Government Automatic Car-

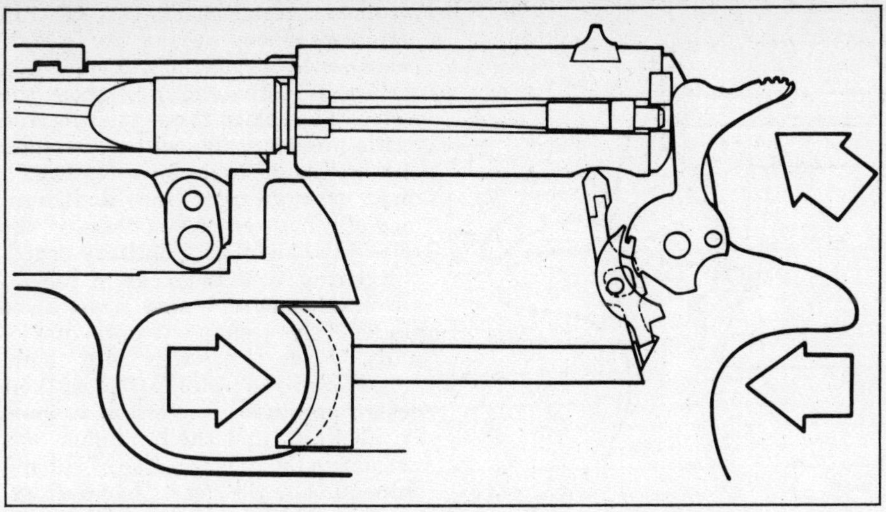

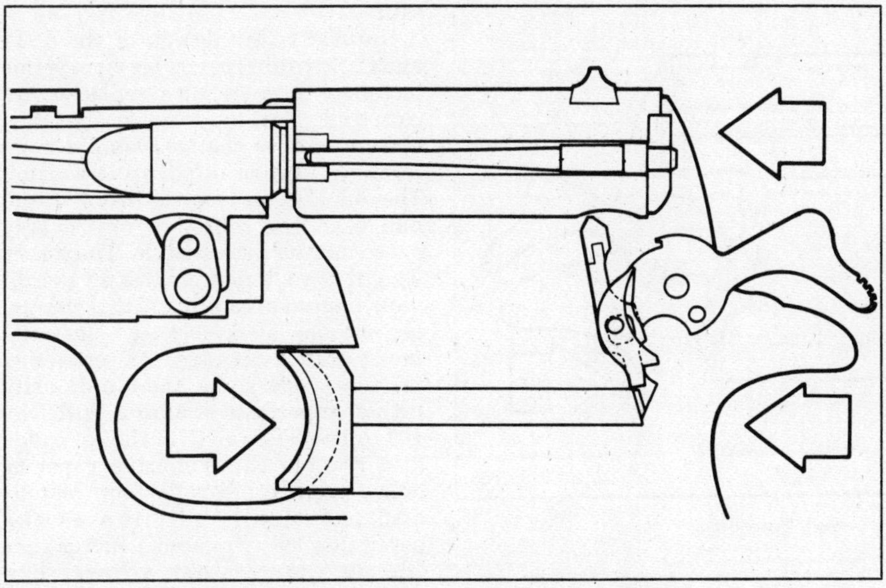

to battery—disconnector will move to ready position upon release of trigger. Notice relationship between sear and disconnector throughout.

tridge was adopted simultaneously with the Colt pistol. This round, carrying a full-jacketed 233-gr. bullet, was developed at Frankford Arsenal from an original Browning design. Although considerably smaller in case capacity than the old 45 Colt revolver cartridge, the 45 Automatic was nearly as powerful, since it was designed for maximum efficiency with smokeless powder.

First Major Test

The new pistol/cartridge combination was used in a series of skirmishes along the Mexican border, and carried into Mexico during the punitive expedition against Pancho Villa's raiders, but the first large scale battle test of the arm followed America's entry into World War One, when U.S. troops arrived in the trenches of Belgium and France. Here, under actual field conditions, the 1911 established its reputation as a rugged, reliable handgun, and also as a dependable man-stopper, despite the rarity of documented enemy casualties that could be attributed to it. Most officers and NCOs were armed with the Colt, however, and no rumors of failure, either of arm or ammunition, ever surfaced.

Criticism of the 1911 did arise during the WW I period, and as a result, certain modifications were later undertaken at Springfield Armory to improve the pistol. These consisted of a widened front sight to better the sight picture; an enlarged spur on the grip safety to prevent pinching of the thumb web during recoil; a shorter trigger and finger cutouts in adjacent receiver areas, to accommodate soldiers with small hands and generally improve trigger control; and a curved mainspring housing, to benefit the pistol's pointing characteristics and afford a superior grip. In 1926 these changes were approved, and the modified pistol was accepted as the M1911-A1. All service pistols manufactured since that date have conformed to the A1 specifications, and the older guns were gradually modified as they were returned to military arsenals. It should be noted that the improvements effected in the A1 version were entirely external in nature; no mechanical changes have ever been made.

The 30-M1 Carbine, adopted upon the very eve of World War Two, was conceived as a replacement for the pistol in the hands of combat troops. In the event, this did not occur. Both weapons were manufactured in huge quantities and equally distributed to U.S. forces in all war zones. The relative value of each was not difficult to assess, since WW II was a long war, and the best documented in history. Combat reports and wound statistics proved the carbine an effective aggressive arm, while the pistol was revealed as a primarily psychological weapon. Times were changing; as shoulder arms became self-loading or fully automatic, the melee was becoming rare. Again, as in WW I, enemy casualties inflicted by the pistol were far flung and few, but its contribution to morale was strong.

The introduction of the German assault rifle during the course of WW II had broad repercussions in the postwar years. The Germans retained full power ammunition for the machinegun and the sniper rifle, but the basic weapon for the infantryman became a short, light, selective-fire rifle, firing a shortened 8mm cartridge of intermediate power and range. This single compromise weapon was intended to replace the full power rifle, the submachinegun, and, it was hoped, the pistol as well.

Russia embraced this concept without reservation, and the power and prestige of the U.S.S.R. carried the idea throughout the Communist World. The pistol could not be eliminated in any of these nations, but its role was downgraded and, in Russia itself, smaller, less powerful handguns were adopted.

With the usual exception of France, the powerful western nations reluctantly followed the lead of the United States in the acceptance of the 7.62 NATO cartridge. This round is a shortened, updated version of the

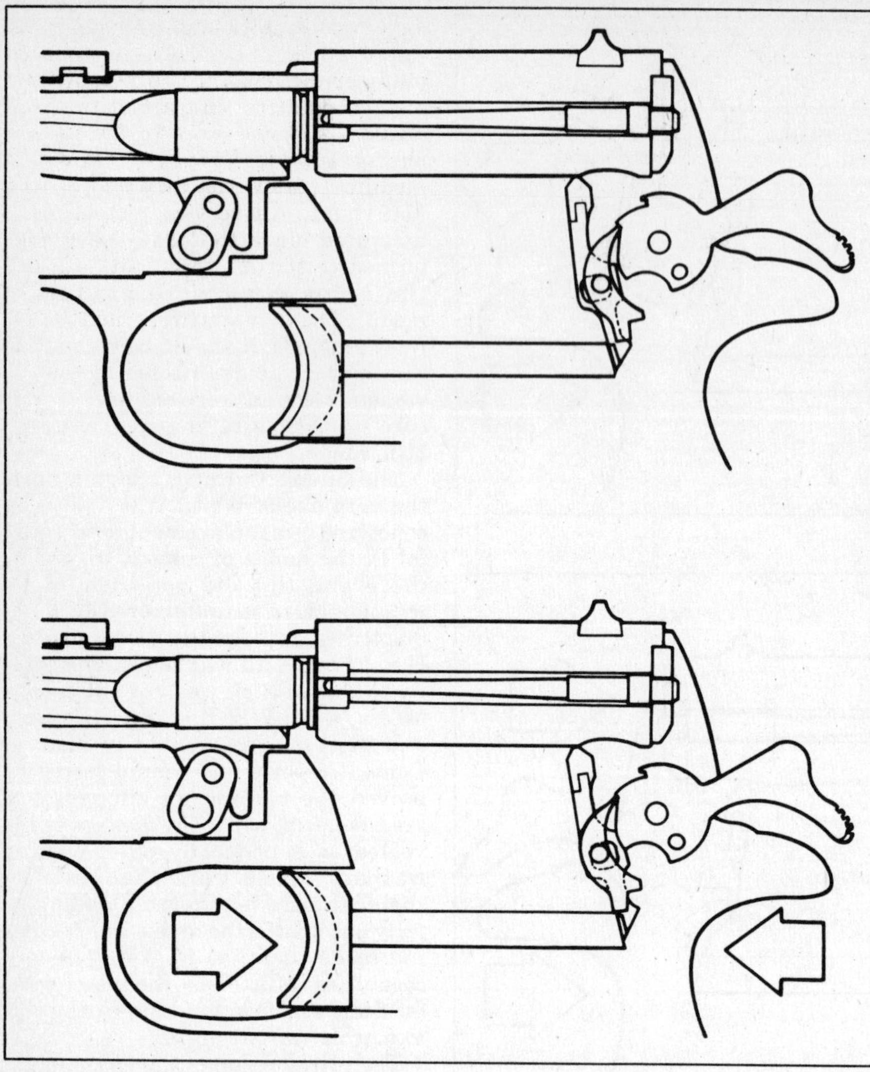

Unlocked slide: Should the slide fail to lock completely (upper), disconnector prevents discharge (lower).

30-06 that differs only slightly in ballistics; a full power cartridge for rifle and machine gun. Our new infantry rifle became the M-14, and the carbine and pistol remained in service.

Successor Rejected

During the 1950s, the U.S. Army explored the possibility of a new handgun. Germany's P-38 seemed to hold the answers to many of the complaints that had been leveled at the 1911 over the years; that it was too bulky and heavy, too powerful, too slow to get into action. In addition, the 9mm Parabellum cartridge had already become the universal choice of the other NATO countries for pistol and submachinegun use. Therefore, a list of requisites was established for a handgun of similar type, including a limitation in bore size of 30 to 35 caliber. Upon Army invitation, several strictly commercial designs were submitted for evaluation, as well as the T3 pistol, developed by the High Standard Company under direct Army contract. A number of these submissions were double action designs, and most were chambered for the 9mm Parabellum. The situation seemed strikingly reminiscent of that which had been obtained in 1892; single versus double action, 45 vs 38 (i.e., 9mm) caliber. The guns and the ammunitions were actually a far cry from those which had figured in that elder challenge, but the findings of the Thompson/La Garde Committee had never been discredited, although they appeared about to be ignored. However, trials were still in process when the decision was announced to retain the 1911, and the pistol testing was abruptly terminated. The reason for this decision has never been publicly revealed, and the preliminary findings of the tests themselves are still classified.

Certainly, a pertinent circumstance was the fact that the nation's armories retained an enormous stock of 1911 pistols produced during the WW II period, even beyond those at present in service in Korea and throughout the world. To replace these existing and battle-proven pistols with a handgun of new design would have required a major expenditure of funds, and this in face of a marked de-emphasis on the role of the pistol as a military arm.

Existing WW II stocks of M3-A1 submachineguns may also have clouded the issue, but only marginally. While these were also chambered for the 45 pistol cartridge, their design permitted conversion to 9mm Parabellum, and their number was not particularly large. Use of submachineguns by U.S. forces had been extensive only among paratroop units, and their future utilization was uncertain.

Naturally, the design of the 1911 and its 45 caliber cartridge were prime factors in the question of replacement. Gun and cartridge were inseparable, since a caliber change would almost certainly have resulted in a new pistol. The 45 U.S. automatic pistol round had been the center of controversy ever since its introduction. The heavy weight of its bullet creates an inordinate amount of recoil, and this characteristic has always caused unsettlement and even fear in military recruits undergoing their ordinarily rather superficial training with the 1911 pistol. The girth of the cartridge also reduces the magazine capacity below that of comparable 9mm pistols, and practically eliminates the possibility of staggered loading that the smaller caliber allows. The superior penetration of the 9mm Parabellum has often been cited as cause for change, since the 45 comes into difficulties against obstructions which the Parabellum pierces with ease. Penetration is of advantage to the submachine gun, an arm of offense, but with the exception of military police duty, the pistol had not been employed as an aggressive weapon since WW I. The role of the pistol had declined to one of a purely defensive arm, whose function consisted of stopping the advance of a determined opponent at close quarters. Stopping power and reasonable accuracy are the primary requirements of a weapon of defense, and these qualities the 45 possessed in full measure. A good man-stopper inflicts instant and massive bodily damage sufficient to break off an attack (not necessarily to kill), and the 45 will almost always achieve this result with a solid hit anywhere in the torso. No current military cartridge came near the 45 in this respect, certainly not the Parabellum.

The Nonpareil—

The 1911 pistol itself was and is much too good to discard unless a prospective replacement could offer irresistible improvements. No pistol has ever surpassed the Colt for utter reliability. It has operated under the most extreme conditions of nature and endured the roughest treatment without failure, and has digested ammunitions of greatly varying chamber pressure without trouble. Any modern military pistol must be capable of field stripping without tools, but the 1911 goes much farther than this. It can be completely disassembled without the use of any tool, excepting only the grips, whose removal is never required. These are attached by four screws and bushings, the only screwed parts used in the gun. Breakage or loss of either or both grips has no effect on the gun's operation, and does not permit the escape of any other part, since all pins are mechanically retained within the pistol independently of the grips. This is an important feature; many of today's military pistols would be put out of action by grip failure.

The pistol's controls are intelligently located for convenience of operation. The hammer is easily thumb cocked, and its contour affords an excellent gripping surface. The safety lies directly above the thumb and operates with great ease. The pushbutton magazine release allows disengagement and ejection of the magazine using only the shooting hand, making this pistol one of the fastest of all automatics to reload. The slide stop works efficiently to signal an empty gun and hasten reloading, and it also permits locking the slide open manually at any time. The Colt's balance is good, and the gun handles well. The weight of the piece and its long sighting radius contribute to steady holding and accurate fire. The presence of the grip safety requires the use of both hands to lower the hammer from full cock. Since manual decocking is the single most dangerous operation necessary to the employment of an automatic pistol, the added control afforded by the mandatory second hand raises the level of safety proportionately.

As a mechanism, the 1911 abounds in excellent features. Its tilting barrel lock remains one of the strongest and simplest of locking systems, and its dual barrel lugs both contact recesses in the top of the slide, dispersing recoil

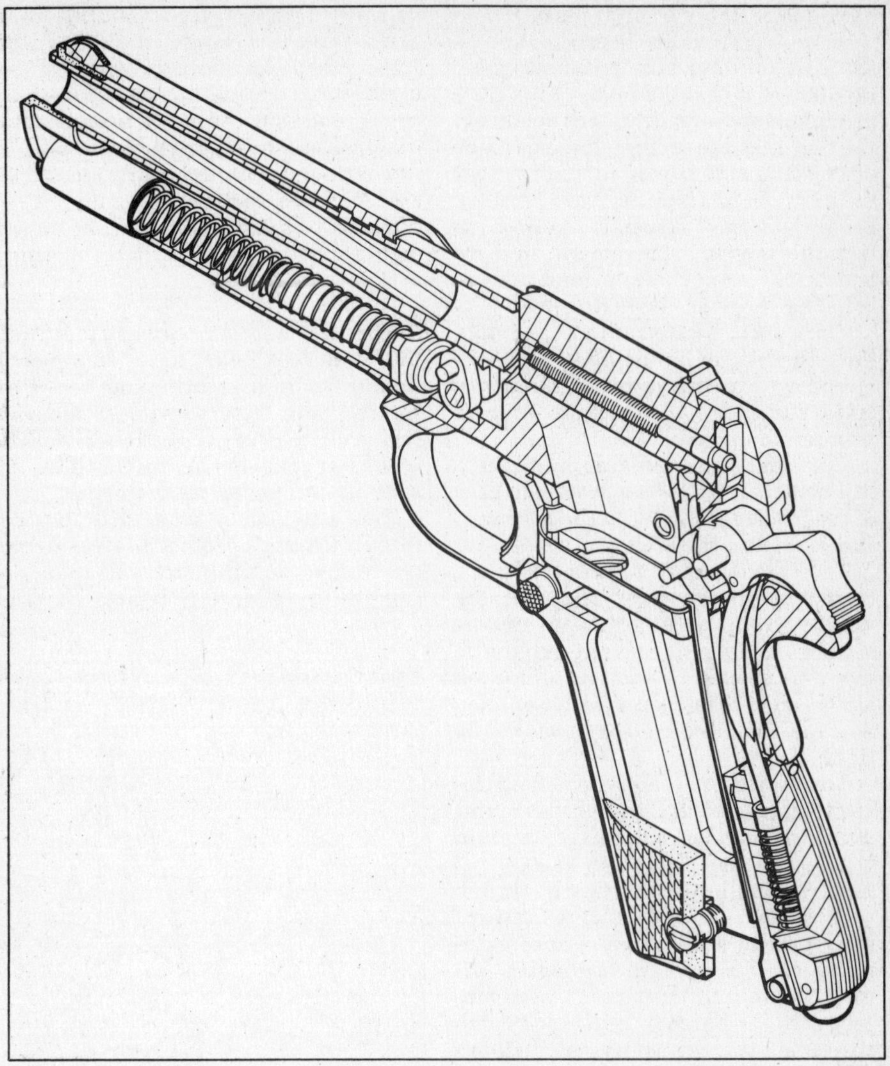

Unloaded and locked, hammer at full cock. Magazine not shown.

forces over a large surface area. The tilting barrel also brings its breech into close proximity with the incoming round from the magazine, and this, plus the barrel tang, affords almost flawless feeding. It is true that a cam system such as Browning used in his later High Power pistol is slightly stronger and more efficient, but this superiority is in degree only; it certainly does not obsolete the swinging link of the 1911.

—Abounds in Excellence

There is no finer extractor in any pistol. It is located entirely within the slide, fully protected against injury or the ingress of foreign matter. Since it does not pivot on a pin and acts as its own spring, it cannot become frozen by rust or hardened lubricant. The design of the feed mechanism is such that the rims of incoming rounds are forced upward behind the extractor, rather than requiring the extractor to snap over them, prolonging the life of the part. However, the extractor is sufficiently flexible to jump the rim of a hand-loaded round as the slide is slam closed upon it. Damage or loss of the magazine does not completely disable the big Colt, since its slide stop, large ejection port, and lack of a magazine disconnector allow handloading and firing in the total absence of the magazine.

The firing pin is an inertia type, affording safe carry with the hammer fully forward over a chambered round. Its long, tapered tip is highly resistant to breakage, while its symmetrical design allows the pin to turn freely, distributing wear. Dry firing is not injurious to the firing pin, because its forward movement in dry fire is arrested by the full compression of its spring, not by a retaining pin.

The firing-pin stop is also a fine feature of the 1911, locking the extractor as well as the firing pin, and affording easy disassembly of both parts.

Some criticism has been directed at the Colt's sliding, stirrup type trigger, because of its vertical play. This play is detrimental only in match shooting; the fact that the trigger does not pivot on a pin is actually of advantage to a military pistol. Neither rust nor any accumulation of debris is likely to affect the trigger's movement, and its operation cannot sweep mud or dirt into the receiver. The trigger and its bar are incorporated into one simple part, the trigger bar being entirely enclosed within the receiver. No other trigger/trigger bar system is simpler or more foolproof.

The safety mechanisms of the 1911 are also very good. Separate surfaces of the manual safety lock the hammer, the sear, and the slide.

The disconnector is completely enclosed by the receiver and operates within a rounded notch on the underside of the slide to prevent automatic fire and discharge with an unlocked slide. Should the gun be assembled without the disconnector, it cannot be fired.

The hammer's safety notch interrupts hammer fall in any circumstance that does not originate from trigger release. The sear enters this notch if the hammer slips in thumb cocking, or the slide moves forward after partial withdrawal, either manually or through an accidental fall upon the muzzle. If the sear loses contact with the hammer's full-cock notch through a jar, the safety notch allows the hammer's recapture before it can complete its stroke. The hammer safety notch is not a half-cock position and should never be so employed, because a blow upon the hammer in this attitude could fracture the sear or hammer notch and discharge the gun.

The grip safety blocks movement of the trigger unless the pistol is held naturally in the hand. Its location at the rear of the grip allows the safety to function without conscious thought, and reduces the danger of accidental self-inflicted wounds.

The Colt's magazine floorplate is permanently attached, in contrast to several more recent designs, whose detachable magazine floorplates allow easy takedown and cleaning of the assembly. Actually, the Colt pattern is preferable from a military standpoint, since this magazine cannot become accidentally disassembled and parts lost, yet its follower and spring may be removed from the top.

The sights are simple, effective, and strong. That they are nonadjustable is advantageous, since their height is calculated for service ammunition at pre-determined range, and they are factory set for windage zero. These sights have no small parts to loosen or break, and they cannot be tinkered out of adjustment. Their very low profile and rounded contours easily clear holster surfaces. Both sights may be replaced in case of damage, or target sights substituted for match shooting.

Few Faults

The 1911 has no really bad features, but it is less than ideal in several areas. The gun is large and heavy in weight, both factors owing to the cartridge it fires. Any reduction in weight would increase the difficulties of recruits in mastering the arm.

The grip safety was incorporated into Browning's prototype 45 at Army request, while the pistol was undergoing its pre-adoption trials. At this time, pistols were carried fully armed in the advance by infantry officers and non-coms, and employed in like manner by mounted cavalry troops. Compared to a shoulder arm, the pistol is difficult to control in a stumble or fall; its small size allows it to turn in the hand and endanger its bearer. An automatic safety reduces such risks, since it tends to engage as the wrist is twisted into an unnatural position. However, the new defensive role of the service pistol largely invalidates this consideration, and the grip safety is at present of small practical value in a military pistol having both an external hammer and a positive manual safety. The Colt's automatic safety causes few problems in its operation, but the safety's inclusion in the design requires a goodly number of additional parts, expensive machining operations, and an additional receiver open-

Action of manual safety. Upper: fire position. Lower: safe position—safety nose raised into slide recess, locking it closed. Separate surfaces of internal boss lock hammer and sear, preventing movement of either.

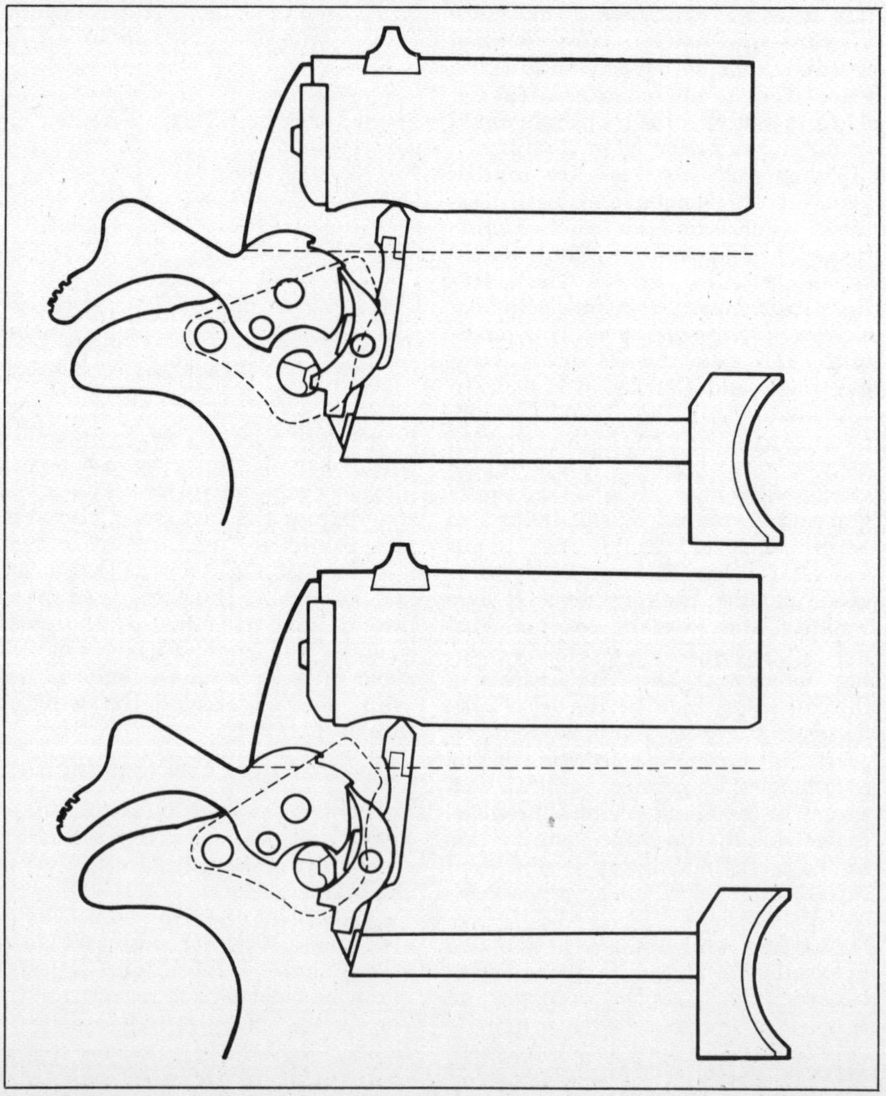

ing, affording entry to water and dust.

A left-handed shooter encounters handling difficulties with the manual safety, but this is unfortunately true of almost all military automatics.

The external location of the safety plunger-tube exposes the safety and slide-stop plungers to water and dirt. The malfunction of either plunger would not put the gun out of action and they are easily serviced, but the arrangement is not ideal. Also, the tube is riveted to the receiver, and any looseness that should develop in these rivets cannot be serviced in the field.

The slide stop does not extend sufficiently rearward to afford good leverage, nor an easy reach for the thumb.

Field stripping of the 1911 is not difficult, but it is rather slow, fairly complicated, and results in more loose parts than could be desired. It should be noted, however, that there is no hazard of kinking the recoil spring during this operation, and that the gun cannot be improperly assembled in a dangerous condition.

The 1911 is not as safe as others whose design affords a mechanical means of decocking the hammer, and is theoretically inferior to a double action pistol, which may be cocked and fired by the application of a long pull on the trigger.

In practice, double-action trigger mechanisms tend to be delicate and complicated. It is doubtful if any such system offers the complete interchangeability of parts enjoyed by the 1911 Colt, and none can match its reliability of function.

For reasons of safety, army regulations require that the Colt pistol be carried with its chamber empty in non-combat areas. Under such restrictions, there is no advantage to a double action pistol, since either type requires manual cycling of the slide before discharge is possible. In combat zones, the Colt is carried loaded, either with safety off and hammer fully down, or with hammer cocked and safety engaged. The first condition requires thumb cocking of the hammer before the gun can be fired, and is slower than the long trigger pull of a double-action pistol. In the second condition only thumb release of the safety is necessary; this operation may be performed and the gun discharged in about the time required to fire a double action design.

An often stated advantage of the double action automatic is its ability to quickly deliver a second blow to a reluctant primer. This may be a valid argument, but it seems equally likely that a soldier would prefer to manually reload the piece immediately upon a failure to fire.

On the whole, the supposed superiority of the double-action pistol is largely illusory. The idea has psychological value but, as a practical matter, an external hammer single-action automatic such as the 1911, having a positive safety properly located and contoured, is no less efficient.

Automatic safety. Upper: safe position—safety nose contacts rear of trigger bar, blocking its movement. Lower: fire position—safety disengaged by pressure on grip.

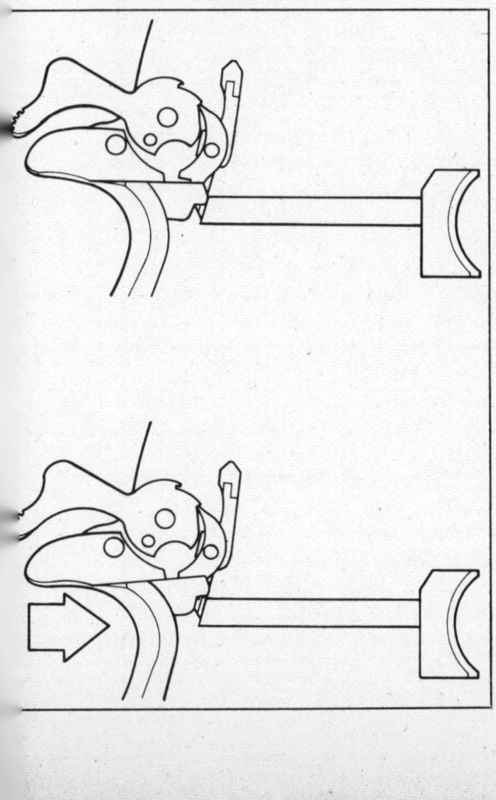

Hammer safety notch. Should the hammer slip during thumb cocking (upper), it is intercepted by the sear (lower) which moves into the hammer's safety notch before the firing pin can be struck.

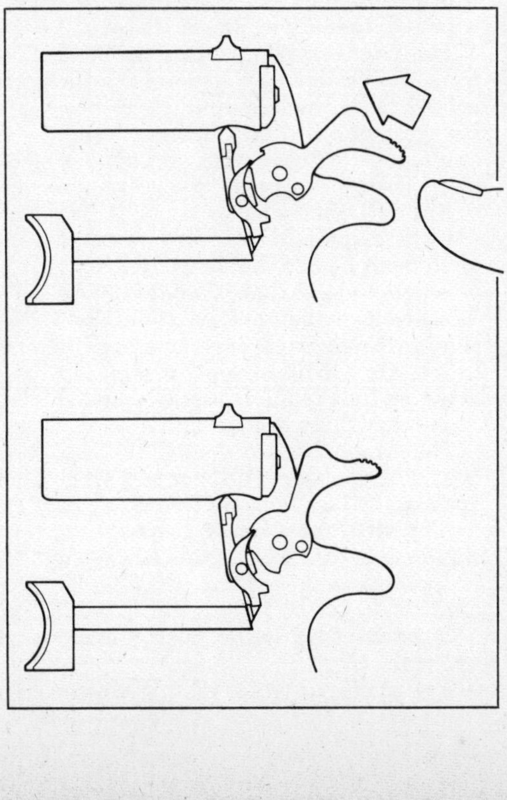

Changes Since Last Trials

In the years that have passed since the abortive pistol trials of the 1950s, significant changes have been made in U.S. infantry weapons. The venerable B.A.R. and the Browning 30 caliber machineguns have been withdrawn from service and quietly replaced by the excellent 7.62mm M60 General Purpose Machinegun, derived from the German FG-42 and MG-42 of WW II design. The jungle fighting in Vietnam called for a high rate of fire and a short, light weapon of intermediate power, a class of arm that fell midway between the M-14 and the M-2 Carbine. Caught in a pinch, the tail wagged the dog, and the services were forced to employ and eventually accept the previously rejected AR-15, with its untried gas system and unconventional design. Deficiencies arose in the field and manufacturing changes were made to counter them; the corrected version was adopted as the M16-A1, a good and serviceable weapon.

Withdrawal of American troops from Vietnam found the U.S. in the position of possessing large quantities of modern service rifles of both full and intermediate power, a luxury enjoyed by no other major nation on earth. The future employment of each has yet to be determined. What proved to be the ideal weapon for Vietnam may not suffice in more open country and under more conventional methods of warfare. In any case, the 30 Carbine and the 45 submachinegun would seem on the verge of obsolescence, and there is apparently no longer any possibility of adopting a 9mm submachinegun.

The nature of the war in Vietnam worked greatly to increase the status of the service pistol. Guerrilla activity in the cities meant that there were no safe areas in the country, and rear-echelon personnel were often dependent on the pistol as a means of personal protection. Carrying it openly reduced chances of attack, and pistols were in great demand, whether authorized or not. Such lessons are not quickly forgotten; the position of the 1911 pistol seems more secure today than it did 20 years ago. The career of Browning's 45 is far from ended. It is as good as it ever was, and that is very good indeed. •

One of these four go-along guns will meet virtually any need for remote country roamings: S&W Kit gun; Model 94 30-30 Trapper; Ruger Blackhawk 357 Magnum; H&R Topper 20-gauge.

PICKING YOUR

THE BEAR was heading for me, that much was sure.

I was examining the remains of a wolf-killed caribou when I looked up to see a sizeable brown bear shuffling onto the scene some 100 yards away. Since a wet wind was at my back, I fully expected him to scram as soon as he got a noseful of me, but bears are hard to figure. This one kept coming upwind, closing the distance rapidly with his rambling gait.

I was in a remote valley beyond Alaska's Chigmit Mountains. There were no trees to climb. The nearest stunted spruce was a day's hike away. Perhaps that bear had never whiffed a human before or maybe my scent was simply masked by the odor of the caribou carcass. Whatever the reason, he was starting to make me feel decidedly uncomfortable.

The bear was 20 yards away now. I guessed he was an eight-footer weighing over 500 pounds. I'd seen bigger, but this one was beginning to look enormous. You don't run from a situation like that. It can trigger an attack. You try to talk it over.

"That's far enough!" I said in the same tone I'd use to admonish my springer spaniel.

I raised my left hand like a traffic cop. My right hand dropped to the 357 holstered on my hip. The bear didn't break stride. It seemed intent on trampling me into the tundra. And it was still 30 feet away when I fired a warning, holding well over its back.

The bear stopped, rolling its head from side to side as if listening to the echoes from the surrounding slopes. Its eyes, small in that massive head, studied me with no apparent expression. Then on he came. I would have to kill him. If I could.

I was gripping the cocked revolver with both hands, holding it close. I was determined that it would not be knocked away before I sent a bullet to the brain via the mouth or an ear. I had little confidence otherwise, in stopping that bear. He would be on me in another three or four steps.

Then anger welled up, overwhelming my rising fear. The bear was surely going to hurt me. He was going to foul up all of the plans I'd so painstakingly made for the summer. It was an irrational thought, but it made me mad.

"GET OUT OF HERE YOU S.O.B!" I raged.

The bear showed expression for the first time. It looked surprised, almost as if it had just awakened from sleepwalking. It halted, one paw upraised, holding the pose for two or three seconds. It seemed like a very long time.

Then that big bear wheeled and ran away. It really ran. Spray spurted from under those huge paws each time they pounded the rainsoaked tundra. My fingers trembled as I reloaded the fired chamber of the Ruger Blackhawk. My knees still felt wobbly as I shrugged the pack back onto my shoulders and headed down the valley.

That was in July of 1976. Dennis Harms of Chugiak had flown me into the region only a couple of days earlier, using his nimble little Super Cub to land on a tiny lake in a high valley. My plan was to camp in the summer range of the Mulchatna caribou herd, hoping to photograph the wolves which followed the cows to the snowfields at calving time.

Upon leaving, I would backpack to the headwaters of the brawling Chilikadrotna River less than 20 miles distant. There Dennis had dropped a rubber raft for me. I would raft more than 100 miles down the Chilikadrotna to the Mulchatna River; then ride the

Author pausing on a portage trail on Alaska's Kanai Peninsula—bear country, for sure.

Surprised in a blueberry patch on a snowy summer morning, this grizzly glared at the author hiking in the Alaska range.

GO-ALONG GUN

by DON L. JOHNSON

Mulchatna's currents some 50 miles to a point above the mouth of the Koktuli River. There Dennis could again land on floats to pick me up. Meanwhile, I was on my own in some of the most remote and breathtaking country left in Alaska.

The gun was not my idea. While packing and repacking for the trip I had decided not to take it. I wanted to minimize the weight I'd be carrying across rugged terrain and by deleting the handgun from the list I felt I could add another camera lens or two.

Dennis, a master Alaskan guide and outfitter, had vetoed that idea. He'd known me a long time and knew I was no novice to wilderness travel, but he'd said he would not set me down in that country without a firearm. The 357 was his minimum.

Other bears were met on that trip and I also had a brief run-in with a hostile mother moose, but that ineffectual shot over the bear's back was the only one I fired. So did I really need a gun?

In retrospect, I think I did. Without it I would still have stood my ground—I really had no alternative—but there would have been more fear. My voice, and probably my odor, would have communicated that. Bears, like dogs and many other animals, surely can sense when we are fearful. They act accordingly. I have never shot any animal in self-defense, but I've had a few other close encounters when the presence of a gun made me feel much more resolute and therefore less vulnerable to attack.

Still, I do not recommend a 357 on every camper's belt. The question of what to carry is complicated by several factors. To illustrate, I'll describe some guns I've chosen to go along with me on wilderness assignments as an outdoors writer-photographer. My choices are not the only appropriate ones, but my reasons may help you decide what's best for you.

I ought to emphasize that I am not a real gung-ho backpacker. I don't savor struggling over rugged terrain, burdened like a burro and spending all my time watching my feet so I won't break a leg. Given a choice, I'll travel by horse, canoe, raft, or dogsled, and I've logged quite a few miles on all of them. However, I've also worn out lots of boots on treks where there were no alternatives. In the final analysis, whatever the main mode of travel, hiking and packing usually constitute some part of a back-country trip. Therefore, the gun which meets the needs of the backpacker well should serve well for all wilderness travel.

We are discussing travelling when hunting is not the primary purpose. On a hunting trip, you carry the appropriate gun for the game you're after. On the other hand, when your basic aim is fishing, photography, prospecting—or just poking around in the wilds for whatever other reason—you want a gun for defense and/or foraging. The choice can be far different from the hunter's.

Let's face it, defense is a consideration whether or not you're in bear country. Even a small handgun in camp can be a comfort, dissuading all kinds of intruders. When laws permit, a good 22 handgun also can put fresh meat in the pot.

To those ends, I have carried a four-inch S&W Kit Gun on many a trail during the past 25 years. It has potted a variety of small game and dispatched a few undesirables, including an aggressive (and probably rabid) skunk which invaded camp one night.

I don't recommend a handgun for serious foraging unless you're good with it. Back when I wrote "Handguns for Hunting" (GUN DIGEST, 1960) I was shooting my sidearms almost daily. I was pretty proficient with that little S&W then. Today, having gotten somewhat rusty, I'm sure I'd eat much better on a camping/foraging trip if I depended upon a 22 rifle instead.

Foraging adds fun and challenge to a wilderness trip. Fish and game have supplemented my rations on treks ranging from Alaska's mountains to the Amazon jungle. A simple 22 rifle is a good choice. It can be an inexpensive single shot, carried on a sling, barrel trimmed to 18 or even 16 inches and the buttstock bored out to reduce weight further. Iron sights should suffice. In real wilderness country, long shots are seldom necessary.

There are many other possibilities. Remington's light, rugged Nylon 66 autoloader is excellent. More specialized is the Charter Arms AR-7 Explorer which stows in its own durable plastic stock and floats, assembled or taken down. I've carried one of those quite a bit in recent years. It's a bit bulky (though not heavy) for backpacking, but it's a dandy for canoe trips.

I want a gun which can be holstered or slung for ready access on the trail. A rifle or a shotgun should be light, short, and just plain rugged. Don't take a fancy gun; it's bound to take a beating.

An old trail buddy of mine favors the Savage Model 24-VS Camper model in 22 and 20 gauge. Another possibility is the Springfield Armory M6 survival gun. The fact is a 22 will suffice virtually anywhere except in bear country. A major advantage is the light weight of the ammo. Even 100 rounds are hardly noticeble in the pack.

So where does the big handgun come in? In North America, the answer ought to be anywhere you might have to deal with aggressive bears. No doubt about it, a handgun is the handiest answer for someone who is carrying loads over long wilderness trails or portages. If you carry a magnum, you can take along some re-

Basic belt equipment on many of author's wilderness treks—a sturdy knife and a Ruger Blackhawk 357 with assorted ammo, including 38 Special loads and Speer shotshells.

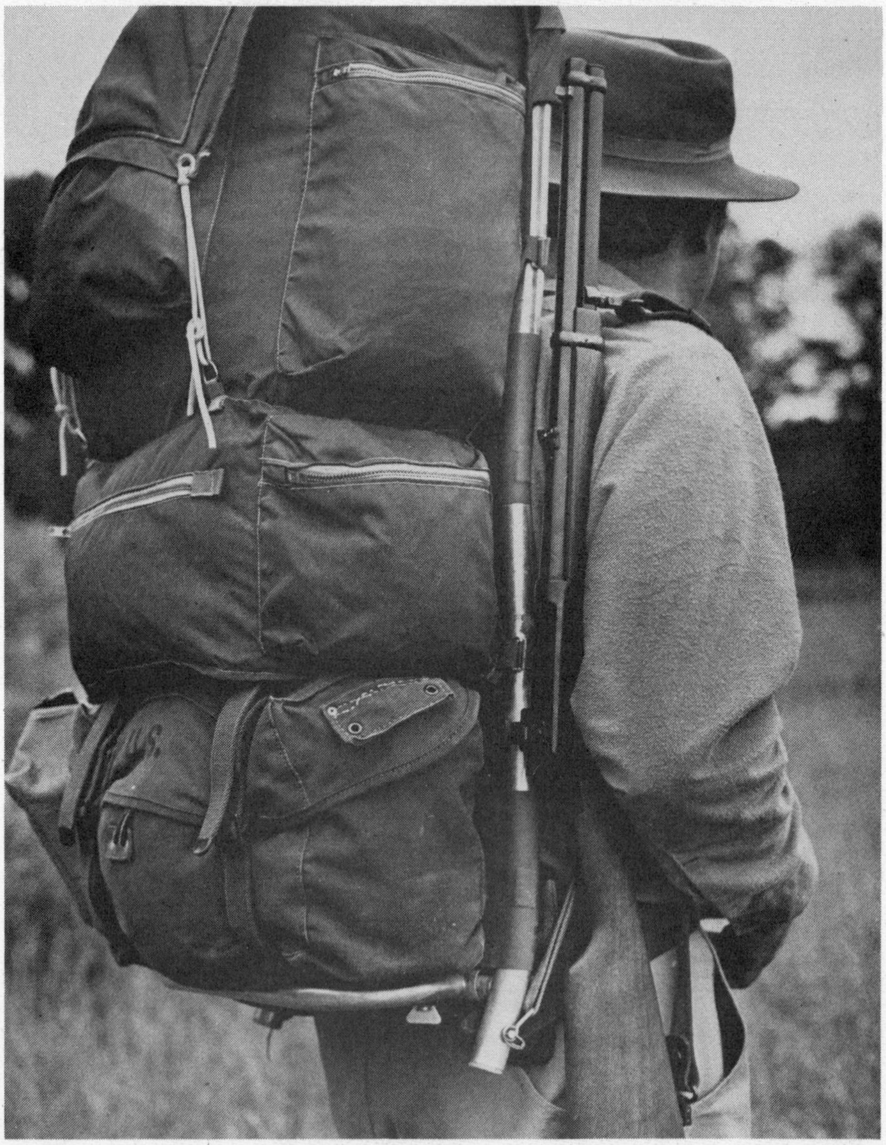

Compact Model 94 Trapper nestles neatly along pack frame; provides ample firepower for emergencies and beats any handgun for bear work.

Equipped with sling swivels, H&R Topper makes a handy and versatile trail companion; Johnson carries both slugs and shot when he goes.

Charter Arms Explorer has many features recommending it as an all-around camping gun, but is at its best on canoe trips—it's waterproof and it floats and is just right on stream-side small game.

duced loads for small game. Shot cartridges, such as the Speers, also can be used to take grouse or ptarmigan at close range.

If any handgun can be recommended for stopping bears, it would be one of the long-barreled Thompson Contenders in a big-rifle caliber. With a sling and Pachmayr grip, they make an appealing package. The single shot aspect doesn't bother me because one good shot is all you're apt to get. I'm not going to start poking at a bear with a handgun while there's a chance he'll change his mind and go the other way.

The problem with handguns is that there's a whole lot of wilderness—all of Canada—where they are taboo. A powerful sidearm may be a good choice in Alaska, but if you plan to drive there, ship your handgun ahead.

It used to be quite easy to carry a handgun through Canada. It would be sealed at the border and checked again upon leaving the country. There might be some circumstances where that is still possible, but I don't recommend trying it. I also urge you not to carry a handgun into Canada undeclared. If you are discovered, it will ruin your day and then some.

Anyway, there are many hundreds of miles of bear country between Alaska and the Lower 48. You'll probably want to camp along the way, perhaps doing some fishing and hiking. You'll want a long gun then.

If I were choosing a gun simply for survival in wild country, it would be an "all-around" rifle in the 30-06 class. Powerful enough to handle any species on the continent, such a rifle can also be used to take small game. I've used reduced loads successfully in a variety of big bores. However, I've also found that I can get by with the same loads for large and small game if a good controlled-expansion bullet is used. You want to hit the little critters in the head or neck anyway. With a good rifle sighted in for 200 to 300 yards you ought to be able to pop a blue grouse or snowshoe hare in the skull at 25-30 yards.

There are good reasons why my 280 doesn't go on non-hunting wilderness excursions. Built on a pre-64 Model 70 action with a stiff 24-inch barrel, it is too heavy and cumbersome. Also, the stock is a creation of the late great Len Brownell. It bears the marks of many hunts, but it's still too pretty to be banging against a pack frame all day.

There are some big-bore rifles better suited for travel though; Ruger's 44 Magnum carbine *(Now discontinued: Editor)* seems almost ideal. It is short, lightweight, and has few obtrusive parts. I regard the cartridge as marginal, so I would regard it as a point-blank weapon. Better, in my opinion, would be a lightweight Ruger 77, Winchester Model 70 or Remington Model Seven in 308. Drawbacks are that bolt rifles do stick out awkwardly in places and those are pretty nice rifles to knock around.

The best big-little bolt action ever made for backpacking in bear country was the Remington Model 600. It was introduced in 1964 and was offered in assorted calibers ranging from 222 to 35 Remington—the latter a pretty fair bear stopper. But, my, it was ugly. I found it easy to resist. Two years later, there was a magnum version which, incredibly, was even uglier. It was chambered for two stubby, belted cases. The 6.5mm Magnum didn't interest me, but the 350 was something else.

That spring of 1967 I was packing for a long assignment which would take me to Kodiak Island and the Aleutians; then into Alaska's interior. For the first part of the trip, which included some hunting, I chose a 300 Winchester Magnum. For my solo trek into the Brooks Range which was to follow, I wanted something handier and the 350 Magnum looked like the answer. It sounded and felt like it, too, when I got hold of one and took it to the range.

I carried the Model 600 on that trip, but never fired it again. I decided not to keep it. I really wish I had. Remington didn't make many and there is nothing else quite like them around. Less than 37 inches long and weighing only 6½ pounds, they were a lot of rifle in a small package. Alaskan bush pilots and other savvy types latched on to most of them. I saw one a couple of years ago in a cabin in Alaska's Kantishna Hills. The owner, an old trapper-miner, said he treasured it because it was handy to take up the creek to work. He added that it also was highly respected by the local bears.

The light Topper 20-gauge is the writer's last-ditch choice—the best compromise he's found.

I've arrived at a compromise when I want to carry something handy and reasonably potent. A few years ago I settled on none other than the venerable Model 94 Winchester 30-30 carbine. In the 16-inch-barreled Trapper version it is just 34 inches long. Fully loaded and equipped with swivels and sling it weighs six pounds. Its slab-sided receiver makes for easy carrying and the time-tested design is reliable. With a Williams aperture rear sight and a Redfield bead in front, I can consistently hold it to four-inch groups at 100 yards.

Never mind telling me about the inadequacies of the 30-30. I know the caliber pretty well, having fooled around with lots of rifles and loads in that number over the years. I've seen a heap of deer taken with 30-30s. Devotees of the caliber also still haul quite a few black bears out of the woods of Wisconsin where I live.

Some people think that magnum handguns are good bear insurance, but believe it's foolhardy to face a grizzly with a 30-30. The facts are different. Ballistically the 30-30 is 'way ahead of a 44 Magnum in carbine or handgun. I won't go grizzly hunting with a 30-30, but if one comes hunting me I think he'll come out second best.

But the most indispensable of my go-along guns is none of the above. The one which I think can do it all is an inexpensive H&R Topper single shot 20-gauge. Mine is a Model 98, a somewhat gussied up version with a nickel-plated receiver and a black-enameled stock. I bought it originally because of its three-inch chamber and a modified choke—just what I needed for field testing some 20-gauge steel shot loads since marketed by Federal Cartridge Co.

Later, I mounted detachable sling swivels to buttstock and barrel and took a rasp to the stock to give it a straight grip. The result was a light (5½ pound), reliable and versatile wilderness companion. It has since made several trips. I carried it across British Columbia, Yukon Territory and much of Alaska in 1980. Snowshoe hares, ptarmigan and grouse were abundant that year and I could easily have survived, if necessary, on small game taken with the Topper.

I also carried some Brennecke slug loads. I have as much bear-stopping confidence in them as in any handgun load. In a GUN DIGEST article way back in 1963 ("A Twenty's Plenty") I made a case for the 20-gauge slug for deer. I've taken large whitetails with both the standard Foster type and the Brennecke slug in that gauge. The penetration of the latter looks pretty persuasive. For that matter, at point-blank range, even an ounce of fine shot is devastating.

Even better than my Topper would be a newer version of the model—the H&R Handy Gun II combo, available in electroless nickel finish. Its 22-inch modified barrel gives the gun an overall length of 37 inches (four inches shorter than mine) and there's a matching 30-30 barrel to boot.

One drawback I can see to carrying any kind of firearm while hiking in bear country is that guns may make some people too bold. They may crowd a bear to take pictures and may shoot (and probably wound) a bear which is only bluffing. People and bears are then needlessly hurt. The gun should be regarded the same as a life insurance policy. You don't really want to use either one.

Avoid taking Old Griz by surprise. In parks where firearms aren't allowed it's an especially good idea to travel noisily through bear country, jingling bells, whistling, or talking. There is usually safety in numbers, too. The average bear is more likely to yield to two or three hikers than to one. Just don't get pushy.

To sum up, the decision on which gun to tote on back country treks depends upon what measure of protection is required and whether or not it will be used to provide provisions. If you're traveling with a companion, the choice gets easier. One of you can carry a pot gun and the other a bear buster without anybody being overburdened.

My choices are based on experience and they work well for me. On the catalog pages in this issue of GUN DIGEST you may find something more exactly tailored to your particular needs.

Personally, if I had to settle on one gun for all such wilderness adventures I guess it would be the 20-gauge single shot. It's rugged and lightweight. It's a good good game-getter and packs a pretty good punch in a pinch. If you think about it, those are all the criteria a good go-along gun has to meet. ●

The Search for Accuracy

by WARREN PAGE

Oklahoman Charlie Jennings is a prime mover in NBRSA activities in Texas and his native state, and one time president of the association. Note simple, effective Beecher tripod.

THE NEED for accuracy in military small-arms fire appears to have swung full circle. Two centuries ago—and this shooting style persisted well into our Civil War—ranked musketeers belched large-caliber balls aimed not at one man but directed generally at an enemy force massed perhaps a hundred grenadier paces away. Not accuracy, but sheer volume of fire carried the field. And today, with automatic weapons squirting bullets by the boxful to blanket enemy positions, the military again rely on sheer weight of metal thrown. But in the sporting weapon, the rifle, there has been no such reversion. Rather have we seen a constant refining of gun and projectile toward the ultimate in rifle accuracy, the ability to hit any target however small over any range at which it can be seen, the basic ability to put every bullet neatly through a single hole.

In September of 1953 the latter of these ideals came within a gnat's eyelash of fulfillment by a gentleman who runs a carriage-trade department store—when he isn't monkeying with tack-driving rifles. From a hundred yards, amid the racket and pressure of competition with over a hundred other riflemen, Colonel Crawford Hollidge drove ten shots into a ragged hole only .2677 inches across the centers of the outermost shots. Bausch & Lomb technicians so measured the group under a binocular microscope. Every bullet from his Buhmiller-barreled 219 Donaldson merely punched larger the hole made by the first 224-diameter bullet. A new world record, under the rules of the National Bench Rest Shooters Association, and any way you look at it a fantastic feat.

On that same weekend, 105 shooters entered the Johnstown matches. Using all manner of rifles and techniques, having all levels of skill, at 100 yards for ten shot groups the whole crowd's average group size was .851 inches, for the ten shooters at 200, only 1.737 inches. In other words, men and rifles firing some ten thousand shots in tense competition subject to time limits, were averaging 85/100th of a minute of angle all the way. The upper crust, the winner group, were cutting that in half and then some. Incredible?

Yet only some 30 years ago, the authoritative *British Text Book of Small Arms* admitted as expectancy for an "accurate" rifle the ability to shoot into three minutes of angle, three inches at 100 yards or nine at 300. That's still good enough for a deer rifle, for big game rifles under most conditions. But the sporting-weight rifle a shootin' man is proud of today will halve that spread, and the varmint rifle he brags about will quarter it. On my rack stands an arsenal of game-caliber rifles that will, when fed proper ammunition, shoot into two inches all the time, an inch and a half most of the time; and the ten or a dozen varmint rifles will hold at least five shots within three-quarters of an inch. What has brought about this remarkable change in our ideas of rifle accuracy?

Birth and Background

A good part of the responsibility belongs to that nation-wide group of gun nuts banded together as the NBRSA, a "new" organization, either seven or ten years old depending on where you hail from. Back in 1944 Puget Sound riflemen organized the Seattle Snipers Congress; but the present organization, which blankets every state in the Union from Maine to Texas, probably stems more directly from the Eastern association formed at Johnstown, N. Y., in 1947. But regardless of whether greater credit should go to New Yorker Harvey Donaldson or Oklahoman Charlie Jennings or Washingtonian Doc Janson, the end and aim of the thousand-odd paid-up members and their host of gun-crank brethren is the same—put 'em all in one hole.

Such dreams of perfection are hardly new. The 16th century experimenters with the rifled bore, the German August Kotter or the Viennese Kollner, were likely tormented by it. But not until the 19th century did the one-hole group seem possible even in fancy. As an outgrowth of back-country turkey shoots, and roughly concurrent with the beginnings of formal schuetzen competition in this country, there came into favor matches featuring "rest rifles." These were percussion monsters at times hefting a full 40 pounds, meant to be fired with the muzzle in a mechanical rest or over a log. In what were essentially gun-accuracy competitions, the rifles made by such artisans as Horace Warner, Billinghurst, Brockway, Lewis and Morgan James at times threw their 35 to 50 caliber lead slugs remarkably close over 20- and 40-rod shooting courses. Some extant groups, then graded by "string measure," run close to an inch and a half across outermost centers.

I briefly owned one of these ponderous rifles, built by Warner with his typical under-hammer sprung by the trigger guard, rigged with a crude optical sight as long as the barrel, a tube octagonal and fully three inches through. It may have been a corker in its day, but I was neither man enough to lug it nor mad enough to consider coping with all the problems of temperamental black powder, the casting and patching of slugs involved in making it really shoot.

Toward the century's end, as black powder was going out in favor of smokeless, came the heyday of the schuetzen expert, of rifle-builders Pope, Zischang, Schoyen, of ballistician Dr. Mann. Experiments searching for the pin-hole offhand rifle led to the use of the bench rest for testing. And the 32-40's and 38-55's of that era shot remarkably well, whether the cast slug was sized in the bore by being started down through a false muzzle, or breech-loaded already seated in the cartridge case after the fashion of today. With Pope rifles, devout experimenters like Sam Clark have in recent years duplicated some of the early records, using modern primers and boosting the black powder loads with light charges of quick-burning smokeless like du Pont 4759. The prime single accomplishment of this era is probably the famous C. W. Rowland group, ten shots recently measured as going into .725 inches from 200 yards. This was shot with a 32-40 Pope-Ballard, from rest, but not under competitive conditions.

Adherents of the golden age of Pope and Schoyen cite such individual groups —never multi-shooter averages—as evidence that today's rifles are no better. But no fanatic however devout has ever entered a Pope or Schoyen rifle in NBRSA matches to my knowledge; nor do I believe that he could compete over any range with today's centerfire equipment, shooting small-caliber pills at better than 3000 foot-seconds and with such accuracy that half a minute of angle only maintains a shooter's self respect.

What has been learned by the experiments of the past seven or eight years that riflemen of high technical skill did not know before? Little, actually, save more details of the basic truth that the secret of accuracy is twofold: precision of manufacture of all components and rifle parts, duplication of every step in the loading, holding, and firing procedures.

From the covered firing point on the Dubois (Pa.) range, rifles can be tested at 100 and 200 yards, 300 meters, on out to 600 yards. The Memorial Day matches at Dubois draw 150 or more riflemen.

The Secret — Uniformity

We have learned how to make superbly precise small-caliber bullets on both an individual and a commercial basis. We know that jacket cups must be of split-thousandth exactness of dimension, absolutely consistent hardness or anneal, that each lead core must be precisely the same form and weight, freed of bubbles by pre-swaging in a "squirt" die. Record-holder Hollidge swears by lead like that used in stained glass windows, not because it is in any way blessed, but because it is pure and uniformly extruded. We know that like good whiskey the two parts of a bullet must be aged in their case to relax internal stresses before they are swaged together, then again aged after forming and before shooting. All evidence indicates that each step in the forming and mating of core and jacket must be taken on the "expanding-up" principle if the bullet is to be homogeneous, balanced in mass. These truths we hold to be self-evident whether the swaging equipment used by the individual is that of R.C.B.S., Biehler and Astles, Hollywood Gun Shop, Pearson, or some gadgetry he has cooked up down cellar.

There is evidence that bullets of equal precision can be made in commerical quantities. Tallying the loading dope of bench resters the country over shows that almost 70% shoot Sierra bullets, about 10% those made by Joyce Hornady, a few Baldwin, Kenru, Jordan and Sisk, and between 10 and 15% projectiles of their own making. Often the best bullet is the one best suited to the whimsy of an individual barrel. In any event, the perfectly balanced projectile is more important than the powder charge behind it. Accuracy fans long ago came to realize that the small variations in powder charges caused by throwing them from a measure, perhaps a tenth of a grain either way, have little effect on the equality of barrel time, which is accuracy magic.

Yet we apparently don't know how to make bullets of greater than .224 diameter to the same levels of accuracy. At least no caliber larger than 22 has to date performed with equal consistency, this despite individual wins and two phenomenal records, the 100-yard and 300-meter five-shot clusters by Dinant and Clarke. The problem is not entirely one of bullets. Recoil increase and a greater tendency toward metal fouling so far have overbalanced the better wind-bucking characteristics of the larger calibers; but bright hopes for the 25's—and of some among us for the 6mm or 243 caliber—have so far not been fully realized.

Better Barrels

We have learned considerable about barrels, chiefly that they must be drilled and rifled to a degree of precision impossible with any but the most modern equipment. We know that there is no gain in hardening a barrel blank to higher than about 24 on the Rockwell "C" scale; that by and large alloy steels containing chrome and molybdenum as well as carbon and manganese make fine-shooting barrels; that while the so-called "stainless" steels (for example those containing 18% chrome, 8% nickel) are definitely tough, resistant to erosion and oxidation at the chamber throat, and hence keep their shooting qualities for many rounds, they are hard to make into tack driving barrels. In every one of these cases the prime consideration has been the relative ease of uniform drilling and rifling.

Many custom barrel makers, craftsmen like Pride, Douglas, Buhmiller, May, Pfeifer, and until recently Gregoire have made splendidly accurate barrels. But these individual tubes can be earmarked as capable of absolute top accuracy only in terms of the makers subjective judgment—his feeling that the blank drilled not only straight but evenly, that it rifled precisely in that the cutter worked smoothly on every stroke, and that a lead slug pushed all the way through with equal pressure gave no evidence of tight or loose spots. And even barrels so selected aren't always top-hole, since the fanatic accuracy bug may try from one to ten selected barrels before he hits on the absolute best.

There's more to be learned about this barrel business, for sure. Possibly modern metal-working methods may someday permit the building up of a barrel by electrolytic methods around a mandrel, to get unstressed homogenous metal and perfect dimensions. Meanwhile there exists a need for fantastically exact equipment for measuring barrel insides, as for example the air-gauge gadgets so far available only to the large arms companies. It can be no accident, by the way, that three 222 Remington rifles, the barrels for which were made and chambered at the same time by one man, "called" before assembly as superbly fine barrels, have been consistent winners all their shooting lives, in the top ten rifles on a national basis in 1952, in the top ten again in 1953.

Those barrels were lapped; that is, they were polished free of tool marks by using a cast lead lap and emery grit of between 125 and 150 mesh, lubricated with ordinary lard oil. The muzzle and breech ends were trimmed back an inch or so to avoid the "bell-mouth" that results from the lap. The chief purpose of any interior polishing, whether by the lap or a bore-honing method, is to smooth out any residual tool marks that would pick up jacket metal and cause lumpy fouling. Opposition to lapping—and it's strictly a job for the expert—has been on the grounds of wearing out the lands before the rifle is shot. But my lapped-barrel 222, which is a venerable graybeard with some 3000 rounds through it at this point—and all fired with the original lot of 60 cases—rated fourth and then third over the national match courses these past two years, have come within a flea's whisker of breaking a couple of records, and I hope to win a match or two with it this season. Can't be that lapping wore it out.

Reloading ammunition at the match is standard procedure for bench rest competitors. Here Warren Page, Field & Stream's Shooting Editor, works up ammo for his 222, a steady winner.

One sure way to ruin a fine barrel blank is by over-enthusiastic turning down to get a desired outside taper. That almost certainly upsets the balance of internal strains and stresses which are literally born in the molecules of the metal, may produce a barrel that is either crooked or becomes crooked as the metal crawls during firing. Hence super-accuracy barrels are usually turned only to smooth up the exterior. Yet we have learned how to taper barrel blanks down easily, cutting very slowly, so that light varmint and even sporter barrels can be as steady as rocks, as tight with their groups as a Scot with his shillings. Witness the half-minute groups, fired with portable, practical-weight rifles, that every accuracy bug carries in his wallet.

Barrel Bedding

We have learned that rifles are as whimsical as women when it comes to bedding. All the experiments of the bench-rest clan, and all the super-scientific oscilloscope-recorder tests of the arms companies prove just that. It now seems reasonable that barrels hung on the relatively stiff Remington 721 or 722 actions shoot their best free-floating, with a full 1/16th clearance between barrel and fore end, judging from the rifles made to date. One secret with these actions, by the way, is to bed the recoil lug absolutely square against its mortise at the rear, but absolutely free of any contact at the bottom or sides. With the standard Mauser action, since it is somewhat less stiff, fore-end pressure should be introduced to suit the individual barrel and its mode of vibration. Exactly where and how much the shooter will have to find out for himself, either by endless monkeying with shims or by using one of the electrical bedding gadgets. We know that any good barrel will shoot at least fairly well when free-floated, that most will tighten or loosen their groups according to the bedding scheme employed, and that a bum barrel won't shoot even if it's bedded in a solid platinum stock on layers of hummingbird down.

Sam Clark and barrel-maker Douglas have experimented with a rig whereby the barrel is clamped into metal blocks which are fastened to the stock, with the clamp a few inches ahead of the receiver so the shooting metal is free to wag at both ends. This has proved little so far; but whether the fault was in the idea, the barrels or the bullets, or in any of the multitudinous variables that affect barrel vibration, the bullet's time through the bore and its flight beyond the muzzle, Heaven only knows.

We have learned that the stock of a super-accurate rifle must be solid and stable. For bench competition it must be heavy, four inches or more broad at the fore end so that it will rest securely on the sandbags and not be twisted around by bullet-induced torque, with as little tendency toward warpage as wood can have when dried down to perhaps 7% moisture content. Elimination of the magazine well, a stunt long practiced by gun-builders Taylor and Robbins, helps stiffen a bench stock; the modern resin-bonded laminations and plastic infusions help balk warpage and make for a heavier handle which moves less in recoil; but your ideas are as good as the next man's when it comes to the ideal buttstock shape for accuracy firing.

Cartridges

There is violent disagreement as to which is the most accurate cartridge—and I for one doubt this hassle will ever be resolved. Fortunately so, too, since to settle it would squash all experiments in cartridge design. The weight of evidence might seem to favor the 219 Donaldson, or, as it is called by Gipson's copyrighted name, the 219 Wasp. In either it is the 219 Zipper case shortened to some 1.760 inches, renecked and fireformed in the chamber to give a neck about .315 inches long, a shoulder taper of 30°, and a body diameter at the shoulder of .406″. The resultant case is meant to burn from 26 to 28 grains of du Pont 3031 and to give 50 and 55 grain bullets of .224″ diameter velocities roughly 200 feet per second less than those practical from the 220 Swift. As of this writing, the 219 Donaldson holds only the world records for ten shots at 100 yards. (.2677 inches) and at 300 meters (1.740 inches); but at one time or another it has borne all the laurels.

The seemingly overwhelming success of this cartridge is suspect, however, when we consider that at bench shoots held east of the Mississippi roughly 60% of the competitors have been shooting rifles chambered for the Wasp, and it is at the Eastern shoots, by and large, where wind and mirage conditions often permit record breaking. Switch to a Western competition, and the 22-250 will number 60% of the gun-bugs on its team. Fathered by Gebby during the early 1920's, although Newton had experimented with a similar version of his 250-3000 even before World War I, this rimless round, which burns only a few grains more powder than the Wasp, is the most popular varmint cartridge among U.S. wildcatters. With a 22-250, Lou Edsall several years ago averaged well under .4 inches for ten 100-yard groups, and it now holds both 200-yard records.

Almost all other cartridge forms experimented with, the standard 250-3000 and its smaller form the 250 Donaldson Ace, the abbreviated form of the 257 known as the 250 Donaldson, the 270 International and others in the larger calibers, the cut-back forms of the 220 Swift—almost all the cartridges successful today in pinhole accuracy firing are of small capacity. We know, or at least have reason to believe, that while extremes of velocity plus adequate accuracy may come with the enlarged wildcat forms, the extremes of accuracy plus adequate velocity come only with the smaller types of cartridge case. Apparently when less powder is burned, but burned in a case which is filled to a high loading density, that powder is completely consumed each shot, the pressures it develops are more nearly the same for each shot, hence the crucial barrel time (the number of milliseconds it takes the bullet to move from cartridge neck to rifle muzzle) is most nearly identical for each shot. Such uniformity, assuming precise bullets and a perfectly bored barrel, means accuracy of the one-hole variety.

All of which may be one reason for the growing popularity of the 222 Remington in this search for accuracy. Only four years old as this is written, the newcomer ranks high commercially, fifth in gross sales among centerfire rifle loads, I understand. Although only two U.S.-made rifles are factory chambered for it, the 222 has caught on equally fast among the accuracy bugs. There were only a couple of these rifles at the benches in 1950, but the 1953 Johnstown competition saw over a dozen 222's brought to the firing line, and four guns in that caliber hit the top ten in national competition. Only two-thirds the size of the famous Wasp in powder capacity, it is capable of driving its bullets, 50, 55, or 60 grains, in the 3000-3200 velocity belt which seems to give minimum wind effect. The pint-sized varmint load may yet be something of a milepost in accuracy research.

You will note that I have carefully omitted reference to the really large calibers in ultra-accuracy terms; and I've had but little to say about accuracy performance over extremes of range to a thousand yards, say. For the same reason in both cases. Big bangs and far shoots mean the inevitable introduction of the human element, in the form of recoil and its needed control with the big-caliber hard-kicking combinations, in the form of judgement of breeze and ability to out-guess mirage when long ranges are concerned. Progress here awaits human development, some sort of super-rifleman, and we can't seem to change men as fast as we can the rifles and cartridges with which accuracy devotees are primarily concerned. But with ragged-hole groups at 100 and 200 yards, accuracy to less than a third of former standards at 300 it is clear that the old measures of musketry are gone with the wind. Closer and closer comes the goal of the accuracy fans, every shot into a single hole.

WORLD ACCURACY RECORDS

100 yards—5 shots—.1057 inch
Paul Dinant, Calif.—250-3000

100 yards—10 shots—.2677 inch
Col. C. Hollidge, Mass.—219 Donaldson

200 yards—5 shots—.3896 inch
Bill Guse, Texas—22-250

200 yards—10 shots—.6378 inch
Frank Cooper, Wash.—22-250

300 meters—5 shots—.6735 inch
Sam Clark, Maine—250 Donaldson Ace

300 Meters—10 shots—1.740 inches
Clair Taylor, Penna.—219 Donaldson

Great Arc of the Wild Sheep Guides

The trophy of trophies, Chadwick's ram, on rock-slide soon after the kill. Frank Golata is on left; Curley Cochrane is on the right. Golata is holding what appears to be L. S. Chadwick's Winchester Model 54 30-06 backup rifle. Chadwick used 404 Hoffman Magnum for the first shots at the ram.

The sheep were up there, and the dudes were down *there* . It was the guides and the outfitters that got them together.

by JAMES L. CARKHUFF

THERE IS A GROUP of sporting heroes, now in their own Hall of Fame, who plied their trade without fanfare far from public accolade, with spectators often only a pair of winded mountain horses and a lone trophy hunter, yet note of their field prowess has come down through the years. The lore wrapping them in legend is zealously maintained. Uniformed in wool shirts, suspendered breeches and rock-nicked mountain boots, they have passed into the annals of sport as master guides pre-eminent in pursuit of the hunter's grail—the heavy-horned mountain ram.

This anecdotal narrative describes the fabled few who, early on, comprised the Great Arc of the North American Sheep Guides. They lived and worked out of mountain-perimeter locations overlaying the Great Arc of the North American sheep.* From the north to south, this vanguard included:

**The Great Arc of the Wild Sheep*, by James L. Clark, a treatise on the distribution and habitat of wild sheep. University of Oklahoma Press, Norman, OK. 1964.

• Eugene and Louis Jacquot of Burwash Landing, Yukon Territory—Dall sheep.
• Frank Golata, Dawson Creek, British Columbia—Stone sheep.
• Roy Hargreaves, Mt. Robson, British Columbia—Rocky Mountain bighorns and some Stone sheep.
• Bert Riggal, Pincher Creek, Alberta—Rocky Mountain bighorns.
• Ned Frost, Cody, Wyoming—Rocky Mountain bighorns.
• Charlie Ren, Sonoyta, Sonora—Desert sheep.

They were mountain men, sheep hunters, horsemen, logistics experts—giants indeed in their field. From the first pulsings of momentum and interest in sheep hunting generated by that great hunter and naturalist Charles Sheldon, in his books *Wilderness of the Upper Yukon* and *Wilderness of the Denali*, they nurtured and developed the infant outfitting business operating into the far sheep ranges.

There were no roads anywhere near most of the areas they hunted. Aerial transportation came only after years of doing it the hard way. Much of the hunting area was only sketchily mapped, if at all.

And even in the "rugged" first decades of this century, not every aspiring sheep hunter was a tuned athlete. The old days had their share of overweight people, much like many of those who can afford today's excursions. So they managed men as well as sheep.

From a work in progress, here are some facts about these great guides, their guns, their clients, their hunts:

Jean and Louis Jacquot

Pursuing Dall sheep in the rugged country around Kluane Lake and the heads of the Generc, the Donjek, and the White rivers from outfitting headquarters at Burwash Landing, provided a substantial living for several decades for two diminutive French chefs. In 1898 these brothers backpacked over the Chilkoot Pass, built a boat on Lake Bennett and floated down the Yukon to the Klondike during the great gold rush. They ultimately sold their Klondike claims in 1904 and moved south to another strike on Burwash Creek, draining into Kluane Lake. And while continuing to prospect, they began trading in furs, trapping supplies, food and dry goods.

They picked up their first big game outfitting and hunting experience through a local named Morley Bones, who outfitted an extended hunt in the fall of 1919 for a party from the States. You can read of it in the classic book, *Alaskan-Yukon Trophies Won and Lost* by G. O. Young.

By the 1930s, the Jacquot reputation was well-established. Their hunts were conducted primarily in the Donjek River basin, prime Dall habitat and fine grizzly country. Trophy aspirants in pursuit of the magnificent Dall rams included hunters from all walks of life and some notables, including General R. E. Woods, Nelson Rockefeller, Richard K. Mellon, and Jack O'Connor.

Capable afield themselves, the Jacquots were possibly the first to see the virtues of employing native guides. They happily watched guides Jimmie Copper Joe, Jimmie Johnson, Johnny Allen, and Jack O'Connor's field mentor, Field Johnson, garner word-of-mouth reputations in their own right.

The Jacquots provided abundant amenities of good camp life. In addition to good tentage, horses and abundant game, the famous quantity and quality of their grub stood on its own. Jacquot-outfitted hunts were gastronomically memorable.

The brothers' recommendation for an all-around mountain rifle centered on the 30-06 with a 180-grain bullet for sheep and a somewhat heavier bullet for grizzly. Such armament was more than adequate also when they wandered towards the White River for caribou and moose. Gene himself carried a 250-3000 and Louis a 30-06 Springfield.

Frank Golata

Frank Golata's present stature did not evolve, certainly, from his physical size but from a spectacular career as British Columbia's most famous sheep guide. Who can forget the classic photos of the 5-ft., 7-in. Golata, in those high laced boots and the distinctive high-crowned hat with its beaded hatband, binoculars raised?

Born in Dunkirk, New York, of Polish parentage, Golata was hung up in the old world custom of collective pooling of wages until *all* the children of the family were educated. After stints as a bellhop, a time clerk, and even a draftsman, his familial responsibilities were concluded in 1912 and he embarked on the long dreamed-of escape to Canada.

In Rolla, British Columbia, not far from Dawson Creek, Golata came under the tutelage of an old-time cowboy named Bill Conn. From him Golata gained an introduction to horses and learned much of his early bush-lore.

Golata acquired a pack string in the early 1920s and perfected his technique packing gear to trappers, and it was not until 1933 that he made his first commercial hunt with a gunsmith from Iowa named Harry Gibson. He liked the job.

On the advice of his trapper friends, in 1935 he made a solo trip into the Prophet River/Musqua River country for a two-month reconnoiter, and in 1936, a local Rolla compadre, Curley Cochrane, accompanied Golata and Roy Hargreaves on the now-famous L. S. Chadwick hunt, on which the world's record Stone sheep was killed.

On this trip, in addition to the record head, Chadwick also took a second ram measuring 39-in. on one horn and 38¼-in. on the other, after it broke 6 to 7-in. of horn off each side in a 250-yard skid down a rock slide. Hargreaves shot for himself a Stone ram

Roy Hargreaves, master outfitter, hunted a paradise for sheep, provided Jack O'Connor with the unforgettable trip of a lifetime, all while making a living.

L. S. Chadwick, Roy Hargreaves and Curley Cochrane with a wolf shot by Chadwick in 1936. Hargreaves is 6-feet tall; Chadwick much taller. The wolf is not small, either.

Mac McGuire with 43-inch Stone's ram taken by Joseph H. Shirk in 1948. It holds 8th place in current Boone & Crockett records. Massive bases measure 15⅝-inch. That's probably Shirk's rifle

Legendary Ned Frost of Cody, Wyoming, carried his old Model 95 carbine in 30-06 up to where they posed these rams as he carried it most other places.

Golata with a pair of Stone rams.

Two of Golata's own trophies and his own taxidermy. His brand is G4.

Classic photo of Frank Golata, in high-laced boots worn in early years, glassing for rams at head of Prophet, circa 1935.

measuring $41\frac{1}{16}$-in. and 42-in.; and another, measuring 38-in. per side, in which he expressed disappointment. That made four trophy Stone sheep in nine days, with the monster $51\frac{5}{8}$-in. head dominating them all.

It was 14 days by packtrain up Bear Creek to the Halfway River, then on to Deadman Lake to get into Frank's base camp at Redfern Lake. Once the Alaska Highway went through, Golata steadfastly refused to book anyone for a period shorter than 30 days. He felt anything less than 30 days in the mountains "shorted" the hunter.

It was as a jack-of-all-trades that Golata shone. He was a trapper and big-game guide supreme; a taxidermist of no mean accomplishment; an artist, working in oil; he did extraordinary bead work; he tanned hides for his own taxidermy work and for his own leather jackets. He made his own saddle and bridle and the distinctive curved pack boxes for sawbuck saddles were an early creation. So also was a special campstove that went into the mountains with him for 30 years.

As a rifleman, Frank was not so unsophisticated as he was unimpressed. To him, a rifle was a tool. In the early years he used a well-worn 30-30 Winchester carbine. Later, he replaced it with a 30-06 Winchester Model 70. His ammunition was off-the-shelf. He did treasure and swear by a pair of 7x50 Zeiss binoculars.

Hunters to the high country with Frank Golata took the world record Stone ram and another Stone sheep taken by Joseph Shirk that still holds eighth place in the Boone and Crockett record book with horn lengths of 43-in. and $43\frac{4}{8}$-in. and incredibly heavy (for Stone sheep) bases of $15\frac{6}{8}$-in. One Golata hunter took a gigantic 72-in. moose. Another, of reported timid personal traits, shot one of the largest of grizzlies, judging by the photograph, before he lapsed into hysteria.

Frank Golata did it all, in professional style, at a time when access into the Stone sheep country was measured not in hours but in trekking *days*.

Roy Hargreaves

Roy Hargreaves and his brothers, of Mt. Robson, British Columbia, operated in eastern B.C. and the fabulous Smoky River country of western Alberta. During much of Hargreaves' active tenure, that may have been the finest game country on earth.

In 1935, L. S. Chadwick, one year before taking the world record Stone sheep in British Columbia, hunted with Hargreaves on a classic. They covered over 800 miles on horseback and made 26 camps. In one day, Chadwick related that he saw 34 nice bighorn rams, 50 ewes and lambs, 25 goats, 7 black wolves and one silver fox.

Hargreaves, in those days, maintained both an Alberta and a British Columbia outfitter's license. In so doing, he harvested the finest trophies on both sides of the provincial border running down the spine of the Canadian Rockies. Locally, despite awesome success with bighorn sheep, Hargreaves came to be known as the Grizzly King because of an uncanny ability to find grizzly bears.

He was born in Gardner, Oregon, on February 17, 1918, but his family soon moved. They went to southern British Columbia, then during the winter of 1912-1913, they moved on to settle at Jasper, Alberta. Roy went to work as a hunting guide for Curley Phillips. In 1913, in Phillips' employ, he found the site of what would subsequently be his Mt. Robson ranch.

For World War I, Hargreaves went off to Europe. He spent 18 months in the hospital after being gassed on the battlefield, but Armistice Day found Roy and his father and brothers back at the spot, with the breath-taking view of Mt. Robson, he had discovered in 1913. The family team cut and hauled logs for the ranch buildings and by 1920 were established ranchers and outfitters.

It was his association with L. S. Chadwick in 1935 and again in 1936 that launched his major following. Incidentally, there is considerable credence to the story that Hargreaves himself actually trailed, caught up with and despatched the lightly wounded monster Stone ram. It may be Chadwick's 404 Hoffman had caused only a hip wound on the record sheep before Hargreaves put it down and into the records forever.

In his account of a hunt with Roy in 1943 down the Smoky River, Jack O'Connor related that it was one of "the great experiences and most successful hunts of a lifetime." On that trip, they saw 180 bighorn ewes and lambs, 35 mature rams, 33 grizzlies, thousands of goats, hundreds of caribou, and a dozen bull moose and about that many mule deer and black bear. It was eight years after Chadwick's account of the region's vast game resources. Sadly, today it is all but gone.

A utilitarian approach to rifles prompted Roy to carry an iron-sighted 30-06 that succeeded a lever action Winchester 30-30. In Alberta, however, it was illegal for a guide to carry a rifle and that particular Model 70 spent a lot of time propped near the wood pile in camp.

Curley Cochrane, an early Hargreaves sidekick, who moved to the Peace River country in 1924 and from there all over the North hunting and trapping, used a 33 Winchester Model 1886 take-down. Cochrane, probably by necessity, loaded for his rifle but Hargreaves bought his ammunition over the counter.

Ned Frost

Ned Frost of Cody, Wyoming, guide to the likes of James L. Clark and Dr. Saxton Pope and Ralph Young, was larger-than-life and difficult to describe. His hunting career got off to a prodigious start when he killed his first grizzly at the age of 7 using a 45-90 Model 1886 Winchester.

Ned Ward Frost was born in 1881. His reputation as a sheep guide evolved through the years from about 1900. Do not confuse him with Nedward Mahlan Frost, or "Chew," his son. Chew was a tremendous sheep guide in his own right, running up a string of 83 sheep hunting clients and 83 successes, but he was Chew, not Ned.

Ned was extremely competent at one of the things which built his reputation—getting hunters to the game. However, his personality also encompassed the roles of ranconteur, public speaker, photographer, promoter and general businessman. He made many trips "back East" in the early days to show his black and white movie footage (shot in the old 32mm format) of the breathtaking scenery around Cody and of the myriad big game resources of the time.

Frost's life included a grizzly mauling while on a hunting trip with the colorful "Phonograph" Jones, and he guided and backed up Pope and Young when they collected, with vintage 1920 archery tackle, 3 grizzly bears in Yellowstone Park for a museum diorama. He also introduced James L. Clark to the world of mountain sheep.

Frost was not a horse fancier. He was a good and efficient packer, sat a horse with the aplomb and assurance of long-familiarity, could shoe and doctor his equine charges but he looked upon them only as a long-legged means to an end. He was more of a firearms enthusiast than most.

Frost used a variety of firearms over the years. The old 45-90 Model 1886 Winchester actually belonged to his father. Later, Ned drifted over to a Remington Model 8, in 35 Remington

(Below) Bert Riggal (R) with client at ease during early fall junket to the high country. Riggal's clients got the best of everything, including gun talk.

An early photograph depicting a hunter Riggal guided successfully to a truly trophy bighorn ram. Note massive horns, the muzzle protector on the rifle, and the walking stick.

A Riggal pack train moving out for a hunt in country north of Waterton Lakes National Park. Getting into untouched country was a matter of weeks on horses in the old days. Most felt that was a good part of the whole idea.

caliber. Finally, he acquired a Winchester Model 1895 carbine in 30-06.

Jessee Frost, Ned's youngest son and a most gracious source of information for this piece, once used the rifle to kill a buck antelope 100 yards away in a coulee. He was instructed to "draw a fine bead" on the antelope's front knee as the animal stood broadside. Jessee did, and the animal fell, shot through the heart. It becomes obvious Ned kept his sheep rifle sighted in for the longer distances.

After World War II, still not sold on bolt-action saddle arms, Frost acquired a slide action Remington 270, and retired the old Model 95. With the exception of the old 45-90 cartridge, Frost did not handload. He bought off the shelf, and stuck to the same bullet weight for which the rifle was sighted. None of his rifles, except for a 222 Sako acquired in the early '50s, ever wore a telescopic sight.

Frost considered himself somewhat of an anachronism. He was frequently heard to remark, "Damn it, I was born 100 years too late!"

Bert Riggal

Bert Riggal was the consummate professional hunter. Born in England, he emigrated to Canada about 1900 and took his first paying client into what is now Waterton Lakes National Park in 1907. He was a naturalist, a noted botanist, a photographer, a mountain climber, a rancher, a most sophisticated gun enthusiast and handloader. He was a student of the Greek classics and an original thinker.

Riggal, the author, was a long-time contributor to *Arms and the Man*, the predecessor of *The American Rifleman*. He occasionally wrote for *Outdoor Life*. And his mountain expertise and intellect, as applied to all phases of outfitting, made him the dean of the western Canada sheep guides. His clients took 66 bighorn rams over the years.

Riggal became perhaps as knowledgeable about sheep habits as any man alive. Andy Russell, Bert's son-in-law and a man who has risen to great heights himself as an outfitter, writer, and naturalist, remembered one uncanny occasion when Riggal, two clients and he were pinned down in a windy saddle most of one day by a band of rams on a rock slide above them. Bert finally announced after hours of studying the leader: "They'll be here at 4:00."

Sure enough, at 4:00 p.m. the band meandered out onto the low end of the saddle and grazed slowly towards the waiting hunters. One took his ram at 30 yards, the other at 50.

Of all the sheep guides, Riggal was far and away the most knowledgeable regarding firearms. Riggal once killed—with a 25 Niedner—a trotting coyote at 492 measured yards. Typically, this rifle was stocked by Griffin & Howe on a Springfield action. The rifle was a joint effort between the NRA and Townsend Whelen, who oversaw its make-up and then presented it to Riggal. Later, the rifle was fitted with a Lyman 5A telescopic sight with a Litschert attachment that converted it to an 8x.

Other rifles ran through the Riggal collection over the years. Among them was a 7x57 Mauser by Greener. The rifle is still around. I have handled it and it has that "live" feel. Riggal's favorite "big game" rifle—read grizzly, moose, and elk—was a 30-06 cut-down Mauser carbine. Originally stocked to the muzzle, Bert cut it back to a half-stock. There was a flat bolt handle and a Zeiss Zielklein telescopic sight. This Englishman-turned-outfitter did not have much use for the hard-kicking magnums, feeling that they were unnecessary.

Bert used interesting paraphernalia. In old photographs, one will see Riggal leaning on his ever-present walking stick; when shooting or glassing, he habitually dropped a pretied loop of sash cord around his knees for steadiness; and he also equipped many of his clients with handmade leather muzzle protectors for their rifles.

Charles Ren

Charlie Ren was a high-achieving master guide, but he is a bit of a mystery. Jack O'Connor, a Ren amigo, could doubtless have shed considerable light, but he has also passed on.

Ren was born in the 1870s in the Jackson Hole country of Wyoming. He worked as a market hunter during the Klondike gold rush. Frank Hibben tells me he remembers Ren working as a guide for Wes Brown on Bucking Horse Creek in northern British Columbia in the 1920s. Given that, we know Ren had experience with Dall rams and with Stone sheep during his association with Brown. It is not too improbable to speculate he knew Rocky Mountain bighorns around his own home stomping grounds near Jackson Hole.

Eventually, from a hunting lodge in Sonoyta, Sonora, Ren outfitted the likes of Jack O'Connor, Grancel Fitz, Elmer Keith, and Doctor Wilson DuComb, who turned up everywhere. As resident desert sheep impresario, Ren was acquainted with both Frank Hibben and George Parker. With the hunting passed, he disappeared.

Ren had a vast store of mountain sheep savvy, gained through years of chasing them, and imparted much of this treasure to one Jose del Rosario, a red-headed Mexican associate. By 1935, Charlie simply drove a specially-equipped open truck in and acted as straw boss, cook and general camp jack while the client and del Rosario hunted.

There is considerable question whether all Ren's hunting in Sonora was strictly "legal." If he *was* a peripheral outfitter, he nonetheless managed to keep his clients out of trouble. Several have written, however, how strange it was to go back across the border, sans sheep head, and then have it magically appear in their hotel room in Ajo, Arizona, soon before their departure.

Probably the most significant factor in Ren's success was his knowledge of the regions he hunted—the Pinacates, the Cubabais, and the San Franciscos. A further strength was his ability to deal with this harsh and arid environment. He took clients into it, hunted successfully and returned safely, withal a logistical and tactical effort not many were willing to tackle.

Charlie's tastes in rifles leaned to the traditional. He touted the 7x57 Mauser or his favorite 300 Savage Model 99 lever action. His weapons were always equipped with rubber recoil pads for rock gripping, as he always used them for alpenstocks.

Charlie operated professionally in a desolate, treacherous, physically and politically inhospitable environment without fanfare. In his life, he saw his footprints over all the continent's sheep ranges. ●

Acknowledgments

The author wishes to acknowledge with heartfelt thanks the cooperation of the following for access to family photo archives and for the kind reconstruction of family history during preparation of this article:

Josie Sais, daughter of Louis Jacquot
Mrs. Frank Golata
Martin Hunter
Murray Cochrane and family
Andy and Kaye Russell
Jessee Frost

For dredging up old memories, thanks also to:
Frank Hibben
and
George Parker.

This 1886 photo shows Geronimo at right with a 45-70 rifle; other warriors are his relatives, carrying 1873 Winchesters and a cavalry carbine. Geronimo also carries what appear to be shooting sticks to help make that first shot count.

FIREARMS IN APACHE TRIBAL USE

In this 1867 photo, a Jicarilla Apache fondles a Henry rifle, which according to the author would have been quite a prize at that time, even with its ammunition problems.

These are Tonto Apache, circa 1882. They had—at least for the photographer—no guns, but they were armed. Apparently, being armed is an Apache habit still in vogue.

How the Apache handled gun problems through 300 years of guerrilla war

by D. C. Cole

FEW NATIVE American peoples enjoyed such a fearsome reputation as fighters as did the Apache of the arid Southwest. For over 300 years the various divisions of the tribe prevented settlement of their mountains and deserts by Spanish, Mexican, and American colonists. During these centuries of warfare, the Apache became the acknowledged masters of the horse, the gun, and the tactics of mobile guerrilla warfare. Recent movies and books relate the activities of such remarkable leaders as Cochise, Geronimo, Ulzana, Chato, Mangas Coloradas, and Massai. Yet, very little has been written of the weapons they used or the sources of ammunition which sustained them in their years of combat.

Apache traditional history stresses the idea of a warrior people. According to the ancient stories, the people were hunters and raiders from the dim mists of their origins in forest Siberia. Part of the Athabascan group of peoples, the Apache were often known as the people of the knife, who also possessed the fearsome Asiatic compound-complex bow.[1] The arrival of these people in the Southwest in pre-European times triggered a 500 year war with the Aztecs and gained them the name Apache, "enemy people," from Zuni antagonists.

When the Spaniards arrived as heirs to the Aztec empire, they blundered into this ancient war and were caught up in it. Spanish viceroys and governors struggled for 250 years to subdue the area they called Apacheria. In the end they failed. The Spanish did, however, introduce the horse and the gun to the Apache.

The first Spanish guns into Apacheria were crude military firelocks (matchlocks); many of them rejects from European service.[2] Slow to load, unreliable, and hopelessly inaccurate, they were inferior as weapons to the bows of the Apache. During this time Apache ignored firearms, concentrating instead upon the speedy acquisition of horses, iron knives and lance tips, and, occasionally, pieces of Spanish armor. As one historian states, the Apache underwent a revolution in technology based on the horse and metal weapons.[3]

The advent of the miquelet lock in the early 16th century brought into being a relatively troublefree and reliable musket lock.[4] It became possible to make a musket of much lighter weight and shorter barrel, thus speeding reloading time without any loss in the weapon's questionable accuracy. By 1700, short-barrelled miquelet fusils became available to the plains dwelling Apache. These came at first by capture from Spanish sources and later through trade from the French colonies in Louisiana.[5] The French influence became a source of considerable worry to the Spanish who sought to end it by making alliances with the Comanche to attack the plains Apache. While this was in part successful, the Spanish were forced to supply their Indian allies with guns which fell frequently into Apache hands.[6] Warriors on horseback came to favor the fusil as the weapon for opening a fight, especially when the fusil was loaded with shot or gravel instead of a single ball.

Late in the 18th century, the Spanish were startled to discover the Apache engaged in manufacture of gunpowder.[7] Crude but functional powder was made from wet and ground willow charcoal, Texas sulphur, and nitrate from the bat-filled caves of New Mexico. Tribal legend holds that the secret of manufacture was learned by an Apache enslaved in Mexico who escaped his captors and returned to share the new knowledge with his people.

By 1779 Theodoro de Croix, the Spanish governor, went so far as to suggest that the Spanish themselves supply the Apache with guns and powder of inferior grade. This, it was hoped, would create dependency, wean the warriors from the bow, and cause them to give up the manufacture of powder on their own.[8] A Spanish expedition of 1780 penetrated to the Chiricahua Mountains for the first time since Spain's Apache wars began. There the Spanish discovered the Apache storing goods and weapons in sealed caves, a practice continuing to this day.[9]

The French had left Louisiana in 1763 and within a generation the supply of miquelet and flintlock fusils and muskets dried up. By 1800 few Apache warriors possessed working firearms. This situation changed suddenly in 1810.

The Mexican War for Independence threw the Southwestern frontier into a turmoil. Spanish officials, rebels, and English and American agents bid for Apache support.[10] These agents supplied the Apache with flintlock muskets, most of which were soon shortened for ease of use. Oddly these new muskets were almost all French. Americans tended to pass on superannuated muskets, 18th century types often called Charleville models supplied to patriots during the American Revolution. British agents passed on weapons captured from France during and after the 1760's. The Spanish, now under Joseph Bonaparte, brother of Napoleon, sent to the frontier French muskets declared unserviceable for use with Napoleon's troops.[11]

During this period a very few British Brown Bess muskets, Spanish fusils, and American-made rifles also fell into Apache hands. Still, the numbers of firearms remained low; few warriors had guns of any variety. After Mexican independence, more flintlock smoothbores came north from the settlements in trade and as spoils of war. These were now primarily British surplus, as England was supplying newly independent Mexico with military weapons.[12]

During the 1820s and '30s, American mountain men trapped in the southern Rockies. They brought with them the typical large bore mountain rifles, usually flintlocks by makers such as Hawken, J. Henry, Leman, and Golcher. The accuracy of the new weapons impressed the warriors of the Apache bands.

Some of these new weapons arrived in trade when James Ohio Pattie and James Kirker worked the Santa Rita, New Mexico, copper mines.[13] More were obtained after trappers turned to scalp hunting for the Mexican government in 1836. When James Gleason massacred friendly Apache at Santa Rita, the war bands virtually annihilated American trappers in Apacheria.[14] In this war of raid and ambush, many large bore, half-stock rifles fell into Apache hands. I remember seeing one of those mountain rifles as a boy. The flintlock still worked, but the bore of soft iron was worn out smooth to about .60 caliber. It was still in use with shot and ball in the 1930s.

Various Texas adventurers entered Apache country during the late 1830s and early '40s. They brought with them rifles and rifled muskets of United States manufacture and issue. Some of these had been converted to percussion cap.

The first large influx of percussion guns came with the Mexican War of 1846-48. During the course of the war,

This is Naiche, an important Apache leader, sitting for a formal portrait, very likely with his wife, and almost certainly with a prop rifle not his own. Many contemporary Apache portraits show prop rifles and handguns—having a gun with them in their pictures apparently seemed fitting to warriors.

Apache fighting men and women noticed the Hall rifles with their effective, but brutal, detachable locks.[15] For the first time revolvers were seen. Previously, Apache had looked with contempt upon pistols and had refused even to take them as booty in raids. The big 44-cal. Walkers and Colt Dragoons with nearly four pounds of heft and deadly accuracy caught the warriors' fancy. It was several years before any Apache possessed one, but they were then treasured above all other firearms.[16]

The turmoil of the Southwest drew many adventurers carrying what seemed to the Apache to be an infinite variety of weapons. Many of these fell into tribesmen's hands. Most common were the converted flint percussion muskets and the newer U.S. percussion rifled muskets.

By this time the Apache had learned to make a sort of percussion cap out of match heads and hammered copper foil. These were marginally effective, giving frequent misfires and hang fires. Powder was readily available in trade. Much of it was supplied by Mexican traders at Janos and by Mormon traders from Utah. Each of these groups held grudges against the United States Army or settlers and gladly supplied tribesmen with weapons.[17] Lead was frequently scarce. On occasion warriors cast slugs from copper or hammered them out of gold and silver. General George Crook remarked in the 1870s that a sure way of predicting an Apache outbreak was to observe warriors gathering scrap cans in order to melt out the lead for bullets.[18]

For nearly twenty years after the Americans seized control of the Southwest from Mexico, the Apache relied on a wide variety of percussion firearms. Revolvers became somewhat more common with the big 44-cal. Dragoons being the weapon of preference. More common were ex-military rifled muskets in 69 or 54 caliber. The most frequently encountered firearms among Apache remained the converted flintlock smoothbore musket, usually shortened to about 44 inches over-all and fitted with crude sights.[19]

Civil War action brought both Union and Confederate forces into Apacheria. Control of the route to California gold fields was the great prize in the Southwest. Activities of Apache raiders effectively denied control of the routes to both sides. Arizona and New Mexico were nearly cleared of white settlement in the process.[20]

Apache leaders tried briefly to face down United States troops with massed forces. This had been successful against Spanish and Mexican soldiers. Zebulon Pike reported years earlier a conversation with a Spanish officer who stated, "Apache cavalry scattered our infantry and it was not to be thought that our cavalry could break a line of Apache infantry."[21] Such was not the case with the Americans, however. Cannon scattered the warriors at Apache Pass. Cochise, Mangas Coloradas, and others resumed guerrilla warfare, never to willingly mass against American troops again.

The battle of Apache Pass pointed up a major weakness in an Apache use of firearms which was never overcome. Due to lack of adequate ammunition for long range practice, the Apache marksmen tended to fire high. In spite of heavy fire in that battle, very few United States soldiers were injured.[22]

Following the Civil War, breechloading rifles began to appear in Apache country in ever increasing numbers. Captain John C. Cremony, who had fought at Apache Pass, stated that Apache warriors were by 1868 well-equipped with the latest Spencer, Henry, and Sharps rifles.[23] This was not actually the case. Some rifles were at that time reaching tribesmen by way of traders from Salt Lake City, but numbers of trade guns were then quite small.

During the 1870s and '80s, increased numbers of lever action

This is Dutchy, a Chiricahua scout, photographed in 1886 with his Mills belt and 45-70 Springfield carbine. Note also the considerable supply of ammunition this Apache on the Army side could carry.

Henrys, Winchester 1866s, and Winchester 1873s came into use by raiders. Most of these guns, likewise, were sold by Mormon traders who took payment in gold gathered from streams in the United States and Mexico.

While the light Winchester repeaters gave their user heavy firepower superiority, the warriors preferred the more powerful single shot rifles of the time.[24] The 1866 rifles with their brazed 50-caliber barrel inserts and Springfield 50-70s Model 1868 and 1870 were widely used. These trapdoor Springfield rifles with the later 1873 through 1884 Model 45-70 rifles and carbines became almost the standard of Apache armament for a generation. These were often obtained from battlefields, but also from traders who purchased the weapons of army deserters.[25]

Also encountered in the war bands were sprinklings of Marlin lever actions, usually Models of 1881 which used the 45-70 load similar to that of the U.S. cavalry carbine.[26] Remington arms were relatively scarce in Apache camps at this time, although a few rolling block sporting rifles were to be found and very rarely a Remington Keene in 45-70. Other repeaters included Colt pump action rifles in 44-40, a Colt Burgess lever action or two, and a few Bullard rifles obtained from Provo and Salt Lake traders.

In the canyon and chapparal country, shotguns were fairly popular with warriors. Cochise had favored a side-by-side silver inlaid gun which was buried with him. This particular gun may well have been a combination rifle/shotgun of German make. British doubles, such as Clayborough and Greener, were seen as were Colt, Remington, and other American doubles of assorted makes. Most were fitted with auxiliary rear sights and used with buck or ball as occasion demanded.[27]

Shot was obtained in raids or by crude manufacture. Lead was melted and poured out into flat sheets. The sheets were then cut into strips with a sharp knife. The strips cut into cubes were either used in that form or rolled round between blocks of mesquite. Alternatively, molten lead was poured into hollow reeds. The reeds were then cut into short strips and rolled round for use. Ten and twelve gauge brass cases were always available and Apache priming methods worked better for shotguns than rifle reloads.

Handy guns with lever-actions still suit the Apache. Here the author's Winchester shows special practical touches: adjustable aperture sights and detachable sling swivels.

Also favored, but rarely encountered, were the big Sharps cartridge rifles, especially when fitted with telescopic sights. Many Apache suffered from poor eyesight which they attempted to rectify with telescopic sights and good field glasses.[28] The preferred Sharps were all various 45 and 50 calibers. Massai preferred 50-cal. Sharps and Springfields. On occasion crude attempts were made to rebore a 40 or 44 Sharps to 45 or 50, usually with the result being ruined accuracy. Various attempts were also made to rebarrel weapons to 45 and 50 calibers. Some of these conversions were functional; others were not. A more useful expedient was to lengthen chambers to accommodate the longest case available in a given caliber. Thus most 45s were lengthened to accept all cases from 2.1 to 3.25 inches in length.

Toward the close of the Apache wars, the preferred repeater, when available, was the Winchester 1876, usually in 45-60 or 45-75 and often in carbine form. Naiche, Geronimo, and others favored this weapon for its sustained firepower and reasonable long-range accuracy.[29] The '76 was, however, a hard gun to keep functioning. Most saw only limited war use before parts breakage rendered them unserviceable.[30]

Throughout the 1870s and 1880s, many Apache scouts were enlisted by the United States Army. These were nearly all armed with standard issue Springfield trapdoor 45-70 rifles and carbines.[31] Some, acting as sergeants, were issued Colt single action army revolvers. The Colts were nearly all 7½ inch barrelled blued weapons rather than the nickel plated pistols issued to plains scouts and Indian police.[32]

Among hostiles any sort of pistol might appear. Geronimo favored a Remington Army 44 cap and ball.[33] Others stuck to Colt Dragoons, 1860 Armies, or Colt conversions. An occasional Smith & Wesson American, Schofield, or Russian might be seen, especially among southern Chiricahua Apache who raided in Mexico. Merwin and Hulbert revolvers, especially the open top single action model of 1876, were popular for a few years as cartridges interchanged with Winchester '73 rifles. Few Colt single action army revolvers came into Apache bands until the 1880's. They were highly regarded, but very scarce.

Many warriors preferred cap and ball weapons due to greater availability of ammunition. Blasting powder could be stolen from mines and railroads in 50 pound kegs. Coarse grained black powder was wet and ground down to smaller size. Fine powder was used as found or, on rare occasion, mixed with corn meal to reduce power.

Cartridge arms, on the other hand, demanded a steady supply of fixed ammunition. Due to the variety of arms in Apache camps, adequate munition supplies were almost impossible to obtain. Raids were often organized to obtain cartridges. Jason Betinez, who rode with Geronimo, told of a raid into the United States made necessary because the warriors were equipped with modern American breechloaders for which ammunition was unobtainable in Mexico.[34]

Traders were much more willing to sell rifles than ammunition. Raiders usually captured relatively few cartridges. Most warriors using cartridge firearms were forced to attempt reloading. Molds for bullets were cut from stone and proved effective. Cases were usually cut off rather than resized, but functioned well. Priming was a major problem. Copper foil and match head primers gave frequent misfires. Cases were often drilled out to accept percussion caps or primers. Even when ignition occurred, the primer was almost always blown and often jammed the action. Ammunition was such a problem that when Chali At Pun of the Mojave Apache surrendered to General Crook in 1873, he merely said, "Demasiados cartuchos del cobre." (You have too many copper cartridges.)[35]

The military was sometimes no better off. Lieutenant John Bigelow, Jr., wrote in *On the Bloody Trail of Geronimo* that soldiers of the U.S. cavalry stationed at Ft. Apache had gone six months without rifle practice.[36] He reported that several men could not shoot at all and that there was not one marksman or sharpshooter in the company.[37] Apache scouts, on the contrary, he reported, used their rifles as frequently as possible and hunted game at every opportunity.[38]

About 1900, these three Apache had Model 1894 and 1873 Winchesters, by then practically the standard article in the Southwest for Indian and white hunters and travelers alike.

This familiar pose and defiant expression is known to most Americans. It's Geronimo, of course, armed with another 45-70. In the end, Geronimo relaxed his fierce defiance sufficiently to ride in Theodore Roosevelt's inaugural parade.

What success the Apache enjoyed with firearms was usually based on hunting habits applied to war. A careful stalk to close range followed by a single well-aimed shot, or a single careful shot from ambush, brought the best results.[39] Subsequent shots were usually wild.[40] Very few Apache became long range marksmen; fewer still were capable of rapid fire hits on enemy personnel.

Apache wars with the United States ended before the 1886 Winchester, or the models of 1892 and 1894, became available in the Southwest. These rifles became favorites for the few reservation hunters who could afford them. Pictures showing warriors with these weapons sometimes are purported to be from the war era; this is in error. Another common error stems from salon pictures taken in 1884 and 1886 by a frontier photographer. Lieutenant Leonard Wood reported in *Chasing Geronimo* that General Nelson Miles and his captives stopped off for photographs.[41] These show many Apache notables against varied backdrops but using the same Frank Wesson single shot rifle as a prop. Field pictures taken during Geronimo's surrender negotiations show warriors with Springfield 45-70 rifles and carbines and Model '73 Winchester lever actions.[42]

Southern Chiricahua Apache in Mexico used many Remington rolling block 7x57mm rifles; the carbine was not favored. In later years the Mauser '93, '95, and '98 in 7x57mm came into wide use. Many of these were obtained from Mexican soldiers and revolutionaries; some were fitted with telescopic sights by their new users.

North of the border the Model '94 Winchester 30-30 was the weapon of choice through the 1950s. Those who could not afford Model '94s purchased Krag Jorgensen 30-40s at $1.50 to $3.50. Boys used Springfield 45-70s which often were loaded with 2½-inch .410 shells. Handloading the Springfield trapdoor was done in the same fashion as in an earlier generation.

Since the end of the Second World War, the guns in Apacheria have changed considerably. Pickup trucks, which have replaced horses, sport Model '70 Winchesters and Winchester Model 100 autoloaders. M1 carbines are seen frequently. Occasionally one encounters Rugers in Models 77 and No. 1. One deputy carries a chopped BAR in his jeep pickup. Pistols now run to Ruger in 357 and 44 magnums. A few Smith & Wesson 44 magnums are to be seen, as are a fair sprinkling of Browning 9mm Hi-Powers.

South of the border in the Sierra Madres, the Chiricahua Apache favor AK 47 in 7.62x39, and Czech M52 light machine guns. These are obtained at $400 to $700 from leftist guerillas who use the money to partake of capitalist luxuries in the cities.

Marksmanship had improved over the years. Two hundred to six hundred yard practice ranges have been marked out here and there. At least one two-thousand yard range is in use. Veterans of the United States Army practice regularly and some are interested in metal silhouette shooting. In both field hunting and guiding sportsmen, the Apache are recognized as first class hunters.[43]

At present many older weapons are being retrieved from arms caches which are in many cases over 100 years old. Numbers of these now adorn racks in modern cottages on the four United States reservations. Some will no doubt make their way into circles of trade and the hands of collectors. Many have seen hard service; others are nearly new. Unlike plains Indians' firearms, almost none of the Apache guns show any gaudy decorations of carving, tacks, beads, or feathers.

Show was never Apache style. Weapons were for use. They still are. Some things never change. •

BIBLIOGRAPHY

Interviews

Geronimo, Robert. ca1955

Documents

The National Archives. National Archives and Records Service. General Services Administration. *Letters Received by The Office of Indian Affairs, 1824-80.* Microcopy No. 234. Washington, D.C.: National Archives Microfilm Publications, 1966.

Books

Basso, Keith H., ed. From the notes of Grenville Goodwin, *Western Apache Raiding and Warfare.* Tucson: The University of Arizona Press, 1971.

Betinez, Jason, with Wilbur Nye. *I Fought With Geronimo.* New York: Bonanza Books, 1959.

Bigelow, John, Jr. *On the Bloody Trail of Geronimo.* Ed. by Arthur Woodward. Los Angeles: Western Lore Press, 1968.

Billington, Ray Allen. *Westward Expansion: A History of the American Frontier.* New York: Macmillan Publishing Company, Inc., 1974.

Chandler, David G. *The Campaigns of Napoleon.* New York: The Macmillan Company, 1966.

Cook, James H. *Fifty Years On the Old Frontier.* New Haven: Yale University Press, 1923.

Cremony, John C. *Life Among the Apaches, 1850-1868.* 1868 Rpt. Glorieta, N.M.: Rio Grande Press, 1969.

Crook, George. *General George Crook: An Autobiography.* Ed. by Martin F. Schmitt. Norman: University of Oklahoma Press, 1946.

Cruse, Thomas. *Apache Days and After.* Ed. by Eugene Cunningham. Caldwell, Ohio: Caxton Printers Ltd., 1941.

Dunn, J. P., Jr. *Massacres of the Mountains.* New York: Archer House, Inc., 1886.

Held, Robert. *The Age of Firearms.* New York: Harper & Row, 1957. Revised ed., Northfield, IL: DBI Books, 1970.

Horgan, Paul. *Great River: The Rio Grande In North American History.* New York: Rinehart & Co., Inc., 1954.

Jackson, Donald. *The Journals of Zebulon Montgomery Pike: With Letters and Related Documents, Vol. II.* Norman: University of Oklahoma Press, 1966.

John, Elizabeth A. H. *Storms Brewed In Other Men's Worlds: The Confrontation of Indians, Spanish and French In the Southwest, 1540-1795.* College Station: Texas A & M Press, 1975.

Kaywaykla, James, and Eve Ball. *In the Days Of Victorio: A Warm Springs Apache Remembers.* Tucson: University of Arizona Press, 1970.

Lamar, Howard Roberts. *The Far Southwest 1846-1912: A Territorial History.* New Haven: Yale University Press, 1966.

Lane, Jack C., ed. *Chasing Geronimo: The Journal of Leonard Wood, May-September, 1886.* Albuquerque: University of New Mexico Press, 1970.

Moorehead, Max L. *The Apache Frontier: Jacobo Ugarte and Spanish-Indian Relations In Northern New Spain, 1769-1791.* Norman: University of Oklahoma Press, 1968.

Opler, Morris E. *An Apache Life Way.* Chicago: University of Chicago Press, 1941.

Parsons, John E. *The First Winchester.* New York: Winchester Press, 1969.

Pattie, James Ohio. *The Personal Narrative of James O. Pattie Of Kentucky.* Chicago: R. R. Donnelley & Sons, Inc., The Lakeside Press, 1930.

Peterson, Harold L. *Pageant of the Gun.* Garden City, N.Y.: Doubleday and Company, Inc., 1967.

Thrapp, Dan L. *The Conquest of Apacheria.* Norman: University of Oklahoma Press, 1967.

———————. *Victorio and the Mimbres Apaches.* Norman: University of Oklahoma Press, 1974.

Utley, Robert M. *Frontier Regulars: The United States Army and the Indian, 1866-1891.* New York: Macmillan Publishing Company, Inc., 1973.

Wellman, Paul I. *Indian Wars of the West.* Garden City, N.Y.: Doubleday & Company, Inc., 1947.

Periodicals

Brady, Bruce. "Elk of the Mescalero," *Outdoor Life,* Vol. 156, No. 2, August, 1975.

Clum, John P. "The San Carlos Apache Police," *New Mexico Historical Review,* 1930.

Larson, E. Dixon. "Rarest Army S. A. Colt Was Nickeled," *American Rifleman,* Vol. 118, No. 5, May, 1970.

It will not be ancient revolvers should the Apache take up arms again. This is the author with his choice in a belt gun—the Model 1911 in 45 ACP.

FOOTNOTES

[1]Morris E. Opler, *An Apache Life Way*. Chicago: University of Chicago Press, 1941, pp. 386-387.

[2]Robert Held, *The Age of Firearms*. New York: Harper & Row, 1957, rev. ed. Northfield, IL: DBI Books, 1970, pp. 38ff.

[3]Elizabeth A. H. John, *Storms Brewed In Other Men's Worlds: The Confrontation of Indians, Spanish and French In the Southwest, 1540-1795*. College Station: Texas A & M Press, 1975, pp. 19ff.

[4]Held, op. cit., pp. 74ff.

[5]John, op. cit., p. 698.

[6]Max L. Moorehead, *The Apache Frontier: Jacobo Ugarte and Spanish-Indian Relations In Northern New Spain, 1769-1791*. Norman: University of Oklahoma Press, 1968, pp. 157ff.

[7]John, op. cit., p. 530.

[8]Moorehead, op. cit., p. 122 and pp. 127-128.

[9]John, op. cit., p. 604, and Dan L. Thrapp, *Victorio and the Mimbres Apaches*. Norman: University of Oklahoma Press, 1974, p. 193.

[10]Paul Horgan, *Great River: The Rio Grande In North American History*. New York: Rinehart & Co., Inc., 1954, pp. 424-434.

[11]David G. Chandler, *The Campaigns of Napoleon*. New York: The Macmillan Company, 1966, pp. 341-342.

[12]Ray Allen Billington, *Westward Expansion: A History of the American Frontier*. New York: Macmillan Publishing Company, Inc., 1974, pp. 484-494. Outlines British support to the Mexican government during this period.

[13]James Ohio Pattie, *The Personal Narrative of James O. Pattie Of Kentucky*. Chicago: R. R. Donnelley & Sons, Inc., The Lakeside Press, 1930, pp. 149ff.

[14]Paul I. Wellman, *Indian Wars of the West*. Garden City, N.Y.: Doubleday & Company, Inc., 1947, pp. 250ff, and J. P. Dunn, Jr., *Massacres of the Mountains*. New York: Archer House, Inc., 1886, p. 315.

[15]Harold L. Peterson, *Pageant of the Gun*. Garden City, N.Y.: Doubleday and Company, Inc., 1967, pp. 120-122.

[16]Keith H. Basso, ed., from the notes of Grenville Goodwin, *Western Apache Raiding and Warfare*. Tucson: The University of Arizona Press, 1971, p. 178.

[17]Howard Roberts Lamar, *The Far Southwest 1846-1912: A Territorial History*. New Haven: Yale University Press, 1966, pp. 342ff, and Thrapp, op. cit., p. 126.

[18]General Crook to General Schofield, Adj. General, Department of the Pacific, 25 January, 1872, *Letters Received by the Office of Indian Affairs 1825-1880* (Washington, D.C.: National Archives Microfilm Publications, General Services Administration, 1966), Microcopy No. 234. (This publication is hereafter referred to as *LROIA*.)

[19]John C. Cremony, *Life Among the Apaches, 1850-1868*. 1868 Rpt. Glorieta, N.M.: Rio Grande Press, 1969, p. 194.

[20]Wellman, op. cit., p. 307.

[21]Donald Jackson, *The Journals of Zebulon Montgomery Pike: With Letters and Related Documents, Vol. II*. Norman: University of Oklahoma Press, 1966, p. 54.

[22]Cremony, op. cit., p. 164.

[23]Ibid., p. 194.

[24]Jason Betinez, with Wilbur Nye, *I Fought With Geronimo*. New York: Bonanza Books, 1959, p. 77.

[25]Robert M. Utley, *Frontier Regulars: The United States Army and the Indian, 1866-1891*. New York: Macmillan Publishing Company, Inc., 1973, p. 23. In 1891 the Adjutant General calculated ⅓ of enlisted men or 88,475 of 255,712 had deserted between 1866 and 1891.

[26]Betinez, op, cit., p. 77.

[27]Cremony, op. cit., p. 194.

[28]Cremony, op. cit., p. 232. Also James Kaywaykla and Eve Ball, *In the Days Of Victorio: A Warm Springs Apache Remembers*. Tucson: University of Arizona Press, 1970, p. 13.

[29]John E. Parsons, *The First Winchester*. New York: Winchester Press, 1969, p. 123. Parsons states that the .45-60 carbine only became available in 1885. Also Peterson, op. cit., pp. 171, 174-175, shows Model '76 .45-60 carbines surrendered by Naiche and Geronimo in 1886.

[30]Parsons, op. cit., pp. 128-130, discusses the sort of damage common to the '76 in hard service.

[31]John P. Clum, "The San Carlos Apache Police," *New Mexico Historical Review*, 1930, p. 69. More than 300 Springfields were issued for the Chiricahua removal of 1876 alone.

[32]E. Dixon Larson, "Rarest Army S. A. Colt Was Nickeled," *American Rifleman*, Vol. 118, No. 5, May, 1970, pp. 22-23.

[33]Discussions with Robert Geronimo, ca 1955.

[34]Betinez, op. cit., pp. 88-89.

[35]George Crook, *General George Crook: An Autobiography*, ed. by Martin F. Schmitt. Norman: University of Oklahoma Press, 1946, pp. 173-179, and Wellman, op. cit., p. 356.

[36]John Bigelow, Jr., *On the Bloody Trail of Geronimo*, ed. by Arthur Woodward. Los Angeles: Western Lore Press, 1968, pp. 104ff.

[37]Ibid.

[38]Ibid., p. 101.

[39]James H. Cook, *Fifty Years On the Old Frontier*. New Haven: Yale University Press, 1923, p. 171.

[40]Bigelow, op. cit., pp. 38-39, and Thomas Cruse, *Apache Days and After*, ed. by Eugene Cunningham. Caldwell, Ohio: Caxton Printers Ltd., 1941, pp. 115ff, discusses the Cibicu fight where hundreds of Apache fired for hours inflicting few casualties.

[41]Jack C. Lane, ed., *Chasing Geronimo: The Journal of Leonard Wood, May-September, 1886*. Albuquerque: University of New Mexico Press, 1970, pp. 111-112.

[42]C. S. Fly, the Tombstone photographer, accompanied the 1886 expedition. See Dan L. Thrapp, *The Conquest of Apacheria*. Norman: University of Oklahoma Press, 1967, p. 343.

[43]Bruce Brady, "Elk of the Mescalero," *Outdoor Life*, Vol. 156, No. 2, August, 1975, pp. 52ff.

by HENRY M. STEBBINS

WHEN 22 AUTOLOADERS WERE YOUNG

There have been 22-cal. autoloaders for 75 years, and a backward look is past due.

QUITE OFTEN then you were the only fellow in town to own a 22 automatic rifle. But after nearly 70 years that gentle surge, its sweep then limited by high gun and ammo costs compared to those of hand-operated repeaters and their grass-roots loads, has become a genuine flood.

Catalog pages of 22 rimfires in the 1979 GUN DIGEST list some 27 autos, 20 bolts, 8 levers, 6 pumps, 8 single-shots and 19 heavy, costly, precision target rifles. Among the light, medium-price 22's a hand-operated one may cost more than an autoloader of equal grade, like the Model 572 Remington pump compared to the Model 522A auto. Well, if the gun itself does most of the work functioning, why isn't it simpler to make?

The variety of these little self-loaders is great in styling, size and price. What salesman, gun-crank or hunter can rattle off their roll-call and not draw breath to think fast?

Commonly misnamed "automatic" from the first, the correct, more formal, clumsier "semi-automatic" would have been recognizable. But a better name was the once-famous "trigger-controlled repeater." It didn't often fit, much less often then than now. The slipping out of two or possibly three shots at one squeeze of the trigger didn't always send a gun to the factory or a 'smith. Quite commonly it was taken in stride until, if it occurred too often, something was done. Stoppages were frequent, compared to the 1,000 shots of today. Cleaning action as well as bore helped prevent stoppages, but perhaps nearly all came from stale ammunition from country or even village stores where stock turnover was slow. This staleness of the often special loads required affected accuracy as well as power. Today's fairly common five in an inch at 50 yards bench would have been almost unbelievable then.

Three pioneer rifles deserve special treatment: The Winchester 1903, Savage 1912 and Remington Model 16 of 1914. Only the Savage and its Long Rifle Dupont Lesmok or King's Semismokeless cartridges were inexpensive. Savage rifles weren't doomed to ruination like the other two, each with its own case design loaded with straight smokeless. But size crippled the Savage, made only till 1915, the factory reports, for it weighed 4½ pounds against the 5¾ of each of the others. It was too light and wavery for adults' good holding, but what a winner it'd have been if made grown-up, with heavier stock and longer, heavier barrel!

Winchester and Remington autos' ammunition each had 45 grain bullets, rarely different even in hollow point or the Winchester "Spotlight," a hollow point with flash powder for the iron targets so much used then. (Even in 22 Short, another size offered thus, they winked, all right.) Remington auto rounds were fair subloads for 22 WRF rifles and pistols (and would work today in 22 WRM chambers), but no other regularly made arm took the much over-sized Win. auto loads.

The Savage had a nearly straight feed off the detachable seven-shot clips, and the other two pioneers fed rounds from stock-tube magazines almost straight forward, not the back-up-then-forward travel that under-barrel tubes now often inflict on auto-rifle feeding processes.

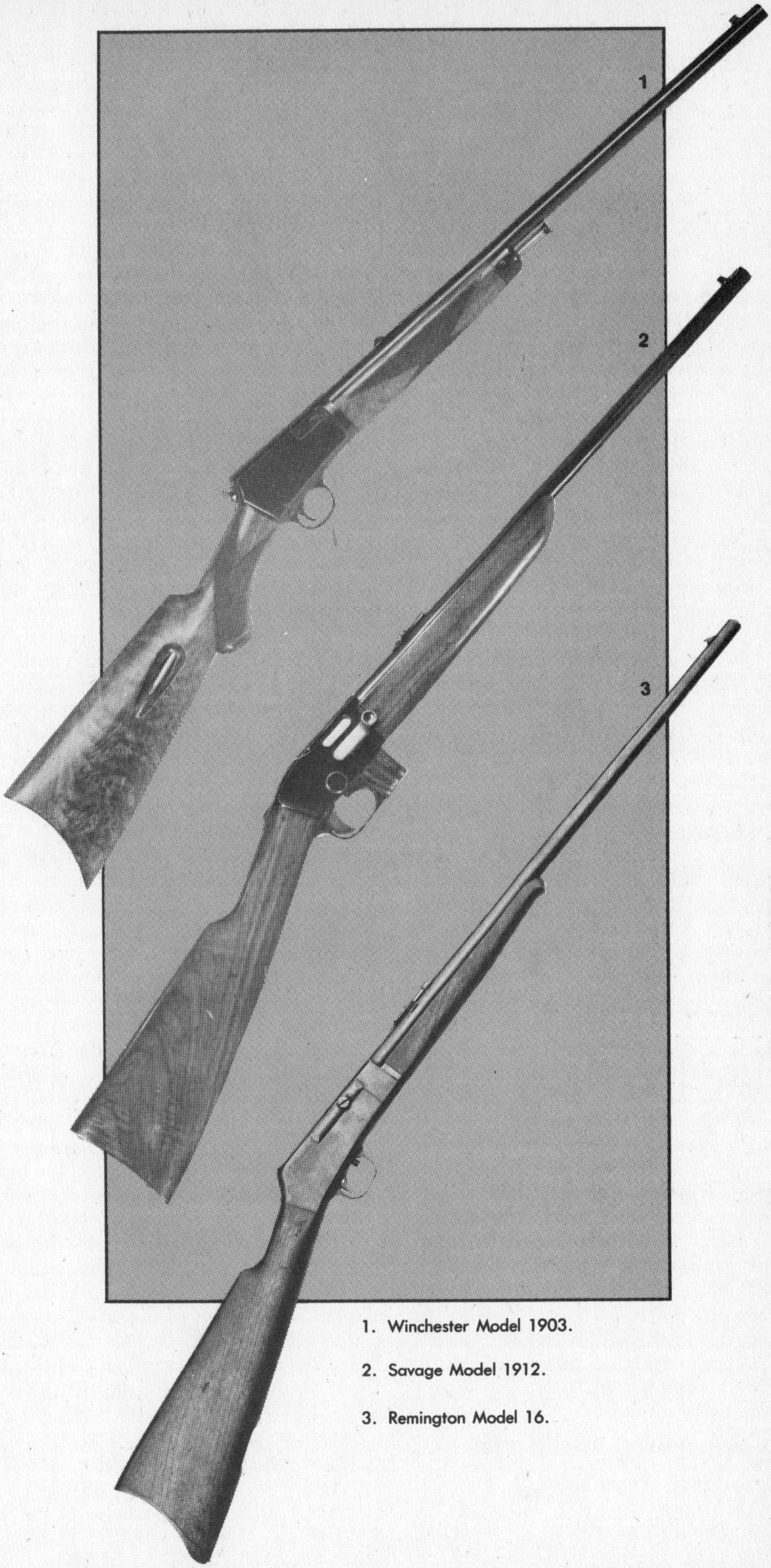

1. Winchester Model 1903.

2. Savage Model 1912.

3. Remington Model 16.

22

Refilling tube magazines took time and attention. (One catalog's text advised us to be very careful to load cartridges with bullets forward!) But these two rifles' system taught a shooter to point the muzzle earthward while reloading. The Winchester's charging slot was in the right side of the stock, as some later autos have them, but the Remington tucked it away almost out of sight in the bottom line of the stock, where it was better looking, maybe, but not as handy.

An at first puzzling Winchester extra was the gravity charger, like an elf-size set of shotgun barrels. Right and left tweaks on it, centered over the stock's loading slot, sent two shipments of five rounds each hustling down the magazine. That gadget went hunting perhaps once before it was retired as too rattly. On picnics it'd have been great!

As non-corrosive ammo got around, 22 auto popularity grew. Now such a firearm is sometimes a youngster's first gun. If faces lengthen at this, we might consider the much wider spread of commonsense in gun-safety, conservation and the need for decent marksmanship before a kid hunts. Hosing lead seldom kills cleanly, but a real shooter who sees the supreme value in placing Bullet No. 1 sometimes has, if he needs it, a second chance with his automatic. Except for the uncommon, never loud ringing of steel, the report of the shot may swallow the rattle of action functioning.

Almost from the first, dealers had realized that an auto's reliability is its most desirable attribute. Then, it depends mostly on a clean, oiled action and fresh ammunition. In little towns, odd sizes like "that automatic stuff" moved less briskly than semi-smokeless long-rifles.

Winchester Model 1903

The 1903 Winchester, a Thomas Johnson development in which factory personnel for years took great pride, was so carefully planned that only trivial changes like less stock drop and the replacement of bronze firing pins by steel ones took place. Much thought went into ammunition design, too, to build resistance when a charge was fired. This made unusually heavy backthrust for a load as mild as the 22 Automatic really was—sometimes more, sometimes less than the Long Rifle—hopefully to operate the simple, rugged little blowback.

The early solid, greaseless bullet was hard, was even called "chillled" by some users. Its long, parallel sides took some push to start in and follow through the snug rifling. It was heavy, the same 45 grains, though alloyed, as those pure-lead 22 slugs of the WRF, WCF, and the two lengths of Maynard centerfires. This made it a "super 22" in weight. Its ogive was a quick taper to the sometimes flat, sometimes rounded nose. This ogive eased its job of reliably nosing its way into the briefly waiting open chamber.

Almost 10 years elapsed before the flat-nosed, soft lead hollow point came out, but it fed as well as the sharply tapered old solid had. Other hollow point 22s were earlier, and it seemed as if the makers were taking no chances on a cave-nosed, flat-pointed 22 Auto. They needn't have doubted. Many of us then paid a bit extra to get the H.P.'s because they were inside lubricated, as later all were.

The taper of the solid's ogive was a strict continuation of that line in the long, heavy crimp, which of course built up recoil and made chamber entry more certain. Sometimes the powder loading helped backthrust. This was simply, and safely, a hard cardboard wad a bit under 1/16 inch thick. It increased loading density.

Cases for both Winchester and Remington autos were built to take it, especially so at the head. Powerful mainsprings drove heavy hammers through long, swinging arcs to the firing pins, and misfires were really rare. I never knew of either of my '03's having a burst case in many years of use, and the Remington 16 had no trouble while it was mine. Neither did I know of a WRF case failure in the extensive use my friends and I gave the Model '90's. Yet perfectly sound rifles for the usual Short, Long and Long Rifle trio seldom had by any means such clean records in the 1920s.

These rimfires with snugly seated, not heel type, bullets have a little appreciated (but so important when it counts) oil- and waterproof quality that centerfires hardly can better, to speak very mildly. Discontinued or not, like the 22 Remington Auto, 25 Stevens Long and Short, and 32 Long Rifle, along with current jobs like the patient old 22 Winchester Auto, 22 WRF and Magnum, and 5 mm Remington—all were or are hermetically sealed.

The 22 auto rifles, especially the early and long-continued Model 1903, not two feet long when taken down for packing, got to the wild places of the world. The '03's long, decidedly hardened early bullet was a killer with properly placed head shots. Deer, jaguar and even moose fell to it. A man I knew told of a moose quickly and humanely killed. "I shot him in the forehead and I don't think he even heard the gun go off."

Up to some 50 yards the hollow point did really well on small game. Compared to the Long Rifle's hunting bullets of 35 to 37 grains we've had through the years, these rounds at least did creditably. They had the weight and length to hold velocity well and keep on plowing through flesh and light bone, and they weren't noisy.

Before Kleanbore, 22 auto cartridges with semi-smokeless powder were asked for often, but never came, and contemporary smokeless rounds were wisely shooed away from Savage's M12. There was a way, hardly known, to clean after smokeless rimfires. That potassium chlorate fouling was called "acid" but really was a salt. So came the swabbing with patches wet with the aqueous, ammonia-strong Winchester Crystal Cleaner, never letting it touch walnut or blued steel. When no dissolved fouling showed on the patches we'd dry the bore and adjacent parts, the rod, too, and swab with oiled patches. Again we'd dry the bore and apply a heavy coating of the forerunner of our RIG, the British Birmingham Small Arms' Saftipaste. We never "shot out the grease," but wiped it out before firing. That made sense and with a high-power might be necessary for safety.

We must comment here on the fallacy that auto rifles, at least blowbacks like these 22s, demand ammunition geared to a set figure of recoil. "Too little jams the rifle; too much wrecks it," has been said. Only in part is this true, though handloaders of centerfire autos never should exceed factories' top loads.

But figures for the '03 auto have ranged widely. The 1904 catalog lists velocity at 1125 f.s. The 1911, 1914 and other listings in that "middle-aged" bracket were 903 and 950, and the modern 1055 f.s. has gone on for years.

Remington Model 24.
Remington Model 241.

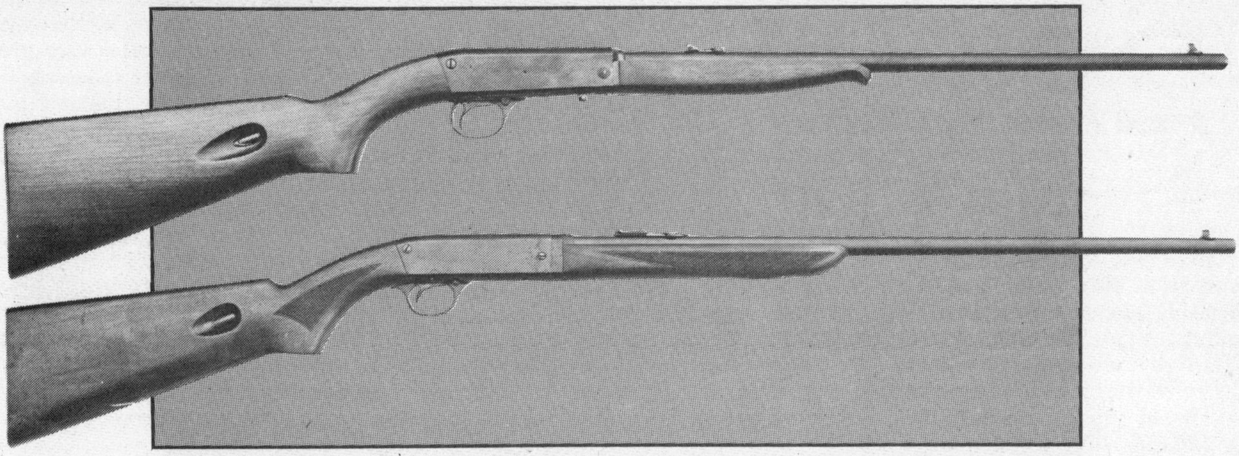

Winchester Model 63.
Long barreled Model 63.

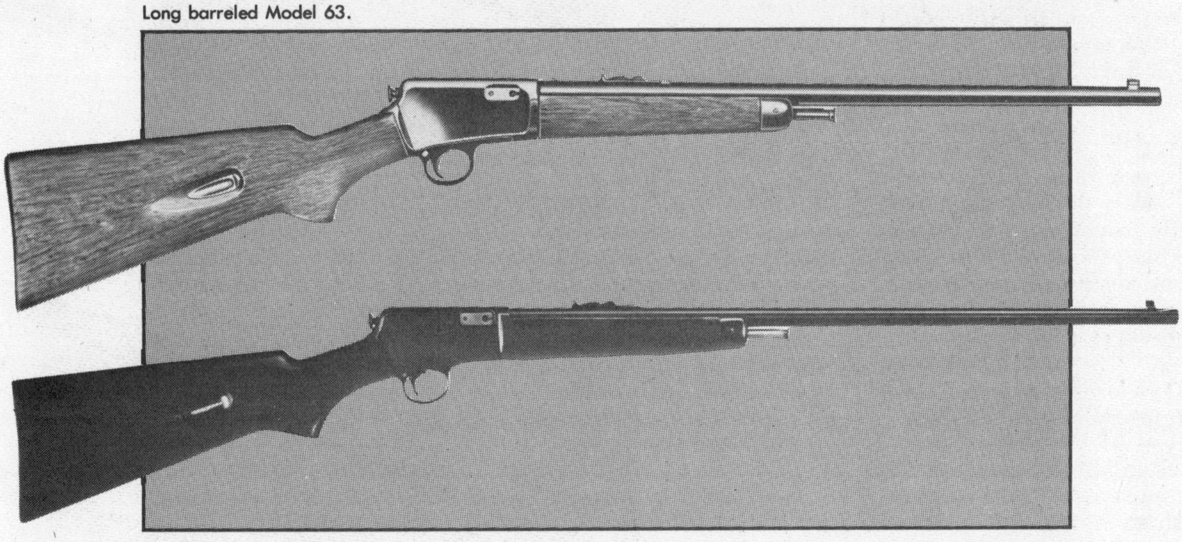

Savage Model 6.

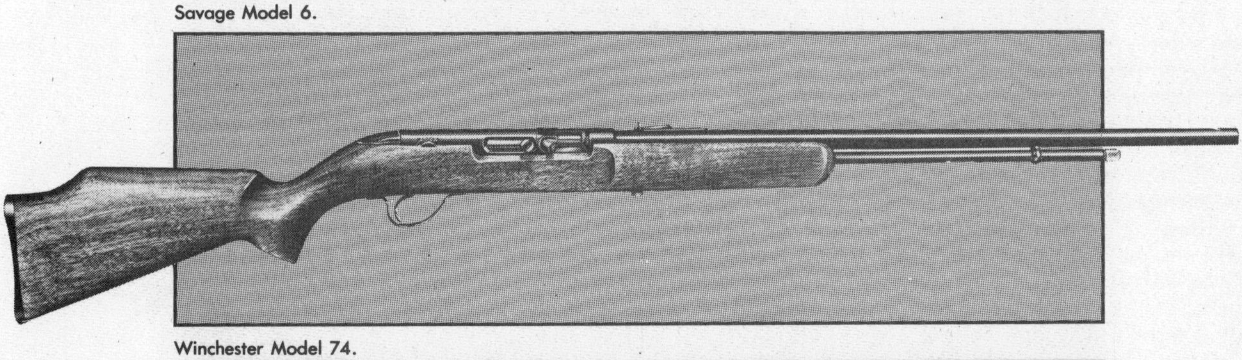

Winchester Model 74.

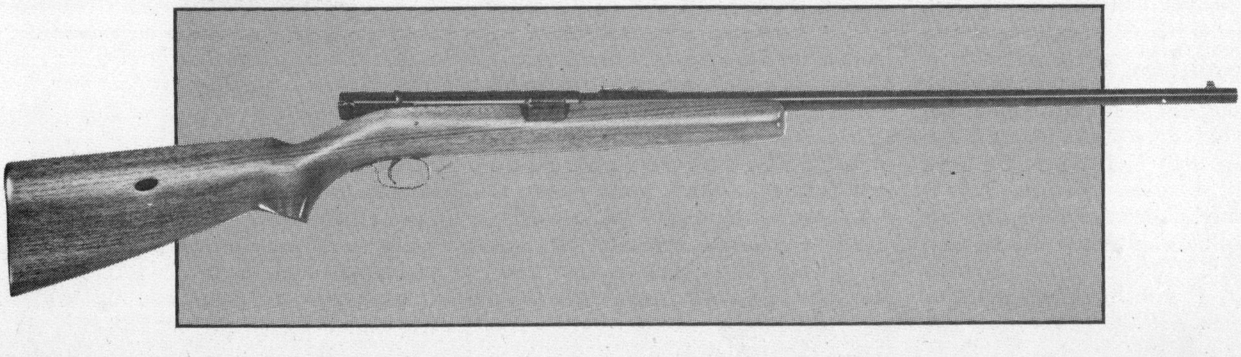

A few 1904-type loads got into my 1920-issue rifle. Major Payne—bless his thoughtfulness, so appreciated by kids—found a stray half-boxful and gave them to me. The difference showed! Old as they must have been, they still ripped out right merrily.

About 126,000 '03's were made—good for a rifle and its ammo that were so costly then. In 1932 this rifle stepped aside for the very similar M63 for Long Rifles, or did it? It stays around, and its ammunition still sells.

The Savage Model 1912

Despite its top-tang safety, high quality and easily found, economical 22 Long Rifle fodder that 4½ pound rifle seemed built for kids, and in that time of often sketchy (if any) junior rifleman safety training, few would have been encouraged to use an automatic.

The M12's use of standard Long Rifles was a mixed blessing. Though semi-smokeless rounds were strongly advised, black and smokeless probably would have sneaked in. The former choked actions not carefully and promptly cleaned; the latter were sure ruin to a bore not fastidiously cleaned, and almost no shooters had heard or read of (and where, pray?) how to deal with the potassium chlorate prime. fouling that did the bad work.

Another early auto may rate a place here, the Baker Gun Company's 22 Short Batavia. About 1912 a flyer on it lay on the County Clerk's desk where we kids sidled up to buy hunting licenses. He let me read about that graceful, long-barreled rifle. "What a dream gun for me!" I thought. And for Shorts only; I could really learn to use it, and on my small allowance. But was it ever made, not just planned?

Remington Model 16

This beautiful smallbore, one of the very best balanced of the whole tribe, now so big, still had the handicap of needing its special, high-priced, straight smokeless ammo. Its 45 grain solid or hollow point started at 950 f.s. and was a bit longer, and of smaller diameter, than the Winchester's round. Those Remington Autos, while they were made, could serve as subloads for most WRF rifles and pistols.

The common 22 Long has been advised as fairly successful in the M16, but the rifle chamber would have been much oversized, and the 16" twist has shown, almost but not quite always, great inaccuracy beyond 50 feet when Longs and Shorts are delivered from it. Maybe an M16 barrel could be cut off at the breech and chambered for Long Rifles. Then either a single-shot for Long Rifles or an auto for shortened LRs might be possible. Plainly, this is one of the little rifles that are "such stuff as dreams are made on."

The M16 was far more than an understudy, which it was, to the Remington high-power Model 8 and 12 gauge Model 11. About all that they had in common was their triggers. You pulled 'em but just once for each shot.

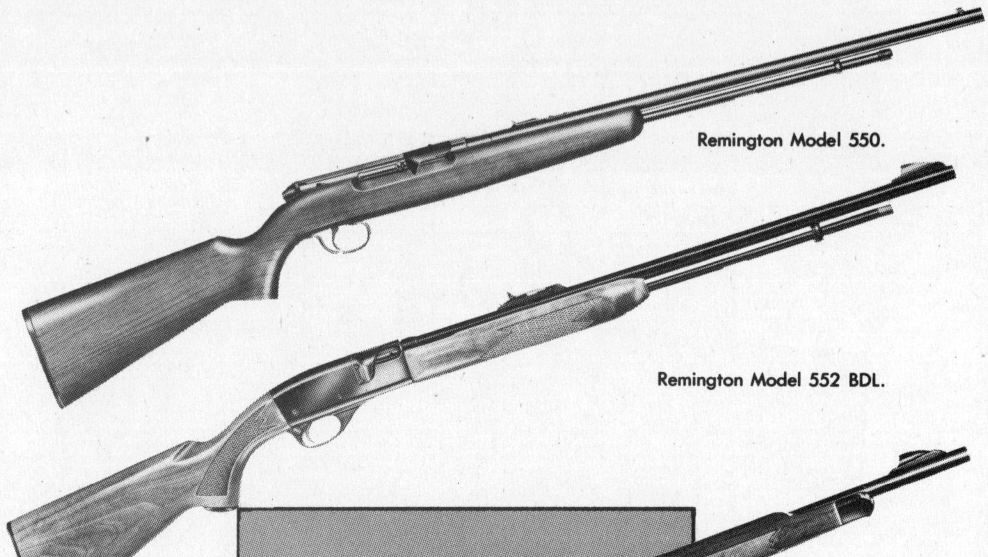

Remington Model 550.

Remington Model 552 BDL.

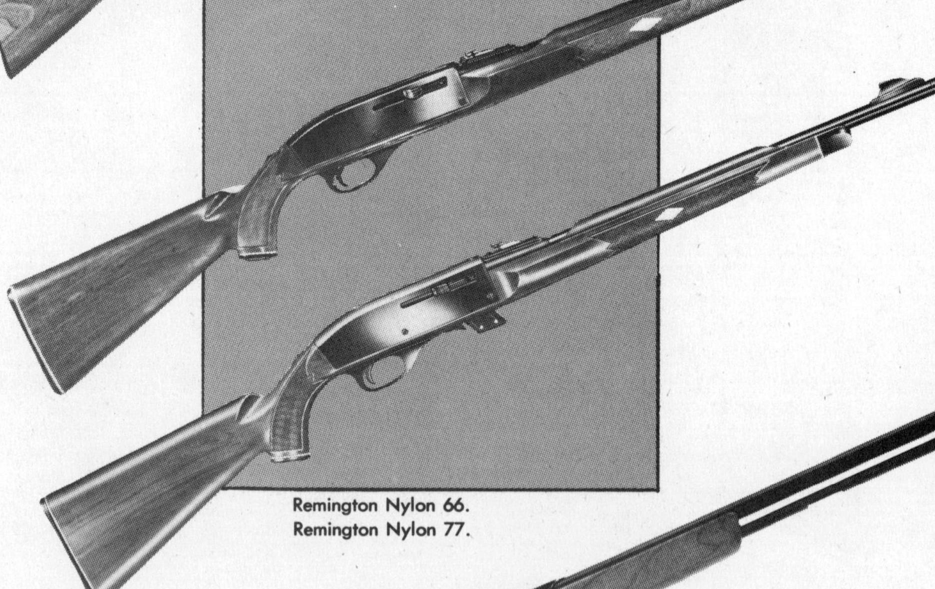

Remington Nylon 66.
Remington Nylon 77.

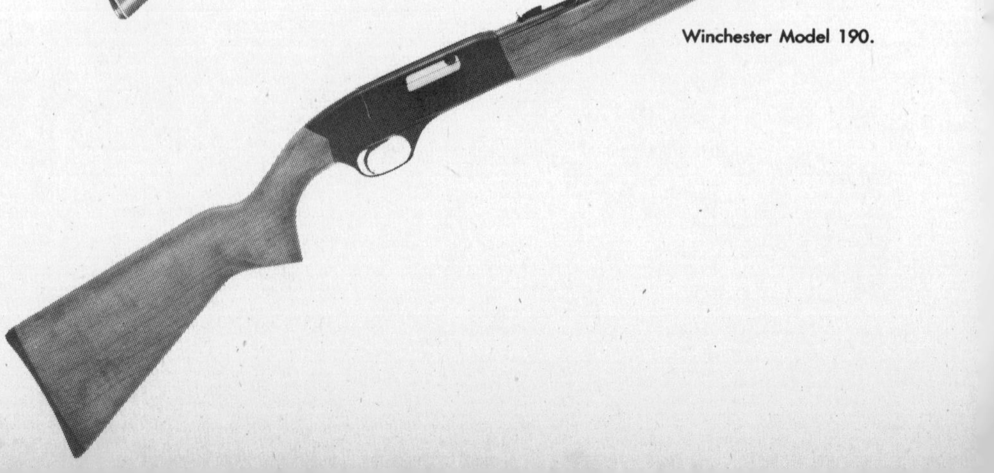

Winchester Model 190.

The safeties were located and operated by entirely different motions of the forefinger or thumb. One had a tube magazine in the stock, one a tube under the barrel, one a single-column box magazine under the breech-bolt. Keeping them all in a rack or cabinet looked and felt good, but you had to look alive—like when you toted one afield. They made a fine trio, and some fortunate owners stacked all three of them side by side or one over the other.

This smallbore was one of the most suitable multi-shot hunting 22's. When the woods were crisp and snow was flying, or when rain slanted viciously down, the inside workin's kept pretty dry. An ejector-slot cover plate that shot back and forth with the bolt saw to that.

Somehow the idea goofed around that rimfires from 22 Short to WRF figured in developing the Remington Autoloading. Mr. C. F. Witsil, well remembered at Bridgeport, denied this, assuring me that Remington autoloading cartridges taking form had been used. So for years to come, the corrosive smokeless rounds had to do. Really, there were but two serious drawbacks: the difficulty in bore-cleaning and the uncertain quality of ammo bought at small-town stores. Some was excellent, but we always wished that two or three others owning and using these guns would stay in town and keep buying their ammunition.

The M16 action seems less rugged than the '03's, though both had the long life of high-grade, precisely made 22's of the time. The Remington recoil and hammer springs were apparently as strong as the Winchester's, but the latter's breech-block, L-shaped and extending halfway up the fore-end, was much heavier. Neither stock could be readily shortened, because of the magazine in the butt, and the Remington at first felt long for shortish riflemen. A quick forward shove and then a pull-back into the shoulder hollow cured this trouble. Actually, the smoothest mounting of any rifle seems to lie in being thoroughly accustomed to it. Reaching that point is a smart spending of time.

Remington, not the originator of 22 automatics, has been outstanding here. Models 24 and the heavier, later 241, 1922-35 and 1935-51, some 186,000 rifles in all, led from corrosive priming and Lesmok to clean priming and smokeless. The Browning-designed actions featured bottom ejection through a receiver port, with solid receiver top and sides keeping weather and trash out. The first rifles took 22 Shorts only, but Long Rifle alternate choices soon came. Making Shorts operate the action was possible partly by using substandard size boring and rifling.

Almost certainly the most arresting development of these ingenious Remington rifles was the loading route from tubular, stock-held magazine to chamber. Near the end of this long magazine it curved down to a short, level path, parallel with the top surface of the receiver and *over the top of the breech-block*. The first round in line took a downward dive into the chamber, from which the empty case of the previously fired load, if any, had been hurled down and out. This may sound complicated but it didn't faze the loads I shot through my 24, and the action, 24 or 241, seems to have been unusually reliable. It wasn't especially "good" to see fine machining and slick finish on a repeating 22 action then because they were *expected*.

The 19-inch barrel M24 was for kids, and far-travelers, but the 241 had a 24" tube and more generous woodwork, so much that it did well in indoor rifle club use, the six pound weight nicely serving young men who'd grow up with it. For an all-too-rare holiday it was as good as ever. It earned the honored position of being a family rifle.

The 550 Remington (1941), thanks to "Carbine Williams" patents, was the first automatic rifle to automate reliably with mixed ammunition, Shorts, Longs and Long Rifles. With Shorts, gas muscled in just beyond the case-mouth and above the floating chamber which was shorter than any case normally used for autoloading in a rifle. The floating chamber therefore was driven forcefully back and the Short empty hopped out triumphantly. The 550 thus became a hunter's rifle and a plinker's delight. Since it came out in 1941 and the depression still hung on, it was good to have a 22 that thankfully lapped up whatever came along. The 550 looked big, went over 6 pounds and still keeps a good-sized following.

The Nylon 66 Remington, much later, is a practical knock-about 22 auto that's pretty sure to work anywhere from Arctic cold to the penetrating dampness of Southern swamps, both having been its owners' proving grounds many times. Internal Nylon bearings that need no oiling, and outside parts chromed to prevent rust aren't just parts of a "gun of the future." The idea is to make the rifle perk right now and keep on doing it. Long-lasting too are the Nylon stock and even its finish. It should mate well with action and barrel bedded in it.

It sells well. The Nylon 66 is the original, the magazine-in-buttstock model. Wisely made for Long Rifles only, this rifle is for business. 66GS is for Shorts only. In 1970, came the Nylon 77 using 5- or 10-shot clips. Otherwise it's much like the Nylon 66. These are little rifles, easily handled, or tossed when necessary, weighing about 4 pounds, smooth when no magazine projects to be snaggy, and really winning in their chummy ways.

Savage Model 6 tubular and 7 box magazine were, at the shooter's will, autos, locked-bolt repeaters or single-shots. Pushing the bolt knob in locked the bolt during firing. Then pulling it outward let the bolt be pulled back. For training, when at least the early firing should be slowed, the system was splendid. It converted the auto into a straight-pull repeater or single-shot.

The Winchester 63 of 1933-58 resembled the 1903 but had a modern pistol grip, shotgun buttstock and used the recommended high-velocity Long Rifles until the shooter got curious and loaded in standard-velocity rounds. Usually no probation period was called for until the 63 had had a chance to show that it handled them, too. About 174,692 of these reliable rifles were made.

The Model 74 Winchester, introduced in 1939 for Shorts, was available the next year in Long Rifle models. It definitely showed that inexpensive autos had a place. The one-piece stock cut manufacturing costs, and still more the tubular receiver did, for it made unnecessary much of the slow, careful, costly machining of the elaborate receivers of pioneer 22-auto days. Such shortcuts had become acceptable, for Model 74 sales records reached 406,574 before the rifle went out of production in 1955. Good Junior Rifleman shots could break Expert with it and be under small or no handicap.

Most rifle makers now have an auto model in 22, and to keep up with the parade they may have several. If tightly assembled against the back-and-forth slam of firing, and blessed with snug bedding of steel into stock and, usually, forestock, these 22's shoot almost if not fully as well as similar-weight bolt guns, benching five shots into an inch, say, at 50 yards, in my experience.

That's good enough. •

The Ones That Shoot Back

"... there was a bellow of rage ... and, out of the trees burst a great silvertip. He was down at the third shot, but I was five years older." An unforgettable experience for O'Connor and one of many told here about the world's most dangerous game.

by JACK O'CONNOR

MY GUIDE and I had seen the big grizzly from the top of a hill. He was about 1500 feet below us and was earnestly engaged in turning over rotten logs for the grubs and mice he found beneath them. Quickly we appraised the situation. A strong wind was blowing directly from us toward the bear. It looked as if we might get up to him if we stayed about 200 yards to one side, worked past him, and then approached up wind. Not far from where he was feeding was a dead fir, the last tree standing of what had once been a heavy forest. But many years before a fire had swept through the woods and all the trees had been killed. Now only this gaunt gray skeleton stood in the midst of the second growth with its patches of muskeg, its yellow grass, its criss-crossed half-decayed trunks, its low berry bushes, its scarlet kinnikinik, and its scattering of pale yellow willows. The big snag would make a fine marker to work back to when we were to hunt up the grizzly.

Scent of Grizzly

When we saw the bear we were above timberline. We ran and slid down a long steep shoulder of the mountain until we came to the flat. We worked beyond the dead tree until we had the wind on the bear. Then keeping the direction of the tree in mind we began to work cautiously up wind.

Presently we found the place where the bear had been working when we first saw him. A log had been torn asunder and his big tracks were fresh in the soft soil where it had rested. I could almost smell bear. The guide plucked a piece of dry grass, tossed it into the air. Down there in the timber the wind was not so strong as it had been on top, but it was still steady, still blowing the way it had been. We sneaked furtively along, putting every foot down with the greatest of care, taking precautions not to put our hob-nail boots down on a dry twig or a stone that might move.

As we worked along up wind the tension mounted, and my thumping heart bounced around in my chest so noisily that I felt the bear must surely hear. I felt an insane desire to cough and I knew that the palms of my hands were sweating. I reflected gloomily that when we saw the bear it would be close and that because of an idiotic Canadian law which forbade a guide to carry a rifle, it was just me and the bear. My clumsy foot broke a half-rotten stick then. It sounded like a rifle shot and my guide turned around to glare at me.

A moment later and about fifty or sixty yards away, I saw something move in a patch of thick, young timber ahead of me. The guide had not seen it. I stopped, raised my binocular to my eyes. Whatever it was had long, dark, silver-tipped hair. It could only be the grizzly. I put down the glass, raised my rifle. I tried to decide just what part of the bear I was looking at. Then my excited imagination drew outlines. That patch of hair I could see through the opening, I convinced myself, was the chest area. Through the scope I simply *knew* it was the chest area. By this time the guide had seen the bear, too, and he watched as I threw off the safety and raised the old 30-06. Afterwards he told me he could see no more than I could. From my actions he assumed I knew what I was doing.

Near Disaster

For a moment the post reticle wobbled around on the patch of hair, but then it settled down, and I squeezed the trigger. The crash of the shot down there in that dark, dank, and lonely forest sounded like a crack of doom. For seconds afterwards I could hear it echo and re-echo from the surrounding hills.

Then from the patch of little trees came a mad and terrible bawling. For a moment it was accompanied by the sound of movement as if something was threshing around. Then there was silence — or almost silence, as I thought I could hear a hoarse and labored breathing.

"You got the sonofabitch," my guide said.

"I'm not sure," I whispered, moving quietly over toward him, as if his presence would shield me from the wrath of a hurt and vengeful grizzly.

"Where'd you hit him?" he asked.

"I thought in the lungs, but I'm not sure."

"Damn it," he jerked. "Never shoot at a grizzly unless you've got him with his pants down."

"I'm sorry," I said humbly.

For two or three minutes we stood there silent. My legs were still weak and trembly. I still wanted to cough.

My guide was getting impatient.

"He's dead," he finally announced. "I didn't hear him run and he quit roaring."

"Let's wait a while." I still thought I could hear an animal's labored breathing.

"Oh, hell . . . he's dead. Look, I'll go over here to the side and see if I can see him."

So he circled around to my left trying to find an opening in the trees that would give him a look at the bear.

Suddenly there was a bellow of rage. The guide whirled and ran at right angles to me and out of the trees burst a great silvertip that to my startled eyes looked as tall as a moose and as heavy as a rhino. I don't think I have ever worked a bolt half so fast in my life. He was down at the third shot, but I was five years older. I'll never be quite the same again. My guide was a bit wrought up, too. He grabbed my rifle from my hand and emptied it into the carcass of the bear and while he did so he was making remarks about grizzlies in general and this one in particular. As I had feared, my first shot had been too far back, had gone through the big bear at an angle and had lightly touched one lung.

From that snafu and near disaster I learned a little lesson that if applied will keep hunters of dangerous game living a long time: *Never shoot at an unwounded head of dangerous game unless you are sure you can kill him or render him helpless.*

It is a good maxim to follow. Generally I have done so. Since that time I have killed eight grizzlies and a couple of Alaskan brown bears. I have never even come close to getting et. I haven't always followed that rule with other stuff and I cannot remember a single time that I have violated it but what I got into trouble.

I also learned something else that day, and that was that the danger associated with a game animal is compounded of two ingredients — himself and the country in which you find him. Before that day I had collaborated on one grizzly. A pal and I found it across a canyon and above timberline in the open. We had accurate scope-sighted rifles and were reasonably good shots. Killing that bear was like shooting fish in a barrel. But taking on a grizzly 200 yards away above timberline and getting in a fight with one at 50 yards or less in timber and muskeg are two different things.

The hunting of dangerous game gives a thrill that nothing else in sport quite equals, and many men are eternally fascinated by it, some to the extent that they find the hunting of anything else a waste of time. I suppose that this is the same impulse that leads men to climb high and dangerous mountains, to drive too fast, to fight bulls, to dally with chorus girls, or otherwise run grave risks. A friend of mine who hunted in Africa recently was left cold by the rare and beautiful antelope such as sable and kudu. What really sent him was the big tough stuff. He managed to get charged by a rhino and chased by a few elephants and when a wounded buffalo came tearing out of the reeds at him with death in his eyes he was delighted.

Buffs and Lions

There are almost as many notions as to which are the world's most dangerous animals as there are animals that can be called dangerous. When I was in Africa I made it a point to pump all the white hunters I ran into as to their choice of the No. 1 tough guy. I have also tried to winnow the opinions of others from books they have written. The only conclusion I could reach is that the individual choice depends almost entirely on the hunter's experience.

Syd Downey, the white hunter's white hunter, is inclined to put the Cape buffalo in first place as a bad actor. He has been run over and tossed by buffalo, as has Myles Turner, another famous African white hunter. Don Ker, who had never had a close shave with a buffalo, but has had trouble with elephants, votes for the tusker. John Hunter, veteran white hunter who wrote the book *Hunter,* thinks the sly and agile leopard is the most dangerous of all. The rhino ranks pretty low on most people's list of bad actors, but Bwana Charles Cottar, the Oklahoma frontiersman who became a famous African guide and ivory hunter, was killed by one.

From what I have heard and read, I am inclined to think the lion is the most dangerous of the African game animals and that lions kill more armed white men than do any other animals. Compared to the thick-skinned rhino and buffalo he is soft of skin, tender, and frail. But the lion can conceal himself in very little cover, and when he charges he comes on like a flash, so close to the ground that it is easy to shoot over him. Unlike the elephant he charges determinedly, and to stop him you have to kill him. A lion does not have to be wounded to be dangerous. He'll charge if he is followed or annoyed.

In his definitive work, *The Book of the Lion,* Sir Alfred Pease places the lion in the top spot. He says there are records of men who have shot hundreds of buffalo without getting into trouble, and he says if they had shot half that number of lions they would have had a good many narrow escapes. Certainly more white men have been killed in Kenya colony by lions than by anything else. When I was hunting there a planter went out to shoot a lion that had killed a cow. He wounded the lion with his first barrel, missed with his second when the lion came for him. He was mauled so badly that he died in a Nairobi hospital. Of the long list of professional hunters who have lost their lives in the bush, the lion has accounted for far more than any other.

Leopard, Tiger, Gaur

If the vicious, crafty, and vindictive leopard were as large as a lion, he'd be the world's most dangerous animal. He charges without a warning growl, and he is cunning and determined. But he is a small animal, so small that he can be stopped with buckshot. My friend, Herb Klein, killed an exceedingly large one when we were in Africa, but I doubt if it weighed 150 pounds. There are records of several men, including Carl Akeley, the sculptor-taxidermist, who have killed wounded leopards with their bare hands.

That world's largest cat, the Indian tiger, has killed and eaten enormous numbers of men, but few of his victims have been armed white men. Most tigers are shot from the safety of machans in trees or even from the backs of elephants. Usually the hunter has a good chance to place his bullet, and if by chance the tiger is wounded he can generally get the help of elephants or of many natives. Those enormous wild cattle, the fairly common gaur and the rare wild water buffalo of India are dangerous, but their reputations are less fearsome than that of the African Cape buffalo.

Rhino and Elephant

The rhino is formidable largely because of his chronic ill temper and his unpredictability. He is an exception to the general rule that animals are dangerous only when annoyed and wounded. The rhino has a grudge against the world and a low boiling point. Many people have been tossed or pounded by rhinos when they were going about their business and had no idea there was a rhino in the country. But the menace of the rhino is lessened by the facts that he is almost blind and not to difficult to dodge and likewise that a shot will generally turn his charge. The rhino is not difficult to kill either – or at least that is what those with a lot of rhino hunting experience tell me.

The great wild cattle of Asia and Africa – the Cape buffalo of Africa, the wild water buffalo, the gaur, and the sladang of India and other parts of Asia, seldom pick a fight. But when they are wounded they are among the most dangerous and vindictive of enemies. The buffalo of Africa is the only animal that would vie with the lion as the most dangerous animal and many put him in the No. 1 place. But he can conceal himself less easily than the lion and he is a larger mark.

Most hunters of wide experience in Africa do not rank the great elephant as nearly as dangerous as either the lion or the buffalo. When a lion makes up his mind to stand his ground and fight only death will stop him, they say. The same thing is generally true of a wounded Cape buffalo. But a heavy bullet slammed almost anywhere into the head of an elephant will turn him. I am also told that it is impossible for an elephant to move with a broken leg or shoulder.

Every member of the African Big Five — lion, rhino, elephant, buffalo, and leopard — can be considered a formidable opponent, but because of the ease with which he can conceal himself, his determination, and the speed of his charge, the lion probably deserves the No. 1 spot.

The only North American animals that can be counted as dangerous are the grizzly and brown bears — and some of them can be tough indeed. The late Ned Frost, famous Wyoming sheep and grizzly guide, felt that when the number of grizzlies and the number of hunter casualties were taken into consideration, the grizzly was a more dangerous animal than the African lion. Ralph Young, the famed brown bear guide of Southeast Alaska, is convinced that under the right (or wrong) set of circumstances the big Alaskan brown bear is the most dangerous animal in the world.

Big Bears

The grizzly and the brown bear are close relatives and there isn't any doubt but they can be bad actors. When white men first encountered grizzlies, the big bears didn't have the least fear of them because they were used to poorly armed Indians. Many a pioneer hunter and trapper was mauled and killed by grizzlies. Even today in true wilderness areas where grizzlies are not familiar with men and rifles they display little fear.

An exceedingly large grizzly will weigh as much as 900 pounds, but the average male will weigh about 500 or 600. The largest of the big browns will weigh as much as 1500 pounds. An African lion that will weigh over 400 pounds is a very large one and a tiger that will weigh over 500 is likewise very large. Since as a general rule the larger an animal is the more difficult it is to kill, the grizzly should be somewhat harder to stop than either a lion or a tiger, and the big brown should be enormously more difficult to pile up.

Those who argue that the grizzlies and the browns are the world's most dangerous animals have much to back them up. Back in the days when I was hunting in the Canadian Rockies and the Yukon every fall and writing a good deal about grizzlies, correspondents used to send me many newspaper clippings and other accounts of killings and maulings by grizzlies. From them I estimated that about a dozen people were killed or mauled by the big bears every year in Canada between the American border and the Alaska line. In Portuguese East Africa a few years ago, one pride of lions killed and devoured literally hundreds of natives and depopulated a whole district. Several hundred Indians are killed annually by tigers. However, African and Indian natives are not often armed, whereas the victims of the grizzlies most often are.

But no matter which of the world's dangerous animals you vote for, any of them can cause trouble if they are poorly handled, and most of the killings and maulings are done by wounded animals. In the fall of 1956 a pair of Montana sportsmen wounded a grizzly and followed it up. One of them was killed. In Alaska in the spring of 1956 a grizzly killed not only the armed hunter but his armed guide — an astounding feat! An account of a terrible mauling in Alaska by another grizzly has recently appeared in OUTDOOR LIFE, and I have on occasion written of the shocking experience of my old Yukon Indian friend and guide, Field Johnson, who was with me when I shot a couple of grizzlies in 1945 and one in 1949. Field was the victim of an unprovoked charge when he was hunting moose near the little Yukon village of Champagne. The grizzly beat him up and buried him. When Field thought the bear had gone, he tried to get out of his grave. But the bear had lain quiet nearby and when he saw Field get up, he mauled him again, dragged him by the feet more than a mile, and buried him once more. When Field regained consciousness the bear was gone and the sun was almost down. Field managed to stagger to the Alaskan Highway and modern antibiotics saved his life. He will never completely recover from the terrible experience.

The placement of that first shot on any game is of great importance, but when the game is dangerous the placement may mean the difference between a clean, easy kill and tragedy. A few years ago an American hunting in India took a shot at a tiger moving through tall grass. Whether his bullet was deflected or whether he did not lead the spot he wanted to hit enough I do not know. The bullet hit the tiger in the abdomen. The great cat went down, got up roaring, charged into the line of beaters. He got one beater down and was mauling him. The hunter fired again, but this time in the melee he hit the beater in the leg. The high velocity bullet so mangled it that the leg had to be amputated. A few days later the tiger was found dead and half devoured by vultures. The hunter will carry a sense of guilt to his grave.

When I was in India I violated my own rule of never firing a shot unless I was sure the bullet would kill the animal or break it down. A few days before, when I was hunting spotted Axis deer (chital) by spotlight, we had seen a tiger about 80 or 100 yards off the road in high grass. The spotlight was not too good and the big cat was pretty well concealed. I could not tell which end of the tiger was which. I had only a 270 with me and I refused to shoot.

The Indian shikari, who had previously seen me down a flying peacock and several running chital stags with the same rifle, was disgusted. The *burra sahib* (that old man — namely, me) was a good shot, he told our outfitter, but when he encountered a tiger he was definitely chicken.

Tiger in Darkness

I still remembered that crack some nights later when this same shikari was with me in a machan high in a tree over a tiger bait. Not long after sundown we heard the tiger calling up the canyon, but it grew dark and the tiger did not come. Stretched out in the machan, with a sweater draped over me and my 375 Magnum with a cartridge in the chamber and on safe beside me, I counted sheep for a while and then began to doze.

I was awakened by a crunching of bones on the bait. I managed to sit up without making a sound.

"Shere (tiger)?" I whispered to the shikari.

"Shere," he said in confirmation.

I had told the English-speaking outfitter that afternoon when we went to the machan to instruct the shikari that when I punched him twice with my elbow he was to turn on the 5-cell flashlight by which I was to do the shooting. I switched off the safety, trained the big rifle on the bait, and then gave my two punches.

I had seen dozens of drawings of sahibs shooting tigers on baits from machans. Always they show the tiger in plain view. But when the light went on I couldn't see a thing. The bait was

lying by a bush and the tiger had approached from behind the bush and had drawn the rear end of the carcass into the bush before he started to feed. In the glare of the light the shadows of the limbs and twigs on the tiger's stripes made perfect camouflage.

"Shere," the boy whispered. "Chute!"

Taking it for granted that he had enough sense to center the bright spot in the middle of the beam on the portion of the tiger I was to hit, I put the crosswires of the scope right in the middle of the bright spot and touched one off. The tiger let out a startled roar and took off like a drunken buffalo bull.

Tiger Jumped

At dawn the next morning I shinnied down a rope to the ground and quickly found a little blood. Until late that afternoon we tracked the tiger. We finally came onto it by a little water seep high in a rocky canyon. He saw me just as I saw him and he had to make one jump to be out of sight in the bordering jungle. I could plainly see that he had only a flesh wound in his cheek. All that day he had lain by the little seep, drinking now and then and soothing his wound by lying with his cheek against the cool, damp sand. If the bullet had been a few inches to the left I would have got that tiger, but I was not justified in shooting.

The tiger I got later was galloping through tall grass ahead of an elephant drive, but I reasoned that I could kill him before he got to cover. I did.

The one African lion I have shot was in contrast a very neat operation. Don Ker and I were out to look at our baits in the gray of dawn. There was a maned lion on our first bait, but Don thought we could do better, so we sneaked off. Baits 2, 3, and 4 were blanks. A lion had been on bait No. 5, so we parked the car and hunted on foot.

Suddenly our Dorobo tracker grabbed my arm and whispered that magic word: *"Simba!"* I followed his pointing finger and could see the head and neck of a fine maned lion about 200 yards away in the grass. He hadn't seen us and was looking back toward the bait.

About 75 yards from the lion was a big termite hill and Don and I crouched and sneaked rapidly toward it, keepit between us and the lion. Once behind it, I poked my head around the side. The big cat hadn't moved. I laid my left hand against the hill and rested the 375 against it. The sight of the crosswires sharp and black against the lion's neck steadied me. I squeezed the trigger carefully and the lion was down, threshing about, roaring horribly. Another shot finished it.

The Best First Shot

The best place for that first shot on most dangerous game is through the shoulder. The crash of a heavy bullet against the shoulder blade seems to transmit shock throughout the system and almost always knocks the animal flat. If the penetration is sufficient and the angle correct, both shoulders are broken and the animal is helpless. That is my favorite shot on a grizzly. It is also a fine shot on a buffalo or a rhino and one that will knock a charging animal head over teakettle. It will even anchor an elephant.

With the same old 375 in my hands

I lay in the rain on a lonely beach on Admiralty Island in the spring of 1956 while a big brown bear rolled along directly toward me. I had made up my mind that when he got to a certain piece of driftwood, I'd let him have it. When he reached that point, I broke his downhill shoulder and tipped him over. I then jumped up and let him have a couple through the lungs. That was it.

The classic shot on elephants is into the brain, with aim taken between the orifice of the ear and the eye, from a broadside position or at an angle to reach the same objective. An elephant so hit will fall as if a rug had been jerked out from under him. However, if the brain is missed a head-shot elephant, I am told, will travel forever. For that reason many white hunters prefer to have their clients shoot for the lungs and then wait until the eleplant drowns in his own blood and falls. Some like the shoulder or heart shot, but whatever it is the shot should be taken with the greatest of care. An angry and wounded tusker is bad business.

Head and Neck Shots

As a general thing head shots are not a good idea. The brain is a small mark, and unless the angle is right the bullet can be deflected by bone. The history of Indian hunting, for example, is full of rhubarbs that came about because some sahib tried to poke a bullet into a tiger's brain and only succeeded in wounding him. A dangerous animal with the side of its face shot off, its nose shot off, or its jaw broken can still do a lot of damage.

The often-used neck shot is a dandy if the bullet breaks the spinal column, but no good if it doesn't. In Africa I once decided to break the neck of a topi, an antelope about the size of a mule deer. We wanted it for camp meat for the crew. I rested my left hand against a tree trunk, then laid the scope-sighted 375 across my wrist. At the shot the topi flattened. The boys shouted in glee, rushed over to *halal* it — cut its throat so it would be official eating for Mohammedans. Suddenly the topi decided it didn't like what was going on, jumped to its feet, and ran for almost 200 yards before it toppled over.

On the other hand the animal with both shoulders broken will be helpless and the one with one shoulder gone will be knocked flat and put out of action for a time. Large heavy animals cannot navigate on three legs.

The type of country an animal is hunted in has much to do with the degree of danger it presents. A grizzly shot in the fall in a big open basin above timberline presents far fewer hazards than the same bear shot in the willow jungle along a salmon stream. If I could take them in the open above timberline I'd shoot any grizzly that ever lived with a 257, but if I had to hunt them in heavy cover I'd want a 375.

Generally speaking, dangerous stuff, particularly in brush, is best hunted with rifles using heavy bullets at moderate velocity. Such bullets are less deflected by brush or turned from their course by bone and they have the momentum to knock down an animal in case of a charge. Syd Downey says that in the case of an unwounded lion the 270-gr. bullet of the 375 Magnum is the world's finest lion medicine, but when a lion is charging he wants the 500-gr. soft point bullet in his double 470. Given a side shot at a grizzly, it is no trick to slip a 130-gr. 270 bullet through his ribs and knock him for a loop. In willows and alders I'd rather have a heavier bullet for a frontal or shoulder shot. Favorite tiger medicine in India is the 450-400, which uses a 400-gr. 40 caliber bullet at 2200 f.p.s., but the 375 Magnum with its 300-gr. bullet at 2450 f.p.s. is gaining on it. For elephant, rhino, and buffalo in Africa the standard cartridge is the 470 Nitro Express with a 500-gr. bullet at 2125 and about 5,000 foot pounds of energy — an exact ballistic duplicate of the new Winchester 458. For American grizzly and brown bear, the hunter should take at least a 30-06 or 300 Magnum with the 220-gr. bullets or better still the 375 with the 270 or 300-gr. bullets.

Proper armament is part of handling dangerous game, but the most important ingredient is what lies in the hunter's head. If he is calm, experienced, cool, he'll take his time and he'll place the bullet just where he wants it. If the animal is moving rapidly or is concealed by brush which may deflect the bullet he'll either postpone shooting or pass up the shot altogether.

I think it is entirely normal for anyone going after his first head of any dangerous game to be somewhat spooky, but if he remembers not to fire until he is *sure* where the bullet is going to land he won't get into trouble.

Just so the hunter is *sure* of that first shot, he doesn't have to get too close. Much of the philosophy of the British white hunter was evolved in the days of black powder and open sights, and many pros try to get their clients far too close. Often this is a mistake. A client that is reasonably calm when he is 125 yards from a rhino, may be jumping right out of his pants if his guide sneaks him up to within 25 yds. Any competent woodchuck hunter should be able to kill a grizzly with neatness and dispatch at 200 yards if he takes his time, gets into a good position, and waits for the bear to co-operate. But if his guide hauls him up to within spitting distance he may come unglued. That has happened many times. It is far better to take a good shot at some distance than to work closer and gamble on having to shoot at a running animal or on the hunter's getting jittery.

Right Spot, Right Shot

Whether it is at 30 feet or 250 yards, that first shot simply must go into the right spot. If it does all is rosy, because a modern rifle with the right bullet makes puny man more than a match for the roughest and toughest animal that walks the face of the earth.

But if it doesn't, then there's trouble.

It's a nerve wracking business — this following up a wounded animal that may launch a charge at any moment. Sometimes the hunter is so jittery and unnerved when the charge comes that he is paralyzed. In the spring of 1955 a New Delhi business man hunting in Northern India's terai country didn't even lift his rifle while a wounded tiger charged fifty yards to maul and kill him.

Once a wounded animal is located in a ravine or a patch of long grass every effort should be made to pin point it by making it move or growl. Sometimes the grass is fired. Often the animal can be got to move by firing rifles or shotguns into a suspected location. In India men are put up trees to pelt brush patches with stones. Sometimes the patch is driven by elephants or a herd of tame buffalo.

But the best thing is never to let an animal be wounded. That first shot is the one that counts!

THE GATLING GUN

The interesting material presented here is from Ernest L. Reedstrom's new book, *Bugles, Banners and War Bonnets*, reproduced with the permission of the author and publisher. This large volume, published in 1977, was edited by Don Russell. Published by the Caxton Printers, Ltd., of Caldwell, Idaho, the big book was among the top three finalists in the annual Spur Awards for Best Western Nonfiction books, this competition held by the Western Writers of America, Inc.

Military historians and armchair Indian War buffs have never quite forgiven Custer for refusing the 3 Gatling guns offered by General Alfred Terry, commander of the Department of Dakota, or the additional force of the Second Cavalry battalion prior to the march to the Little Big Horn. Custer refused the Gatling guns, it is said, because they were drawn by condemned horses, and would slow and impede his march.[48] More likely, Custer's refusal was not because the Gatling guns were hauled by condemned horses, but because of the terrain which he confronted. Second Lieutenant W. H. Low, 20th Infantry, had problems with the Gatlings upsetting several times on the march. Custer sought and obtained permission to have the battery of Gatling guns detached from his regiment and the battery was accordingly ordered to join General Gibbon on the north bank of the Yellowstone.[49]

The Gatling gun had proved itself and played a decisive part in a fight against Comanches and Kiowas on August 30, 1874 at Mulberry Creek in El Llano Estacado, the "Staked Plains" of West Texas. From ambush, some 200 Indians charged Brevet Major General Nelson A. Miles' Indian Territory Expedition, almost destroying an advanced party of scouts in the first assault. Lieutenant James W. Pope, commanding a Gatling gun battery, moved into action swiftly, scattering the attacking warriors. On other occasions, the Gatlings were reported to "have done splendidly" in brief encounters with Indians.

The Little Big Horn terrain was quite different. Much of the area shown on maps studied by Custer was unsuited for wagons, or for wheeled Gatlings pulled by condemned cavalry horses and their ammunition limbers. The ground was hilly and the trail was undetermined. Like wagons, the Gatlings might straggle behind, placing the command in a dangerous position. Every seasoned officer knew that mobility was the key to Indian warfare. In order to fight Indians, you had to find them. One of the main reasons Custer ordered pack trains instead of wagons to carry food and ammunition was because of the fast pace needed. He proved his point by arriving at the Little Big Horn on June 25 instead of the proposed June 26.

General Terry's confidential telegram to General Sheridan, July 2, 1876, reads in part:

"The plan adopted was the only one that promised to bring the infantry into action and I desired to make sure of things by getting up every available man. I offered Custer the battery of Gatling guns but he declined it saying that it might embarrass him;

Gatling Gun at Washington Arsenal viewed from the rear, May 26, 1866. *Courtesy National Archives.*

Custer in parley with some Indians. *Art by E. L. Reedstrom.*

that he was strong enough without it."[50]

Custer's attitude toward Gatlings was different in 1874, when he commanded the expedition into the Black Hills. In a letter to a friend, Custer wrote:

Fort Lincoln Dakota, May 19th, 1874.
My Dear Laurence . . .
. . . I will have ten full companies of the best Cavalry in Uncle Sam's service, a detachment of Indian scouts taken from (sic) friendly to the whites and hostile to the Sioux, and a section of Gatling guns, the latter capable of being fired fifty times a minute.[51] I will tell you candidly that we will have contests with the noble red man but my friend Laurence need feel no anxiety on that score as he can remain an impartial witness of the battle and be exposed to no danger whatever.[52]

Many officers had objections to the Gatling gun, even though its firepower was that of two companies of infantry while it took the services of only four infantrymen to operate it. However, training of gun crews was often inadequate. During the late 1860's and early 1870's, target practice was infrequent because of objections to extra expenditures for ammunition. It was said that the weapon was clumsy and hard to conceal. The operators were exposed to enemy fire,[53] in a stationary position, and the weapon would soon lose its effectiveness with several men wounded.[54] Officers cautioned the operators to keep their heads down when firing, but, towering above the men was the Gatling's gravity-fed ammunition case. A stray bullet might slam into the feed case, rendering it useless or exploding several cartridges within it.[55]

In swinging the gun about to change firing positions, two men were exposed, one at each wheel; one man would push one wheel forward, the other pull back on the opposite wheel. This lateral roll gave the Gatling a wider field of fire power, but exposed the men operating it.

It has commonly been assumed that the Gatling guns of the Little Big Horn expedition were of 45-70 caliber, the standard carbine and rifle ammunition of 1876. Unimportant as this might seem, it has confused the subject. Dr. Gatling had made various improvements and a new patent was awarded in 1865. After a number of tests and inspections, the battery was approved and 100 guns were distributed to various commands.[56] Gatlings were shipped by rail to Fort Sully, Fort Rice and Fort Randall.[57] These weapons were of the modified model of 1866, and in both .50-, and 1-inch calibers. The report of the War Department, 1876 (Vol. 2, Part 3, p. 700) refers to "A battery of three half inch Gatling guns, (.50 caliber)[58] commanded by Second Lieutenant W. H. Low, Twentieth Infantry," substantiating that the .50-caliber was in use instead of the 45-70 caliber.

Dr. Richard Jordan Gatling did not have an opportunity to see his "battery gun" in action during the Civil War. It was introduced too late to be used in many campaigns. However, it had been put to many practical tests by officers of the Ordnance Corps, who spoke of its performance in high terms. At the beginning, Gatling's gun was called a "novel engine of war" that would prove useful in guarding bridges, fords and roadways. There was little recoil to affect the accuracy of its aim, and, once sighted on a target, it can be fired day or night from an aimed position. Lieutenant Maclay, U.S. Ordnance, reported: "The advantages claimed for this gun are: 1st. There is no escape of gas at the breech. 2d. There is no recoil, which can destroy its accuracy. 3rd. It performs the operations of loading, firing, and extracting the case, by simply revolving the crank. 4th. Accuracy. 5th. Rapidity of fire." The report concludes, "All parts of the gun work well."[59]

Army plans placed the Gatling in the artillery arm. It was contemplated that in campaigns against the Indians the gun could be used to advantage as a "flank defense gun."

Two sizes of Gatlings were manufactured by the Colt's Arms Company, Hartford, Connecticut, one of 1-inch caliber, capable of being fired 100 times a minute, and one of .50 caliber, which could be fired 200 times a minute. Copper-case primed cartridges were used in both guns. Each gun had 6 steel rotating barrels. The reason the Gatling had little recoil is that gun and carriage were of sufficient weight to overcome the recoil of each discharge without movement and therefore no time was lost in sighting after each fire. If an operator other than the one who was cranking moved a wheel forward or backward, the gun was given a lateral movement while firing, to sweep a sector of any circle within its range.

An order for 100 Gatling guns was issued to Talbot, Jones & Company of Indianapolis, Indiana, August 24, 1866. Fifty .50-caliber, or half-inch guns, and 50 1-inch caliber guns were ordered by General A. B. Dyer. Each weapon had 6 steel barrels, all rifled. The wooden field gun carriages were to be of seasoned white oak, with all iron or steel parts blued, with the exception of the gun barrels which were to be browned, a blue-black rusting process.

The weapons that Custer declined were of the 1866 improved models, chambered for the 50-70-450 centerfire infantry cartridge, interchangeable for rifle. The weight of the machine, not including the carriage and limber, was 224 pounds. Total weight of carriage, omitting the gun, was 202 pounds. The limber (empty) weighed 200 pounds. The smaller sized gun had a range up to one mile, while the larger gun had a range up to two miles. Of course, the extreme ranges would seldom produce accurate hits.[60] Open sights were located centrally upon the breech housing; when the sights were not used, they could be

At the Washington trials, May 8, 1866, three Gatling guns are posed on the banks of the Potomac; the 50-cal. and 1-inch guns have all passed severe tests. *Courtesy National Archives Records Group, Wash. D.C.*

retracted into the case. Elevation was attained by use of a jackscrew in the trail.

The mobility of the Gatling gun had not been criticized by other commands. The gun and its carriage, compared to other artillery, was light in weight and could be drawn by two horses.[61] Four horses or six were required for field guns. The lives of three or four men at the most need only be exposed; and the results attained can only be measured by the exposure of as many as a hundred men armed with ordinary rifles.

The men of the Seventh U.S. Cavalry had already found uses for the Gatling gun. One company, returning from the Hancock Expedition in 1867, ran into a large herd of buffalo while escorting a wagon train on the Smoky Hill route. When the buffalo threatened to stampede the wagon train, two companies of cavalry dismounted, knelt and fired volleys into the oncoming herd. This only frightened the animals and they headed straight for the train. Two Gatling guns then came into position and began firing. After a number of buffalo were killed, the rest of the herd broke around the wagon train. A detailed group of soldiers went forward to cut the hind quarters of the dead buffalo, loading them into the wagons for garrison consumption.[62]

The Gatling gun manual and firing tactics in battery formation are as follows:

The New Battery Manual
of the Gatling Gun

Positions of the Cannoneers in Battery

Figure One

Nos. 1 and 2 on the right flank of the piece, No. 1 opposite the cascabel, No. 2 opposite the rear end of the hand spike, and both facing towards the piece, 18 inches outside of the face of the nave of the wheel, Nos. 3 and 4 on the left flank piece, No. 3 opposite the cascabel, No. 4 opposite the rear end of the hand spike, both facing toward the piece, 18 inches outside of the face of the nave of the wheel.

A feed-drum has been placed on the piece, the crank and traversing apparatus has been placed in action, and the hand spike has been placed at the end of trail.

At the command PREPARE TO FIRE, No. 1 places himself in position to turn the crank with his right hand, No. 2 directs the piece and seats himself on the trail seat, prepared to elevate or depress the piece. No. 3 goes to the feed-drum, and attends it, No. 4 goes to the limber, and gets a second feed-drum all ready to relieve No. 3. At the command FIRE, No. 1

Footnotes

48. Custer would have known these horses were condemned because of their brands "I.C.," which means "Inspected and Condemned," E. B. Custer microfilm, Roll 6, No. 6427, Custer Battlefield.
49. Narrative of First Sergeant Hugh A. Hynds, Sergeant of the Gatling gun battery which General Terry offered Custer and he declined. Hynds mentions four Gatlings, two .50 calibers or ½-inch guns and two .100 or one-inch guns. On file at the Custer Battlefield Museum Library. Also see Research Review, Little Big Horn Associates, Vol. VI, Winter, Number 4.
50. For full text see: The Custer Tragedy, by Fred Dustin, privately printed by Edwards Bros. Inc., Ann Arbor, Mich., 1936, p. 197.
51. The Gatling Gun, by Paul Wahl & D. R. Toppel, p. 30, includes a report by T. G. Baylor, Captain of Ordnance, Ft. Monroe Arsenal, Virginia, July 14, 1866, "I had the oil rubbed off this gun, drenched it with water, and then exposed it for two nights and a day to rain and weather, but though it was quite rusty, it was fired 97 times in a minute and a half, one man turning at the crank."
A short time after the Gatlings were delivered to the Army, it was noted that, when cranking at top speed to attempt the firing power of two hundred shots in one minute, shots occasionally struck the front cross bar of the frame, throwing lead and parts of metal back into the crew. This could very well be the reason for Custer's mention of 50 shots per minute. See "The Gatling Gun," p. 32.
52. From the collections of the Manuscript Division, Library of Congress (AC. 11700), Ghent Collection.
53. Infantry Uniforms, Book No. 2, 1855-1939, p. 210, Robert and Christopher Wilkinson-Latham; MacMillan Co.
54. See this chapter for "The Gatling Gun Battery Manual" for duties of each man.
55. Army and Navy Journal, Feb. 21, 1874, p. 443.
56. Army and Navy Journal, Aug. 20, 1870, p. 6.
57. Ibid., Aug. 3, 1872, p. 813.
58. Author's note. See reference No. 49 in this chapter: Narrative of First Sergeant H. A. Hynds who states two Gatlings were .50 calibers, and two were one-inch. I am more inclined to take the War Department's word of three Gatlings in the .50-caliber; the fourth in the one-inch caliber.
59. Army and Navy Journal, July 13, 1867, p. 741.
60. Author's Note: A good example of this particular model can be found in Francis Bannerman Sons, Military Goods Catalog, Illustrated and Descriptive, 1931, "Cannons . . . p. 134 . . ." Gatling Rapid-Fire Guns, Cal. 50; the breech mechanism was encased in a bronzed jacket with four-foot wheels.
61. General E. S. Godfrey had four Gatlings hauled by two mules during the fall of 1867. Guns were receipted to Godfrey from Ft. Harker. Winners of the West, March 30, 1930.
62. Elizabeth Custer microfilm, Roll 6, No. 6402, Custer Battlefield.
63. Army and Navy Journal, June 15, 1872.
64. Narrative of First Sergeant Hugh A. Hynds, on file at Custer Battlefield Museum.
65. Ibid.
66. Ibid.
67. Records of U.S. Army Continental Commands, 1821-1920, Fort Abraham Lincoln, Special Orders, Vol. 83; Special Orders 48, 1876, Record Group No. 393.
68. Record Group No. 156, Records of the Office of the Chief of Ordnance, Letters Received, 1875.
69. Records of the Office of the Chief of Ordnance, Letters Received No. 2520, 1876, Record Group No. 156.
70. Record Group No. 156, Records of the Office of the Chief of Ordnance, Letters Received, No. 2520, 1876.

turns the crank, No. 3 attends the feed-drum, seeing that the cartridges are fed regularly, No. 2 sees that the piece is properly aimed. When the feed-drum is nearly exhausted, No. 3 warns No. 4 by calling out, "Drum," when No. 4 brings up a loaded feed-drum, and when the first drum is exhausted, No. 3 lifts it off, takes it to the limber chest, and gets another loaded feed-drum ready. No. 4 at the same time takes his feed-drum on the piece, and takes the duties previously performed by No. 3. He is in turn relieved by No. 3, and so on. At the command CEASE FIRING, No. 3 or No. 4, as the case may be, keeps the feed-drum stationary. No. 1 turns the crank until the loose cartridges are fired. All then take the positions "in battery."

When feed-cases are used instead of feed-drums, the duties of the cannoneers No. 1 and No. 2 are not changed. The duties of the cannoneers No. 3 and 4 are to supply the piece with the feed-cases. At the command PREPARE TO FIRE, No. 3 inserts the lower end of the feed-case in the hopper, and No. 4 stands by ready to insert a filled case when the first is exhausted. At the command FIRE, No. 3 sees that the cartridges feed regularly, withdraws the case when it is empty, and No. 4 inserts at once a filled case, and is in turn relieved by No. 3, and they too keep up a constant supply of cartridges. At the command CEASE FIRING, Nos. 3 and 4 remove the feed-cases to the limber, and place them in the chest. At the command LIMBER TO THE FRONT, No. 1 fastens the crank, ungears the traversing apparatus, and goes to the end of the trail. No. 3 and No. 4, as the case may be, takes off the feed-drum and places it in the limber chest, where the other feed-drums, ready for use, are also placed. No. 2 unships the hand spike, keys it in its place on the trail, and places himself at the end of the trail opposite No. 1.

The limber is brought to the front of the piece, passing it on the right, and No. 1 and No. 2 bring the piece to the right about, limber up and key the pintle. All then take the positions "in battery," except that Nos. 1 and 3 are opposite the naves of the wheels of the piece, and Nos. 2 and 4 opposite the naves of the limber wheels. At the command LIMBER TO THE REAR, the actions of the cannoneers are the same as in the last command, except that the limber is brought to the rear of the piece and is brought to the left about, and the piece is limbered and keyed, but not brought to the right about. On the march, the cannoneers march in the places indicated in the last two commands. At the command CANNONEERS-MOUNT, Nos. 1 and 3 mount on the rear side of the limber, Nos. 2 and 4 on the front side. The piece being limbered, and on the march, at the command IN BATTERY, the piece halts, the cannoneers, if mounted, dismount. Nos. 1 and 2 unlimber the piece and bring it to the right about. The limber is brought to the left about, is taken 20 paces to the rear, and is again brought to the left about. No. 1 frees the crank and gears in the traversing apparatus. No. 2 detaches the hand spike, places it on the trail, and gives the general direction to the piece, and notes whether the traversing apparatus works properly. Nos. 3 and 4 go to the limber and get out two loaded feed-drums. No. 3 takes one to the piece, places it on the pintle, and gets it ready for feeding. Then all take the positions of the cannoneers "in battery". The foregoing instructions apply to pieces of ordinary musket caliber, and mounted as small field-pieces.

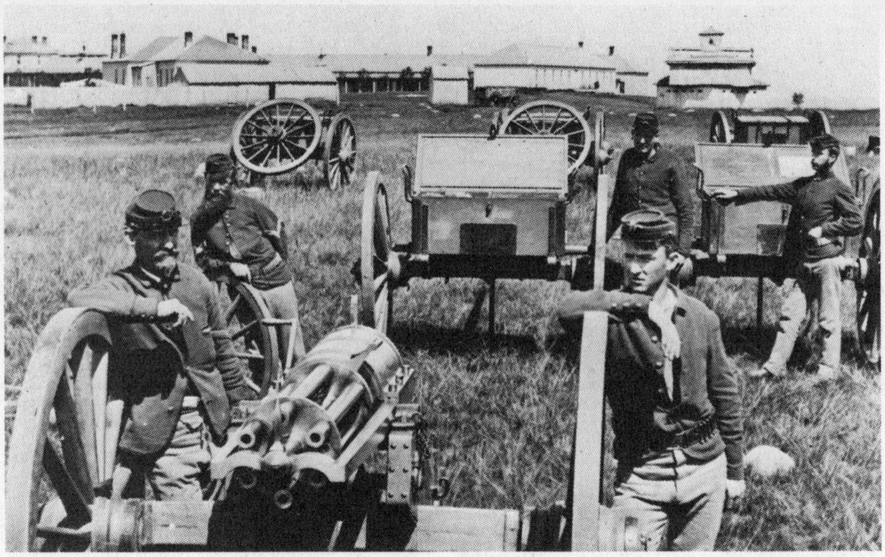

At Fort McKean, North Dakota, in 1877, members of the 20th Infantry stand at ease next to caissons and 1-inch Gatling guns. *Courtesy Custer Battlefield Museum.*

For the large calibers, the feed-drums are so heavy that two men will be required to handle them. An additional man must therefore belong to each piece, who may be called No. 5, and whose position "in battery" will be in the rear of the limber box, and on the march midway between Nos. 3 and 4. His duty will be to assist Nos. 3 and 4 in getting the feed-drums in readiness, and in carrying them to and fro between the limber and the piece, and in packing them in the limber chest. He must be mounted with the other cannoneers on the front of the limber chest or on a caisson if there be one.

With the guns of musket caliber disposed for transportation on animals' backs (camel guns), the number of cannoneers will be the same as that given above for small field-pieces. Any intelligent officer can make the modifications that the case requires, thus No. 2 should arrange the tripod for field-carriage and keep the gun accurately pointed. No. 1 should adjust the crank and traversing apparatus, and Nos. 3 and 4 should see that the supply of cartridges is kept up. Nos. 1 and 2 will remove the gun from the back of the animal and adjust it on the carriage. With guns of caliber larger than that of the musket, it will be advisable to have a sixth cannoneer, whose duty it shall be to relieve No. 1 at the crank.

In drilling at the school of the cannoneer in garrison or camp, it will be well to remove the locks, to prevent the unnecessary snapping of the springs, and the cartridges can then be run through the hopper at will, familiarizing the men with the use of the gun without waste of ammunition or injury to the locks.[63]

Second Lieutenant William Hale Low and Second Lieutenant Frank X. Kinzie arrived at Bismarck, Dakota Territory, March 20, 1876 with 32 half-frozen men from the 20th Infantry[64] with orders to report to the commanding officer of Fort Abraham Lincoln and organize a Gatling battery for an expedition against hostile Indians. Some of the men remembered seeing General Custer driven in an ambulance to a railway terminal at Bismarck, en route to Washington, D.C., to give evidence in the Belknap case.[65] The snow had drifted into huge banks, swept by the winds, making travel difficult by foot or wagon. After reaching the fort, Low began to train his men with the Gatling guns awaiting them. Within 6 weeks they would be ready to march. May 10, the command moved to Cannon Ball Creek, 3 miles south of the fort on the west bank of the Missouri River. Here organization of the expedition was completed and troops were put under canvas until the march began on May 17.[66]

Orders to Lieutenant Low were:

Headquarters, Fort Abraham Lincoln, D. T., March 18, 1876.

Special Orders No. 48[67]

Article 8. Upon the arrival at this post of the detachment of the 20th Infantry under command of Second Lieutenant Low of that regiment the officers and men of the Detachment will be provided with quarters at Infantry Barracks and under the direction of Lieutenant Low will be organized and drilled for service in the field with a Gatling gun battery consisting of four pieces.

As soon as the weather will permit horses to be kept on the picket line at night the Post Quartermaster will turn over to Lieutenant Low for services with the Gatling

CUSTER'S LAST SHOT

BY
ERNEST L. REEDSTROM

"Tom Custer and his brother George—at the final hour."
Courtesy Dr. Larry Frost/art by E. L. Reedstrom.

gun battery such numbers of horses as may be suitable and may be required to supply the battery, not including mounts for the cannoneers. Two horses will be supplied for use of officers serving with the Battery. The officers and men composing the Gatling gun detachment will not be required to perform any duty at this post which will conflict or interfere with their organization and preparation for the field.

Lieutenant Low will fully instruct his men in the duties pertaining to the Gatling Gun service in the field and render them as familiar as practicable in the proper care and management of horses.

By order of
Brevet Major General Custer
(Signature) W. W. Cooke
1st Lt. & Adjt. 7 Cavy.
Post Adjutant.

The lighter 45-70 Gatling guns could have been available for the Little Big Horn campaign, had not it been for a delay in communications among department headquarters in Chicago and Washington Ordnance offices, which held up requisitions for the distribution of the weapons for 5 months. We would have to wade through a tide of letters, telegrams and second- and third-endorsements to pin down the responsibility.

On November 17, 1875, Brigadier General S. V. Benet, Chief of Ordnance, Washington, D. C., announced that 45-70 Gatling guns at various arsenals were available, and asked what disposition the Lieutenant General wished to make of the guns. The weapons could be requisitioned by commanding officers of posts needing them most. There were 10 Gatlings at the San Antonio Arsenal to be issued to posts in the Department of Texas, 5 guns at Fort Union Arsenal for the Department of the Missouri, and 17 guns at Rock Island Arsenal, of which 8 were to be allotted to posts in the Department of Dakota and 9 to the Department of the Platte. With each weapon, a sufficient supply of ammunition would be furnished with harness for 2 horses. It was noted that these guns were much lighter than the 1-inch caliber and 1/2 inch, or .50 caliber, already serving garrisons in many departments.[68]

Five months dragged by before communications from officers reached General Benet's desk in Washington; meanwhile, Benet sent a second communication:[69]

Ordnance Office
War Department
Washington, May 5th, 1876

Captain J. W. Reilly, Chief Ordnance Officer Military Division of the Missouri, Chicago, Illinois

Sir:
Referring to my letter of November 17, 1875 (copy enclosed) directing you to advise to this office, what distribution the Lieutenant General of the Army desired to make of the 17 Gatling guns Cal. 45, on hand at the Rock Island Arsenal, I infer that as this information has not yet been furnished, it may have been overlooked.

Respectfully
Your obedient servant,
(Signed) S. V. Benet
Chief of Ordnance

Captain Reilly had reported:

Headquarters Military Division of the Missouri, Office of Chief Ordnance Officer

Chicago, Illinois,
April 6th, 1876

Chief of Ordnance U.S.A.
Washington, D. C.

Sir,
I have the honor to inform you that your communication of November 17th, 1875, relative to the distribution to Troops in this Division of certain Gatling Guns in the possession of the Ordnance Department, was referred by me with an Endorsement to the Lieutenant General November 20, 1875. I recommended that the 10 at San Antonio Arsenal be issued to Posts and Troops in Department of Texas. Five at Fort Union Arsenal be issued to Posts and Troops in Department of Missouri. Nine at Rock Island Arsenal to Posts and Troops in Department of the Platte. Eight at Rock Island Arsenal to Posts and Troops in Department of Dakota. The Commanding Generals of the Departments were instructed by the Lieutenant General, if they desired these Guns to designate, their disposition in the proportion I recommended. Reports have been received from Generals Terry and Crook; and Generals Pope and Ord have today been directed to forward reports at once.

The delay in returning the complete papers to your office, has been caused by the failure of the latter named officers to answer the communication. The matter will now however be pushed to a conclusion . . .

Very respectfully
Your obedient Servant
(Signed) J. W. Reilly
Captain of Ordnance
Chief Ord. Off. Mil. Div. Mo.

Eventually, all department commanders replied. General Terry designated the companies to receive the 8 guns allotted to his department. General Crook stated that he did not wish the guns. General Pope designated posts to receive the 5 guns at Fort Union Arsenal and requested 3 additional guns. They were allotted from those apportioned to the Department of the Platte. General Ord designed the disposition of 8 guns at San Antonio Arsenal, but asked that 2 remain there for emergencies. The 6 guns remaining at Rock Island Arsenal were retained there for possible use in the Department of the Platte.[70] •

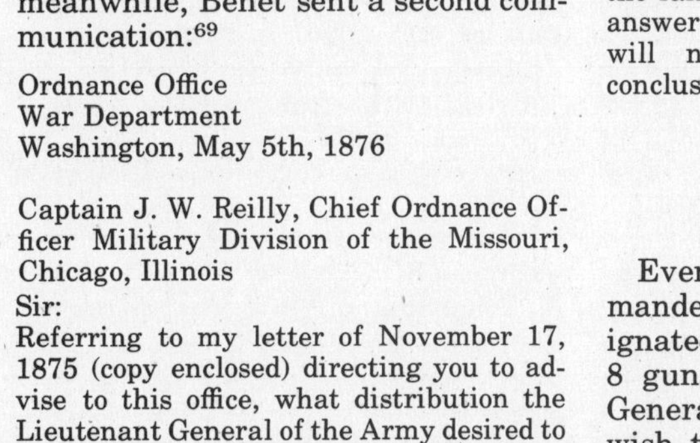

Although Custer favored the early Gatlings on a previous expedition he refused to have the battery accompany him to the Little Big Horn.

A GOOD

For a handy fellow, can be a

by RAY ORDORICA

MOST OF US HAVE felt pangs when a good gun comes back from a hunting trip with new scratches. Some, who spend only a small amount of time in the outdoors, can put up with a few nicks in a fancy gun to enjoy its company. Those who spend a lot of time outdoors with a rifle may often be better served with a rather plain companion.

The 1893 Mauser, also called the Spanish Mauser, is one of many that offer advantages to those in need of a good down-and-dirty working rifle, not the least of which is a usually modest price. They cock on closing, which is not really a problem; they are usually chambered for the 7x57 round, an effective all-round cartridge. It is factory loaded to moderate pressure levels and adequate ballistics. The rifle has one of the best forms of extractor, and with luck or a little tuning, the two-stage military trigger can be very good. You *can* fit custom triggers and sights and safeties, but for the best bargain, use what's on it. All the standard issue equipment has been proven in war, the hardest test of a rifle.

The little rifle pictured here is an example of a good working tool that fills a need and didn't cost much in either time or money. Other than the checkering and time for the finish to dry, it took less than two hours to complete, starting from a military configuration. It cost me less than $50 and I even got some ammo with it.

Years ago, back in Michigan, a friend gave me the idea of having an alternate rifle for use in the really bad weather that so often accompanies hunting season in Michigan. He uses some pretty fancy rifles, but always keeps a rough weather rifle handy. It is usually some form of Mauser, with most of the military trim left on: a good weapon underneath some protective wood and unfancy iron that, if dinged up or banged around, will not be any major cause for alarm.

In succeeding years I spent a lot of time hunting in Michigan, Colorado, and Montana, and put my share of nicks in various rifles, and even broke the stock of one when it (and I) went over a cliff, but I never got around to a rough-use rifle. Looking back, I admit I could have used guns lots less fancy and I would have done just as well in my hunting efforts.

We are often, for example, obsessed

Rough work, if it's solid, is OK on a rifle expected to take a beating. Writer did not waste time on this ramp.

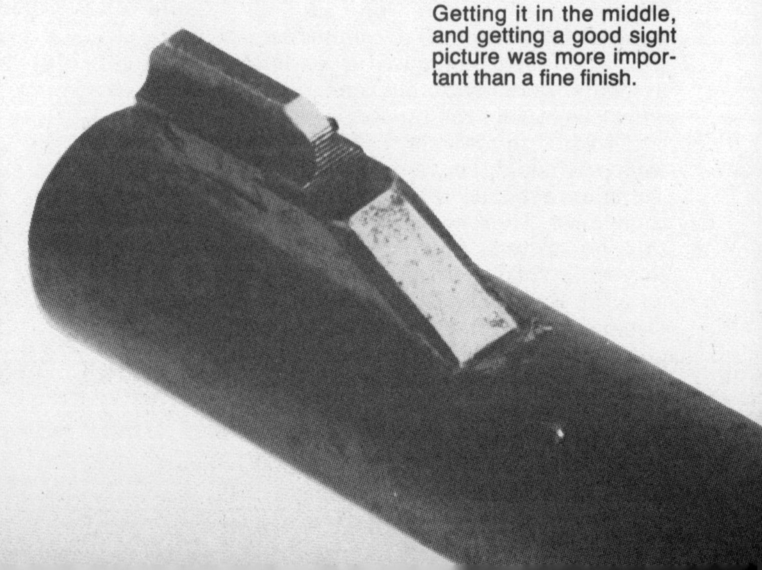

Getting it in the middle, and getting a good sight picture was more important than a fine finish.

ROUGH RIFLE

nearly any military rifle sound trail companion.

with a desire for accuracy in a rifle that will never be needed. I am as guilty as anyone of the unreasonable desire for less-than-MOA rifles, but I have now come to admit that a whole lot less accuracy than that will do just fine for most of my shooting needs.

When I came to Alaska to live I brought nice rifles along. Shortly after I got settled, I started living the outdoor life with a vengeance. I was spending most of my time outdoors in the company of one or more firearms, and I discovered that none of my rifles was at all suited to the rough use of such a life. I cared too much for them. They were all too nice to endure the vicissitudes of a long Alaskan winter riding a thousand miles or more on a snowmobile under my foot.

We use snowmobiles some seven months out of the year as our main form of transportation in the Alaskan bush. I wanted a rifle along at all times for use against fur critters, and in case I came upon a grizzly or black bear while exploring some new country, so I started looking for a rifle to use for this rough work.

One day, a friend hauled this Mauser up from the floor of his pickup truck and handed it over to me to examine. He had no more use for it, and thought I might like to buy it. The rifle looked like it had spent its entire life in places a lot worse than the floor of my friend's pickup, especially the bore. I said so, but was told in good faith that the rifle shot very well indeed. I took that with a grain of salt, but its origin—Deutsche Waffen und Munitionsfabriken, or DWM—and a

Editor's Note:** Writer Odorica has been living in the Alaskan bush where one learns to weld and use a chainsaw and make a snowmobile go, or one moves to town. Readers with less training or aptitude for metalwork who want a rifle like this should see they hire a gunsmith for the following chores: Cut and crown barrel; install ramp front sight; drill and tap for receiver sight; bend bolt handle. With no polish or finish needed, these shouldn't be expensive. **K.W.

good trigger pull decided the matter. I gave him $40 and got the rifle with most of a box of ammo.

It was in pretty much original military trim with 29-inch barrel and a bolt handle that stuck out at a right angle to the stock, pointing east if you

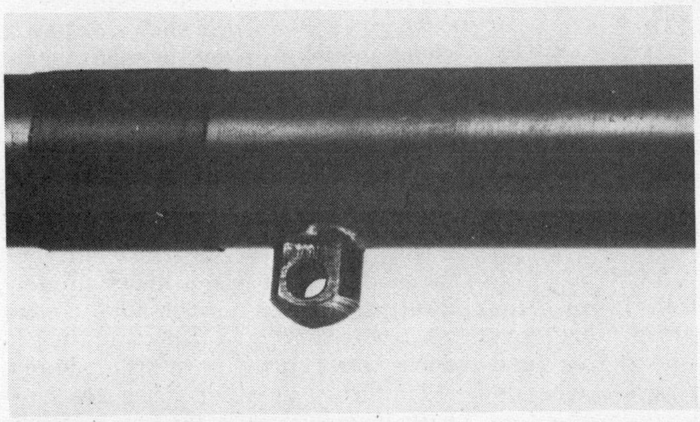

The front sling lug, silver-soldered in place, was made from a standard one, cutting off the screw and shaping the base with a file. That's muzzle tape behind it.

This old Lyman aperture sight is the kind of thing gun people keep just in case, and before your very eyes is a case.

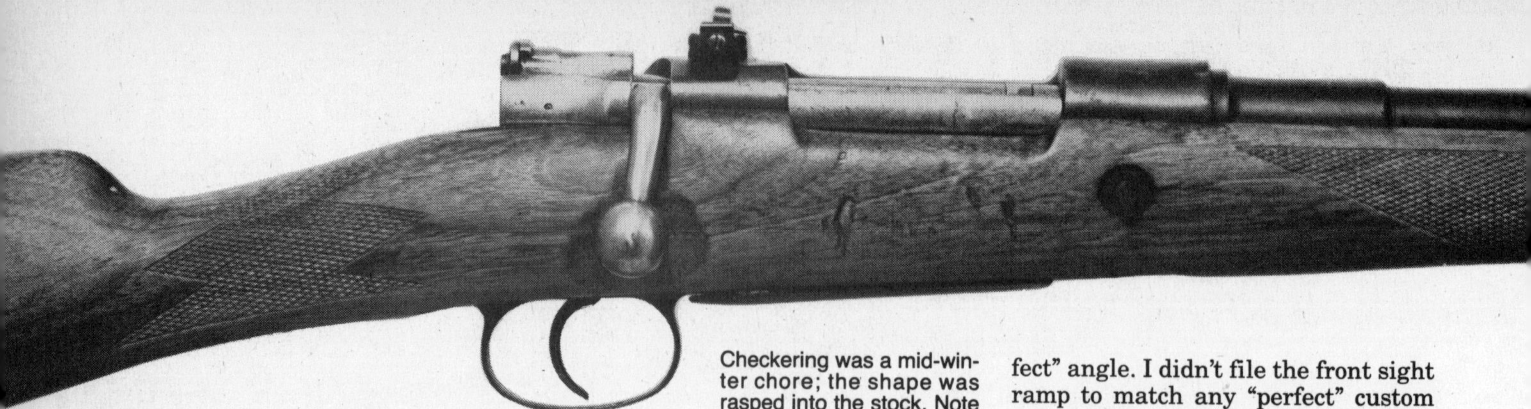

Checkering was a mid-winter chore; the shape was rasped into the stock. Note the cut-down area at the ejector port.

Rear view shows the tight bolt bend, which makes a slim rifle. Military safety is retained: there's a good-sized aperture in the sight.

faced north. It had the original military tangent rear sight and barleycorn front. With hacksaw, files, and an oxy-acetylene torch, a piece of scrap steel for a front sight ramp, and a few odd parts that I had scrounged over the years I made what you see.

I cut nine inches off the barrel, bent the bolt down, fitted aperture rear and sourdough front sights, and trimmed the military stock to a handy size. Metal parts were touched up with cold blue. I didn't spend a lot of time making the bolt bend to the "perfect" angle. I didn't file the front sight ramp to match any "perfect" custom ramp. And I didn't spend hour after hour sanding and whiskering and finishing a fancy stock or polishing metal. I knew that this rifle would get rusty, scuffed, and scratched and did only enough busywork to make the rifle a little handier, so it would therefore tend to always be there.

I got lucky with the rear sight, in that I already had a unit that was custom made for slipping over Mauser bolt releases with very little fitting required. I picked it up years ago at a gun show, figuring it might come in handy someday. It is a Lyman unit, patented in 1905. Iron sights are far less likely to break than even the most durable scopes, and never fog up. I gave the stock a quicky oil finish using Lin-Speed. Then, after the rifle had seen a little use and I knew it was worth the effort, I did a simple job of checkering it during some long Alaskan winter nights.

None of this "custom" work was at all difficult to one accustomed to working with hand tools. There are certainly plenty of suitable old rifles around. In fact, many of these would be used more with this treatment in place of costly rebarreling and restocking. There are many barrels prematurely consigned to the scrap heap that could provide years of acceptable service. As long as the basic unit is sound and the barrel at all usable, why not have at it? A few inquiries at used gun parlors, gun shows, or pawn shops should give you the makings in short order. The military stocks are excellent walnut and fine practice pieces for the beginning checkerer.

If in doubt as to the suitability of a rifle, take it to a qualified gunsmith for a careful appraisal. He can tell you if the gun in question will be suitable for modification into a knock-around hunting rig, and may be able to suggest some short cuts to getting the job done. One caution is in order: Many old military or other rifles are now valued collector items, and either your gunsmith or perhaps a collector friend can tell you if you plan to cut up a museum piece. Make haste slowly.

Fears concerning my rifle barrel's rough condition were groundless, and the little rifle shoots fully as well as I can hold. This is my second custom rifle based on this action. The first was a 257 Roberts I traded off, but I think this new one will be with me for a long time.

Testing it at a remote Alaskan lake with a good hill to back up stray bullets, I picked out a rock some 300 yards away just above the shoreline. The rock sat in an area where I could spot hits against a dirt bank. Now 300 yards was stretching both this rifle's sights and my eyes to the limit. However, I was able to keep all my shots within an area that would approximate the vitals of a deer or caribou at that range.

Continuing my testing at targets of opportunity at closer range, I rediscovered the great speed possible when using a large rear aperture combined with a good visible post front sight. Picking out a tomato can or a clump of dirt at 25 yards, I'd throw the rifle to my shoulder, put the post on the target, and cut loose, trying for a good combination of speed and accuracy. The little M93 was fully up to it, and when the front sight was on target as the shot broke, the target broke. I saw no bear, but it took my share of ptarmigan and rabbit, all I asked of it.

It is always there at the side of my snowmobile in its scabbard with a piece of tape over the muzzle to keep out water, and a bread wrapper loose around the action to keep it from freezing shut. I don't worry about rust, stock damage, or a fogging scope. While it is no Rigby Mauser, this working tool does have a certain amount of elegance in its simplicity of form and function. It does a job I'd never ask of any fine and valuable custom rifle—day in and day out service under very harsh conditions.

You don't have to run an Alaskan trapline to have a need for such a handy little rifle. You can do a lot of hunting, fun shooting, practicing, and even instructing with a good solid and plain Mauser. Part of the money you save over a more costly rifle can be used for loading dies, powder, and bullets and you can therefore get in lots of shooting with the rifle. A bit of regular practice will go a long way toward overcoming any accuracy deficiency the rifle may have. Military Mausers deserve a lot of consideration if you are in the market for a good rough rifle. ●

This clip-loading hump was filed down to clear the unique old Lyman sight. The lever unlocks it.

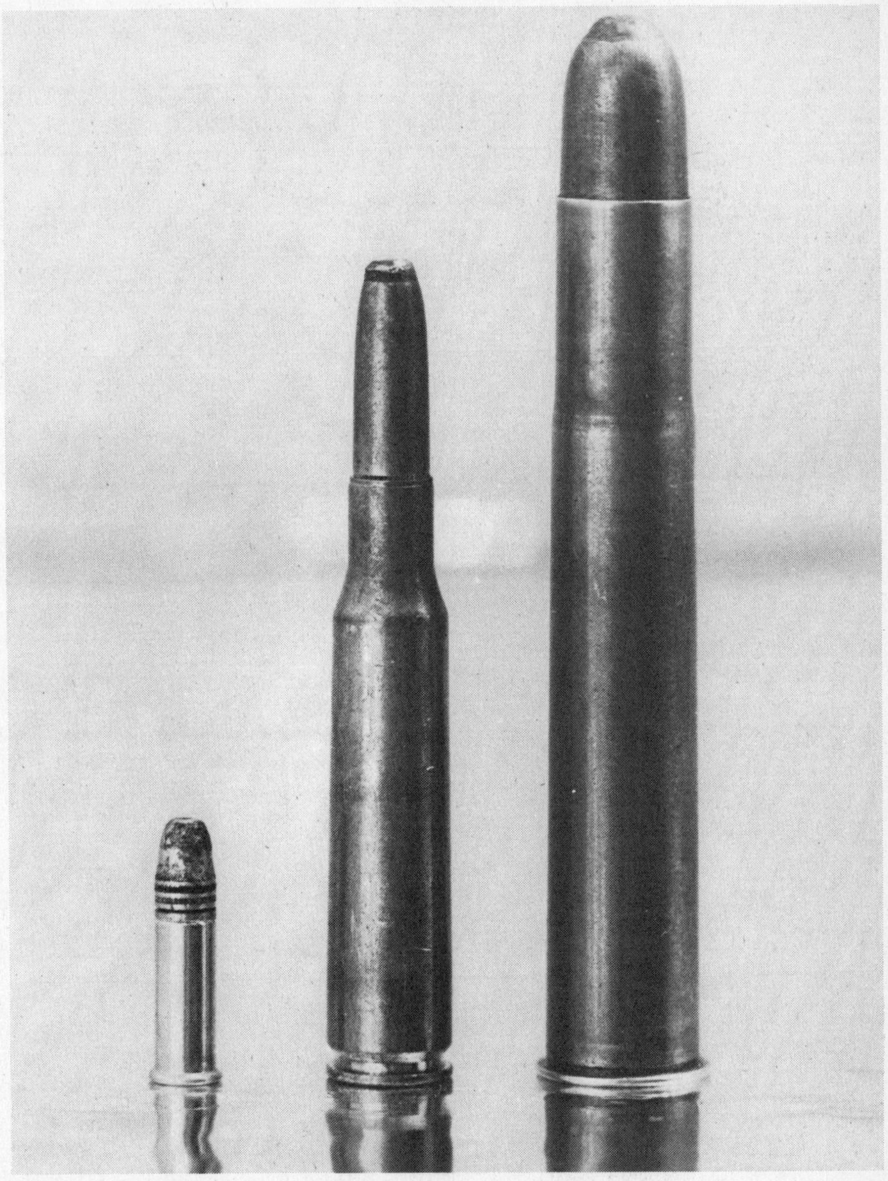

The 7x57mm at center overshadows both the 22 Long Rifle and the 470 Nitro when it comes to versatility. It's enough gun for Alaska's bush.

the HOLES in

by **LEON DAY**

STOPPING POWER THEORY

No one who already knows he knows the truth should read this.

FROM HUNTERS talking about stopping power, you get simple and direct ideas derived from their experiences. They will tell you that the movement of the game after it is hit depends strictly on the damage done to relevant parts of the critter's anatomy. No hunter of any experience will pretend for a second that a deer shot through the guts or the left hind leg will fall down in a swoon and wait for a second shot—rather, they think it will try to run off.

This is not the attitude you find in policemen and soldiers. Many of them think that their human targets are very different, and that certain calibers or bullet weights or bullet constructions or velocities will produce nervous collapse and prostration even if nothing essential to fighting or fleeing is damaged. I used to think so, myself.

Everybody who has reflected on it realizes that bullets—especially handgun bullets—don't have any knock-down power. Our projectiles are fine for punching holes in things, but lousy for pushing them around. The impact of a bullet is of too short a duration to overcome the inertia of anything heavy. The momentum of the bullet and that of the recoiling weapon are roughly the same, so any firearm that could knock down your attacker would certainly floor you at the same moment. Finally, the experience of men wearing body armor shows that so long as the bullet doesn't penetrate the skin most men can run, shoot, and do anything else needed in a fight.

If an animal moves violently when shot, that's the animal moving, not the slug moving the animal. I noticed this with the first rabbit I shot. The critter turned a backward somersault that any gymnast would be proud of and wound up pointed south instead of north. Since I had shot from the east, it was plain that my bullet hadn't *pushed* the beast through this gyration. I soon found that I could depend on this dramatic display whenever I hit a rabbit just behind the head. But if I shot at a dead rabbit, or a sandbag of the same weight, my 22 wouldn't produce more than a twitch. This was a novelty to a 12-year-old, because shooting at tin cans had led me to expect that things shot would bounce around some.

While few people believe in "knock-down," quite a few brilliant men have believed in "stopping power" or "shocking power." The best of these in recent times is Carroll E. Peters, author of *Defensive Handgun Effectiveness*. Peters' work is a mathematical elaboration of the formulas of Julian S. Hatcher. Hatcher's work, in turn, is designed to agree with the experimental test firings of Major Louis Anatole LaGarde and Captain John T. Thompson, who tried some of the weapons available in 1904 against live steers.

All these authorities deserve more than a casual salute. Thompson was the developer of the Thompson submachine gun; LaGarde wrote *Gunshot Injuries,* which remained the primary medical text on the subject until well beyond WW II; and Col. (later Major General) Hatcher brought ballistic science to millions of practical shooters in a series of interesting and well-written works.

Popular articles on handgun stopping power are easy to find, but a serious student really needs Hatcher's *Textbook of Pistols and Revolvers,* where his theory of stopping power is presented in detail. Since it is long out of print, we should review the theory briefly.

Hatcher's first effort at a stopping power theory was presented in 1927 in his book *Pistols and Revolvers and Their Use*. Hatcher ranked pistol cartridges by multiplying their cross-sectional area by their muzzle energy by a shape factor accounting for the form of the bullet. This produced an evaluation of pistol ammo that in general, substantiated the common experience that bigger is better, but the exceptions were bothersome. Hatcher had two accounts of the Thompson-LaGarde tests, one from LaGarde's *Gunshot Injuries,* another from an article by Stephen Trask in the magazine *Arms and the Man*. Neither gave good marks to 30 Luger and 30 Mauser, but by the energy formula those rounds ranked above 38 S&W and nearly equaled 38 Long Colt. Further, 9mm Luger came in ahead of *all* contemporary 38-cal. revolver loads. This worried Hatcher more than somewhat.

So, in 1935 in *Textbook of Pistols and Revolvers,* Hatcher published a revised formula—cross-sectional area times *momentum* times shape factor. This put all those foreign cartridges in their place. In spite of its flat point, 9mm Luger was now slightly below 38 Super Auto. In spite of their high energy, 30 Luger and 30 Mauser were now ranked barely superior to 380 ACP. The theory was now in line with conventional wisdom.

No additions were made to stopping power theory for 17 years. In 1952, the Medical Corps produced a volume of theoretical and experimental studies titled *Wound Ballistics*. By animal tests, cadaver tests, and gelatin studies the GI doctors established that the actual damage done to an animal was proportional to the energy lost by any projectile in its impact with the body.

Basing himself on these findings, medical examiner Vincent J. DiMaio published in *FBI Law Enforcement Bulletin,* Dec., 1974, "A Comparison of Wounding Effects of Commercially Available Ammunition Suitable for Police Use." This study by the Southwest Institute of Forensic Science was simple and straightforward. The medics shot at 6-inch blocks of flesh-simulating gelatin. The speed of the bullet was measured going in, and measured going out again, and the difference in energy was taken as a figure of wounding effectiveness. Simple.

This study provoked some controversy. By 1974, jacketed hollow-points were popular in all calibers, and many cops probably supposed that some 38-cal. loadings were as good as some 45 loadings. But few uniformed or civilian shooters were prepared to believe that a 22 revolver could do as much actual damage as a 44 Special with the standard round-nose bullet. Many marksmen were plainly dismayed by the idea that from now on a ruler would be insufficient for making a choice of weapons. Slide rules and calculators were beating on the doors of people who were uncomfortable with even the basic mathematics of Hatcher's Relative Stopping Power formula.

Less than a year later, the Department of Justice released its study *An Evaluation of Police Handgun Ammunition*. This document brought a new wave of shocks and surprises to everyone who thought they understood bullets. The humble 38-cal. wadcutter loads, intended for nothing more hostile than a piece of paper, ranked about halfway up the list of 142 tested loadings. They were fully three times as effective in wounding power as the 38 158-grain lead round-nose loads that most police departments still carried on duty. The paper-punchers also dumped nearly twice the energy in a 6-inch gelatin block as the much-honored 45 ACP. The tests also revealed that many expanding bullets never did, and the ammo manufacturers consistently fibbed about how fast their slugs would go.

Many denounced the new tests, but others, more scientifically inclined, screened the results with great interest. Those who had really studied Hatcher's Formula had long realized

MORE ON NUMBERS

BULLET/grs. Round-Nose Hardball 45-cal.	VELOCITY feet-per-second	ENERGY foot-lbs.	HATCHER SCORE	PETER'S IMPULSE
500	391	169	62.5	.692
400	488.75	212.2	"	.774
300	651.6	282.9	"	.894
230	850	369	"	1.02
180	1086.1	471	"	1.15
140	1394.4	606	"	1.31
60	3258.3	1414	"	2.0

Here are seven loads, some real, some only possible. They all have the same Hatcher score—62.5—though they vary from sedate to frantic in velocity and energy. Few would believe they had the *same* stopping power, but Hatcher's formula says they do.

Hatcher disregarded energy entirely, although that is hard to tell in the welter of calibers, point forms and momentums. And something else: Hatcher said "stopping power" doesn't apply to very scared or angry men, which seems to mean that it disappears at the moment of need. Peters' rankings show a steady progression and is a description of relationships that might be useful.

Leon Day

that its weakest point was the form factors assigned to different bullet shapes. The new data seemed to them an opportunity to discover *actual,* not approximate, figures. The best of these researchers was Carroll E. Peters.

Peters' book, *Defensive Handgun Effectiveness,* is an inspiring *individual* achievement. With no government grants, and no impressive equipment except his mind, he has made it practical for a shooter to know in advance the momentum loss in any thickness of flesh, the energy loss, the penetration in soft wood, and the recoil of nearly any bullet at common velocities. Any shooter can sit down with the book and a hand calculator and learn nearly as much about the combat utility or any current or hypothetical load as the Justice Department discovered in 1975 with a million dollar laboratory.

Because Peters' book lets us figure out how our slugs will act in flesh, it will be extremely useful even if Hatcher's Theory is *wrong*. Hatcher thought that stopping power was proportional to the momentum the bullet lost in the human body. He did no tests himself on live animals which could either verify that there was any such phenomenon as stopping power, or that momentum was the key to it. Rather, he constructed his theory to agree with what he knew had been established by the Thompson-LaGarde handgun tests of 1904. He believed those firings against live steers to be extensive and definitive, and saw no purpose in repeating them.

Thanks to the Old Army Branch of the National Archives, I now have a copy of the original Thompson-LaGarde Report. Of the 13 cattle shot, not one collapsed from anything resembling our modern conception of "stopping power." Nor did the live animal firings justify that board's recommendation that any new service pistol should be at least 45 caliber. *(Editor's Note: That's right. The hoopla of 75 years has been based on 13 dead beef animals. Why, I have shot nearly that many myself. KW)*

Hatcher apparently never had this document. In his book, he refers only to a chapter in LaGarde's *Gunshot Injuries* and a description of the tests in *Arms and the Man* by Stephen Trask. When I saw that there were discrepancies between the two accounts, I decided that I needed the original and set the Archives searching.

My suspicions about stopping power and shock effect were also aroused by Hatcher's extensive use of what doctors call "anecdotal material." We all like to hear stories about gunfights, and there are enough in *Textbook of Pistols and Revolvers* to please anybody. But if a 45 failed to stop its target, some excuse was always made for the cartridge. None were offered for 32s and 38s. In fact, at one point it is suggested that anybody who drops from a non-lethal hit with a small caliber must be a sissy quitter, or must have been totally surprised. Thus the reader was encouraged to discount any incident in his knowledge when a small caliber was successful. In the following paragraphs, it was explained that people who were excited or desperate wouldn't be stopped by anything less than a hit to heart, brain, or spine. Any failure of a fat slug was thus discounted at once.

So we got a bunch of entertaining war stories, but we were not encouraged to sort them out in any way that contradicted the approved theory.

I'll now describe and summarize the tests themselves. First, a word about the cartridges, many of which are now justly obscure. The 476 Eley did not throw a 48-caliber bullet. Rather, .476" is the diameter of the case body. The *bullet* is very like a 455. This is important because both Hatcher and Peters assume in their calculations that .476" is the diameter of the slug, assigning it a larger cross-sectional area. The four large-caliber bullets in the Thompson-LaGarde tests don't differ appreciably in diameter, only in weight, speed, shape, and energy.

Of the 13 animals shot, a total of eight were attacked with the four 45-cal. cartridges. The 30 Luger was used on two critters, and 38 ACP, 38 Long Colt, and 9mm Luger got to show their stuff on one beast apiece. Of the 45s, two types had bullets designed to expand. Both expanded in the testing. Of the smaller calibers, none were constructed to expand without striking bone, and none did.

On the first day, eight animals were shot. The scene was the killing floor of the Nelson Morris Co. Union Stockyards, Chicago. Range was 3 feet. Every effort was made to shoot cattle in non-vital areas, so as to measure stopping power instead of wounding effect. In these summaries, we have rearranged the firings according to caliber, and eliminated unnecessary detail in the autopsies.

(Editor's Note: From the official report, what follows is what happened in 1904. It's middling ugly. There doesn't seem to be an honest way around publishing it. KW)

• 476 Eley

288-grain lead round-nose, 729 fps, 340 ft. lbs.

1st animal: Stag, 4 years old, 1200-1300 lbs. (A stag is a critter castrated after maturity.)

Two shots were fired through the lungs, left to right. The impacts were 4 inches apart. Did not fall for 4 minutes, was dead at 5 minutes.

4th animal: Stag, 1300 lbs.

Shot through the intestines, once. After 2 minutes, shot through intestines again.

After 70 seconds, (3 minutes and 10 seconds from first shot), shot through intestines again.

Still standing at 6 minutes and 10 seconds, the beast was shot twice in the head.

Standing at 7 minutes and 15 seconds, shot in the ear.

Standing at 8 minutes and 15 seconds, shot behind the ear.

With no effect noted, the animal was killed with four blows of a sledgehammer to the head. Autopsy showed that no slug had reached the brain.

• 455 Man-Stopper

lead cylinder, hollow point, hollow base, 218.5 grains, 801 fps, 312 ft. lbs.

8th animal: Stag, 1250 lbs.

Shot once through lungs left to right.

After 1 minute, shot again through lungs.

At 2 minutes and 10 seconds, shot through intestines

At 3 minutes and 15 seconds, shot through intestines.

At 4 minutes and 15 seconds, showing "no particular manifestation of pain or shock" animal was killed with hammer. The bullets recovered from the abdomen, where no bone was struck, were uniformly expanded.

• 45 Colt

220-grain hollow point, 700 fps, 239 ft. lbs.

6th animal: Cow, 1000 lbs.

One shot through lungs.

At 1 minute, shot through lungs again.

At 2 minutes, began to fall and was shot through the abdomen twice.

Both bullets shot through the lungs struck ribs and expanded. Only one bullet was recovered from the abdomen, and it was undeformed.

• 45 Colt

250-grain lead bullet with small flat on point, 720 fps, 288 ft. lbs.

7th animal: Bull, 10 years old, 1300 lbs.

Shot through lungs.

At 1 minute, shot again through lungs.

At 2 minutes, shot again.

At 2 minutes 35 seconds, shot through abdomen and fell.

At 2 minutes 45 seconds, shot again through abdomen, *got up,* then fell again—tried to regain his feet for 70 seconds—and was killed with the hammer.

• 38 ACP

130-grain round-nose full metal jacket, 1107 fps, 354 ft. lbs.

5th animal: Steer, 1100 lbs. (A steer is a bovine castrated before having any fun at all.)

Shot through lungs.

At 1 minute, shot through lungs again.

At 1 minute 35 seconds, shot again, same way.

The animal fell only after four blows with the hammer. The two bullets recovered had struck ribs and were slightly flattened. The last struck no rib and was lost.

• 38 Long Colt

148-grain round-nose lead, 723 fps, 191 ft. lbs.

3rd animal: Stag, 1200 lbs.

Shot through lungs, scampered about.

Two minutes, 30 seconds; shot through lungs again, jumped around.

Three minutes, 20 seconds; shot again, staggered for 30 seconds and fell.

This critter had a 16″x18″ tumor of the right lung. Further, it was discovered that the last shot had punched through the aorta.

• 30 Luger

92.5-grain full-jacket flat point, 1420 fps, 415 ft. lbs.

2nd animal: Stag, 1200-1300 lbs.

Shot through lungs left to right; dropped 30 seconds later.

Autopsy showed that bullet cut posterior aorta, left body and was lost. Contusion surrounding the wound track described as "not quite so extensive as with 476 revolver."

At the end of the first day's tests, Thompson and LaGarde could not have been very happy. They had shown that bullets through the aorta led to prompt collapse from bleeding, that shots through the lungs led to *eventual* collapse by suffocation, and that shots through the intestines might fell the foe the next day through peritonitis and hemorrhage. Nothing like Stopping Power or Shock Effect had happened. Sometimes the animals had showed fright; sometimes blood flowed from mouth and nose as a result of bleeding in the lungs, but on the first day no critter fell promptly with any non-lethal wound. Not only did these shootings fail to show the superiority of the 45s, they did not demonstrate that "stopping power" existed at all.

So, on the second day, a new procedure was adopted. Animals were now to be shot as fast as possible, until they fell, or until they had been hit 10 times. It was hoped that the shock to the nervous system was additive, and that the number of shots needed to floor an animal would reveal the relative merit of the cartridges being tested.

On the second day five cattle were shot.

• 476

12th animal: Bull, 1100-1150 lbs.

Dropped after sixth shot. All shots through lungs.

• 455 Man-Stopper

13th animal: Bull, 1150 lbs.

Five shots through lungs.

After 30 seconds, three more shots through lungs.

After one more minute, two more shots through lungs, animal began to fall and two more shots were fired through abdomen.

Abdominal shots mushroomed to .70; all others were deformed to some extent.

• 45 Colt

flat point

9th animal: Cow, 950 lbs.

Shot through lungs, fell at the sixth shot.

Free hemorrhage from one exit wound; four bullets recovered, considerably deformed.

• 9mm Luger

FMJ, flat point, 123.5 grains, 1048 fps, 301 ft. lbs.

11th Animal: Cow 1100 lbs.

Shot twice through lungs.

After 1 minute, (there was a jam) shot six more times through lungs.

After reloading break, shot twice through abdomen and twice through lungs.

Killed with hammer.

• 30 Luger

10th animal: Cow, 950 lbs.

Shot through lungs, three times.

After 1 minute, (to clear jam) shot five times.

After reloading break, shot twice; then killed with hammer.

On the second day, two of the five animals fell promptly. The bull hit with 455 Man-Stopper had stood for a minute and a half, taking 10 lung hits before collapse. The two Luger rounds couldn't be fairly compared to the revolver loads, for their jams had given the targets a considerable intermission for recovery. And if the felled steers had dropped from shock effect, why not from wounding effect? Shock effect is hypothetically cumulative, but wounding effect is certainly cumulative. The lesser calibers were not given a fair test, and *still* the 45s didn't look very good.

In their report to the Ordnance Department, Thompson and LaGarde recommended that any new service pistol be at least 45 caliber. They maintained that *caliber* was important, not velocity or energy. But they hedged their conclusions thusly:

". . .the Board is of the opinion that soldiers armed with pistols or revolvers should be drilled unremittingly in the accuracy of fire, and that the vital parts of the body, their location and distribution in the organism, should be intelligently explained. Based upon the distribution of the vital parts, and parts of the body which when hit insure sudden stopping of an adversary, the Board hopes, in its complete report, to furnish a target of a shape to include the more essential points to be hit in the body . . . The Board has been prompted to refer to this point because of the prime importance of decisive shooting at close quarters, and of the large amount of the target area of the human body which *offers no hope of stopping an adversary by shock or other immediate results when hit.*"

You may think a 45 slug through the abdomen or the muscles of the arm will make you fall down in a swoon. Maybe it will, especially since you *think* it should, but Thompson and LaGarde did not believe it. They wanted soldiers trained to make head, heart, and spine shots.

Neither Col. LaGarde nor Stephen Trask remembered the tests rightly in later years. Trask says of the quick-firing test:

" . . .the steers shot with 38 ACP and 38 Long Colt dropped after six or seven shots . . ."

But, as we have seen, neither of these cartridges was used in the quick-firing.

"With the 45 Colt revolver the steers dropped after the fourth or fifth shot . . ."

But as we have seen, no critter dropped before six hits.

"With the 455 and the 476, they dropped after the third or fourth shot . . ."

Which didn't happen.

Harder to understand is the way Col. LaGarde misquotes himself in *Gunshot Injuries:*

"The animals invariably dropped to the ground when shot from three to five times with the larger caliber Colt's revolver bullets . . ."

But in truth, both 476 and 45 Colt needed all six. And 455 needed 10.

The remarks for 45 Colt—"free hemorrhage from one exit wound"—suggest an artery hit. But this was not investigated.

You can't prove anything about stopping power from the Thompson-LaGarde live animal tests. Maybe it exists, but not at handgun energy levels. Maybe it exists in people, but not in animals. And maybe it doesn't exist at all, and every combat shooter should use his handgun as deliberately as a surgeon wields a knife.

A modern experimenter would do things very differently. He would shoot more critters—say, 10 for each load. He would take pains to have all of them about the same age, weight, sex, and glandular condition. He would assign the same number of beasts to each cartridge. He would test a wider variety of cartridges, and make sure that expanding bullets were available in each caliber. All these things Thompson and LaGarde could have done, but they neglected them. They did not get Man-Stopper slugs for 38 Long Colt, or hollow-points for 30 Luger, 9mm, and 38 ACP. They did, however get 476 Eley from Britain and have a Colt New Service chambered for it. And 32-20, 38-40, and 44-40 were available at the corner store, but they were not tested.

So the work of Hatcher—and to some degree the work of Peters—is based on a false understanding of both the quality and the results of the live animal tests of 1904. If anyone wishes to claim that stopping power is some phenomenon independent of wound effect, he will have to prove it some other way.

In the cadaver testing there was much better uniformity among the targets: All were dead. These human bodies were hung by the head and shot with various loads at various ranges—3 feet, 37.5 yards, and 75 yards. The amount the corpses swayed when hit permitted the board to estimate (they did not measure) the momentum imparted to the target.

A little anatomy: Between the joints, human bones are hard, strong, and brittle; sort of like glass tubes. At the joint ends, the bones become much thicker to provide a large bearing area, and though the hard outer layer—the cortex—is thinner, it is backed up by a thick layer of spongy honeycomb. So we should expect a bullet to have different effects in different parts of the same bone.

When flesh alone was hit, only the hollow-points—45 Colt HP and 455 Man-Stopper—produced any sway at all. When the joint ends of bone were hit, all loads made a pretty similar twitch, though 455 and 476 seemed somewhat better.

When the hard shafts of bones were fired on, there was enough difference in the amount of sway for the researchers to put numbers on it. However, you must remember that these are not *measurements,* but subjective impressions.

38 Long Colt lead round-nose	50
30 Luger, flat point FMJ	60
38 ACP, round nose FMJ	60
30 Luger FP-FMJ, *tip filed*	60+
38 ACP soft-point	70
38 ACP RN FMJ, *filed*	70
9mm Luger FP-FMJ	80
45 Colt, lead small flat	80
45 Colt, lead hollow-point	85
455 Man-Stopper	87
476 (really 455) lead round-nose	100

The impressions don't line up according to caliber. The 30 Luger FMJ flat-point did better than 38 Long Colt, and equaled 38 ACP RN-FMJ. 9mm Luger FP-FMJ matched 45 Colt lead flat-point.

In wounding effect against the bones, all these rounds were *tactically* equal. All could easily produce a compound fracture of shin or thigh bone, making it impossible for a man to run, and difficult for him even to stand.

Directed at the softer joint ends, all but one round punched simple holes that would not always be prompt handicaps. The 455 Man-Stopper would fracture joint-ends at 3 feet, but failed even to penetrate them at a distance.

LaGarde did observe that the revolver fractures were more complex, and would take longer to heal. This isn't relevant to gun-fighting. The break may knit in 6 weeks, or it may take 10—gunfights don't last that long. Six weeks after the fight, the survivors are sitting around the fire telling lies—oops, *anecdotes*—and the losers are rarely present to correct exaggerations or offer their own.

The live animal testing provided no sound basis for any estimate of stopping power. The cadaver testing proved you could have fine wound effect with the 9mm flat-point, or 38 ACP with a similar bullet. In neither test series did the results justify or support the Board's conclusion that *caliber,* rather than energy or bullet form, was the important factor.

Why did LaGarde make recommendations that his tests would not sustain?

I don't know. It is interesting that the flat-point 9mm recently adopted by the U.S. Air Force is very like the one tested in 1904. We have taken 76 years to come full circle in the design of 9mm military ammo. Louis Anatole LaGarde had a lot to do with that delay. ●

If you think a repeater is too bulky, and can't afford a good double, you might . . .

TRY A SINGLE

by **KEN WARNER**

I GAVE UP my search for the good moderately priced double gun when the dealer cost on the cheapest new gun I could find that came anywhere near the ideal rose above $1000. You—you, the hunter and reader—cannot get what us "experts" think is a good new double for less than $1500.00 to $2000.00.

There are cheaper doubles to be had, of course. They are sturdy, heavy, and often clubby tools, by and large, that offer the *procedural* benefits of double guns, but not what the printed wisdom of the years has perceived as *shooting* benefits. For a time I contemplated altering such guns into the state of balance and weight needed, and that is possible, but not really practical.

So, a couple of years ago, at about the same time as a colleague, Gough Thomas of the British *Shooting Times*, I came to contemplate the single barrel gun as a viable route to the highly-touted shooting graces of the fine double gun. He has discussed the matter in a couple of his trenchant columns, but he operates in the United Kingdom, where brief dalliance with numbers of guns is not simple, and his standards are indubitably higher than mine.

I simply acquired a couple dozen cheap and not so cheap single barrel guns and looked them over, tried them out, lived with them. I tried to confine all my personal shooting to singles for a couple of seasons, but that wasn't wholly possible, and had it been, it wouldn't have made much sense because they were not great seasons.

The idea was to discover if the single barrel gun, suitably employed, offered the procedural and shooting advantages of the fine double without sacrificing too much. I believe it does. That is, unless you are an unusually fine shot you may be disappointed on any single day, but you'll probably bring as many birds to bag over a mixed season with a single gun as any other; after a season or so, your cartridge-to-bird ratio will improve greatly; you will all the while enjoy some other advantages over cheap doubles or expensive repeaters.

And those are the ideal gun advantages you have read of in this and other journals for 30 years or so: the easy management, light weight and simple handling to a quick and hitting shot long considered the sole province of the good double. You don't get the second shot and you can't pay more than $100 or so for one here in the States, so they don't run to refinement in fit and finish. All the rest of it is there when time comes for the shot—a six-pound 12-bore, say, lofting 1⅛ oz. of shot at standard velocities, with much of the weight between your hands.

It's a dead-straight gun, of course, with cast neither on nor off, but that's not much of a trial to American shooters who shoot dead straight guns their whole lives. Pitch and pull length and other buttstock dimension and proportion start as average and can be adjusted to suit as with any gun, perhaps most easily by installing a recoil pad.

There is almost universally a hammer to manage, but that's not the worst of systems, really. The top snap may be a thumb button instead, or even the trigger guard pulled to the rear. And, generally speaking, whatever is in the chamber is ejected when the gun is opened, fired or not. Triggers are, in most current models, crisper than they used to be, and manageable. There may be zinc or sintered or even nylon parts, but what will you? These are the 1980's.

And then, inescapably, there's the look of the currently available singles. They are not ugly, not in a world which includes pump guns and autoloaders. In the main, though, they're ordinary. They are not really sleek or trim, except to the hands. Handsome, when it comes to available single guns, just has to be as handsome does.

My notion of procedural advantage distinct from shooting advantage concerns all that time when one has the gun in hand but is not shooting: one is walking, preparing to shoot, travelling or has arrived home with a gun to clean and store. I have been accustomed to repeating shotguns for 40 years, but find them procedurally far more difficult than the break-open gun.

That is, one pushes or pulls or levers some reasonably obvious appurtenance and the break-open gun breaks open, revealing all—it is either loaded or unloaded, and either way it is out of action. One pops a cartridge (cartridges) into the only fitting place (places) in sight, and shuts the gun.

One soon discovers whether or not one must subsequently unlatch some other mechanism called a "safety" or cock an exposed hammer in order to shoot. Having shot, one need only repeat the process to shoot again. When it's all over, the break-open gun is easily separated into three pieces, which are easy to clean and pack and store.

These are procedural advantages and all the U.S. single guns discussed here have them.

Over the months and years I have been acquainting myself with single-barrels, I have acquired some rather broad opinions of the various brand names and models. Throughout here, when required, I have examined the details, but I do have a general opinion of each sort of shotgun:

First, there is little functional choice among them. The strength of one model is counterbalanced always by a weakness and so on. For me, the realities of weight and gauge and feel are more important than brand name, construction detail or basic design.

The Winchester guns are all sturdy guns of full weight. They are more comfortable to shoot in cold blood than all the rest. They are done up nicely and present a good appearance, but there are some anomalies. For instance, the Model 37 Winchester in 28 gauge furnished to me is built on a full 20-gauge frame, it seems, and the barrel has very thick walls. The gun weighs 7¼ pounds and really does not make a lot of practical sense.

The Winchester Model 37 Youth gun is the choice for the sturdy youngster with good shoulders and arms. It is heavier by 19 ounces at 6 lb., 7 oz., than its Stevens counterpart. The standard Model 37 12-bore, with 30-inch barrel, makes the most immediate pick-it-up-and-go-hunting gun, although obviously it is not suitable for all shooting. It weighs 6 lb., 7 oz., carries very nicely, and delivers a genuine full choke pattern to the point of aim.

On balance, the Winchesters are the most conservative in most respects of the generally available single shots; certainly, a great many people would consider them the most handsome.

The Stevens-Savage guns seem more to be to be built for hunters who walk a lot and carry guns more than they shoot. They seem in general to be quicker to the shot; obviously, because of their lighter weight recoil is more of a factor. Their checkering is pressed checkering; the stock finishes over hardwoods are somewhat syrupy looking; but the guns really do perform.

The Savage Model 94 Youth gun has the right dimension and the right weight for even a relatively small kid, but any parent who tried to teach a child to shoot using this gun without using very light-recoil handloads would be doing both the child and the sport a disservice. Once that hurdle is passed, the Savage Youth gun for an accomplished youth shooter would provide an excellent field companion.

The shape and balance and the stock measurements of the Savage-Stevens line, which has several different breech and opening mechanisms, seem to be right down the center line of American need. Comb drop and drop at heel and pitch are all esoterica, to be sure, but they really count in gun feel; the Savage-Stevens guns have good gun feel.

The Harrington & Richardson guns strip away all the non-essentials and deliver handy working guns in all of the right combinations. A Harrington & Richardson 28-bore, for instance, weighs just five pounds, and is as lively a shotgun as one could find, no matter the price. The Topper 12 and 20-bore slug specials are particularly well suited to the utility role. In practice, the functioning of the H&R guns in the hands—the mechanics of loading, cocking, firing, unloading and reloading—are very straightforward and people learn them easily.

One day a friend came by my place about 2:30 and suggested we run about an hour down-country and shoot some doves. I grabbed the most recently shot single-barrel and a box of shells and a stool and left. It came on to rain, but I got seven legitimate shots and picked up five birds. The gun was an H&R 20-ga. Buck Special with rifle sights and cylinder bore and the loads were Skeet 9's and I was left with hardly a thing to say.

Those are the three mainstream American brands. Possibly equal to at least two of them in sales are the guns imported from Brazil by F.I.E. These guns are made in two factories and are two very different guns. One of them, called the CBC by people who know, is made by the Remington subsidiary in Brazil, and we are told, in fact, that it is marketed outside the U.S. as a Remington. The other is the ERA, which is very much a Brazilian-style utility gun, but it has some specific virtue. Certainly, for the money, these guns represent very good value, although their construction details and general design are distinctly imported. Where money is important—even though where we're talking just about a very few dollars—the imports are functional guns. Where extreme light weight is likely to be useful, one or two of them are very good choices. In general, their chokes are exceedingly tight. Galef brings in a familiar pat-

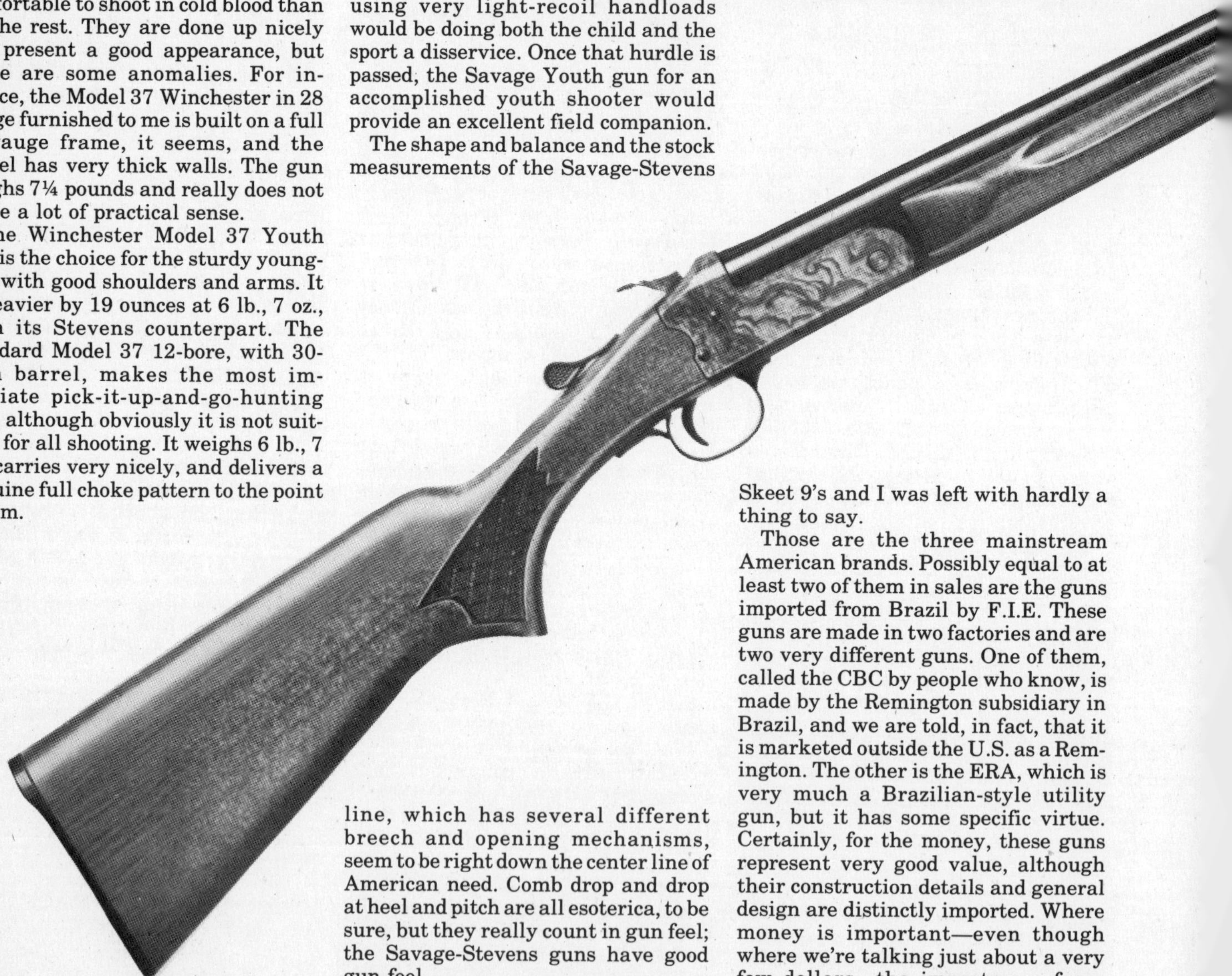

Most typical current single-barrel is probably the Savage Model 94, with top-lever, case-hardened receiver, relatively light weight, in choice of four gauges.

tern of gun—the folding shotgun—and it has much to recommend it. including its being a true hammerless design. And there are a number of Russian models around also.

One British single gun that has

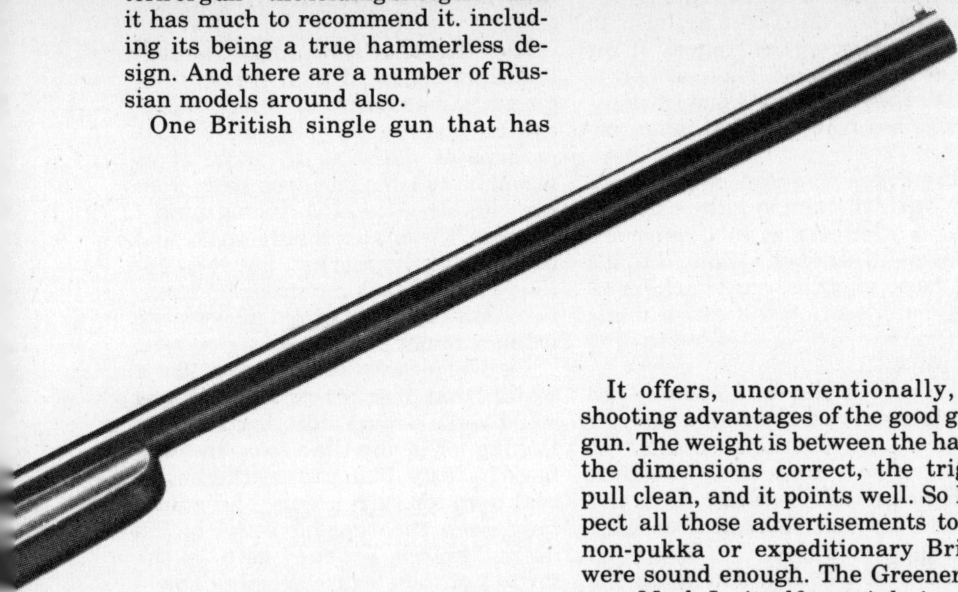

received a certain amount of American attention in print is the Greener GP gun, GP meaning General Purpose, no doubt. This is a sturdy mechanism, a large Martini action, that yet permits a six-pound gun. Gotten up with British ideas in stocking, it has long—decades and decades and decades—been touted in the U.K. as the useful expedition gun for rough service and as sound enough for use by the lower echelons of overseas British wherever there is shooting.

Getting one was not so simple in 1979 and in the end I had to prevail on a friend to import three and pay a stiff price. When it arrived it proved to be a Mark I, not a GP, and quite a bit different in manufacturing detail from the GP I knew of, but the same gun in broad general terms. It was fun to shoot and I shot it well, but really it's a different story—its management, though no problem at all, seems to me enough different from the rest to take it out of consideration here.

For the record, the gun weighs 6¼ pounds, has a 27½" barrel with full choke. It never even hiccuped. Once you learn to manage this underlever action, its manners are very good indeed. I did get it onto the wrong dove field and can tell you it is not the right machine for 20-yard doves because that choke is really tight and my reputation in southern Arizona will never recover, but it was all in the interest of science. (Ordinarily, I have little compunction about reaming out unnecessary choke, but in the case of this Greener, it is so extraordinarily tight I thought I'd wait and examine that separately.)

It offers, unconventionally, the shooting advantages of the good game gun. The weight is between the hands, the dimensions correct, the trigger pull clean, and it points well. So I expect all those advertisements to the non-pukka or expeditionary British were sound enough. The Greener GP—or Mark I—itself certainly is.

Taking the general availabilities into account, it ought to be obvious in this short description that any man with access to a full display of the commonly available single shots can, within the limit of the single shotgun idea, suit himself. He will have barrel work to do, of course, if he wants anything but a full choke or modified, and he might want to spend a little money or time getting a recoil pad, not so much because a recoil pad is required, but that it affords the opportunity to give the gun the proper length and pitch, but all that aside, there is a single gun in the United States to suit any pocketbook and most sporting uses.

There is one unmitigated joy to the American single-barrel shotgun. One can go to the field with his tested choice, and can leave in the car a second gun, identical or different, as a back-up without undue concern over its physical safety or the investment involved. These days, investment in an entirely suitable second single does not amount to two or three days' pay for a laboring man. They offer, therefore, peace of mind on money, at least, and surcease of worry in the rain.

One ought not buy a single-shot gun and head merrily out to hunt. I recommend shooting at least 100 rounds quickly so one can detect incipient or actual malfunctions while the gun dealer still remembers his name. It has not been my experience that singles malfunction or are mis-manufactured anymore than ordinary American factory arms. They are made for the mass market, however, and they are not all perfect.

Beyond that, the firing of 100 rounds does a great deal to smooth out the inevitable burrs, relieve the crankiness of new parts, and familiarize the new owner with his new possession. That first 100 rounds, by the way, does more to accomplish this than all the subsequent firing, although with use and in the hands of the man that knows it, almost any single barrel becomes a rapidly worked and comfortable shooting tool. The experience of those of my colleagues who do a great deal of testing is that the bulk of malfunctions to be discovered in any firearm are found in that first 100 rounds.

In the current case, I left all but one of my 25 or so single shots just as they came from the box and shot them that way. There is not world enough or time to work over a dozen guns to suit. I did do that one, though.

In pursuit of knowledge and a good gun, I took a standard 28-inch barreled $70 (at the time) Savage Model 94 12-gauge and spent $55 in gunsmithing on it. (Well, that is what it would cost to have the same work done by a fellow of equal talent to the fellow who did my work.) I didn't do much. I had a first-class recoil pad installation accomplished to put the pull length at 15 inches, which is an eighth-inch longer than I am told is perfect for me, but I intended this gun for a shirt-sleeve gun anyway. The other work involved removing all but .006-inch of choke.

At that point, ready for the woods, I had a 5¾-pound, very fast, very positive slim shoulder arm that proved to be very efficient in the harvesting of feathered game. It was a great pleasure also to carry, was about as safe a mechanism as a firearm can be in the hands of a man in the field, and its management and manipulation was at no time, even the end of the day, difficult. I don't even think the gun is bad-looking, although it is not anything like my Churchill-style AyA, a handsome Brescian hammer 20 I own, or a Westley Richards that has my allegiance. Perhaps handsome really is as handsome does. And more certainly, alongside those excellent repeaters and doubles I own, this Savage 94 will always have its place.

I found a number of things using it and about three other singles extensively over a period of time. Except when I missed, I found little to fault with any of them, and some things to praise.

One hidden benefit of single-barrel guns is the considerably reduced load of ammunition one need carry. For instance, in a hard day of Pennsylvania pheasant hunting, one is really unlikely to get fair shots at more than 10 birds. If one carries a single-barrel gun, he therefore need carry no more than 10 shells. A confident marksman might carry no more than three or four shells where the limit is three birds, but I have never—not to remember—seen a marksman so confident.

Most fellows who straggle off away from their cars in the uplands carry, if they intend to be gone for the morning, the best part of a box of shotshells if they shoot magazine guns. The single-gun gunner would be planning glorious sport indeed were he to load his pockets with more than 10 cartridges.

Quite naturally, then, some of the other accoutrements of sport become unnecessary. You certainly do not need a shell vest, and if you claim you need it to carry the game, then that is because you have too heavy a gun. The veteran single-gun shooter knows very well that he can carry two-thirds of a pheasant limit in one hand and his gun in the other and be none the worse for it. In all, as these things are added up, the single shooter may leave pounds and pounds of gear at the gate, compared to his multi-shot brethren.

When the time comes to shoot, it is marvelous how uncluttered the mind is for the single-shooter. It isn't so much a deadly grim determination to succeed in spite of having only one shot, nor is it a fear of failure, but rather a calm realization that what is happening right now is what has to be dealt with, because what happens next is not going to happen for five or fifteen seconds.

I know because I have enjoyed playing a little game with a couple of friends which we call "single-barrel Skeet." It is played just as we shoot regular Skeet, except for the doubles. The doubles are thrown as singles just five seconds apart. That is, the shooter calls for the first bird and, willy-nilly, hit or not, ready or not, five counts later the other birds comes out of the other house. One learns with this game how to load a single barrel quickly and I have been treated to watching a good friend break 24 birds in a single-barrel Skeet round. He had, I might add, the full and complete attention of all the other members of the squad throughout the entire performance.

Concerning technique, we found no single way to success in the quick-loading of a single-barrel gun. That is, one fellow gets along with an extra shell tucked in his hatband; the next must carry the shells he intends to load in his left hand out along the forend; and the third does better with one shell between the fingers of his right or trigger hand. There are probably 16 other ways to get the job done, so, as so much in shooting, it all depends.

If the doves or ducks or geese are flying well, the single gun is no bad handicap whatever so long as you're only going to shoot one limit. If that's three geese, or six assorted ducks or 12 doves, you'll get them all with a single gun if you're shooting well and they're flighting well.

The same is true on good days in good pheasant country with a three or four-bird limit, and the circumstances of most good grouse and woodcock cover mean there's really only one good shot per flush. On called turkeys, the single works fine.

The fellow who can double on the flush of a quail covey—well, the single puts him out of it. The joy of the right and left is gone wherever it existed. After a time, it might be replaced by long strings of days with, say, six or seven birds in bag for each ten shells, which has its own satisfactions, particularly on the days when it's eight birds.

To a degree, perhaps, we choose our guns and enjoy them on the basis of the identities carried with them. It would be easily possible to carry this thought to a ridiculous degree, since functionality and price and many other factors also enter into the selection of a gun for purchase or a gun for use on a given day.

Nevertheless, I am just as happy setting off to the hedges for, say, pheasants with a single-barrel shotgun that costs maybe $80 even in these inflation-ridden times as I am with a Westley Richards ejector double. And I own both guns. Maybe that means the day in the field is what counts with me; it may also be that I care just as much about the stereotype of a farm boy kicking out the home brush rows with a hammer single as I do for the stereotype of the tweedy connoisseur of fine guns, dogs and fast automobiles who shoots the expensive double.

Your reporter, and a colleague overseas, and doubtless some other people, would like to see a very nicely done single barrel gun for sporting use. It would have a selective ejector, a hammerless top-snap action, some grace of line, and a suitable choice of barrels and chokes and ribs and the like. It would be light for gauge and, as all of us collectively see it in our minds' eyes, it would be altogether a thing of grace and beauty. And it would cost lots less than an equivalent double gun.

Now that I have acquired this shallow experience with a great many single guns in a number of different situations, I agree wholeheartedly that perhaps as many as 15 or 20 of us would buy such a gun each year, were it available. After a very long time, I am sure, the quality single would find its place in the market, but it is unlikely anyone but a pioneer and venturesome capitalist would invest what it takes to put one there.

That capitalist would have, for a while, that market to himself and could make a mark in it, but I am not looking for it any time soon. In barefaced honesty, I have to say there is no real need for such a gun. The guns I have been shooting have few of the desired graces, but they do have the virtues of the elegant sporting gun—they are easy to carry, quick to swing, reliable in function and they shoot where aimed.

The fellow who would take the trouble to acquire one of these, alter its choking and barrel length and stock dimension to suit him, and use it in the field with the success I know he can reach has something else entirely in mind if he insists on a hammerless top-snap action, perhaps with a little engraving, and some high-priced touches including excellent walnut, rust blueing, perhaps a chaste little rib to glance his eye along. That man is looking for some form of social acceptance.

Oh, perhaps that is unfair. There is no doubt that such a gun would be handsomer and therefore nicer to own than even a much refurbished American hammer single. And a fellow who is really looking for that, in my mind, could probably get it by taking some extra time and trouble working with knowledgeable gunmakers somewhere. However, it would cost a lot more than seems sensible. For not much more, he could have a rather nice double, and nothing here says that a good single beats a good double.

I don't think the nice single is in the cards.

As in choosing a partner for life, one cannot always expect to get passion, good looks and competence in the same package, but two out of three ain't bad. So me and my Savage Model 94 12-gauge and some other singles will still, each year, travel to the bushes together and enjoy the experience. I shall acquire the social acceptance I deserve, no doubt, by my bearing. And what I don't hit, I'll miss, same as with any gun I ever fired. •

Two Inches of Pleasure and Problems

by PETER BARRETT

Getting the ultra lightweight Holland & Holland double gun to shoot safely and effectively with homemade shotshells wasn't easy, but teamwork and perseverance paid off.

The 2-inch chambered Holland & Holland in its original oak-and-leather case.

EVERY GROUSE AND WOODCOCK hunter enamored of fine double guns dreams of acquiring the perfect shotgun—one that flies to the shoulder effortlessly, swings like a dream and seems to point by a special instinct of its own. Of course, there is no perfect shotgun because there is always some little thing wrong or that displeases. Nevertheless, we search. And one wintry day in 1974 I picked up a dream gun, swung it a few times, hefted it and fell in love.

The place was Gary T. Herman's Safari Outfitters, on Route 7 north of Ridgefield, Conn.—a barn-red old house with white trim whose lower floor is crammed with handguns, rifles and shotguns. There's every grade of firearm at Herman's, but the emphasis is on top-of-the-line guns in good to fine condition.

The gun I'd picked up and swung was a 12 bore Holland & Holland side-by-side with its original lightweight leather case and accessories. Most of the casehardening colors on the full-sidelock plates remained, and there was minimal blue wear. The stock had been expertly refinished and, I'm sure, the checkering recut. The gun closed with an elegant *thunk!* and was absolutely tight.

I was not happy that there were two black spacers at the butt instead of one. Yet the Holland fitted me so well it nearly brought tears to my eyes.

We put it on Gary's scale and I could hardly believe the reading of $5\frac{1}{2}$ pounds, for this was a 12 bore with 28-inch barrels. It was then that I took a hard look at the rib and read: "Centenary—For 2 Inch Cases Only."

This brought me up sharp. "What kind of a load does the gun shoot?" I asked. Herman wasn't sure but thought 1 ounce, maybe $1\frac{1}{16}$ ounces. I considered this information. If I were to shoot 1-ounce loads I'd be practically using a 20 gauge, though the patterns and shot string might be a bit better. But $1\frac{1}{16}$ ounces is only about 25 pellets below $1\frac{1}{8}$ ounces in $7\frac{1}{2}$ shot.

Quandary

You can see how my mind was working. I *wanted* the gun and wanted to justify getting it. I recalled that when I'd shot driven grouse in Scotland for one glorious week, those of us with 12 gauges shot British ammo loaded to $1\frac{1}{16}$ ounces, which was very effective when the gun was pointed right.

Then I got to musing about some WW2 experiences in England. I'd bought a used field-grade Jeffery 12 gauge for an amazingly low $65. This gun had $2\frac{1}{2}$-inch chambers, and we in the Air Force had nothing but $2\frac{3}{4}$-inch Skeet shells loaded with 8s. Regardless, I bought the gun, tied it to a table and shot 10 rounds through it, pulling the triggers with a long string. The gun didn't burst and I was to shoot some hundreds of $2\frac{3}{4}$-inch paper shells through it.

After the war I took the gun to

H&H 2-inch chambered shotgun weighs just over $5\frac{1}{2}$ lbs.

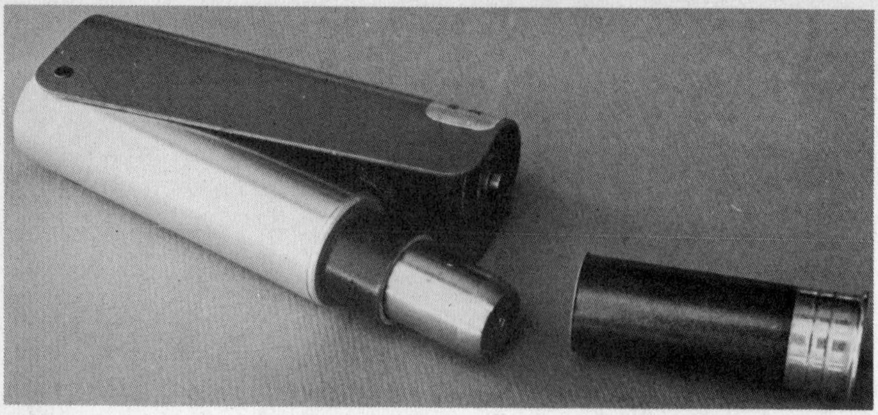

The Lyman hand trimmer was adjusted to cut a 2$^{3}/_{16}$". Severed cut case sections are on mandrel.

Finished 2$^{3}/_{16}$-inch shell sits beside same-length case in P-W shortened shell holder.

Judson S. Darrow, my gunsmith at Woodbury, Conn., and asked if he could lengthen the chambers to 2$^{3}/_{4}$". "No problem," he said. "There's plenty of metal and I've done this several times."

So, I thought, *Maybe Jud can stretch these 2-inch chambers a bit.*

Now I asked Gary Herman to measure the chokes. "About improved cylinder," he announced. "The left barrel could be a hair tighter."

Later that day, after telling my wife at lunch that I was going to swap some guns for one that cost as much as a new car (in 1974, remember), I parted with a pair of 12 gauge over-under S03 EL Berettas which I'd come to consider a bit on the heavy side, and an exquisite 28 gauge top-grade Zoli. I'll regret losing the latter till my dying day. But at the time I reflected I was out of pocket for only half the price of the Holland.

Now the problems began.

I couldn't find any 2-inch cartridges in the New York area. A salesman in Abercrombie & Fitch called the Chicago branch, then shook his head. "The Eley factory in England blew up recently," he remarked. "There's no telling when they'll be back in business."

I called Gary Herman. Yes, he had a shipment of British ammunition but it was tied up in a dock strike.

In desperation I wrote to Malcolm Lyell, Director of Holland's in London and a friend. My gun was made in 1936, he wrote me, and continued: "The shot load for 2-inch cartridges is $^{7}/_{8}$-ounce. It would certainly not be safe to have this gun chambered for 2$^{1}/_{2}$-inch cartridges."

What had I done?

My next move was to take the gun to Jud Darrow who made a cast of one of the chambers. To our mutual surprise this proved to be 2$^{1}/_{8}$ inches long. After doing some careful measuring Darrow finally decided he could lengthen the chamber by $^{1}/_{16}$-inch only, and ease the angle of the forcing cone which he said was rather steep.

Cartridge at Last

In the interim Gary Herman's British ammo arrived and I picked up 10 boxes. Nowhere on Eley's boxes was there mention of the weight of the shot charge, though in the fine print on the back there was an obscure reference to proofing at $^{7}/_{8}$-ounce. Back home, I cut open a shell and weighed its No. 6 pellets (about the size of our 7$^{1}/_{2}$s)—$^{7}/_{8}$-ounce on the nose. Sonofabitch!

I knew in my heart when I decided to have the chambers lengthened that I was going to have to take up shotshell loading, and the Eley loads (only ordered by Herman in 6s) reinforced this. I took a box of them to Darrow's when the gun was ready and we fired two shots in his yard, then measured the paper hulls. They were 2$^{1}/_{8}$-inches long.

Jud was looking hard at the mouth of the fired case and smiling. "Notice how thick the wall is?" he said. "Well, the Federal paper case is only about half as thick so there'll be more room for shot. I'm sure we can load 1$^{1}/_{16}$ and maybe 1$^{1}/_{8}$."

So I took the plunge and ordered a Ponsness-Warren Model 375 Du-O-Matic loader with 20 and 12 gauge tooling. I'd long been a reloader of centerfire cartridges and could now look forward to making conventional-length shells with loads unobtainable from the arms companies—such as 12 gauge 3-1$^{1}/_{4}$-8$^{1}/_{2}$s for early-season woodcock—as well as 2$^{3}/_{16}$-inch minis.

The Du-O-Matic, an expensive outfit, would be easy to adapt for short shells, Darrow felt. We ordered an extra 12 gauge shell holder to shorten, and two 6-point crimp starters, one to lengthen and reach down to 2$^{3}/_{16}$-inches. A 6-point crimp starter is usual for paper shells, 8 points for plastic.

Right from the start we decided against using a roll crimp and card atop the shot for fear of ruined patterns. The 2-inch Eleys have a roll crimp and their 6s patterned well, I was to find. Still I don't regret using a folded crimp and doubt there is much difference in shot capacity between the two systems.

We ordered Federal paper shells because paper is much easier to trim by hand than plastic. For this operation Darrow altered a Lyman shotshell trimmer to cut exactly at 2$^{3}/_{16}$. I was to find the trimming job surprisingly fast.

After Jud Darrow had altered my loader, he set about assembling a 1$^{1}/_{8}$ ounce load after finding room for the shot above modest wadding. An experienced shotshell loader himself, he checked several individuals and sources, including the first edition of the excellent Lyman Shotshell Handbook.

First Handloads

"Aren't they neat?" he said when I arrived. Jud was holding some newly made minis. "And believe it or not, it wasn't hard to get 1$^{1}/_{8}$ ounces of shot in there."

He showed me how to work the loader and I built several shells right there. It was downright easy. I bought some bags of shot in different sizes from Jud and went home.

Here's the load Darrow had worked up:

Federal paper shells with Federal 209 primers.

Alcan P.G.S. overpowder wad and Winchester $^{1}/_{4}$-inch fiber wad.

An alternate load substituted the Federal 12SC100 plastic shot cup for the $^{1}/_{4}$-inch fiber wad. This shot protector is nothing more than a flat-based shot cup with side cuts, by the

Comparing crimps—Eley roll on left, author's 6-point pie at right.

From left—Eley 2-inch, W-W $2^3/_4$-inch and author's handload.

way, and no cushioning of any sort at its base. The protector sits atop the P.G.S. (for plastic gas seal) wad. There is no room for even a slim card wad inside or outside the shot protector unless the shot load is reduced, which I was against.

It was now the middle of August, 1974. I loaded some shells with 8s (since this is what I'd use first come fall) in both styles—with and without the shot protector. Then I patterned the gun at 40 yards and at some closer distances.

There were two surprises. The $5^1/_2$-pound Holland was quite comfortable to shoot in shirtsleeves with the $1^1/_8$ load and was, of course, even milder with the Eley shells. The unprotected-shot patterns were the tightest. Here's how the gun patterned at 40 yards:

Protected shot	Unprotected shot
Right—32%	Right—38.3%
Left—34.4%	Left—41.1%

The Eley patterns were exceptionally even but, since I wasn't planning to hunt with these shells much, I did not figure their patterns. As to the patterns being more open with shot-cup shells, I figured the culprit had to be the lack of cushioning—many soft-lead pellets deformed inside the cup at the instant of firing.

At this point you may well think: *He got away with stuffing $1^1/_8$-ounces into those little shells. No need to read further.* Wait! This was only the beginning.

I loaded some $8^1/_2$s in protected loads (the widest shooting) for use in the right barrel for early woodcock, plus a good supply of 8, $7^1/_2$ and 6 unprotected-shot (tighter shooting) shells.

The gun proved a delight to shoot and I downed the first ruffed grouse I fired at. Somehow the 28-inch barrels did not prove cumbersome in woods and brush. At a preserve shoot, using 6s, the gun did well for me on pheasants and helped me perform beyond my normal ability on flighted ducks.

Seasons passed and about half a case of my minis went through the Holland. Last winter I prepared to write this article and John Amber said, "We must have pressure and velocity figures on the Eley and your shells. Would you mind sending a box of each to Mike Bussard of Federal who has kindly offered to help?"

The Bad News

In time I had a call from Mike, who is director of public relations for Federal Cartridge Corp. in Minneapolis. "We tested the shells," he told me, "and the Eleys are about normal—1280 fps and 7100 LUPs."

There was a pause, LUP is the abbreviation for lead units of pressure and the recommended safe average limit is 10,500.

Mike Bussard went on, "Are you sitting down?"

I said I was.

"The velocity of your handloads is 1153 fps, but you are getting 15,600 LUPs average. Some went over 16,000."

Mother of God! More than 50 percent above the safe limit!

I would like to have called Jud Darrow about this but he has gone to that wonderful place where a gunsmith never drops anything, screw heads don't get buggered and where all parts fit the first time. Instead I asked Mike Bussard for advice.

In essence, he felt I was overly ambitious in trying to cram $1^1/_8$ ounces into such little shells and also hope for acceptable pressure and a desirable velocity. "Go to a cooler primer, say the Remington 97*," he advised, "and try Green Dot, a slower-burning powder." He recommended a charge of no more than 19 grains. Finally he added, "That PGS overpowder wad in your particular load is probably a big factor in your pressure problem."

That weekend I frantically searched Connecticut for fiber wads of different thicknesses, and card wads. There were none! One-piece plastic wads had made cardboard and fiber combinations obsolete. Winchester had quit making such, but I learned that Federal still made components.

Next I cut open an Eley shell to check its makeup, which consists of two overpowder .085" card wads and one $^1/_2$-inch brown felt wad. I noticed that the shell wall was not nearly twice as thick as Federal's, as Jud had thought. The *mouth* of a fired Eley fluffs out, giving the false impression that the wall is thicker than it is. So I now found I didn't have as much volumetric room to play with as I'd thought I had.

Luckily Jud had made for me a $1^1/_{16}$-ounce shot bushing by slightly boring out a 1-ounce bushing and I decided to use this. Following Mike Bussard's suggestion, I made some Green Dot loads using two $^1/_4$-inch Winchester wads and $1^1/_{16}$-ounces of shot, which just fitted. The pressure checked out at a mere 6900 LUPs, but the velocity was only 1000 fps., too low.

I also modified the original 15,600 LUPs load, substituting for the PGS wad a $^1/_4$-inch Winchester wad (now there were two), and dropping from $1^1/_8$-ounces of shot to $1^1/_{16}$. Pressure was now 9900 LUPS average, velocity 1166 fps. Perfect!

Meanwhile, I've acquired some Federal $^1/_2$-inch wads—the discontinued brown fiber cushions and the current gray counterparts. I also learned about a specialist in hard-to-find components—Ballistic Products, Inc., 17610 19th Avenue N., Wayzata, Minn. 55391. Phone 612/473-1550.

All's Well

In the interest of presenting a load with available components, here's how one checked out: Federal paper shells with Remington 97* primers, $20^1/_4$ grains Green Dot, Federal $^1/_2$-inch gray fiber cushion wad, $1^1/_{16}$-ounces shot—9800 LUPs, 1079 fps. The velocity is a touch low, and there were considerable swings in pressure, from 8900 to 11,800, not exactly ideal. A different wad might smooth out the pressure swings, so I'll try again.

I'll also try some $^1/_2$-inch wads in the 700-X load, against the day when I run out of $^1/_4$-inch Winchester fiber wads.

Meanwhile, thanks to John Amber's insistence on pressure and velocity figures, I'll not be shooting proof loads through the Holland this fall. As for the shot reduction from $1^1/_8$ to $1^1/_{16}$-ounces, there are nevertheless 383 No. $7^1/_2$ pellets average in my new mini shells (a magnum loading by British standards). I'm sure they'll do the job when my Holland points itself for me in my grouse and woodcock covers. •

INDIAN GUNS

Contrary to popular opinion, the Plains Indians were "Good shots, good riders and the best fighters the sun ever shone on," said General Benteen. Here is the story of their firearms and their shooting ability.

by Norman B. Wiltsey

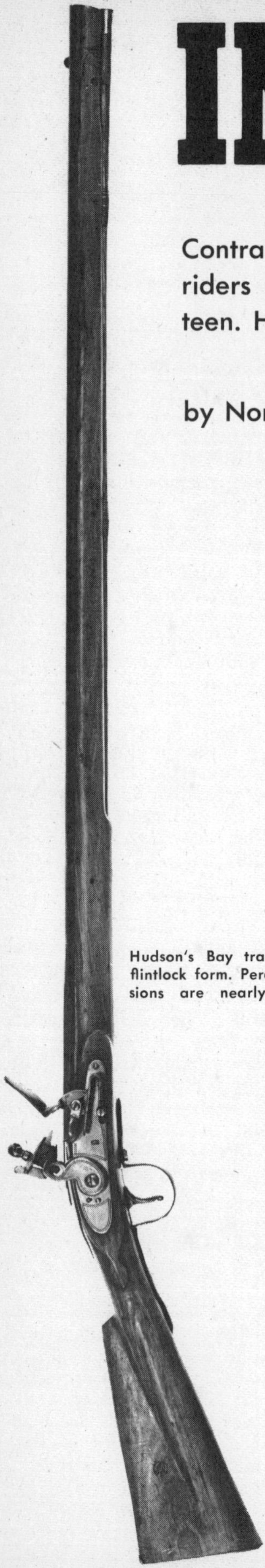

Hudson's Bay trade gun in flintlock form. Percussion versions are nearly identical.

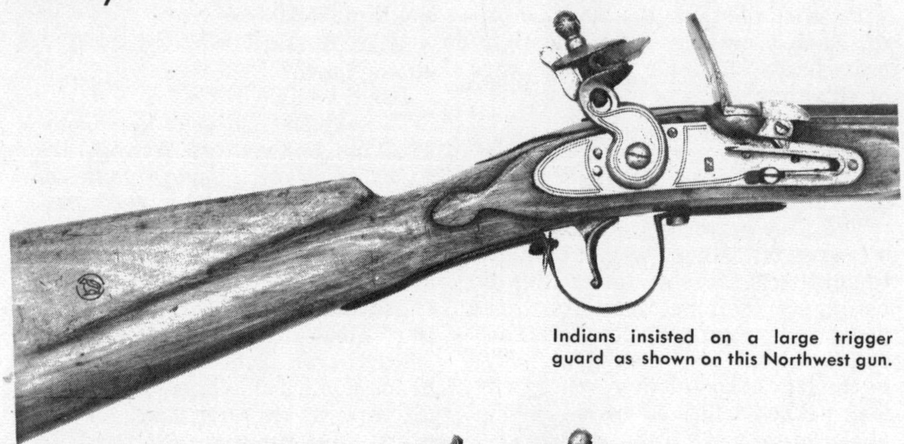

Indians insisted on a large trigger guard as shown on this Northwest gun.

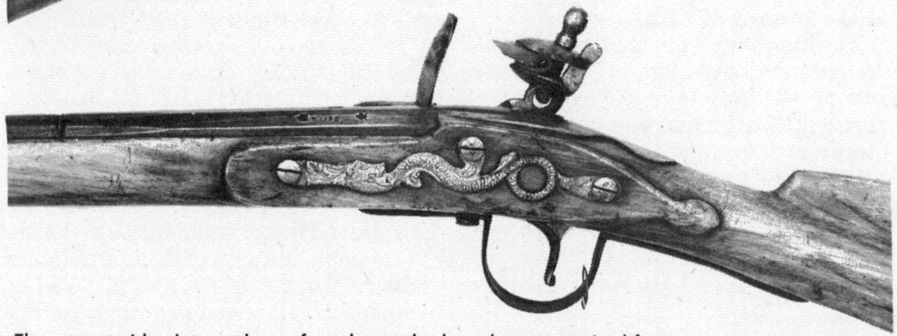

The serpent side-plate and proof marks on the barrel were required features of Northwest guns to assure acceptance by bargaining Indians.

THE AMERICAN INDIAN, after recovering from his initial awe and amazement at first contact with the white invaders' firearms, was not much impressed with the cumbersome wheel-lock and matchlock muskets of the enemy. His own bow-and-arrow, silent, deadly and faster firing, was a far more efficient weapon. Not until the lighter, handier and comparatively accurate flintlock arrived in the New World, about the middle of the 17th century, did the Indian show much interest in acquiring the white man's "thunder stick."

& GUNFIGHTERS

The first Indians to obtain the new flintlocks in appreciable quantities were the Huron and Algonquin allies of the French in New France — the Canada of today. The powerful Iroquois Confederacy, implacable foes of the French since 1609 — when Samuel de Champlain, accompanying a war party of Algonquin, Huron and Montagnais braves, killed two of their chiefs with his arquebus near what is now Ticonderoga — countered by trading beaver skins for flintlocks with the Dutch at Fort Orange (Albany, N.Y.) and Rensselaerwyck on the Hudson. The canny Dutchmen received 20 prime beaver pelts for one gun and a correspondingly high price for gunpowder. Later the price for both coveted items was sharply reduced by order of the Dutch government as a necessary measure to retain the friendship of the Iroquois and prevent, if possible, their trading with the French.

The guns sold to Indians by both French and Dutch traders were short, light snaphances known as *fusils*, the term later corrupted to *fusees*. When the English took over New Amsterdam from Peter Stuyvesant in August of 1664, they quickly found that the Iroquois expected them to continue the fair trade practices belatedly established by the Dutch. The latter continued in business for many years after the English take-over and gradually became assimilated with the conquerors. Stuyvesant's Dutch province became the property of the Duke of York and his beloved New Amsterdam became New York.

The haughty Iroquois could not have cared less about all these territorial shifts by the whites. Ruling the great forests from Canada to Tennessee and from Maine to Lake Michigan, they were the balance of power between the rival French and English and they never let either faction forget it. They hated the French, but would trade with them if trade suited their purpose. They distrusted the English, but cynically allied with them to keep the French and their Indian allies north of Lake Champlain. Heavily armed, with flintlocks supplementing their bows and tomahawks, the warlike Iroquois (the Five Nations) had crushed in turn the mighty Huron Confederacy—themselves comprised of tribes of Iroquoian people—and the People of the Panther, the hard-fighting Erie. The major battle of the last campaign, in 1654, saw less than 2,000 Iroquois opposed against nearly 4,000 of the Erie.

In 1666 the French mounted a full-scale military invasion of Iroquois territory, burning towns and crops, ruthlessly dealing what they believed to be a death-blow to the Five Nations. Further decimated by a deadly epidemic, the tenacious Iroquois grimly met a new challenge from the Susquehanna to the south. Defeated in the first battle of this new war, the beleagured Iroquois Confederacy received unexpected assistance when an epidemic similar to the plague that had ravaged their own ranks struck the Susquehanna. European settlers along the borders of the Maryland and Virginia colonies helped out by banding together and attacking the weakened Susquehanna. The appreciative Iroquois, moving in, mopped up almost without opposition.

This, the last of the major Indian-against-Indian wars on the Eastern frontier, left the Iroquois holding the future destiny of the nation in their hands. They were ideally situated to capitalize on their favorable position, and astute enough to do so. The adroitness of Iroquois statesmanship is amply illustrated by the remarks of La Grande Gueule (Big Mouth), noted Onondaga orator, to a French governor in 1684: "We Iroquois will go where we wish, allow passage through our country only those who seem to us good, and will buy and sell with whom we please."

So the Great League flourished for nearly a century more. The Five Nations became Six Nations with the addition of the Tuscarora around 1720. Four of the six—the Mohawk, Onondaga. Cayuga and Seneca—sided with the English in the Revolutionary War; the Tuscarora and the Oneida decided to aid the Colonists. Thus the Great League, after more than 300 years of existence, came to an end.

We get a glimpse of the type of arms furnished by the British to their Indian allies in Carl P. Russell's carefully documented book *Guns of the Early Frontiers*. Russell cites a request from the English governor Benjamin Fletcher, to the British Committee of Trade in London in 1693 for "200 light fuzees from their Majesties to the Five Nations of Indians; they will not carry the heavy firelocks I did bring over with me, being accustomed to light, small fuzees in their hunting."

Fletcher received more than the 200 "fuzees" requested, as the wealthy Lords of Trade in London knew well the economic importance of keeping on friendly terms with the Iroquois.

Geronimo, War Chief of the Apaches, shown with a Sharps rifle in this famous photograph by A. Frank Randall which is now in the collection of the Smithsonian Institution.

These weapons were undoubtedly the short, lightweight flintlocks in use by European cavalrymen of the period, commonly called musketoons or carbines. After 1675 practically all guns in the New World were of the true flintlock variety, but in the loose terminology of the times these continued to be designated as snaphances. Musketoon, carbine and fusee—or "fuzee"—derive from the French *mousqueton, carabine* and *fusil-court*, as the French short, light musket preceded the English version.

Effectively blocked from direct southern expansion down Lake Champlain and the Hudson River by the English and their Iroquois allies, the French moved westward from New France into present-day Michigan, Wisconsin, Minnesota, Indiana and Illinois. Traders went right along with the intrepid *coureurs de bois*, seeking to strengthen the ties with their own Indian allies with guns, powder and ball, pots, kettles, vermillion, hatchets,

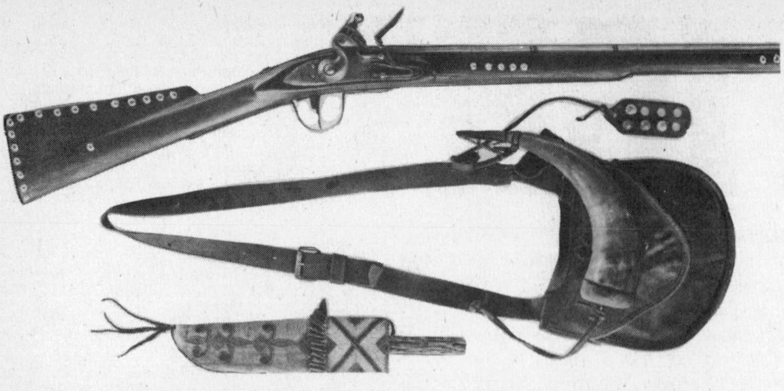

The Northwest flintlock was popular as a trade item throughout western Canada and the American West; it was made and used for a hundred years or more.

knives, beads and mirrors. Russell states: "In the last decade of the 17th century, French muskets were in use by natives everywhere from Lake Winnipeg to Lake Champlain and south to the mouth of the Mississippi."

The French weapons, so liberally distributed to the Indians, were inferior to English arms. Many warriors were killed or injured when a fusee burst upon firing. Most of these accidents were doubtless caused by

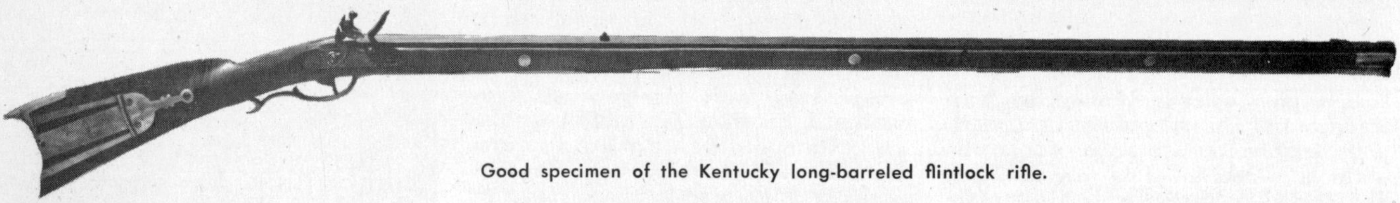

Good specimen of the Kentucky long-barreled flintlock rifle.

overcharging, since at first the naive red man operated on the theory that if a little powder and one musket ball was effective, then two balls and a double charge of powder would do twice as well.

Raid and counter raids between the hostile factions finally resolved into the six-year French and Indian War, beginning May, 1754, and ending in September of 1759. New France officially ceased to exist one year later when the Governor de Vaudreuil surrendered Montreal and all of Canada to the English general, Amherst.

Russell estimates that 200,000 muskets had come from the French factories during France's more than a century of struggle against the English and Iroquois for control of the New World. About 80,000 French military muskets were supplied to the Colonists during the Revolution. Many of these arms may be found in American collections today, but hardly a trace remains of the thousands of French trade-guns sold to the Indians. What happened to them is one of the fascinating mysteries in the history of firearms.

Swedish colonists, who settled in what is now Delaware and southeastern Pennsylvania from 1638 to 1655, evidently used Dutch or English guns for their trading with the local Delaware, Susquehanna and Mahican Indians, for no guns of Swedish manufacture have been traced to that period.

The Spanish invasion of the New World contributed little to the acquisition of firearms by the Indians; all gun trading was outlawed.

Whatever guns the sullen tribesmen in New Spain acquired were received from French and English traders. Creek, Chickasaw, and Cherokee braves, armed with French and English guns, assisted the English colonists in a bitter four years' war against the Spanish in Florida, following a formal declaration of war by England in 1739. In 1763, Spain ceded Florida to England.

In the Southwest, encroaching French traders bartered their inferior flintlocks in New Mexico and Texas early in the 18th century. Hard-riding Comanches, armed with French fusils, conducted raid after raid upon Spanish settlements until, by 1759, all of north Texas was abandoned by Spanish soldiers, settlers and missionaries. With the rout of the enemy from northern Texas, the insatiable Comanches turned to harrying the New Mexico towns.

Rated by early frontiersmen as the greatest horsemen of all the Plains tribes, the Comanches were trained in warfare from childhood. One trick of horsemanship, which few white men were ever able to master, was the spectacular stunt of swinging over the "off" side of a mount, using the horse's body as a shield. By hooking a leg over the horse's back, and hanging in a rope loop attached to his saddle or plaited into his horse's mane, the warrior had both hands free to use gun or bow, or to pick up a wounded comrade. When using a muzzle-loader on horseback, these early-day pirates of the prairie carried a powder horn and a mouthful of balls. The powder charge was poured by guess at full gallop, a wet bullet spat into the muzzle and the ball settled by a thump of the hand against the butt. The trick was to fire the gun when the barrel was level, but before the ball rolled out.

The English Hudson's Bay Company, attempting to take over all trading with the Indians of the Northwest after the fall of New France, discovered that the French traders were still much in evidence. Nine different French companies had combined by 1784 to form the North West Company in direct competition with HBC. Grace Lee Nute writes in *The Voyageur* that she found 2,431 voyageurs represented in the government licenses issued at Montreal and Detroit for the year of 1777. These rugged adventurers, other traders already afield, plus the employees of the Hudson's Bay Company and the American traders from the new United States, brought the total of traders to "5000 men sprinkled from Montreal to the Rocky Mountains and from Hudson Bay to the Gulf of Mexico." Guns and ammunition provided the best trading bait to swap for furs with the more than 300.000 Indians roaming this vast territory.

Short, light fusils continued to be the favorite arm of the red men. Not

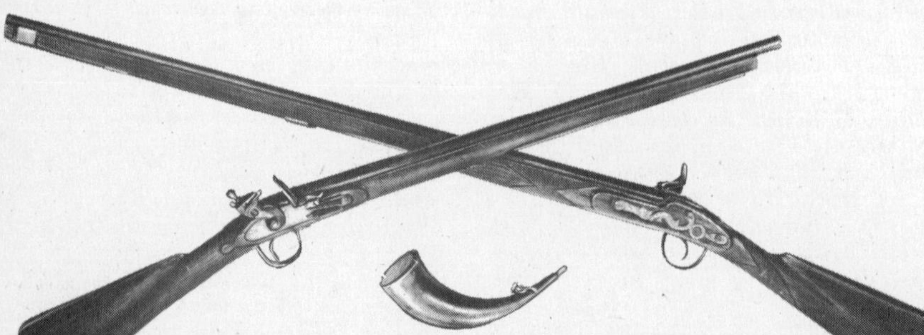

Indians often cut down the barrels of their guns for easier handling when hunting buffalo. Caplock gun, shown at right, was made in fewer numbers and in later years of production.

until around 1805 was this type of weapon generally recognized as the "Hudson's Bay fuke," the "Northwest gun," or the "Mackinaw gun." Russell describes it as: ". . . light in weight, often short of barrel, and cheaply constructed. Commonly it was gauged to shoot a one-ounce ball; that is, it was 16-gauge, or about 66 caliber, although some were smaller. The trigger guard was clumsy in appearance and was large enough to permit access to the trigger even though the trigger finger was enclosed in glove or mitten."

Many of these distinctive Northwest guns were made by Barnett or Bond, British gunmakers. Most, if not all, carried a brass dragon-pattern sideplate on the left of the stock. Many such guns traded by the Hudson's Bay Company were further distinguished by the figure of a seated fox superposed on the initials TB or EB on lockplate and barrel. The fox is still part of the company crest.

W. Chance and Son; J. Hollis and Son; Ketland; Lacy and Company; Parker Field and Company; Robbins and Martin; Sargent Brothers; and Wilson, all British firms, contributed guns for use in America, in addition to Barnett and Bond.

Leman of Lancaster; Deringer of Philadelphia; Henry of Philadelphia and Boulton, Pennsylvania and the C.H. & S. Co. of New York are among the American gunmakers known to have turned out facsimiles of the Northwest gun for the Indian trade. The U.S. government got into the field by building over 1,200 "Indian muskets" during the years 1807-1810. Most Indians rejected these substitutes for the Northwest Gun, and in 1848 nearly 700 of the guns were still in storage at the Springfield Armory where they had been manufactured.

In the middle 1820s the redmen became aware of the superior accuracy of the rifle over the smoothbore, and began to demand them in exchange for furs at the annual rendezvous of the American Fur Company. Deringer, Henry, and Tryon of Philadelphia all made rifles for the Indian trade; some used the new caplock ignition system, but many warriors still preferred the tried-and-true flintlock. The famed Goulcher family of gunsmiths — the name was also spelled Golcher — made both flintlocks, percussion locks and rifle barrels in their shops in New York City and Philadelphia for the Indian trade.

During the early 1800s the Plains Indian enjoyed a transitory reign of glory as the "Noble Red Hunter of the Prairies"—the perfect "Child of Nature," according to the Eastern press. But the telltale signs pointing to his down-grading to the status of "ruthless savage" were beginning to appear. The vast territory west of the Missouri, despite Lewis and Clark's expedition to the Pacific in 1805-07, was still designated on most maps as "The Great American Desert," but already the greedy white man was beginning to covet the Indian's virgin lands. Under the terms of the Indian Removal Act, signed into law by President Andrew Jackson in 1830, all tribes east of the Mississippi River were to cede their lands in exchange for territory in the West. It goes without saying that the land to which they were banished was arid, infertile terrain which the whites did not want for themselves. The Choctaw, the Chickasaw and the Creeks were the first to be forced from their ancestral home-land; the Cherokee the last of the four great southeastern tribes to leave. In the spring of 1838 the sad migration known as the "Trail of Tears" cost the lives of 4,000 of the 13,000 Cherokees on the fearful journey west to what is now Oklahoma.

The Seminoles of Florida, operating under the brilliant leadership of Osceola, defied the removal order and battled the Army to a standstill in a war (1835-1842) that cost the lives of 1,500 soldiers and $20,000,000 in military expenses. Only after Osceola had been captured and imprisoned through treachery did the war peter out. Most Seminoles eventually moved west to Indian Territory, but a few bands moved deep into the shadowy Everglades, and easily eluded the Army's clumsy efforts to root them out. The descendants of these dauntless ones live there today, still as independent as ever, and proud of the fact that they have never signed any form of peace treaty with the government of the United States.

War between the Indian and the white man on the Great Plains became inevitable with the virtual disappearance of the beaver trade, the consequent acceleration in the slaughter of the buffaloes for hides, and the appearance of the settlers' wagon trains west of the Missouri. The Plains Indian had welcomed the fur traders who brought the guns and ammunition he wanted and the trinkets craved by his women-folk; he had tolerated the mountain men who were hunters and wanderers like himself; but the hide hunters who destroyed the buffalo, and the settler who fenced off land and called it his, were entirely a different proposition. Clashes inevitably occurred between Indians and the Forty-niners and the pioneers heading

Sitting Bull, shown in ceremonial dress, is holding his later favorite weapon, an 1873 Winchester. Probably one of the few, if any, 73s used in the Custer fight.

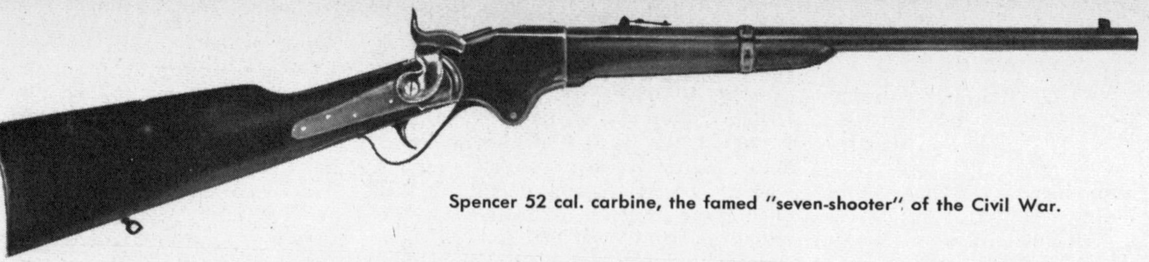

Spencer 52 cal. carbine, the famed "seven-shooter" of the Civil War.

west over the Oregon Trail, yet—in the curious manner of Indian warfare —the tribesmen lost no opportunity to trade for guns with the whites. The warriors were avid for modern rifles to replace their ancient trade guns; not for hunting game but for killing white men.

George Bird Grinnell, noted recorder of Indian history, in his book *The Fighting Cheyennes*, observes: "American Horse (a Cheyenne chief) has told me that the emigrants passing up the South Platte River to the mines between 1858 and 1865 were largely armed with the Sharps military rifles, and the Indians secured many of them in trade from these travelers. They were useful arms. The Indians also had some old-fashioned cap six-shooters, and during the year 1875 (the year before the Custer debacle on the Little Bighorn) there was a good deal of trading done for improved rifles.

"The method by which the Indians kept themselves supplied with ammunition for firearms, not only loose ammunition but also fiixed, has always been more or less mysterious, but they explain that in those war days they were constantly purchasing powder, lead, primers, and also outfits for reloading cartridges. They carried with them as part of their most prized possessions sacks of balls they had molded and cans of powder. So far as possible, they saved all the metal cartridge shells they used or found, and no doubt became expert reloaders of shells."

The late Stanley Vestal, University of Oklahoma professor, famed Western historian and close friend, before his death in 1957, of the Sioux, compiled a box score of 12 major engagements between redman and white, including the Custer fight. In these engagements a total of 10,356 Indians fought 5,249 whites. The results: Indians, 69 killed, 28 wounded; whites, 383 dead, 102 wounded.

The list appeared in an article Vestal—who was actually Professor Walter S. Campbell—wrote in *Guns Magazine* for December, 1956. "Other than the astonishingly low number of casualties on either side," Vestal said, the battles, "reveal an important trait of the Sioux campaigns. The Indians, like Napoleon, fought as a rule only when they had the advantage of numbers. . . . They did this with hardly half enough guns to go around under the best conditions, and with no cannon at all."

Today's Western television fan stubbornly believes that the average Indian warrior was a lousy shot compared to the average U.S. Cavalry trooper. This, too, is part of the glamorous mystique of the Old West, for when we turn to the men who actually traded shots with hostile braves we find that, gun for gun, the Indian was more than a match for the soldier. More than that—and this, also, may come as a shock to the die-hard Western buff—the Indians not only outshot but outrode their cavalrymen foes.

Major Walsh of the Royal Northwest Mounted Police declared them "superior to the best English regiments." One of General Crook's staff officers described them as "the finest light cavalry in the world." General Charles King rated them "foemen far more to be dreaded than any European cavalry." Major Anson Mills, a captain at the Battle of the Rosebud in 1876, declared, "Their like will never be seen again." General Frederick W. Benteen, also a captain in 1876, gave the red riders of the Plains this high accolade: "Good shots, good riders, and the best fighters the sun ever shone on."

General George Crook, in an official report to the Secretary of War in 1876, stated: "When the Sioux Indian was armed with a bow and arrow he was more formidable, fighting as he does most of the time on horseback, than when he got the old-fashioned muzzle-loading rifle. But when he came into possession of the breechloader and metallic cartridges, which allows him to load and fire from his horse with perfect ease, he became at once 10,000 times more formidable." Crook added: "I have seen our friendly Indians, riding at full speed, shoot and kill a wolf, also on the run; while it is a rare thing that our troops can hit an Indian on horseback, though the soldier may be on his feet at the time."

Corroborating Crook's view of the Indian in warfare,.General Nelson A. Miles gave this coolly professional opinion of the Indian's proficiency with improved arms: "The Indian's marksmanship is very accurate within the range to which he is accustomed in killing game, say within 200 yards. But in the use of the long-range rifle, where he must take account of the elevated sights, the distance and the effect of the wind upon the flight of the bullet, he is inexperienced and in no way a match for his more intelligent enemy."

Miles, however, neglected to amplify his statement by admitting that very few rifles with elevating sights came into the hands of the redman, and that he wasted mighty little of his precious ammunition in target

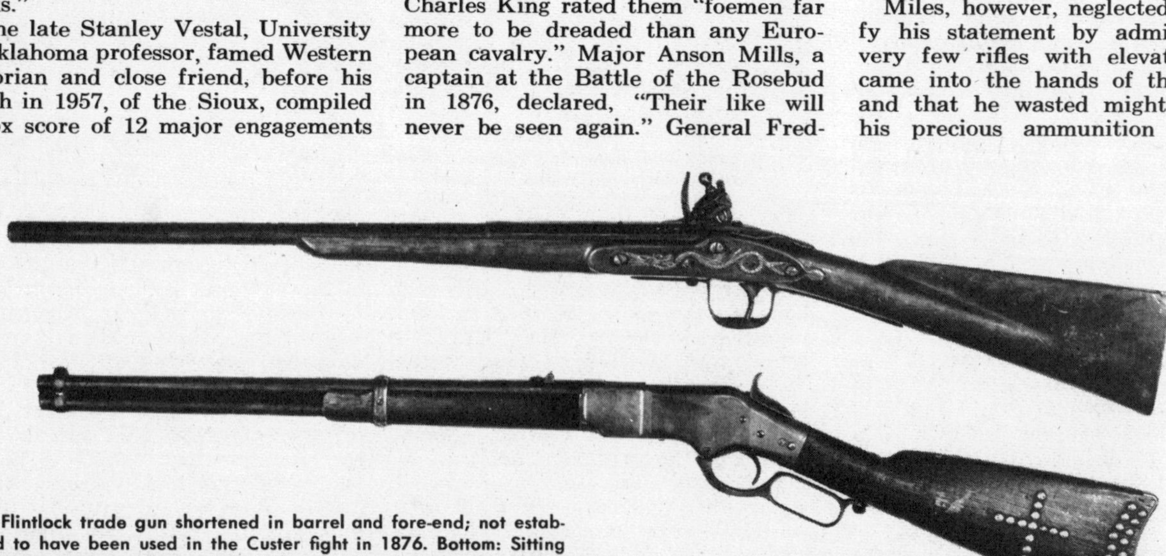

Top: Flintlock trade gun shortened in barrel and fore-end; not established to have been used in the Custer fight in 1876. Bottom: Sitting Bull's Winchester carbine, Model 1866, in Major Brotherton collection. This gun was surrendered to Major Brotherton, C.O. at Fort Buford on the Missouri River on July 19, 1881, by Sitting Bull.

practice; the battle-field was the Indian's rifle range.

In 1866, in the Fetterman fight at Fort Phil Kearney, the Sioux acquired 79 Sharps carbines and Springfield muzzle-loaders from the bodies of the slain soldiers. Two frontiersmen killed in the fight carried 16-shot Henry repeating rifles, caliber 44. These were the first repeating rifles ever taken by the Sioux. A good idea of how the hostile tribesmen were equipped with firearms before this scrap may be obtained from Grinnell, who notes: "Only six of the 81 white men (killed in the Fetterman fight) bore gunshot wounds."

In that year of 1866 a law was passed "allowing any loyal citizen, or proper citizen, to trade with Indian tribes." And so—since guns were what the Indians wanted most—guns were what they got. But there were never enough guns to arm all the fighting men of all the tribes, and even after whipping Crook on the Rosebud on June 17, 1876, and capturing a number of carbines from the troops, only about half the Indians had guns for the climatic struggle with Custer 8 days later. Grinnell wrote that ". . . the guns were of many sorts—muzzle-loaders, Spencer carbines, old-fashioned Henry rifles, and old Sharps military rifles. The Sharps were probably the best guns they had, except those recently captured from the soldiers."

In Thomas B. Marquis' book *Wooden Leg's Story*, the narrator, a Cheyenne, declares: "Guns were not plentiful among us. Most of our hunting had been done with bows and arrows. Of the Cheyennes, Two Moons and White Wolf (chiefs) each had a repeating rifle. Some others had single-shot breechloading rifles. But there was not much ammunition for the good guns. The muzzle-loaders usually were preferred, because for these we could mold the bullets and put in whatever powder was desired, according to the quantity on hand. I believe the Sioux, in proportion to their numbers, had about the same supply of firearms that we had. The Waist and Skirt people (a tribal division of the Cheyennes) had few or no guns; were in every way poor. My muzzle-loading rifle had been lost with my other personal effects when we were driven out and our lodges burned on Powder River." (here Wooden Leg referred to Colonel Reynolds' attack on a Cheyenne village on March 17, 1876).

"6 or 8 guns, I suppose, had been taken from soldiers at the Rosebud fight. I recall seeing only two, a rifle and a revolver, among the Cheyennes. Both of them used cartridges . . ."

"My cap-and-ball six-shooter was my warring weapon. I had plenty of caps, powder and lead for it. I had a bullet mold to make its bullets from the lead. I kept the bullets and the caps in two small tin boxes. The

After the massacre at Wounded Knee, Big Foot lies dead and frozen in the snow.

powder I carried in a horn swung by a thong from my shoulders."

In his statement, Wooden Leg pinpoints the reason why the Indians were so poorly armed in comparison to the soldiers; economics. As Vestal has pointed out, ". . . only rich Indians could afford to buy repeaters, and rich Indians were no more numerous per capita than rich white men are."

The going price for even a single-shot breech-loader was 20 buffalo robes or several horses; the price for a repeater three times that. So, unromantically, the lie is given to the persistent myth that the Indians at the Little Bighorn were all armed with Winchesters as opposed to the soldiers' 45-70 single-shot Springfield carbines. The myth began at the Military Court of Inquiry after the disastrous 20-minute battle in which Custer and 206 troopers of the Seventh Cavalry were killed. Major Reno—scornfully called The-One-That-Ran-Away by the Sioux—answered interrogation as to the Indians' armament thus: "The Indians had Winchester rifles and the column made a large target for them and they were pumping their bullets into it."

Question: "The Indians, so far as you observed, were armed with Winchester rifles?"

Answer: "Yes, sir."

Question: "Do you know that they had any other arms?"

Answer: "No, sir."

Lieutenants Varnum and De Rudio backed Major Reno, at least in part. Both officers were cross-examined as to the Winchesters' range, after Varnum had mentioned them in his testimony.

Below the rank of commissioned of-

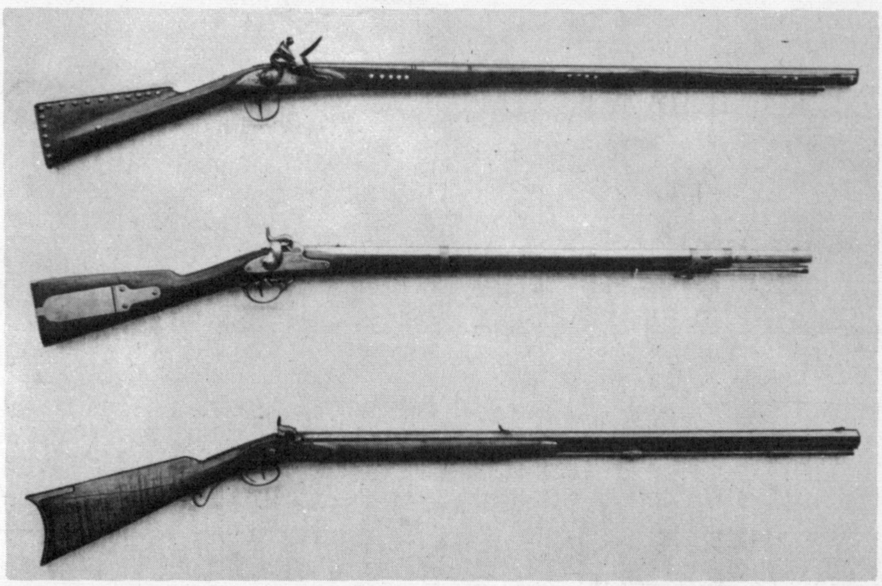

Typical of guns used in the early Canadian West are, from top: flintlock Northwest trade gun; Mississippi rifle, a favorite of land-seeking pioneers and miners in the 1800s; half-stock caplock rifle of Samuel Hawken's pattern.

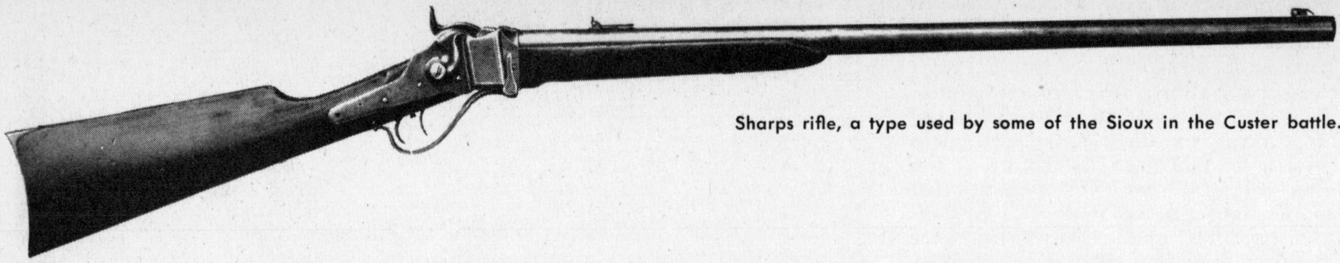

Sharps rifle, a type used by some of the Sioux in the Custer battle.

ficer, the "Winchester story" was considerably different. Sergeant Windolph, in the book *I Fought With Custer,* by Frazer and Robert Hunt, had this to say on the subject:

"It has been generally accepted that all the red warriors were armed with the latest model repeating Winchester rifles and that they had a plentiful supply of ammunition. For my part, I believe that fully half the warriors carried only bows and arrows and lances, and that possibly half of the remainder carried odds and ends of old muzzle-loaders and single-shot rifles of various vintages. Probably not more than 25 or 30 percent of the warriors carried modern repeating rifles."

Sergeant Windolph's estimate is far more logical and reasonable than that of Major Reno. Granting this, it is still improbable that about 500 braves were armed with repeaters. Of 284 long guns turned in by Sioux and Cheyennes in 1877, some 160 were muzzle-loaders according to Army Ordnance records; included in the lot were 94 percussion rifles by H. E. Leman, six Hawkens, and a weird assortment of Kentuckys, old Springfield and Tower muskets, and one flintlock smoothbore. The balance were cartridge weapons. Thirty-nine repeaters were included in the batch of 124 breech-loaders. In six different calibers, they included four Henrys, 12 Winchesters and 23 Spencers. 123 revolvers were turned in, all but one cap-and-ball. The Ordnance report listed the condition of these weapons in these terms, "would be classed as 'unserviceable' at an arsenal."

Don Rickey, of the Custer Battlefield National Monument Museum, told Stanley Vestal: "On the Custer Battlefield, we have found several types of empty cartridge cases—of other than Army issue. They are mostly 50 caliber (for the Sharps, like the carbine we have that was used by Spotted Wolf, a Cheyenne) and for other 50 caliber arms such as the 1866, 1869 and 1870 models of the Springfield carbine and rifle, which were retired from Army service by the introduction of the 45-70 Springfield in 1873-74. I have one 50 case that has been purposely altered at the primer pocket end, to enable a hostile to re-prime the cartridge with a common percussion cap—the usual method. It was originally a civilian, Berdan-primed cartridge. We have also found many 44 copper rim-fire cases that would have fit either the Henry rifle or the 1866 Winchester rifle or carbine. Other dug-up items include: a 58 caliber mould for the Minié type bullet used in the Civil War muzzle-loaders (dug up at the site of an Indian village, Little Big Horn valley), two percussion revolvers, and an 1873 Winchester 44-40 carbine."

Rickey did not mention finding any centerfire cartridge cases for the '73 Winchester, which would seem to dispose of the persistent tale that hundreds of braves were armed with this famous rifle in the Custer scrap. Sitting Bull's own Winchester, surrendered to Major Brotherton at Fort

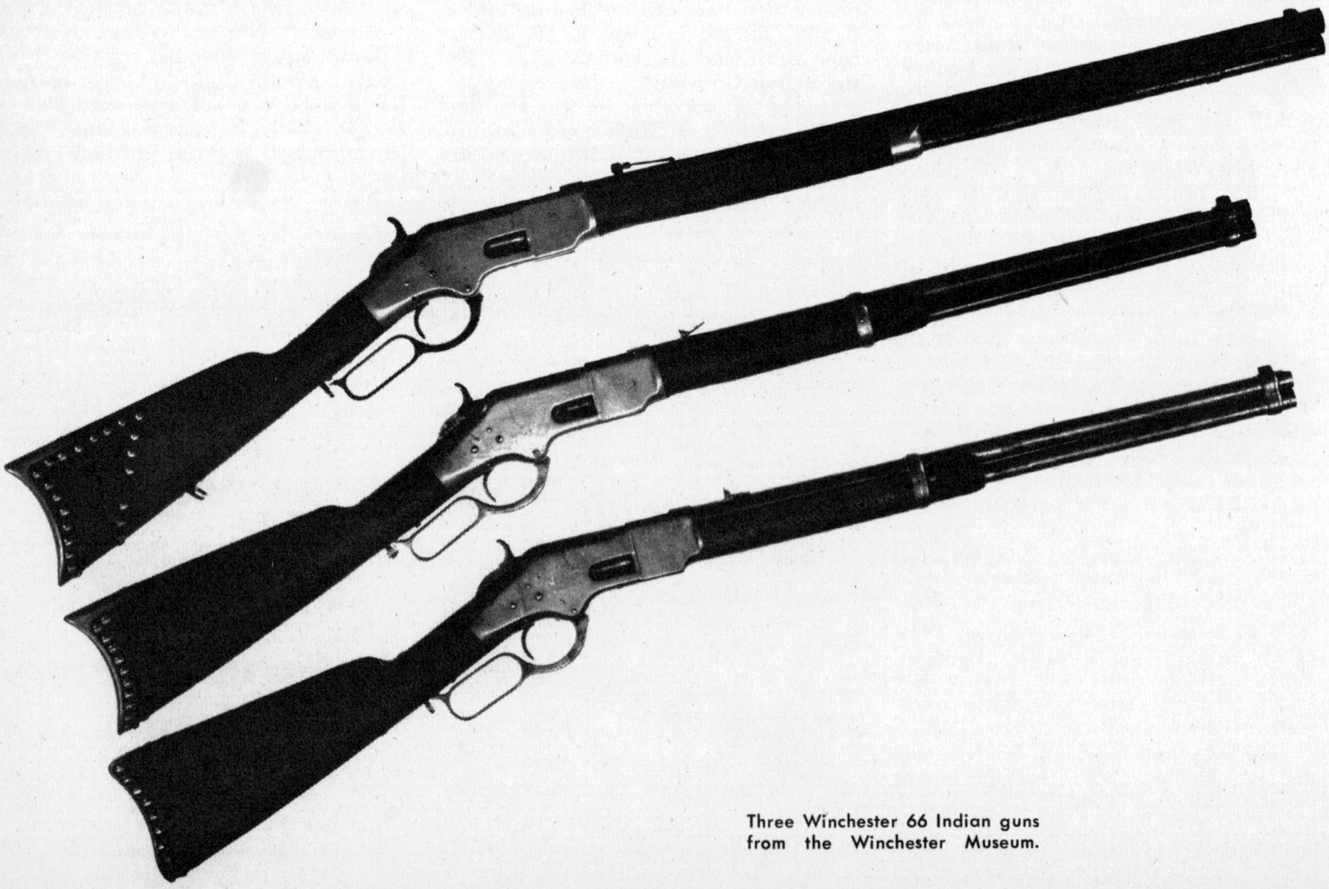

Three Winchester 66 Indian guns from the Winchester Museum.

Reproduction of a color painting by John Barsotti of Columbus, Ohio. The Indians are Apaches.

Buford, July 19, 1881, was a Model 1866 carbine, caliber 44 rimfire, serial number 124,375. This weapon is now in the Major Brotherton Collection at the Smithsonian Institution. The old Bull was reported to have carried a Winchester '73 at the Little Bighorn but, if the story is correct, he parted with it before surrendering to the Army five years later.

The fiery war leader of the Oglala Sioux, Crazy Horse, carried a Model '66 Winchester, as did a few of the other chiefs. Colored pictographs of the battle drawn by Indian participants show lever action rifles with bronze or brass frames in the hands of some of the warriors. Clearly, these weapons were 1860 Henry rifles and Model 1866 Winchesters.

Vestal notes that "when the Army used Gatling guns and Hotchkiss cannon, as at Wounded Knee, the Indian wars came swiftly to an end."

Wounded Knee, to which Vestal refers, is a particularly tragic incident in the annals of the Indian wars; it resulted from an attempt by the Army in 1890 to suppress the so-called "messiah craze," which was causing some unrest among the Sioux in South Dakota. The craze was a sort of religion marked by glorification of the past, ancestor worship, and the belief that an Indian messiah would appear and lead the Indians to victory over the white man. When the Army arrived, many Indians fled their reservations. The Army pursued them, killed Sitting Bull for resisting arrest on Dec. 15, 1890, and attacked a large party of Indians at Wounded Knee Creek, So. Dak., on December 29. Killed were some several hundred men, women, and children. This slaughter was the last "battle" of the Indian wars in the United States. Within a short time the surviving runaways were captured and returned to the reservations.

Even before the brutal massacre of 300 Sioux men, women and children at Wounded Knee in December of 1890, the Apaches had discovered that the White Eyes' "wagon-guns" were sheer murder. When Geronimo ended the 50-year Apache war with the whites by surrendering to General Miles in 1886, the chief laid his hand on a Gatling gun at Fort Bowie and growled: "Heap bad medicine! God-dam—sumbitch!"

The Ghost Dance craze, the murder of Sitting Bull, and the shocking tragedy of Wounded Knee ended the "Indian trouble" between the Mexican and Canadian borders. The last stand of the American Indian in Canada was made in 1897 by a sharpshooting young Cree named Almighty Voice, who was sentenced to 30 days in the guardhouse at the Duck Lake Post of the Northwest Mounted Police for shooting a settler's (some versions say government-owned) steer. Almighty Voice escaped, fleeing into the desolate northern wilderness. During the ensuing chase, and until the ultimate death of Almighty Voice, 4 Mounties were killed and several wounded. Only after some 61 Mounties had cornered the Cree did their 7- and 9-pound field guns write an end to the saga of Almighty Voice.

So, in a blaze of red raw courage, ended the American Indian's 300 year struggle against the all-conquering white man. Not until World Wars One and Two did the conquerors appreciate the unique fighting qualities of the conquered, when young men of all tribes distinguished themselves in all branches of the Armed Forces. Today, in the steaming jungles of Vietnam, Indian specialists in American uniforms are instructing the Vietnamese in the guerrilla warfare practiced by their ancestors. ●

Bibliography

Guns of the Early Frontiers, by Carl P. Russell, Berkeley, Calif., 1957.

American Heritage Book of Indians, American Heritage Pub. Co., New York, N. Y., 1961.

Firearms in the Custer Battle, by J. E. Parsons and J. S. Dumont, Harrisburg, Pa. 1953.

I Fought with Custer, by F. and R. Hunt, New York, N. Y., 1947. (Story of Sgt. Windolph)

Wooden Leg's Story, by T. B. Marquis, New York, N. Y., 1928.

Report of Major Reno to Chief of Ordnance, *Army & Navy Journal,* Aug. 19, 1876.

On the Border with Crook, by Capt. J. G. Bourke, New York, N. Y., 1896.

Fighting Indian Warriors, by E. A. Brininstool, Harrisburg, Pa., 1953.

Carbine and Lance, by Col. W. S. Nye, Norman, Okla., 1937.

Sitting Bull, by Stanley Vestal, New York, N. Y., 1932.

The Voyageur, by Grace Lee Nute, New York, N. Y., 1934.

When it comes time to fight, the Afghan likes to be looking down their throats, and the terrain helps. These three fighters all have SMLE's. Wide World photo.

The workman at the right, in Darrah, is stocking a hill-made Martini. His sidekick appears to have an early SMLE copy.

THE AFGHAN AND HIS SMLE

He likes the bolt gun, the old 303, and makes his own when he has to, and his tactics and riflery make the Afghan hills tough nuts to crack.

by JACK LOTT

As the sun crept from its place of ambush behind the sawtooth peaks lining the Khyber Pass, an eagle soared over the bone dry ridges flanking the little Afghan valley below, seeing all, including a herd of strange metal creatures groaning and whining up the camel track towards the watchtowers of a fortified tribal village. Malik Yousef Ali Khan, the village headman and chief of his clan's guerrilla band, awaits the approach of the Russian armored column with a deadly patience born of a two-thousand-year heritage of defending these hostile barren mountains against foreign invaders, including Alexander the Great, Genghis Khan and the Imperial British of Kipling's time.

Wearing coarse homespun baggy trousers and shirt under a sleeveless sheepskin coat, Ali Khan had swept the loose part of his turban over his face until only the fierce black eyes of the hawk-faced Pathan (pronounced "Ptahn") showed. His hands clutched an Afridi tribal-made copy of Britain's World War I battle rifle, the 303 Lee-Enfield Mark III (SMLE), its stock patina the result of years of handling and shoulder-slung rubbing against homespun. A bandolier of 303 Mk. VII ammo smuggled in from India crossed his chest, and in a homemade flap holster on his belt hung an original Webley Mk. VI 455 British Army revolver, the fruit of a trade with an Afridi involving a camel and the Webley, which the Afridi's father had taken from a fallen British subaltern in 1938. In deference to an older tradition, Ali Khan kept a 12-inch straight-bladed "Pesh-Kabz" dagger in his belt with its camel bone grip and heavy ridged back and reinforced point, originally for piercing chain mail. The dagger is quite useless for skinning ibex, but the thrifty Pathans do not waste expensive 303 ammo on wounded enemies.

Crouching behind Ali Khan are a dozen fierce-looking rangy bearded giants, type-cast by nature for the role they were born to and prefer to play. All watch and listen for the column of Russian T-62 tanks and BTR-60PA armored personnel carriers to round the rocky promontory just downhill on the torturous road of broken stones. The armor is on the way to the village to reduce it to rubble for spawning a series of successful raids on truck transports supplying a remote Afghan puppet troop garrison to the north. Unknown to the Russian column commander and his Russian and Afghan officers and men, the road behind them, their only escape route, was closed after they passed by an avalanche of boulders launched by Gul Mustafa's men, who are part of Ali Khan's "lashkar" (fighting group). What the Russians also cannot see is that in the track below Ali Khan's "Mujahedeeni" (holy warriors) a second roadblock, an appalling chaos of boulders, blocks the upward track to anything but ibex and the agile Pathans.

As the lead tank confidently approaches the place of ambush, it is killed by the blast of two captured Russian TM 57 anti-tank mines with their combined charge of thirty-one pounds of TNT. This is the signal for Ali Khan's men to attack the stalled column with Molotov cocktails and grenades quickly wedged in the treads. Two guerrillas are killed by automatic fire during this audacity, but the rest are too quick, and in seconds three tanks at the rear are burning and immobilized, stalling the column.

There it is: In this man's face, you can read all you need to know about what the Russians face in the Afghan hills. Wilfred Thesiger photo.

The rear of the trapped column is under attack by Gul Mustafa's men. It takes but a brief interval for turret lids to open and for other tanks to lay down a withering fire, but the tribesmen provide few opportunities. The Russian tank commander in the lead tank emerges, Makarov pistol in hand, only to be killed instantly by a sniper's 303 from the hillside. He is quickly pulled down out of the way by the panicked Afghan and Russian crewmen whose raised hands obtain no mercy from the Pathans, who give no quarter and ask no quarter.

The fight lasts no more than 20 minutes. The mainly Afghan crews succumb to the compelling wisdom of fear – fear of an enemy and neighbor whose implacability and fighting skills were their childhood legendry. It is a case of familiarity which does not breed contempt. Those Afghani puppet troops who shout "Allahu Akbar" (God is Great) quickly enough are spared, quickly disarmed and tied and blindfolded, to be marched to a cave outpost and "encouraged" to join the "Mujahedeeni."

The Pathans waste little time and ammunition on the Russians, who are invariably killed with the "Pesh-Kabz" to save 303 ammo. Most tribesmen reload their SMLE copies for any encore, while other more old-fashioned types clean their soiled blades on Russian uniforms. The Russian prisoners all die bravely, but their eyes betray a stark animal fear of an enemy even more brutal than themselves. Even these Marxist-programmed peasant soldiers cannot refute the simple justice: In Afghanistan, it is bad manners to come to a war when you're not invited!

"Inshallah" (God is bountiful) and the tribesmen sling their 303's and begin the looting. Once more the old favorite had justified a faith forged in 50 years of Frontier warfare. The Soviet gunship arrives too late to save the armored column, as the Pathans bound up the rocky hillsides with their own rifles, captured AK's, RPK's and PKM's, ammo, grenades and a few rocket launchers and rockets. The gunship descends as low as possible for maneuvering within the narrow confines of the defile, its 6,000 r.p.m. electronically driven "Gatling" delivers a cloudburst of leaden rain, mainly to the boulders, but also to a few visible darting figures of Tenth Century men in homespun, clutching burdens of booty, like overloaded ants departing an untidy campground. Two overburdened tribesmen drop their prizes for an instant, fumble trying to save their loads, and die on the spot. Most work up into the giant rocks they know as the eagle knows his eyrie.

The gunship circles continuously to lay down a full measure of fire power, but bulletproof and visible rocks are many, and visible rebels few. Napalm and incendiary are ineffective when there is little but rock to burn. One tribesman in an outburst of elan and outrage fires his 303 impotently at the armored underbelly of the Russian pterodactyl, and for this instant of bravura is crumpled into a pitiful bloodstained heap of homespun.

From a natural "sangar" (rocky emplacement) a thousand or more feet above the still hovering and spitting gunship, Nazar, Ali Khan's younger brother, aims an old but still serviceable 303 Bren gun captured years before from the British by Afridis across the Durand Line in what was then India. Serving the Bren is his young cousin Ahmed, while Ahmed's brother Suleiman, 14, works his Lee-Enfield copy like a veteran. The gun-wise tribesmen hadn't forgotten to load some Indian tracers, and the Bren now spits them out at the gunship below. Suleiman empties his magazine in aimed rapid fire and clip reloads another ten Mark VII's. The faces of the three young Pathans, though adolescent, glare at the gunship with a hardness born of centuries of fighting heritage as they feed the ravenous Bren with spendthrift indifference. The deadly parabola of 303's arcs gracefully down at an angle of 50 degrees, the tracers catching up fast. Suleiman's SMLE finds the cockpit bubble in the copter's topside, its unarmored sticking place. Nazar's final burst completes the job begun by Suleiman's rifle, and in a blinding explosion, the gunship commits suicide with its own fuel supply. Obsidian Pathan eyes watch with grim satisfaction as the copter disintegrates.

Ali Khan and his men rendezvous and rest, then await nightfall for a final salvage operation for anything usable and unburned. The bodies of the five fallen comrades are removed for burial, the wounded handed over to the women for nursing. The Russians will not be returning for a while, and when they do, there is more weaponry available to repel them. So long as the Pathans do not try to defend fixed positions, drawing concentrated Russian air and ground firepower, the tribesmen retain the initiative, and as always, the night belongs to them.

The eagle circles above the smoking wreckage, uninterested in the inedible metallic creatures as it seeks marmots or a strayed village lamb. An ibex ram gives a haughty glance at the strange spectacle below, then casually turns and rounds the ridge, a hoof catching a stone which tumbles crazily down the canyon, loosening others in turn, until all reach bottom, where there is only death in a disorderly shambles of steel and blood. No other sound breaks the silence, and for a while, a peace of sorts returns to the valley and its people.

That's what's happening and here's some background:

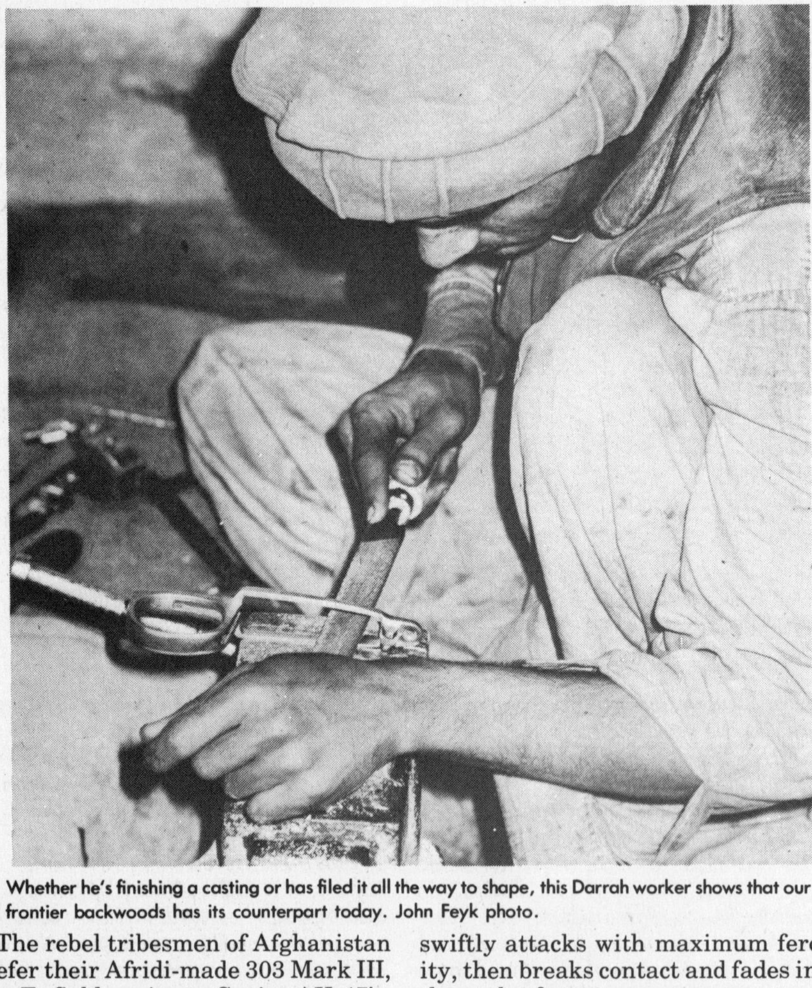

Whether he's finishing a casting or has filed it all the way to shape, this Darrah worker shows that our frontier backwoods has its counterpart today. John Feyk photo.

The rebel tribesmen of Afghanistan prefer their Afridi-made 303 Mark III, Lee-Enfield copies to Soviet AK-47's. They are, by tradition and experience, mountain guerrilla snipers, relying mainly on aimed fire from strong natural positions. When surprise and ambush have immobilized an enemy for even a brief interval, the Pathan swiftly attacks with maximum ferocity, then breaks contact and fades into the rocky fastness.

This is "Jihad" (Holy War) in defense of the Moslem faith as much as of native mountains and a way of life combining feudalism and barbarism with the gentlest hospitality to friends who come in peace to share their humble fare. Loyalties are first to the family, clan and tribe, the law of blood feud, the Khyber knife and the 303, and criminal use of a gun is rare within the tribe.

The arrival of the British in the 19th Century meant some losses for the tribesmen, but they regarded that colonial warfare as "sport," and the British conceded the Pathan's independence in Independent Tribal Territory, and only reacted forcefully when raided outside that sanctuary. This war is different, and there is no respect or romantic aura such as inspired Kipling's poetry. There is only a bottomless hate for the invader.

Though obviously a "nation of riflemen," the Pathan is not exactly "the boy next door" with a turban and a 303! His love of freedom, family, tribe and land, finds a sympathetic understanding among Americans. Americans, however, do not think highly of beheading prisoners, of cutting off a wife's nose "to spite her face" when she has flirted, or flaying alive especially hated enemies, or wearing daggers, SMLE's and bandoliers like three-piece suits. They are not asking us to accept their sometimes frightful customs, only to understand their right to freedom, and their ability and determination to fight to the utmost with what they have—or can make, which includes rifles.

The Afridi tribal rifle industry began in 1910 in Independent Tribal Territory in Kohat Pass. A "Malik" (headman) of the Adam Khel tribe of Afridis disassembled a Martini-Enfield rifle he had taken from an Indian Sepoy (soldier) he had killed in a fierce skirmish between his lashkar (fighting group) and a withdrawing picket of British Colonial troops. The old Martini falling block action with a 303 Enfield barrel was issued to native troops then. Sher Din Shahabuddin, the Malik, admired the rifle's rugged simplicity and understood its working principles. He reasoned that its manufacture, aside from rifling, was no more difficult than that of a flintlock "Jezail."

In Bombay and Sialkot were workmen who had experience in British Indian arsenals, some retired, some unemployed. A tribal council gave tentative approval. At first railroad tracks were ripped up to make actions; eventually crude wooden lathes and rifling machines produced the barrels.

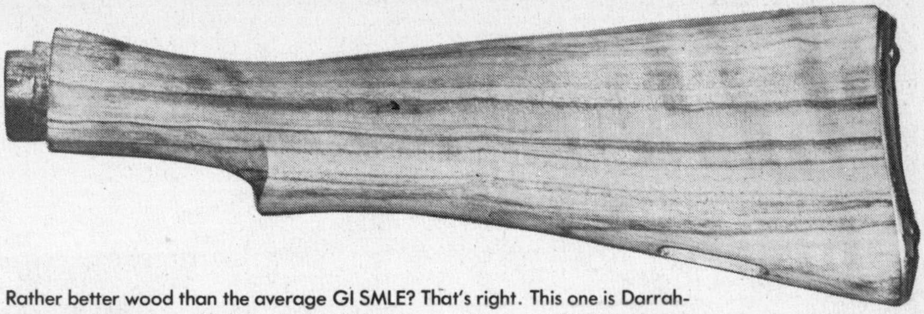

Rather better wood than the average GI SMLE? That's right. This one is Darrah-made, perhaps even whittled out while held between the toes. John Feyk photo.

They make Mauser copies in Darrah, too, and now and then, someone shoots one and this fellow is doing just that.

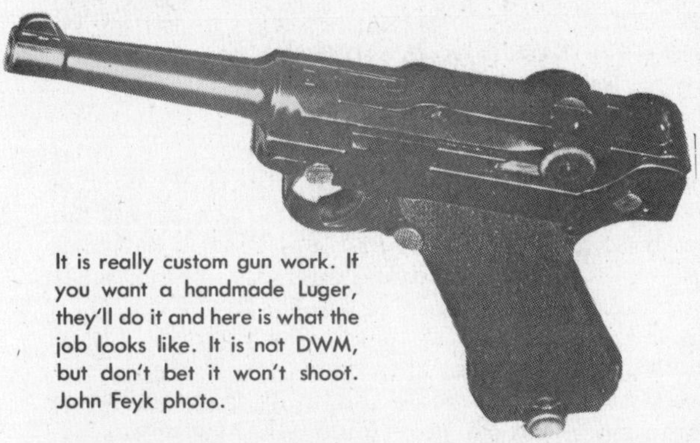

It is really custom gun work. If you want a handmade Luger, they'll do it and here is what the job looks like. It is not DWM, but don't bet it won't shoot. John Feyk photo.

Hillmen don't have much, but they do have essentials: sandals, headgear, a rifle and ammo, and doubtless a knife under there somewhere.

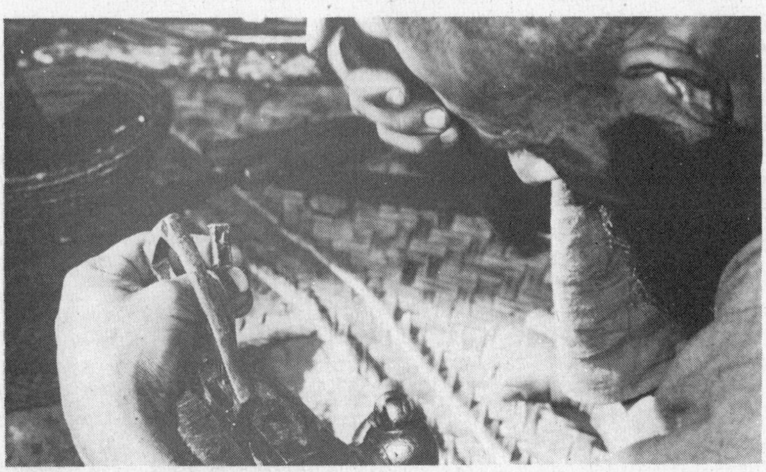

If it takes a cold chisel, that's what they use in Darrah, where this man is chiseling out a revolver frame. The gun will work, too. John Feyk photo.

Wind-toughened native walnut provided material for the stocks, inletted and shaped while held between the toes.

Later, more workers were imported from Sialkot and steel from Bombay. Gone was the day of ripping up railroad tracks. Ammo was now a problem, but there were British ammo convoys plying the Khyber and Kohat Passes. When ambushes of ammo convoys became expensive in men and rifles, Sher Din and his sons thought again.

The result of this thinking was a

This pile of rocks in a sangar, virtually invisible, and the three gentlemen within carry on SMLE, on AK-47, and RPK machine gun sans bipod. This is at Barikot in Kurnar Province late last year and these men had targets in sight. Wide World photo.

decision to experiment with reloading the empty fired cases. Ordinary wooden matches made in India used a simple fulminate, easy to make, so a similar compound was applied to the cups of fired Berdan primers with the indentations hammered out. Narrow punches were used to drive out the primers through a flash hole. Highly inflammable nitro-cellulose motion picture film was imported and shredded into a sort of unstable and vicious flake powder whose loading data would never grace a Lyman handbook or be sold by Bruce Hodgdon. By cut and try, fire and fly, the ammo improved until the 303's wounded or killed more enemies than firers.

A tribal industry had been born, and on Sher Din's death his five sons inherited a thriving business. They soon argued and with economic attrition were reduced to three separate firms from an original five. In 1925 a Darrah-made Martini-Enfield cost four hundred rupees ($128). Each year, production increased an increment or two and prices became more competitive with the British-made original, which was more expensive both in terms of money and the other terms which the British and their Colonial troops invariably demanded and received in "payment."

The Russian invasion of Afghanistan has now created a big boom in Darrah's small arms industry and a sympathetic reaction among related tribes in Pakistan. Sharing the same religious, ethnic and linguistic background, the Paks need no encouragement. Rebel groups filter across the border at night for resupply and to convey wounded and refugees to hospitals in Peshawar. Captured Russian AK's and other small and not so small arms are traded, bought and sold. Arab oil money pours into the Frontier, much of it going for the weaponry of Darrah.

Sajad Ahmed in his mid-twenties runs a factory in partnership with his three brothers, and produces 40 rifles a month, including fake SMLE's and '98 Mausers for $300 apiece. Waiting time is four days. The favorite rifle of the "Mujahedeeni," the 303 SMLE copy, sells in Darrah for between $200 and $300. It is difficult for any but the expert eye to distinguish the Darrah copy from the genuine. Earlier copies of the SMLE were softer and cruder, so that the tribesmen preferred the British product, but Darrah has come of age, and generally, the Darrah product is battle-worthy. Even their ammo is usually serviceable, but of course, imported arsenal ammo is preferred—and more expensive—up to $3 per round when supplies are tight, but cheaper when a new lot arrives by camel caravan.

One Darrah gunmaker stated the case thusly for the local product: "They serve us well (SMLE's) and every man with a gun is a free man. The Pakistani government offered to build us a textile mill and all kinds of other things a few years ago if we would give up our autonomy and our guns, but we value our freedom and our guns more than anything."

Indeed, there is little crime in Darrah and no police, since individual responsibility is the law as dispensed by tribal Jirga and the word of the Prophet Mohammed as written in the Koran.

My knowledge of Darrah-made rifles is first-hand, based on onetime ownership of a fine Martini-Enfield

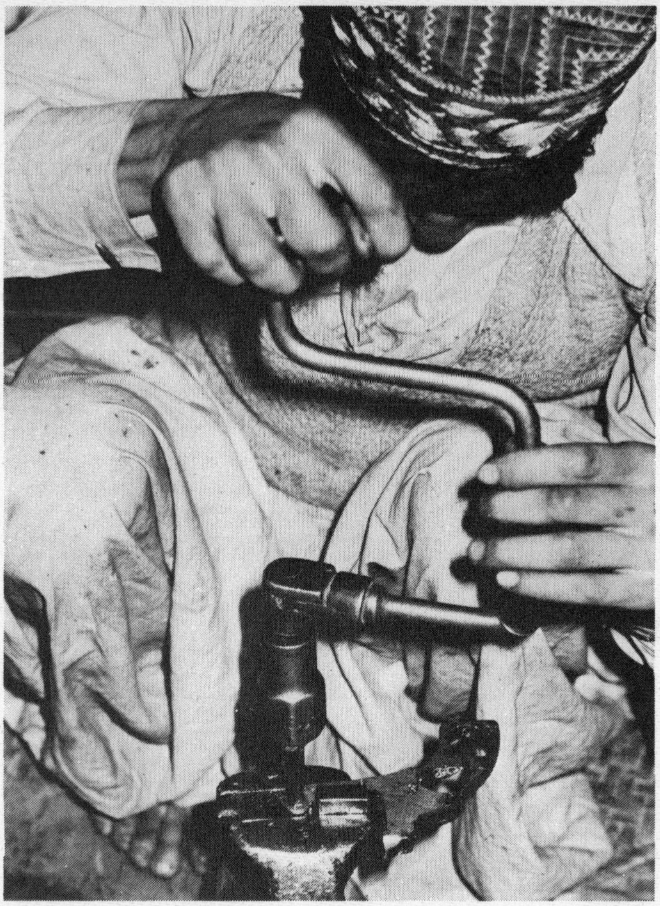

Tools from anywhere is the motto in Darrah. This one looks British and is being used to ream the hole for the hinge-pin in a Webley revolver look-alike. John Feyk photo.

The Afridi understand hot metal and with a hand-pulled bellows will forge-weld and harden drill bits and reamers. John Feyk photo.

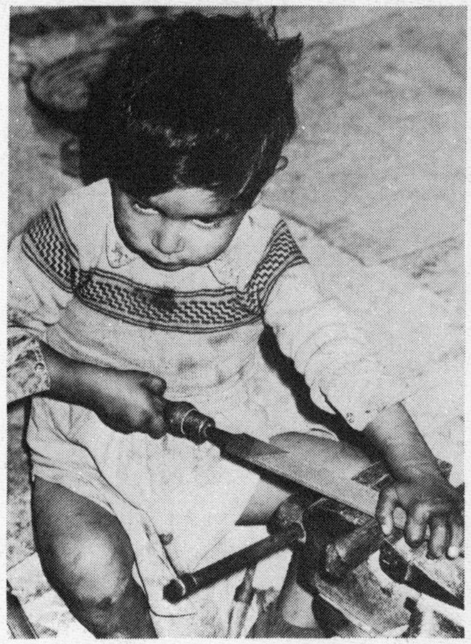

Fat as he is, this is no underpriviledged child. He's playing with a purpose, learning the family business as his fathers before him in Darrah. John Feyk photo.

copy. Proof of its excellence is that the proprietor of the gunshop where I purchased it, an expert, didn't know it was a copy. The hand-engraved range markings on the elevator sight were, on close scrutiny, not the work of an Enfield artisan, and the stock walnut was simply too fancy and "Circassian" to be British issue.

The tribesmen produce a variety of heavier arms, including 20 mm antitank rifles, mines and grenades, and many thousands of rounds of 303 and other ammunition are produced from imported and fired brass.

The Russian invasion is unlikely to inspire such poetry as Kipling wrote, but a certain timelessness is apparent. A comment from the official British India yearbook of 1930 gives the British view of the Pathan:

"The trans-border tribes are in communication with each other from north to south, as well as with tribes beyond the Durand Line, and military operations against any one of them are apt to produce sympathetic effects among the others. And containing as they do some of the most magnificent fighting men in the world, it is only picked and highly trained troops who can compete with them on anything like equal terms in their own hills."

Indeed the Russians and their Afghan puppets have their work cut out for them, and they know it enough to remain in their bases at night. All hands are against them, and to stall a vehicle for more than a few minutes, or to be left wounded or to be in the wrong place for more than a few minutes means instant death. The Pathan equates freedom and the rifle with life and the air he breathes, and every Pathan man, woman, and child now knows why the textile mill and similar incentives to drop small arms production was a bad bargain. •

Editor's Note:

It may be, sadly, that the Soviets will succeed in the Afghan hills. If they do, it will be with weapons other than artillery, air power and small arms. With such, the hillmen can contend and even win.

There are other weapons, noxious ones, in the Soviet arsenal. They have demonstrated their willingness to use them; what has not been demonstrated is the effectiveness of gas attack in the hills. No one knows if determined riflemen cannot figure a way to beat such weapons.

It was thought until recently that helicopter gunships were a sure cure against guerrilla groups. It now appears that when the targets shoot back, accurately and quickly, gunships are vulnerable. Perhaps it will be so with other weapons.

However it goes in the end, riflemen alone have shown the world, and most certainly the Soviets, they ought not be counted as other men.

K.W.

FINE GUN STEELS

An eminent gun designer discusses in clear terms the availability, properties, and treatment of special steels useful to the professional gunsmith and the home craftsman.

by PHILIP R. LICHTMAN

IN FIREARM ADS WE often read phrases such as "made of the finest steels." Many of us have paused to wonder what this means. There are thousands of "analyses," or compositions, of steel. The wealth of information about steels and their heat treatment is so staggering that it would take a lifetime of study to assimilate it.

Nonetheless it behooves us to learn as much as possible about steels, since—after all—nearly every part of a gun is made of some type of steel. A modicum of metallurgical knowledge is essential for the designer, experimenter, restorer, and gunsmith. This article, more practical than theoretical, has four purposes. First, we will briefly examine those basic properties of steel that relate directly to gun parts. Second, we will run through the vocabulary of heat treating. Third, we will take a look at four specific steels and their appropriate heat treatments. Although not the cheapest, I am confident, based on personal experience, that they are entitled to be listed among "the finest steels." Finally, we shall learn where these steels can be purchased, and where they can be heat treated properly.

Some Properties of Steels

One can describe a steel in many ways. A property of great significance is "tensile strength." Not only is tensile strength intrinsically descriptive of a steel, but also many other important properties are directly or inversely related to it.

The tensile strength of a steel is determined by literally pulling apart a test bar of the material. A massive machine firmly grips each end of the test bar and stretches it like a piece of taffy. At first the bar stretches elastically, so that it would return to its original size if the machine were to relax. Next, the bar yields plastically (in other words, becomes permanently stretched). The point at which plastic deformation occurs is called the "yield point." The testing machine relentlessly continues until the bar actually breaks in two, this point being known as the "ultimate tensile strength."

Tensile strength (by which I mean ultimate tensile strength) is what holds a gun's chamber together at the instant of firing. When gases expand against the chamber wall, the outward force causes each region of the wall to stretch away from its neighboring regions. This is conceptually the same as the tensile strength test itself. Tensil strength is measured in psi (pounds per square inch). For example, the popular barrel steel 4140, when tempered at 1,000°F., has a yield point of 143,000 psi and a tensile strength of 156,000 psi. Tearing apart a square inch cross-section of 4140 therefore requires a pull of 156,000 pounds. Although this is a tremendous force, gun parts are rarely one square inch in cross-section. A typical part, 1/10 inch square, has a cross-section of 1/100 square inch. A force of 1,560 pounds is sufficient to break it. Much larger forces are generated in firearms! By comparison, the strongest aluminum alloys have tensile strengths of about 80,000 psi, which explains in part why aluminum is rarely used for highly stressed gun components.

Tensile strength varies greatly with the alloy and with its heat treatment. But, picking a gun steel is more difficult than specifying the highest obtainable tensile strength. A crucial factor is "impact" or "shock" resistance—the ability of the metal to remain intact when subjected to sudden shock loads. A steel that performs creditably under static conditions may fail when used for a gun part due to the shock transmitted to the piece with each firing. Because shock resistance generally goes down as tensile strength goes up, one must strike a careful balance between the two properties.

Impact resistance is measured in several ways. Comparisons among published figures are hard to make because the readings vary according to the method employed. One common procedure is the "Charpy V-notch test," in which a test bar is given a deep, specially shaped notch which acts as a stress concentration point much as a crack in a piece of glass serves as a focus for further damage. The test bar is struck a blow hard enough to crack it, and the energy of the blow is recorded. Because gun parts are never completely free of machining or grinding marks, each of which can cause a concentration of stress, the Charpy V-notch figures are meaningful indications of shock resistance in firearm applications.

Another important property is the steel's hardness, which is directly proportional to tensile strength. Hardness is frequently measured by the "Rockwell" test, which impresses a tiny diamond point into the surface of the steel. The penetration for a given force determines the Rockwell hardness. Drills and milling cutters are Rc (Rockwell hardness on the C scale) 62 to 64. Punches are 56 to 60. Springs are 46 to 54. Rifle barrels are 32 to 38, and an ordinary unhardened drill rod is about 20. Hardness is a vital feature of gun parts, necessary to resist abrasion and surface wear and also to prevent "brinelling" or indenting of the pieces due to the constant pounding of one part (such as a pistol slide) against another (such as the frame).

A word commonly used to describe steel is "toughness." Toughness can be thought of as the opposite of brittleness. Clearly, toughness and impact resistance are intertwined, and we should perhaps consider shock resistance as toughness when faced with sudden loads. Semantics aside, choosing a gun steel is satisfactorily accomplished when one arrives at the optimum combination of tensile strength, shock resistance and hardness. The production engineer is confronted by many additional considerations such as cost, machinability, and availability. However, these are secondary matters to us.

Principles of Heat Treatment

Just as steels differ from each other in their properties, so do the properties of the same steel vary according to heat treatment. Steels are furnished in the annealed, or soft, condition for ease of machining. After pieces are fabricated the steel is heat treated to reinforce its good properties. Heat treating generally comprises two processes: hardening and tempering. (The word "drawing" is used synonymously with "tempering.")

Steel changes its internal organization, although not its chemical composition, as it is heated. After cooling from high temperatures steels change into a phase characterized by extreme hardness and brittleness. The hardening process begins by heating the metal above this critical temperature. Then by rapid quenching (cooling) the steel is transformed into its hard, brittle phase, where it remains even after returning to room temperature. Fully hardened steel is almost as brittle as glass and therefore quite useless for gun parts. In the tempering process the steel is baked well below the hardening temperature, which "draws" back some of the original toughness of the alloy, at some expense of tensile strength and hardness. The higher the drawing temperature, the softer and tougher the steel becomes. One selects a drawing temperature that produces the best combination of tensile strength, toughness (hence shock resistance), and hardness.

Some steels lend themselves to case hardening, more properly known as carburizing, an operation by which carbon is added to the surface of the metal to produce—upon rapid cooling—an extremely hard, wear resistant outer case while retaining a relatively soft, tough core. Steels so treated are noted for their shock resistance, since the brittleness of the outer case is compensated by the toughness of the core. Case hardening entails heating the parts in the proximity of carbon compounds, which causes carbon to enter into the surface of the steel. Since higher carbon content leads to greater hardness

Barrel cam pins. Pin at left, made of 0-1 tempered at 450° F. (Rc 58), broke immediately. Pin at right, machined from S-7 tempered at 600° F. (Rc 55), will last indefinitely.

This pistol slide fractured after several hundred rounds due to repeated impact against the frame abutment. The alloy is A-2, an air hardening die steel, double tempered at 1,100° F. The same heat treatment applied to S-7 produced an unbreakable slide.

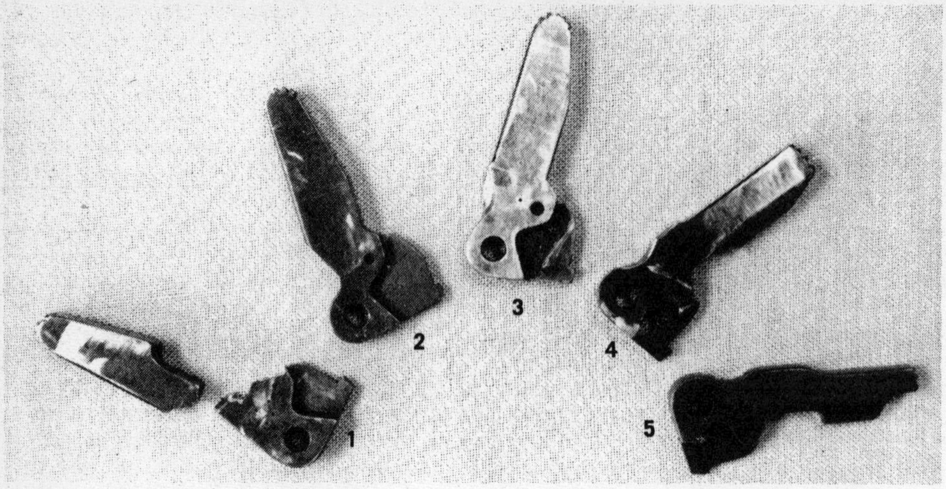

An array of pistol hammers. From left—(1) S-7, carburized to .005" depth, through hardness Rc 60. This hammer cracked after 1,389 rounds, indicating need for more shock resistance. (2) S-7, carburized to depth .005", through hardness Rc 56. Narrow sear contact surface rounded over, evidence of insufficient surface hardness. (3) 8620, a case-hardening steel, carburized to depth .005". Case hardness Rc 60. Sear contact surface failed from insufficient "back-up," or core hardness. (4 and 5) AMS 6263, carburized to depth .040". Case hardness Rc 61; core hardness Rc 44. These hammers are still working well after extensive testing.

upon quenching, the case becomes much harder than the core (although there is no clear line of demarcation).

The case may be only a few thousandths of an inch thick or it may extend inwards one-third the thickness of the piece. Case-hardened parts can be made of inexpensive, low carbon steel; consequently case hardening is preferred to "through" hardening for economic reasons in many high volume applications. However, there are also technical reasons for specifying case hardening in some situations.

Details of Heat Treatment

Through-hardened steels are often classified according to the media in which they are quenched during hardening. Therefore we speak of air-hardening, oil-hardening, and water hardening steels. The quenching medium determines the rate of cooling. Although alloying elements such as nickel, chrome, and molybdenum affect hardenability, in general the faster the cooling, the harder the quenched steel tends to be. Brine (salt water) quenches the fastest and, when used with water hardening steel, produces spectacularly hard pieces. Ordinary water quenches very rapidly. Oil, the most common quenching medium, cools at medium speed, while air cools slowly. It is extremely important that steel be quenched in the proper medium, because if a piece is cooled too rapidly it may develop stress cracks before the part is ever used; if cooled too slowly, it does not achieve the desired hardness.

The reason for considering air-hardening or oil-hardening alloys, when water-hardening steels are capable of such great hardness, is simple. Air-hardening steels (and oil-hardening steels to a lesser degree) are much less prone to warpage during quenching than are water-hardening alloys. A good air-hardening steel is not quite as hard after quenching as its water-hardening counterpart. But it is hard enough for any gun component. Furthermore, the air-hardened part retains its shape during heat treatment, while the water-hardened piece may distort to such a degree that it needs reworking. Premachining a hardened part is a chore to be avoided if at all possible!

Air-hardening steels normally require higher hardening temperatures than do oil- and water-hardening grades, which leads to the formation of scale on the surface of the hot metal while in the furnace. To combat this problem many metallurgists heat air-hardening steels in a vacuum, which completely prevents scale formation. Parts so treated have the same appearance as before treatment, notwithstanding their exposure to temperatures of 1,700 or 1,800 degrees F°.

Case hardening is performed in several ways. The oldest method is "pack carburizing;" parts are heated in a box of coke or charcoal. Some of the carbon migrates into the surface of the steel, raising the carbon content of the case, which after quenching becomes harder than the low carbon core. The carbon can also be imparted by heating steel in a liquid salt bath (such as cyanide), or in a gaseous medium (such as natural gas).

Tempering of either through-hardened or case-hardened steel is much simpler than hardening, because the temperatures are considerably lower. Once the parts have been quenched most of the work is done. To avoid the formation of stress cracks, the steel is tempered immediately after quenching. If tempering has to be postponed, the parts are stress relieved at a moderate temperature to forestall cracking.

The foregoing—although necessarily technical—is the bare minimum of information necessary to understand the specific recommendations that follow.

O-1: A Steel You Can Heat Treat at Home

There is a wide range of alloy steels used in making tools, dies, machine parts, and jigs. Known as tool steels, perhaps the most commonly used alloy is "O-1." The O stands for oil hardening. Oil-hardening drill rod is customarily O-1, as is most precision flat-ground stock. Industrial hardware stores carry many sizes and several shapes of O-1. I favor Starrett No. 496 flat-ground stock, which is obtainable from any Starrett tool distributor in a vast array of widths and thicknesses. The material comes fine ground on all sides except the ends, and thickness is held to within .001". An equally good brand is Carpenter Steel's "Stentor," which is designated "O-2" and is treated similarly to O-1.

The advantages of O-1 are its availability, ease of machining, and simplicity of heat treating. O-1 is perfectly adequate for gun parts that are so large in cross-section or so lightly loaded that failure due to overstressing is virtually impossible. For example, a dovetailed rear sight is very unlikely to fracture. Even if it were to break, the functioning of the weapon would remain unimpaired and damage to the shooter would be improbable. Such a part made of O-1 might be

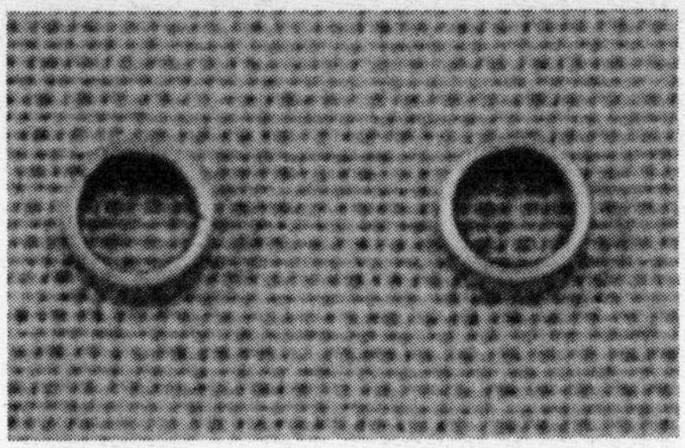

Two tiny rollers for a double action searage. They look identical, and are both tempered at about 400°F. The roller at left is turned from 52100, a bearing steel, and cannot last. The roller at right, made of S-7, will survive.

hardened and then tempered at 450° F. for a hardness of Rc 58 to 60. The corresponding tensile strength is about 280,000 psi, far above the requirement of the part. However, the high-tensile strength is intimately linked to the hardness, which is needed to resist denting of the sight due to its inevitable maltreatment with a hardened drift punch.

The greatest disadvantage of O-1 is its relative lack of shock resistance. We would not (except in an emergency) use O-1 for a firing pin. A firing pin made of O-1 at Rc 58 would have the right hardness but could break unexpectedly unless it were of a very large cross-section. On the other hand, an extractor could well be made of O-1 because the hardness requirement is much less—say, Rc 48 to 50—well within the so-called "spring temper" range of O-1. O-1 drawn at 800°F. would do the job. Its tensile strength of around 240,000 psi would exceed the requirement and the extractor would be tough and springy, with considerable resistance to impact. The key to the acceptability of O-1 for an extractor, but not for a firing pin, is the lesser hardness requirement of the extractor. Concomitant with the lower hardness is greater toughness, hence shock resistance.

A receiver, frame, slide or barrel made of O-1 would be a risky proposition. Frames are typically of hardness Rc 40, corresponding to O-1 tempered at about 1,100°F. At this hardness tensile strength drops to about 170,000 psi, which is still plenty, and impact resistance is fair. However, frames, slides, and barrels are costly pieces whose failure can damage the weapon and shooter. Much better steels are available for such important parts. O-1 should be reserved for emergencies or for pieces subjected to low stresses and shock. Indeed, a great many gun parts fall into this category.

So let's examine the heat treatment of O-1 steel. O-1 is treated by heating to 1,475°F., quenching in warm oil, and tempering between 350°F. and 1,100°F. to achieve desired properties. Ideally the steel should be heated in an electric furnace having an accurate temperature gauge. But few of us own such equipment. (Possibly the least expensive furnace is made by Thermolyne, of Dubuque, Iowa, whose Model No. F-D1525M sells for about $330.00) Therefore we shall see what can be done with a torch and regular household equipment.

The first step, hardening, requires a torch (oxy-acetylene, or—for small parts—a simple propane torch), some firebricks or concrete blocks on which to place the hot work, a household oven, and a pot of thin oil. There are excellent quenching oils (such as Mobil's Therm-Rex V), but they must be purchased in fairly large drums. Thus for occasional work light automotive oil—10W-30 at the heaviest—will have to do. It is imperative that the oil be warm, and for this purpose a household range or small hotplate works well. Heat the oil to about 120°F., which is warm to the touch but not scalding. Make sure that the volume of oil is very large compared with the pieces to be hardened. Situate the firebricks and the workpieces immediately adjacent to the oil, and proceed to heat the parts with the torch. This is the difficult part, because even experts cannot agree upon the exact shade of red heat that signifies 1,475°F. As a rule, heat the steel until its color is just beginning to change from red to orange. Then, without allowing the steel to cool, roll the parts off the firebrick into the warm oil. As soon as the pieces are cool, test the hardness with the flat of a fine file. The file should skitter across the surface without biting into the steel, since at this stage the pieces ought to be harder than the file. Leave the parts in the warm oil until they can be tempered, which should follow immediately.

The kitchen oven works admirably for most tempering. 450° is a good tempering temperature for pins, sights, spring plungers, detents, bushings, and rollers, yielding with O-1 steel a hardness of about Rc 58. (An oven thermometer should be employed, because oven dials are frequently inaccurate.) The procedure is simply to place the parts on a piece of aluminum foil in the hot oven, where they remain for one hour.

O-1 parts subjected to moderate stress—extractors, triggers, trigger bars, magazine catches, and screws—should be tempered at about 800°F., which exceeds the capacity of the household oven. With practice the torch can be used. To ensure some minimum degree of toughness, initially temper the parts at 550°F. or as high as the oven can attain. Then, polish as much as possible of the steel so that smooth bright metal is visible. As the parts are gently heated with the torch their color changes: first light straw appears, then dark straw, followed by brown, purple, and dark blue. The dark blue soon gives way to light blue, and finally the metal becomes almost steel-white again. At this point the parts have been exposed for at least a short time to about 800°F.

After tempering, the steel can be immersed in a glass of muriatic acid, which is commonly used for cleaning

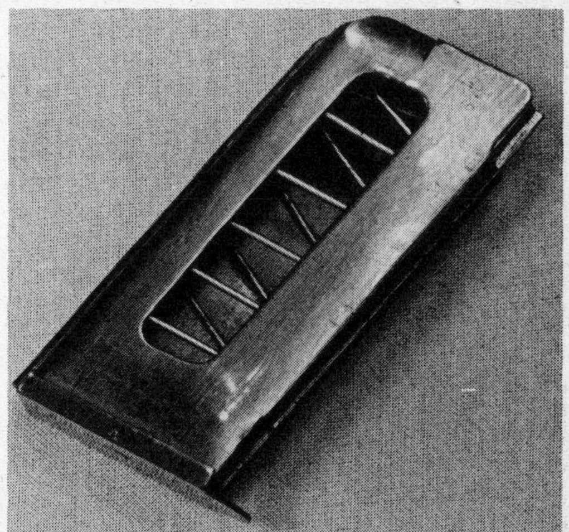

An experimental double-row pistol magazine. The body is formed from dead soft annealed 1075, using hand tools. After hardening and tempering at 700° F., the part is hard yet retains a springlike resilience. The buttplate and follower are machined from 0-1 tempered at 450° F.

masonry and is available at hardware stores, to clean off any remaining scale or color. To avoid any possibility of hydrogen embrittlement of the steel, bake at 350°F. to 375° for several hours after acid cleaning. (This is particularly important for pieces that have been subjected to plating!)

These steps produce hardened pieces that serve well in non-critical applications. The pitfalls are many. In particular, overheating during hardening can cause excessive brittleness, while underheating results in inadequate hardness. Nevertheless it is sometimes necessary to fabricate and install parts in a hurry, and in these instances a piece of O-1 steel and a little practice with home workshop hardening can save the day.

For highly stressed parts O-1 will not do and we shall now consider a few truly excellent steels that can be used successfully in almost any firearm application.

1075—A Fine Spring Steel

The uses of 1075 are manifold: flat springs, side plates, and magazine bodies are typical applications. 1075 is obtained in "dead soft annealed" sheets which can be bent almost as easily as soft aluminum. Annealed 1075 can be bent into sharp right angles without fear of breakage and can be cut with simple hand tools. It is an ideal steel for making sheet metal parts that must be readily formed or machined but which require hardness and springiness after heat treatment. 1075 is readily available from many steel warehouses. An outstanding variety of thicknesses and widths is carried by the Ward Steel Division of National Steel, Randolph, Mass. The minimum charge is steep, but 1075 is such a handy material that it is worth having a few thicknesses—say, .015, .025, and .031—on hand. It is important to specify "dead soft annealed," since 1075 can also be found in the hardened and tempered mode. The "75" connotes a carbon content of .75, or 3/4, of one percent. If 1075 is unavailable 1060, 1070 or 1080, which are nearly the same steel, can be substituted.

1075, an oil-hardening alloy, is the steel of choice whenever parts have to be fabricated from formed and bent sheet stock. 1075 distorts surprisingly little during heat treatment, so that complicated shapes can be bent and welded together with little fear of their "moving" during treatment. 1075 can be repeatedly annealed, reshaped, and rehardened. While 1075 can be treated in the home shop identically to O-1, parts made of 1075 are usually thin and relatively fragile. Accordingly, professional heat treatment is recommended. Any competent heat-treating house can process 1075, and instructions to the heat treater would typically read:

"3 pieces 1075 steel furnished in dead soft annealed state. Please harden and temper at 700°F."

The tempering range of 1075, insofar as gun parts are concerned, is from 600°F. to about 800°F. 600° is considered a hard spring temper, producing a hardness of Rc 53 and tensile strength of 255,000 psi. 700° gives a medium spring temper; the figures are Rc 47 and 230,000 psi. 800° is a soft spring temper, having Rc 44 and 205,000 psi. It is better to err on the soft than on the hard side; shock resistance increases as hardness decreases. Furthermore a soft piece, if bent, can be straightened and re-hardened whereas a hard piece, if broken, cannot be salvaged.

Bearcat S-7
A Multipurpose Super-Steel

In recent years several tool steels have been developed for extreme shock resistance. Bearcat S-7, a product of Bethlehem Steel, is probably the best example. The "S" stands for "shock resisting." Bearcat is so superlative a steel that if I were permitted to use only one alloy for all purposes, Bearcat would be the unquestioned choice. Bearcat has an unusual combination of toughness and hardness. Furthermore Bearcat, an air hardening steel, undergoes virtually no distortion in heat treatment; complex parts can be finish machined and polished prior to heat treating. Bearcat machines more easily than ordinary O-1 drill rod.

Bearcat S-7 is available in drill rod and fine ground precision flat stock, as well as ordinary flats and rounds. A broad range of sizes is stocked by Bethlehem tool steel distributors, my favorite source Lindquist Steel of Stratford, Conn. Bearcat was developed for such tools as welding chisels for nuclear reactors. In this application a chip broken from a chisel point can contaminate the reactor, yet the chisel has to be hard enough to retain its edge. This correlates with firearm applications, where pieces must be hard to resist abrasion and pounding but cannot be allowed to fracture. Bearcat is stronger than 4140, and can be used for receivers, barrels, frames, firing pins, strikers, and virtually any other heavily stressed gun part. In certain applications a case hardened part can withstand more shock, but these instances are few and are discussed below. For all practical purposes, Bearcat S-7 is an everyday super-steel and should be stocked by all gun part makers.

The heat treatment of S-7 is a job for professionals. The hardening temperature of over 1,700°F. demands special protection of the surface. Typical heat treating instructions are:

"2 pieces Bearcat S-7 tool steel furnished in the annealed state. Please harden in *vacuum furnace*. Inert gas quench. *Double* temper at 400°F."

The reason for double tempering is to eliminate the last traces of so-called retained austenite or untempered martensite, left over from hardening, which might induce brittleness. The treatment above is excellent for firing pins, hammer blocks, and other severely shocked pieces demanding high hardness. It results in a hardness of Rc 58 to 60, which is very hard indeed, and tensile strength of over 300,000 psi; yet this steel withstands repeated high shock loads without breaking.

The use of Bearcat is becoming more widespread and it should be easy to find a local supplier for this treatment. My source is Industrial Heat Treating of Quincy, Mass., who treat Bearcat on a routine basis.

For frames, receivers, and slides, which require much less hardness, a good treatment is identical to the above except that the double tempering is carried out at 1,100°F, yielding Rc 47 and 230,000 psi. With this treatment Bearcat is extraordinarily tough and can withstand extreme shock.

Drawing at 1,100°F results in surface color and scale. Although many heat treating firms use vacuum furnaces for hardening, very few of them temper in vacuum. One can protect the surfaces by copper plating the parts between the hardening and tempering operations. First, the Bearcat is hardened in the usual way; then it is stress relieved at about 350°F to prevent cracking prior to tempering. The parts next are plated with 1/2 thousandth of copper, and are returned to the heat treater for double tempering at 1,100°F. After tempering, the copper plate is stripped, exposing the original bright steel surface. If scale and discoloration are immaterial, as is the case if post-hardening grinding or lapping are

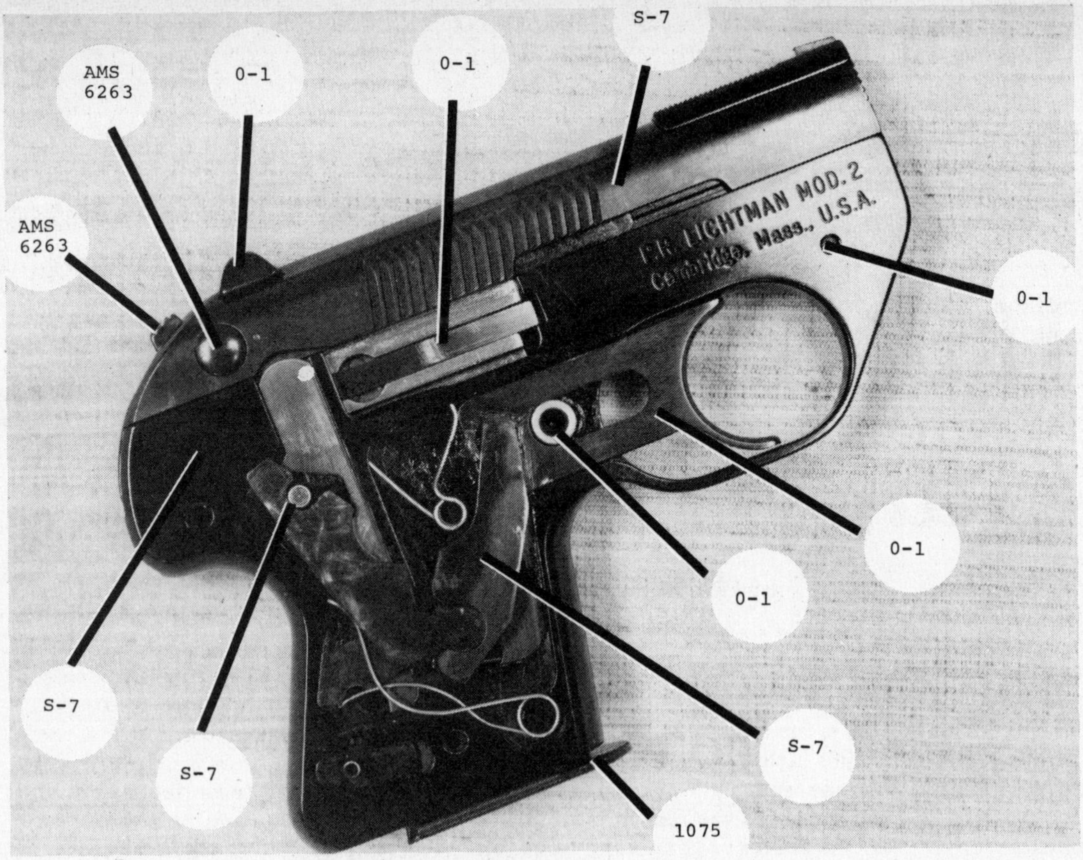

An experimental pistol with cover plate removed to show materials used for various parts. See text for details of these number-indicated metals.

planned, the copper plating process is unnecessary.

AMS 6263
A Tough Carburizing Steel

Only a few gun parts are critically important to the functioning of the firearm and the safety of the shooter. Sometimes these parts require high surface hardness, such as hammers and sears, whose rubbing edges must not wear. For such parts one does well to select AMS 6263, a carburizing steel used for military tank transmission gears and other severe applications. (Because tank gears are subjected to very great shock, yet must be hard to minimize wear, their problems are similar to those of hammers and sears.) AMS 6263 is the aircraft certified version of a relatively common steel, 9315, which can be used in place of AMS 6263 if the latter cannot be obtained. Numerous steel warehouses carry 9315, and I have purchased AMS 6263 from Bowsteel of Linden, NJ. AMS 6263 is difficult to obtain except as round bars, but a variety of diameters can be had and flat shapes can be cut from rounds without much difficulty since this steel machines very easily.

When high surface hardness is not needed, Bearcat S-7 tempered to medium hardness has as much or nearly as much shock resistance as carburized AMS 6263. For sears and hammers, though, AMS 6263 is superlative. The treatment is fairly exotic, sample instructions being:

"4 pieces AMS 6263 (aircraft grade 9315) furnished in annealed condition. Please *gas* carburize. Cool to room temperature. Re-heat for hardening. Oil quench. Deep freeze. Temper for case Rc 60-62, core Rc 44. Hold distortion to a minimum. Case depth to be .030-.040 in."

This treatment was recommended by, and is performed at Bennett Heat Treating of Newark, NJ, although other sources can be found.

Case depth is a crucial element. As a rule, the core must not be less than 1/3 the total thickness of the part. However, parts vary in thickness from point to point, and one has to determine case depth based on the thinnest section of the piece. Otherwise the hard case might completely penetrate the thin areas, leading to excessive brittleness and premature breakage at those places. Case depth is the only variable I recommend in the treatment above. A core hardness of Rc 44 is needed to back up the hard case. If the core is too soft, forces acting on the hardened surfaces can crack the case by permitting it to flex against the soft core.

Conclusion

At least one of the four steels we have examined is appropriate for practically any small-arms part. O-1 is not particularly strong or shock resistant, but it is almost always available and can be treated without delay. 1075 is a soft, easily bent sheet stock that hardens into a tough, springy steel. S-7 is a superb general purpose shock-resistant alloy. AMS 6263 is a tremendously tough carburizing steel. As a group these steels represent a useful range of properties that should keep any well-designed gun intact. ●

EDITOR'S NOTE: Readers should understand that misuse of materials in firearms can be harmful to the weapon and perhaps dangerous to the shooter. The publisher and author cannot assume responsibility for accidents and damages arising from use of unrecommended materials or faulty firearm construction.

World's Handiest Gun

by FRANK de HAAS

A FELLOW ONCE bought a second-hand gun from me and he paid for it by writing out a check. When he got to the part on the check that read "For . . . . .," he hesitated a moment and then wrote "Rat Poison."

"That's for the income tax boys, and besides that is just what it's for," he told me. That was all right with me, he had bought a lot of rat poison in that gun; but more than that he'd also bought the handiest, most versatile gun made anywhere in the world today, the Savage 24.

This little Savage is voted the number one utility gun by a great host of shooters, and the reason is simple; it is two guns in one, a very desirable combination of two of the best liked and most widely used cartridges ever made, a 22 rimfire and a 410 rifle-shotgun wrapped in one low-cost package. Both the 22 rimfire and the 410 shotshell have always been extremely popular in single shots, but put them both together in a single arm, one that looks and feels like a gun, and the combination goes to town.

No newcomer, the little piece is now a tried and true gun. Stevens first made it in 1939, when it was known as the Stevens 22-410, and when Savage took over Stevens, they called it the Savage 24. It remains the only 22-410 on the market, and no other gun even resembles it. Describing it, I'd say it is a regular 410-gauge single barrel shotgun with a groove milled in the top of the barrel, and into which is brazed a slim 22 caliber tube. Then the breech is raised for the 22 firing pin and a little lever added in the frame for the firing selector. Add a pair of rifle sights, and we have a single-triggered over-under combination that is gaining new friends daily.

The author's son Mark, armed with the customized 22-410, waits out a squirrel.

Best for Farmers

As a gunsmith serving a rural area I know that the appeal of this type and caliber of gun is very great. For the farmer a 410 shotgun and/or a 22 rifle is almost a necessity around the place, so what could be better than to have both in one handy gun? Farmers use the 24 for everything — employed on livestock for butchering, on sick and injured animals, on starlings and sparrows, the little gun is pointed at and kills more varmints than anything else, such as rats, stray cats, weasels, and a raft of other pests. Although neither the 22 nor the 410 is considered gun enough for the larger pests, many of them — fox, bobcat, badger, etc. — have found themselves a little too close to the muzzle of this over-under. If within 25-30 yards, most pests are killed with the 410 load; beyond this range the 22 caliber slug will prove the better killer. With adequate and correctly adjusted sights, the 22 range can be extended up to 75-100 yards. Leave it to the farmer to get the most out of a gun — he'll have this one handy near the back porch or barn for any and all unwelcome critters, but he'll shoot little game.

Most of the other owners of the 24 bought them, like the farmer, for pest shooting. My main interest in it, and that of many others, is for small game shooting, largely rabbits and squirrels. It's the ideal gauge for a cottontail rabbit gun, bar none, and is used by bunny hunters from young to old. Shot at short ranges, they are easy to kill, and the 410 will seldom fill the meat with a lot of fur-balled shot as the larger gauges often do. I have stopped a lot of bunnies with my Model 24 in ditches and brush patches at ranges up to 30 yards with only one or two pellets doing the work, using the short 2½-inch shells with 6's. However, most of my rabbit shooting is done with the 22 top barrel of this gun, taking only head shots at ranges seldom over 30 yards, about the same as the 410 range. This is done when there is snow on the ground — I spot them sunning themselves near their burrow entrances or on the edges of brush piles and small groves. Even if the shot is missed, the 22 Short doesn't bother them much and I can usually get in the second shot. But if he runs, a flick on the selector button and the 410 catches him if he is still in range. For this shooting, when the ranges are close, I prefer the 1x scope sight on the gun over any other sights.

Squirrel hunting is tougher, but the Savage 22-410, with proper sights, is right up to the task. There are two types of squirrel hunters, those who favor the shotgun and those who prefer the 22 rifle. The 24 is the only gun made that fills the needs of both. I am an in-betweener, taking squirrels with either bore as the occasion warrants, though preferring always to take the squirrel with a 22 head shot. On most hunts I never use the 410. However, on a few hunts, when they were wild and ran directly to the den tree, I'd not have nailed any without that 410 barrel. For squirrels I like a 2½-power scope with plain crosshairs; the 1x scope lacks definition to pick out and sight on a squirrel's head beyond 25 yards, camouflaged as they are most of the time in branches and leaves.

I derive much pleasure from a gun in the Fall, when the closing weeks of the fishing season coincide with the opening of the squirrel and rabbit season; Fall catfishing and squirrel hunting along a wooded river is usually very productive. At that time the 22-410 brings home more meat than the fishpole. The little gun is also a good companion on summertime fishing trips along the river to kill water snakes and snapping turtles.

The barrels of the Model 24 are 24 inches long, and they're equal in performance to other guns of the same caliber and quality. I've never had to complain about the accuracy of the 22 barrel, with proper sights, of course, for it is securely brazed to the 410 barrel, thus making it as stiff as a heavy target barrel. On all the 24's on which I have installed new and better sights, testing them for accuracy revealed that the 22 Long Rifle cartridge could be counted on to hit the head of a rabbit at 50 yards and of a squirrel at 35. That's as good as you'll get from any other 22, single shot or

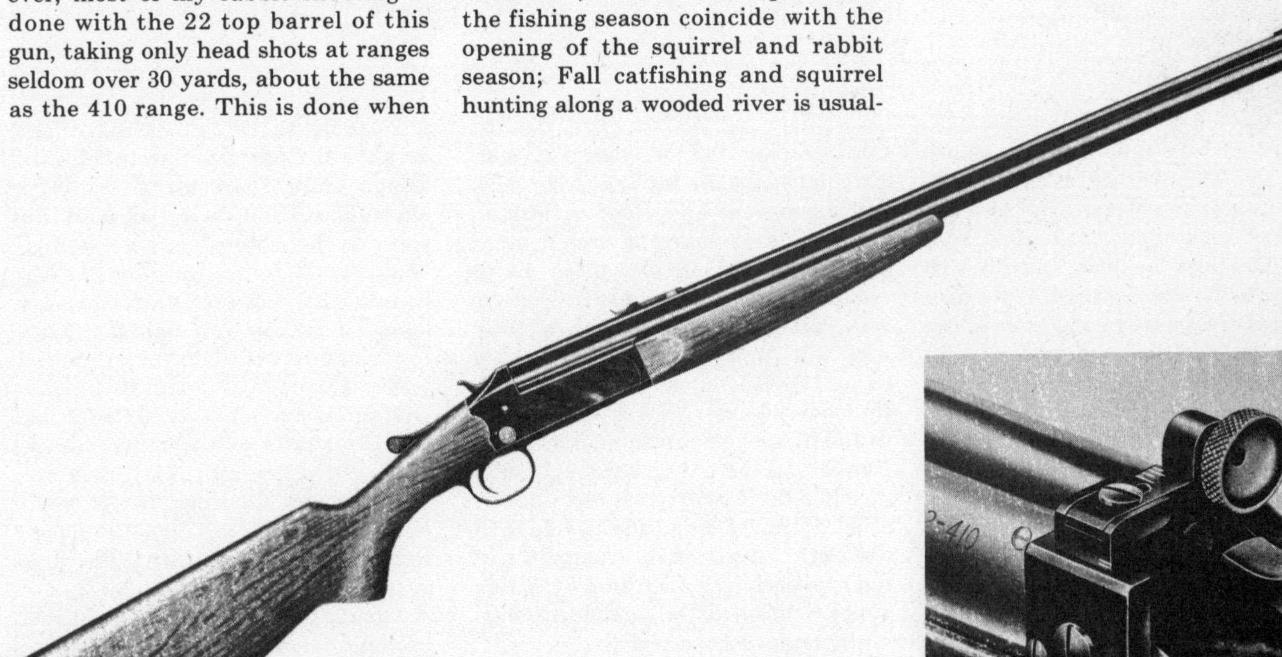

The Savage Model 24 combination 22 rifle and 410 shotgun, the handiest gun made in America today, is a light, low cost favorite with farmers, campers and small game hunters.

The 22-410, fitted with Lyman 55 peep, is more accurately aimed, but the sight does interfere with fast shots from the 410 barrel.

repeater, in the lower price class. A couple of these 24's tested were very accurate, especially when fitted with a 4-power scope (for testing only) and the trigger honed to a lighter pull. You can thus expect the accuracy to be far better than normally required of this rifle. The factory sighting arrangement on the rifle barrel hides much of this little gun's potential accuracy — more about this later.

The pattern and range of the short 410 barrel is also normal and will compare favorably with other 410's in this respect. In testing patterns with the M24, I found a couple that gave larger than average spread, but this may be an advantage if the gun is used mostly on pests. Any 410, at its best, is still a very short range shotgun, regardless of all the tall tales from many 410 fans. Beyond 30 yards, the 410 pattern rapidly becomes too thin to be effective. Number 7½ shot is best, with 6's next, in either the 2½- or 3-inch shells. 410 rifled slug loads can also be had, but they're highly ineffective — they are *not* deer loads. Muzzle energy of the 410 slug is a mere 460 foot pounds; at 100 yards it's only 225, while the 12-gauge slug figures are 1995 and 1165. The 410 slug, energy-wise, is in the same class as the 25-20 and 32-20 rifle cartridges, and neither are deer loads. In a dire pinch and at close range, when the shot can be well placed, they will down a deer. I know a butcher who used 410 slugs to slaughter cattle, but that is no guarantee, for he could have done the same with a 22 Short.

Remodeled Mossberg scope mounts carry the 1x Weaver, clamped over the 22 barrel of the Savage 24.

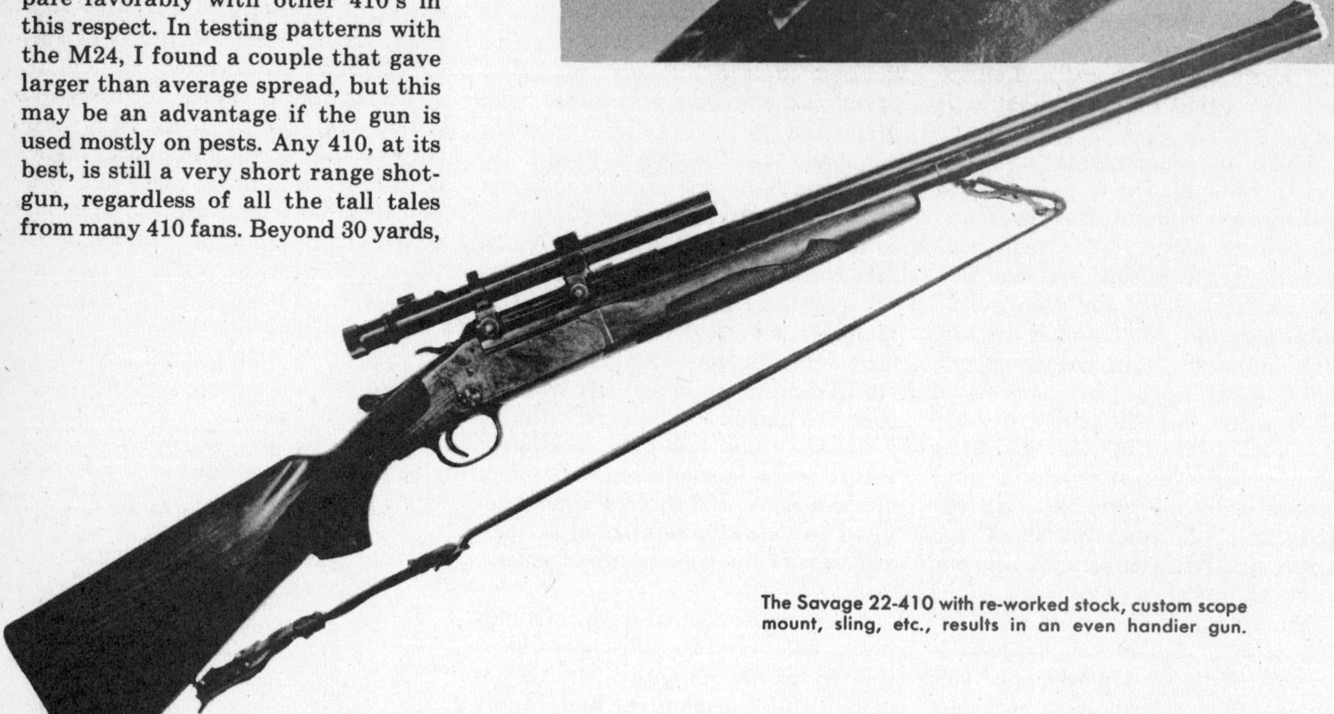

The Savage 22-410 with re-worked stock, custom scope mount, sling, etc., results in an even handier gun.

Soon after its debut, the Model 24 became very popular, especially so as a farm gun, where they really got used a lot. Quite a few were brought in for minor repairs, which generally consisted of replacing broken firing pins, 410 extractors and selector button screws. But something much more serious showed up also. The major complaint from most of the owners was that they could not hit a thing with the 22 barrel, therefore having to use the 410 almost entirely. Inspection quickly revealed a loose sight problem, often both front and rear; frequently the entire rear sight was missing or it was so loose that it could be moved from side to side with the slightest pressure. I usually put the rifle back into operation by fitting a new sight or the original one, sweating it in place to keep it there.

Only Real Flaw

Right there, in the rear sight as the factory installs it, is the major fault and weakness of the Savage 24. It is actually the only real flaw in its entire design. Sure, there are a few other things that could be better on it, but this one thing stands out so glaringly that I can't figure out why Savage hasn't long ago remedied this. The fellow at Savage who figured out how to put the 22 barrel on the 410 barrel, who dreamed up the two firing pins-one hammer action, was no slouch, but not so with the gent who drew up the specs for attaching the open rear sight. Even a TV script writer would have known the tiny weak dovetail wouldn't be worth a darn. The fault is not so apparent when the gun is new, but after some use the sight soon becomes loose, thus giving the top half of this wonderful little gun a bad break. An entire new rear sight should be designed, then securely fitted to the barrel.

The front sight is on a very small

ramp held in place with one tiny screw, which appears solid enough at first glance. The aiming part is a small square-topped blade and for me it is as near ideal as I'd want. However, many shooters prefer a slightly higher sight with a small bead of some sort. Being as small as it is, the whole ramp and sight does not interfere with quick aiming as a shotgun and is rugged enough to stand a lot of abuse — if it were only fastened on better. The little screw that holds it in place will shake loose and sometimes come out, for the gun is often carried on a tractor. It should be sweated on, in addition to the screw, and then it is on to stay.

Even with the factory sights sweated down, they are still a long way from being entirely satisfactory for precise aiming of the rifle barrel, which is capable of very accurate shooting. The next improvement that the shooter can make towards better sighting accuracy is to remove the factory rear sight and fit Lyman's #55 receiver sight to the frame. I used a Model 24 so equipped for several years and the rifle barrel accounted for a lot of small game. As good as it was, though, the peep sight spoiled the usefulness of the 410 barrel because the peep disc and arm seemed to get in my way when sighting for a fast shot at running or flying game.

The Lyman #55 sight is the only such sight made for the little over-under, but it is, unfortunately, poorly constructed. No stronger than the factory open rear sight, it can be moved and bent by thumb pressure alone. It is even more vulnerable to bumps because its arm has no support at all. Thus, though the peep sight does allow more accurate rifle aim, the advantage is more than offset by the fact that it slows up the shotgun and it lacks ruggedness. A good receiver peep sight featuring a flip-over disc could be designed for this rifle-shotgun that would be both rugged and handy. The disc would be up when the rifle is to be used and flipped down out of the way when the shotgun is fired, ideally with the flip arrangement tied in with the selector button so that the correct sight would appear when choosing the barrel to be fired.

Until such an aperture sight is available, I have abandoned all iron sights in favor of a scope sight as being far superior for any and all types of shooting with the 22-410. The 1x Weaver scope (no longer made), correctly mounted on this gun, will make it even more versatile and handier than you could possibly imagine. It really comes into its own when so equipped. The old style Weaver scope, which has a ¾-inch tube, is just the ticket if both the rifle and shotgun bores are used equally; the finest and best suited sighting equipment to be had, it provides an accurate and fast means of sighting for both barrels. The latest 1-power K Weaver scope would do even better although the larger 1-inch tube might look somewhat out of place on such a small gun.

When this gun is used mostly for game shooting, as it is in my case, and

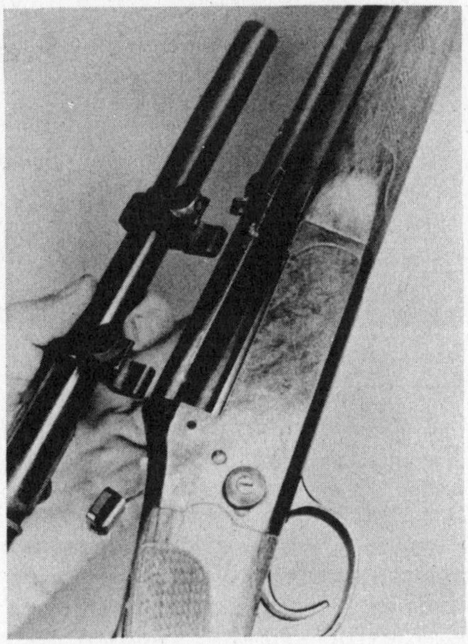

Knurled nuts let the custom mount slip off the gun, can be replaced in seconds with scope still in zero.

the hunter wishes to place meat on the table that is not all shot up, he'll naturally be using the 22 barrel more than the 410. In this case, a small 2½-power scope might be a better choice, because it affords more precise aim, say, when shooting at a squirrel or a grouse's head. A good quality 2½ x scope will not slow the shotgun shooting much, if any, especially if you are accustomed to using scopes. The Weaver J2.5 scope would be a good choice. My present Model 24 is fitted with an old Weaver 330 scope, about 2½ power, with plain crosshairs. The scope is sighted-in with the 22 barrel and the 410 will then, or very nearly so, throw its pattern around the center of the reticle.

Selecting the scope is relatively simple, but mounting it is something else again. No one makes a mount for the Savage 24, so attaching the scope will have to be a gunsmithing job of adapting an existing mount or making an entire new one. Although the 22 barrel is quite small in diameter, the easiest solution is to cut two shallow grooves along the top of the barrel (an easy milling operation) to accept the Weaver tip-off mount or other mounts on the same principle, such as the Mossberg. I have fitted a couple of Model 24's this way with complete owner satisfaction. A minor objection to the Weaver tip-off mount is that it is too long to attach without first removing the factory rear sight. Other than these low cost tip-off mounts and the necessary groove cutting, any other mounts must be tailor-made to fit the gun and scope.

Making a mount for this combination gun is not too difficult for a careful metal worker, and the gun is already provided with natural anchoring grooves where the 22 barrel joins the 410 barrel. Designing and making the mount requires provision for rings to hold the scope tube, with clamps to fit into these grooves. Utilizing this natural "dove-tail" where the two barrels join, I have designed and made several types of mounts that were satisfactory in every way. The latest one, illustrated on my own 22-410, is by far the best, featuring quick detachability. It is small and light, yet strong enough for the roughest use, and is easily and quickly removed and replaced without changing its zero. The scope and the entire mount are removed as a single unit, leaving nothing on the rifle — no bases, pins, screws, or holes. The original rear open sight stays on the gun, enabling it to be used when the scope is removed.

Equipped with a scope, the hammer cannot be easily grasped with the thumb to cock it, but the Williams Gun Sight Company makes a large hammer spur for the 24 that solves the problem. Even without a scope on the gun, this wide spur is helpful in pulling the hammer back easily and quickly.

One would think that this small-bore over-under would make an ideal gun with which to teach youngsters something about rifle and shotgun shooting, or as their first gun for hunting. In principle it is just that because it has a safe break-open type of action, is easy to load and unload, and has everything plainly visible at all times. The exposed hammer, which automatically rebounds to the safety notch, always has been considered safer than any so-called safety ever devised. Yet, I must reluctantly say, action stiffness will prevent youngsters much below 12 years old from using it safely. If a boy or girl can't close an opened Model 24 without resting the muzzle on something, or cannot easily draw the hammer to full cock and let it down again, then it's not safe for them to use. My son could handle the 22-410 when he was 13, but not when he was 11.

That hard closing, much too difficult for young arms, especially with a new gun, is caused by the stiff hinge and because the closing of the action must also compress both 410 and 22 extractor springs. Gunsmithing can relieve this stiffness somewhat and some of the stiffness also works out after the gun has been used a great deal. The main trouble lies in the fore-end fastening, which has a very stiff spring exerting a lot of pressure on the hinge surfaces. Savage claims this fore-end fastener will positively prevent the gun from shooting loose; true, but it also keeps the gun from closing easily. A stiff mainspring is necessary for the desirable short hammer fall, but young fingers have trouble cocking the hammer easily. These difficulties are of no consequence to older shooters, but until your youngster can readily manipulate the Model 24, it is best not to give him one.

With the squirrel and fishing seasons both open, chances are the 22/410 will take home more meat than the fishpole.

Marble's Game Getter Compared

The predecessor to the Model 24 Savage combination gun was the famous (or infamous) Marble's Game Getter, a skeleton stocked short barreled 22-44 or 410, half pistol-half shotgun-rifle combination over-under. The early advertisements made many claims for it, such as shooting a host of cartridges from all the 22 rimfires to a mess of 44's and 410's in both shot and ball. It was also credited with killing moose, bear, and other large game by backwoodsmen and trappers. The name "Game Getter" was well suited to this holsterable weapon. The Federal Firearms Act put the damper on it because of its short barrels and folding stock. Years later, during and after World War II, our armed services adopted a similar weapon and called it the Survival Gun, chambered for the 22 Hornet and the 410. While the old Game Getter did have a lot of merit (more so than its modern counterpart, the equally odd looking Survival Gun), they were strictly tools and designed as such. The Savage 22-410, however, is a sporting gun, looks and handles like a gun should, yet it's able to do the utility work of the Game Getter and do it better.

The only competition that the Savage 24 has ever had existed for a couple of years or so, back around 1941, when Marlin made one similar to it, built on their Model 90 over-under shotgun action. Besides 22 Long Rifle chambering in one barrel, it could also be had in 22 Hornet or 218 Bee, all in combination with the 410 shot barrel. It never became popular, chiefly because the then-Stevens 22-410 sold for the ridiculously low price of about $15.00, while the Marlin gun was tagged at over $40.00. That was a lot of difference in those days and the Marlin was not that much better. Today the Savage sells for the inflated price of about $40.00, but that 40 bucks cannot buy a handier gun anywhere, or one that can be used and enjoyed as much.

There has not been a single major change made in the Savage 24 since it was first introduced. If the gun had a little competition today we might see some alterations for the better made in it, for it can well stand some basic improvements by the factory. Besides new sights, they could cut down the hammer rebound so that a lighter mainspring could be used, thus making the hammer and trigger pulls lighter. The hammer spur could also be reshaped for easier thumbing. The

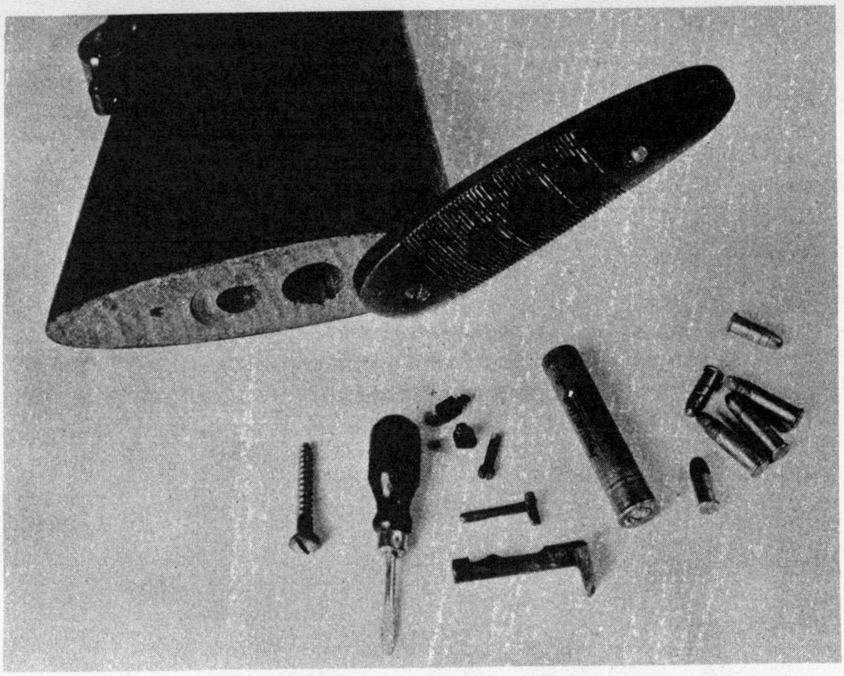

Spare parts, plus some emergency ammo, could come in mighty handy some day.

earlier guns, they at least were superbly fitted, shaped, finished and checkered, and the amateur gunsmith (or professional) could not do better than to copy these in reshaping the present wood stocks and fore-ends. Then sand, refinish and checker as desired. A light ⅞-inch sling is very useful on this gun and is easily added. Screw one swivel in the butt stock and clamp the proper Phil Judd barrel band swivel on the 410 barrel.

Besides the small game hunter and the farmer, there are many others who will find the Savage 24 ideal. On trips into the wilderness any place on the globe (the gun is exported to many places all over the world), whether camping, hunting, exploring or whatever, the 22-410 is the handiest gun to have along, bar none. Ammunition can be purchased anywhere and it is light and easy to carry. Taken down, it can be stuffed into a duffle bag, bed roll or suit case. With barrels only 24 inches long, it packs into spaces few other guns can enter. Even fully assembled it is only 40 inches long, with utility packed into every inch. I know a missionary who took one of these Model 24's into the wilds of the Pan-American countries, and no one was ever more pleased with any one gun. For any extended trips into the wilds, the gun should be revamped as outlined above to make it more rugged, reliable and easier to carry. Besides this gunsmithing, a few spare parts, wrapped in waxed paper, should be taken along, placed in the hole in the stock under the butt plate. They are: firing pins and extractors for the 22 and 410 barrels, one each; a selector button screw or two, plus a small screw driver that will fit the head of the firing pin retaining screws. These are the parts most often broken or lost. With these six small parts, there is still room for a few waxed matches, some 22 cartridges and a 410 shell, emergency items that could spell "survival."

If I were limited to just one American made gun, that gun would be the little Savage Model 24. I'm an average shooter who does some small game hunting and pest shooting, a lot of plinking and informal target shooting, who just likes to have a gun along when out-of-doors, and for these several purposes, this combination rifle-shotgun suits me right down to the ground.

selector lever could be a bit heavier and with a slightly longer up and down movement, and a non-rotating selector button attached with a larger screw. (Savage informs me that the selector mechanism is in line for revamping and will correct this weakness. Perhaps other faults will be corrected later.) A new steel trigger guard, even a stamping, would be better than the pot-metal one it now has. The fore-end latch could be changed so that the gun would open and close easier. Lastly, the gun should be made with less drop in the stock. The drop varies from gun to gun, not so much because the stocks differ, but because of the way the barrels are fitted to the frame. From all this, it may seem that I'm running down the 22-410 unnecessarily; far from it, for even with the bugs cited, it is still the most versatile gun we have today. But after about eighteen years of personal acquaintance with these guns, in using, repairing and remodeling them, I think some changes are overdue and, if made, would further boost its popularity.

Amateur gunsmiths can do some fixing on the Model 24 and they'll like the way it responds to the simple gunsmithing and remodeling needed to make it look, feel and shoot better.

Here's how to sweat that rear sight in place: remove the sight, polish the bottom and also brighten the slot in the barrel. Then tin both with regular solder, using a small torch. Drive the sight back into place, carefully sight-in, and then reheat with the torch until the solder melts to join the dovetails. The front sight ramp should be done at the same time.

Tuning Trigger

The trigger pull may be lightened to about 3 or 4 pounds by carefully honing the sear, but the sear engagement must not be reduced as the main spring is very stiff. The pull required to cock the hammer can be reduced slightly by grinding about one-half turn off the mainspring. Removing a full turn or coil will make it too weak to fire reliably. The opening and closing of the action can be made a little easier if the hinge bearing surfaces are polished and oiled, and the breech face also polished smooth where the 410 extractor rubs.

To improve the looks and to make it feel and handle better, the excess wood on the fore-end, especially on the late models, should be trimmed down until it is flush with the frame and more pleasingly shaped, thus killing its pot-bellied lines. Since the pistol grip on the buttstock is unnecessarily long, a half-inch can be cut from the bottom of the grip, the grip then capped and shaped as it should be. While I did not care for the Tenite stocks and fore-ends that were on the

The Miquelet Lock

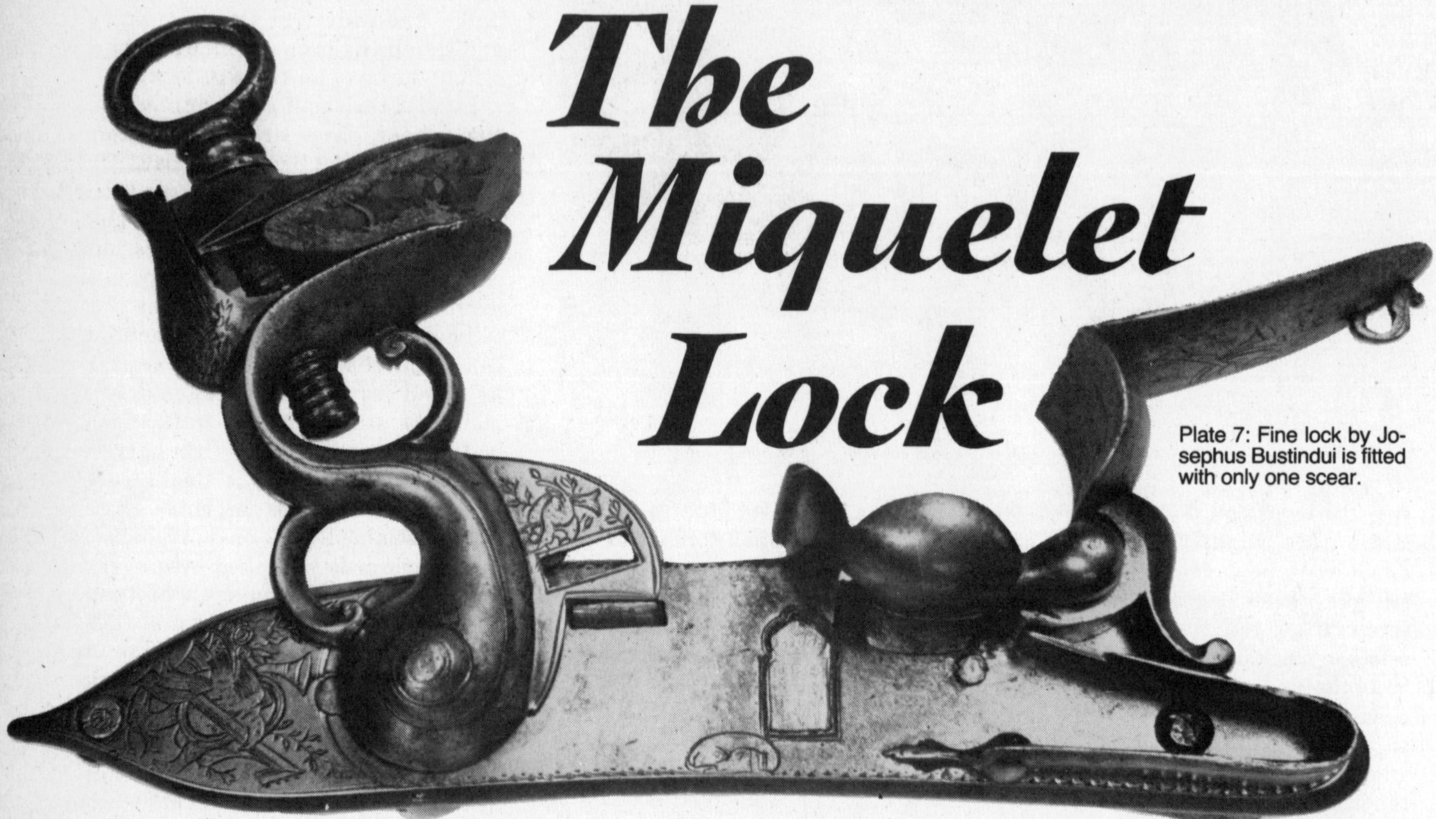

Plate 7: Fine lock by Josephus Bustindui is fitted with only one scear.

by MAJOR NOEL CORRY

Interesting and decorative, it follows its own rules.

IN 1588, King Philip II of Spain sent his Armada to invade England and, as every British schoolboy learns, a great storm blew up and the Spanish ships were blown northwards to be wrecked on the shores of Scotland. Many members of the crews managed to scramble ashore, and amongst these unfortunate invaders there must have been at least one trained armourer on each ship. Doubtless, when captured, several were made to work at their trade in return for their keep. They must have had a hand in producing some of the very earliest Scottish pistols — rare early examples exist which are fitted with miquelet locks of the general types we show here.

How else can one explain the geographical gap? While this form of lock was probably invented in Spain during Philip II's reign (1556-1598), it is virtually never found on any English or French flintlock arms. In any event, the lock was rapidly superceded in Scotland by the English type of flintlock action.

The name probably originates from a diminutive of the Spanish Christian name Miguel. It was to spread from Portugal, along the north coast of Africa into Southern Italy, and much further East into Turkey, Persia and Southern Russia. The miquelet lock is to my mind by far the most interesting and decorative of all the gun locks made after the wheel-lock and nearly to the breechloader.

I imagine it is safe to say that the majority of gun collectors think of the miquelet lock as easily recognizable because it alone has an outside mainspring. This is not the case.

Actually, conventional flintlocks are to be found with the mainspring outside the lockplate. This sometimes occurs on multi-barreled sidelock arms where there is not always room to fit the mainspring in the conventional inside position.

The real definition of a miquelet lock to my mind is "a lock in which the scear(s) operate at right angles to the barrel, through the lockplate." The important word in this definition is "through." Miquelet locks have one or two holes in the lockplate, through

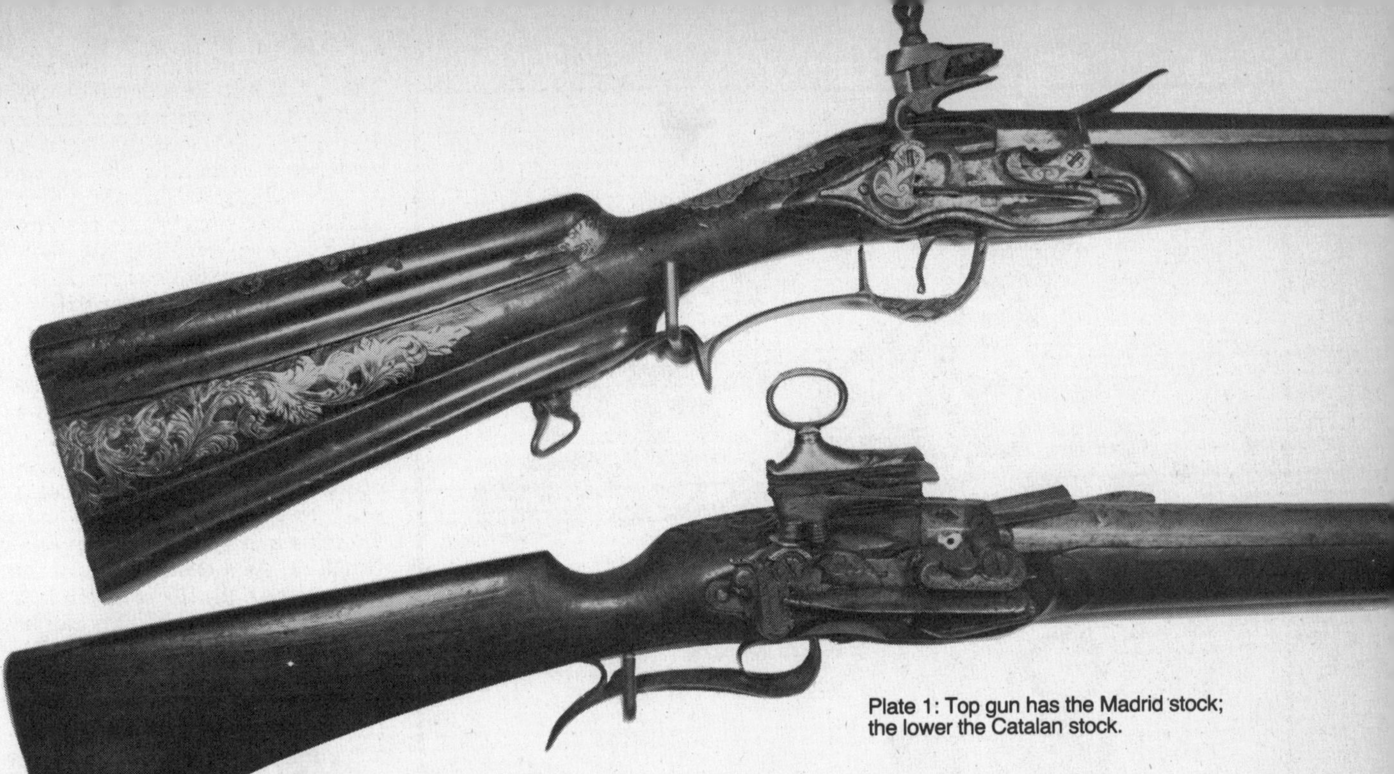

Plate 1: Top gun has the Madrid stock; the lower the Catalan stock.

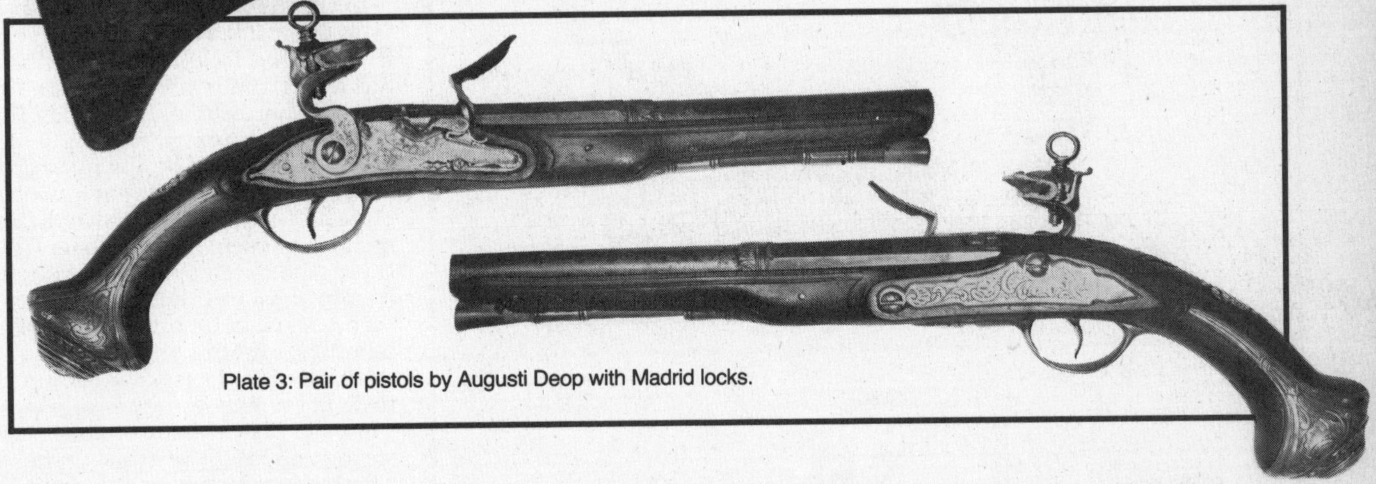

Plate 3: Pair of pistols by Augusti Deop with Madrid locks.

which the scear(s) operate. The scear itself may be defined as "the part which comes into play when the lock is cocked and which the trigger presses up against when it is required to fire the gun." Normally in a miquelet lock the secondary scear holds the hammer at half cock, and the primary scear holds it at full cock. The trigger in a miquelet lock always presses the tail of the scear backwards and not upwards, as is the case in an ordinary flintlock. (Editor's Note: "Scear" is a spelling for the word "sear" which American editors permit English writers to use.)

Plate 1 shows two typical Spanish shotguns, the upper has a barrel over 43 inches long. It is fitted with engraved brass mounts which include a grotesque mask beneath the trigger-guard. The lock is marked CARLA; the stock is the Madrid type. The lower gun is shorter with a barrel of 29 inches and was made by Francisco Anuada and is dated 92 (1792). Its stock is the Catalan type. I believe these stock classifications are from W. Keith Neal's book, *Spanish Guns and Pistols*. Both guns are fitted with the commonest type of miquelet lock with two scears operating on the toe of the hammer. Both are 16 bore.

Plate 2 shows the action of a Portuguese flat-stocked miquelet lock arm which may date as early as 1650. The stock is more reminiscent of a wheel-lock cheek stock, but the gun can in fact be fired from the shoulder. The 21-inch barrel is of 5½ bore. The rare feature on this lock is that the outside mainspring operates downwards on the toe of the hammer, in the same way as an ordinary flintlock mainspring does. The weapon is shown at half cock, the second scear, consisting of a steel rod, has popped out through its hole in the lockplate, below the toe of the hammer. When the lock is fully cocked, the first scear slips out just above the hammer heel and holds it down until the trigger is pressed. This first scear is made in the shape of a small rectangle. The pierced steel bridle covers up both these scears and it is not possible to photograph them. The scears are pressed through the lockplate by two long straight springs. This rare lock is in some ways similar to a commoner type of Italian miquelet lock. When the trigger on this specimen is pressed, the action is as smooth as that on many rifles in use today. The lock embodies a typically Spanish feature — the large ring in the top jaw screw, which allows the flint to be replaced without the use of a screwdriver, since any suitable rod or large nail can be inserted into the ring and used to unscrew the top jaw.

The frizzen or feather spring in

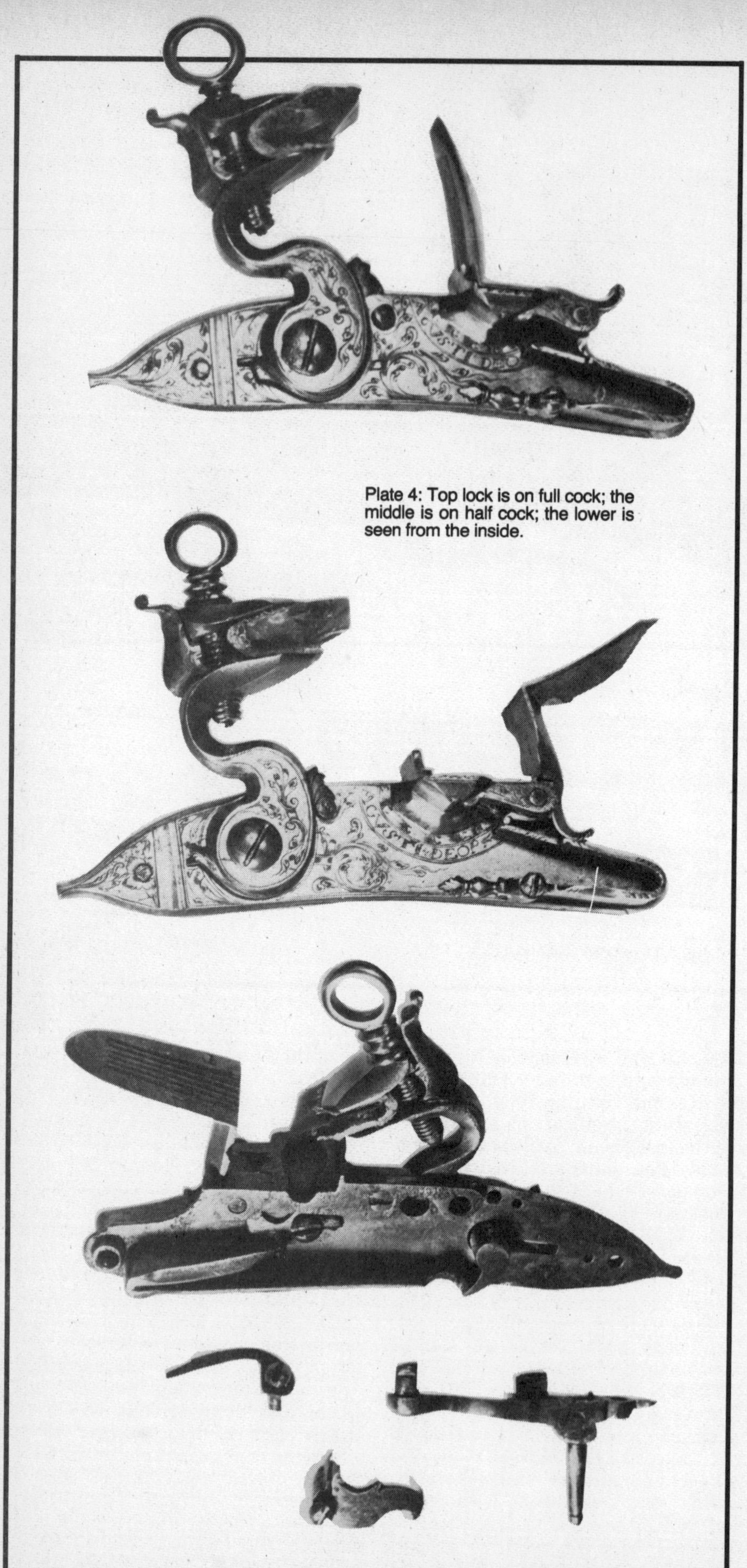

Plate 4: Top lock is on full cock; the middle is on half cock; the lower is seen from the inside.

Plate 2, it will be noted is straight for half its length and then curves slightly under the toe of the frizzen. The method of attaching the hammer to the lockplate, with a pin which goes through the square at right angles to the hammer, avoiding the need for a hammer screw is also typically Portuguese. It was most interesting to me to discover this after many trips to Spain followed by two visits to Portugal in search of antique weapons.

In Plate 3 we see a fine pair of brass-mounted "Madrid" lock pistols. Made by Augusti Deop *circa* 1750, the escutcheons and grotesque masks of the butt caps are of silver. The frizzen springs are typically conventional flintlock. At a casual glance, this appears to be a flintlock, but in fact, it is a true miquelet lock. This can best be explained by reference to Plate 4 which shows the two locks from these pistols detached, together with a third from another similar pistol by the same maker, shown from the inside.

In the Madrid lock, the mainspring is on the inside but the scears operate through the lockplate. The hammer has a small spur sticking out in front and another behind, both being flush with the lockplate. The top lock in Plate 4 is at full cock, the rectangular first scear has come through the lockplate and has engaged above the spur behind the cock. In the middle lock of three, the round scear is holding the hammer at half cock. The second scear is sticking out in front of the hammer, and fits under the spur on the front of the latter. The bottom lock in Plate 4 has been photographed from the inside and the scear, scear spring and bridle have been removed. The scear is below on the right, the toe which is pressed back by the trigger is pointing towards the bottom of the photograph. The middle projection on the top side of the scear holds the weapon at full cock, while the projection at the top left end of the scear controls the half cock position. The scear is lying on its side here, but when in position the toe will stick out towards the reader. The small curved spring seen on the left of the scear is screwed into position through a hole at the right end of the scear, and this spring presses down on the center projection which comes through the lockplate when the hammer is fully cocked. The screw referred to holds the spring, and the scear in position. The piece right at the bottom of the photograph is the bridle and screw, which fits over the scear in the same way as a bridle operates on a conventinal flintlock. Today, the Madrid lock is exceedingly uncommon.

Plate 8: Roman locks fit close to their barrels and require less wood to be cut away from the stock.

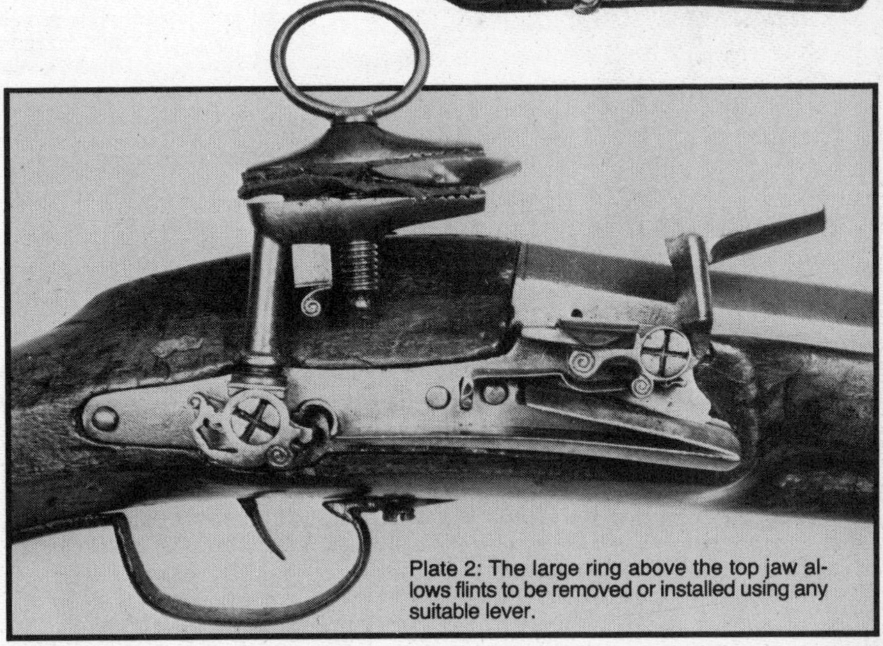

Plate 2: The large ring above the top jaw allows flints to be removed or installed using any suitable lever.

Plate 5 illustrates the inside of a detached conventional miquelet lock (flint), removed from a good quality pistol. The arrangement of the two scears, which are quite separate, is described below. The top of the frizzen is in this case rounded, though a flat top is much more commonly found. The two round ends of the short arm of the mainspring may be seen (given a close look) projecting through the inside of the lockplate below the pan. The projection on the left just below the screw head and slightly to the right of this screw is held in position with a small steel pin. This screw head referred to holds the first scear in position. The pin is missing from the projection on the right. The screw in the right end of the lockplate holds the second scear in position.

Incidentally, this straight first scear spring is kept under constant strain when the weapon is uncocked and often becomes weak through the years, so weak the weapon appears not to be in working order. This can very often be remedied by removing both scears and giving the inside of the lockplate a good clean. The spring should then be carefully bent by holding one end in a vise and gently pressing the other end.

Another typical feature of the miquelet lock is clearly seen in Plate 5. That is the serrations cut down the inside of the frizzen. These enable almost any flint picked up from the road to be used, there thus being no need to carry a supply of specially knapped flints.

Plate 6 illustrates a small Spanish pistol fitted with steel mounts and inscribed in silver on the barrel "Ano d 1821." The lock on this pistol is probably the final development of the miquelet before the percussion era. I say *probably* as it is always possible that another variation of this fascinating lock may be found. The screw holding the hammer and the frizzen in position are inserted from the inside of the lockplate, the frizzen spring itself has become completely visible and is not covered up by the box cover over the pan. Also, there is a spur running up behind the hammer jaw.

In Plate 7 we see a detached lock that is a real gem. I was lucky to find this in the Rastro in Madrid one Sunday morning and believe the shopkeeper must have been slightly hungry. (The Rastro is a large antique market where there are literally dozens of small shops massed into one area. They normally do not bother to open except on Sunday mornings, and then as a general rule the prices are very high, unless, as I was, one is lucky.) This lock was made by Josephus Bustindui, one of a very famous family of Spanish gunmakers. It is in some respects similar to that in Plate 6, but was made some 50 years earlier. Bustindui obviously had seen examples of locks made in France. There is a rainproof slot cut into the rear end of the pan, but the really interesting feature is the fact that there is only one scear. This may be seen holding the hammer on full cock, while the hammer itself has a slot cut into it through which the scear slides when the lock is on half cock. Bustindui's gold *poincon* may be seen on the lockplate.

The two locks illustrated in Plate 8 are both made in what is termed the Roman form, and were in fact made in Italy. The top one from a gun is inscribed Vinovio Sagnollis and is dated 1735, while the delightful little pistol lock beneath it is signed C.A. on the inside. Both scears operate through the lockplate, half cock holding the projection on the front of the hammer whilst full cock is maintained by the square projection which holds the tail of the hammer down. A feature on all miquelet locks that have their main-

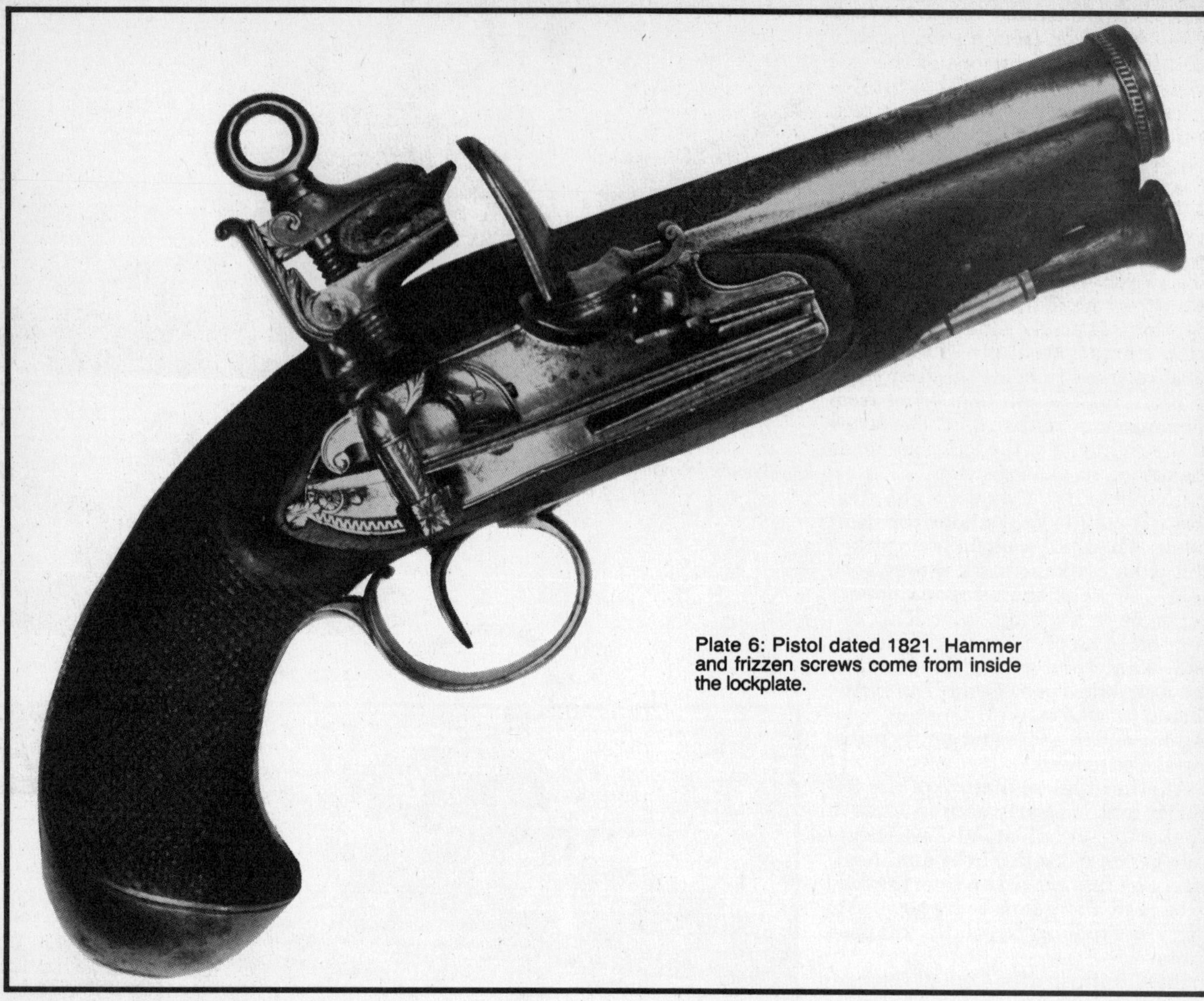

Plate 6: Pistol dated 1821. Hammer and frizzen screws come from inside the lockplate.

springs on the outside of the lockplate is, of course, that they can be more easily positioned right up against the touchhole, without cutting away anything like so much of the stock, as is the case of a lock with the mainspring inside the plate.

We now turn to the percussion era in this description of the miquelet lock.

The pistol shown in Plate 9 is a brass-mounted Spanish arm, originally a Madrid lock holster pistol made about 1750. The maker's name as usual appears in a gold *poincon* on top of the barrel, but, as is often the case, it is not possible to make it out. The gunsmith who converted it to percussion has made a very interesting job of it. The considerable amount of filing necessary to remove the pan left the front half of the lockplate blank; to counteract this blank patch he left the flat side of the engraved percussion hammer head blank. The pistol measures 16½ inches over-all; the forward half of the 17-bore barrel is 16-sided.

Plate 10 shows a single-barrel 16-bore shotgun made by Ybarazabal in Eibar. The lock is signed "ORTIZ" in gold and there is much gold inlay. The hammer takes the form of an animal eating the nipple; he has an elaborate tail which is of course used as the thumb piece. The heel of the hammer is fitted with a roller wheel which reduces friction to a minimum. Only the very highest quality Spanish firearms were fitted with these roller bearings; even in really good quality guns, they are scarce.

Plate 11 illustrates a pair of Spanish percussion pistols with lion's head hammers. The upper one is on half cock and the lower on full cock. These pistols are of 16-bore and have on the barrels, inlaid in gold, "En Eibar Ano 1856". The barrels are 8½ inches long and the over-all measurement is 13 inches. The lion was the commonest of all the animals utilized when the early percussion gunmakers made their hammers so decorative.

The pair of pistols illustrated in Plate 12 are fitted with barrels signed by Jacob Kuchenreuter, who was one of a famous family of German gunsmiths and worked, according to Gardner, from about 1740-1770. It is very unusual to find arms made in Spain without Spanish barrels. The tendency was distinctly for Spanish barrels to be exported to other countries, and not German barrels to Spain.

The locks on these pistols are signed F.B. and the mounts are of silver. These fine pistols were made in the period 1830-1840. It is difficult to say whether they, and the hosts of European pistols of a similar type, were made with duelling or target shooting

Plate 5: Note serrated frizzen which does not require a specially knapped flint.

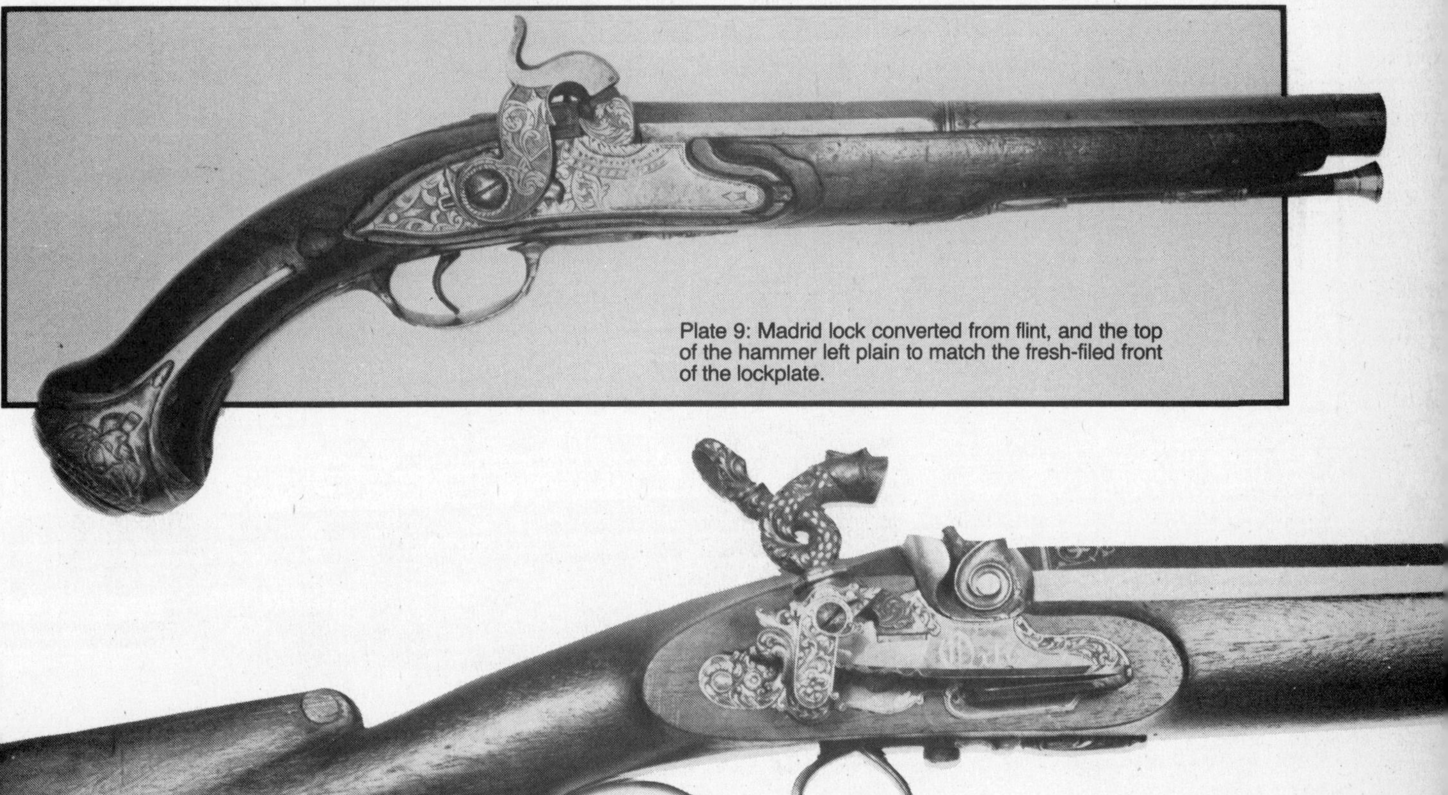

Plate 9: Madrid lock converted from flint, and the top of the hammer left plain to match the fresh-filed front of the lockplate.

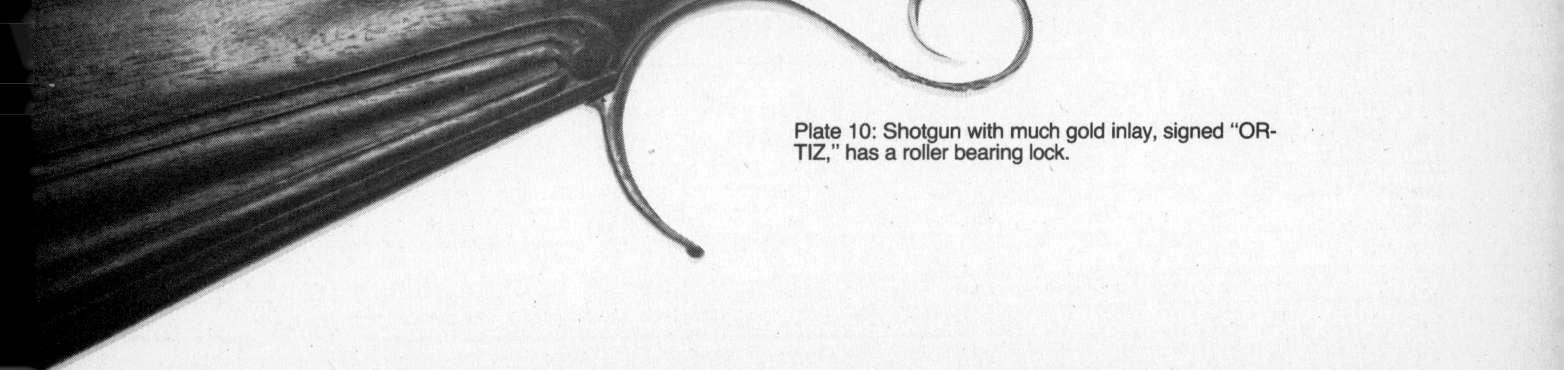

Plate 10: Shotgun with much gold inlay, signed "ORTIZ," has a roller bearing lock.

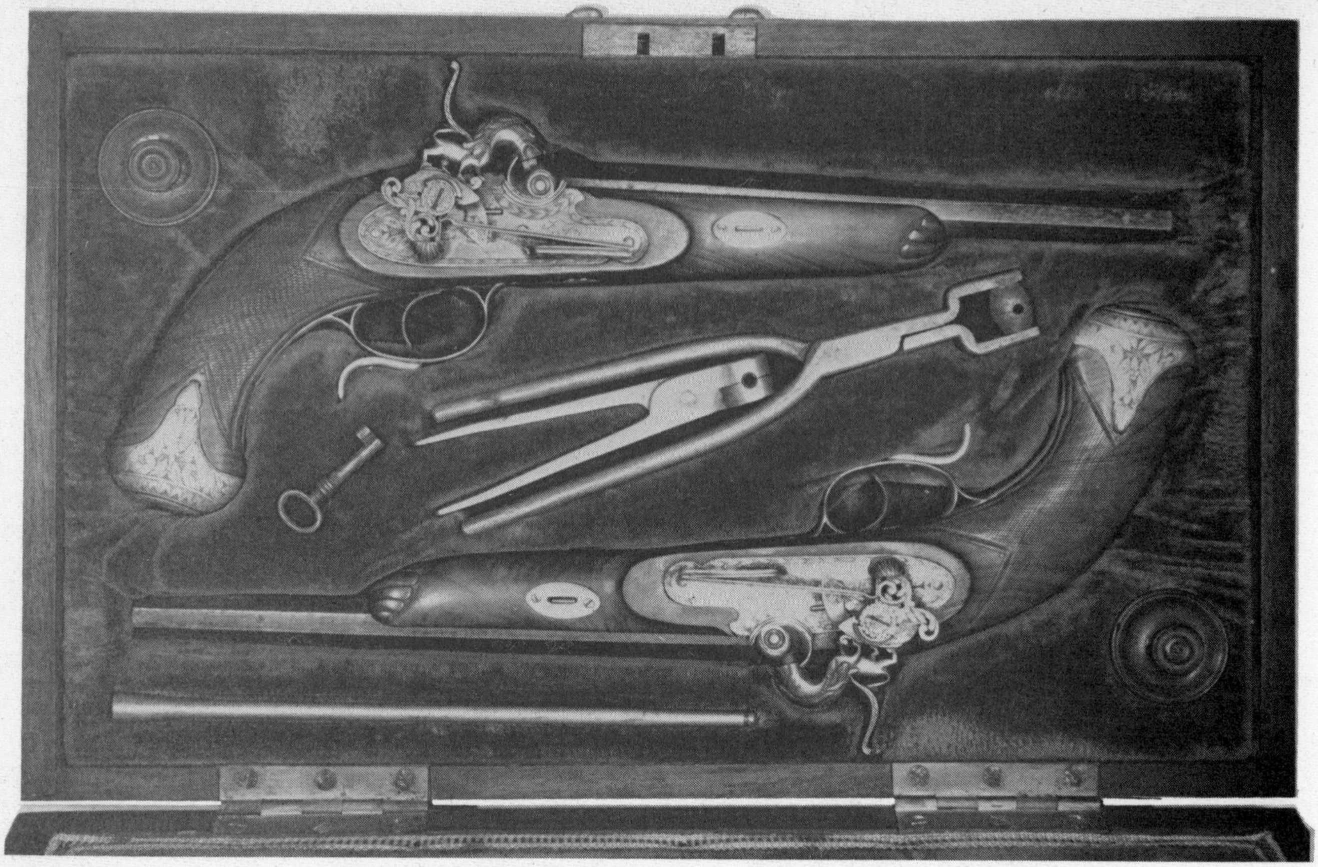

Plate 12: Cased pistols with German barrels by Kuchenreuter.

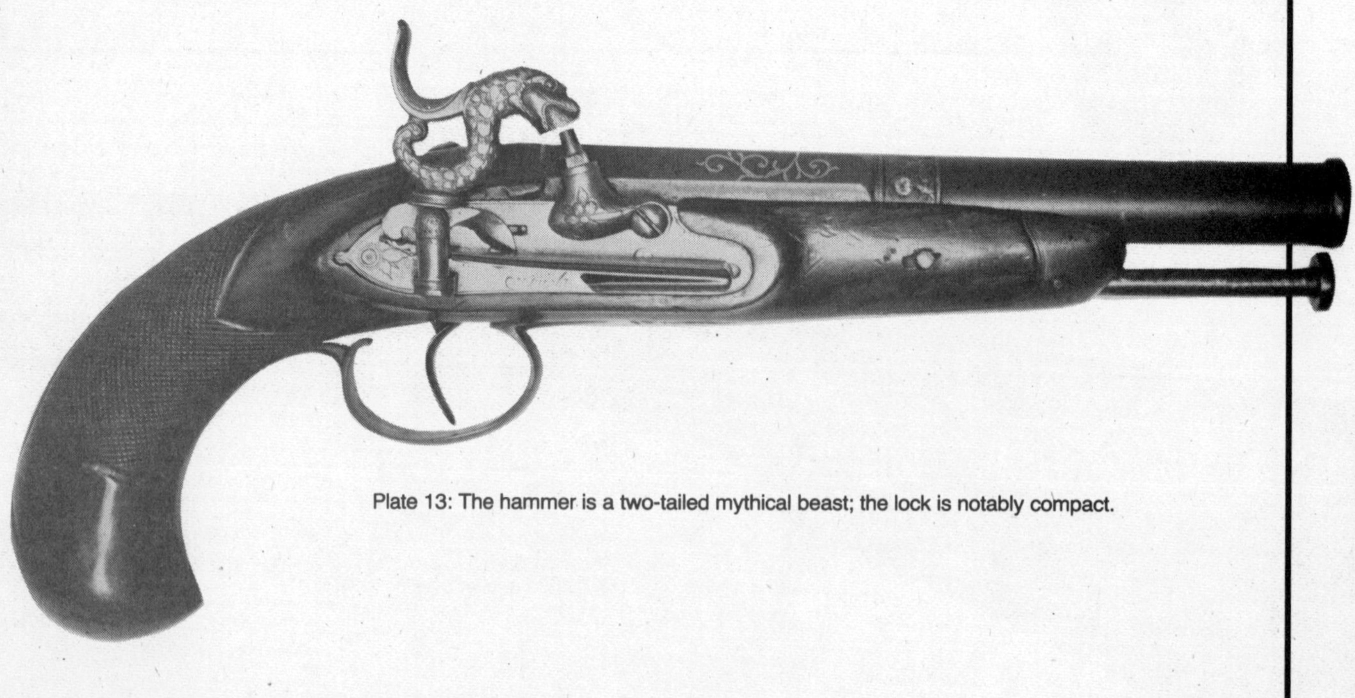

Plate 13: The hammer is a two-tailed mythical beast; the lock is notably compact.

Plate 11: Pistols made in Eibar in 1818 with lion's head hammers.

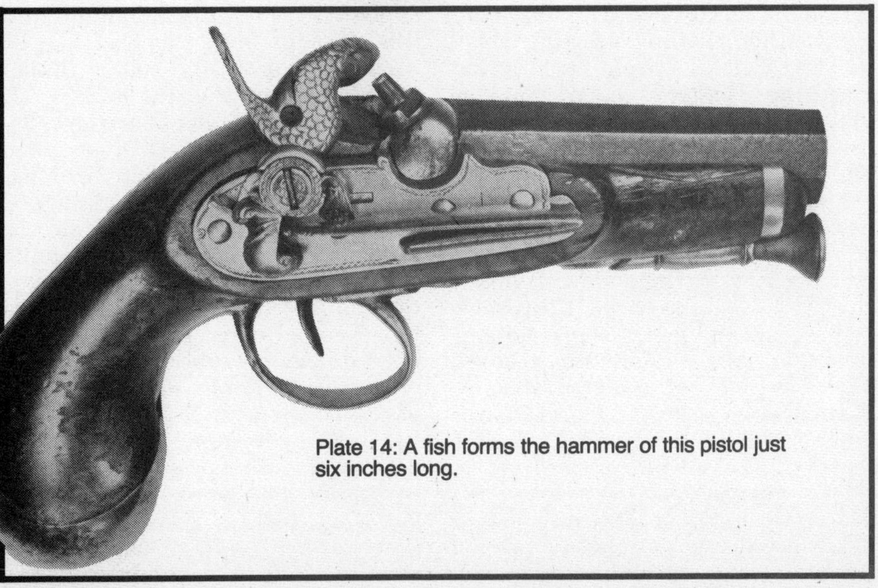

Plate 14: A fish forms the hammer of this pistol just six inches long.

in view. The trigger guards are fitted with spurs intended for the second finger to counteract "jump" at the shot. The pair are fitted in a blue velvet-lined case with two bullet moulds, steel ramrod, and two turned wood boxes, one for caps and the other for bullets. There is no provision for a powder flask in the case. The lid is elaborately carved with the initials C.P. Cased pairs of Spanish pistols are rare items.

An interesting Spanish pistol is seen in Plate 13. It has been converted from flintlock, being most probably of the usual style of miquelet lock. It will be noted, however, that the hammer is secured by a screw from inside the lockplate. The animal forming the hammer is very unusual, though these animals or grotesques form an interesting study on their own. The portion holding the nipple fits over the lockplate as seen, and the screw on the right of this piece must be removed before the barrel can be tapped out. The barrel must be lifted clear before the lock can be withdrawn. The barrel is inlaid with a quantity of silver wire.

My last photo, Plate 14, illustrates yet another hammer, this one made in the form of a fish. This little 24-bore pistol is only 6 inches over-all; it has no markings or decoration other than the brass strip near the tip of the stock.

It is of course quite impossible in an article of this length to show more than a few of the different types of miquelet lock. However, I must try and put one misconception right: Poor little Albania, a mountainous country on the Adriatic coast, south of Yugoslavia and north of Greece, is even today credited with having made an enormous number of rat-tailed miquelet lock pistols by most top British auctioneers. It is not the source of those pistols.

Several years ago, my wife and I tried to get into Albania to check this, hopefully to find piles of such pistols all going for a song. Of course, it was not to be. In those days tourists were only allowed to make a brief visit if in a group of 20 and accompanied by guides.

Later, on a visit to the Military Museum in Istanbul, what I then knew was the real truth about "rat tailed pistols" was confirmed in no uncertain terms. They are, of course, Turkish. In the Museum, there are considerable numbers of figures in the traditional dress of various periods; each has a rat-tailed miquelet pistol in its belt. ●

These justly famed cartridges have suffered sharp criticism over the years. Here's a ringing defense of their many merits by a long-time user of them both.

A PAIR OF ACES

by JOHN JOBSON

HOLLAND & HOLLAND, an elegant establishment in the refined West End of London, is famous for its double barrel rifles, double barrel shotguns and repeating rifles—all so functional, so tasteful, so elegant that many connoisseurs class them as the equal of any—nay, the superior of most. It has been said in some exalted circles of firearm knowledge that a Holland double rifle shades the field, and that a Purdey side-by-side fowling piece noses out the rest of the group in a tightly packed finish. Yet feuds have been started by yet another man (a knowledgeable gent, for that matter) stubbornly pontificating that a Rigby double rifle is superior to all others and that a Holland shotgun is the ultimate. Like straight malt Scotch whiskey, all first-quality British sporting arms have been good—the *creme.* But in any such seminars you'll hear the name Holland & Holland (or the more familiar "Holland") loud, clear and frequent.

Eyeballing any Holland piece (apart from a few hastily-done postwar bolt actions) would make even Bigfoot realize he was looking at sheer, unadulterated class. Their honest, meticulous craftsmanship (true artistry), the restrained, graceful, quite lovely line and form, combine to produce a treasure to use and handle. A thing of grace and beauty.

Holland has, over the years, made many other fetching sporting rifles besides doubles—triple A-1 grade magazine sporters on commercial Mauser actions, though they've also used other actions. Beautiful sliding-block single shot rifles similar in appearance to the famed Farquharson, but different internally. Once I feasted my avaricious orbs on a cased and matched set of Holland & Holland stocked rifles, the wood Circassian walnut and the metal engraved and inlaid—a pair of '76 Winchesters! That was *some* outfit, and all the guy wanted was a paltry eight grand. No, Clyde, I didn't buy 'em. I don't think I had even $8 in my poke at the time.

Of greater interest to us here, however, is the fact that this conservative old firm was, at one time, known for its enterprising get-up-and-go, its virile promotion of several radically-advanced cartridges they'd designed. Though their excellent 465 Nitro Express cartridge may be looked on as a logical follower of the India-banned 450, I refer here, for one, to their sizzling hot bolt action rifle cartridge, the 244 Belted Magnum. This was a potent little package even by Yank standards, its 100-gr. bullet reaching 3500 fps at the muzzle, 'tis said. Another excellent cartridge, my personal favorite of all the belted 7mms, is their voluptuous 275 Magnum. This first of the 7s, dating to around 1912, took some years to be recognized in the U.S. commercially (though the old Western Cartridge Company loaded it in the '30s) and Roy Weatherby recognized its merits in producing his superb 7mm Weatherby Magnum. My own 275 H&H Magnum is a genuine cased-complete Holland, right from London, and I dote on it like a father with his first boy child. Its best shot is a 160-gr. bullet at 2950 fps, carefully chronographed. With 175-gr. bullets it is most accurate at a sedate 2700 fps,

My fetchingly fascinating genoowine Holland & Holland-made 275 H&H Magnum.

and it gooses the 139-gr. most accurately at a hair over 3100. The 160-gr. is most accurate at maximum velocity, something to do with the alchemy of interior barrel dimensions, twist, groove depth, land shape, barrel vibration, and so on. Why? I really don't care – the fun is in finding out.

The 375 H&H

Holland & Holland struck gold in magazine-rifle cartridges with the design of their nonpareil 375 belted case and the 300 belted to a somewhat lesser degree. The belted case design was designed and patented by Hollands in 1907, the 375 H&H as we know it appearing about 1912.

Seldom has more benign fortune smiled upon sportsmen than when H&H produced this duo of superlatively excellent, outstanding, effective cartridges. The 375 H&H is so versatile it will perform with ease far out of and above its class. It is a penetrater, a stunner, a shocker, like nothing else resembling it. Anyone who has used the 375 H&H extensively *in the field,* not an armchair theorist, knows this. That has been my experience and, of more importance to the reader, that of many old African hunting buddies who use it. John Taylor, writing of his controversial "knock-down" formula,* says that although his figures give the 375 H&H a "Knock-out" value of only 40 points, he must "regretfully" admit it doesn't do justice to the cartridge. In "actual practice the stopping power of the 375 H&H warrents a higher classification," he observes, and then adds, "The full-patch 300-gr. bullet has, I think, deeper penetration than any other bullet I have ever used." He goes on to say that it is a sound and intensely satisfactory round to use against any animal, anywhere, and that he had shot over 5,000 rounds of 375 H&H *at game,* from elephant on down. He adds one significant observation (with which I fully agree): "Excluding head shots which missed the brain and only stunned. . . . I have never known of an animal brought down by this rifle *to get to his feet again.*" (My emphasis.)

One amateur had the gall to call the 375 H&H insufficient for African lion (for heaven sakes). The belted 375 H&H is too small for lion about like George Foreman is too small to take on Mickey Rooney.

If one had to use only one rifle for worldwide use (and it could, alas, come to that some day) – North

**African Rifles and Cartridges,* Georgetown, S.C. 1948

The Al Biesen-made Model 70 rifle, caliber 375 H&H, mentioned in text.

This is one grizzly that actually did charge. If you want a sure stopper, try the 375 H&H—you won't regret it. The hunter is my late pal, Terry Stone.

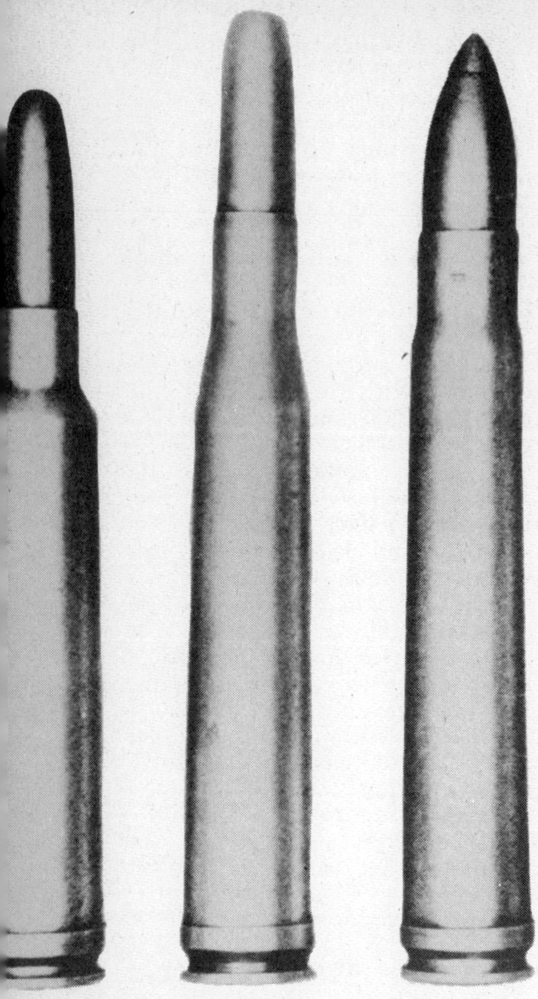

Relative sizes and shapes of three H&H cartridges, all in belted rimless form. From left—275, 300 and 375.

America, Africa, Asia—the choice is ridiculously uncomplicated. For most genuinely experienced-in-the-field hunters, it will be the great, the mighty 375 H&H.

Not a steam-roller, crusher type of caliber, though it has such power, it is an accurate, flat-shooting load (trajectory a bit flatter than the 30-06 with similar sectional density bullets), delivering a terribly shocking, knockout punch. At close range it hits like a sledge, as deadly as a scimitar wielding executioner. Its penetrative powers are phenomenal. I have (more than once) shot completely through the head of an African elephant and (more important) have shot through Cape buffalo from stem to stern—and I mean *clear* through. I have shot through the shoulders of American bison bulls and heard the soft point bullet whining away (!) against the next hillside. Though it has well over 4000 pounds of muzzle energy most of us don't find the kick all that bad. Its recoil I have never, ever found ferocious. Once, in front of witnesses I shot my 9-lb. 375 Biesen 105 times at one sitting from the bench—and a bench is no place to shoot a "ferocious" kicking rifle. Yes, that was too much, and I did have a bit of a headache, but some tests had to be completed.

My wife, just under 5 feet tall, has shot a 375 H&H many times and had no broken shoulder. Not even a bruise. Kristin Sergel, a comely wee lass who used to work for *Sports Afield,* preferred the 375 over any other rifle for her dangerous game hunting. In fact she wrote an excellent piece extolling its killing abilities that appeared in the April, 1948 *American Rifleman,* its title "Make Mine a Magnum."

Besides its superb penetration, the 375 H&H clearly seems to have a peculiar property in its inexplicable shock value. Bullet diameter, weight, velocity combine and blend to make a super cartridge, one so excellent it is, I firmly believe, unique.

My own beguiling 375 H&H started life as a factory pre-64 M70 Winchester. Al Biesen trimmed the barrel to a more elegant lightweight contour and shortened it to 23 inches. He installed a ramp carrying a Sourdough front sight, with a British-style wide shallow V rear, sighted in for 50 yds. The floorplate's button release is in the trigger guard, now nicely streamlined. The bolt release was built up a bit and checkered. Trigger pull is a dream, and the action was carefully honed and fitted. It has a Griffin & Howe left-side removable scope mount, the scope a Leupold 3x with Duplex reticle. It is handsomely and meticulously stocked in hard-as-bone French walnut, the recoil pad of red rubber. I wouldn't trade it for a house and lot.

The 300 H&H

Sadly, the truly good 300 H&H Magnum has suffered in this country, though not in Africa, from an unjust and misinformed press. Over the years this writer has copied that one, with the result that a lot of biased, poorly-researched pieces have been published—and believed by too many. But those who own and shoot the 300 H&H know the versatile jewel they have. Back in the 1920s, when it all began, an otherwise sensible and capable writer took one quick look at the new and wicked looking long case, a potent proposition for those innocent times, and nearly fainted. He rolled his eyes back in his head, turned pale, frightened his wife into hiccups and, when he emerged from this catalepsy, interpolated, guesstimated (setting the path for many gun writers who followed), and laid down the edict that this monster would recoil so much it might well bust your shoulder. At the least, it'd dislodge your bridgework and glaze your eyes. His fans believed him, ex-

Left—Lyle Corcoran (of Hollywood loading tool fame) and his good shooting 300 H&H Magnum. Center, gunstocker Leonard Mews, at right the author.

My friend Yakima Canutt—famed movie stuntman and director—with his pet lightweight 375 H&H—short, handy, and deadly. The Model 70 Winchester was stocked and altered at Alex Kerr's shop in Beverly Hills, California.

cept for a few "show me" riflemen who quietly obtained one and *shot* it. The recoil of a properly stocked 375 would not wreck the hair-do of a lissome maiden of 104 pounds. In spite of its bad notices, more and more 300 H&Hs appeared in the hands of advanced rifle buffs and shooters, men who often scraped and saved and pillaged the egg money to get one. Flossy sporters from Griffin & Howe, Hoffman, and other custom makers then cost packets of folding money. But in 1937 Winchester offered (hosanna!) the 300 H&H and 375 H&H chamberings in the then-new long-action Model 70, and anyone could have one who truly wanted it—the price was low! Even today, as far as the barrel and action are concerned, there are no better rifles around in those calibers than those old M70 faithfuls, as most any old hand in Africa will enthusiastically tell you. Some will trade you a spare daughter for one. I refused $2650 for my 375, and by no means is over two grand inconsequential to me. In 1937 the bite for one of these lovelies was $61.25.

Because the design of the 300 H&H was erotic—whoops, I mean exotic—and "different" the bush league handloaders and cracker barrel ballisticians (those not *owning* a 300 H&H) began sniping at the cartridge. The brass "flowed," they said, and "thickened the neck" so you couldn't reload it. Target shooters who loaded and shot thousands of rounds annually never complained to me of this, or over the equally ludicrous thought that the case "funnels" American powder down the bore so devilishly that it emerges from the muzzle largely unburned! Sure, with some slow-burning powders most any rifle will occasionally eject a few grains of unburned, or still-burning powder, but I've never seen the 300 H&H do it any worse than most others.

The greatest myth of all, though how it got started I cannot say, has been widely accepted as Holy Writ over the years. This calumny—cribbed, parroted, plagiarized and otherwise disgustingly copied by lesser talents and even a few major ones—insists that the 300 H&H offers no greater velocity than the 30-06 does, shooting the same bullets. This is a crockful of imposing proportions. I've owned, loaded for, and shot a hell of a lot of each. I still own some. The 300 H&H will beat the bejesus out of the 30-06, and don't let anyone tell you it won't. Not only that, it does so with a lost less pressure. Pressure in smaller cases is what moves identical bullets fast.

It is true that the 300 H&H case capacity and bore size needs a 26″ barrel, and that the 30-06, with its lesser case capacity and bore size (same), can get by very well with a 22″ barrel—thus making the '06 in some ways a more suitable sporter for North American hunting. The 300 H&H's 26″ barrel is no handicap in Africa, however, and that's the hunting area it was designed for primarily. It also ain't bad for long range 30-caliber target shooting, as Ben Comfort discovered in winning the Wimbledon Cup match at Perry years ago.

300 H&H versus 30-06

Anyway, alas, this hoary old rumor that the 300 H&H will scarcely beat the 30-06 is still taken as gospel in some areas. Now, just to take some recent figures from the latest loading manual, the Nosler, listen to this: In a 26″ barreled 300 H&H M70 Winchester, 65 grains of H-205 (a potent powder, not to be confused with the now-gone Norma 205) shows a MV of 3006 fps for the Nosler 180-gr. Partition bullet; in a 22″ M77 Ruger 30-06 the same bullet, fired by 57.0/H-205, gave 2821 fps at the muzzle. That's a difference of 185 fps, and that's enough to make a big difference out at 300-400 yards, where the old H&H masterpiece shines. Here's another comparison, using this time my favorite bullet weight and, in truth, a favored bullet—the 165 gr. Nosler Partition Spitzer: The *Nosler Manual* lists 3161 fps as MV for the 300 H&H (and it showed "best accuracy," too) against 2968 fps for the 30-06—both rifles as before. The MV difference here is 203 fps.

In my loading experience these 300 H&H figures can be bettered over the 30-06 (I've done it, if admittedly pushing the loads a mite), but this much is *clear*—anything the 30-06 can do can be beaten by the 300 H&H.

My beauteous little 375 H&H at Bonnet Plume Lake, far north in the Yukon Territory, a smidgin from the Arctic Circle and the Northwest Territory border. That's Bill Fraser, my outfitter, admiring it.

Sure, some will argue that a couple hundred additional foot seconds doesn't mean a damn thing, citing that old and tired chestnut that the elk (or whatever) will never know the difference. If that twisted thinking were to apply, then the whole exercise of handloading, the effort to obtain maximum velocity (read *optimum* MV, too, in many cases) would be pointless, null and void, not worth the (considerable) effort.

When I lived in Los Angeles and shot regularly at the now defunct Burbank rifle range, it was a seething hive of advanced riflemen, all reloaders. Many of them—target shooters and world-famed big game hunters—used 300 H&Hs. Claude, the rangemaster, had a lovely pre-war M70 with a Sorenson springboard mount and a big Ajack 4x scope. He was murder with it—I once saw him hit a coyote, trotting in front of the 1000-yard targets, that must have been almost that far off. He never mentioned having any trouble with the 300. He had two National Match Springfield 30-06s too, but when he shot the 1000-yard Wimbledon course, he used the 300 H&H.

Many professional hunters in Africa are partial to the 300 as a camp-meat rifle, perhaps most often using the less-potent-than-ours British loads. (That comment may need some explaining, and what I'll put down now applies to the 375 H&H equally, maybe even more so.) Their theory, as told to me, is that the 300 H&H has the happy if hard-to-explain characteristic of placing its bullets accurately, effectively, even pleasantly, at a pace that is not too fast, and not too slow. That last clause may well hold the key to the uncanny success story of the 300 H&H—and the 375. Velocity can sometimes be too high, especially if certain bullets are used, bullets that were designed to open up properly and adequately at predetermined terminal (read game ranges, say 200-300 yards for the 300 H&H) velocities. The same bullets, driven too fast and perhaps used at shorter ranges, may easily blow up too soon in flesh., may fragmentize and fail to penetrate desirably. Certainly the same performance phenomenon appears to exist among a few other cartridges among them the 7x57 or 7mm Mauser.

Still, maybe in contradiction, there comes a time in the life of a 30-cal. bullet when a mere 300 fps will turn it from a routinely efficient game load into a stupendous killer. A deadly executioner which, if not in the same league as the 375 H&H, does its job efficiently, capably, without fuss, bother, or complications. Sometimes only 200 fps more will do it at certain levels. The 300 H&H Magnum is such a cartridge.

Holland's belted 375 and 300 Magnums are two worthwhile, genuinely good, eminently satisfactory cartridges that, happily, are still on the scene. For their intended purposes I don't think they have an equal. Surely not the 375 H&H, and I feel much the same about the 300 H&H.

They're a duo of beauties!

Better than a pair of queens.

Better than a pair of kings.

A pair of aces, that's what they are. ●

I heard the other day that this very thing happened to Bill Jordan. Famed as a hand-gunner primarily, Bill is a long-time, successful big game hunter as well, not to mention his excellent bird shooting ability.

On a recent safari in Botswana Bill used his old 22-inch barreled 375 Mashburn, a big belted magnum. Jordan loaded the new Sierra 300-gr. boat-tail soft points to about 2700 fps, he thought, though they weren't chronographed. The powder charge was 88 grains of 4350. Accuracy was very good, but he ran into trouble in killing Cape buffalo—out of three shots fired, from a mere 25 feet to 125 yards, only one jacket could be recovered, the lead core completely gone. One core was found, too, but without its jacket. The buff required some further shooting!

These 300-gr. Sierras were, in his example, simply failing to hold together properly. It could be argued that, at a lesser MV, they might have held together better.

Speculation, of course, but it is a fact that the 375 H&H does a great job (usually) when its 300-gr. bullets leave the muzzle at around 2500 fps.

Poor Man's Double

No, it won't perform like a Westley Richards double rifle, but converting a double-barreled shotgun to big game use can be relatively inexpensive, simple and straightforward, effective and lethal at short ranges.

by HAROLD O. DAVIDSON

IF YOU'RE AMONG the unfortunates who get turned on by the looks and feel of an English side-by-side rifle, but turned away by the price, take heart—here are glad tidings. Admittedly they don't tell of a Westley Richards warehouse sale, or of a newly discovered supply from the Chinese Peoples' Republic. The truth is there's no new discovery involved, but rather a re-discovery that you can get many of the features of a 375 H&H double for around a tenth the cost.

To learn the secret for yourself stop by the library, dig into some old books on African hunting, and check the record of smooth-bore doubles on top game animals. Remember, too, that the normal big game loads in those days were black powder and ball. You'll find the 8-bore (with a two-ounce lead ball) and the 10-bore were most commonly used. However, 12s were included in many hunters' battery and were used effectively on heavier game, including elephant.

The fact is that a 12-bore has ample power for any North American big game within the range of reasonably accurate shot placement. Moreover, the 12s effectiveness with such modern ammunition as the S&W "sabot slug" is far better than it used to be.* The S&W projectile is in fact a tremendous improvement over the conventional shotgun slug and, in my estimation, puts the 12-bore in the same class as the 45-70 and 450 Martini.

The reputed superiority of doubles over repeaters is based on three factors: better "handling" qualities (carrying and getting on target), a fast second shot, and reliability in the form of positive extraction and—in a sidelock—two separate firing mechanisms. These qualities are most important when hunting dangerous game in thick cover where the accuracy advantage of rifled barrels over smoothbores is largely academic. On thick-skinned, heavy-boned game, however, the superior penetration characteristics of full-patch rifle bullets over conventional shotgun slugs would be a decisive advantage. Though hunting experience with the S&W slugs is too limited for final judgments at this time their superior penetration characteristics have been proved in tests for police applications, and there's no doubt in my mind that they'll perform well on heavy game.

The merits of smoothbores for thin-skinned dangerous game are already established. Among jungle hunters a 12-bore with double-O buck loads has been considered one of the better insurance policies for use against tigers and other large cats in heavy cover. It could also be the gun you'd choose to take into an alder thicket after a wounded grizzly.

In this discussion I've been talking about short and very short ranges—generally under 50 yards and in no event greater than 100. At medium-to-long ranges the double rifle has it hands down over a smoothbore. But remember this: a poor man's double *plus* a scoped bolt action together will cost only a third or less than a double rifle. Now toss in the fact that my smoothbore can do double duty as an upland bird gun (within limits) and varmint eliminator, and you have the essence of an argument that the PMD could find a niche in many a sportsman's kit.

"Grip" carry of PMD emphazises light weight and good balance as author looks for grouse on portage trail.

Where to Get One

I haven't yet said exactly what this poor man's double or PMD is, but the reader should get a pretty good idea from the illustrations—what they show is a short 12-gauge double with rifle sights, sling, and Monte Carlo pad. You don't find this kind of rig in the gun catalogs, of course, so the "where do you get one" question is in order.

*S&W has recently discontinued the sabot slug loads. Let's hope someone else will pick up the ball, or perhaps someone will make moulds available. JTA

Muzzles of PMD showing epoxy/steel filler between ribs and Williams ramp installation.

The answer: you make one yourself, in a half-dozen hours or less using basic hand tools. Of course, you've got to start out with a suitable shotgun; and that's where the poor man's double might seem to be the "impossible dream." Obviously you don't want to mutilate a collector's grade Parker or Smith, but neither do you want a bargain-basement clunker if you're planning to use it in serious hunting; perhaps on dangerous game. The solution is a patient search of ads and gun shops for a good quality 12 bore with damaged muzzles and whatever exterior-finish condition you're willing to live with. As with cars, appearance affects the market price.

What's wanted is a sound action with about 20 inches of good barrel ahead of it, a serviceable stock, and an attractive price. My own PMD was a bargain-priced Parker Trojan lacking most of its original blue and the muzzles looking quite sad with their splits and pits. The important thing was that it had some 22 inches of bright, sound tubes and an action as snug as the day it left the factory. The stock was sound and in good condition despite a floor-varnish finish applied by some former owner.

How About Accuracy?

You may be wondering how you can tell whether the two barrels will shoot slugs closely enough to the same point of aim after you've trimmed off the damaged muzzles. Unfortunately, there's no way to tell until you finish the job and shoot it. You may be lucky and get acceptable groups to nearly 100 yards. The odds are, however, that your effective range will be less than that, using a single aiming point for both barrels. In other words, you should expect to find an appreciable difference in the impact points beyond 50 yards and be prepared to live with this as a fact of life.

I chose the approach of sighting in to give a correct point of impact for one of the two barrels. Based on the inherent grouping ability of the gun this gives me a maximum effective range of about 75-80 yards with the right barrel. At this range the left barrel shoots to the same elevation but about a foot left. Therefore, at maximum range I've got to crank in "Kentucky windage" to shift the center of impact

Rear sight fitting entailed tapping two holes in rib, then use of steel-epoxy to fill gap between concave rib and sight base. Davidson later filled sight "ears" level with top of notch.

for the left barrel. At short ranges the difference can be neglected. Needless to say, it's immaterial when using buckshot loads.

There is no aiming problem with either approach in close-range "desperation" situations. At 20 yards and less, both barrels shoot to the same point of impact for all practical purposes.

Painless Remodelling

An "easy" remodelling job sometimes turns out to be one that you start yourself and turn over to a professional to finish. Not so in this case. The poor man's double really is a simple job that an amateur gunsmith can do with a minimum of hand tools and skills. You'll need a hacksaw with fine-tooth blade, a 10" mill cut file, a few taps and tap drills for sight and sling mounting, caliper, rule, machinist's square, scribe, and center punch.

The first step is to cut off the damaged muzzles. Make the cut as square as you can to minimize later filing effort, and be sure to allow a little surplus metal for the final squaring and finishing. The question of barrel length must be decided first, of course. The extent of muzzle damage sets an upper limit on barrel length and the law sets the lower limit at 16 inches. Between those limits it's a matter of personal choice. I decided on 20 inches for good balance and ease of carrying in brush, car, and boat. Disassembled and put into a light canvas case the PMD stows easily in or across most frame packs and pack baskets.

Ballistically, there's no need for barrels longer than 18-20 inches. Because of the lower muzzle velocity and faster burning rate of the powder there will be less muzzle flash with these barrels than with a 24-inch barrel on a 30-06. In fact, there just isn't any to speak of. The average muzzle velocity loss in cutting back from standard shotgun barrel lengths is also negligible.

Finishing the Muzzles

When you've got the muzzles cut off you'll probably find some gaps between the top and bottom ribs and the barrels which were filled with solder at the original muzzles. These gaps are easily filled with a steel powder/epoxy compound packaged in a pair of tubes and available at most hardware stores. When the epoxy's hardened dress the muzzles off square with a mill file, then polish with fine emery cloth.

To attach a front swivel base wood screw type was shortened (lower left) and remainder of thread roughened with hack saw or file to inprove bond. Lower rib is drilled and tapped for two small machine screws to give mechanical reinforcement to bond. Steel-epoxy was then flowed around screws and short base.

PMD versatility. From left—aerial signal flare, birdshot load, buckshot load, and the S&W-Fiocchi "sabot-slug" load which puts the 12-bore in class with 450 Martini and 45-70. "Police" designation indicates slug is of hardened alloy designed for high penetration. Compare S&W projectile (shown here with only half of its plastic sabot) with conventional slug of same weight but much lower ballistic efficiency on far right.

This method of carrying PMD can also be adapted to cars and planes. Brackets are made of aluminum bar stock padded with foam rubber and buckskin, sewn and cemented in place. Gun is retained in grip bracket by a loop of shock cord, with a rawhide pull for quick release.

Fitting the Sights

I fussed around with several schemes for fitting sights and finally decided that the simplest arrangement would be a Williams Shorty Ramp front (screw-on type) and a Williams Open Guide rear. The former is available only with a concave underside to fit normal rifle barrels. I chose the lowest available height of ramp with the largest underside radius, then filed away surplus metal to obtain a profile matching the upper surface of the rib (see photo). The mounting hole was then located, drilled, and tapped in the rib, positioning the front edge of the ramp even with the front edge of the rib.

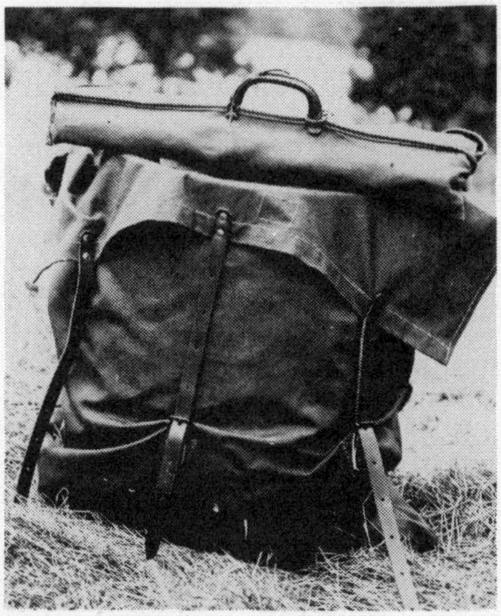

PMD in canvas case stows in or on most back packs.

The Williams Guide rear sight was obtained with a flat base. I located the base's rear surface 1.8 inches from the breech face; then located, drilled, and tapped the mounting holes. Instead of contouring the base by filing I decided it would be easier to build it up with the epoxy-steel compound. To do this I coated the rib surface and the mounting screws with the parting agent used for glass-bedding actions and barrels. I then applied the compound to the underside of the sight base, screwed it down on the rib, and wiped off the excess that had squeezed out. This resulted in a perfect fit of sight base to rib yet allows for easy detachment by removing the two screws.

The next step was selection of a front blade of proper height. This was done by setting the rear sight at its lowest position and measuring its height above the center line of the bore. The difference between this height and the height of the ramp (also above bore centerline) was the required blade height.

Finishing Touches

These sights raised the line of aim by such an amount that the Parker would no longer point well with its original stock. This problem was solved with a lace-on Monte Carlo pad. I'm partial to slings for field guns, so this became the next task. Williams has a special front swivel, both conventional and "QD" style, which screws to the under rib of a double barrel gun and makes a very neat installation.

Quail, Anyone?

That's the story of the poor man's double, except that in talking about sights I forgot to mention that I drilled and tapped a second hole in the rib ahead of the mounting hole for the Williams ramp (which covers this second hole). It takes only a few minutes to remove the front ramp (one screw), put the original bead in that second hole, remove the rear sight (two screws), and slip off the Monte Carlo pad. And there, you may be sure, is one heck of a quail and thick-cover grouse gun.

There's no denying that the performance of my PMD at 100 yards and beyond is just not in the class of a Westley Richards 375. You might say it's like a pick-up truck in the Gran Prix. On the other hand, when have you seen a 375 double that will throw improved cylinder patterns with an ounce of 7½s or 8s? ●

Short over-all length (36") of PMD makes it easy to carry in hunting car. Simple bracket consists of butt rest secured to floor, and a velcro fastened barrel strap attached to door post. A block of wood, padded with carpeting, is used with strap to keep gun from rubbing against car trim. Gun is released quickly by one sharp tug on loose end of strap.

GENERAL JOHN JACOB and his ECCENTRIC RIFLE

by GARRY JAMES

This gallant brigadier apparently never let a fact change his mind, once he was sure.

A soldier of Jacob's Rifles as envisaged by their founder. It is highly unlikely that the unit was issued the double rifles that were ordered for it from England.

Brigadier-General John Jacob, commandant of the Scinde Irregular Horse and inventor of the double-barreled rifle that bears his name.

ON THE OUTSKIRTS of Jacobobad on India's Northwest Frontier in the 1850's Brigadier-General John Jacob, Commandant of the Scinde Irregular Horse, erected an elaborate range at which he tested a new rifle and explosive bullet. Barrels of gunpowder were set at distances in excess of 1000 yards and the indefatigable Jacob went through the process of blowing them up with his percussion "shells," which, with characteristic overstatement, he termed "the most formidable missile ever invented by man."

Jacob, known chiefly today to historians as the man who tamed and kept order in the turbulent Scinde region in the years just before the Indian Mutiny of 1857, was typical of that breed of adventurer who expanded Britain's frontiers during the 19th century. Called by Major-General Sir Charles Napier "the Siedlitz of the Scinde Army," Jacob could be at once charming, opinionated, bellicose, and boorish. A stammer which made him appear somewhat shy in no way affected his self-image. He was one of India's most able administrators and military leaders.

He was considered absolutely fearless on the battlefield, and he was addicted to romantic poetry. Firearms had interested him from an early age, and though his practical knowledge of ballistics was somewhat indifferent, his skill as a mechanic and outright enthusiasm for the subject, coupled with a substantial income, allowed him to carry on the experiments which are the subject of this article.

Jacob was born in 1812, the son of a Wiltshire vicar. At 14, he enrolled in the Honourable East India Company's training school at Addiscombe where he noted that the entrance examination involved nothing more than to perform "an easy sum in vulgar and decimal fractions and to construe a few lines of Caesar."

Upon graduation two years later, he was granted a second lieutenancy in the Bombay Artillery. During the First Afghan War (1841) he was attached to the Scinde Irregular Horse, where his riding ability, natural leadership qualities and easy manner with the native troopers under his command drew the attention of authority. Thus, in late 1841, Jacob was recommended to command the regiment, a post he accepted with alacrity.

The Scinde Irregular Horse was what was termed a *sillidar* regiment. This meant that the native Indian cavalrymen or *sowars* received a greater rate of pay than did their counterparts in regular units and were required to supply and maintain their own equipment and horses. The East India Company provided only ammunition and firearms. Everything else, including rations, fodder and medical care, was the responsibility of the trooper.

Upon enlistment the soldier normally paid an *assami* for a horse and uniform. When he left the regiment this was returned to him. His pay was subject to levies which allowed him to build up an account to replace his mount and equipment when necessary. Should a horse be killed on active duty, it was replaced using money from a regimental fund, subscribed to by the men.

Naturally, the lack of encumbrance inherent in such a system, allowed the unit to travel lightly and swiftly, attributes which suited Jacob's mercuric temperament ideally. He felt that military units should "be able to move far and fast at a moment's notice, and to be as self-contained and independant of the 'regular' transport as possible."

His men figured heavily in the conquest of the Scinde in 1843, and throughout the middle years of the 19th century they were constantly involved in skirmishes with border tribesmen. Jacob's star ascended and his renown spread throughout Northern India. He greatly improved the living conditions of the people in the area in which he was stationed and in recognition of this the town of Khangur was officially renamed Jacobabad in 1851.

Even while on campaign, Jacob worked on ways to improve the military service rifles of the period. From 1837 until 1851, rifle units of the East India Company and those of Crown troops, were issued the Brunswick rifle, one of the most controversial arms of the period. The Brunswick system involved a bore cut with two deep spiraled grooves into which a mechanically fitting .704 caliber "belted" ball was loaded. The girdle on the bullet corresponded to the width and depth of the grooves, and when the gun was fired, a spin was imparted to the projectile. Brunswicks could keep most of their shots in a two-foot circle at 200 yards.

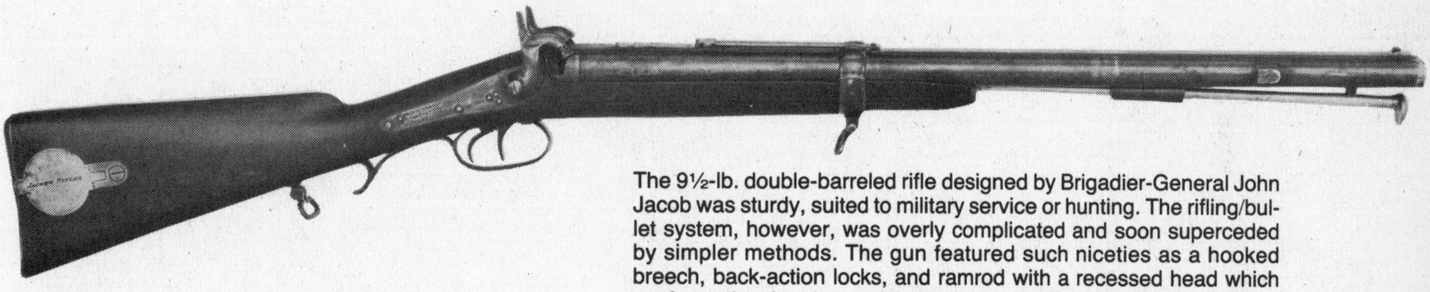

The 9½-lb. double-barreled rifle designed by Brigadier-General John Jacob was sturdy, suited to military service or hunting. The rifling/bullet system, however, was overly complicated and soon superceded by simpler methods. The gun featured such niceties as a hooked breech, back-action locks, and ramrod with a recessed head which conformed to the shape of the bullet nose. Crown copyright photo.

The arm was damned by most of those who had to use it, one officer commenting, "The loading of this rifle is so difficult that it is wonderful how rifle regiments can have continued to use it so long. The force required to ram down the ball being so great as to render a man's hand much too unsteady for accurate shooting."

Jacob had seen the gun in use in India and was also unimpressed. While he felt no particular animosity toward the concept of a mechanically fitting projectile, he correctly surmised that the irregularity of the Brunswick bullet was not conducive to superior accuracy.

He proceeded to design a barrel which increased the Brunswick's two grooves to four. This allowed him to fire a symmetrical ball, cast with a pair of crossing belts.

The rifle was extensively tested by Jacob, according to Lieutenant Hans Busk, first lieutenant of the Victoria Rifles, in his book *"The Rifle and How to Use It."* Jacob's range was a level

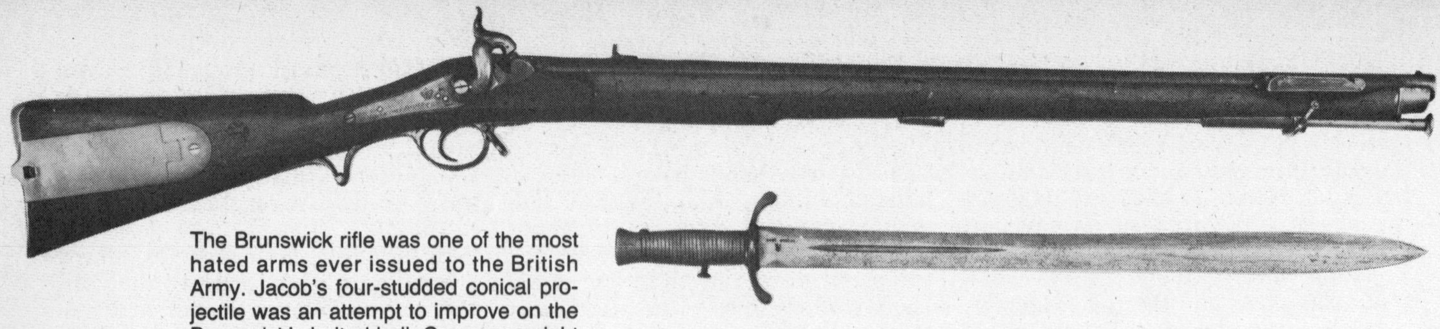

The Brunswick rifle was one of the most hated arms ever issued to the British Army. Jacob's four-studded conical projectile was an attempt to improve on the Brunswick's belted ball. Crown copyright photo.

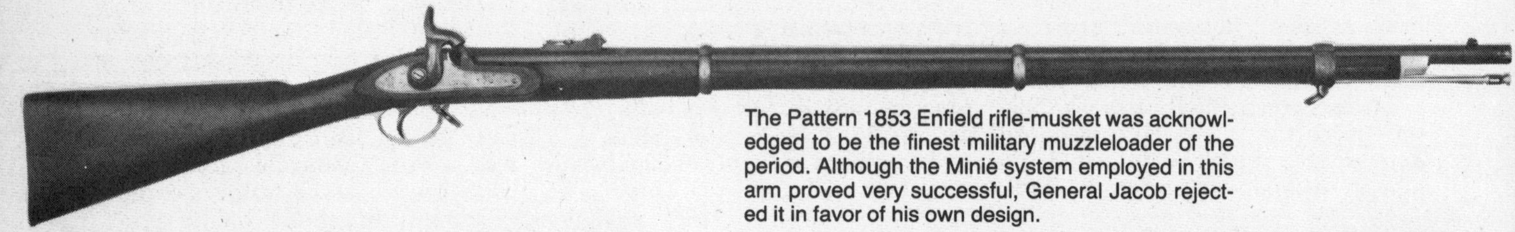

The Pattern 1853 Enfield rifle-musket was acknowledged to be the finest military muzzleloader of the period. Although the Minié system employed in this arm proved very successful, General Jacob rejected it in favor of his own design.

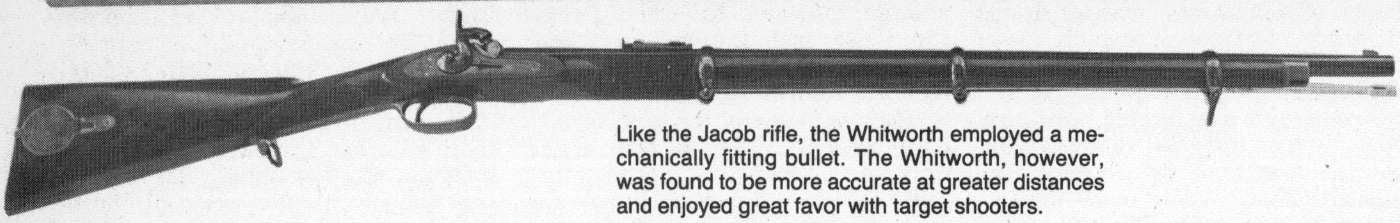

Like the Jacob rifle, the Whitworth employed a mechanically fitting bullet. The Whitworth, however, was found to be more accurate at greater distances and enjoyed great favor with target shooters.

plain "studded with numerous targets and stretching far away into the sandy desert in front of the lines of the Scinde Irregular Horse, near Jacobabad."

Busk further described the "practice ground" as having massive "targets, thirteen in number, costing many hundred pounds in their construction . . .of sun dried brick almost as hard as stone, and placed at various distances from the shooting shed, so as to afford ranges varying from 100 up to 2000 yards. . . .the surface of each target is whitewashed, and marked with circular bull's eyes, increasing one inch in radius and raised one foot from the ground for each hundred yards of increased range."

Experiments were so encouraging that Jacob offered his improved rifle to the East India Company, who flatly rejected him stating "the two-grooved rifle, which is thought good enough for the Royal Army, is good enough for the soldier in India."

Undaunted, Jacob continued his experiments. He next tried a conical bullet with a pointed nose, round base, and four studs to engage the rifling. Accuracy was markedly superior to that of his belted ball and he claimed he was able to hit targets regularly out to 800 yards. Jacob also noticed that the heavy conical bullet required less powder to do the same job the round ball did.

About this time (1851) the French-designed Minié rifle, using hollow-based bullets which were expanded into the riflings by the main charge, was adopted by the British government. Early Minié bullets employed iron cups in their bases to aid in the expansion, although because very often these cups were blown through the bullet, they were eventually replaced by boxwood plugs.

As events later proved, the Minié rifle was one of the soundest, most accurate muzzle-loading rifles ever issued to the common soldier, but Jacob, after what he claimed to be exhaustive testing, rejected it outright, and proceeded to design his own, a severely pointed projectile *sans* expansive cup (in this he was in advance of the authorities) and with the addition of four studs to engage the rifling in the manner of his previous design.

The results were impressive, Jacob said, with good accuracy attained out

The back-action lock on our test Jacob rifle was stamped with the maker's name, Swinburn & Son, and the date 1860. Specimens of this gun have been found dated from 1859-1861.

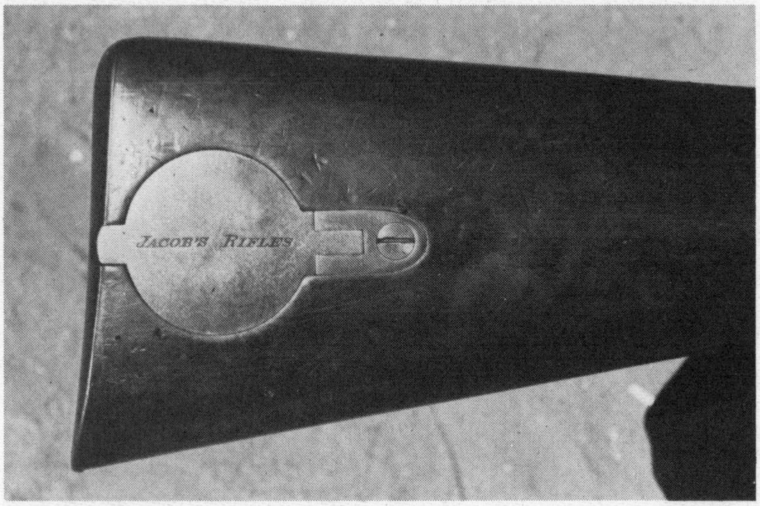

The butt boxes of Jacob's rifles were engraved with the name of the unit for which they were intended.

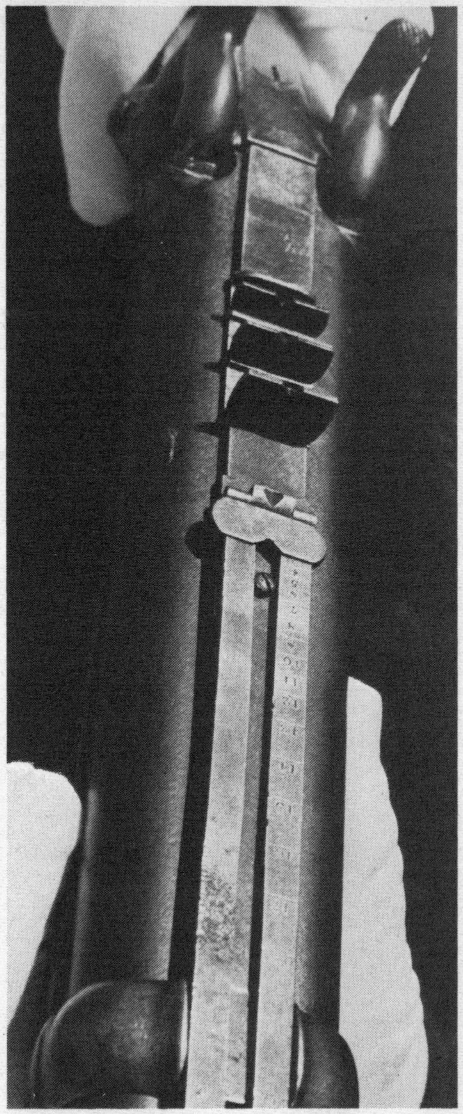

The sights of the Jacob rifle were quite sophisticated for a military arm, consisting of express sights to 300 yards and a 5-inch high "ladder" graduated to 2000 yards.

to 1200 yards. The bullet was further "refined" by elongating it to 2½ diameters and eliminating the hollow base. Jacob was still locked into the concept of a mechanically fitting projectile. As the projectile was developed, so was the rifle. Specimens reflecting Jacob's changing concepts were ordered from England from the best makers, which included Witton and Daw, John Manton, and Swinburn & Son.

During his trials, Jacob became infatuated as well with the concept of the double rifle and turned his attentions toward its further development, and to the perfection of the explosive bullet.

The "rifle shell" was not original to Jacob, having been thought up by Captain Norton of the 34th Regiment of Foot. Both Norton and Jacob recognized the value of a bullet which could be used to explode enemy artillery caissons at great distances, although as noted by Busk, "a solid acorn-shaped shot fired from a common rifle will expand for half its length, but will not carry its point foremost during the whole of its flight, unless the centre of gravity be in the fore part of the shot." It was imperative that the point of the bullet, containing the explosive compound, strike the target first.

To this end Jacob designed his "perfected" bullet with the dimensions noted earlier. It was available in two forms, solid and "shell." The General also conceived his own explosive devices which consisted of pointed percussion tubes, "made of copper, and

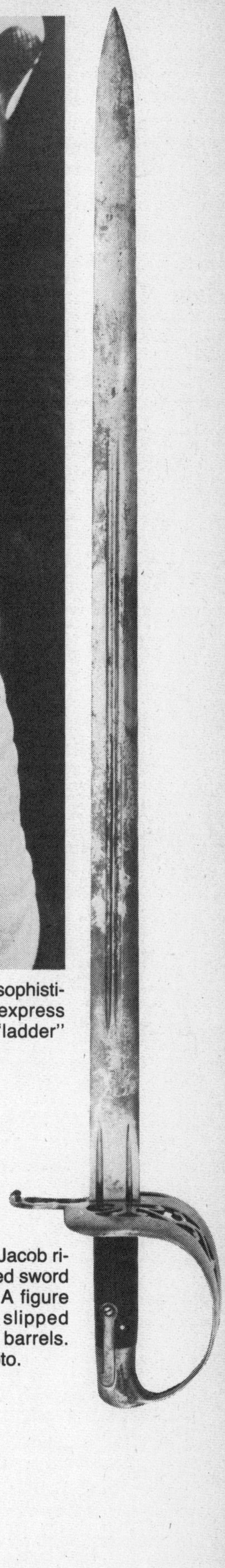

The bayonet for the Jacob rifle was a basket-hilted sword with 30-inch blade. A figure "8" ring in the hilt slipped over the gun's twin barrels. Crown copyright photo.

which fit into the fore part of the shell. Each tube, about the thickness of a quill, and three quarters of an inch long, is closed at one end, terminating in a cone that contains the fulminating powder; the rest of the tube is filled with fine gunpowder, stopped with a cork or plug varnished over."

All the while the "ideal" rifle was being perfected. Finally, Jacob felt confident enough in its design to describe it:

"Double—32-gauge—4-grooved—DEEP grooves, of breadth equal to that of LANDS, to take four-fifths of a turn in the length of the barrel—barrels the best that can be made, twenty-four (24) inches long, weight of pair of barrels alone about six pounds, NOT LESS: the ends of the lands to be rounded off at the muzzle—patent breech—no side vents—first sight EXACTLY PARALLEL to the bore—the muzzle sight being raised if necessary for this purpose—four points to be inserted inside the barrel near the breech for tearing open a blank cartridge when rammed down whole—full stock, well bent, of the best heart walnut wood, attached to barrel by bands—best plain case-hardened mountings—folding sights attached to the barrel twenty inches from the muzzle, five (5) inches long, secured by spring below, protected by projecting wings when lying flat on the barrel, the slide of this sight to be well secured by springs at its back, so as never to work loose—the slide to come down quite low on the sight, the top of the sight, etc., to be strongly made and nicely finished, marked and engraved for distances, say up to 1500 or 2000 yards—leaf sights folding flush for 100 and 200 yards—muzzle sight to be fine. Best locks, strong mainsprings, and heavy cocks. Half cock half an inch above nipple (not less). Triggers easy to pull, plenty of play in the cocks, external vents in nipples to be small—six spare nipples of each size to fit Eley's No. 13 and No. 26 caps—one mould for balls and two for Jacob's shells, flat ended, two-and-a-half (2½) diameters long—moulds to be made of good steel, to open in the middle of one pair of bands—the balls and their bands of size and depth to fit the barrel nicely but easily with a patch, exact diameter of the bore in thousandths of an inch .529—of shell or ball .524—plugs of shell moulds to fit Jacob's shell tubes ('long 16-gauge,' as made by Eley)—plugs or cores of shell moulds to have wooden cross-handles."

Apparently experimental versions of this rifle were manufactured for Jacob by George H. Daw, who later advertised sporting models of the piece. A writer of the period described shooting a gun made on this pattern:

"The recoil is by no means pleasant. The gauge is 32. This rifle does not seem to have any advantages at sporting ranges; but for military purposes it has been strongly recommended, especially in reference to the explosive shells which are used with it. In 1856, a report on General Jacob's rifle was

Due to the weight of the gun (9½ lbs.) recoil was not prohibitive. Accuracy, while adequate for a military rifle, was not phenomenal, and regulation proved to be something of a problem.

made to the Indian Government, which states that at ranges from 300 to 1200 yards the flight of the shell (used with this rifle) was always point foremost, and the elevation at the extreme range inconsiderable. The shell which struck the butt invariably burst with full effect; and practice was made by the many officers who attended, at distances which could not have been attained with any other missile. The shells alluded to in the report require a short stout barrel, and cannot be used with a long thin one, like the Enfield. For killing large animals, like the elephant or rhinoceros, they are particularly qualified; and I should strongly recommend elephant hunters to examine the merits of this rifle, as made by Mr. Daw, of Threadneedle-Street London."

Lieutenant Busk, a strong supporter of the Jacob system did have some reservations about the efficiency of a double rifle, however. He recognized the expense and difficulty of manufacture as well as the problems of regulation. Loads had to be carefully measured and bullets cast perfectly to insure that both barrels would strike in the same place at a given distance.

"General Jacob states that 'the double rifle is found to perform better than the single'," wrote Busk. "This I confess myself at a loss to understand. Speaking from personal experience, the result of many thousands of experiments, I certainly had arrived at an opposite conclusion. Nor was I surprised at the circumstance because every pair of rifle barrels, in order that one sight should serve for both, must converge; consequently at some point, however remote, the lines of trajectory of the two barrels must inevitably cross."

By this time Sir Joseph Whitworth's hexagonally-bored rifle, using "smallbore" (.451) bullets of great sectional density, was receiving considerable acclaim as a long-range target gun. Granted, Jacob has never intended his short-barrelled double to have pinpoint accuracy, however now even his claims of superior range were being challenged.

Although Jacob was not directly involved in the Indian Mutiny—his command belonged to the Bombay Army and it was primarily the Bengal Army that revolted—there are oblique references to one of his single barrel rifles and explosive shells being used by an officer to blow up an Indian artillery caisson at a distance of over 1000 yards.

Despite being an outspoken critic of the rebellion, Jacob was realistic enough to be aware that, "to attempt to keep the natives of India or the soldier of the Indian Army in darkness and ignorance, in the hope of increasing power over them will be as contemptible and base as it would be unwise and useless."

Perhaps bearing this in mind, he decided in 1858, while the Mutiny was still raging, to raise a battalion of native riflemen to be armed with his double gun. The men were also to be issued an unusual sword bayonet which Jacob described as "Best double-edged straight sword with blade thirty inches long, to attach to rifle by

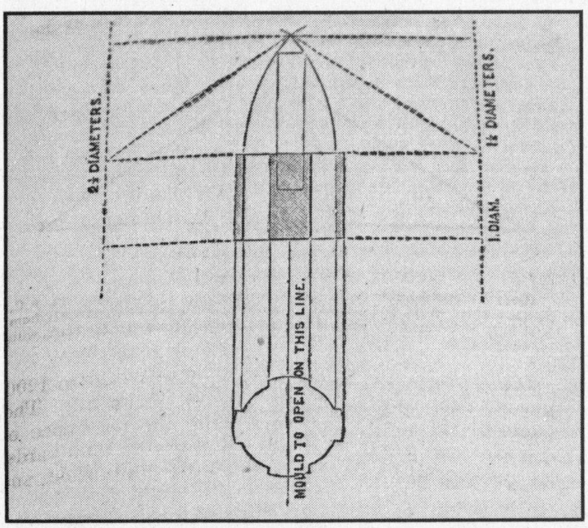

The Jacob projectile, as pictured in Lieutenant Hans Busk's treatise, *The Rifle and How to Use it.* Note the cavity in the nose of the shell for the explosive percussion tube.

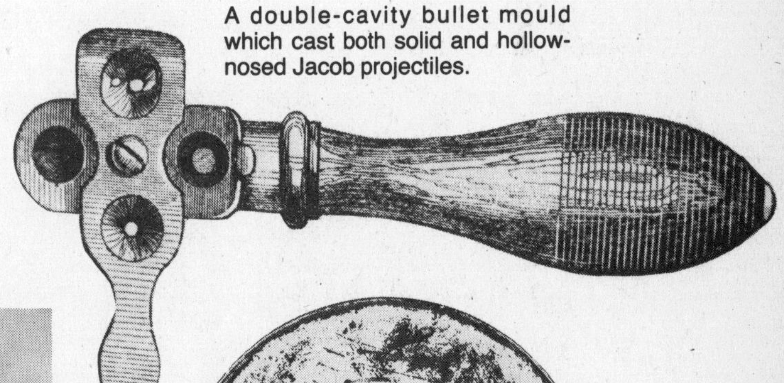

A double-cavity bullet mould which cast both solid and hollow-nosed Jacob projectiles.

The Jacob bullet (second from left) and its competitors (left-right) 577 Enfield "Pritchett" Minié bullet, hexagonal Whitworth "bolt," and Brunswick belted ball.

A tin of percussion tubes produced by Eley for Jacob's explosive shells. The projectile found favor with hunters for use against big game.

To fire the Jacob rifle at extreme ranges, the butt must be held against the shooter's chest for proper sighting.

As per original specifications, the test Jacob rifle was charged with 2½ drams (68 grains) of FFg black powder.

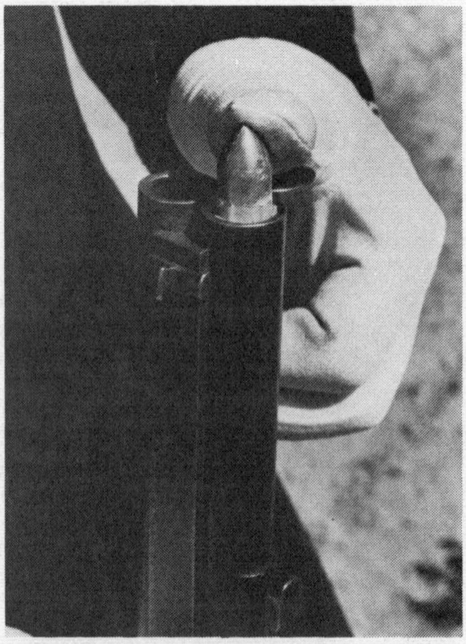

Test bullets cast from an original mould were lubricated with a beeswax/tallow mixture. While they slid easily down the bore, there was no room for a patch.

ring around the muzzle of both barrels, as well as by spring socket, with scabbard and belt complete (scabbard of strong wood covered with leather, case-hardened mountings riveted on. . . . The sword to be made with good steel, or case-hardened iron. Half basket hilt."

Jacob's Rifles, as the unit was to be called, was to be organized on the *sillidar* system, like the Scinde Irregular Horse, and would number about 1000 officers and men, over 900 of whom would have to be armed with very expensive and complicated rifles.

It is at this point that the history of the Jacob rifle becomes hazy. Jacob died of "exhaustion" on December 5, 1858, but apparently not before he was able to place an order with Swinburn & Son for the requisite number of guns. These arms, along with their swords, were produced, for a number of examples of both still exist. They follow Jacob's descriptions very closely, with the exception that it was apparently felt prudent to dispense with the cartridge-breaking studs in the chambers. Each gun had the date of manufacture (varying from 1859-1861) engraved on the back action locks and the legend "Jacob's Rifles" emblazoned on the cover of a round iron butt box on the right side of the stock.

The unit, redesignated the 3rd Baluchi Rifles in 1861, and later the 30th Bombay Native Infantry, had a long and distinguished career; however, there is no indication they were ever issued their originator's weapons. The most probable reason for this was that following the Mutiny, the Peel Commission decreed that native soldiers were not to be armed with weapons as up-to-date as those carried by Crown troops. To this end there was even a pattern of smoothbore longarm authorized for sepoys which had the external appearance of the P-53 Enfield Rifle-Musket.

The General's years of insistence upon the marked superiority of his weapon apparently had been taken to heart in some quarters, and without his strong advocacy the authorities felt it wise not to equip native troops with such a "sophisticated" weapon. The men were more than likely given old Brunswicks until the adoption of the Snider breechloader in 1866, after which they received muzzle-loading Enfield rifles.

It is curious however that, although the decision to rearm the Indians with inferior weapons was made quite early, Swinburn & Son continued to produce Jacob rifles until at least 1861.

Perhaps official vacillation kept the makers hoping the guns would, in fact, finally be accepted.

Concurrently with the production of the rifle, Swinburn was also manufacturing a double-barreled smoothbore carbine (with a marked resemblance to the rifle) and a double-barreled pistol, both for the Scinde Irregular Horse. These arms *were* issued and continued to be carried by the *sowars* for a good number of years.

Swinburn must eventually have accepted the inevitable and overstocked with a number of costly double rifles, offered them to sportsmen or militia units. In any event, the number of Jacob rifles that have turned up in England indicate that few ever left the island, except perhaps for hunting expeditions. In fact, Daw had already had some success marketing single and double-barreled Jacob rifles for such purposes. At any rate, his explosive shell experienced considerable vogue amongst hunters for use against large, thick-skinned game.

Though currently Jacob rifles are scarce and desirable collectors' pieces, we managed to locate a specimen in good shooting condition, along with a number of bullets cast from an original mould. Our rifle followed Jacob's description, with the exception that there were no cartridge tearers in the breech, and the nipples were of the standard Enfield variety to accept large musket caps.

The gun was carefully cleaned and the tubes found to be about perfect. A preliminary fitting of bullet to bore showed very little windage, certainly not enough to accept the "patch" noted in *The Rifle and How to Use it*. The chosen charge was, as per Hans Busk, 2½ drams (68 grains) of FFg black powder. Bullets were lubricated with a period mixture of 40 percent tallow and 60 percent beeswax. The rifle was carefully loaded, insuring that the bullets, while firmly seated atop the powder, were not deformed in any way.

Our first pair of shots, fired at 100 yards, were disappointing, with hits six inches either side of the target. The gun was then loaded and fired again with even more distressing results, as the bullets expanded their error by about two feet each. A fifth round produced our first hit on the target, but alas, it had keyholed.

The bores were now scrupulously cleaned and gun fired again with the first pair of shots duplicating the premier experience. Again the gun was scrubbed and fired with similar results.

Our sights were now raised to 200 yards and the rifle aimed at a 2½-foot diameter gong at that distance, both rounds elicited a satisfying reverberation as the 600-grain bullets unerringly found their mark. This feat was repeated a number of times, although it was necessary to brush and swab the tubes after each discharge. About 75% of the shots struck the target, with the right barrel being the most accurate. The vent on the right barrel's nipple was quite eroded, indicating that it had been used more frequently than the left.

Long range firing (out to 500 yards) produced groups similar to those achieved by Busk in the late 1850s. Thirty rounds were loosed at a 6-foot by 3-foot white cardbooard target. All but six projectiles hit, with the majority of them grouping in about 3-feet on the lower left of the rectangle. A half dozen bullets, however, had the temerity to dot the target at distances approaching five feet from one another. It was necessary to set the sight slide at 700 yards to strike the board.

Unfortunately no appropriate ranges were available to try the gun at anything over 500 yards. Based upon our experience, however, 2000-yard shots would be extremely optimistic. In fact, when the arm is to be fired at this extreme distance, it is necessary to rest the butt on one's chest in order that it be properly sighted.

Although a number of charges were tried during several separate outings, 2½ drams was found to produce the most consistent results. Because of the weight of the arm, recoil was not prohibitive.

The Jacob rifle and its creator remain enigmas. While the gun performed well enough under carefully controlled conditions, it was in no way markedly superior to the standard P–53/58 Enfield service rifle. Granted, a rifle that could find its target at the long distances encountered in India's Northwest Frontier, was an attractive proposition. However, the time-consuming care that had to be taken to insure the Jacob rifle's proper functioning far offset any advantages it might have had.

As has been noted by a number of his critics, General John Jacob's tenacity on the battlefield was only matched by his narrow-mindedness in other matters. He was the sort of person who, though an innovator, could become enamored with his product to the exclusion of all else. A considerable private fortune was spent to promote the Jacob rifle to no avail. Time and technology simply overtook the concept. ●

The author wishes to thank Dave Cumberland, The Old West Gun Room; John Fabb, A.R. Fabb Bros., Ltd; and Val Forgett, Navy Arms Co., for their assistance in the preparation of this article.

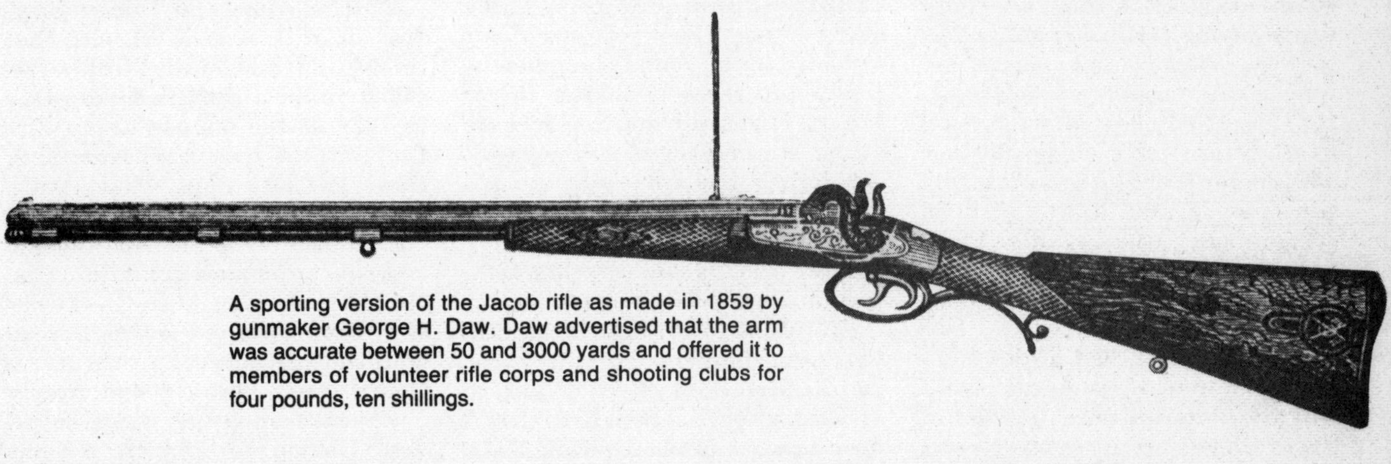

A sporting version of the Jacob rifle as made in 1859 by gunmaker George H. Daw. Daw advertised that the arm was accurate between 50 and 3000 yards and offered it to members of volunteer rifle corps and shooting clubs for four pounds, ten shillings.

A day's sport near Webster, Dakota Territory, sometime in the 1880's. *Courtesy Bettmann Archive*

The guns of 19th century market hunters threw less lead than today's magnums—and our dwindling wildfowl population reflects the difference.

IN JULY, 1958, I was shooting at our venerable Memphis, Tenn., Trap & Skeet Club, when my gifted gunsmith friend, Mr. H. L. Highsmith, one of the nation's top-bracket riflemen, shotgunners and stockmakers, arrived for a bit of special skeet practice with a strange piece. 12's, 16's, 20's and 410's were already rapping out from our four fields. Mr. Highsmith's weapon du jour was a 10-gauge Purdey hammer double, exquisitely engraved, with a deft, side-slip opener beneath its trigger guard. Its stock, a thing of beauty and a joy forever to any gun collector's eye, couldn't have missed my own gun's measurements (14¼"-1⁹⁄₁₆"-2¼") by more than skeletal fractions anywhere along the line. The Purdey's 32-inch tubes of lovely flowered Damascus were, of all things, bored true cylinder. Probably made before choke boring happened in Great Britain. 9½ pounds, it handled fast.

Mr. Highsmith had loaded himself a bagful of 10-gauge hulls with only 3¼ drams of black powder in some, semi-smokeless in others, and the equivalent in smokeless for the rest. Using 1⅛-8's ahead of such propellants, the combination was almost too light for a 10-gauge. But Mr. Highsmith's was a crash investigation of a lot of gunning's adages and priorities ballistically. He was out to enjoy an afternoon's pleasant "boom-and-bust" on a shotgunning Renaissance. He broke a 23x25 at skeet, mixing the loads indiscriminately, to the amusement and amazement of his squad-mates, equipped with 12-bore doubles, over-unders, pumps and autos. Some were using muzzle gadgets. Mr. Highsmith then turned his 10-bore Purdey over to Robert Sheffield, one of our region's best all-round shotgunners, and he proceeded to shatter 25x25. Messrs. Highsmith and Sheffield are young, strong fellows, so the heavy old Purdey was apparently no adverse factor, even at station 8, which, in this writer's opinion, is a silly trick shot. Birds shot at such ridiculous range would be pulped.

Everybody enjoyed the Highsmith-Sheffield exhibition and quite a few members tried the Purdey just to say that for once in their lives they'd fired a charge of black powder. Mr. Highsmith, a student of magnum shotguns (early and late), has a gift for restoring "grandpa's" old fowling pieces. Too, aside from his knowledge of ballistics, he can practice what he preaches, from goose-pit or duck-blind. When it comes to stockmaking, he is an artist with a deep, keen knowledge, not only of woods and world-models in stocks, but of what should be found *in* those woods—for perfect grains, burls and quality of inlays that only perfect wood will allow. In short, in his chosen profession, Mr. Highsmith is a double-actioned, delicate artist.

Watching him and Robert Sheffield shoot 96% at skeet with that lovely, old fashioned Purdey, recalled for me a Fathers & Sons Day in 1928 at the famous Camp Fire Club, up the river from New York City. The late Capt. Paul Curtis, then the famed gun editor of *Field & Stream*, had invited me and the late and equally famous gun critic, Col. Harold P. Sheldon (then Chief Conservation Officer of the U.S. Bureau of Biological Survey) to shoot the Club's newly installed and freshly discovered shooting game called skeet. Having been Director of Game Restoration for the Western Cartridge Company, I was in charge of

ARE WE SHOOTING 8-GAUGE GUNS?

by NASH BUCKINGHAM

its trapshooting activities when the originator of skeet, the late William Harnden Foster, of Andover (Mass.) brought it to Western and saw it adopted by them first. I had also served several terms on the National Skeet Board, but had had literally no experience at the game.

Magnum at Skeet

I had been live pigeon shooting at the Philadelphia Gun Club and had with me a brand-new 10-pound, 32-inch, over-bored 12-gauge magnum (with Askins-Sweeley type boring by Burt Becker) from which I had been firing Western's latest 3-inch case with copper coated shot. In 1928 Burt Becker was acknowledged the world's master-borer. The Fox-Becker magnums had been in production approximately five years and Western had developed their first loads and copper coated pellets. At the Camp Fire Club, though, I was using standard trap loads. Col. Sheldon was using a beautiful 20 double just sent him by the late Bob Owen, the British gunmaker, who was later employed by Winchester, and who had something to do with the development of their famous Model 21. The colonel and I were patiently briefed by Capt. Curtis as to the game's rigmarole and how to swing and lead and behave ourselves at each station. Then, squadded with the captain and two other club-members, we "lit out!" There was covert eyebrow-lifting and subtle snickers at my magnum and for the colonel's 20-bore and his quail loads. If I recall correctly, in those days, at station 8, instead of snapping at the incomer, you could face about and fire at the target as it went away. I broke 98x100 and the colonel 97 – the first time he'd ever shot skeet! Captain Curtis accounted for 95x100. We got bawled out as thieving ingrates but we held it over Paul for many a day. Especially about how a magnum 12 could be put to a good many uses, on the basis that you have to first hit something, no matter what you're using.

It is a great satisfaction to me now to recall both Sheldon and Curtis as two of the soundest field and wildfowl shots I've ever encountered, and comradely sportsmen as well.

From that day at Camp Fire I was to shoot that 12-bore Becker magnum at practically every species of North American wildfowl and upland game – except quail and snipe. I shot it steadily for twenty-one years until, in 1948, an examining game agent forgot to put it back where he found it in the automobile – somehow it was never recovered.

With that gun I fired every 12-gauge combination from 3-dram 1-ounce loads to the heaviest charges in 3-inch cases. Long since, I have come to realize that while the good big gun will nearly always beat the good little one, it is the gunner himself who must toe scratch and point the weapon rightly – or be penalized with a miss. You either hit or miss, hit and kill, hit and cripple – and recover, maybe, provided you work hard or have a good retriever – the last named being the best magnum I've ever seen. When you discuss "long range shotgunning," with magnum guns and loads (neither is worth a hoot without the other), meaning anything past 50 yards for lethal falls, you had best have a good retriever at "sit" beside you in blind or boat. Or else go over your stock of alibis very carefully.

By the time I was fifteen, in 1895, I was no stranger to the magnums. We didn't know 'em by that name then, such appellations applying to champagne bottles of greater capacities, vintages and voltages. The 20-gauge was virtually non-existent sportingly. 14 gauges were still around and 16's frequently encountered: in fact that was our first double – a 16-bore hammer Parker for my older brother. 12 gauge was definitely standard, but for wildfowl there were many 10's and quite a few 8's in use. My father used 12-bore double hammer guns by E. Smith, of England, for quail, snipe, woodcock and plains game. For wildfowl he shot a W. W. Greener side bolt, 11-pound, 32-inch 12-bore, bored for 3¼-inch cases – if need be! Its stock specifications would fit me today. Until a few years ago I still had one of those long Winchester cases he fired from the big Greener. Made with a reinforced base, it was loaded, according to its topwad, with 44 grains of duPont powder and only one ounce of 6's, the load made famous by the late Fred ("Old Fritz") Gilbert, of Spirit Lake, Iowa. Fred was employed by duPont as a professional trap shot, and I have a cup won in 1915 celebrating his 20th anniversary with that company. My parent used many cases of those "Gilbert loads," so, naturally, I fired a great many of them. In those days the loading companies would put up for jobbers these "favorite loads" of famous market hunters, live-bird and clay pigeon champions. A favorite duck load for the Wapanoca Outing Club of that day, at what is now Turrell, Ark., consisted of a 12-gauge combination of 3¼-1-6 chilled. Members bought them lavishly. Duck bag limits were fifty a day, market hunting was strictly legal and, with plenty of fowl around, it was a pleasant load to shoot from both double guns and the increasingly popular repeating shotguns.

Four club members used 10's and 8's by W & C Scott, of England, all sweetly handling double hammer guns. I was permitted their use when the owners were not around, and as I was then five-foot ten and weighed 185 pounds, recoil was no problem. There were worlds of swans and geese available and men didn't have to consider the word "magnum" then—big guns for flock shooting at longer ranges, or in closer for bag-limit results, were simply matters of course. There was no specialization at long range, so to speak. There was little or none of what is known today as "sky-busting." There was no need for it.

The use of those 8- and 10-bore guns in my earlier years left me an experience that stood me in good stead in after years of controversial discussion about the Federally legal aspects of their banning or regulation. There has never been a more misunderstood and humorously garbled ballistic field, from the conservational or industrial slant, than the furored forensics by gun editors (some of whom never fired an 8- or 10-bore in their lives) and official Washington, charged with such contentions under the Migratory Bird Law's rulings. One paragraph should cover that historical era.

In the early 1890's, first lever- and then trombone-action repeaters by Spencer and Winchester, carrying six shells, made their appearances and quickly infiltrated the ranks of sportsmen and market-hunters. About 1905 the first autoloading 12-bore appeared to further accelerate the pace of national waterfowl destruction. By 1912-1913, when the Weeks-McLean Bill and the Lacey Act appeared, it had become obvious that waterfowl populations (whipsawed by upped fire-power and the northern breeding grounds' agricultural attritions) were doomed unless remedial measures were taken. Federal bag limits of 25 ducks a day and 8 geese, with 90-day open seasons, were clapped on. To make assurance doubly sure, from the market shooting slant, the poor old 8-bore got banned. The lighter, faster-shooting pumpguns and autoloaders, were allowed to continue. KO'ing the 8-gauge probably seemed the right thing to do to those earliest swivel-chair Federals and equally innocent conservationists who knew little about such matters.

This ballistic travesty, begun then, continues—a 3-shot magnum 12, pump or autoloader, carrying three of today's maximum charges, gives the user equal if not more fire power than the old double-tubed 8's of my youth. (We'll go into this later.) Nor, in those days did we have the tiny 410 gauges with which to cripple game. Failure to ban these little guns on Federal migrants has long pointed an accusing finger at the integrity of Washington. Gun editors and ballistic writers have long known and panned this obvious official deviation from conservational principles, but there is where we stand today.

Today, using "muzzle gadgets" successfully designed to permit all degrees of restriction, the gunner, by a mere twist of the wrist or a tiny wrench, can select the pellet density he deems best for an approaching upland bird or wildfowl shot. Or for the type of flushed game covert he's tramping, thick or wide-open walk-up. The mental processes channeled by such decisions constitute today's fascinations for hunters the country over. If they miss, it was the gun's faulty choke; definitely not any faulty lead.

Lakes of ink, mountains of paper and earth-girdling typewriter ribbons have been dedicated to man's fancy for sporting weapons and their ballistic developments. I have listened by the hour to heated discussions on the "killing power" of guns of varying weights and chokes, on various loads of propellants and shot. Lead and hitting, in such arguments, become vague inconsequentials. I have heard more simon pure bunk spilled about magnum shotguns and their loads than the law should allow.

W. W. Greener and Fred Kimble produced "restrictions" or choke-boring in shotgun barrels a decade before I was born.

According to Mr. Kimble's memoirs it was not unusual for him, during his market-gunning days along the Illinois, Mississippi and Little rivers, to boat two hundred or more assorted ducks per day. He used his favorite, personally choked 6-gauge (Tonks of Boston finished up several such weapons for him) with a stiff charge of powder in the heavy piece's single, muzzleloading tube, and an ounce and a half of what he called "St. Louis 3's." In a delightful and voluminous correspondence with me during the late 1920's, when, at an advanced age, he was living in retirement in California, he described how, in those early times, he made his own powder. "It was," he wrote in an exquisitely copper-plate hand, "of a slow-burning texture similar to today's new-fangled progressive-burning powder. I cooked it up myself on the back of my kitchen stove, from personally compounded ingredients costing but a few cents per pound." (I would like to own that recipe today.) He had frequently, he said, made long runs on single mallards of 50 to 60 straight, flighting timber at 60 to 70 yards. "I came to realize that to shoot a long way, it takes a cannon, so, for my duck shooting, I tried to get the closest thing to one."

To really appreciate such bags and feats of marksmanship, think of the

Top—Custom built M50 Winchester 12 autoloader with two sets of ventilated-rib barrels. Weight fully loaded, 9.2 lbs. Handles very fast with 26-inch tubes on quail and snipe; with the full-choke tube shoots a dense, even pattern with author's wildfowling load of 4 drams, 1⅜-ounces of copper-coated 4's. Shot in all weathers, it's never failed to function. For the "one barrel" gun pointer, for all-round use on all species, this is about the ultimate.

Center—Custom built and hand bored magnum 12 double by Burt Becker. Bored for 3-inch cases, it weighs 10 lbs. loaded, and with its F and F 32-inch tubes it swings and balances beautifully. This was the last magnum built by Mr. Becker, now living in retirement near Aurora, Ill. He also made and engraved some of the fine old Remington doubles exhibited at the St. Louis World's Fair in 1904. Later, with the Fox Gun Company, he bored (and helped develop) the Askins-Sweeley magnums. Col. H. P. Sheldon called him "the greatest borer of shotgun barrels on earth." This gun, with 1⅜-ounces of coppered 4's, patterns about 90- and 92 per cent ahead of 4 drams. It also handles from 3-1-8 to 4½-1⅞-4, the maximum.

Bottom—Custom built and stocked Winchester 21, with 32-inch full-choke tubes and extra set of barrels. Weight, magnum loaded, 8.4 lbs. This gun has been shot thousands of times and handles especially fast on flighting game, such as doves. These three weapons have accounted for all but about three of North American migrant and upland species. Their stock measurements are identical—14¼"-1$\frac{9}{16}$"-2¼".
Beyond light trap loads for quail and snipe, the author uses but two loads for the vast majority of his gunning—the 1⅜-4's just described, and the magnificent modern load of 3¼-1¼-7½. You can take those three combinations and kill off all the wildlife remaining in field and marsh.

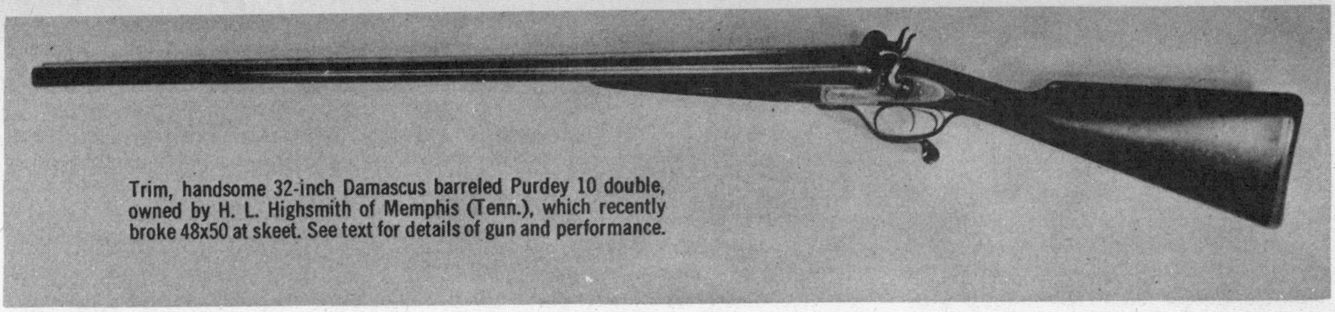

Trim, handsome 32-inch Damascus barreled Purdey 10 double, owned by H. L. Highsmith of Memphis (Tenn.), which recently broke 48x50 at skeet. See text for details of gun and performance.

physical labor expended, not only to paddle or row a heavy boat all day and gather one's bag, but to muzzleload for that many ducks (many of which were undoubtedly missed) day in and week out. Such results were obtained, Mr. Kimble wrote, "by the trial and error basis." This means, in effect, having to learn gun yardage the hard way.

Having sat at Mr. Kimble's knees for fifty years, I know that this means sizing up an approaching goose or duck and saying to yourself, "The last time I saw a chance like you, I shot about yonder." And, suiting brain reflex to action, you try to swing and hit "yonder." You try to hit a moving spot ahead of that duck, just as you tried to before, at such a distance. Each chance becomes a hazard in gun yardage. The mallard, meanwhile, is carried in your subconscious mind. You can't intercept it by firing at a fixed spot out ahead—your gun must be moving. You know what happens to your swing or golf yardage when you fail to follow-through? In shotgunnery, it is proper forward allowance—or else. And it takes many an "or else" to make a real, bang-up game shot. It also takes absorbed energy to lethalize game and put it on your table. In a gunning way, never send a boy on a man's errand. The use of a magnum means, simply enough, "getting there firstest with the mostest." But get it out of your head that simply because you buy a magnum you have to shoot heavy loads out of it at everything. If your wildfowling's wild and rough, use the maximum charge you personally prefer to shoot. If the shootin's in the woods over decoys, the pigeon load of 3¼-1¼-7½'s will knock 'em for loops. I've killed many a limit of doves with my magnum using a 3-dram 1-ounce charge. Magnum or no-magnum, gunning's law is, "You've got to hit 'em—first." And lethally, again. That's absorbed energy. Remember that.

From a gunning and ballistic angle I am, as the old song goes, "right back where I started from" sixty-eight years ago, when I was ten years old. I sometimes sit appalled and all but cringe at blue-sky advertising which claims that clean kills can consistently be made with certain 10-bore magnums at 100 yards, using a heavy powder charge and two ounces of 2's. That's the length of a football field. Have you ever paced off a full 100 yards? Would you try for a goose at that range with any gauge gun or load—or even a guided missle? Advertising can take shotgunnery from ad astram *to* ad nauseum.

Between early-day big bores and comparatively modern magnum shotguns lie two main differences in American wildfowling. During the reign of the big bores (6-, 8-, and 10-gauge singles and doubles) there was so much game and populations were so sparse, that the wildlife hucksters rarely expended an unnecessary charge. They water-huddled or "flat-shot" fowl and boated as many as possible with one or two wallops. Seven-tubed muzzleloaders hurled thousands of pellets into night-rafted concentrations. I've seen it done, too often. If and when they fired at a single flying duck, they had it, so to speak, "where they wanted it."

Market hunting stems from the earliest shooting on New England's coastal fresh water ponds. Village shoemakers built camouflaged shore blinds and cobbled footgear behind such brushed-up hides while crude goose decoys floated out front. When honkers dropped in the cobblers let them huddle and then unleashed hails of hand-moulded pellets, cut-up horseshoe nails or gravel from their smoothbored, flintlock muzzleloaders. Their "Goodies" plucked the slain for featherbeds and pillows and roasted them for the community.

Later, wealthier sportsmen fashioned elaborate lodges camouflaged seaward to match tidal levels; in adjoining watch-towers game keepers trained and released goslings to fly out as "greeters" to coastal migrants. With parent fowl in restraint (the keepers having sighted flocks headed down-coast) the gaggle of greeters winged forth and vocalized welcome to safe-harbor. When the visitors were "lit," the trained young stooges ducked under the gate-pens and rejoined the old folks. Afront the clubhouse hide was a spring-latched window

Albert M. Day with battery of illegal guns. *F. & W. S. Photo by Rex Gary Schmidt*

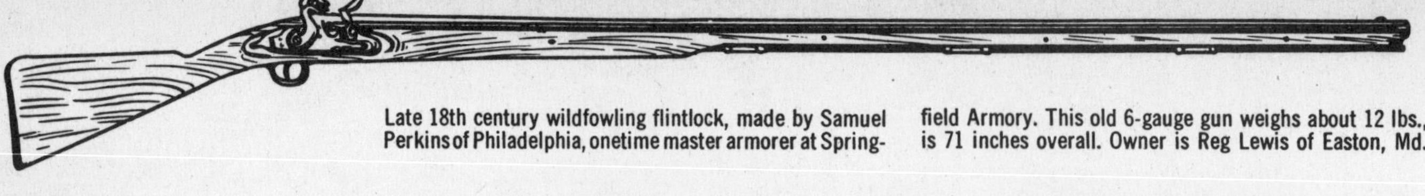

Late 18th century wildfowling flintlock, made by Samuel Perkins of Philadelphia, onetime master armorer at Springfield Armory. This old 6-gauge gun weighs about 12 lbs., is 71 inches overall. Owner is Reg Lewis of Easton, Md.

opening onto a big stool of floating lures. The keeper-lookout, pressing a buzzer that interrupted the card game and sent the players to the window with 8- and 10-bores, pulled the dead-fall. Up-lashed the window and there, right under the sportsmen (?), were the victims. B o o o o o m ! Pure slaughter.

I am writing about what I have witnessed. By the time live decoys were banned, many autoloaders and pumpguns had found their ways into these goose-hides and displaced the big bores.

With pumpguns and autoloaders in use (despite the banned 6's and 8's) recession came swiftly to our basic waterfowl stocks. Market hunters, armed with magazined 12-gauges shot killing loads faster than they could have with the 8's and 10's. Sportsmen were also easy prey to advertising that said, "shoot faster, shoot more and kill more." This way-paving to the demise of wildlife resources soon began revealing the barrel's bottom. In those days access to choice waterfowling centers was difficult. Market hunters and sportsmen killed only about as much game as they could carry, pack and ship. Some duck clubs, foreseeing the evil day, clapped on daily bag limits—usually 50 ducks and as many geese as one could gun. In the light of today's regulations, almost unbelievable.

Today, the sale of other than legally banded and pen-reared products (in some states) for public use, is strictly forbidden. The fact remains that if, tomorrow, the United States suddenly found itself dependent upon the food values in quantity of its wildlife resources, there would be just about enough for two square meals. As of now, however, we have not even approached, much less solved, the problem of combining decency afield with game production of a controlled or managed nature. In this country, the public's first reaction to any game law is not how it can be best obeyed or enforced, but how it can be evaded or, worse, violated. An unhappy but true situation.

Conservation, in its many fields and ramifications, made no move toward the restriction of magazine guns until the early 1920's. There had been mutterings through the years, but these were stifled by the gunmakers who had seen the big bores banned by the Migratory Bird Law, the Treaty Act with Great Britain. At that time *Field & Stream* (and its publisher, Eltinge Warner) boldly challenged the autoloaders, only to be badly beaten. Soon, however, a new force arose which called magazine guns and their manufacturers to an accounting. Begun in 1929 by the American Wildfowlers, a small foundational group that eventually emerged as More Game Birds in America and, later, as Ducks Unlimited, the battle terminated in 1934-35 when an executive order, by the late Franklin Roosevelt, restricted magazine guns to 3 shots. The various states then passed equivalent legislation, many of them outlawing guns of more than three shots on upland game species. It is now freely admitted that had this not been done we would not, today, be shooting wildfowl. It is also worthy of note that practically every major benefit attained by this nation's wildfowl and upland game resources has been due to conservationists' brains in conceiving such measures and fighting for them with lethargic congresses and villainously exploitive commercial interests.

Let's examine some of the old big bores, strictly from their records, then compare them with today's 12-bore magnums, in both double and magazine guns. All targets were one-foot square.

Fred Kimble's 6-gauge, 36-inch barrel, muzzleloading shotgun, hand choked by Fred Kimble.

6 drams, 1½ oz. 3's at 40 yards.
79 struck, or 44.7%.
6 drams, 1½ oz. 2's at 40 yards.
55 struck, or 36.6%.

J. Kelley's 8-gauge, single barrel muzzleloader. Rugh of Peoria, Ill., builder. Hand choked by Fred Kimble.

Nash Buckingham

5 drams, 1½ oz. 1's at 60 yards.
40 struck, or 33.75%.

Long's 10-gauge double, 32-inch barrels, breechloader. Maker, Schaeffer.

5 drams, 1½ oz. 2's at 40 yards.
58 struck, or 38.6%.
4½ drams, 1½ oz. 2's at 40 yards.
59 struck, or 39.2%.

Only one pellet struck outside of 25 inches.

These, then, were the guns that made history in the art of choke boring, a boring that permitted powerful charges of powder and heavy shot loads for lengthened kills. They endured until, in 1912-13, a well-meaning Federal assumption of waterfowl protection banned gauges larger than 10.

Now let's look at today—forty-some years later. My own field and wildfowl artillery will suffice:

M21 Winchester, magnum, 32-inch tubes.

M50 Winchester auto, 30-in. barrels.

Burt Becker, 10-pound, 12-bore magnum (Askins-Sweeley) for 3-inch cases. See photo caption for details.

It is possible, from a 3-inch chambered 50 Winchester or any similar type (one of which, the Browning autoloader, is now factory bored to handle 3-inch cases), to fire three magnum shells each containing almost five drams of powder and one and seven-eighths ounces of shot—thus giving the user almost 15 drams of powder and five and five-eighths ounces of shot! If the old big bore users had had such outfits, chances are our waterfowl populations might have been wiped out earlier.

Today, with a Federal bag limit nationally of less than six fowl per day, on the average, it matters little what type of gun and load the fowler uses, provided it is of sufficient power to not be too little (as is the 410) and thus invite indiscriminate crippling of migrants or upland game. The more shot, the more penetration, the more absorbed energy, the less chance to cripple. The magnum trouble is this: the American gunning public has, as usual, been "over-exposed," as the ad men have it, rather than "over-gunned." The novice hunter, hearing about those fantastic kills, buys himself a magnum and the most powerful hulls to be had. Then, by merely pointing his great gun in the quarry's direction, he expects he'll see it collapse per the advertisement's claim. If the advertisers had stressed the fact that a magnum armed hunter is never undergunned; *that a magnum isn't a special gun shooting 3-inch shells only, but can handle any length shell and bag its fair share of game, close or distant—* if it's hit—*the shooting world would be a cleaner place in which to live. That's the one, big, important thing, magnum or not—you've got to connect!*

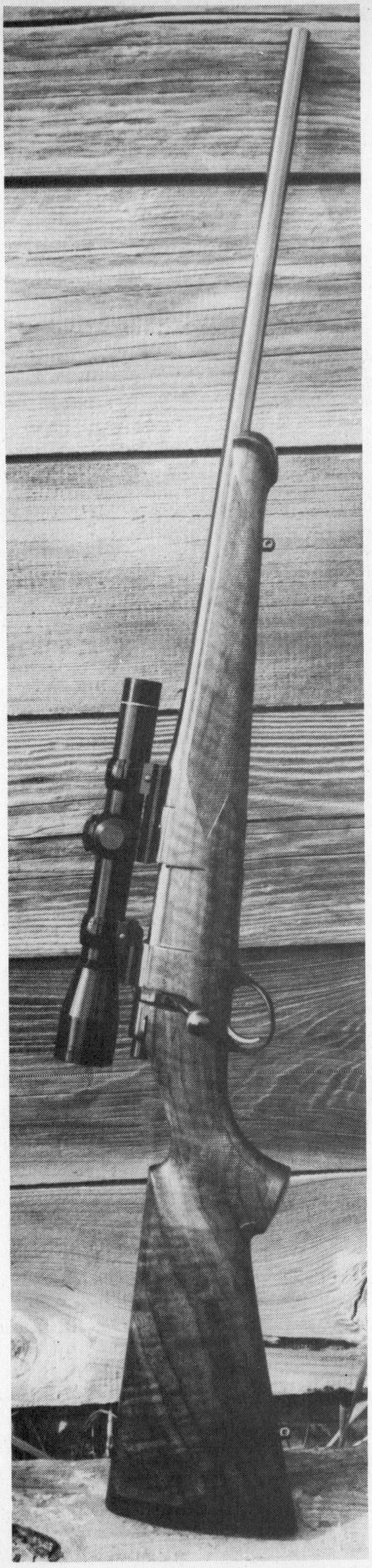

Milady's Rifle

How do you come up with a deer rifle suitable for a small and trim girl? Have it custom made? Make it yourself? Here's what the doctor ordered.

by DR. SAM FADALA

NO THINKING MAN would consider fitting his favorite lady into a dress four sizes too large, baggy hose, and a hat big enough to cover a watermelon. But, unwittingly, each year many would-be huntresses are burdened with rifles that suit them about as well. Expecting the woman shooter to do well in the woods lugging a rifle she cannot wield is like hoping for prices to go down. It isn't likely to happen.

The men who recognize that their favorite hunting rifle fits the lady nimrod something like a bazooka often try to compensate for this by giving her the short and not-too-heavy Model 94, or some counterpart. The trouble with this slab-sided little carbine, good as it is in a saddle scabbard, is its thin-stocked, small-buttedness, which often rears back to smack the woman shooter right in her pretty chops.

Finding this out, the interested male looks for a more suitable lady's rifle, only to find that no major arms company makes one. In the past low sales might have justified their not making such a rifle, but I am not so sure the same situation exists today. Lady shooters are taking to field and range in ever-increasing numbers. Maybe women's lib has had impetus here. I can't say, but the gals can be great shooters.

Of course, even with enthusiasm and perseverance working for her, the rifle still has to fit, whether for hunting or for punching holes in paper. Assuming we could talk a manufacturer into building a lady's hunting rifle, what should we ask for?

First, the rifle would be shorter than the men's version—shorter in barrel length, perhaps, certainly in stock pull. The action, too, should be shorter than the standard bolt action designed around 30-06 and longer rounds. Weight should be kept down, the fore-end made a bit slimmer than usually, the buttstock just thick enough to offer support for the face and a generous shoulder area to absorb recoil. The rifle would function smoothly, be easy to load and fire, and have a trigger light and crisp. The caliber would be big enough to get the job done, but not a shoulder pounder.

Since no such fortunate combination exists commercially now, how does the female shooter get a rifle she can handle with facility, carry without undue strain, shoot with comfort and hit what she's aiming at? Two obvious possibilities come to mind: A) a rifle can be made from scratch by a competent gunmaker and, B) an existing man's version can be cut down to fit the girl shooter.

I found myself facing just such a problem a few years ago. With the kids old enough to keep camp going, and a bit of time to spare, my wife took a serious interest in the hunt and in rifles, both of which had been latent interests previously.

After the first few times out she found as much game as I did; today, in fact, she finds more than I do because she has twice the patience when glassing the country. And she could shoot. Fitted into anything she could use with confidence the target, tin can or bullseye, was in trouble. Fortunately, I foresaw that if this trend continued she'd need the best possible equipment—not only boots and clothes and binoculars, but rifle as well.

Obviously Nancy could never enjoy firing the author's 7mm Magnum Ruger 77—the rifle is too long, too heavy, has too much recoil.

Nancy's custom made Sako L-461 rifle fits her well. The length of pull is correct, as is the scope's eye relief, and the near-22" barrel makes for good balance.

First Effort

Before it was all over with, the rifle turned out to be two rifles. She needed one that would drop a deer-size critter out to a maximum of 200 yards, another that could knock over a larger animal at about the same range. The problem was taken to a local gunbuilder, Frank Wells, of Tucson, Arizona. Frank and I sat down to many a cup of coffee before Nancy's little rifle began to take form. We came to one agreement early in our discussions—if we could match the ballistics of the old but proved 250 Savage cartridge she'd have power enough for deer-sized game out to 200 yards, and the light recoil wouldn't bother her.

We also wanted the smallest possible rifle for Nancy, a small-sized girl herself. "What we need," Frank said one day, "is that 250 Savage or something like it chambered in the Sako L461, the small action that handles the 222." I agreed, but we knew that the 250 or one of its 6mm counterparts would be too large for that little action.

That thinking brought the little 6mm/222 to mind. We considered the 6mm/223 as well, but after a good bit of testing we decided that the standard 6mm/222 would fill the bill—and it did indeed. The strong L461 action was fitted to a 21½" 6mm/222 barrel, set carefully into a nice Claro walnut stock graced with checkering but no frills. Functionality was the byword. Nancy was fitted to that rifle with more care than if she were having a gown made up for the Governor's ball!

The results were pleasing to the eye as well as showing a surprising performance. Frank had turned a Douglas blank down so that it matched stock and action dimensions. The rifle goes only 40" from butt to crown, weighs 7½ lbs. with scope and sling, and the stock pull is 13," the trigger crisp at 3 lbs. A neat package, indeed, and one that put 5 shots into 1¼" at 100 yards.

Eight head of game went to the freezer in the first few seasons of the little rifle's life, both in Nancy's hands as well as the hands of those who had to try it to see if we were bragging too much about its merits. All bullets but one totally penetrated those deer and antelope. That one, a bullet designed more for varmints, lost its jacket about halfway through an antelope, requiring a second shot.

Those who tried the rifle or saw it in use, including a game warden and one guide, said they wouldn't mind having one of these little "lady rifles" around as a venison getter. Most of the calls Wells subsequently got to build the little rifles came from men, too! The ease of placing its bullets made the little rifle deadly above its apparent capability.

As for those ballistics, the 80-gr. bullets perked along at just under 3,000 fs (foot seconds) as measured by two Oehler chronographs, the Chronotach and the Model 11, one used to verify the other's findings. Muzzle energy was 1,578 fp (foot pounds). So we really did duplicate *factory ballistics* of the 250-3000, though it is true that the 250 can generate more energy than the 6mm/222 with handloads. Still, the 80-gr. 24-cal. bullet has a small edge on the 87-gr. in 25 size via the 6mm's higher sectional density.

Pressures are probably high with the 27 grains of BLC2 used behind the 80-gr. bullet, but the cases have lasted well, held reloaded primers in place, indicating no drastic stretching in the head area, and resizing has been no problem.

The largest thing Nancy knocked off with her 6mm/222 was a good sized whitetail buck, shot while she was trying out a new load—the 87-gr. Hornady with 26.0/BLC2, which chronographed 2,875 fs. The near-200 yard shot put the bullet a few inches behind one shoulder, breaking the other on its way out.

The Other Rifle

As I said, Nancy ended up with two rifles. When she started making plans for elk and moose, the 6mm/222 was suddenly deficient. Frank and I sat down and started all over again.

The 7mm Mauser seemed about right, but then our eye caught a Ruger

The 7½ primer (left) shows a bit of cratering, but cases are long lasting and there is no measurable head size change with the loads mentioned in the text. Obviously, each rifle differs in chamber size and must be loaded differently, starting with mild loads and working up. The primer on the right shows that is is softer than the 7½. Both were fired with same exact load, except that the R-P case was loaded with one (1) grain less powder due to slightly different case-wall thickness. This difference can be two grains and more in larger cases of different brands, but the little 222 case differences are almost negligible. In later loadings no separate powder charges were used for different case brands. *Kenn Oberrecht photo.*

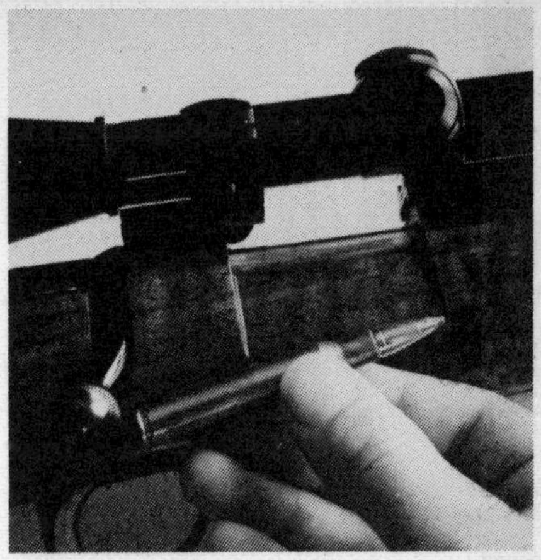

Now the 6mm/222 wears its 4x Leupold scope. Here the 30-06 round contrasts with the little Sako L-461 action. *Kenn Oberrecht photo.*

The 30-06 cartridges loom large against the 6mm/222 loads. *Kenn Oberrecht photo.*

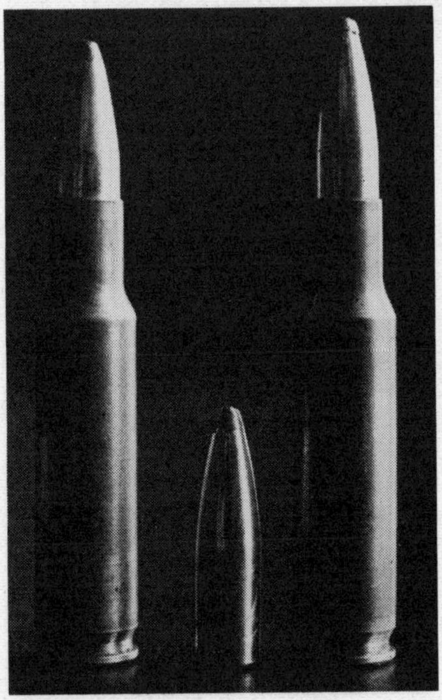

Though hardly perceptible here, the cartridge at left would not chamber properly because the sizing die was set all the way down—adjusted by the book. The area below the shoulder expanded too much, preventing full entry. Moral—adjust the die progressively, tailoring the case to the chamber dimensions. *Kenn Oberrecht photo.*

M77 bolt action in caliber 284 on the shelf. Here was a shorty case and a short action, velocity and energy a tad more than the 7x57. With a bit of stock thinning and shortening the 22-inch barreled rifle might be just about right for Nancy's elk rifle.

Leaving the barrel alone, we slimmed the stock, chopped the butt to 13″ with a recoil pad, and worked the trigger over as best we could—but it still has some creep. We loaded all manner of 7mm bullets and, in our testing, we discovered no adverse effects from seating bullets deeper than normally. Nearly all reloading pundits contend that pressures invariably rise if this is done. We were not, of course, trying to develop super loads in the first place.

Here are several "best" loads, though other powder/bullet combinations were tried:

56/IMR4350/140-gr. bullets,	MV 2,950
57/IMR4831/160-gr. bullets,	MV 2,890
54/IMR4831/175-gr. bullets,	MV 2,675
57/IMR4831/154-gr. bullets.*	MV 2,900
58/IMR4831/150-gr. bullets,†	MV 2,950

*Hornady †Remington

The 160 Speer Mag-Tip bullet offered a special bonus because of its truncated lead tip. It didn't have to dip into the powder space as much as did pointed projectiles—which the magazine governed. We chopped the lead points off other bullets, too, seating them less deep as well, but we found no change in accuracy or point of impact with these nose-less bullets.

I refinished the Ruger stock, finding under the factory finish a very nice piece of wood. Nancy's interest in the rifle went up after that face-lifting. The 284 weighs a pound more than the 6/222, part of the price we paid for power.

As for glassware, the 6/222 wore two scopes—a Bushnell 2½-8x for those long-range small-target trips, and a Leupold 4x for big game. The 284 looked just right with a Leupold 3x.

There are, naturally, other routes to selecting a lady's big game rifle—and one arm could suffice. The 7x57 or 284 would be ample for deer on up to larger game, and for small stuff with the right handloads. A dozen others would also fill the bill. If she doesn't mind the push, and some women apparently don't, bigger calibers might be looked into. But the main problem always is fit.

Perhaps some arms company will eventually offer a rifle designed for the ladies, perhaps one more or less like the lighter one described here.

The caliber should be 24 or 25, the case just big enough to drive a 24/25 bullet of about 90 grains to some 3,000 fs at the muzzle. Looking at the little Russian M43 7.62x39mm the other day, I wondered what it would do necked to 24 or 25. ●

Remington's 721-722: THE STORY OF A SUCCESS

This is Remington Model 721 rifle No. 0000001.

by **STUART OTTESON**

REMINGTON today stands well out front as the leading maker of sporting long arms in the world. Their Model 700 bolt action enjoys the same position among high power rifles. It's been that way for so long we sometimes take it for granted.

Matters were once far different. Between the World Wars, Remington's gunmaking operations came perilously close to following the likes of Newton, Standard, Lefever, and Ross into the history books. Impressive physical facilities existed at Ilion, thanks largely to their World War I activities, but not many guns were being shipped, and those that were often as not sold at a loss to the factory. Remington kept going during those years mostly on profits from the cartridge division in Bridgeport.

When DuPont took over in 1933, Remington was running a poor third in gun sales behind Winchester and Savage. DuPont's Board of Directors planned to close down the firearms end of the business, but as a matter of routine they first dispatched a team of DuPont engineers headed by a Mr. George Read to Ilion to determine what if anything was worth salvaging. In the course of his survey, Mr. Read fortunately became a convert. On his return to Wilmington he made such a strong appeal on Ilion's behalf that he is now credited with almost single-handedly saving the factory.

Despite new DuPont investment which followed, things didn't really turn around at Ilion for some time. New machinery and processes were set up, but DuPont encountered a lot of resistance to attempts to modernize the design of the guns themselves. The problem was mostly how the guns were made, not how well they shot.

Remington's product line had evolved without much continuity over the years, a situation which can play havoc in volume arms manufacture. Each gun was an individual, and while most worked well enough, their manufacture was slow and inefficient.

An example was the Model 720, the immediate predecessor to the 721 and 722 rifles. It listed at $97.40 just before the war, certainly no bargain basement price. Though put together from a lot of leftover military parts, it was costing more than that to make and sell. The extremely fine Model 37 target rifle was known around the plant as the Model $37 because that was roughly what Remington was losing on each one.

Under such circumstances, morale throughout the organization was understandably very low, and even with DuPont's help, Ilion's future continued to look dim. The Second War reversed things almost completely. This was not because of the enormous arms contracts, because profits on these were relatively meager. In fact, overbuilding and overexpansion could easily leave a company like Remington in worse shape than it started. The First War certainly hadn't yielded any lasting economic benefits.

World War II created an opportunity, or excuse, if you will, to "clean house" and modernize at Remington that didn't exist during normal times. DuPont instituted a far-reaching program in anticipation of post-war conditions. Officially titled *Reconversion and Modernization,* it was known around the plant as simply R & M. The 721 and 722 rifles were slated as the vanguard project of this R & M program, and were expected to pave the way for what was to eventually be a whole series of successful new Remington firearms. They were thus extremely critical to Remington's future in the DuPont corporate structure. In turn, success or failure of the new bolt rifles became in large measure the responsibility of one man, Merle (Mike) Walker.

Walker is a native of Iowa, and got an engineering degree from Iowa State in 1934. This was the depth of the Depression, and so almost any job was a welcome blessing. Thus, Walker was more than happy to be working for Dow Chemical in the late 1930s, although he had little desire to finish out his career there.

One might wonder how a person makes the transition from organic chemist to one of the world's top firearm designers working for Remington. Surprisingly enough, Walker simply answered an ad in *The American Rifleman* magazine. He went to Ilion for an interview in April, 1942, and came on board as part of Remington's Research Department three months later. There were a lot of new faces then, as DuPont was assembling a large engineering staff to meet their massive wartime arms commitments.

The new centerfire rifle project officially began on August 12, 1942, with an authorization of $200 to prepare a project outline, the first "paperwork," so to speak. Later that year, the head of the Research Department, a Dr. R. Hentchel, used another $11,500 for some preliminary background research. That was as far as things got until Walker took over the project two years later.

During 1942 and 1943 Walker was busy on war jobs, ranging from the development of buttoned rifle barrels manufactured (for Springfield rifles, but later, of course, with industry-wide application) to an optical sighting-in device for the Springfield rifle (which bore some resemblance to the collimators now used by gunsmiths). He even worked up a 4,250 feet-per-second artillery round capable of defeating the Nazi Tiger tank, though some other method was found and used by the military. Regularly producing 15-inch groups at 1,000 yards, performance of this last item was something even today's long-range target shooters don't scoff at.

In August of 1944, with the Springfield rifle contracts completed, Walker was given $35,000 to begin making drawings and building prototypes of a new rifle. While designers from other projects were to make important contributions, the actual 721-722 "team" consisted of only three other men; Dana McNally, Leon Rix, and Knute Reed. McNally was an engineer; the other two men assisting Walker working strictly on the boards as draftsmen. While you won't hear them mentioned again, these three in fact bore the yeoman's share of work in getting the new design drawn up and into prototype form.

The paper studies done in 1942 pretty well established what was desired: a light fast-handling rifle which could be made at low enough cost to market successfully and make some money for Remington. Volume would be the key to success. Thus, the new rifles were not primarily targeted to compete with Winchester's Model 70, the leading bolt action of the day, but rather with the Winchester Model 94, Marlin Model 36, and Savage Model 40, which together represented the biggest market for centerfire rifles. Remington gambled that if they could offer a stronger and more powerful rifle, which still handled as well and sold as cheaply, it would cut deeply into that market.

What makes the 721-722 story worth recounting now in some detail is not simply the fact that the rifles became a commercial success and met the specifications, but that they exceeded them to such an extent that the rifle design remains a leader today, more than 30 years later, and seems to grow stronger each year in the marketplace. It thus, I believe, deserves special recognition alongside other enduring firearms such as the Model 1898 rifle of Paul Mauser, the Colt single-action revolver, and John M. Browning's lever-actions.

Walker's crew had the first drawings of the rifle ready by the end of 1944. They pretty accurately depicted what was to become the production 721, except at the breech. Walker's "counterbore" pattern was one of the last elements of the design to fall into place, and the rifle was originally drawn up with a 35-degree cone breech. Considering that Remington had used a cone pattern since at least 1920, and Winchester still used one, and would in fact for another twenty years, that's not surprising. The 722, when it was later drawn up, differed from the 721 only in length, measuring exactly 0.85 inches less through the magazine and loading port.

Design

It might be useful at this point to examine some of the principal mechanical features of the 721-722.

Mike Walker in 1951 with 722 rifle chambered in the then new 222 cartridge.

The most costly single component of a bolt action is its receiver. Thus in cutting costs and production times, Walker had to get away from the traditional forging with its intricate machine work. He was not the first to build a high power rifle from barstock. Savage had done so for many years. His contribution instead lay in utilizing a very simple round receiver which did not finish to look like an overgrown rimfire rifle.

The receiver was carefully proportioned for a trim 1.355-inch diameter, thus making use of standard 1⅜-inch barstock. Instead of special grooves or slots, the tooling jigs and fixtures indexed directly in the boltway. Much effort also went into multiple tooling cuts. Those underneath the tang and bridge, for example, were made on a single pass with three cutters bolted together. A simple bracket blanked from steel plate and clamped between the receiver ring and barrel served as the recoil lug.

The bolt was also "modernized." Besides very large and solid locking lugs, and a bolt handle shaped for low-mounted scopes, its construction was carefully planned for volume manufacture. The "standards" at the time for quality high power bolt action rifles definitely called for a one-piece forged assembly. But such parts were not only very slow and costly to make, the end result wasn't necessarily precise. Walker fabricated his bolt, induction brazing the bolt handle in place with silver solder, and also making the bolt head separate. With the head and body of the bolt machined from barstock, extreme precision and concentricity was possible, while the furnace-brazed joint between them used a copper alloy that for practical purposes yielded one solid piece of steel. As extra insurance, a sturdy steel dowel fits cross ways through the joint.

Besides barstock and screw-machine parts, stampings were used where strength and wear weren't critical. This included the magazine and much of the "fire control unit." To avoid the need for inserts, adjusting screws in this latter assembly threaded directly into the sheet metal by means of 90 degree bends and partial threads cut into opposing interior walls of the trigger housing.

In writing up an incentive award for Walker in 1948, his supervisors noted that whereas the Model 720 bolt and receiver had required a combined total of more than 250 machine operations, the Model 721 required approximately 60. Beyond pure numbers, perhaps a more accurate gauge of Walker's contribution is the fact that his design allowed the Ilion workforce to produce truly precision parts in volume, and without the high degree of individual skill and workmanship that previously would have been needed.

Cartridges in the new rifle were extracted after firing by a small circular spring inside the bolt head. If any single part played a key role in the 721/722, it was this extractor. Not until it was certain that it worked in a high power rifle, and equally important that it could be successfully mass-produced, could Remington proceed with the final pattern of the bolt and barrel, and the all-important breech formed between them.

When developed by John Howell in 1945 for an unsuccessful autoloading rifle, the extractor's object was not so much a safer and stronger breech, but rather a cheaper part capable of a surer grip than conventional extractors. It was a crescent-shaped spring with a claw formed in its middle. Instead of being pivoted or collared to the bolt, it snapped into a peripheral groove milled inside the bolt face. Being thus trapped and contained within the counterbore itself, rather than fastened externally, it was less disposed to slippage, and enormous extracting power was potentially possible. Remington later ran advertising claims of double normal strength , based on tear-away tests in which the new extractor held up to around 300 pounds, compared to 150 pounds with conventional types.

But forming the necessary claw on this springy little part very nearly proved its undoing. The machined prototype versions were far too expensive for mass production. The problem was well known throughout the Research Department, and it wasn't until one of the toolmakers, Homer Young, devised a method for coining the claw that this novel extractor could be safely counted as part of the new rifle.

The ejector also occupied the bolt face rather than penetrating from outside. But here the way was shown by our World War II combat rifles, and Walker simply adopted the spring-loaded pins used in the M-1 rifles and carbines.

With everything nestled within the bolt face, it was now possible to ring the cartridge with a solid and unbroken belt of steel. The breech devised and patented by Mike Walker went further than this by also closely counterboring the end of the barrel to accept the bolt nose. Thus the cartridge was not only enshrouded by the bolt, but both were then enshrouded by a barrel flange. If a cartridge tried to rupture, pressure could expand the belt on the front of the bolt only far enough to fill the recess in the barrel.

Attached to the opposite end of the receiver is the fire control unit, more commonly known as the trigger and safety. For the Models 30 and 720, Remington had merely dressed up the existing military triggers. When Winchester introduced a superb new trigger in the Model 70, Remington had little choice but to follow suit. They had fortunately by then acquired a first rate trigger design of their own from a California inventor named John Sweany, and had experience with using it in the Model 37 rimfire target rifles since shortly before World World War II.

Walker took the somewhat bulky Sweany layout and reshaped it into a

ABOUT THE AUTHOR

Stuart Otteson once nearly withdrew from human society when, through no personal fault, he lost access to 1500 acres of Virginia groundhog pasture that had been his private preserve. He is a rifle nut. He is also 42, a mechanical engineer, and the writer of **The Bolt Action,** *just about the best book done on rifle actions. If Otteson still could shoot that 1500 acres, we probably wouldn't have the work he does for* **Rifle** *magazine, or this piece. K.W.*

slimmer easy to manufacture unit. It is fully adjustable and has a special spring loaded "connector" piece between the trigger and sear to allow a cleaner pull and the virtual absence of overtravel or "slap."

Hinged to the trigger housing is a two position side-mounted safety. It uses a cam to block the sear, a fact that caused the Research Department some unanticipated grief shortly before the rifles were to be released.

The patent attorneys in Bridgeport discovered during a final check of the rifle that this arrangement might infringe the safety in Winchester's Model 52 target rifle, and thus a redesign was ordered. Phil Haskell, a young engineer from the Aberdeen Proving Grounds, got the last-minute assignment. Like Walker, he had arrived via an ad in *The American Rifleman,* although about four years later. After several weeks of pondering the subtleties of such an infringement problem, Haskell split the sear into two side-by-side stampings, one for the trigger and the other for the safety cam.

No one today can fully explain why this change satisfied the attorneys, or even if they originally had that much of a problem. The only sure thing is that a lot of gunsmiths through the years have puzzled over what Remington was up to. In any event, once this "solution" was accepted, the thousands of guns already in the warehouse were uncrated and returned to the factory for refit with two-piece sears.

The rifle's bolt stop also underwent last minute revision. It originally consisted of a stop lever only, so that like the units fitted many years later to Remington's economy-line Model 600 rifles, something like a small screwdriver or jacknife was needed to get the bolt out. This was generally recognized to be a pretty cheesy arrangement by most Remington employees who handled the early pilot rifles. One of them, Charles Morse, volunteered to devise a linkage release system fitted to the trigger housing (ironically enough, it was Morse who would later develop the Model 600). This proved a very auspicious change, as the "new convenient bolt stop" became a major marketing feature of the new rifles.

While, according to Walker, there were literally "thousands" of problems and delays getting the rifles finished up and into production, the only other one he clearly recalls now involved heat treatment. Both to speed production and reduce warpage, the receivers in the first pilot rifles were hardened at the front only. But a color line appeared in the blueing, forcing Remington to start heat treating the entire part. Too much warpage then occurred, however, to allow using close fitting precision bolts. The problem was only solved by going to chrome moly steel and an *austempering* process where a hot salt quench subjects the final machined receiver blank to much less temperature shock and thus less warpage than conventional oil or water quenches.

Barrels and Sights

The 721 and 722 rifles were fitted with six-groove barrels, rifled by the button system developed by Walker during the war. The standard outside contour was a double taper of medium weight, closely resembling the barrels in the Winchester Model 70. A short distance forward of the receiver ring a swell was formed to serve as the base for the rear sight assembly. Behind this swell, the barrel tapered 0.110 inches per inch, while forward to the muzzle the taper was only one-tenth as steep, 0.011 inches per inch.

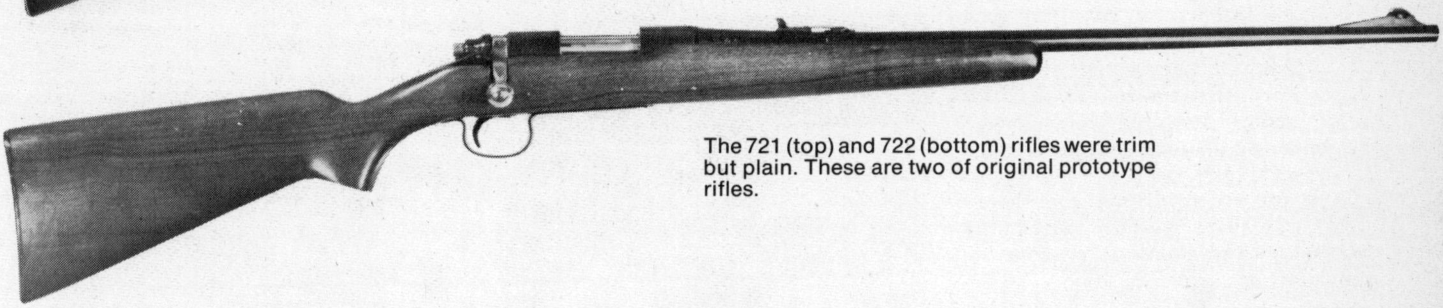

The 721 (top) and 722 (bottom) rifles were trim but plain. These are two of original prototype rifles.

Although the original 721-722 drawings show four barrel lengths, ranging from 20 to 26 inches, the rifles were introduced in 24 and 26-inch lengths only. The 26-inch length was reserved for 300 H&H (at least until the 222 Remington version was added a couple years later). The magnum barrel was also heavier than the standard contour, the combination increasing the rifle's over-all weight by about one pound. In later years, 22-inch barrels were offered in some calibers.

The receiver was drilled and tapped for scope bases and receiver sights. Some of the very first production rifles lacked holes on top of the bridge for a rear scope base, but this was very quickly corrected after complaints from the gun writers who tried to use them.

Each rifle had a white metal bead front sight dovetailed into a matted ramp brazed to the front of the barrel, and a step adjustable V-notch rear sight dovetailed into the integral swell near the rear of the barrel. Unlike the Winchester Model 70, this swell did not also serve as the base for a barrel screw, for the 721-722 rifles had semi-floating barrels screwed only to the receiver.

Weight and Handling

While action strength perhaps made the 721-722 rifles famous, their light weight and good handling also drew praise. The 721 and 722 weighed 7¼ and 7 pounds, respectively, very favorable figures for a high power rifle at that time. In comparison, Winchester's Model 70 listed at 7¾ pounds, at least until 1952 when their 6½ pound "Featherweight" version came along. And the custom rifles being put together at that time on surplus military actions often tipped the scales at 8 pounds or more.

The stock, although very plain and lacking either checkering or sling swivels, generally met with favor also. Cut from American walnut, it had a good pistol grip and a full semi-beavertail forearm. A shotgun type metal buttplate fitted to the back was nicely checkered to prevent slippage. While normally coming in an iron sight version (dropping 1⅞ inches at the comb and 2⅞ inches at the heel), a high comb stock (drop at comb of 1⅜ inches, and at heel 2 3/16 inches) more suitable for scope use accompanied the 222 rifle and was optional at no extra cost in other calibers.

Cartridges

After culling out a few "oddballs" suggested by marketing, such as the 30 Remington, Walker ended up with a lineup of six cartridges for the new rifles. The 721 was slated for 30-06, 270 Winchester, and the 300 H&H Magnum, while in the 722, 220 Swift, 257 Roberts, and 300 Savage chamberings were planned.

During some test firings in 1946, a defective Swift cartridge let go in a 721 rifle Walker was using. While no real damage or injury resulted, the experience nonetheless left a strong impression. Since Walker hadn't been all that anxious about tooling for a special slanted magazine for the Swift anyway, it took only a couple days to decide to kick it from the lineup, leaving only five chamberings at the time the rifles were introduced.

In 1950 a brand new varmint cartridge was developed. Labeled the 222 Remington, it is sometimes assumed to have been developed part and parcel with the new 722 rifle. According to Walker, however, that wasn't the case and there was no tie-in with his earlier decision to drop the 220 Swift.

The 222 modified earlier experimental cartridges developed at Bridgeport to utilize .30 Carbine cup blanks. The original cartridges, while suitable for single shot rifles, were too short to feed in the 722. Walker put a steeper shoulder on the cartridge, lengthened the neck, and then stretched the whole thing out by about 3/10 of an inch so it could better bridge the gap between the magazine and chamber. In the process, velocity was boosted from 2800 to 3200 feet per second with a 50-grain bullet.

Even lengthened, feed with the 222 was less than ideal. But instead of giving up, or going to a different type of magazine and feed system altogether, as Winchester had done for the 22 Hornet, Remington (more specifically, Phil Haskell) kept tinkering with the angles and dimensions of the 722 magazine until it finally digested this little cartridge with some reliability. Also of concern was whether the bullets were too solid for small varmints. After spending a good part of his summer shooting woodchucks with the new cartridge, Walker convinced Bridgeport to swage the bullets from thinner jackets. Thereafter, the cartridge quickly gained popularity, still universal today, and greatly complemented sales of the 722 rifles.

Cartridges were, of course, added, and dropped, from the rifles' chamberings in subsequent years. For the 721, the 280 Remington and 264 Winchester Magnum became available, while the 308 Winchester, 244 Remington, 222 Remington Magnum, and 243 Winchester appeared in the lineup for the shorter rifle.

Tests

The 721 was probably subjected to a more grueling series of tests than any commercial firearm before or since. Wayne Leek, another Aberdeen recruit, ran Ilion's newly formed Test Department. He introduced a lot of military methods, applying them with a vengeance to his first victim, the new 721 rifle.

These included a dust test, ice test, rain test, and blow-up test. An automatic fixture was built which put the rifles through 50,000 cycles to check wear of the bolt and firing system. Leek also placed the 721 prototypes in an "iron lung" for gas-leak tests using white blotter paper and cartridges filed down to the point that their heads would open up and spill gas upon firing. The rifle came through this latter test pretty well, except that the cocking piece was somewhat disposed to blow back through the unshrouded bolt sleeve. While it never got completely away, it did exhibit a nasty habit of cocking on the receiver.

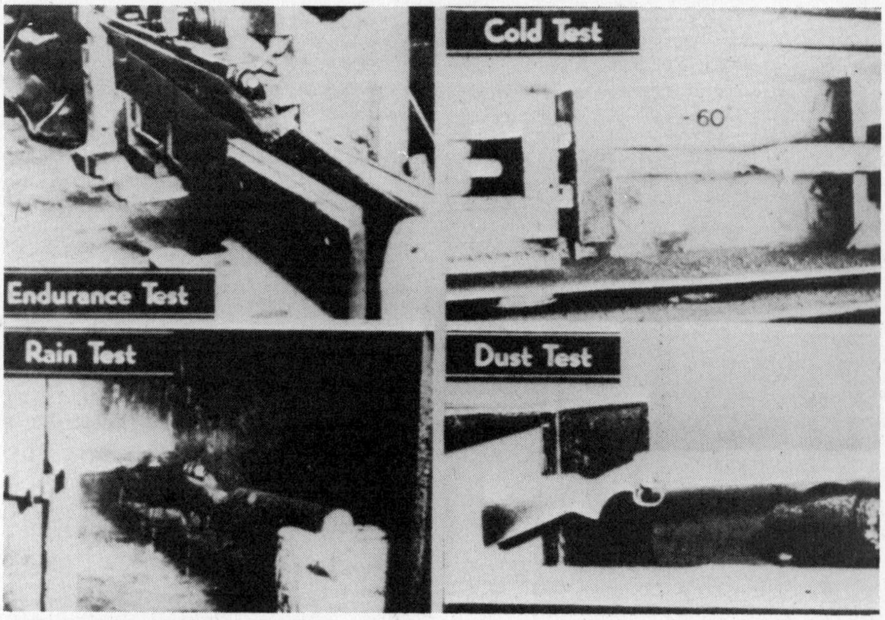

Excerpt from Remington literature shows stress marketers laid on factory tests of the new rifles.

When loaded with dust, a perhaps unrealistic criterion for a non-military arm, the cocking piece also tended to bind with the sear. To overcome this, the flat area of contact between these two pieces was relieved by cutting serrations into the top of the sear. For production, the same result was gained with less expense by simply lathe-turning the cocking piece to yield a radiused contact surface with the sear below.

The blow-up tests were the big thing, and the most publicized. They were run on two 721 rifles chambered for 30-06, which Walker considered the worst cartridge from a blow-up standpoint. Starting with a proof cartridge, 220-grain bullets were progressively lodged in front for each shot until the rifles no longer functioned. By the fifth extra bullet, the bolt head had expanded into the barrel counterbore so tightly in both rifles that the bolt handles were broken off trying to open them. But because the enshrouded cartridge heads remained intact through it all, no further damage occurred and the only gas to escape came through the primer.

Such conditions far exceeded anything that a brass cartridge head could withstand alone. According to Remington, the two 721 pilot rifles were subject to pressures estimated as high as 300,000 pounds per square inch. Conventional rifles tested alongside them for comparison all turned to scrap at much lower pressures.

Patents

Besides the button rifling patent (no. 2,383,356 issued August 21, 1945), three others related specifically to the 721-722 rifles. Number 2,473,373, covering John Howell's extractor, was filed on January 30, 1946 and issued a little over three years later on June 14, 1949. The next (no. 2,514,981), for Walker's redesign of the Sweany trigger, plus Haskell's work on the safety, was filed on February 12, 1948 and issued July 11, 1950.

The last, number 2,585,195 covering Mike Walker's *counterbore* breeching mechanism, wasn't filed until January 8, 1949, almost a full year after official announcement of the new rifles, and at a time when many thousands were already in circulation. Thus there was great difficulty with the application. Remington's attorneys and the Patent Office went around and around on the invention, the Patent Office seemingly determined to throw just about every patent they could lay their hands on against it, particularly the just-issued Howell patent.

Remington not only had to come up with depositions establishing when, where, and who did what on the new rifle, they pulled out all stops to convince the people in Washington of its overwhelming technical merits. Copies of the many favorable gun reviews were furnished. Twice the Remington attorneys lugged down all the rifle specimens used in the blow-up tests, the wrecked Mausers, Springfields, Winchesters, etc., as well as the unscathed 721s. They once even took the head examiner over to the Arlington Rifle Club for an afternoon's shooting with the new rifles.

By going back and blowing up a 721 rifle with the barrel flange machined away, Remington finally convinced the Patent Office that it was not Howell's bolt face alone that accounted for the new breech's remarkable strength, but that in fact the barrel flange was the real key which allowed continued support of the cartridge under the most extreme pressure conditions. The Patent Office thereupon relented, and issued Walker's patent on February 12, 1952.

Mike Walker around 1952 testing one of first 222 benchrest rifles. Mike and his wife Olive were among leading stool shooters in the '50s and '60s.

Introduction and Delivery

While development of the 721-722 was a well kept secret at the factory, a select group of gun writers examined pilot rifles in the spring of 1947, and soon rumors of a new Remington rifle were surfacing. Those actually shown rifles probably didn't do too much talking, however, at least in specifics, because rumors centered on a commercialized version of the Springfield.

Considering the million-plus

Remington 721/722 Specifications

Caliber	Rifle	Magazine capacity	Over-all length	Weight	Barrel length
30-06	721	4	44¼	7¼	24
270	721	4	44¼	7¼	24
300 H & H	721	3	46¼	8¼	26
300 Savage	722	4	43¼	7	24
257 Roberts	722	4	43¼	7	24
222 Remington	722	5	45¼	7½	26

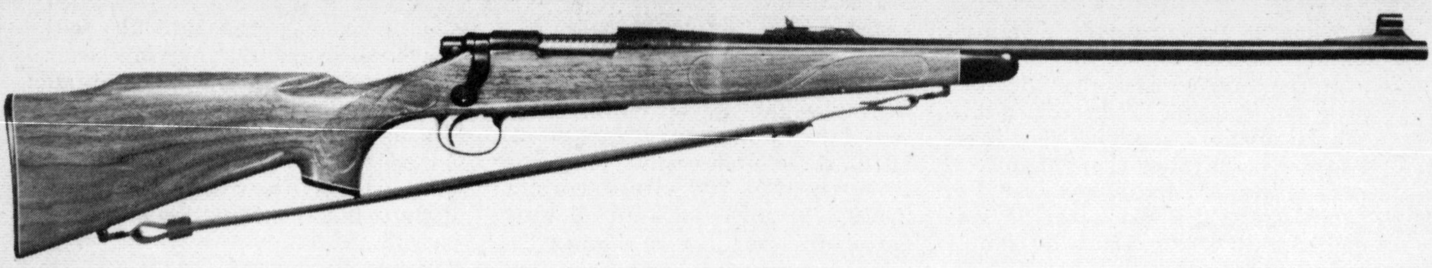

The 1962 Model 700, a major facelift of the 721-722, came in two grades. The 700BDL (at top in short action) featured fancy-pattern pressed checkering, tips on forearm and pistol grip, white line spacers, hinged floorplate, and sling assembly. Standard grade 700ADL (bottom in long action) had simpler checkering pattern and blind magazine.

Springfield rifles Remington had just finished cranking out for the Army, such a conclusion wasn't irrational. In fact, there were those at Remington who had originally leaned strongly in that direction. But once Mike Walker took charge, there was no further hesitation about going to a completely new rifle. He had carefully studied Remington's pre-war experiences, and well knew that even though development costs might be much lower, making converted military rifles was not profitable in the long run.

Marketing had originally scheduled announcement of the new rifles for January, 1947. Since that committed them to a wholly impractical timetable, Walker and the rest of the Research staff got a little stirred up, to put it mildly. Even 1948 presented a lot of problems, but an announcement date of January 21, 1948 was finally agreed on.

The 721 and 722 were cataloged at $79.95 and $74.95 respectively, compared to $59.50 for Winchester's Model 94, $58.75 for the Marlin Model 36, and $52.40 for the Savage Model 40. While thus falling a little short of the original pricing goals, they were still comfortably below the $106.00 that the Model 70 was commanding at the time. To their advantage, the 722 offered U.S. shooters the first true short-actioned production bolt rifle in some 20 years.

It was also very helpful that deliveries of Model 70 rifles following the war were so slow that it was often difficult to lay hands on one at almost any price. Many shooters were turning in desperation to custom rifles built on surplus military actions, running $175 and up for decent specimens. The market was ripe for an eighty-dollar rifle with state-of-the-art performance.

The first small lot of production guns was distributed to writers for evaluation in the fall of 1947. Deliveries to wholesalers were scheduled to begin by caliber as follows:

30-06 Springfield .. March 1948
300 Savage .... May 1948
270 Winchester and 257 Roberts .... July 1948
300 H&H Magnum .... September 1948

The rifles were officially designated the 721A and 722A to denote a "standard" grade. "Fancy" grades were also offered, the B (Special) with a checkered stock of selected walnut and sling swivels, and D (Peerless) and F (Premier) grades which featured even better wood, plus engraving. There were also later designations such as the 721AC-722AC and 721BDL-722BDL, but in practice even Remington marketing seldom used suffixes, and the guns were invariably referred to simply as Models 721 and 722.

Sales

Sales of the Model 30 and 720 rifles which preceded the 721-722 had totalled a scant 25,000, roughly 1,000 rifles a year. Thus DuPont knew that the new rifle had nowhere to go but up. The big question, of course, was how far? Development of the rifles cost $175,000, and tooling roughly another million. New high-volume guns coming out today routinely cost a lot more, but that was an unprecedented investment for the time, and an enormous pile of pre-1950 dollars.

DuPont gambled that the low retail price made possible by the new machinery and processes would generate enough sales volume in the post-war market to recover the investment. The break-even point was figured to be approximately 15,000 rifles per year. Considering Remington's dismal pre-war sales record, the whole thing obviously required some confidence on management's part.

An opportune juxtaposition of a good rifle, low retail price, and booming post-war demand for high power hunting rifles brought an acceptance and sales volume that took even Remington by surprise. Favorable articles and evaluations began pouring in so fast that the Marketing Department compiled a 23-page booklet entitled "What The Experts Say About the New Remington Models 721 & 722 Big Game Rifles." It contained twenty writeups which appeared in print during the first four months of 1948, ranging all the way from a brief announcement in the *New York Times,* to an exhaustive dual evaluation in *The American Rifleman* by the esteemed team of Julian Hatcher and Al Barr.

The following summary of the "experts" reactions shows they liked a lot more things about Remington's new rifles than they disliked:

Features acclaimed:

1. Light weight and good balance.
2. Strength.
3. Safety.
4. Speed and smoothness of operation.
5. Good stock lines and proportions.
6. Convenient and noiseless safety.
7. Convenient bolt stop.
8. Extractor strength.
9. Low selling price.
10. "Miracle" trigger.
11. Bolt handle shape and safety location for low-mounted scopes.
12. Smooth and clean receiver lines.

Two men who actively contributed to 721-722 project: Wayne Leek (left) tested the rifles; Homer Young figured out how to manufacture the little spring clip extractors.

Features criticized:

1. Lack of scope base holes on bridge (immediately corrected).
2. Non-detachable sheet metal floorplate and trigger guard.
3. Plain uncheckered varnish-finished stock.
4. Lack of sling swivels.

Most of the complaints about "austerity" were tempered by a recognition that the very favorable retail price of the new rifles forced Remington to keep some things basic. The lack of checkering on the stock was a good example. Even at the labor rates then, hand checkering would have boosted the rifles' retail price by between $10 and $15, bringing it up closer than Remington wanted to be to the Model 70.

The first full year's production (1949) was approximately 42,000 rifles, and that was more a manufacturing limitation than anything else, because for the first couple years the factory was working day and night and Remington was selling everything they could ship from Ilion. Sales in 1950 topped 50,000.

But the rifle's engineering virtues could sustain this level of sales only so long. Very plain and unexciting lines limited its ultimate sales potential. While it certainly wasn't ugly, neither could anyone ever accuse it of winning any beauty contests against the Model 70, or even the many custom-built Mausers, Springfields, and Enfields, for that matter. In 1951 sales began to cool off, thereafter settling down into the 30,000 range, although there were one or two more 50,000-rifle years.

Such sales continued to make many at Remington very happy, but they didn't satisfy Walker, and he had a completely restyled rifle ready for 1952. Remington's management, loth to tamper with success, vetoed the change. The same thing occurred in 1960.

Meanwhile, in 1958 another rifle with obviously close ties was briefly added to the Remington product line alongside the 721 and 722. The Model 725 originated on "the other side of the house" insofar as Remington's engineering organization was concerned, being designed under Wayne Leek, who had by then come up from the testing department to become a design supervisor, mostly for shotguns and rimfire rifles.

While the 725 had a slightly swept back bolt handle, releasable floorplate, and checkered stock, it also tended to harken back to Remington's pre-war rifles, in the process requiring some expensive extra machining cuts. Sales were poor, about 10,000 rifles total, and it was discontinued after three years.

The commercial failure of this rifle obviously helped persuade management finally to approve Walker's redesign of the 721-722. In 1962 the Remington Model 700 came into being, superseding the 721 and 722. At the same time sales began to take off, climbing back into the 50,000 to 60,000 category in the first year of production. They have been on the rise ever since, eventually surpassing 100,000 per year and making the Model 700 (which is really still just a prettied up 721/722) easily the best bolt-action seller in the world, today pursued seriously only by Ruger's Model 77. •

ACKNOWLEDGEMENTS

Several current and former Remington employees helped gather material for this article. I want to thank Ted McCawley, Clark Workman, Mike Walker, Larry Goodstal, Phil Haskel and, most particularly, Sam Alvis, former Chief Engineer at Ilion and, in retirement, Ilion's untiring historian and archivist. *Stuart Otteson*

Alex Henry

and his falling block rifles

ON APRIL 17TH, 1865, Alexander Henry of Edinburgh (Scotland) petitioned for British patent protection and was granted patent No. 1071 on an outside hammer, underlever, falling-block rifle. There is little doubt that Henry's action design was patterned after the earlier American Sharps system, Henry borrowing the basic falling-block and underlever; but the rest of Henry's action was such a total redesign and improvement that it bore little resemblance to the Sharps.

Many variations were produced, the early rifles closely following the patent drawings, but improvements followed until the design settled down to become the rifle so familiar to collectors and shooters today.

His final design used a large and graceful outside hammer, with a typical back-action lockplate let into the buttstock. The breechblock, at right angles to the bore, is connected by a short link to the finger lever. Before the action can be opened the hammer must be drawn to half-cock. A locking catch on the end of the finger lever is pressed and the finger lever is pushed forward and down. This lowers the breechblock until it contacts a short extended arm on the Martini-type extractor, which withdraws the fired case. The extractor, spring loaded, reseats itself when pressure on the finger lever is released. A flat spring does the reseating.

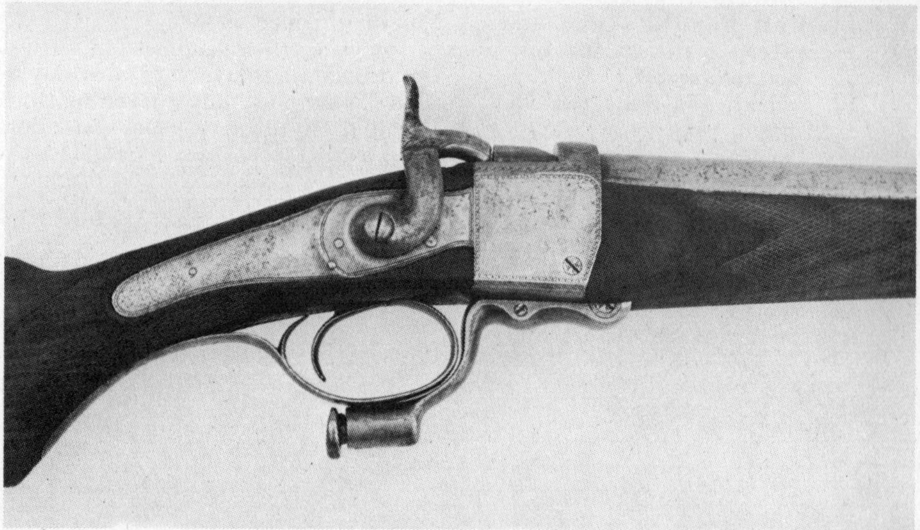

Fig. 1—This quite plain Alex Henry is without the bolting lever, and its caliber is 577/500, a scarce chambering. Serial No. 1672.

Early production rifles followed the extractor shown in the patent drawings. A plate was soldered to the underside of the barrel and an extractor fitted that slid in line with the barrel. The finger lever was extended ahead of its pivot pin and provided with a short arm. As the action opened fully this short arm was raised to contact the extractor's front end. Final pressure on the finger lever forced the fired case from the chamber, the extractor extending over the top of the breechblock 3/8"—much farther than the usual falling-block extractor travelled. Many other rifle designs barely started the case from the chamber.

Henry had trouble with this extractor, however, when his rifle was rejected from the British Army trials. These trials were set up to find a successor to the 577 Snider, then the standard British service arm. One complaint concerned the soldered plate holding the extractor to the barrel, another was made because a cartridge could be seated ahead of the extractor, thus jamming the piece. Modifications of the sliding extractor quickly followed, and Henry finally settled for the Martini extractor type, which has its own pivot pin with a flat spring provided to reseat it.

While we are on extractors, most Henrys show cartridge rims rebated into the barrel, but a few have the rim rebate in the breechblock face.

Three Locking Systems

Patent drawings show three lock systems that could be used with the falling block. Apart from the familiar back action lock, Henry's patent covered a front action lock with the lockplate and working parts within the buttstock, extending through the action body and into the fore-end. The patent drawing also shows a shotgun using a horizontal firing pin within the standing breech. The interesting point is that the standard back action lockplate is shown, but with a completely enclosed hammer fitted onto the usual back action pivot. This variation could, of course, have been used with his falling block action, and Henry thought enough of it to improve on it in patent No. 511 of February 1869, four years later.

Henry was granted many patents for falling block rifles, hammerless and hammered. I've seen one other variation of this 1869 patent. One wonders how many of each were made and in what numbers they exist today.

Much confusion exists over the back action lock used by Henry. Some collectors have contended that all sporting rifles had right-side locks and that all military rifles had left-

A detailed and fully documented report on the beautifully built single shot cartridge rifles made by the great Scottish gunmaker.

by WAL WINFER

Fig.2—This untypical Alex Henry, caliber 360 Nitro, was built (probably) on the thin-trigger Jeffery action which, in fact, looks much like a Farquharson action, at least externally. Serial No. 7197.

side locks. Others feel that the right-side action is much rarer on a rifle that was basically a left-side hammer type. A serial-number study, together with the rifles on hand, shows that most early rifles had left-side hammers, safety bolted behind. Later rifles had right-side hammers, front bolted. Why the change was made I don't know. Nothing is certain and nothing can be taken for granted with British rifles, for there was no real standard. You could order what you wanted—and get it. A few right-side hammer types will be found among early rifles, and by the same token, a few left-side ones occurred in later production. Henry also supplied barreled actions to the trade, firms which stocked them and fitted their own locks; some had safety bolts, some none.

All of the bolted-hammer Henrys I have seen could only be bolted with the hammer at half-cock. This was considered a safety feature when carrying the rifle at half-cock in the bush. A trailing vine or branch could catch the unbolted hammer, draw it slightly out of the half-cock notch until it slipped, broke out the notch on its return, and continued on to fire the cartridge. The serial-number study showed that the bolt change occurred between number 3,800 and 4,100, roughly, or about half-way through total production. There are few exceptions to this rule.

Now consider the thought that went into the hammered back-action design. This hammer, quite heavy and powered by a strong V-type mainspring, is arranged to increase the power of its blow as the hammer falls, through its hook up to the hammer. At the moment the hammer nose strikes the firing pin the hammer's heavily-constructed flat underside comes to rest on the long action top, thus the blow delivered (more than is needed to fire the cartridge) is absorbed along the action top, eliminating the battering of firing pin, bush or hammer nose—quite neatly done.

Only two action sizes are known to me. The small-frame type could, perhaps, be called rook size but, in the 10 or so I've seen, all were chambered for the 360/2¼″ black powder cartridge.

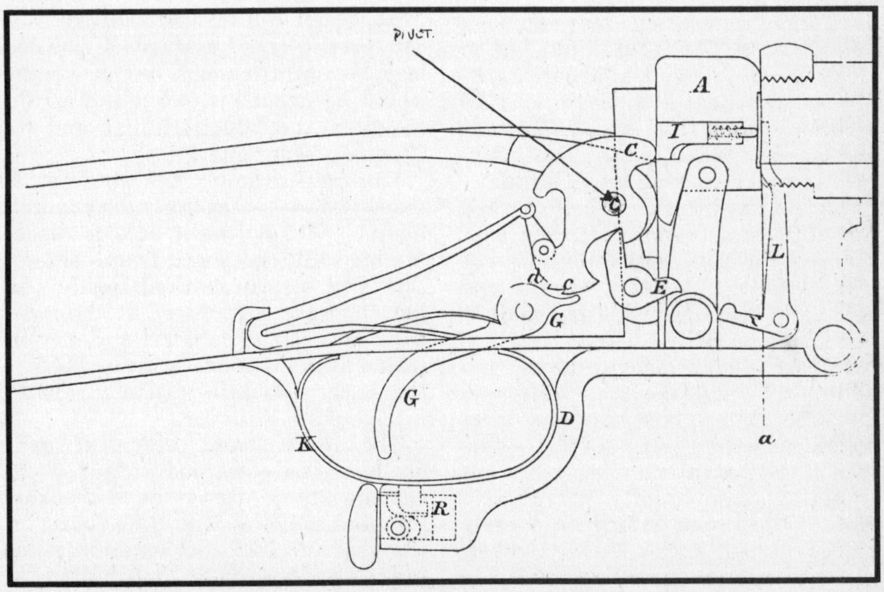

This is Alex Henry's 1869 patent, No. 511. See text for details of this system, which appeared well before the John Farquharson patent.

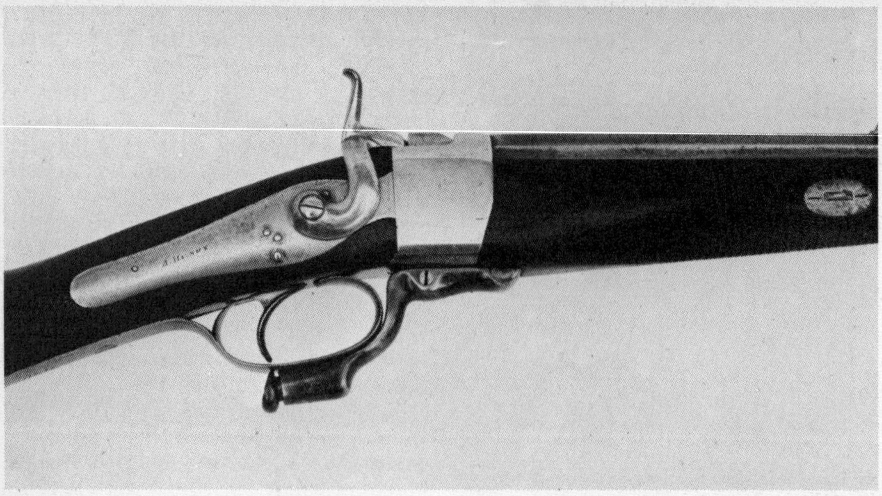

Fig.3—Another plain-grade Alex Henry—caliber 360, built on the light-frame action, and made without hammer locking lever or bolt. Serial No. 4120.

Fig.4—This Alex Henry rifle, chambered for the 450/3¼-inch cartridge, is fully engraved in floriate/scroll designs, and has the safety bolt ahead of the hammer breast. Serial No. 4327.

This cartridge, of about 30-30 head size, was loaded with 150-gr. bullets ahead of about 60 grains of black powder; later the bullet weight was increased to 190 grains and, later again, it carried a 300-gr. jacketed bullet ahead of smokeless Cordite powder. (Do not use smokeless loads in such rifles, even though they will fit the chamber, unless the rifle is proved and so-marked for the much more powerful nitro load.)

Small Frame Henrys

The small action, quite light and neat, is essentially a scaled-down version of the larger action. All small-frame rifles I've seen have been rather plainly finished, had straight grip stocks and border-line engraved at most. Most of them have a 26″ gradually-tapered full octagon barrel—a few will be round—with a matted or cross-hatched top flat. Rifling will be typically Henry type—7 flats and a small ridge between each pair of flats. The front sight, put in from the muzzle end, slides in a narrow front-to-rear slot. Some may be secured with a tiny screw. The rear sight is dovetailed in the usual manner, across the barrel. It will ordinarily have a fixed standard leaf marked for 100 yards, and a folding leaf marked for 200 yards. Both leaves usually have a platinum line inletted vertically below the wide and shallow V, a common British usage. The barrel should show Henry's name and address, behind the rear sight and ahead of the receiver ring; and, most times, his patent and a number—this is not the patent number, note, but the usage-number of a barrel with Henry's patented rifling. All early rifles will have such a barrel number, also an action number engraved on a small flat atop the receiver ring, and the rifle's serial number on the lower tang. Later barrels don't usually carry the barrel number, perhaps because the patent(s) had expired.

These small-frame rifles were quite light, about 5-6 lbs. on average. Recoil, even with a heavy black powder load, is mild, though more weight would be needed if one found a rifle handling the 300-gr. bullet and its Cordite powder charge.

The small-frame rifles were not, it seems, made with the safety-bolted hammer. I have been able to disassemble only one small-frame action. The lock was unmarked inside and did not have a fly fitted at the half-cock position. The lock and action inside finish was every bit as good as the most elaborate specimen examined to date, however.

The buttstock and fore-end are generally of finely-grained walnut, without cheekpiece. Henry liked checkering, and much of it will be found on the grip and fore-end, extending unbroken on both sides and bottom of the latter. Very well done, too. The fore-ends do not have the typical Henry tip shape found on his bigger rifles, being rounded and usually not capped. Buttplates are of steel or horn, most of them steel. Fore-ends will be cross-bolted (or keyed), as are all Henrys I have seen except the take-down models.

Large-Frame Henrys

The large action—by far the most common of the two sizes, if either could be called common—will generally, but not always, carry the finest of stock wood, finished to perfection with faultless inletting. The lock, action, barrel and furniture look as if they have been nailed to a tree and the wood grew around them, so expert is the fit. Many are superbly engraved in the very best manner, but a few rifles by Henry were unadorned, as were quite a lot of those fitted up by other markers using Henry's action.

Alex Henry was certainly one of the best—if not *the* best—gunmakers in the British Isles in the late 1800s. He built many of the highest quality single and double barrel rifles of his day. Everything he made was handsomely crafted; even his plainly-finished rifles received as much handwork and attention to detail as the most elaborately engraved specimens. The balance of Henry rifles is near perfection, even though they vary in stock length, shape, barrel diameter and weight. All Henry's I've had the pleasure of handling swung, pointed and balanced almost as if alive.

Henry was, apparently, particularly fond of cheekpieces, as time wore on, and most of his later-period pistol grip models on the large-frame action have them, well placed and undercut in the best manner, with a neat fillet behind the back edge of the grip. Early rifles—for the most part—lacked cheekpieces, but about midway through production, 1880 or so, saw them gaining in favor.

A few straight-grip stock rifles were also made, generally unengraved, and having much plainer stock wood. Cheekpieces were absent on these and they were generally plainly finished. Nevertheless, the same degree of skilled handwork went into them, for quality was always a watchword with Henry.

Left-hand hammer Alex Henry rifle, cal. 450/3¹/4". Its 28" barrel has broad file-cut full length rib. Receiver sides, hammer, lockplate, etc., fine scroll engraved, receiver top reads "PATENT NO. 756," and the rifle number, 2774, appears on the lower tang.

Recoil and Castoff

The British learned early that to save one's face from the recoil of a heavy-caliber rifle or gun called for a stock with castoff—meaning that the vertical centerline of the buttplate was offset to the right about ¹/4" to ³/8"—for a right-handed shooter. That allowed the rifle to slide away from the face in recoil, and the buttplate to fit more neatly—depending on the individual—into the hollow between shoulder and arm, not on the muscles of the arm. The heavy-cheeked shooter benefitted most from castoff. A final touch often seen on British firearms is the placement of the stock's toe a little farther to the right than the heel. This also helps place the buttplate in an area best able to absorb recoil with the least discomfort to the shooter.

Apart from the straight-grip military rifles, most large-frame Henry's seem to have been pistol-grip stocked; these grips will be capped in horn or in steel, the latter often having a trap or small hinged-lid compartment. The neatly-fitted hinged cover lifts up, revealing space for a spare front sight, firing pins or other small parts or springs, items one could have ordered with the original rifle. These steel trapped gripcaps are often so well made that in a couple of engraved specimens I have seen it is impossible to detect the seams unless they're pointed out.

Fore-ends carry the well-known Henry shape—so well liked by Bill Ruger that he adopted it for his sporting No. 1 single shot rifle. Forearms are cross bolted (keyed or pinned) and, together with the pistol grip, carry profuse and finely-executed checkering.

Round barrels, nicely tapered and made with the top flatted at the breech, seem to be standard—if anything can be called "standard" on early British falling-block rifles. Some round barrel rifles have a full-length matted rib, hand filed to a cross-grooved appearance and thereby reducing glares. These ribbed barrels will have sights put on the same way as do the small-frame octagon-barrel rifles. Non-ribbed round barrel rifles have sights on small and neat ramps at breech and muzzle via the same methods of fitting. Engraved on the small ovalled flat atop the receiver ring will be found "PATENT" and a number; early rifles may carry "HENRY'S PATENT" followed by the *action* number. The serial number, as before, is found on the lower tang. Yet earlier barrels have barrel number and action number engraved following Henry's address. Later barrels carried only the barrel number and, still later, this barrel number was left off, presumably when his patent expired. However, this action number, in the receiver top, was used to the end of production.

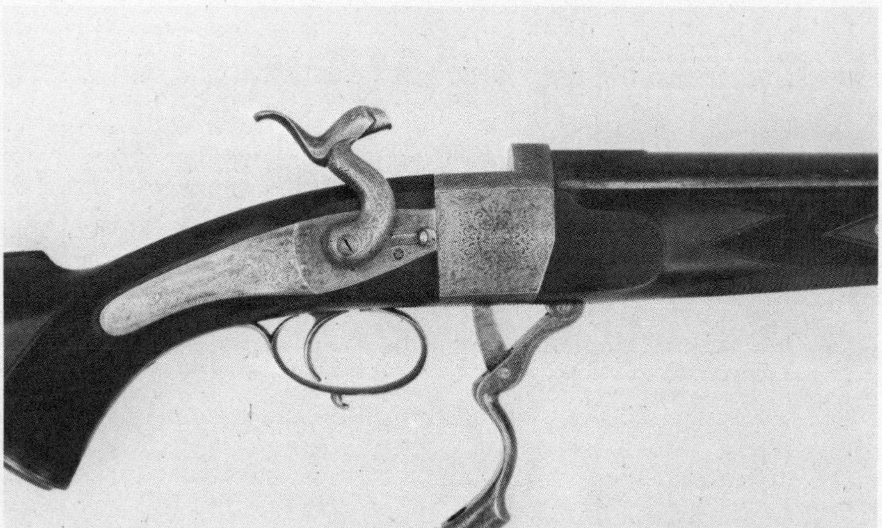

Fig. 5—The same 450/3¹/4-inch rifle pictured in Fig. 4, here with operating lever fully open and hammer cocked.

The typical Henry military rifle, full length or carbine style, is unmarked as to barrel, action or serial numbers, so we don't know if these rifles were included in Henry's numbering system. If they were included and *not* numbered it would mean that far fewer sporting rifles are around than the numbering system would indicate.

Henry supplied rifle actions and barrels to the trade, too. I have seen Henry hammered-action rifles carrying such names as Purdey, Holland & Holland, S. Alport, Dickson, et al—again the question, were these actions—without his number—included in Henry's numbering system or did he number only his own production? The only exception I've seen was a 450 BP rifle by E. M. Reilly which had "HENRY'S PATENT" stamped on the *rounded* receiver ring—no flat—and an indistinct number. Its left-side lock was unbolted, the hammer large and ungraceful, the work generally not up to Henry's standards.

It is not generally known that Henry made take-down rifles on a unique system, using the large frame action. He might also have made them on the small-frame system, but I don't know of any.

The barrel shank is unthreaded and is made with a taper of about 6°; a corresponding taper is formed within the receiver ring. The underside of the barrel is milled out fore-and-aft for about 1¼" and a heavy lug is inserted and silver soldered or brazed in place. The action body has a large integral bracket extending about 2" forward from the action face. This extension is milled out to take the barrel lug just noted. All three sides of the barrel lug are sloped outward, away from its leading edge; the recess in the receiver or action bracket is similarly treated and shaped to match. The front quarter or so of the receiver extension tapers in slightly, in line with the barrel. On one side there's a pivoted latch and, being fitted on the slope, it has some camming power. Similarly a slight cam surface is formed on the back edge of the barrel lug. To seat the barrel it is pushed into its mating seat within the receiver ring and then rotated downward until the barrel lug enters the bracket extension. At this point the barrel is seated on two tapers and, to hold the rifle together, the lever latch is rotated upward until its short end overlaps the barrel lug and cams it tightly within the seat. The system is sturdy and solid. I cannot vouch for its durability after much shooting, but because the mating surfaces are large I see no reason to suspect that oft-repeated assembly/disassembly could wear the parts appreciably.

This take-down rifle has a rounded-tip fore-end, not of the typical Henry shape, and attaches to the barrel via a side-swinging lever pivoted a few inches back from the tip. This lever operates an internal cam surface mating with a slotted lug formed on the underside of the barrel. The forearm is detached by swinging the small neat lever to the right; returning it to straight ahead effectively cams and locks the forearm tightly to the barrel. A tiny stud, formed on the metal seat below the lever, mates in a hole provided in the underside of the spring-tempered lever.

All large-action barrels seen have Henry's typical rifling—7 or more flats with a sharp ridge raised in the corner of each pair of flats, the 7-flat type giving a 14-point bearing surface to the bullet. Larger bores had more—my 577 has 11 sets. Some Henry rifles had gain-twist rifling; these start at the breech end with a slow twist, or pitch, the pitch gradually becoming faster. Many barrels were also slightly choke bored, being about .002" smaller internally at the muzzle. Both ideas, it was argued, increased accuracy. This may have been true (Harry Pope did it also) but when the British Government adopted the Henry barrel and Martini action in 1871 a standard or steady twist was used. However, such barrels were still choke bored and used Henry's form of rifling.

Big Action Marks

Various markings appear on early Henry barrels—and also on barrels by other makers who used Henry's patented rifling system—amongst them Westley Richards, Soper, Holland & Holland and a host of smaller makers. "Henry's Patent" will be found stamped or engraved close to the proof marks as will the letters A & T with a winged spear surrounded by two coiled snakes. There may be numbers present also. All of these marks will be found on the left-hand side of the barrel just above the fore-

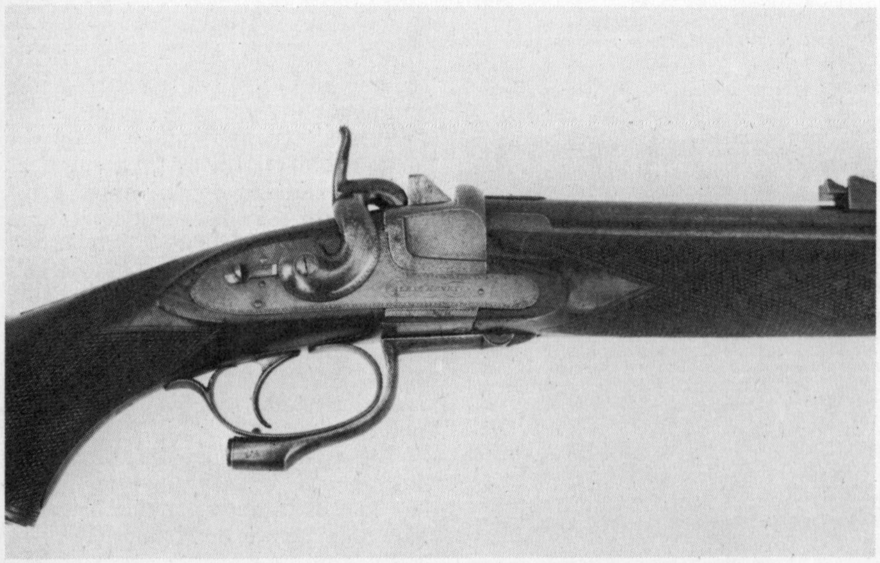

Fig.6—A relatively early Alex Henry rifle, this specimen is chambered for the 2-inch 577 cartridge. Note the quite different profile of lockplate (a bar action rather than a back action), breechblock and operating lever, and the half-cock safety bolt behind the hammer. Serial No. 1437.

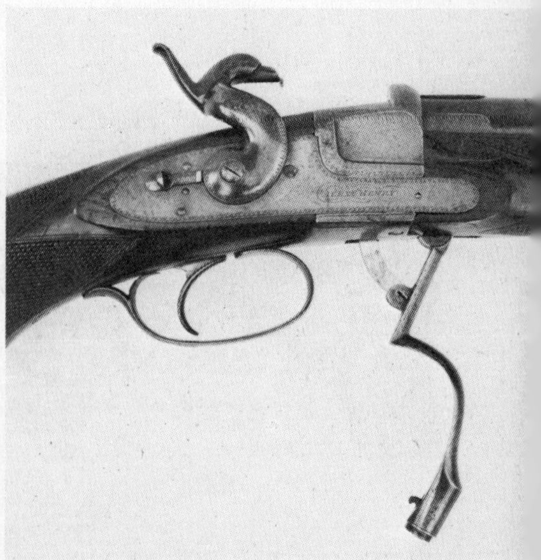

Fig.7—The same 577/2-inch Henry rifle seen in Fig.6 to show different form of the opened lever and the hammer profile.

end. (Someone out there may know what all of these markings mean; if so I'd like to hear from him.) I have no concrete evidence, but I'd guess that the letters and numbers belong to the barrel maker. I am assured that Henry did not actually make barrels at this time, which would in no way be unusual. Many British gunmakers, even large ones, bought their barrels, mostly from Birmingham. This was also true with locks, for very few makers of rifles or shotguns made their own locks, preferring to buy them from such as the famed J. Brazier (The Ashes, Wolverhampton) who specialized in such work. Though the rifle builder's name appeared on the outside of the lockplate, the inside of the plate will often show a different name.

I pulled the locks from 4 Henrys to check this. A small-frame 360 rifle was unmarked inside, nor was a 500/3¼" straight numbered 6128, hence a quite late production piece. The small-action rifle is numbered 4120, thus made about 10 years before. Both 450/3¼" straight rifles were marked "J. BRAZIER" on the inside. All locks had "ALEX. HENRY" engraved on the outside. The three large locks were identical internally as to pin placement, parts, shape, finish and general expertise. These three had large-bolted locks and a swinging hammer-fly at the half-cock position. The small rifle lacked fly or bolt.

Buying barrels and lockwork, even sidelocks, is still practiced in Britain today. I think few British gunmakers ever made a *complete* rifle or shotgun.

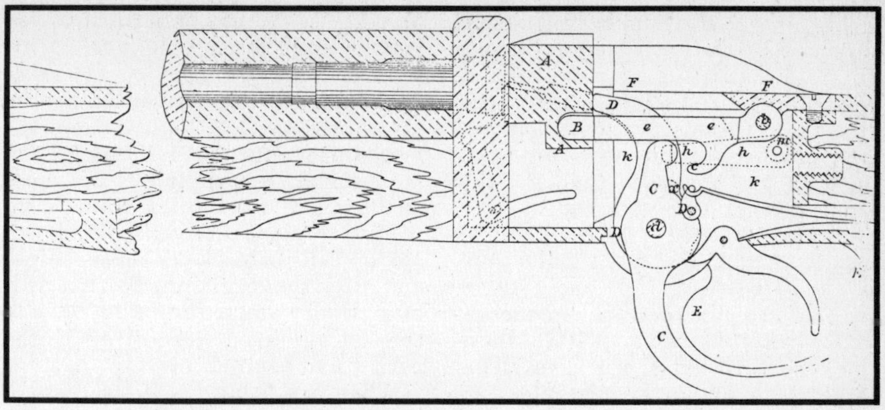

Shown here is one view of Alex Henry's patent of 1870, No. 2769, and illustrating a very early hammerless design.

Getting back to Henry and the winged-spear device, which seems confined to early production, other numbers and letters will be found stamped on action parts, the front face of the receiver and the underside of the barrel. Some of these are inspection marks or assembly numbers.

Three proof marks will usually be found on Henry BP rifles, these appearing on the left side of the barrel just in front of the action. A single proof mark will be found on the action body adjacent to the barrel proof and also one on the breechblock. This is no place for a study of proof marks but it should be pointed out that the number stamped between the barrel proof marks is the gauge or bore size in round balls. If the number is 52 (balls to the pound) it will be of 450 caliber. For the 360 gauge figure is 105; the 577 is 25 gauge; 39 is the 500 bore.

A study of the serial numbers, action numbers and barrel numbers makes collecting Henrys an even more interesting undertaking. (Gibbs and Fraser each had a similar numbering system.) By cross-checking these various numbers it is possible to get at least a rough idea of when these rifles were made. Also, assuming Henry did indeed make barrels, any that did not go into falling blocks must have gone into double barrel rifles or were sold to the trade. Thirdly, a number of British rifles were made up for presentation, most of these having a dated presentation plate in or on the stock. Such dates give us an almost certain year of manufacture and, using this and other numbers, the year(s) of production of fall-block rifles can be approximated. I know it is dangerous to stick my neck out, but it seems clear from my study of action and serial numbers that about 32% to 38% of Henry's production was falling-block rifles.

The Production Years

Henry made these from about 1865 to the late 1890s, perhaps to about 1905 at the latest, judging from the serial numbers of his hammered falling-block rifles. Around 1900-1905 he made some rifles on the Jeffrey Farquharson action and on a later, larger Farquharson action said to have been made in Belgium for the British gun trade—it is a near Jeffrey-action copy with a top tang safety.

For many years Henry had been

Fig.8—This Alex Henry rifle, otherwise conventional, is a rare take-down version. See fig.9 for details.

trying to get his hammerless action accepted by the shooting public and, from 1869 to 1873, he obtained patents on more than 24 action designs. Several of these actions reached limited production, but he never managed to capture more than a quite small portion of the market.

Henry persisted with his hammer action, though, and some 2,500 were produced between 1865 and 1900 or so. Toward the end of production Henry was making about 100 of these fine sporting rifles per year. This might seem low to the general collector but it was considerably more than Gibbs made; he managed less than 1,000 rifles on the Farquharson patent, but he made many other guns, of course. These hammered Henry rifles seem to have been made into the high 6,000 serial range at least, and perhaps beyond. The Jeffrey and Belgian Farquharson actions start showing up in the 7,000 serial range and it looked—at this stage—that Henry had given in on the popular Farquharson action.

In 1872 Henry and Farquharson went to court over the Farquharson action, which both men claimed to have invented. Farquharson was found by the courts to be the inventor and an embittered Henry licked his wounds. There is today considerable doubt about Farquharson being the inventor of such a highly ingenious mechanism due to his total non-mechanical upbringing, and more doubt arises when Alex Henry's inventive genius is considered in developing falling-block designs before and after the legal suit. Be that as it may, Henry started to build rifles to the Farquharson design, since the patent had expired.

When one measures the success of Henry's hammered falling block against the hammerless actions of his competitors one may be forgiven for wondering why all the fuss was made over the need for a hammerless action. The hammerless action, of course, was the coming thing and none of the many makers busily perfecting the falling block could see the bolt-action rifle just around the corner. If the turn-bolt rifle had been delayed just 10 more years the question of a hammerless falling block would have been vital to Henry.

The success of Henry's falling block hammer rifle is not hard to understand. It was not until the early 1870s that a successful hammerless action was evolved; it had a reasonably short life (about 35 years) and it was made when 95% of the rifles offered had a large exposed hammer. Shooters of that age were slow to see any advantage in concealed-hammer rifles; they required a safety of some kind, hence there were additional parts, some rather complicated, so more could go wrong. Shooters were long familiar with a large outside hammer, they could see at a glance if the rifle was cocked, and thus it appeared safer to them. These points, coupled with a high workmanship Henry bestowed on his rifles, left little reason to make the change.

Henry's Patents

Evidence of this reluctance to change is seen in the patents taken out by Henry in the late 1860s and early 1870s for various improvements, designs that were only accepted much later (and used by other makers when the patents had expired). Henry's detachable-barrel patent (2158 of 1873) used two lugs formed on the barrel, these mating with matching recesses formed within the breech. Only a quarter-turn was needed to detach the barrel. This system was copied and used by Westley Richards as late as 1912, perhaps later, on rifles in 577, 425 and 600 Nitro built on their underlever falling-block action.

Henry patented the round breechblock (2158 of 1873) later used by Webley in their small-frame rook rifles of about 1902 and in calibers at least up to 32-40. Patent No. 2540 of 1872 covered, in part, a spring-loaded catch to hold an underlever closed. Later on Field used this same system on his side-lever falling block patented in 1877, No. 1927.

Perhaps Henry's most interesting patents covered an improvement to the back-position rifle. This 1877 patent (number unknown) used an extended trigger situated halfway along the fore-arm, at which point a seperate pistol grip was formed on much the same lines as the grip on a submachine gun.

The regular pistol grip and trigger were kept, the grip much deepened. The buttstock, behind the grip and between the buttplate, was deeply hollowed to fit over the shooters shoulder thus the stock would fit well and the extended rear pistol grip would take the recoil. The forward grip and trigger allowed the right arm to stretch out fully, allowing the rifle to be shot in the back position,

This is an Alex Henry double rifle, cal. 450-400/3¼", in hammerless underlever form. Each lockplate has "COCKED" inlaid in gold ahead of the cocking indicator levers. Ahead of the tang safety is "SAFE," also inlaid in gold. All action area metal is profusely engraved in fine scroll work. The 26" barrels carry a broad file-cut rib.

The receiver top shows "HENRY'S PATENT NO. 173" and the rifle's serial number, 6334, appears on the lower tang. This rifle is cased (oak-and-leather, red felt lined) and among the usual fittings are a case sizing die with ram and knockout rod, a powder measure (not a flask), etc. Several tools are missing, however.

Fig.9—The same rifle seen in Fig.8. Note tapered barrel breech (inverted) and barrel lug that mates with matching recess in action extension. Pivoted lever on extension moves upward to lock barrel. See text for further data.

yet not cramped or uncomfortable.

Many Henry falling blocks were cased outfits, usually furnished with loading details, such reloading tools as case sizers, neck reamers, steel bullet moulds (numbered to match the rifle and including an ebony-handled hollow-nose plug to fit the mould). Powder measures were also supplied, again with ebony handles as were the set of screwdrivers—or turnscrews as the British call them—and a special key to take out the firing pin. Spare firing pins, a bridle (or link) and small springs were often included as were full sets of cleaning gear, rods, special non-spill white metal oil bottles, in fact everything needed to keep the hunter shooting, down to the jointed cleaning rods and leather wallets to hold the brass brushes used.

These Henry cases were usually of oak and leather, lined with red or green felt or baize, the better ones covered in pig skin. Walled compartments around the rifle permitted the proper stowing of each piece of reloading and cleaning gear.

Besides giving a superb rifle, the best it was possible to build, we owe Henry thanks for cutting his chambers to take the standard cartridges of the day—nothing special or 'way out in case sizes or bullet diameters, so that today we can obtain brass cases and shoot our Henrys again.

Shooting the Henrys

The 450 straight is nothing but the earlier black powder version of the 450 Nitro Express; the 500 straight preceded the 500 Nitro and the 577 BP can be made from the 577 Nitro. Cases for the 450/400 can also be made from 450 Nitro. The 360/2¹/₄″ can be formed from 30-30 brass but as it will be a little short it is better to use the 9.3x72R, a case ideal as to head size; only trimming to length is needed.

Please note—in all of Henrys I've tried the 450 N.E. will fit the 450 B.P. chamber, the 500 N.E. fits the 500 B.P., and the 577/3″ Nitro will fit 577/3″ chambers made for black powder only, and in some cases will even fit 577s with 2³/₄″ chambers. *Under no circumstances,* however, should nitro rounds be fired in black powder rifles. This is a highly dangerous way to get empty cases, and it could result in a blown-up rifle and perhaps, loss of life. At best it will be quickly shorten the life of a good rifle, for the steels of 1870 were not like those of nitro express days. Most actions of that black powder period were made completely of wrought iron in one form or another.

The best bullet I have found for the 450/3″ and 3¹/₄″ B.P. rifles is Winchester's 300-gr. 45/90 bullet, Lyman number 456/191. The 500/3″ and 3¹/₄″ B.P. uses the 360-gr. Lyman 509/134. Bullets for the 577/2³/₄″ and 3″ can be about 530 grains.

All of the early B.P. loads used a deeply hollow-pointed bullet that was light in weight for its bore size. Thus high velocity was obtained—1700 to 1900 fps—and flat trajectory out to about 200 yards, the maximum useful range for these fast-stepping rifles. Beyond 200 yards the light bullet lost most if not all of its moderate accuracy.

We needn't worry about hollow point bullets for our needs. The tigers are long gone, and we don't need the smashing blow such bullets delivered. Solid bullets of the weight suggested will work well, and we use a caseful of black powder, which was the standard charge. Use FG only, nothing finer. It is important to "slug" barrels to ascertain actual bore-groove size, for many old rifles have varying dimensions. There was little standardization as we know it today. As noted before, many rifles were put out with bullet moulds that fitted such variant bores. No rifles will shoot well with undersize bullets and it should be noted that many old rifles have oversize bores. I have one 577 that slugs .585″, a 360 that is .375″ and a second that is .385″. As the latter is a rook, break-open rifle, and by a maker not well known, it worries me a little. Bullets should be cast rather soft, using a little tin to help the melt flow better—about 1 to 40 or 30 would do. Harder bullets can be used but there is not much point unless one has worked up light loads of smokeless powder—such loads don't do so well in large cases. There is too much air space, wads and fillers do not help much and I am loath to use larger charges of slower powder for fear of damaging the many fine bores found in these rifles. The point is not how much the action will safely stand but rather how much damage hot smokeless powder gases in large doses do to fine rifling in soft steel barrels.

Henry rifles command large prices these days, the better ones selling for more than the famous Farquharson. At times justly so, too, for most Henrys exhibit fine fitting, magnificent stock wood, and simply superb engraving—nothing could better them. A cased Henry lying surrounded by its full set of tools and accessories is a sight not easily forgotten by any real rifleman. •

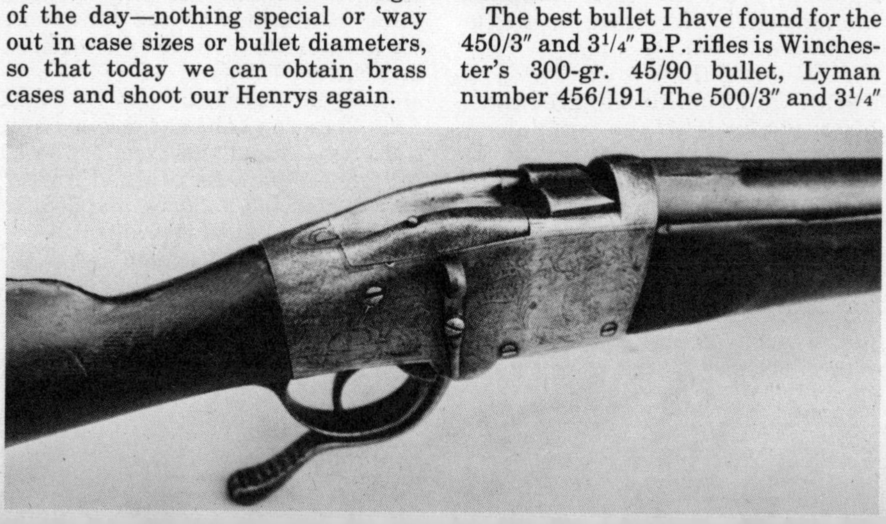

Fig.10—This view shows an Alex Henry hammerless single shot, falling-block design, probably made after Henry's patent 2769 of 1870.

by **E. B. MANN**

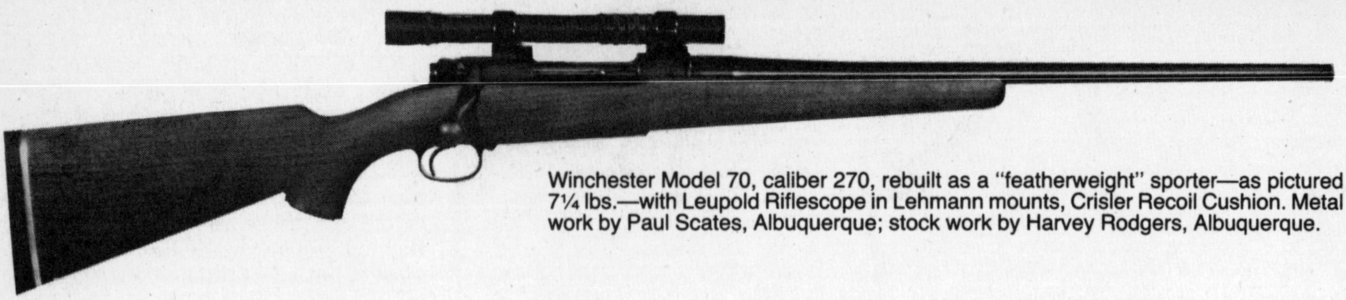

Winchester Model 70, caliber 270, rebuilt as a "featherweight" sporter—as pictured 7¼ lbs.—with Leupold Riflescope in Lehmann mounts, Crisler Recoil Cushion. Metal work by Paul Scates, Albuquerque; stock work by Harvey Rodgers, Albuquerque.

When Bev Mann wanted to go light and hunt happy, way back when, he came up with . . .

A FIRST FEATHERWEIGHT

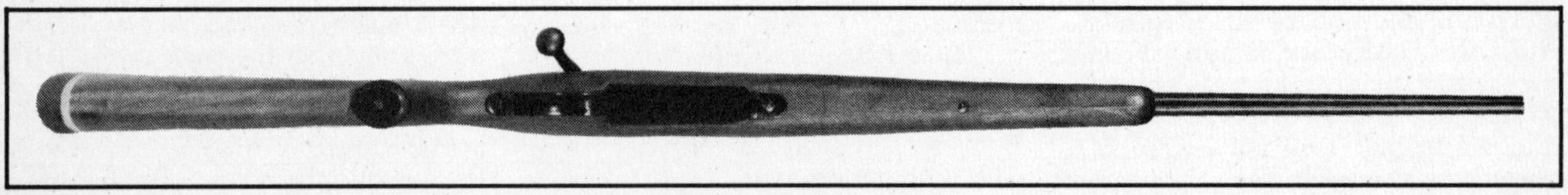

This sort of slimming is as important as profile changes when it comes to losing ounces and gaining feel in a hunting rifle.

IT ALL BEGAN in the mid-1940s at one of those Seminars in which certain firearms manufacturers showed off their new or improved products to such gun writers and editors as Elmer Keith, Charley Askins, Jack O'Connor, Warren Page, John Amber, and other similarly interested parties. We learned a lot in those sessions, both from our hosts and from each other. Differences of opinion were common enough, but we were usually tolerant of each other, and friends notwithstanding.

It takes some remembering, but there weren't any lightweight rifles for big game then, and on this occasion I was complaining about having had to tote some 11 pounds of artillery for nearly a week over some of New Mexico's roughest country. I didn't see why, I said, a rifle couldn't be whittled down to where, even with telescopic sights and a sling, it would weigh approximately the same as a lever-action 30-30 and still get the job done on anything smaller than, maybe, moose; and we didn't see many moose in New Mexico.

O'Connor's snort of derision was utterly lacking in tolerance! First, it couldn't be done. Second, if it were done, the rifle would be ruined: short of both range and accuracy; too much recoil; too much muzzle blast. And, anyway, hell's bells, if a man ain't man enough to carry a big game rifle, he shouldn't hunt big game!"

Somebody, I think it was Page, answered him: "Wouldn't make those 500-yard-plus shots you write about, eh, Jack?," and the laughter that followed prevented any comment I might have offered.

But the question was right on target. At an earlier Seminar, I had made some derogatory remarks about long range shooting being poor fodder for magazine articles which would be read by less expert hunters who would take them as excuses for shooting at anything they could see through a 4x scope.

But O'Connor's words rankled. What if I could prove him wrong? Having a rifle customized would cost something, but maybe I could write an article about it and get some of the money back. I knew the people who could do the work for me: Paul Scates, a fine gunsmith who had done work for me on rifles sent me for testing; and Harvey Rodgers, one of the best stockers in the country—so good that Ellis Christian Lenz had devoted half a chapter to him in his excellent book, *Muzzle Flashes*. So I talked it over with Scates and Rodgers, and bought a Winchester Model 70, caliber 270.

Next, I chose a Leupold scope, for several reasons. I had tried several of them, and liked them. Optically excellent and mounted low in rigid ring mounts, with a dot reticle subtending three minutes of angle, it would be perfect. And it weighed only 6¼ ounces.

Recoil in a hunting rifle is mostly in the mind of the shooter, but O'Connor had mentioned it specifically, so I chose Crisler Cushion Pads; pads plural because they came in pairs, one thick and one thin to adjust for the difference in "reach" caused by summer or winter clothing. I don't think they are on the market now, which is too bad. They were good looking, effective—and they weighed only 4¼ ounces; a trifle less in fact, when trimmed to fit my slimmer stock.

Meanwhile, Scates was working on the rifle. New, it had weighed 8¼ pounds, as advertised. First, he cut 4 inches off the barrel. That disposed of the front sight and sight ramp, so we discarded the rear sight too. The scope would be the only sight I wanted or would need. Then Scates lathed what was left of the barrel (20 inches) in a long taper from the receiver forward. The rear sight bulge disappeared and the barrel, finished and crowned, looked like something designed for space travel.

We discussed slimming the action, too, cutting magazine capacity by one cartridge. But Rodgers objected. "You won't gain much in weight, and it would spoil the lines of the rifle, making it look weak in the middle." There was no use begging Harvey to do something that would spoil the lines of the rifle, so we bowed to wisdom.

Meanwhile also, Rodgers was rebedding the barrel, shortening and tapering the forearm, thinning and shaping the stock, lifting the curve behind the trigger guard to produce a full pistol grip, and finally, believe it or not, drilling half-inch holes deep from the butt forward and covering the holes with a white liner and one of the black Crisler butt cushions. When we seated the metal into the wood, it looked—well, as pretty as a picture, and here are pictures so you can see for yourself.

The question now was: will it shoot?

We did some sighting-in shots at 25 yards. Then we moved out to 100 yards and adjusted blanket and bedrolls for prone shooting. I asked Scates to shoot first; I had buck fever, and Scates was a better rifleman than I was.

His first three shots centered at one o'clock, two inches above point of aim, measuring a hair under an inch, center to center. The ammunition was 130-grain Western Silvertip Expanding Super X.

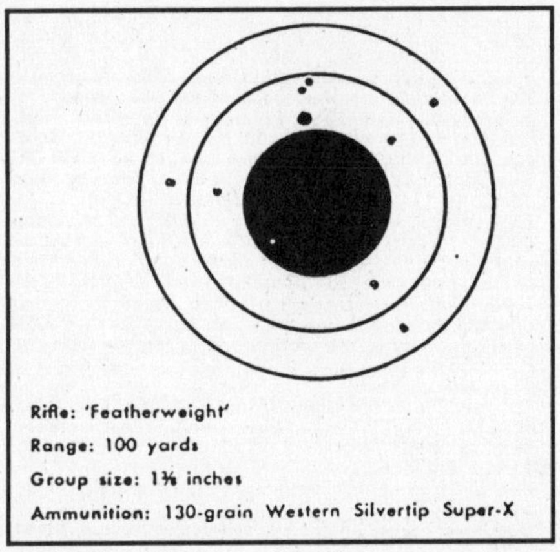

Here's how *The American Rifleman* showed off Mann's new rifle's potential.

I let my fingers come unclinched.

"I'd like it centered, 3½ inches high at 100, Paul," I said. "That will keep them within a 4-inch rise or fall out to around 300 yards, and that's as far as I will ever shoot it. Move it over one click and up one, and try three more."

He made the adjustments. The next two shots were where I had requested, 3½ inches high, centered, with ⅜ of an inch between them. When the third was fired Scates called it "Low, damn it. Just a little low, but centered." His call was correct: the group measured 1⅜ inches.

I did some shooting then, to make sure that Paul and I were seeing alike. We were not; my groups were low and left, about seven o'clock, due to my funny vision. My three best groups were 1½ inches.

(I have been asked, "Why did you fire only three-shot groups?" My answer: "When did you ever get more than three shots, if that many, at a game animal? If three shots don't get him, ten to one it wasn't because of the rifle!")

We shot it later at 200 and 300 yards, prone, with rest. Our best groups at 200 were around 2½ inches; at 300, just under 4 inches. Good enough, we thought, for a hunting rifle. Neither muzzle blast nor recoil were noticeably worse than those of standard rifles fired for comparison.

I carried the "shorty" on a couple of hunts, then wrote my article. *American Rifleman* bought it. When it was published I got a letter from Winchester: "We enjoyed your article. It was of particular interest in the matter of design, and many of the points brought out deserve further study. Would it be possible for us to examine the rifle?"

Needless to say, I sent them the rifle. Considerably later it came back to me with their verdict: "It will do everything you said it would do."

I sent a stat of that letter to Jack O'Connor. It came back to me with a question scrawled across it: "But what will it do at 500 yards?"

The question was hardly worthy of Jack; given the data furnished, any ballistics table would tell him what it would do at other ranges. I simply scrawled my answer under his: "Who the hell cares?"

I carried that rifle over a lot of miles and it did everything I asked it to do; no spectacular 500-yard kills, but who needs them? I did put a variable-power scope on it for a time, and the gunsmith who mounted it did, as a favor to me, some other work that I hadn't asked for; a favor that cost me a day of re-testing to make sure the rifle had lost none of its accuracy. It hadn't. But I had to replace the old mounts and scope when I sold it; the buyer demanded that the rifle come to him in exactly its original condition, matching his copy of the "Rifleman" article.

There are many "featherweight" rifles today. The Winchester Model 70 ("The Rifleman's Rifle") is now offered as "The Rifleman's Carbine,"—20-inch barrel, weighing as little as six pounds. A scope sight and sling would add at least a pound to that, but the comparison is obvious. New materials have made it easier to produce a light rifle; fiberglass stocks, for example. They have advantages; but I still like walnut better!

No, I did not invent the featherweight hunting rifle; I only happened to build one of the earlier ones. The trend was already in process. My rifle cost me $373.95. It was a profitable venture, dollar-wise. But most valuable to me was its dozen years or more of impeccable performance. ●

EDITOR'S NOTE

You can find, if you look, the name E. B. Mann high on the mastheads of gun magazines back a long way. He delighted me 20 or more years ago by buying photography and even articles from me, and not so long ago by being my roommate at some of those seminars he mentions.

So, like another fellow we both knew, if Bev Mann tells you he was there, he was there. And if he tells you it shot, it shot. No doubt about it—even if it was all the best part of 40 years ago. *K.W.*

Gun Digest Index

1944—1987

PART ONE: AUTHOR INDEX

[1] = Used in GUN DIGEST TREASURY, 1st ed.
[2] = Used in GUN DIGEST TREASURY, 2nd ed.
[3] = Used in GUN DIGEST TREASURY, 3rd ed.
[4] = Used in GUN DIGEST TREASURY, 4th ed.
[5] = Used in GUN DIGEST TREASURY, 5th ed.

PART TWO: SUBJECT INDEX

1. ANNUAL ARMS SURVEYS

1a. Ammunition

1b. Foreign Arms

1c. Handguns

1d. Rifles—Shotguns

1e. Testfire—Shooters' Needs

1f. Black Powder

2. ARMS LIBRARY

3. BALLISTICS

4. BULLETS & EFFECTS

5. CLUBS—SAFETY—YOUTH

6. CIVIL WAR

7. COLLECTING

7a. American Repeating Rifles

8. COMBINATION GUNS

9. COVER ILLUSTRATIONS

9a. Back

9b. Front

10. COVERS, INSIDE

10a. Inside Back

10b. Inside Front

11. CUSTOM GUNS

12. ENGRAVING

13. EXPLODED DRAWINGS

14. FANCY SHOOTING

15. FOREIGN WEAPONS

16. GLOSSARY FOR GUNNERS

17. GUN CARE

18. GUN CATALOGS IN FACSIMILE

19. GUNSMITHS—GUNSMITHING

20. GUNSTOCKS

21. HANDGUNS

21a. Combat-Hunting-Plinking

21b. Revolvers

21c. Target

21d. Handgun Miscellany

22. HUNTING

22a. Africa—Asia

22b. American Big Game

22c. European

22d. Small Game

22e. Varmint

23. INVENTORS-GUNMAKERS

24. MACHINE GUNS

25. OUTFITTING

26. PELLET AND AIR GUNS

27. PHOTOGRAPHY

28. PROOF IN EUROPE

29. RELOADING

31b. Doubles

31c. Magnums

31d. Military

31e. Muzzleloaders

31f. Small Game

31g. Target—Benchrest

31h. Wildcats, Varminters, High Velocity

32. SHOTGUNS

32a. Chokes—Patterns

32b. Hunting

32c. Shotshells

32d. Trap—Skeet

32e. Shotgun Miscellany

33. SIGHTING IN

34. SIGHTS AND SCOPES

35. MISCELLANEOUS

Handloader's Digest Index 1962—1984

PART ONE: AUTHOR INDEX

PART TWO: SUBJECT INDEX

1. BALLISTICS (Internal & External)

2. BEGINNERS

3. BLACK POWDER

4. CAST BULLETS

5. CHRONOGRAPHS, CALCULATORS & COMPUTERS

12. PROPELLANTS

13. RIFLES

14. SWAGING

15. SHOTGUNS

16. TOOLS

17. WILDCATS

Guns Illustrated Index 1969—1987

PART ONE: AUTHOR INDEX

PART TWO: SUBJECT INDEX

1. ANNUAL ARMS SURVEYS

1a. Ammunition

1b. Black Powder Check-Out

1c. On The Firing Line

1d. Shooter's Review

2. AUTOMATIC WEAPONS

3. BALLISTICS

4. COVER ILLUSTRATIONS

4a. Front

4b. Back

4c. Inside Front

4d. Inside Back

5. COLLECTING

6. FOREIGN GUNS

7. GUN CATALOGS IN FACSIMILE

8. GUNSMITHS—GUNSMITHING

9. HANDGUNS

9a. Combat-Hunting-Plinking

9b. Revolvers

9c. Target

9d. Handgun Miscellany

10. HUNTING

10a. Big Game

10b. Small Game

10c. Varmint

11. PELLET GUNS

12. RELOADING

13. RIFLES

13a. Big Game

13b. Military - Para-Military

13c. Small Game

13d. Target-Benchrest

13e. Muzzle-loaders

14. SHOTGUNS

15. SIGHTS & SCOPES

16. MISCELLANEOUS

Gun Digest Hunting Annual Index 1984—1987

PART ONE: AUTHOR INDEX

PART TWO: SUBJECT INDEX

1. AFRICA

2. ANTELOPE

3. ARCHERY

4. BLACK BEAR

5. BLACK POWDER